# CONSUMER BEHAVIOR

KU-619-912

WILLIAM D. WELLS
University of Minnesota

DAVID PRENSKY
Trenton State College

JOHN WILEY & SONS, INC.

New York   Chichester   Brisbane   Toronto   Singapore

ACQUISITIONS EDITORS   Tim Kent, Petra Sellers
DEVELOPMENTAL EDITOR   Rachel Nelson
MARKETING MANAGER   Leslie Hines
PRODUCTION MANAGER   Charlotte Hyland
ART DIRECTION   Dawn L. Stanley
DESIGNER   Jenkins & Page
MANUFACTURING MANAGER   Mark Cirillo
PHOTO EDITOR   Hilary Newman
ILLUSTRATION COORDINATOR   Anna Melhorn
OUTSIDE PRODUCTION MANAGEMENT   Ingrao Associates
COVER ART: "The Magic Eye" © N. E. Thing Enterprises, Inc. Reprinted with permission of Universal Press Syndicate. All rights reserved.
PICTURE RESEARCH: Carousel Research, Inc.: Laurie Platt Winfrey, Beth Krumholz, and Jennifer Goerk Lyden

This book was set in 10/13 Century Old Style by Ruttle Shaw & Wetherill, Inc. and printed and bound by Donnelley/Willard. The cover was printed by Phoenix Color Corp.

Color separations were handled by Professional Litho.

Recognizing the importance of preserving what has been written, it is a policy of John Wiley & Sons, Inc. to have books of enduring value published in the United States printed on acid-free paper, and we exert our best efforts to that end.

The paper on this book was manufactured by a mill whose forest management programs include sustained yield harvesting of its timberlands. Sustained yield harvesting principles ensure that the number of trees cut each year does not exceed the amount of new growth.

*Library of Congress Cataloging-in-Publication Data*
Wells, William, 1926-
    Consumer behavior / William Wells, David Prensky.
        p.    cm.
    Includes bibliographical references.
    ISBN 0-471-59641-8 (Cloth : alk. paper)
    1. Consumer behavior.    I. Prensky, David.    II. Title.
HF5415.32.W45    1996
658.8'342—dc20                                95-45409
                                                CIP

Printed in the United States of America

10   9   8   7   6   5   4   3   2   1

Books

WITHDRAWN

WILLIAM WELLS

After receiving an A.B. degree from Lafayette College, and MA and Ph.D. degrees from Stanford University, Bill Wells joined the faculty of the Psychology Department of Rutgers University in 1954. At Rutgers, he taught both graduate and undergraduate courses in psychology and psychological research and, with Professor George H. Smith, established one of the first master's degree programs in Consumer Psychology. While at Rutgers, Bill served as a consultant for the Benton & Bowles advertising agency and for the New Jersey Bell Telephone Company.

In 1966, Bill joined the faculty of the Graduate School of Business of the University of Chicago as Professor of Psychology and Marketing. While on the Chicago faculty, he served as a consultant for the Leo Burnett Company, the American Dairy Association, Market Facts, Inc., Miles Laboratories, Sears Roebuck & Company, the law firm of Jenner and Block, and the Federal Trade Commission. In 1974, Bill joined the Needham, Harper and Steers advertising agency as Vice President and Director of Corporate Research. In 1991, he retired from DDB Needham Worldwide as Executive Vice President and Director of Marketing Services.

In 1992, Bill joined the faculty of the School of Journalism and Mass Communication of the University of Minnesota as the first Mithun Land Grant Professor of Advertising. There, he teaches a course in communication research and a course in persuasion and conducts basic and applied research on substantive and methodological topics related to advertising.

Bill is the co-author, editor, or co-editor of five books, including *Advertising: Principles and Practice* and *Planning for R.O.I.: Effective Advertising Strategy,* both published by Prentice Hall, and *Lifestyle and Psychographics,* published in 1972 by the American Marketing Association. He is also the author or co-author of more than 60 journal articles and numerous presentations at meetings to business and professional organizations.

Bill has served on the editorial review boards of the *Journal of Consumer Research,* the *Journal of Consumer Psychology,* the *Journal of Advertising Research,* the *Journal of Marketing,* the *Journal of Marketing Research, Psychology & Marketing, Marketing Research,* and *Current Issues and Research in Advertising.* He has been elected a Fellow of the Association for Consumer Research and a Fellow of the American Psychological Association and has served as President of the Association for Consumer Research, and President of the Consumer Psychology Division of the American Psychological Association. In recognition of his numerous achievements, he has received the Distinguished Professional Contribution Award from the Society for Consumer Psychology and the William F. O'Dell award and the Paul D. Converse award from the American Marketing Association.

DAVID PRENSKY

David Prensky is a faculty member in the School of Business at Trenton State College, where he teaches courses in advertising, consumer behavior, and marketing management, principles, and research. He received his Ph.D. in Sociology from the University of Chicago, his M.A. from Indiana University, and his B.A. from the University of Pennsylvania. While at Chicago, Dave concentrated in research methods and organizational behavior and completed a dissertation that identified the segments among organizations that were active in health policy debates. He held a National Science Foundation Graduate Fellowship and a National Institute of Mental Health Training Grant and was a Fellow of the Center for Social Organization Studies.

After receiving his Ph.D., Dave worked in advertising and marketing research. He began his career at Needham Harper Worldwide, where he had the pleasure of working with his co-author, Bill Wells. Dave worked in Needham's Marketing Decision Systems Group producing strategic marketing analyses for such agency clients as Anheuser-Busch, General Mills, Ramada, and Shasta. He then moved into the new product development and testing area, serving as a research manager for Yankelovich Clancy Shulman and as Associate Director in the Assessor Group at Information Resources (IRI). Before returning to academia, Dave wrapped up his full-time industry career as Marketing Planner for NW Ayer, where he produced strategic, marketing, and media allocation plans for such clients as General Motors, Gillette, and Sterling Drug.

Dave has published a number of articles and papers in a wide variety of professional and academic settings. His work has examined integrated marketing communications; media, consumer values and advertising; and the history and sociology of marketing research. Over the years, he has led numerous seminars and professional workshops on issues including multilevel analysis, network and structural analysis, and employment in business and government settings. His current research focuses on interactive marketing communications; organizational issues in marketing management; and media, consumer values, and advertising.

Bill Wells (left), Dave Prensky (right).

# PREFACE

When we sat down to begin writing this book, we reviewed the leading consumer behavior textbooks and realized that they contained very few vivid images of consumers—lots of ads, but few consumers. We felt it was like reading a book about fish that includes a lot on fishermen/women but very little about fish. The books focus on theories and research but rarely discuss how consumers actually behave. While theories are useful, they are insufficient by themselves. Students must marry knowledge to skills that will allow them to analyze and influence consumers' behavior in the real world. It is our contention that students cannot understand consumer behavior without comprehending the things that real consumers, marketers, and public policy actors do. Too often, consumer behavior texts leave students mystified about *why* consumers behave as they do and *how* marketers and public policy actors use their knowledge of consumer behavior in their work. Students must do more than just memorize theories and examples to spit back on exams. They must be able to integrate these theories and examples into the marketing activities they learn about in other courses in order to apply consumer behavior principles to marketing problems.

In this book, we focus on the skills students require in order to participate more effectively in marketing-related activities. We propose to teach students these skills by emphasizing how consumers actually behave and then showing how marketers, consumer activists, and public officials influence their behavior. Our approach emphasizes how marketers and others *apply* consumer behavior theories, as distinguished from an emphasis on the theories themselves. We use text, examples, and extensive video material to illustrate the behavior of real consumers and provide opportunities for students to develop their analytic knowledge through guided questions and activities.

## ▼ A CONSUMER BEHAVIOR TEXTBOOK WITH A DIFFERENCE

*A textbook in consumer behavior should face outward toward the real world rather than inward toward academic research, researchers, research methods, and theories.* Research, methods, and theories are unquestionably important, but they are means, not ends—they are useful only insofar as they lead to genuine pragmatic understanding of how consumers actually behave.

*A textbook in consumer behavior should include the full range of consumer decisions.* It should focus on life-altering decisions, such as purchasing a home, planning a wedding, or deciding whether and when to have child. It should also address less momentous decisions, such as buying a soft drink, choosing a breakfast cereal, or going to a movie. These latter choices are equally important to a study of consumer behavior, for two reasons—consumers make them many times each day, and they are vital to the large industries that market products and services of this kind.

*A textbook in consumer behavior should address both the pleasures and the dark side of consumption.* Consumers derive many benefits from their purchase and use of products and services—music and movies provide entertainment; checking accounts afford a means of budgeting one's income. At the same time, consumer behavior has a dark side—alcohol and drug addiction, pollution of the environment, eating disorders, compulsive gambling, and overuse of credit are striking examples of consumer behavior gone awry. Such behavior damages its victims and is the focus of all those who try to help.

*A textbook in consumer behavior should include the full range of consumers.* Consumers are old and young, rich and poor, male and female, black and white. Some consumers work full-time; some are retired. Consumers live in Pennsylvania, Florida, and California; India and Peru. Some consumers are homemakers who acquire products for their families; others are students who buy for themselves.

*A textbook in consumer behavior should include all the participants in the marketing process.* Consumers, advertisers, marketers, and media executives represent a portion of the participants in the marketing process; they are joined by consumer advocates and local and national government officials, who influence these parties. Students who study consumer behavior may choose to enter careers in any one of these fields. A solid understanding of consumer behavior will enable them to work effectively in their chosen profession.

*A textbook in consumer behavior should provide experience in doing rather than memorizing.* Students must learn how to make rational personal consumption decisions, create convincing advertising, evaluate local and national marketing plans, develop and test new products, and prevent marketers from injuring consumers or damaging a fragile environment. While they cannot be expected to do any of these things as well as experienced professionals, they should be expected to make credible and interesting attempts. After all, learning without doing is the same as not learning.

## ▼ THE DEVELOPMENT PROCESS

In developing this project, we conducted some of our own market research to ensure that we could help you meet the objectives noted above in the most efficient way for the ultimate consumer—your students. Early on, we conducted focus groups of instructors of consumer behavior to discuss the use of media technology in the classroom. We found that existing video series are sorely lacking in quality. You told us that you want something more than strings of broadcast commercials. You want to be able to show your students real-world applications of consumer behavior in action—the decisions ordinary consumers make every day. *We delivered.* You told us you preferred to stay away from corporate talking heads espousing the virtues of Fortune 500 companies. *We concurred.* Based on this feedback, we developed a prototype for the video series and conducted a second focus group at the Association for Consumer Research meeting a year later. You told us what you liked and what we could do better. You suggested ideal time frames, quantities, and concepts. *We responded.*

Having established criteria for the video component of the package, we set to work developing the manuscript. Once a first draft was complete, we bought together a group of professors at the Marketing Educator's Conference in San Francisco for a reviewer conference. Working with the authors and editors, the group poured over every page of the manuscript, praising its virtues and critiquing its weaknesses. For two days, we drank coffee, ate sandwiches, and debated, and at the end of the second day, we shook hands, compiled our notes, and went back to the drawing board and revised. We took your comments to heart, and we thank you for your candor and your guidance.

No market research is effective if it does not involve the ultimate consumer of the product. Through a series of focus groups on business disciplines, we turned to the ultimate user of our product—the student. We discussed pedagogy and design—what works and what doesn't, what draws attention and what is disregarded. We discovered some new ways of doing things—replacing the tired review questions at the end of each chapter with self-tests reminiscent of the type found on exams—and better ways of treating existing features—embedding boxed material more closely into the content of the text, adding definitions of key terms to the margin running glossary. Through these discussions, we feel that we have developed a pedagogically sound product that serves as both a source of information about consumer behavior and a teaching and learning tool for successfully completing a consumer behavior course.

## ▼ FEATURES OF THE INSTRUCTIONAL PACKAGE

Our package portrays consumers as individuals, as family members, as influential friends and neighbors; it depicts marketers, media executives, consumer activists, and government officials at work. It does so by extending the traditional focus on consumer behavior theories to integrate real consumers, marketers, and public policy actors into the discussion, in both the body of the text and the pedagogical elements described below.

**Consumer Snapshot**    Each chapter opens with a photo of a real consumer the authors have interviewed. The photo is accompanied by a brief autobiographical caption of the consumer—his or her name, age, occupation, marital status, and place of residence. These consumers are also featured in the accompanying video series.

**Eye on the Consumer**    Portions of the consumer interviews are recounted in chapter-opening vignettes. Eliot Spiegel describes the Harley subculture as a way of life. Trupti Niak chronicles her decision to major in mechanical engineering at the University of Minnesota. Dorothy Sinclair recounts her experience with credit card debt. These are real people, from across the country. They represent different demographic groups. They live their own lifestyles. And they are all consumers.

**Fact or Fiction**   The Consumer Snapshot is followed by a series of statements for the student to consider. The student must decide whether these statements are true or false—fact or fiction—based on his or her existing knowledge: Are David Letterman's Top Ten Lists considered a part of American culture? Does home shopping eliminate most of the situational influences on purchasing? Throughout the chapter, as these concepts are addressed, the Fact or Fiction statements are revisited and answers are provided.

**Chapter Objectives**   A numbered list of chapter objectives follows the Eye on the Consumer vignettes. These objectives identify the core concepts of the chapter, providing an overview of the key topics and preparing the student for the discussion.

**Thematic Boxes**   Three core themes are highlighted in anecdotal boxes throughout the text—the pleasures of consumption, the dark side of consumption, and public policy issues. The Pleasures of Consumption boxes cover such topics as the growing popularity of Christian music and the pleasures of exercise. The Dark Side of Consumption boxes grapple with such controversial issues as the portrayal of negative role models in the media: Do television programs like *NYPD Blue* portray too much sex and violence? Do movies like *The Program* encourage teenagers to imitate dangerous behavior? Are models like Kate Moss responsible for anorexic behavior in adolescent girls attempting to emulate the "waif" look? The Public Policy boxes take these concerns one step further and examine the ethical and moral implications of such issues and the role of local, national, and federal law makers in legislating against them. For example, one Public Policy box discusses FCC legislation of 800 numbers that aren't free of charge but imply that they are. Another questions the responsibility of marketers who distribute the popular children's game Pogs—Are these marketers encouraging gambling behavior in children? Do they have a responsibility to restrict the images portrayed on pogs and refuse to sell those that carry pornographic or satanic figures? Every box throughout the text concludes with a series of thought-provoking questions for the student to consider.

**Running Glossary**   Every boldfaced key term is called out and defined in the margin in a distinctive purple box, creating a running glossary throughout the text. These *key terms* are listed again at the end of the chapter, along with page references, so the student can find them easily in the body of the text when reviewing the material for exams.

**Summary**   Each chapter concludes with a narrative summary, broken down into the numbered objectives posited at the beginning of the chapter. Each of these chapter objectives is revisited and developed in the chapter summary, providing a detailed overview of the key points of the discussion.

**Skill-Building Activities**   End-of-chapter skill-building activities ask students to apply the concepts discussed in the text by completing an assignment, conducting an investigation, or defending the role of a consumer, a marketer, or a public policy advocate in a specific situation. The student may be asked to take the role of a government official interested in discouraging teenagers from smoking and to incorporate various learning processes to do so. Or, the student may be asked to watch an hour of evening network television and count the number of violent acts that are shown and consider the effects this behavior has on consumers. Some of the activities can be conducted as in-class group projects, while others may be given as individual assignments.

**Self-Tests**   End-of-chapter self-tests provide sample test questions for students to use to prepare for exams. The questions are organized into multiple-choice, true-false, short answer, and application exercises reminiscent of the type students may be given in class. Answers to all self-test questions are included in the back of the book.

## ▼ THE ILLUSTRATION PROGRAM

In keeping with the modern, cutting edge feel of the text, we selected an art studio to generate the dynamic three-dimensional illustrations featured throughout the pages of this book. Thunderbolt Graphics delivered an art program that is as bold and vibrant as the discipline of consumer behavior itself and the countless examples we encounter every day. Complementing these dynamic illustrations is a collection of striking print advertisements and storyboards. These ads have been selected to enhance the textual discussion by visually delineating the concepts introduced in the text; none are extraneous or incidental. Together with the editors, illustrators, and photo researchers, we have succeeded in developing an art program that uniquely complements this text and facilitates the education of today's visual learners.

## ▼ ORGANIZATION OF THE BOOK

The organization of this book is rather unique. We have organized the chapters into four parts—an Introduction, Background Characteristics, Behavioral Processes, and Consumer Behavior and Marketing. The *Introduction* presents the framework we have used to organize our discussion of consumer behavior. In the first chapter, we provide an overview of consumer behavior by discussing the roles played by consumers, marketers, and public policy actors. In the second chapter, we furnish a framework for the analysis of consumer behavior which emphasizes the *background characteristics* on which consumer markets are segmented and the *behavioral processes* consumers use to complete their purchase processes. In the third chapter, we focus on marketers. We review the basics of marketing strategy—segmentation, positioning, and marketing mix—and the vital role analysis of consumer behavior plays in formulating marketing strategies.

Part 2, *Background Processes,* introduces the most common background characteristics on which consumers may be segmented. This part includes chapters on culture and values; demographic subcultures; personality, lifestyle, and psychographics, and reference groups, communities, and families.

Part 3, *Behavioral Processes,* presents the behavioral tools consumers use to complete the purchases process—motivation, perception, learning, attitude formation, and decision making. We present background characteristics before behavioral processes because marketers and public policy actors segment markets on the basis of these characteristics and then examine the different ways consumers in distinct segments use the processes. Chrysler might distinguish between men and women because they have different attitudes towards minivans, for example, while the Federal Trade Commission monitors advertisements aimed at children more closely than those targeted at adults because children's perceptual and learning skills are less developed.

Finally, in Part 4, *Consumer Behavior and Marketing,* we consider the application of consumer behavior insights to some key consumer and marketing activities. The chapters included in this section discuss purchase and usage behavior, on the part of the consumer; forms of marketing communication, including integrated marketing communications; the effects of interpersonal communication and opinion leadership on consumer behavior; and new product planning, on the part of the marketer.

## ▼ TEACHING AND LEARNING PACKAGE

**Video Library**   This textbook comprises just one component of an entire package designed to enhance teaching and learning. The book itself is packed with relevant information, useful concepts, real-world case histories, and skill-building activities. Regardless of how eloquently we present written examples, however, visually observing activities can provide insights that can't be captured in any other way. Accordingly, we have developed a video library consisting of over 50 video segments selected from more than 40 hours of interviews with real consumers. While students are, naturally, acquainted with their own behavior as consumers, they have little first-hand contact with consumers whose behavior is different from their own or with the marketing activities that produce advertising and retail sales efforts.

Our video segments are significantly different from the "talking heads" of television news commentators or the promotional films of national marketers. We have conducted the interviews and shot the video footage ourselves in six different geographic areas around the country. In doing so, we are able to bring you examples of consumers in their natural settings. We take you into their homes, their histories, their lifestyles. We show you why some consumers elect to join health clubs; how television advertising affects certain people and not others; why some people feel violence on television should be regulated by the government; how having children has changed the consumption habits of a young couple . . . the topics are endless. *This* is consumer behavior.

**DDB Needham Lifestyle Survey**   An important component of consumer behavior is lifestyle analysis—How does a consumer's lifestyle affect his or her consumption patterns? Do people with similar lifestyles have similar consumption habits? DDB Needham Advertising is famous for its Lifestyle Survey, developed by former Director of Research and co-author of this text, William D. Wells. Portions of this survey are available on disk. Instructors can have their students complete the lifestyle survey and tally the results for their class using the software provided. These results can then be compared to the national average to assess the similarities and differences among the populations.

**Additional Supplements** This teaching and learning package includes a number of other important ancillaries. Each of these suppements is a vital component of a sound teaching and learning system that provides information and insight about real consumers, marketers, and outsiders.

Written by Larry Anderson, of Long Island University—Post, the *Instructor's Manual* includes sections on historical foundations of consumer behavior theories, additional references, and a description of the lifestyle survey and guidelines for implementing it in class. In addition, each text chapter is broken down into a chapter outline, a summary, tips for implementing the skill-building activities in class, and additional group activities.

A *Video Guide* is available, corresponding to the four hour-long tapes that make up the *Consumer Behavior* video series. Written by Lara Carls-Lissick, who videotaped the consumer interviews, the video guide contains written transcripts of all of the interviews contained in the text as well as previewing questions for classroom discussion; summaries of the consumer profiles, along with text page references; and suggestions for how to incorporate the videos in class.

Prepared by Dorothy Ranson of Wichita State University, who contributed the self-tests found at the end of each chapter, the *Test Bank* contains between 75 and 80 multiple choice, 20 true-false, 3 to 4 short answer, and one application question per chapter. The multiple-choice questions are identified as either factual or applied. Those questions identified by an asterisk are adapted from the self-tests found in the text; the remainder of the questions are brand new. The test bank is also available in a computerized version, MICROTEST, for use on IBM compatible computers running on MS-DOS.

All of the full-color line drawings from the text are available as transparency acetates. Black-and-white *transparency masters* of the figures are also included in the back of the instructor's manual. For your reference, Wiley also has a Web site (www.wiley.com). We invite you to visit our site and watch for additional information and announcements.

▼ TO THE STUDENT

Consumer behavior texts cover a wide range of approaches and expository styles. Some attempt to provide an exhaustive reference to all the theories academic consumer researchers use in their work. Others provide an abridged reference to the key theories and adopt a more approachable style. Whether the treatment of theory is exhaustive or abridged, the focus tends to be more on the theory than on the behavior of actual consumers.

This book is our attempt to provide you with another alternative. Instead of offering a condensed version of the exhaustive reference works, we have at-

# BRIEF CONTENTS

**PART ONE**
Chapter 1

**INTRODUCTION**
An Introduction to Consumer Behavior, 1

Chapter 2

A Framework for the Study of Consumer
Behavior, 35

Chapter 3

Marketers and Consumer Behavior, 65

**PART TWO**
Chapter 4

**BACKGROUND CHARACTERISTICS**
Culture and Vision, 99

Chapter 5

Demographic Subcultures, 129

Chapter 6

Personality, Lifestyle, and Psychographics, 169

Chapter 7

Reference Groups, Communities,
and Families, 199

**PART THREE**
Chapter 8

**BEHAVIORAL PROCESSES**
Consumer Motivation and Needs, 225

Chapter 9

Perception, 255

Chapter 10

Learning, 285

Chapter 11

Attitude Formation and Change, 311

Chapter 12

Consumer Decision Making, 341

Chapter 13

High and Low Involvement Decision Making, 371

**PART FOUR**

Chapter 14

**CONSUMER BEHAVIOR
AND MARKETING**
Purchase and Usage Behavior, 395

Chapter 15

Marketing Communication, 425

Chapter 16

Interpersonal Communication and Opinion
Leadership, 455

Chapter 17

New Product Planning, 483

# CONTENTS

▼ CHAPTER 1
AN INTRODUCTION TO
CONSUMER BEHAVIOR                                  *1*

Fact or Fiction?, *1*
Eye on the Consumer, *2*
**What is Consumer Behavior?,** *4*
   Consumers, *5*
   Exchange, *5*
   Products that Satisfy a Need, *7*
**An Approach to the Analysis of Consumer
Behavior,** *8*
**Consumer Behavior Actors,** *9*
   Consumers, *10*
*The Dark Side of Consumption: Life Imitates
Entertainment, 12*
   Marketers, *13*
   Public Policy Actors, *17*
**Watching Television as Consumer Behavior,** *22*
*Public Policy: NYPD Blue: Sex and Violence
on Television, 23*
**Public Policy Issues and Ethics,** *24*
   Areas of Public Policy, *25*
**Consumer Behavior and Its Multiple
Perspectives,** *26*
   Psychology, *27*
   Economics, *28*
   Sociology, *28*
   Organizational Behavior, *29*

**Consumer Behavior Actors and Perspectives,** *29*
**Summary,** *30*
**Key Terms,** *31*
**Skill-Building Activities,** *31*
**Self-Test,** *32*

▼ CHAPTER 2
A FRAMEWORK FOR THE STUDY OF
CONSUMER BEHAVIOR                                 *35*

Fact or Fiction?, *35*
Eye on the Consumer, *36*
**Consumer Purchase Activities,** *37*
   Recognize Needs, *37*
   Search for Alternatives, *40*
   Evaluate Alternatives, *40*
   Purchase and Use the Product, *40*
   Evaluate the Consumption Experience, *41*
   Provide Feedback, *43*
   End the Consumer Purchase Process, *43*
**Variations in Purchase Behavior,** *44*
   Consumer Background Characteristics, *45*
   Behavioral Processes, *46*
**Consumer Background Characteristics,** *46*
   Demographics, *48*
   Personality, Lifestyle, and Psycho graphics, *50*
*The Pleasures of Consumption: The Pleasures
of Exercise, 51*
   Reference Groups, *52*

**Behavioral Processes,** *53*
    Motivation, *53*
    Perception, *54*
*Public Policy: Aren't 1-800 Numbers Free?, 54*
    Learning, *56*
    Attitude Formation, *56*
    Decision Making, *58*
**Using the Key Components to Analyze Consumer Behavior,** *59*
**Summary,** *59*
**Key Terms,** *60*
**Skill-Building Activities,** *60*
**Self-Test,** *61*

▼ CHAPTER 3
MARKETERS AND CONSUMER BEHAVIOR    *65*

Fact or Fiction?, *65*
Eye on the Consumer, *66*
**The Role of Consumer Behavior in Marketing Strategy,** *67*
    Components of a Marketing Strategy, *68*
    The Benefits of Using Consumer Behavior in a Marketing Strategy, *70*
**Market Segmentation,** *71*
*Public Policy: When Does Segmentation Become Discrimination?, 72*
    What is Segmentation?, *73*
    The Results of Segmentation, *74*
    Selecting Target Market Segments, *79*
    How Marketers Use Consumer Behavior to Segment Markets, *80*
    Segmentation Strategy, *83*
**Product Positioning and the Marketing Mix,** *87*
    Product Positioning, *87*
*Pleasures of Consumption: It's Fun to Have a Party with a Friend, 88*
    The Marketing Mix, *90*
**Marketers, Consumer Behavior, and Marketing Strategies,** *93*
**Summary,** *94*
**Key Terms,** *95*
**Skill Building Activities,** *95*
**Self-Test,** *96*

▼ CHAPTER 4
CULTURE AND VISION    *99*

Fact or Fiction?, *99*
Eye on the Consumer, *100*

**Culture,** *101*
    The Nature of Culture, *101*
    Subcultures, *104*
    Consumption of Culture, *105*
*Pleasures of Consumption: Selling Christianity, 107*
**International Marketing Strategies,** *113*
    Cultural Similarities, *114*
    Cultural Differences, *114*
    Segmentation Strategies in the International Market, *115*
    Cross-Cultural Analysis, *117*
**Core Values and Their Measurement,** *120*
    The Research Value Survey, *121*
    The List of Values (LOV) Approach, *121*
    American Core Values, *122*
*Public Policy: The Wal-Mart Story, 123*
**Culture, Values, and Subcultures,** *124*
**Summary,** *124*
**Key Terms,** *125*
**Skill-Building Activities,** *125*
**Self-Test,** *126*

▼ CHAPTER 5
DEMOGRAPHIC SUBCULTURES    *129*

Fact or Fiction?, *129*
Eye on the Consumer, *130*
**The Bases of Demographic Differences,** *131*
    Tangible Attributes, *132*
    Intangible Attributes, *132*
**Gender,** *134*
    The Female Market, *134*
    The Male Market, *136*
**Age,** *136*
    Children, *138*
*Public Policy: Kids and Their Pogs, 138*
    Generation X, *139*
    Baby Boomers, *141*
    The Mature Market, *143*
**Race and Ethnicity,** *144*
    The African-American Market, *145*
    The Hispanic Market, *147*
    The Asian-American Market, *148*
**Religion,** *149*
**Social Class,** *150*
**Geography,** *152*
    Geodemographics, *153*
**Household Characteristics,** *154*
    Family Life Cycle, *157*
    The Gay Market, *161*

**Public Policy and Demographic Subcultures,** *162*

*Dark Side of Consumption: College Drinking, 163*

**Summary,** *165*

**Key Terms,** *165*

**Skill Building Activities,** *165*

**Self-Test,** *166*

▼ CHAPTER 6
PERSONALITY, LIFESTYLE, AND PSYCHO-
GRAPHICS                                              *169*

Fact or Fiction?, *169*

Eye on the Consumer, *170*

**Personality, Lifestyle, and Psychographics,** *171*

**Personality,** *172*

   Personality Traits and Types, *173*

**Theories of Personality,** *174*

   Freudian Theory and the Development of
   Personality, *174*

   Trait Theories and Personality Types, *179*

   The Self-Concept, *182*

**Lifestyle and Psychographics,** *185*

**Lifestyle and Psychographic Approaches,** *188*

   Activities, Interest and Opinions, *188*

*Pleasures of Consumption: Citizen Environmentalists, 189*

   VALS, *190*

**Public Policy, Lifestyle, and Psychographics,** *191*

*Public Policy: Is Your Lifestyle Private, 192*

**Background Characteristics, Lifestyle, and Psycho-
graphics,** *192*

**Summary,** *193*

**Key Terms,** *194*

**Skill Building Activities,** *194*

**Self-Test,** *195*

▼ CHAPTER 7
REFERENCE GROUPS, COMMUNITIES, AND
FAMILIES                                              *199*

Fact or Fiction?, *199*

Eye on the Consumer, *200*

**Why Select a Reference Group?,** *201*

   The Role of Groups in Consumer Socialization, *203*

*Pleasures of Consumption: Consumption
Communities, 206*

**Types of Reference Groups,** *207*

   Group Dimension, *207*

**The Influence of Reference Groups,** *211*

   Bases of Influence, *211*

   Influential Types of Reference Group, *212*

   Does Reference Group Influence Vary By
   Product?, *216*

**The Family as Reference Group,** *217*

**Public Policy: Television Advertising and
Children,** *219*

**Reference Groups,** *220*

**Summary,** *221*

**Key Terms,** *221*

**Skill Building Activities,** *221*

**Self-Test,** *222*

▼ CHAPTER 8
CONSUMER MOTIVATION AND NEEDS          *225*

Fact or Fiction?, *225*

Eye on the Consumer, *226*

**Motivation,** *227*

   Needs, *228*

   Goals, *229*

   Conflicting Goals, *232*

**Approaches to Consumer Motivation,** *236*

   Maslow's Hierarchy of Needs, *236*

**Identifying Consumer Benefits,** *239*

   Motivational Research, *239*

   Means-End Chains and Laddering, *242*

   Consumer Benefits and Marketing, *243*

*Pleasures of Consumption: Americans Love to Join, 243*

**Motivation and Levels of Involvement in Decision
Making,** *244*

**Do Marketers Create Needs?,** *246*

*Public Policy: Does Kate Moss Cause Anorexia?, 248*

   The Mirror Controversy, *248*

   Motivation, *249*

**Summary,** *250*

**List of Key Terms,** *250*

**Skill-Building Activities,** *251*

**Self-Test,** *252*

▼ CHAPTER 9
PERCEPTION                                            *255*

Fact or Fiction?, *255*

Eye on the Consumer, *256*

**Defining Perception,** *257*

*Pleasures of Consumption: The Magic Eye, 258*

**Perceptual Selection and Organization,** *260*

   Selective Perception, *262*

Organizing Input From the Senses, *265*
Perceptual Organization, *266*
*Public Policy: Don't Flatter These Marketers by Imitating Them!, 268*
Subliminal Perception, *269*
**Interpreting Marketing Imagery, 271**
Perceived Risk, *271*
Risk Reduction Strategies, *272*
Positioning and Brand Image, *275*
Perceived Quality, *276*
**Public Policy and Perception, 277**
Deceptive Advertising, *278*
Product Packaging and Labeling, *278*
**Selecting, Organizing, and Interpreting Stimuli, 279**
**Summary, 280**
**Key Terms, 281**
**Skill Building Activities, 281**
**Self-Test, 282**

▼ CHAPTER 10
LEARNING     *285*

Fact or Fiction?, *285*
Eye on the Consumer, *286*
**Learning, 287**
Characteristics of Learning, *288*
*Public Policy: How Much Alcohol in That Beer?, 290*
**Behavioral Learning Theory, 290**
Classical Conditioning, *291*
Instrumental Conditioning, *294*
The Reinforcement Schedule, *295*
**Cognitive Learning Theory, 296**
Information Processing and Memory, *296*
Storing and Organizing Knowledge, *297*
Retrieving Knowledge, *298*
**Marketing Applications of Consumer Learning, 300**
Rewards, *301*
*Dark Side of Consumption: The Rewards of Gambling, 301*
Repetition, *302*
Stimulus Generalization and Discrimination, *302*
Experience, *303*
Signs and Symbols, *303*
**Public Policy and Information, 304**
Unlearning—The Effectiveness of Warning Labels, *304*
**Learning, 306**
**Summary, 306**
**Key Terms, 308**
**Skill Building Activities, 308**
**Self-Test, 308**

▼ CHAPTER 11
ATTITUDE FORMATION AND CHANGE     *311*

Fact or Fiction?, *311*
Eye on the Consumer, *312*
**Attitude Formation, 313**
Attitudes Are Learned, *313*
The Functions of Attitudes, *314*
**Attitude Models, 319**
Tricomponent Attitude Models, *319*
Multiattribute Models, *321*
Attitude-Toward-the-Ad Models, *325*
**Measuring Attitudes, 325**
Observation, *326*
Qualitative Investigations, *326*
Attitude Scales, *327*
**Changing Consumer Attitudes, 328**
Attitude Consistency, *328*
Influencing Consumers' Attitudes, *329*
*Dark Side of Consumption: Don't Kill the Dolphins for a Tuna Sandwich, 331*
**Public Policy and Attitude Change, 332**
*Public Policy: Cloth or Disposable Diapers?, 334*
**Attitudes, 335**
**Summary, 336**
**List of Key Terms, 337**
**Skill Building Activities, 337**
**Self-Test, 338**

▼ CHAPTER 12
CONSUMER DECISION MAKING     *341*

Fact or Fiction?, *341*
Eye on the Consumer, *342*
**Levels of Decision Making, 343**
Influences on the Level of Decision Making, *344*
Extensive Decision Making, *345*
Limited Decision Making, *347*
Routine Decision Making, *347*
**The Decision Making Process, 347**
**Search for Alternatives, 349**
Sources of Information, *349*
Types of Search Activities, *351*
*Public Policy: Campus Crime, 352*
The Results of Search, *353*
**Evaluation of Alternatives, 354**
Evaluative Criteria, *354*
Decision Rules, *356*
**Marketers' Influence on the Decision Making Process, 361**

Search for Alternatives, *362*
Evaluation of Alternatives, *362*

**Public Policy and Decision Making,** *364*

*Public Policy: Do You Know What You're Eating?,* *365*
Consumer Decision Making, *366*

**Summary,** *366*

**Key Terms,** *367*

**Tasks and Activities,** *367*

**Self-Test,** *368*

▼ CHAPTER 13
HIGH AND LOW INVOLVEMENT
DECISION MAKING                    *371*

Fact or Fiction?, *371*

Eye on the Consumer, *372*

**Motivation and Involvement,** *373*
Factors that Affect Involvement, *374*
The Effects of Involvement, *377*

**High Involvement Purchases,** *378*
Recognize Needs, *378*
Search for Alternatives, *379*

*Public Policy: What* Does *a Car Cost?,* *380*
Evaluate Alternatives, *381*
Purchase and Use the Product, *381*
Evaluate the Consumption Experience, *381*
Provide Feedback, *382*
End the Consumption Process, *384*

**Low Involvement Purchases,** *385*
Recognize Needs, *385*
Search for Alternatives, *386*
Evaluate Alternatives, *386*
Purchase and Use the Product, *387*

*Pleasures of Consumption: Trade in Your Coffee for a Soft*
*Drink at Breakfast,* *389*
Evaluate the Consumption Experience, *389*
Provide Feedback, *389*
End the Consumption Process, *390*

**Involvement and Decision Making,** *390*

**Summary,** *391*

**Key Terms,** *391*

**Skill Building Activities,** *392*

**Self-Test,** *392*

▼ CHAPTER 14
PURCHASE AND USAGE BEHAVIOR        *395*

Fact or Fiction?, *395*

Eye on the Consumer, *396*

**Activities in Purchase and Usage Behavior,** *397*

**Influences on Purchase and Usage Activities,** *398*
Situational Influences, *399*

*Dark Side of Consumption: What's My Credit Line?,* *400*
How Marketers Influence the Situation, *404*
Usage Influences, *405*

*Public Policy: Don't Drink and Drive!,* *407*

**Post-Purchase Activities,** *409*
Preparing to Buy Again, *409*
Consumer Satisfaction or Dissatisfaction, *411*
Product Disposal, *417*
Purchase and Usage Behavior, *419*

**Summary,** *420*

**Key Terms,** *421*

**Skill Building Activities,** *421*

**Self-Test,** *422*

▼ CHAPTER 15
MARKETING COMMUNICATION           *425*

Fact or Fiction?, *425*

Eye on the Consumer, *426*

**The Communication Process,** *427*
Source, *428*
Message, *429*
Medium, *429*
Receiver, *431*
Feedback, *431*

**Two Perspectives on Consumers,** *432*
The Hierarchy of Effects Model, *432*
The Brand Experience Perspective, *434*

**Integrated Marketing Communications,** *436*
Advertising, *437*
Direct Response, *438*

*Pleasures of Consumption: 30-Second Ads Bore, 30-Minute*
*Informercials Entertain,* *439*
Publicity, *440*
Personal Selling, *442*

**Strategies for Effective Marketing**
**Communication,** *442*
Message Strategy, *443*
Media Strategy, *447*

**Public Policy and Marketing Communications,** *448*
Fairness, *448*

*Public Policy: Was that an Ad?,* *449*
Equity, *449*

**Marketing Communication,** *450*

**Summary,** *450*

**Key Terms,** *451*

**Skill-Building Activities,** *452*

**Self-Test,** *452*

▼ CHAPTER 16
INTERPRESONAL COMMUNICATION AND
OPINION LEADERSHIP                               *455*

Fact or Fiction?, *455*

Eye on the Consumer, *456*

**Interpersonal Communication,** *457*

**Word-of-Mouth Communication,** *457*
  Information Content, *458*
  The Receiver's Purpose, *458*
  The Source's Purpose, *459*
  Source Credibility, *459*

*Pleasures of Consumption: Saturn Dealers Treat Customers Right?, 461*
  Type of Communication Partner, *461*
  Type of Product, *462*

**Theories of the Flow of Communication,** *464*
  The Two-Step Theory of Communication, *464*
  The Multistep Theory of Communication, *465*

**Opinion Leadership,** *466*
  Authorities, *467*
  Trend Setters, *468*
  Local Opinion Leaders, *468*

**Measuring Opinion Leadership,** *469*
  The Self-Designating Method, *469*
  The Key Informant Method, *471*
  The Sociometric Method, *471*

**How Marketers Use Interpersonal Communication,** *473*

*Public Policy: Why Did You Recommend That?, 474*
  Creating Word-of-Mouth and Opinion Leaders, *474*
  Simulating Word-of-Mouth and Opinion Leadership, *475*

**Consumer Gather Information From One Another,** *477*

**Summary,** *477*

**Key Terms,** *478*

**Skill-Building Activities,** *478*

**Self-Test,** *479*

▼ CHAPTER 17
NEW PRODUCT PLANNING                               *483*

Fact or Fiction?, *483*

Eye on the Consumer, *484*

**Types of New Product Innovations,** *485*
  Dimensions of Innovation, *486*
  Continuous Innovations, *487*
  Dynamically Continuous Innovations, *487*
  Discontinuous Innovations, *489*

**The Diffusion of an Innovation in a Market,** *489*
  Categories of Adopters, *489*
  Marketers' View of Diffusion, *491*

**The Adoption Process,** *492*
  Traditional Models of the Adoption Process, *492*
  Rogers' Model of the Adoption Process, *493*
  Factors that Affect Adoption, *495*

*Pleasures of Consumption: Window Shop Before Buying, 497*

**Barriers to Adoption,** *498*
  Usage, *499*
  Value, *499*
  Risk, *501*
  Psychological Barriers, *501*

*Public Policy: Fill...I Mean Charge It Up, 501*

**Consumers and New Products,** *502*

**Summary,** *503*

**Key Terms,** *504*

**Skill-Building Activities,** *504*

**Self-Test,** *505*

**Answers to Self-Tests,** *AN-1*

**Glossary,** *G-1*

**Footnotes,** *F-1*

**Illustration Credits,** *IC-1*

**Photo Credits,** *PC-1*

**Company Index,** *CI-1*

**Name Index,** *NI-1*

**Subject Index,** *SI-1*

# 1

# AN INTRODUCTION TO CONSUMER BEHAVIOR

◉ Consumer Snapshot   *Barbara Hawkins is a 66-year-old homemaker living in Denver, Colorado, with her husband, Bill. She is the mother of five grown children, Janice, 43, Nancy, 42, Douglas, 40, Mary Ann, 36, and Brian, 29.*

## FACT OR FICTION?

◉   Most consumer behavior involves purchases.

◉   Selling is the central concept in consumer marketing.

◉   Products can be tangible or intangible.

◉   Most consumers are affected by the dark side of consumer behavior.

◉   "Let the buyer beware" is also knows as "the marketing concept."

◉   Large businesses, small businesses, nonprofit organizations, and government agencies all employ the marketing concept.

◉  When you watch a television program, you are exchanging something of value for something you need.

◉  Public policy debate focuses on the effects of consumer behavior on the larger society.

◉  Economists assume that consumers use information to make rational choices that satisfy their needs.

## EYE ON THE CONSUMER

Barb Hawkins was watching the news on television and saw a report on a new chip that could be included in television sets to allow parents to program their sets to prevent their kids from watching shows that contain too much violence. The broadcasters would have to label programs containing violence, and the chip would automatically prevent children from watching those shows even when their parents aren't home. It's certainly a different world than when Barb's children were young, she thought. She remembered when she began to notice that the kids were hitting each other more than they used to—poking their fingers in each others' eyes and slamming each others' heads. She realized that they were imitating *The Three Stooges*, which was one of their favorite shows. So she didn't let them watch the *Stooges* anymore and, after a month or so, they stopped poking and slamming each other nearly so much. And when she and her husband decided to buy cable television service, her 14-year-old son started to watch a lot of MTV. Barb didn't like the immorality and sexual content of the music videos he was watching, so they canceled their cable subscription.

Barb doesn't like the idea of censorship, though—she considers it just another example of the government regulating everything and infringing on personal choices. She feels that television stations should police what they broadcast and that parents should exercise their parental authority and choose the programs and movies their children watch. Maybe more parents need to know about the effects of violence and sex on television on their kids' behavior; then they won't let them watch those kind of programs. On the other hand, a device that makes it easier for parents to prevent their children from viewing what they shouldn't see might be a good idea too.

This book has been written with two objectives in mind. The first is to help you analyze any instance of consumer behavior in two ways—(1) by identifying the relevant consumer behavior *concepts*, and (2) by applying them to your *analysis* of the behavior. The second objective of this book is a more personal one: This book is intended to help you get an "A" in this course. We offer some hints about how to use the book to achieve both of these objectives in the box entitled "How to Get an 'A' in This Course" on page 3.

To become a skilled analyst of consumer behavior, you must first be able to identify all of the actors who have a role in the consumer purchase process and then apply perspectives that will give you insight into their behavior.

After reading and thinking about this chapter, you should be able to:

1. Analyze the roles that consumers, marketers, and public policy actors play.
2. Recognize the needs that motivate consumers to buy and use products.
3. Identify the consumers for whom consumption can be harmful and examine the effects of that consumption on other consumers.
4. Determine the tools that marketers use to influence consumers' behavior.
5. Identify the impact of public policy actors on consumers and marketers.
6. Examine the fairness, equity, safety, and social implications of a consumer behavior problem.
7. Apply the perspective of each discipline to your analysis of a consumer behavior problem.

## How to Get an "A" in This Course

You have chosen to take this course and bought this textbook to help you meet a need: You want to learn about consumer behavior. If you are like most students, however, you also want to get an "A" in this course. As good marketers, we want to help you satisfy both of these needs. We have designed this book with a number of features to help you to master the material and earn an "A."

We believe that the only way for you to learn the key *concepts* of consumer behavior is to apply them to the *analysis* of consumer problems. That is, to truly master the key concepts of consumer behavior, you must apply the concepts to develop the analytic skills you use to understand the real behavior of consumers, marketers, and public policy actors. To help you integrate knowledge and application, each chapter contains the following features:

- **Fact or fiction statements** appear in the beginning of each chapter to give you the opportunity to test your prior knowledge of the concepts that are presented. Each statement will be identified as "fact" or "fiction" at the point in the chapter where the concept is introduced.
- **Opening vignettes** entitled "Eye on the Consumer" describe the behavior of an actual consumer in the context of the topic of the chapter. By beginning with a real-world example of consumer behavior for you to analyze, you will see a reason to learn the concepts. It is much easier to learn concepts when you know *why* you are learning them.

- **Chapter objectives** describe the *analytic skills* you will use to understand consumer behavior. Each of these skills is based on a key concept from the chapter.
- A **running glossary** in the margin of the text is provided to draw your attention to the key concepts necessary for understanding consumer behavior. These glossary terms can serve as a useful study guide for quizzing yourself on the definitions of key terms and concepts.
- Three types of **embedded boxes** provide current real-world applications of key concepts on the following topics (1) public policy, (2) the pleasures of consumption, and (3) the dark side of consumption. The boxes are embedded both in design and application to the textual discussion. Each concludes with a series of thought-provoking questions concerning your own opinions and thoughts on these issues.
- A chapter-ending **summary** of the objectives of the chapter reviews the major points of the chapter and shows how the concepts are used by consumer analysts to understand the behavior of consumers, marketers, and public policy actors.
- **Skill building activities** at the end of each chapter require you to apply what you have learned about consumer behavior concepts and analysis to real-world assignments. The tasks ask you to assume the role of consumers, marketers, or public policy actors so that you can gain firsthand experiences of consumer behavior.
- Chapter-ending **self-tests** give you the opportunity to verify the knowledge you have gained about the material presented in the chapter and help you prepare for examinations by answering multiple-choice, true–false, short answer, and applications questions related to the chapter material.

# What Is Consumer Behavior?

" Consumer behavior" encompasses a wide variety of actions and reactions. You buy a bottle of Dawn dishwashing detergent or pay another student to tutor you in calculus. You look at a variety of cars with your parents in order to convince them to make the down payment on a Saturn as an early graduation present. You complain to the Saturn dealer when the car breaks down after only three days. You browse through the edition of *Rolling Stone* magazine you bought yesterday or turn on the Fox network to watch *Melrose Place* while you avoid doing your marketing homework Monday night (Figure 1.1). The common element of all of these activities is that they are part of the wide variety of steps that surround the purchase and consumption of a physical good or something less tangible, such as a service or an idea.

■ FIGURE 1.1
Watching television is a form of consumer behavior.

The discipline of **consumer behavior** is the study of *consumers* as they *exchange* something of value for a *product or service that satisfies their needs*. You can think of consumer behavior as the study of the processes involved in selecting, purchasing, using, evaluating, and disposing of products and services that will satisfy a person's needs. It includes the ways in which (1) consumers decide to spend their time and money to buy and consume products and services that will satisfy their needs; (2) marketers try to offer products and services that will satisfy consumers so that they will buy from them; and (3) public policy actors try to influence consumers, marketers, and the laws and regulations that affect consumers and marketers.

> **Consumer behavior** is the study of consumers as they exchange something of value for a product or service that satisfies their needs.

## FACT OR FICTION REVISITED

◉    It is *not true* that most consumer behavior involves purchases. Consumer behavior includes browsing, influencing others, using the product, returning the product or complaining, if necessary, disposing of the product, reading magazines and watching television, and many other activities.

## ▼ CONSUMERS

Consumers are the key element in consumer behavior. Consumers *recognize* that they have needs; *search* for a product that can meet their needs; *use* the product to satisfy their needs; and then *dispose* of the product once it has met their needs. To understand consumer behavior, we must first comprehend how consumers complete each of these activities. In doing so, there are a number of fields that focus on human activities at our disposal, including psychology, economics, sociology, and anthropology. Throughout this book, we will present insights from all of these fields to help deepen your understanding of the activities in which consumers participate to satisfy their needs.

## ▼ EXCHANGE

*Exchange* is the central concept in consumer behavior and marketing.[1] Imagine a world in which you could satisfy all of your own needs by yourself. As soon as you recognize a need—say a weekend in an exotic destination—you would produce whatever is necessary to satisfy the need without expending any time or effort— transportation to the French Riviera (Figure 1.2). There would be no reason to

■  FIGURE 1.2

Taking a vacation is a need that is satisfied through the generalized exchange of money for transportation, hotel accommodations, and anything else that provides the consumer with the vacation.

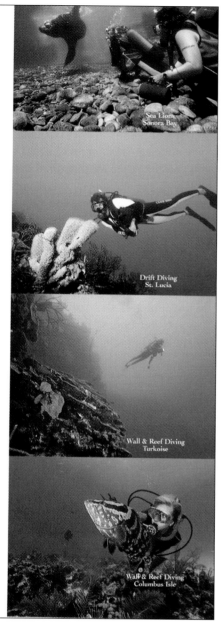

search for alternative ways to satisfy your need—such as comparing airlines, talking with a travel agent, or researching the best place to go; to decide which of the alternatives is most appealing—a bustling city or a secluded island; or to buy and use that alternative to satisfy your need—a first-class plane ticket and a reservation in a four-star French hotel. In reality, however, you can't produce all of the things that you need by yourself, so you look to "the market" for others from whom you can get them.

To get what you need from others, you exchange things that will help them satisfy *their* needs, such as time or money. You might exchange something that takes your time to produce for something that someone else has created. For example, if you are good at repairing cars, you might spend some time repairing a friend's failing transmission in exchange for her building bookshelves for your apartment. This trading, or bartering, requires that you have something specific that your friend wants from you. Since this is unlikely most of the time, you more typically use *generalized exchange*, which gives you the freedom to offer something that is valuable to everyone. Money is such a generalized exchange medium. Money allows you to buy products that will satisfy your needs without having to provide a specific item in exchange. It also enables marketers to specialize in a kind of product that meets a particular need without having to require a specific item in return from consumers. The relationship is simple: You pay money for the things that you purchase, and the marketers from whom you purchase can use your money to exchange with others who can meet their needs. That is, you pay marketers, who then pay the firms that supply them with raw materials.

## FACT OR FICTION REVISITED

◉ Selling is not the central concept in consumer marketing; exchange is the central concept.

▼ PRODUCTS THAT SATISFY A NEED

A **product** is anything that satisfies a need, be it tangible or intangible. The most tangible products are physical goods, such as sodas, computers, and cars, which you use or consume to satisfy your needs. You buy a can of Pepsi because you are thirsty; an Apple Powerbook because you need to write a number of papers for history class; or a Hyundai Excel so you can travel to see your girlfriend on the weekends. There are also less tangible products that satisfy consumer needs. These include (1) people, (2) places, (3) events, (4) ideas, and (5) services. These kinds of products offer *experiences* that satisfy needs. Even though *people* and *places* are physical things, you don't actually buy them. But just the experience of watching Joe Montana throw a football or listening to Sting's latest CD gives you the opportunity to feel comfortable, entertained, or fulfilled. You might even buy memorabilia carrying an athlete's or musician's name or picture because they remind you of those feelings. *Places* offer the same kinds of feelings, so you travel to Paris to experience the feeling of romance it invokes in you.

*Events* are activities that satisfy needs by offering an experience. You can participate directly in an event, such as playing softball in a campus league, or you can observe an event, such as watching the Dallas Cowboys play the New York Giants on television. *Ideas* can also be satisfying by evoking feelings or providing you with knowledge that you use to meet your own needs. For example, you might support smokers' rights because Philip Morris and other cigarette marketers advertise ideas such as personal choice and individual liberties as part of their efforts to combat antismoking regulations. Or you might actively campaign for a gubernatorial candidate because you like her stands on crime and welfare reform (Figure 1.3). Finally, *services* are tasks performed by others that meets your needs, such as an accounting service that completes your income tax return. To simplify matters, we will use the term "product" to refer to *anything* that satis-

> A **product** is any object—whether a tangible, physical product, or an intangible object—that satisfies a consumer need.

■   FIGURE 1.3

A political candidate's stand on an issue reflects a consumer's ideas and may determine if the consumer will support that candidate.

fies a consumer need, whether it is a tangible, physical product, such as a Champion sweatshirt or a Jeep Cherokee, or something less tangible, such as a television program or a cleaning service.

### FACT OR FICTION REVISITED

◉   It is true that products can be tangible or intangible. Tangible products include inexpensive grocery and drug store items and expensive durables. Intangible products include a wide range of services.

## AN APPROACH TO THE ANALYSIS OF CONSUMER BEHAVIOR

This book adopts a specific approach to the analysis of consumer behavior. Throughout this text, we will analyze the actions of three types of actors—consumers, marketers, and public policy actors—and the roles they play. An individual or organization can play several roles at different times. One person can consume some products, market others, and have an interest in the public debate about all of these products. When you order cable television service, you are acting as a consumer, but when you complain to your mayor or city manager about the price of cable television service, you are taking the role of a public policy actor.

Several perspectives are available to help you analyze the actions of these actors. These come from (1) psychology, (2) economics, (3) sociology, (4) anthropology, and (5) organizational behavior. Each of these perspectives offers unique insights into the way humans behave, and combining these views will give you an even more accurate and complete understanding than can any one by itself.

If you only wanted to learn the *concepts* behind consumer behavior, you could just study the fields that provide perspectives on consumer behavior. And, although you should study those disciplines (and may even do so in your college curriculum), that would not be enough to learn how to *analyze* consumer behavior. In order to do so, you must *apply* those concepts to actual consumer behavior using the set of analytical skills you will learn throughout this course.

# CONSUMER BEHAVIOR ACTORS

Any complete analysis of consumer behavior must identify three types of **actors,** the most important of which are consumers. **Consumers** are the individuals that identify a need, buy and consume products or services to satisfy that need, and then dispose of the product or service when they are through with it. The definition of consumer behavior dictates a focus on consumers and the steps involved in consumer exchange. But consumer behavior also involves other parties whose actions affect consumer exchanges. **Marketers** are individuals or organizations that play a direct role in an exchange with consumers. Marketers are in business to satisfy the needs of consumers, and they do so in exchange for money from consumers. The local accountant you pay to complete your tax forms and the multibillion-dollar bank that loaned you the money to buy your car are both marketers.

Consumers and marketers also play the role of public policy actors at times. **Public policy actors** are individuals or organizations that are involved in the public debate about the activities of consumers and marketers. When you complain to your Congressperson about the price of cable television service, you are playing the role of a public policy actor. When the NBC television network sends its executives to testify at a Congressional hearing, it is acting as a public policy actor. Public policy actors have an interest in the way consumer exchanges are completed, even though they may not be directly involved in the exchange. Their interest stems from the fact that exchanges can affect others that are not directly involved in them. In addition to consumers and marketers, policy makers such as Congressional members and officials in the executive branch of government are

> An **actor** is an individual or organization that plays the role of consumer, marketer, or public policy interest.

> **Consumers** are individuals that identify a need, buy and consume products or services and then dispose of the product or terminate the service.

> **Marketers** are individuals or organizations that satisfy consumer needs in exchange for money.

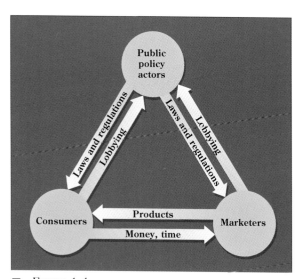

■ FIGURE 1.4

The relationship among consumers, marketers, and public policy actors.

**Public policy actors** are individuals or organizations that have an interest in the consequences and implications of the exchange of products or services between consumers and marketers.

**Organizational buying** is the consumer behavior that occurs in businesses, nonprofit organizations, or government bodies.

public policy actors. Figure 1.4 shows the relationship among the three types of actors involved in consumer behavior.

### ▼ CONSUMERS

Consumers can be individuals or groups of individuals. It then follows that some of your consumer behavior is individual—when you're sitting alone in your room looking for something to pass the time, you may choose to turn on the television and watch *Oprah Winfrey*—whereas other consumer behavior involves groups—if you are choosing a movie to go to this weekend, you would consult with the friends who are going with you; all of you would consider the movies that are showing nearby and reach a group decision.

Furthermore, the purchaser and consumer of a product may not be the same person. For example, you might purchase a gift for a friend or relative. Children often use everyday items, such as clothing and toys, that others have chosen for them. When you were a child, you might have told your mother and father what television programs or movies you wanted to see, but the decision was ultimately made by your parents. Similarly, most of the foods you ate and the clothes you wore as a young child were chosen by your parents. As shown in Figure 1.5, marketers often aim their ads at such decision makers. Even as adults, oftentimes one person in a household controls the choice of television programs that everyone watches.

In this book, we will focus on consumer behavior that involves the purchase of products for personal use or for the use of others with whom the buyer has a more personal relationship. Therefore, **organizational buying**—the consumer behavior that occurs in businesses; nonprofit organizations, such as churches, colleges, trade associations, and social action groups; or government bodies—is beyond the scope of this text. Although the individuals and groups that make up an organization actually make the decisions, they act as purchasing agents under the guidance of organizational procedures and acquire products for the organization as a whole. Much of what is purchased is for the use of others in the institution whom the purchasing agents may not even know. Your purchase of textbooks is an example of organizational buying. Although you actually purchase and read the texts, your professors make the decision about which books will be used in each course. In some large schools, a committee of professors chooses the book for a large introductory course, and individual professors may not know the students who are in other sections of the class.

**The Pleasures of Consumption and The Dark Side of Consumption**    Consumers recognize that they have needs, search for a product that can meet their needs, and then use that product to satisfy their needs. Some needs are biological, such as hunger and thirst, while others are psychological and social, such as self-esteem or peer approval. Using products provides benefits that satisfy consumers' needs—eating a peanut butter and jelly sandwich provides calories to ease hunger, and watching *Home Improvement* on television elicits emotional responses to entertainment. In other words, *satisfying needs gives consumers pleasure.*[2]

But for some consumers, there is a "dark side" to consumption. This dark side reflects obsessive consumption that can be harmful to the consumer, to those around him or her, or to society at large.[3] Consumption that is pleasurable to some people may be viewed quite differently by others. You may be able to eat wonderful desserts that give you great pleasure, but other people may suffer from serious health problems that are aggravated by eating that same rich cheesecake. You might enjoy watching television programs or movies that portray violence, like *NYPD Blue* or *Natural Born Killers* (Figure 1.6), but others may feel that the depiction of such violence in the media encourages violent behavior in real life.

# FACT OR FICTION REVISITED

◉    It is true that most consumers are affected by the dark side of consumer behavior. All products and services can be misused, and many are, in one way or another. And even consumers who do not misuse products or services must bear the costs of regulation.

■   FIGURE 1.6

The depiction of violence in the media is a public policy concern that reflects the dark side of consumer behavior. A prime example is the film *Natural Born Killers,* which was heavily criticized for its violent content.

The dark side of consumer behavior encompasses a small part of the consumption of many consumers and much of the consumption of a few consumers. Many of you recognize that some of your consumption is not what you would like it to be. You eat too many Hershey bars, or you don't save enough money, or you spend more of your time than you really want to watching *Beavis and Butthead* on MTV. While these are not particularly dark consumption habits, they could ultimately have serious consequences. If you continue to eat too many Hershey bars, you may become seriously overweight. If you don't save any money, you may end up in debt, losing your car or your home. If you watch MTV all evening the night before your marketing exam, you stand a good chance of failing it.

It is important to identify the dark side of consumption because it is often the reason that public policy actors become interested in a consumer behavior issue. Public policy actors do not usually object to the pleasures a consumer experiences from consuming a product. Instead, they object to a person's consumption if they view it as detrimental to the consumer or to the larger society. For example, the groups that condemn violence on television and in movies don't dispute the fact that watching violent programs gives pleasure to those who watch them. However, they feel that the programs also distort the viewer's perceptions of violence and make them more likely to commit violent acts themselves.

## THE DARK SIDE OF CONSUMPTION

### Life Imitates Entertainment[4]

On October 15, 1993, Mike Shingledecker watched his high school football team play and then went out with several of his friends to have some fun. Later that night, the boys lay down on the dividing line of a local highway as a test of their courage. When one car narrowly missed them, two of the boys got up, but Shingledecker and another buddy stayed on the road for another chance. The next vehicle struck both of them, killing Shingledecker. The teenagers had been imitating a scene depicted in the film *The Program*, in which college football players were shown lying down in the middle of a busy road as a test of their mental strength. In addition to Shingledecker, another teenager was killed and several others seriously wounded imitating the movie scene. Touchstone Pictures, a division of Disney, responded by removing the harrowing scene from the film.

On October 6, 1993, five-year-old Austin Messner set his bed afire with a cigarette lighter, burning down his house and killing his younger sister. Austin's mother had already removed his bedroom door so that she could keep an eye on him because he had started playing with fire after watching a prime-time episode of *Beavis and Butthead* which showed the cartoon characters playing with matches. In this instance, MTV agreed to remove the *Beavis and Butthead* cartoon from prime-time viewing hours and to show it only during a late-night time slot.

Very few teenagers who viewed *The Program* or children who watched *Beavis and Butthead* tried to imitate the things that they saw, and the marketers of these stories did not intend that they be imitated. Do you think that such dark side consumption is the responsibility of the few consumers who choose to imitate what they view or the marketers of the films and television programs that depict such behavior in the first place?

## ▼ MARKETERS

The underlying philosophy of marketing is the **marketing concept**, which states that a firm is in business to satisfy consumer needs and that the only way for a marketer to profit from its exchanges with consumers is by satisfying their needs.[5] This makes sense: If you buy a Sony Walkman that breaks after the first month, chances are, you won't buy another Sony Walkman. Of course, both you and the marketer would like every exchange to satisfy you as a consumer. Both of you would benefit in this case: You would avoid the need to search for another portable cassette player, and Sony would gain financially when you purchase another Walkman as a gift for your sister.

Unfortunately, the marketing concept doesn't tell marketers *how* to satisfy consumers. Consequently, marketers must *analyze* consumer behavior to learn what products will satisfy them. Indeed, the need of marketers to understand consumer behavior was the biggest impetus in the development of the field of consumer behavior. Throughout the first half of this century, marketers employed psychologists, economists, and sociologists to advise them about consumers. The field of consumer behavior grew out of the interaction among men and women trained in these fields as they tried to provide a comprehensive picture of what consumers really wanted. As we mentioned earlier, consumer behavior adopts the perspectives of many academic fields and continues to embrace new insights from many different sources.[6]

> The **marketing concept** states that a marketer must satisfy its consumers' needs in order to gain a long-term profit from its exchanges with those consumers.

## FACT OR FICTION REVISITED

⊙   "Let the buyer beware" is *not* also known as "the marketing concept." The marketing concept states that the only way to market for a profit is to satisfy consumers' needs.

## Table 1.1

### MARKETING STRATEGY ACTIVITIES

| Activity | Examples |
|---|---|
| Segment consumers and choose a set that can be satisfied | Proctor & Gamble chooses women as its target for Secret deodorant |
| | Gillette chooses men as its target for Right Guard |
| Design the product | Mercedes Benz designs its cars to be luxurious |
| | Hyundai designs its cars to be functional |
| Price the product | Rolex watches are high priced |
| | Times watches are low priced |
| Communicate about the product | Nabisco advertises Oreo cookies in magazines and on television |
| | The American Cancer Society appeals for donations through direct mail |
| Deliver the product | Compaq sells computers through retailers |
| | Dell sells computers directly to consumers by telephone |

**Marketing strategy** is the approach to satisfying a clearly defined set of consumers by designing a product that satisfies them, pricing it at a cost they will pay, communicating about the product with them, and delivering it to them. Defining the set of consumers who can be satisfied is called **market segmentation**, whereas the product design, pricing, communication, and delivery are called the **marketing mix**.

**Nonprofit organizations** are organizations that meet the needs of consumers but do not do so for a profit.

Once marketers understand the behavior of consumers, they must devise ways of satisfying them. Marketers refer to this step as developing a **marketing strategy**—an approach to satisfying a clearly defined set of consumers by designing a product that satisfies them, pricing it at a cost they will pay, communicating about the product with them, and delivering it to them. Defining the set of consumers who will be targeted is part of the **market segmentation** process. The product design, pricing, communication, and delivery are called the **marketing mix**. Table 1.1 shows some examples of marketing strategy activities, and we will discuss these activities in more detail in Chapter 3.

Many organizations and individuals play the role of marketer. The large, traditional marketing organizations are the most obvious examples. McDonald's, Nike, Federal Express, Sears, and NBC are all large organizations that market to consumers in an attempt to satisfy their needs (Figure 1.7); each organization might satisfy different kinds of needs, but they all exist for the same purpose. Many small businesses also play the role of marketer; the local convenience or video rental store are two examples. Some businesses represent both large and small marketers. The local McDonald's in your town, for example, could be a franchisee of the colossal national organization. The smallest businesses are individuals, perhaps an independent accountant or attorney.

Many other organizations meet the needs of consumers, but not for a profit. Colleges and universities are one example of such **nonprofit organizations;** charitable organizations, such as the American Cancer Society, are another. Nonprofit organizations often face a complex marketing task. An organization such as the American Cancer Society must satisfy the needs of its contributors so that

"My husband swears by their submersible pumps."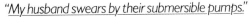

"But I prefer the suede ones."

Red suede pumps, $26

Come see the softer side of **SEARS**

■ FIGURE 1.7

Sears is an example of a large, traditional marketer that advertises its products as satisfying a number of consumer needs, from electronic appliances to children's clothes.

they feel that they are doing something worthwhile. At the same time, it must satisfy the public's need to learn healthy habits, such as quitting smoking.

## FACT OR FICTION REVISITED

◉ It is true that large businesses, small businesses, nonprofit organizations, and government agencies all employ the marketing concept. Examples include McDonald's, Nike, local retailers and professionals, the Public Broadcasting System, and regulatory agencies.

**Traditional Marketing Organizations** Traditional marketing organizations are those large firms that are prominent players on the corporate landscape. These firms have a long tradition that emphasizes marketing, and they have a clear marketing orientation.[7] Managers of such firms have worked hard to understand consumer needs and to develop products that satisfy those needs.[8] Marketing organizations often compete in many markets and therefore market many dif-

■ FIGURE 1.8

Nike's advertising has become so prominent and distinctive that much of it omits the company name altogether.

A **strategic business unit (SBU)** is a part of a large marketing firm that markets a set of homogeneous products to a set of homogeneous market segments.

ferent products to different kinds of consumers. Consequently, they have instituted formal planning processes to develop marketing strategies, to implement those strategies through the marketing mix, and to evaluate the success of the implemented strategies. Such firms spend significant amounts of money on consumer research and product development. They have established well-known brand names for themselves and promote these names through extensive advertising. For example, Nike's advertising is so prominent and distinctive that most people recognize a Nike ad without having to see the Nike name itself. In fact, some recent Nike ads do not use the company name at all; they just display the familiar company logo, as illustrated in Figure 1.8.

These large firms are also organized in a way that supports their emphasis on marketing. They are typically organized into **strategic business units (SBUs)** that market a set of homogeneous products to a set of homogeneous market segments. Obviously, "homogeneous" is a relative term. For instance, in television broadcasting, a firm might have different business units for news and sports because these two kinds of programming require different skills to deliver them and appeal to different viewers. The firm would not divide sports into separate units that focused on football, basketball, and baseball, however, because the viewers of those sports are typically similar to one another, as is their consumer behavior. Instead, each sport might have a different manager who is responsible for its specific programming and marketing.

**Small Businesses**   Small businesses are very common, particularly among the local retailers and professionals from whom you purchase goods and services. Figure 1.9 shows a newspaper advertisement from a local retailer. Because of the size

■ FIGURE 1.9

An ad for a local retailer.

of their firms, small business owners often focus on a limited range of products and consumers. For example, your local pizzeria offers a limited menu and delivers only within a certain vicinity. Traditionally, small businesses are less formal about the marketing strategy process and the research methods they use to gather information about their consumers. Their knowledge of consumer behavior often comes from their everyday experience with consumers rather than from the elaborate research methods used by large marketing organizations. This is changing, however, as small businesses continue to adapt newly developed sources of consumer information and the concepts of strategic planning and research. These concepts are vital to business success in today's competitive markets and can readily be applied in an appropriate scope.

**Nonprofit Organizations**  Nonprofit organizations also attempt to satisfy consumers, but, as noted above, they do not intend to make a profit from their efforts. Instead, they are often motivated by an intense desire to provide consumers with a particular kind of product or service they feel is appropriate or important, as shown by the advertisement in Figure 1.10. In television, for example, nonprofit firms such as PBS, "public television," and the Children's Television Workshop produce programs in which they believe strongly. For example, PBS broadcasts public affairs and cultural programs that attract small audiences with very focused interests. Its nonprofit status allows PBS to produce such programming with less concern about whether it will satisfy enough consumers to earn a profit.

■  FIGURE 1.10

Nonprofit firms such as PBS produce programs they believe will provide consumers with a valuable service or message.

## ▼  PUBLIC POLICY ACTORS

Public policy actors have an interest in the public debates about the way consumers purchase and use products. Public policy actors try to influence the behavior of consumers, as shown in Figure 1.11, as well as the strategies of marketers as they enter into exchanges. They also attempt to influence the legal and regulatory environment in which consumer behavior occurs. For example, a public policy actor could advertise to consumers to change their buying habits (e.g., stop buying fur coats), boycott a firm to influence it to change its pricing (e.g., reduce cable television fees), or lobby for new laws that regulate the actions of con-

17

**■ FIGURE 1.11**
Public policy actors attempt to influence the behavior of consumers. In this public service ad, the American Cancer Society advises women to have regular mammograms to help detect breast cancer early.

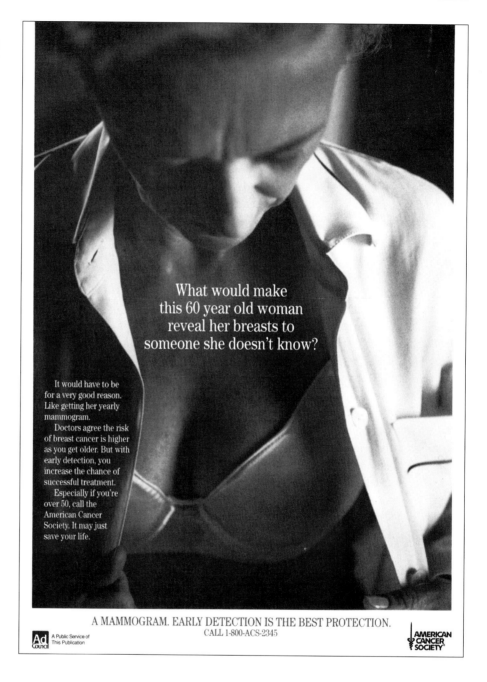

What would make this 60 year old woman reveal her breasts to someone she doesn't know?

It would have to be for a very good reason. Like getting her yearly mammogram.
Doctors agree the risk of breast cancer is higher as you get older. But with early detection, you increase the chance of successful treatment.
Especially if you're over 50, call the American Cancer Society. It may just save your life.

A MAMMOGRAM. EARLY DETECTION IS THE BEST PROTECTION.
CALL 1-800-ACS-2345

Ad Council — A Public Service of This Publication

AMERICAN CANCER SOCIETY

---

**Policy makers** are government officials who have the authority to create and enforce legislation and regulations.

sumers and marketers alike (e.g., restrict the portrayal of violence on television). We will now take a closer look at examples of different public policy actors.

**Policy Makers** Government **policy makers** are obviously interested in consumer behavior because of the very nature of their job; they have the authority to create and enforce legislation and regulations concerning consumer behavior. As a result, they are often the target of others who want to influence those laws and policies. To identify the policy makers who are involved in a consumer behavior problem, you must discover all of the government bodies that have jurisdiction over the area. These include legislators and regulators in executive and administrative positions at the national, state, and local levels of government. A number of policy makers are active in the debate about violence on television, for example. In 1990, the Senate passed the Television Violence Act, which allows the television networks to cooperate on reducing the level of violence without violating antitrust laws. In addition, a number of Congressional hearings about violence on television have been held recently, and the Attorney General has criticized the networks for their lack of voluntary compliance. Finally, the Federal Communications Commission (FCC) has the ultimate authority to regulate the television industry.

**Social Action Organizations**   Consumers themselves try to influence public policies concerning the products they buy and use. In this role, consumers are interested in the way consumer exchanges occur in general, not in the individual purchases they make to satisfy their own needs. Others may be interested in the *results* of purchase and consumption, even though they are not directly involved in the consumer exchanges and do not use the product themselves (see Figure 1.12). For example, some groups are interested in eliminating advertising for cigarettes and alcohol because they feel that such advertising encourages children and teenagers to use these products.

**Social action organizations** are groups that are formed to influence public policies, individuals' actions, and marketers' strategies in areas that interest their members. These organizations represent both consumers who buy and use products and others who are interested in the effects of this behavior. Identifying all of the social action groups that have an interest can be a difficult process because of the wide purview of many of these organizations. The task involves painstaking research into the particular issue to specify the organizations that are involved. Because of the central role played by legislators in public policy issues, many of the groups lobby or testify at Congressional hearings on relevant issues. For example, television violence is an important issue to a wide variety of organizations. The Citizens Task Force on Television Violence is an umbrella organization of such groups as the International Association of Chiefs of Police, the American Medical Association, the National Council of Churches, the American Psychological Association, and the National Association of Elementary School Principals. The Task Force uses such methods as lobbying and circulating petitions to influence television programmers and policy makers. The American Family Association encourages individuals to boycott marketers that advertise on programs that contain violence, whereas the American Civil Liberties Union criticizes laws it feels will curb First Amendment rights of free speech.

**Marketers and Trade Associations**   Marketers also attempt to influence public policy, either individually or by joining with their competitors in a **trade association** that lobbies legislators or tries to influence public opinion, as shown in

**Social action organizations** are groups that form to influence public policies, consumers' actions, and marketers' strategies in areas that interest their members.

A **trade association** is a social action organization formed by marketers in an attempt to influence legislation or public opinion.

■  FIGURE 1.12
National Heart Savers Association is an example of a social action organization. In this ad, it warns consumers about the negative effects of drinking low-fat milk.

Figure 1.13. Marketers intend to influence the laws and regulations that apply to their industry so that they can develop and implement marketing strategies that will satisfy consumer needs and, at the same time, be profitable for them. For example, food marketers recently lobbied Congress as it debated changes in nutrition labeling laws. These marketers were concerned about the reaction of consumers to the nutritional content of their products and the expense of analyzing the products and changing the design of the labels.

Identifying these actors requires enumerating the marketers who are involved in consumer exchanges, as well as potential competitors. Competitors

■ FIGURE 1.13
The National Cable Television Association is a trade association bent on preventing the networks from charging additional fees to cable subscribers.

may include firms that produce the same kinds of product, as well as **generic competitors**—firms that satisfy the same consumer need. For example, railroads are interested in regulation of the airline industry because both industries satisfy the consumer need for travel; regulations imposed on the airline industry may lead to similar regulations on railroads in the future.

**Generic competitors** are independent firms that satisfy the same consumer need.

# WATCHING TELEVISION AS CONSUMER BEHAVIOR

The act of watching television fits the three-part definition of consumer behavior presented earlier in this chapter. Each time you choose to watch a television program, you exchange something of value for a product that satisfies your needs. When you watch a particular program, you have an entertaining experience, or learn some new ideas, or avoid feeling anxious about the French test for which you might be studying instead. You may also feel close to your friends when you watch a program with them or discuss it with them the next day in the dining hall. Thus, watching television provides benefits to meet your needs as a consumer.

## FACT OR FICTION REVISITED

◉   It is true that watching a television program involves exhanging something of value for something the viewer needs. The "something of value" is the viewer's time and (indirectly) money. The "need" may be information, entertainment, or relaxation.

To identify the consumers that must be considered in a consumer behavior analysis, you must look at all those individuals who are involved in the process, directly and indirectly. For example, when young children watch television, others are involved in the consumption process as well. The children's parents may decide what programs are acceptable for them to watch. For example, Barb Hawkins stopped her kids from watching *The Three Stooges* because she was concerned about the violent behavior they were imitating. In this case, an analysis of children's television viewing would have to include both the parent and the child. Similarly, when you watch television with your friends, each of you has a say in what program you watch, so you must all be included in the analysis.

Television also involves generalized exchange among many different parties. You don't actually go to the office of the production company that made the program and operate a camera one day each week in exchange for watching it, or answer the telephone for a few hours at your local cable company in exchange for delivering the program to your house. Instead, you *indirectly* exchange time and money for the positive experiences that satisfy some of your needs. The time you exchange is spent watching advertisements. You don't actually pay to watch most television programs; the advertisers do. Advertisers pay local television stations to place them in programs; the television stations in turn pay the production companies to create the programs that carry the ads; and you pay the advertisers by buying the products that you have seen advertised. This an example of generalized exchange: Time and money are the general currency used, and the exchanges are generalized among all of the parties rather than as specific two-way trades among pairs. For some cable channels, such as Home Box Office (HBO), the exchange is more direct: You pay cash to your cable operator for this channel, and the operator pays HBO. Consequently, there are no ads on these channels.

Now that you have identified the consumers and the medium of exchange, you must identify the marketers involved in satisfying the consumers' need to watch television. The first step is to identify the consumer's direct exchange partners. Because consumers use generalized exchange, you must then identify each subsequent exchange partner as well. In the example of television viewing, following the trail of exchanges leads you from consumers to the local cable operator and television stations, to television networks, production companies, and advertisers. Because marketers spend a great deal of time and effort analyzing consumers, segmenting their markets, and, ultimately, satisfying consumers' needs through the marketing mix, you must analyze the marketing strategy they employ to structure their exchange with consumers.

Many parties, besides advertisers, are interested in the television programs you watch and may try to influence your viewing patterns. Your parents chose the shows that you watched when you were young, for example, and may even try to recommend programs for you to watch today. More likely, your friends influence your choices now; you want to watch whatever programs your friends are talking about on campus so that you can participate in, say, the Friday morning discussions about the latest *Friends* episode.

Other parties you may not even know of try to influence what programs are available for you to watch. To identify such public policy actors in a consumer behavior issue, you must consider all of the reasons that someone may be interested in public policies about the purchase and use of a product. For example, the government—both legislators and the FCC—regulate the television industry; the television industry regulates itself, through both its own internal standards and practices (the network censor) and the local stations that may refuse to air network shows they think their viewers will find objectionable; and a variety of social action groups try to influence consumers, television stations, advertisers, and government regulators about television programming.

Many marketers and trade associations are active in public policy issues concerning sex and violence on television. The production companies that create the programming for television, the broadcast networks, cable broadcasters, local television stations, local cable system operators, and marketers who rely on television to carry their advertising are all interested in the issue. Acting both individually and through their trade associations, these parties testify at Congressional hearings, lobby policy makers, and try to influence consumer opinion so that they can market their products as they would like.

 ## PUBLIC POLICY

### *NYPD Blue:* Sex and Violence on Television[9]

In September 1993, *NYPD Blue,* an urban police drama, aired on ABC. The series follows a group of New York City police detectives through both their professional and personal lives and contains obscene language, partial nudity, sex, and violence. It elicited a wave of reactions from public policy makers about the seemingly offensive nature of the program. Some consumer segments have found the show to be satisfy-

ing television viewing; others feel it contains too much sex and violence to meet their entertainment needs. However, individual consumers do not always have the choice about whether to "buy" the program or not—some local affiliates chose not to broadcast *NYPD Blue*, and some marketers refuse to buy advertising time on the program.

Many groups have been involved in the controversy over *NYPD Blue*, including the ABC television network, the 225 affiliate stations in local areas around the county, Steven Bochco (the producer of the program), advertisers (and potential advertisers) on the program, and social action groups that have either favored or opposed the program. The ABC network chose to broadcast the show, but the local affiliates have the power to preempt the program if they believe it will not be viewed by their local consumers. Initially, about one quarter of the local television stations did not show the program, but some of those stations began airing it during the following months.

Social action groups, such as the American Family Association, strongly protested against the program's sexual content from the very beginning by targeting the local affiliates. The organization encouraged its own members to protest to their local stations and produced newspaper ads that encouraged other consumers to protest as well. It also encouraged consumers to complain to those marketers that bought advertising time on the program. At the end of the program's first year, the American Family Association launched a $3 million campaign to dissuade those advertisers from supporting the program. It continued to encourage consumers to complain and announced plans to boycott the marketers who continued to buy advertising. At the same time, other groups, such as Viewers for Quality Television, opposed such efforts and encouraged viewers of the program to write letters of support to local stations and advertisers alike.

The controversy surrounding *NYPD Blue* exemplifies the range of groups that can become involved in a public policy debate as well as the need to consider a wide range of potential actors in an analysis of any consumer behavior problem. Some of those who played public policy roles were consumers and marketers; others were social action groups that wanted to prevent other consumers from viewing the program because they felt it had harmful effects. Some consumers, such as Barb Hawkins, were able to control their families' television viewing. Is it still possible for consumers to ensure that they and their families don't have access to programs that they find offensive? Do you think that social action groups should be able to influence the television that other consumers watch?

# PUBLIC POLICY ISSUES AND ETHICS

Since our social and political environment gives every citizen the right to appeal for public intervention in consumer behavior and business, it is critical that, in analyzing consumer behavior, you consider the role of public policy. This intervention usually takes the form of legislation or regulation about particular consumer or marketing activities. There is often significant debate about government intervention in terms of (1) whether it is justified, (2) what it is designed to achieve, and (3) how it is implemented. Consumers, marketers, and public policy actors all participate in this debate because consumers' behavior, marketers' strategies, and policy makers' laws and regulations are all affected by the results.

## FACT OR FICTION REVISITED

⊙ Public policy debate does indeed focus on the effects of consumer behavior on the larger society. This focus distinguishes public policy issues from exchange issues.

Consider the significant ongoing debate about the legislation and regulation of violence on television. Congress is considering passing legislation to require television broadcasters to identify violent programs with a code that could be recognized by a chip that manufacturers would build into all new televisions. Parents like Barb Hawkins could then program their televisions to prevent their children from watching these shows.

A wide variety of public policy actors are involved in this debate. Consumers participate through their social action groups. Some, such as the National Parents–Teachers Association (PTA), are directly involved because they don't want their children to watch such programs. Others, such as the American Medical Association, are fearful of the effects on the larger society. Marketers of violent television programs are also interested and participate both directly and through their trade associations. Policy makers, both members of Congress and such executive agencies as the Attorney General and the National Institute of Mental Health, are also active in this debate. For example, Attorney General Janet Reno testified before Congress in October 1993 that the Department of Justice and Congress should step in to regulate television violence if the broadcasters wouldn't do so themselves.

This issue illustrates an important point about public policy and consumer behavior: Public policy debate focuses on the results of consumer behavior on the larger society, not just on the consumers and marketers who are directly involved in the exchange. This does not mean that public policy ignores individual satisfaction; rather, it considers individual gratification as just one element in the larger societal picture. For example, you might enjoy watching "shoot-'em up" Arnold Schwarzenegger movies on television, but public policy debate considers the effects of such programming on everyone from young children to senior citizens. Therefore, public policy debates often concern the dark side of consumption. Even if you like to eat a lot of sweets, smoke cigarettes, or watch violent television programs, public policy actors debate the effects of your consumption on society as a whole.

▼ AREAS OF PUBLIC POLICY

Public policy issues cover four major areas in consumer behavior: (1) fairness, (2) equity, (3) safety, and (4) economic and social welfare.[10] *Fairness* addresses your opportunity to satisfy your needs in exchanges with marketers. To satisfy your needs, you should be able to gather unbiased information about your alternatives, choose your preferred alternative without harassment, and change inadequate products. Deceptive advertising, high-pressure sales techniques, and responsiveness to complaints are instances of fairness issues. For example, consumer advocacy groups are protesting pharmaceutical company programs that compensate pharmacists who advise their customers to switch medications.[11]

*Equity* issues probe whether all segments of the population have access to the same products and are treated the same way by marketers in exchanges. The most extreme kind of inequity is to deny some consumers the right to buy a product. Preventing particular ethnic or age groups from buying houses in a certain neighborhood or denying access to cable television in certain communities are two examples. Other kinds of inequity are discrimination against minority patrons in restaurants and sexual stereotyping of women in television programming and advertising.

*Safety* examines whether a product is physically dangerous to consumers. It includes such issues as product design, a marketer's responsibility to recall products that are later discovered to be defective, and the amount of information that should be provided to consumers during the purchase process. Examples include controversies over the safety of cars and trucks and the health effects of cigarettes. Recently, a jury awarded a McDonald's patron a multimillion-dollar settlement because she was burned by coffee that was hotter than that served in other restaurants.[12] Because most people believe that products should be safe, some public policy actors try to define many consumer public policy issues as safety concerns. For example, critics of television violence try to define the issue as one of public safety because of the residual effects of actual violence on members of society.

*Economic and social welfare* issues concern the widest effects of consumer behavior on the general satisfaction of consumers. Public policy debates in this area address how consumer exchanges affect your own general social and economic welfare, as well as the welfare of others in society. Consumer education is an example of this kind of issue. If you had been taught how to evaluate products and make purchase decisions when you were younger, your consumer behavior as an adult would likely be more satisfying to you. Another example is *social marketing*—the marketing of areas that are not traditionally commercial. If the government encourages water conservation during a drought, for example, you may not satisfy a need in a specific exchange, but your community will be better able to fight fires using the water you have saved collectively.

# Consumer Behavior and Its Multiple Perspectives

Any examination of a consumer behavior problem requires adopting many perspectives, each of which offers you some additional insight into consumers, marketers, and public policy actors that you can integrate to complete your analysis. These perspectives are not competitive; they are complementary. Together, they give you a more comprehensive, accurate, and perceptive understanding of the issue you are studying. Furthermore, each perspective focuses more on particular behavioral processes and less on others.

This is similar to the way you do your academic work. You focus on some subjects and pay less attention to others. Your professors probably tell you that you should use information from all of the perspectives that you have studied. They may even force you to include a financial statement in a marketing plan or to consider the effects of personnel decisions in your strategic management plan. You won't be a successful marketer unless you know something about accounting and finance; similarly, you won't be a successful consumer behavior analyst unless you understand psychology, sociology, anthropology, economics, and organizational behavior.

Once you have identified each of the actors that plays a role in your consumer behavior problem, examine them from each of the perspectives. Apply psychology to understand the consumer's motivations, perception, learning, and attitudes. Use economics to investigate the decision making process used. Employ sociology to examine the influence of family, business colleagues, friends, and others on the consumer, marketer, and public policy actor. Consider anthropology to understand the actors' culture and values. Finally, look at the organizational issues that affect the way marketers and public policy actors do their jobs.

The most important reason to consider all of these perspectives is that each of the aspects they emphasize separately is strongly related to the others in consumers' minds. Whereas psychology and economics focus on the individual processes all consumers use to deal with their worlds, for example, these processes are affected by the social structures sociology examines and the cultural factors anthropology stresses. Similarly, both social structures and cultural values are affected by individual psychological and economic processes. For example, someone may watch *Seinfeld* or *Frazier* in order to talk about the programs with his or her friends; at the same time, that person's choice of friends is influenced by personality and social background, so he or she is probably attracted to the kinds of people who watch *Seinfeld* or *Frazier* in the first place.

Only by looking at the consumer behavior problem from all of these perspectives can you completely understand it. When you apply all of these perspectives to the problem, some will offer greater insight than others. You can then focus on the most powerful insights and use the other perspectives as background. But unless you have considered all of the perspectives, you won't know which are most important for analyzing your problem.

Throughout this book, we will be elaborating on these perspectives. For now, however, you want to be able to identify each perspective and to know how it would apply to a consumer behavior problem. Table 1.2 lists the perspectives and gives examples of the kinds of consumer behavior questions on which each perspective might focus.

## ▼ PSYCHOLOGY

*Psychology* focuses on the individual processes you use to interact with your world. They include (1) motivation, (2) perception, (3) learning, (4) attitude formation, and (5) decision making. Psychology focuses on the internal processes

*Table 1.2*

**CONSUMER BEHAVIOR PERSPECTIVES**

| Perspective | Questions on which they focus |
|---|---|
| Psychology | What motivates consumers to watch violent television programs |
| | How consumers learn about new products |
| Economics | Why consumers repond to a rebate for the purchase of a new car |
| | How income affects choice of a public versus private college |
| Sociology | Why peer groups affect the purchase of clothing |
| | How dual-career couples choose vacation spots |
| Anthropology | How rituals affects the choice of a location for a wedding |
| | Why consumers get tattoos |
| Organizational behavior | How organizational culture influences a marketer's design of a car's safety features |
| | Why a trade association's staff's work histories affect its ability to lobby for changes in regulations |

you use as you buy and consume. It emphasizes your thoughts, feelings, and attitudes, and the way they develop, and accents the importance of personality and personal experiences. These individual processes affect your specific reactions to marketers and public policy actors.

### ▼ ECONOMICS

*Economics* investigates the decision making processes you use to make your consumer choices. The underpinning of economics is the assumption that you use the information available to you to make rational choices that will maximize the satisfaction of your needs. Thus, economics focuses on the way you evaluate your alternatives and make your choices about which products to purchase and use. It tries to determine the criteria that you use to decide among the alternatives that are available to you as well as the financial constraints that arise from limited budgets.

## FACT OR FICTION REVISITED

◉   Economists do assume that consumers use information to make rational choices that satisfy their needs. In fact, this is one of the fundamental assumptions of economic analysis.

### ▼ SOCIOLOGY

*Sociology* emphasizes the way your social arrangements affect your consumer behavior.[13] You are a member of many social groups, including your family, friends, and co-workers, as well as general social categories, such as your age and ethnic group. All of these groups combine to form your social structure, and sociology examines the impact of that structure on your consumer behavior. Sociology also looks at the trends in social arrangements and the impact of those changes on your individual consumer choices. For example, the growth in the number of families in which both parents work has caused consumers to increase their purchase of food products that are easy to prepare.

## ▼ ANTHROPOLOGY

*Anthropology* concentrates on the effects of culture and values on consumer behavior.[14] Each of the social groups to which you belong has its own cultural traditions and ways of enacting its values. These values are influential in the consumer choices you make, both directly and symbolically. They affect you directly by shaping your tastes in food, clothing, entertainment, and other areas. They also indicate symbols of membership that you purchase to show your allegiance to the group's values. For example, you may wear clothes touting the name of your college, fraternity, or sorority, or dress in flannel shirts and baggy, ripped jeans to demonstrate the kind of person you are.

## ▼ ORGANIZATIONAL BEHAVIOR

*Organizational behavior* offers a useful perspective about the behavior of marketers and public policy actors in business firms, government organizations, and social action groups. So many of the actors that try to influence consumers work in organizations. Consequently, you must understand the organizational structure and culture in order to analyze the role these actors play in your consumer exchanges with them.

# CONSUMER BEHAVIOR ACTORS AND PERSPECTIVES ◄

Barb Hawkins is an example of a consumer who is concerned with violence on television. She believes that the television stations should monitor what they broadcast, but that parents should also take responsibility for what they watch. She opposes government censorship, but recognizes that some public policy actor will have to show parents the effects that violent shows have on their kids.

Barb's opinions illustrate many of the concepts we have introduced in this chapter—the three types of actors that are involved in a consumer behavior issue and the perspectives that are useful in analyzing such issues. Consumers, marketers, and public policy actors will all play a role in Barb's solution to the consumer behavior problem. She may not be familiar with the perspectives, but she has used all of them. Psychology, economics, sociology, and anthropology can all contribute to an analysis of the reasons that kids want to watch television programs that their parents view as bad for them. Insights from organizational behavior can show why the marketers and public policy actors argue over censorship and regulations that would require television marketers to sell the proposed video chips.

The rest of this book will present the skills and concepts that are necessary to analyze issues such as this one. We will discuss the roles of consumers, marketers, and public policy actors in detail so that you can understand how consumers seek to satisfy their needs, how marketers try to influence consumers to use their products to satisfy those needs, and how public policy actors try to influence the exchanges between consumers and marketers.

# SUMMARY

1. **Analyze the roles that consumers, marketers, and public policy actors play.** These three types of actors all participate in any instance of consumer behavior. Consumers and marketers are direct participants — consumers exchange money with marketers, who provide products that satisfy the consumers' needs. Public policy actors participate by trying to affect consumers, marketers, and the environment in which exchanges occur.

2. **Recognize the needs that motivate consumers to buy and use products.** Consumers buy and use products that satisfy their needs. These needs range from basic biological needs, such as hunger and thirst, to such social needs as peer approval. A Big Mac or an expensive dinner at L'Orangerie will satisfy hunger; keeping up with the latest soap opera or donning bellbottoms and tie-died t-shirts may get you in with the "in crowd" on campus.

3. **Identify the consumers for whom consumption can be harmful and examine the effects of that consumption on other consumers.** Some individuals consume products that cause them harm. This can occur if consumers use a product "inappropriately," such as consuming too much alcohol or watching violent or sexually explicit television programs. Public policy actors are particularly interested in such "dark side" consumption because of its effects on other consumers—drunk drivers can cause car accidents; teenagers might imitate violent acts they have seen on television. There is much controversy about many of these issues as consumers, marketers, and public policy actors debate just how "dark" some of these products really are.

4. **Determine the tools marketers use to influence consumers' behavior.** First, marketers must use their analytic skills to understand consumer behavior. Once marketers understand consumers' behavior and what kind of products will satisfy their needs, they devise a marketing strategy, which has two major components: (1) a market segmentation that defines the set of consumers who have similar needs and will respond similarly to the marketer's efforts, and (2) a marketing mix which communicates that the marketer can deliver a product designed to meet consumer needs at an attractive price.

5. **Identify the impact of public policy actors on consumers and marketers.** Public policy actors try to affect the exchanges between consumers and marketers as well as the environment in which those exchanges occur. They can influence consumers' buying behavior through advertising and publicity and marketers' strategies through public appeals and boycotts. They attempt to influence public policies by lobbying policy makers to create and enforce laws and regulations that define what consumers can buy and how marketers can sell their products.

6. **Examine the fairness, equity, safety, and social implications of a consumer behavior problem.** Fairness, equity, and safety are characteristics that affect the con-

sumer who is involved in the exchange process. Consumers are involved in a fair consumer exchange when they can buy a product that will satisfy their needs without facing any deception or pressure from the marketer. Equity exists when every consumer has access to the products that he or she needs and is treated the same way as are all other consumers. A safe product is one that will not cause any injury or harm to a consumer who uses it responsibly. The social implications of consumer behavior concern how the purchase and use of a product will affect the economic and social welfare of the wider society.

7. **Apply the perspective of each discipline to your analysis of a consumer behavior problem.** Every consumer behavior problem will benefit from the combination of different perspectives offered by psychology, sociology, anthropology, economics, and organizational behavior. Consumer behavior is affected by many factors, and each of these disciplines is necessary to achieve a complete understanding. Psychology focuses on the individual consumer's characteristics; sociology and anthropology emphasize the social and cultural influences; economics stresses the decision making that must occur under financial constraints; and organizational behavior describes how marketers and public policy organizations choose their courses of action.

# KEY TERMS

Consumer behavior, *p. 5*
Product, *p. 7*
Actor, *p. 9*
Consumer, *p. 9*
Marketer, *p. 9*
Public policy actor, *p. 10*
Organizational buying, *p. 10*
Marketing concept, *p. 13*
Marketing strategy, *p. 14*
Nonprofit
    organization, *p. 14*
Strategic business
unit (SBU), *p. 16*
Policy maker, *p. 18*
Social action
    organization, *p. 19*
Trade association, *p. 19*
Generic competitor, *p. 21*

# SKILL-BUILDING ACTIVITIES

1. Think of a product you purchased within the past week. Trace your consumer behavior through problem recognition, search, purchase, evaluation, transmission of this evaluation to others, and end.
2. How would you have been able to obtain that product if money had not been invented?
3. Think of a service you purchased within the past week. Trace your consumer behavior through problem recognition, search, purchase, evaluation, transmission of this evaluation to others, and end. How did those steps differ from the steps in activity 1, above?
4. For either the product or service you've chosen, how was the consumer behavior process influenced by:
   a. the consumer (you)    b. the marketer    c. public policy actors
5. Describe an incident in which a person you know has been affected by the dark side of consumer behavior.
6. As the owner of a local video rental outlet, how would you apply the "marketing concept" to your business?
7. Spend one hour watching evening network television and count the acts of violence that are shown. How did you define "violence"? How many acts of violence did you count? What effect (if any) do you think watching this violence has on viewers?

8.  Suppose that your violence count were available for a large, representative sample of television programs. Make a list of the parties who might be interested in these findings. For each party, explain why.

9.  For the purchase you described in (1) or (2) above, analyze any fairness, equity, safety, and economic or social welfare issues that might be involved.

---

# CHAPTER 1 SELF-TEST

## ▼ MULTIPLE CHOICE

1.  The study of consumers as they exchange something of value for a product or service that satisfies their needs is the definition of
    a.  sociology
    b.  marketing research
    c.  consumer behavior
    d.  psychology

2.  A complete analysis of consumer behavior should identify three types of actors: marketers, public policy actors, and most importantly _____ .
    a.  advertisers
    b.  employees
    c.  consumers
    d.  suppliers

3.  When Don calls the local utilities commission about the high cost of water, he would be considered what type of consumer behavior "actor"?
    a.  public policy actor
    b.  marketer
    c.  economic actor
    d.  consumer

4.  _____ are individuals that identify needs, buy and consume products, and dispose of products.
    a.  Public policy actors
    b.  Marketers
    c.  Exchangers
    d.  Consumers

5.  The marketing concept states that the only way for a marketer to profit from an exchange with a consumer is by
    a.  producing large amounts of advertising
    b.  manufacturing products that are inexpensive to make
    c.  satisfying the consumer's needs
    d.  providing large dividends to company's stockholders

6.  The American Marketing Association is an example of what type of public policy actor?
    a.  trade association
    b.  social action organization
    c.  policy maker actors
    d.  citizen action coalition

7.  Any study of consumer behavior includes _____ since that perspective concentrates on the effects of culture and values on consumer behavior.
    a.  psychology
    b.  anthropology
    c.  biology
    d.  economics

8.  Large firms often divide their organization into groups or _____ that market a set of homogeneous products to a set of homogeneous market segments.
    a.  market segments
    b.  policy groups
    c.  administrative sections
    d.  strategic business units (SBUs)

9.  _____ organizations are groups that influence public policies, individuals' actions, and marketers' strategies in areas that interest their members.
    a.  social action
    b.  Professional action
    c.  community action
    d.  Universal protection

10. Manufacturers of cassette players are considered _____ competitors of manufacturers of compact disk players since both firms satisfy the consumer need of playing recorded music.
    a. facilitation
    b. general
    c. generic
    d. support

## ▼ TRUE/FALSE

1. Consumer behavior only includes the actual purchasing of products.  T or F
2. Most exchanges that occur between marketers and consumers are considered generalized exchanges.  T or F
3. An experience such as riding on a roller coaster is not considered a product.  T or F
4. The purchaser and consumer of a product is not necessarily the same person. T or F
5. Purchasing and consuming illegal drugs would be an example of the dark side of consumer behavior.  T or F
6. Small businesses do not need to develop marketing strategies since their customer base is so small.  T or F
7. Public policy focuses on the results of consumer behavior on the larger society. T or F
8. Buying a luxury car or an economy car are both examples of products purchased to satisfy the consumer's needs. T or F
9. United States senators have no role in consumer behavior.  T or F
10. In most cases, satisfying needs give consumers pleasure.  T or F

## ▼ SHORT ANSWER

1. List and describe the four major areas in consumer behavior that are pertinent to the development of public policy.
2. How is organizational buying different from consumer buying? Give an example of an organizational purchase and an example of a consumer purchase.
3. Describe the unique challenges that nonprofit organizations experience in their marketing efforts.
4. Discuss the roles psychology and sociology play in the study of consumer behavior.

## ▼ APPLICATION EXERCISE

You are a member of the marketing department of a large consumer products firm that manufacturers children's toys. The firm is considering introducing an action figure toy that can shoot miniature arrows. As one of your responsibilities, you have been asked to analyze the probability that this product will be successful in the marketplace. Assuming you and your organization are playing the "marketer" in consumer behavior analysis, describe what you believe to be the consumers and public policy actors who will play a role in this product's success or failure.

# 2

# A FRAMEWORK FOR THE STUDY OF CONSUMER BEHAVIOR

◉ Consumer Snapshot    *Carol Beutel is a 28-year-old Territory Manager of Industrial Sales. She is divorced and lives in Rivervale, New Jersey, with her 9-year-old son, George.*

FACT OR FICTION?

◉   Information search is the first step in the consumer purchase process.

◉   Consumers spend more time and effort on information search when they purchase high involvement products than when they purchase low involvement products.

◉   Consumers who share the same values generally enact them in the same way.

◉   Values affect the evaluation of alternatives and the feedback offered after a choice has been made.

◉ Most consumers have more than one reference group.

◉ Everything that occurs in the consumer's environment must first pass through his or her perceptual process before the consumer can make any sense out of it.

◉ Most consumer attitudes change very quickly.

◉ When consumers choose among alternatives, they identify options, establish criteria for evaluating these options, develop methods for combining the criteria into rules, and apply those rules when they decide how to act.

# EYE ON THE CONSUMER

Carol Beutel decided to join a health club after her divorce. She thought she should get into better shape and that a gym might be a good place to meet people—new friends and maybe some men. She looked into the health clubs in her area to see what they were like, restricting her visits to coed gyms because she wanted to meet both men and women. On her visits, Carol asked about prices, checked to see how clean the facilities were, and tried to get a feeling for the atmosphere. A friend took her as a guest to her gym, and since it was one of the cleanest and was priced about average for the places she saw, she joined.

In the beginning, Carol went four times a week. She attended some classes, used the Stair Master, and even did some light weightlifting. After a time, rushing to make the classes while balancing work and the time she spent with her son caused too much stress, and that didn't make much sense when one of the things she wanted to get from exercise was relaxation! So she stopped taking classes and spent more time on the StairMaster. But one summer day, as Carol and her son were riding their bicycles around town to drop off the dry cleaning, some library books, and videos they had rented, she realized that she was getting exercise just running errands. She felt it was silly to drive 15 minutes to the gym when she could ride her bicycle and start exercising as soon as she left the house. And then there was the gasoline she was wasting, particularly when her son was always reminding her to be more environmentally and socially conscious. So now Carol doesn't go to the gym much anymore at all, and the only exercise she gets on a regular basis is a bike ride every other week or so.

The purpose of this chapter is to provide an overview of the consumer's role in consumer behavior. As introduced in Chapter 1, consumers go through a series of activities as they purchase and use products to satisfy their needs: They recognize a need, they look at the various products available to satisfy that need, they choose one of the these products, purchase it, use it, and then dispose of it.

For example, you might recognize during fall semester of your senior year that you need something to wear on your upcoming job interviews. You might talk with your professors, friends, and family about appropriate business attire and stores at which to buy such clothes. You would go to a couple of stores to see their selections and prices, then buy a business suit. A couple of years from now, after you have been on the job for a while, you may give that suit to a younger cousin or donate it to a charitable clothing drive.

In this chapter, we will first outline these purchase and usage activities; we will then present a framework within which to analyze them. We will illustrate this framework through a simple analysis of the activities you would use as a consumer in choosing to join a health club. In Chapter 3, we will turn to the marketer's role in this framework, continuing the example of choosing a health club, this time from the marketer's perspective.

After reading and thinking about this chapter, you should be able to:

❶ Identify the activities consumers carry out during the consumer behavior process.

❷ Distinguish among the activities carried out by diverse consumer segments during the purchase and use of a particular product and recognize the factors that cause the different patterns of activities.

❸ Determine which of the background characteristics distinguish among the diverse segments that complete the purchase activities in different ways.

❹ Analyze how consumers use the behavioral processes to help them complete the activities involved in buying and using a product.

# CONSUMER PURCHASE ACTIVITIES

The wide variety of activities consumers complete as they seek to satisfy their needs can be categorized into a series of steps. As a consumer, you (1) recognize that you have a need to satisfy; (2) search for alternatives that might satisfy that need; (3) evaluate the alternatives and choose the best one; (4) purchase and use the chosen alternative; (5) evaluate how successfully your need has been satisfied; (6) provide feedback about your evaluation to others; and (7) end the consumer purchase process. Figure 2.1 illustrates these seven steps, highlighting the effect of feedback on Steps 2 and 3. Table 2.1 presents some common examples of the activities that occur at each step.

## ▼ RECOGNIZE NEEDS

Recognizing needs is the first activity in any act of consumer behavior.[1] Consumers have many different kinds of needs that may be recognized in various ways. A person may feel hungry, want to be entertained, hope her friends think

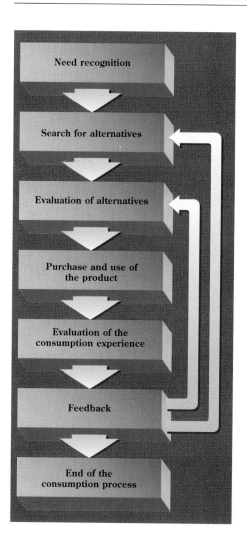 

■ FIGURE 2.1

Steps in the consumer purchase process diagram.

she is a talented musician, or want to be successful in a chosen career. Needs range from simple, physical desires to complex, socially based ideas about what is important to be successful in the eyes of others. As consumers, we may recognize some of our needs on our own, or others may spur us to recognize them. Most of us recognize when we are hungry, but the desire to try a particular new restaurant may be provoked by friends who tell us that it's "the place to go." Figure 2.2 is an example of an ad that is designed to spur need recognition.

What are some of the needs that might motivate you to join a health club? You may want to look good on the beach in Florida during Spring break. Perhaps you tire easily when you play a set of tennis and decide that you want to improve your physical condition. Maybe you have heard that the snack bar in the health club is a great place to meet new people. Your parents may have very different reasons for joining a health club. Your father wakes up one morning and decides that he wants to look like he did 15 years ago. Your mother's physician tells her that exercise will help prevent the onset of osteoporosis. As you can see, people seek to fulfill differ-

## Table 2.1

### STEPS IN THE CONSUMER PURCHASE PROCESS

| Step | Examples of Activities Occurring in Each Step |
|---|---|
| Recognize needs | Feel hungry<br>Acknowledge that you weigh 20 pounds more than you should |
| Search for alternatives | Try to remember the great new restaurant that your heard about<br>Look up health clubs in the Yellow Pages |
| Evaluate alternatives | Check *Consumer Reports* for the article on bicycles<br>Visit the local health club for the one-day free trial |
| Purchase and use the product | Buy a Snickers bar from a vending machine<br>Go to the health club three times a week during the first month of your membership |
| Evaluate the consumption experience | Decide if the Big Mac you ate filled you up<br>Ask your roommates if they think the health club is doing you any good |
| Provide feedback | Renew your subscription to *Rolling Stone* for another year<br>Complain to the health club manager that the pool is too cold |
| End the purchase process | Put your Coke can in the recycling bin<br>Cancel your health club membership |

■ FIGURE 2.2

This ad for The Vertical Clubs is designed to spur consumer recognition of the need to work out in order to look good in a bathing suit this summer.

ent kinds of needs—vanity, health, and companionship, to name just a few. Motivation and need recognition are discussed in more detail in Chapter 8.

## FACT OR FICTION REVISITED

⊚    Information search is *not* the first step in the consumer purchase process; the first step is recognition of a need.

**THESE CHIPS WON'T GO TO YOUR HIPS.**

NATURE VALLEY. LOWFAT CHEWY GRANOLA BARS NEW

THEY'RE LOADED WITH BIG CHOCOLATE TASTE BUT LEAN ON FAT. JUST 2 GRAMS PER BAR.

■ FIGURE 2.3
General Mills alerts consumers to its new lowfat granola bars by placing the word "new" directly on the label.

### ▼ SEARCH FOR ALTERNATIVES

Once a need has been recognized, it is necessary to search for alternate ways to satisfy it.[2] One method is to search one's memory for ways in which the need has been satisfied in the past. This is the source of consumer habits. You develop the habit of going to swim at the pool in the student recreation center at 7:00 every morning, for instance, because you know that you can always find an empty lane. Another option is to contact friends to find out how they have satisfied a similar need. A third alternative is to look for publicly available sources of information, such as The Yellow Pages or magazine ads. The ad in Figure 2.3 is designed to alert consumers to a new alternative.

If you decide that you need to find a new health club with a pool so that you can swim every morning before class, you could search for alternatives in a variety of ways. You may try to recall if you drive past any health clubs on your way to school every morning, or you may look for signs of a health club the next time you head in that direction. You may ask people you know whether they swim and find out where they go. You could look in the telephone book for health clubs, check the school newspaper for ads, or refer to the directory of local businesses your advisor gave you during new student orientation.

### ▼ EVALUATE ALTERNATIVES

After searching for alternatives, the consumer must take the time to evaluate each one and choose that which will best satisfy his or her needs.[3] This evaluation process can be very complex. Before alternatives can be evaluated, criteria must be chosen. That is, individuals must decide what standards are important to them in choosing a particular product (see Figure 2.4). In our example, in choosing a health club to join, is proximity important to you? Is cost even more important? What about cleanliness? Will you consider the health club that is closest to your apartment, the cheapest one that you can find, or the one with the cleanest Olympic-size pool? If several criteria are important to you, you must decide how to prioritize or combine them. You might decide that you will evaluate location and price but that you will only consider health clubs that have an Olympic-size pool and monthly membership dues. As long as the club offers a big pool and short-term memberships, you will consider its location and price.

### ▼ PURCHASE AND USE THE PRODUCT

Once all the options have been weighed, the individual is able to purchase and use the preferred alternative. Purchase is the heart of consumer behavior; it in-

■ FIGURE 2.4
Consumers compare prices, brand names, and capabilities, among other criteria, before choosing a product like a computer.

volves the exchange of something of value to the individual for a product that will satisfy his or her need. Purchasing the product can involve logistical issues, such as locating a store from which to buy a product, as shown in Figure 2.5, or meeting with the person who will actually sell the product to the customer.[4] To buy a health club membership, you may have to go to the health club during particular hours to give a check to the manager and then wait several days for your check to clear. If you charge the membership on your credit card, you would be able to start using the club immediately because the manager can be sure she will be paid. You also have the option of stretching out your payments over an allotted period of time. Once you have acted on any one of these options, you can begin to use the product to satisfy your need for physical fitness, or social interaction, or whatever has motivated you to join a health club in the first place.

### ▼ EVALUATE THE CONSUMPTION EXPERIENCE

Once the product has been purchased and used, the consumer will typically evaluate his or her experience with it and decide how successfully the product has satisfied the individual's needs.[5] This evaluation is very important because the individual will remember his or her level of satisfaction when it comes time to search for alternatives to solve the same need the next time it arises. Evaluation of some products can be quite simple: If the socks you just bought fit, you feel positive about them. Others can be much more complex, such as your appraisal of your health club membership, which involves using more complicated criteria to choose

■ FIGURE 2.5
Tretorn provides the names of various retailers carrying its sneakers, including Lady Foot Locker, enabling consumers to find a convenient location.

■ FIGURE 2.6

This advertisement emphasizes the quality of Ford vehicles so that their owners will attribute any problems they may experience to bad luck or wear and tear instead of poor design.

## OUR DESIGNS ARE CONSTANTLY CHANGING BUT

## OUR *PHILOSOPHY* REMAINS THE SAME.

*Ford Designers: Soo Kang, Robert Bauer.*

*At FORD MOTOR COMPANY, we work with one basic premise: the design of a car or truck must go beyond how it looks. This philosophy has taken many shapes over the years, from the Model T, to the Continental, Taurus, Explorer, and Mustang: cars and trucks celebrated for their design. Which might explain why FORD MOTOR COMPANY has five of the ten best selling vehicles in America today. Right now we're applying the latest technology and the most DETAILED CRAFTSMANSHIP to every aspect of every automobile we create. By working with the automotive industry's most powerful supercomputer, our worldwide design team are indeed becoming the CRAFTSMEN OF THE FUTURE.*

FORD · FORD TRUCKS  LINCOLN · MERCURY ·

## QUALITY IS JOB 1.

among alternatives. Evaluation of a product also depends on whether it satisfies the individual's expectations (see Figure 2.6). Even though the health club you've chosen has an Olympic pool, for example, you may be disappointed because you did not make any new friends while swimming there.

▼ PROVIDE FEEDBACK

Once the individual has decided whether or not the purchase has been satisfactory, it is important to communicate the results of that experience to many people.[6] Feedback may be provided to whomever sold the customer the product and can occur face-to-face, in writing, or by telephone. It can take the form of complaints or compliments. Complaints are usually intended to change the terms of the exchange. The individual may want the value of what she exchanged for the product to be reduced, either by refunding some of the purchase price or by compensating her for other expenses. In our extended example, you may want your health club to refund part of your membership fee because the pool was closed for repairs for an entire week. Or, the individual may want the seller to change the product to increase her satisfaction. In our case, you may ask the health club manager to open the pool at 6:00 A.M. rather than 6:30 A.M. so that you can get there earlier and have more time to get ready for your first-period class.

Individuals also tell others about their experiences with products. You may tell your friends about how much you like swimming at the new club and try to persuade them to join. If you do not like the health club, you may complain to your friends about your experience and try to discourage them from joining. In some cases, consumers may even try to tell strangers about their experience. An individual may write a letter to a local newspaper or a magazine, either praising or condemning the use of a certain product or service. Magazines that specialize in a particular kind of product, such as cars, stereo equipment, or computers, often publish such letters.

▼ END THE CONSUMER PURCHASE PROCESS

Ultimately, the consumer ends the purchase process. In some cases, the individual simply stops using the product and disposes of its packaging and any remaining product.[7] As environmental concerns continue to grow, product disposal has become a more salient issue in consumer behavior. To dispose of a cereal box, a simple trip to the trash can solve the problem. For a bottle of soda, disposal means cleaning the bottle and placing it in a special recycling container. For an old car, disposal is even more complex. You can trade in your old car for part of the purchase price of a new one; the dealer will then market this used car to another consumer whose needs it will satisfy. If your old car is in such bad condition that no one else will buy it, you may have to pay to have it taken to a junk yard (see Figure 2.7).

With some products, particularly intangible ones, formal steps must be taken to end the consumption process. Fans have to leave the stadium after the football game is over; subscribers must notify the local newspaper if they want to end their home delivery service. Consumers often continue

■ FIGURE 2.7

European car makers have increased the number of automobile parts that can be recycled instead of sent to the junk yard.

to use a product that requires such formal steps because they must exert effort to end the exchange; it may be easier to continue to use the product than to try to dispose of it. If your health club requires you to notify them 30 days in advance that you want to end your membership, you may continue your membership longer than you have intended to because you haven't had a chance formally to quit the club.

# VARIATIONS IN PURCHASE BEHAVIOR

The steps described above are not set in stone and do not apply to every act of consumer behavior in the same way. Rather, there are variations in the actions a consumer might take to purchase different products and in the purchase activities that different people use to buy the same product.[8] Consumers may skip steps in the purchase process, or they may jump back and forth among them. For example, you might just buy a Kit Kat bar "on impulse," without searching for information about different brands of candy you might have chosen. You may not even have a conscious set of criteria you use when you think about which brand of candy bar you like best. Or, you may buy a Packard Bell personal computer because several of your friends have chosen that model, and then compare its specifications with other models to justify your choice.

In general, individuals spend more time and exert more effort to buy products that are particularly important or relevant to them than on products that don't matter as much. This concept of **involvement** describes the importance or relevance the consumer purchase process for a particular product has for a consumer.[9] A person's involvement in any consumer purchase is influenced by his or her needs and background. In turn, involvement level will have a significant impact on the effort a person exerts to complete the purchase activities.

> **Involvement** is the importance or relevance the purchase process for a particular product has for a consumer.

## FACT OR FICTION REVISITED

◉   Consumers do indeed spend more time and effort searching for information when purchasing a high involvement product than when purchasing a low involvement product.

No individual will go through all of the consumer purchase activities for everything he or she buys and consumes. For example, you may be very particular in choosing the best workout clothes, since you will wear them a lot, but not care at all about buying a formal outfit that you expect to wear infrequently. Furthermore, people may concentrate on particular activities when buying one product but emphasize different steps for another. For instance, you may spend more time searching for alternatives when you are buying a health club membership than when buying a pair of athletic shoes because you haven't learned much about health clubs in your area and you already know a great deal about the sneakers you plan to wear based on personal experience or preference.

People also differ in the amount of time and effort they devote to each of these activities. You may not put a lot of thought into choosing a health club, as long as it is co-ed, while your more health-conscious friends may spend a great deal more time and effort evaluating the equipment available in various fitness centers. You may decide very quickly that you need to join a health club to get in shape by the summer and start looking into available options right away, whereas your parents may spend a great deal of time trying to deny that they have a need to exercise before learning about the health clubs in their area. It is the existence of these differences among people and products that requires sophisticated consumer analysis. We will discuss the concept of involvement more fully in Chapter 8 when we talk about consumer motivations and needs.

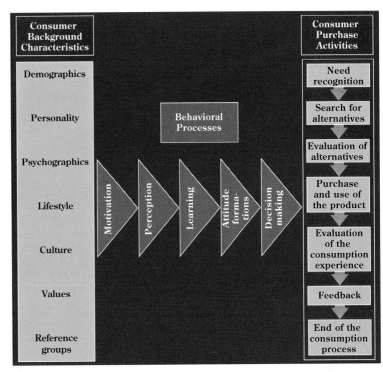

■ FIGURE 2.8

How consumer background characteristics and behavioral processes affect consumer purchase activities.

Once we have identified the actions individuals take to satisfy their needs, we can begin to analyze them. To do so, we must first identify the underlying factors that affect these actions and then analyze how these factors affect consumers as they complete the various steps discussed above. To simplify matters, we divide these underlying factors into the two broad components that are the key parts of our framework for consumer analysis: (1) consumer background characteristics, and (2) behavioral processes. Figure 2.8 illustrates how these components affect consumers' purchase activities.

## ▼ CONSUMER BACKGROUND CHARACTERISTICS

**Consumer background characteristics** are an innate part of a consumer's makeup. These are the things that consumers *are*—the way that individuals describe themselves, and the way they label others. These characteristics are stable aspects of a consumer's life that cannot be changed. Demographic characteristics, such as gender, age, or ethnic background, are examples of background characteristics. When senior citizens evaluate health clubs, they may be influenced by such advantages as senior citizen discounts for retired consumers who can exercise during midday. You cannot change your age at will, so this discount won't influence your choice of a health club, unless you are a senior citizen.

**Consumer background characteristics** are the innate, stable characteristics of a consumer's life that are based on the consumer's cultural background and values and demographic, psychological, and social attributes.

### ▼ BEHAVIORAL PROCESSES

**Behaviorial processes**
are the motivational,
perceptual, learning, attitude formation, and
decision making tools
consumers use to complete the activities that
satisfy their needs.

The second component of consumer behavior comprises the **behavioral processes** consumers use to interact with their world. These are the tools people use to recognize their feelings, gather and analyze information, formulate thoughts and opinions, and take action. For example, learning is a tool people use in many parts of their lives. You learn the lyrics to the latest Pearl Jam song before attending their concert; you learn traffic laws to be able to drive a car; or you learn exercise routines to strengthen the shoulder you injured playing basketball.

Unlike background characteristics, behavioral processes can be affected by a person's environment because they are applied on specific occasions. For example, if your roommate belongs to the Columbia House music club, he could help you learn about new musical groups more quickly by sharing the compact disks he buys through the club with you. Marketers and public policy actors are particularly interested in these processes because they offer opportunities for them to exert their influence over consumers. Music labels give their compact disks to music reviewers and radio stations so that consumers will learn about new releases quickly. In some cases, public policy advocates take offense at the lyrics of some music and attempt to persuade radio stations not to play such songs over the airwaves and music stores not to stock the offensive material.

# CONSUMER BACKGROUND CHARACTERISTICS

As noted above, background characteristics are the unchangeable or stable aspects of a person's life. They describe the traits and attributes individuals possess and the place they occupy in their social structure and environment. These characteristics fall into four main categories: (1) culture and values; (2) demographic characteristics; (3) personality, lifestyle, and psychographics; and (4) reference groups. Some, such as gender or race, can never be changed; others, such as geographical residence, lifestyle, or reference group, require a complete reorientation of a person's life to change them; whereas still others, such as age and stage in the life cycle, evolve gradually as the individual matures.

### ▼ CULTURE AND VALUES

**Culture** is the essential
character of a society
that distinguishes it
from other cultures.

**Values** are the underlying beliefs that are
shared by the members
of a society and that indicate how they should
act, think, and feel.

**Culture** is the essence of a society—the essential character of its people that distinguishes it from other cultures. The defining element of a culture is its **values**—the underlying beliefs shared by a society that indicate how its members should act, think, and feel. Values are the core views people hold about the way life should be lived and about what constitutes appropriate behavior. For example, ideally, all Americans share certain beliefs about the rights of the individual citizen, personal freedom, and the right to better oneself through hard work, as illustrated in Figure 2.9. Such values give meaning to people's activities and the objects they encounter in their environment.

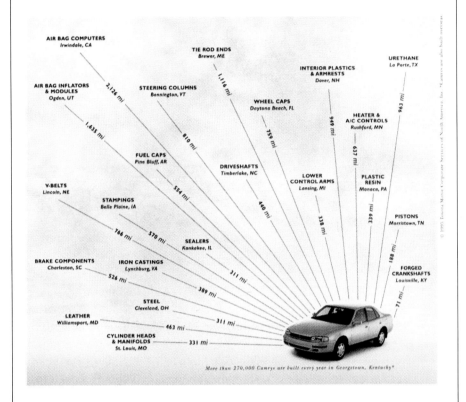

■ FIGURE 2.9
Toyota appeals to the American value of patriotism by promoting the fact that many of its parts are bought and manufactured in the United States.

Although culture and values are shared by most members of a society, they are enacted differently by members of different subcultural groups. *Value enactment* is the way shared values are translated into attitudes and behavior. For example, although many Americans believe that they should exercise in an effort to maintain health and fitness, that value is enacted quite differently by senior citizens, for whom a brisk walk is appropriate, and young adults, who may think that a daily five-mile run is necessary. Members of both groups would say that they value exercise, but they have chosen different ways to enact that value. Sociologists and anthropologists investigate how activities and objects gain their social value and why different social groups develop disparate enactments of commonly held beliefs.

## FACT OR FICTION REVISITED

⦿   Consumers who share the same values generally *do not* enact them in the same way. In fact, the same value may be enacted in many different ways, depending on background characteristics such as age, gender, income, personality, reference groups, and so on.

Culture and values help define how group members participate in consumer exchanges.[10] To begin, need recognition is significantly affected by a person's values. Some young adults view fitness as vigorous activity done on a daily basis, for example, and recognize the need for a place to exercise that offers, say, Stair Masters and a running track. In contrast, the elderly person who views fitness as more restrained physical activity will recognize the need for a safe neighborhood in which to walk.

Values also affect the evaluation of alternatives and the feedback offered after a choice has been made. If your values dictate that equality among social classes and ethnic groups is essential for a society to function properly, for example, you will place more importance on joining a health club that is made up of a diverse group of people than one that is attended primarily by members of a specific social class or ethnic group. Your willingness to complain about your consumption experience could also be affected by the value you place on fairness. Whereas another dissatisfied health club member might simply cancel her membership, you would consider it important to warn others about the treatment they could expect as a member of the club and might actively voice your concerns.

## FACT OR FICTION REVISITED

⦿   It is true that values affect the evaluation of alternatives as well as the feedback offered after a choice has been made.

**Demographic characteristics** are the physical, geographical, social, and economic attributes of consumers that are innate components of their day-to-day lives.

## ▼  DEMOGRAPHICS

**Demographic characteristics** are the physical, geographical, social, and economic attributes of individuals that are innate components of their day-to-day lives.[11] The study of demographics is a traditional part of sociology since these characteristics represent a person's place in the larger social structure. Your demographic characteristics offer a quick, easy way to place yourself and others in your environment. The actors portrayed in advertising typically provide cues as to who is the targeted consumer of a particular product, as shown in Figure 2.10.

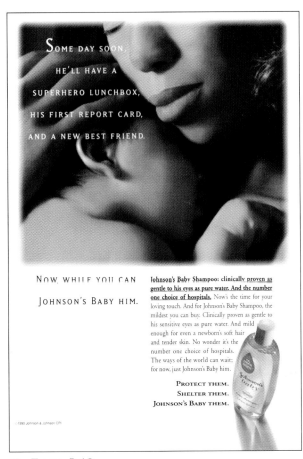

■ FIGURE 2.10

Johnson & Johnson targets African-American and white mothers by using models from each of these ethnic groups in its advertising.

Individuals are expected to act in particular ways because of their demographic characteristics, and we expect people who share demographic backgrounds to act similarly.

Awareness of demographic characteristics can help make social interactions more effective and efficient. While exercising at the gym, for example, you see a pair of middle-aged men in baggy sweatsuits walking on adjacent treadmills discussing what to do about the poor performance of the sales manager in their district. You would probably classify them as local business executives and may try to get to know them to see whether they are hiring new college graduates for entry-level sales jobs. You might view them differently than you would two women in their twenties dressed in leotards on adjacent StairMasters. You must be careful not to let these kinds of classifications evolve into stereotypes that prejudice your expectations about other people, however. If you assume that all individuals who share demographic characteristics are completely similar to one another, or that these characteristics will determine all aspects of their behavior, you run a

49

great risk of unexpected consequences and missed opportunities. The two women may be successful local recruiters for a firm in your area.

Demographics play a prominent role in all of the consumer purchase activities. For example, a person's search for alternatives often involves asking friends about the options they know of. Your circle of friends probably contains people who share your demographic characteristics. They are around your age, live nearby, and come from a similar class background. Consequently, they will recommend similar sets of products. This may be exactly what you are looking for if you want to join a health club and exercise with people like you. But if you are looking for someplace different in order to meet new people from different backgrounds, you would have to widen your search.

The demographics of a club's membership could also affect your evaluation of alternatives if club membership is one of your primary criteria. You may have an idea of the kind of people you want to be around when you exercise, and you look for them in choosing a club to join. The "kind of people" an individual seeks out may vary from product to product, and different consumers may have different expectations. Like Carol Beutel, you may want your fellow club members to be members of the opposite sex who will be interesting to talk with while you exercise and possibly spark a romantic interest. Someone else may want to exercise in the company of members of the same sex to avoid embarrassment or the pressure to flirt while exercising.

## ▼ PERSONALITY, LIFESTYLE, AND PSYCHOGRAPHICS

**Personality, lifestyle, and psychographics** represent an attempt to describe the essential psychological characteristics that affect a person's behavior. Personality classifications measure a person's underlying traits or psychological characteristics, which determine and reflect how the individual responds to his or her environment. It is difficult to measure these innate, deeply rooted traits, however, and to distinguish people who have them from those who do not. Whereas personality affects many consumer activities, it is not easy to detect a person's psychological characteristics in the outward signs of one's everyday consumer behavior.[12]

To address these psychological characteristics in a more useful fashion, psychologists and sociologists have developed ways of classifying consumers that identify the day-to-day expression of these traits. That is, instead of trying to measure their psychological characteristics directly, lifestyle and psychographic classifications identify an individual's current activities, interests, and opinions as indicators of his or her underlying characteristics.[13] *Lifestyle analysis* has traditionally emphasized the social and cultural settings that reflect a group's set of shared values or beliefs, and *psychographic analysis* emphasizes the individual psychological components of these opinions.

To illustrate the distinctions among personality, lifestyle, and psychographic analyses, consider a person who is innovative, craves novelty, and wants others to recognize these traits in her. Although these specific traits are hard to detect, consumer analysts have found that certain observable opinions, activities, and interests indicate whether someone is likely to be this kind of person. If the individ-

**Personality, lifestyle, and psychographics** represent the essential psychological characteristics that affect a person's behavior. Personality measures underlying psychological characteristics, whereas lifestyle and psychographics use consumers' current activities, interests, and opinions as indicators of the underlying characterics.

ual says that she is eager to be the first to try new exercise programs or if she attends high-impact aerobics classes and enjoys bungee-jumping, she is more likely to be the type of person described above than one who joins new programs only after his friends have tried them first, walks for exercise, and plays chess. All of these factors represent the same underlying psychological traits. Lifestyle analysis concentrates more on the social activities in which the traits are exhibited and often forms the basis for the activities portrayed in advertising, as shown in Figure 2.11. Psychographic measures focus on personal opinions. In practice, lifestyle and psychographic analyses are usually completed together.

A person's underlying psychological traits will affect the way he or she proceeds through the consumer behavior process. If you are impatient or quick to make decisions, you will probably move quickly through the search and evaluation steps. Your friend, who is painstaking in everything she does, may take quite a bit longer to complete her search and evaluation of a new health club. Your purchase decision would be very different as well. You would make up your mind after a quick visit to each club, and your friend might try a week's trial membership at several of the clubs before deciding. You might also be more likely to make a quick evaluation of your experience with the health club you've chosen and provide immediate feedback to all of your friends. In contrast, your friend may take longer to decide how she really feels about the place and will not want to influence her friends' opinions by offering any feedback just yet. The Pleasures of Consumption box below provides descriptions of exercisers and nonexercisers to illustrate lifestyle and psychographic differences among consumers.

■ FIGURE 2.11
This Evian ad is designed to appeal to young women who include exercise as part of their lifestyles.

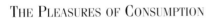 THE PLEASURES OF CONSUMPTION

**The Pleasures of Exercise**

Some Americans enjoy exercise and some do not. Hsiaofang Hwang[14] recently compared American adults who exercised frequently with those who do not and discovered many interesting lifestyle differences. She used information from a national survey of adults from the DDB Needham Lifestyle Survey to compare the lifestyle and psychographics of the 16 percent of Americans who engage in specific exercise activities most frequently with the 18 percent who exercise the least. She also conducted personal interviews with exercisers and nonexercisers. She found that exercisers typically view exercise activities as an integral part of a way of life that provides them with physical, psychological, and social benefits, whereas nonexercisers consider it a byproduct of work or household chores. Exercise is part of a lifestyle for those who do it but is viewed as a boring activity by those who don't engage in a specific exercise program.

Exercisers are typically more health conscious than nonexercisers. They are more likely to avoid cholesterol, fat, salt, and additives and to eat low-calorie foods, low-fat ice cream and yogurt, green salads, and fresh fish and seafood. Exercisers are more likely to select foods with added vitamins, to check ingredient labels, and to use recipes from magazine advertisements. They are also more likely than nonexercisers to be optimistic, self-confident, outgoing, and concerned about the environment. Finally, they are more likely to read *Newsweek* and the *Wall Street Journal*, whereas nonexercisers are more likely to watch *America's Most Wanted*, *Unsolved Mysteries*, and game shows.

Many people begin exercise programs with the best intentions, only to stop in a few weeks or months. Does this support the notion that exercise is an underlying lifestyle or psychographic trait? Think of someone you know who began to exercise regularly after years of inactivity and has continued for a long time. What caused the change?

## ▼ REFERENCE GROUPS

> A **reference group** is the set of people a consumer uses as the standard of reference for his or her behavior.

A **reference group** is an individual or group that serves as the standard of comparison for one's values, attitudes, or behavior.[15] A person's reference group has a significant effect on his or her beliefs, evaluations, and actions. Furthermore, an individual can have many reference groups and may look to different groups for models of different kinds of behavior. The group that you employ as a reference for a particular product will influence the way you use the behavioral processes. For example, if you adopt your wealthy aunt's attitudes about restaurants, you may perceive Burger King as an inappropriate place to have dinner. But if you mirror your roommates' attitudes, you may think that Burger King is great anytime.

At different times, people may choose to make a group to which they already belong their reference group, or they may make a conscious effort to behave differently than the members of a certain group. A person can also adopt the standards of a group to which he or she *wants* to belong. These groups can be defined in a number of ways. Individuals who share demographic characteristics, lifestyles, or a way of enacting values, or who live or work together, can form a reference group. For example, you may use the students at your school as your standard of reference for the clothing you wear on campus today but refer to the models in *GQ* when buying a suit to wear on an interview for a job on Wall Street after graduation.

### FACT OR FICTION REVISITED

⦿   It is true that most consumer have more than one reference group. Reference groups may be based on family, friends, co-workers, teammates, role models, and many other associations.

# BEHAVIORAL PROCESSES

The second component of consumer behavior comprises the general behavioral processes consumers use to satisfy their needs. These are the tools people use to identify their thoughts and feelings and to plan and implement their actions; they allow individuals to interact with their environment. These thoughts, feelings, and actions are generated by the social and psychological processes of motivation, perception, learning, attitude formation, and decision making, which serve as the bridge between consumers' background characteristics and the consumption that satisfies their needs.

*Motivation* is the psychological process that allows consumers to recognize their needs. *Perception* is the process consumers use to gather information from their environment, and *learning* is the tool they use to organize and remember that information. When consumers evaluate that information in light of their needs and background characteristics and then choose a product to buy, they are using *attitude formation* and *decision making*. These behavioral processes are the key tools that consumers use to complete the consumer exchange activities.

## ▼ MOTIVATION

**Motivation** is the internal process that impels individuals to recognize their needs and initiate action to satisfy those needs. Once the motivation process has identified a need, the individual can begin the steps in consumer exchange, using the processes of perception, learning, attitude formation, and decision making.[16] Some are innate biological or physiological needs, such as the hunger for a Big Mac (see Figure 2.12). Other needs have been acquired during past psychological and social experiences, such as Carol Beutel's need to find a place to make friends for social companionship. Many different needs can motivate consumers toward the same consumer behavior. For example, you may have joined a health club to fulfill your need for physical exercise, but another member may have joined to meet new people to fulfill his need for social interaction.

> **Motivation** is the process by which consumers recognize their innate or acquired needs and initiate action to satisfy those needs.

Because motivations vary from one individual to another and for the same consumer under different circumstances, the benefits consumers seek will also be different for different people and in different situations. As a result, different evaluation criteria may be used. For example, if your motivation to join a health club is exercise, you will look for health benefits and emphasize the quality of the facilities over anything else. But if another consumer's motivation is to meet new people, she is seeking social benefits and will focus on the kinds of people who belong to the club.

Consumers recognize that some of their needs are more important or relevant than others. Such important and personally relevant needs are called *high involvement needs*, while less important needs are *low involvement needs*. The more motivating, higher in-

■ FIGURE 2.12

McDonald's hopes that showing a Big Mac in an advertisement will motivate hungry consumers to buy one.

volvement needs elicit stronger feelings and require greater thought throughout the consumer purchase process. Consequently, a person naturally invests more time searching for and evaluating alternatives to satisfy a high involvement need. For example, some consumers may be more involved in choosing their health club than their dry cleaner, even though they spend the same amount of money each year on these services. This is because they have stronger feelings about the way their bodies appear and function than they do about their clothes.

## ▼ PERCEPTION

**Perception** is the process by which individuals select stimuli or objects in their environment, gather information about them, and interpret the meaning of the information to give them a coherent picture. Perception allows individuals to identify the people and products around them, providing a link between the individual and the outside world. As a result, everything that occurs in the environment must first pass through the individual's perceptual processes before he or she can make any sense of it or use it.

> **Perception** is the process consumers use to select stimuli or objects in their environment, gather information about them, and interpret the meaning of the information.

### FACT OR FICTION REVISITED

⊙    It is a fact that everything that occurs in the consumer's environment must first pass through his or her perceptual process before the consumer can make any sense out of it.

Perception is most useful in the consumer exchange steps that require consumers to glean information from their environment—searching for alternatives, evaluating them, and conducting a postpurchase evaluation.[17] Furthermore, the act of searching for alternatives only identifies those options the individual can perceive. That is, a person's ability to perceive an alternative is affected by both the individual's perceptual tools and the visibility of the option. You may drive past a health club every day on your way to campus, but you don't notice it until someone else points it out to you. Likewise, that health club may not display a sign or advertise its services, so it will be less visible than competitors that do both. Ultimately, you only evaluate those clubs that you interpret as viable alternatives. If you look at a health club more closely and identify it as inappropriate because it doesn't have a pool or some other important criterion, you won't even bother to evaluate it. Consumers' perceptions can also influence the way information is interpreted. For example, most consumers assume that any 800 numbers they dial will connect them to a free service (see Figure 2.13). As the Public Policy box below illustrates, this is not always the case.

 PUBLIC POLICY

**Aren't 1-800 Numbers Free?[18]**
Consumers use their perceptual tools to gather information during their search for and evaluation of a new product or service. Most consumers interpret a "1-800" num-

Model 735i

## Introducing
## BEL 735i Plus

*with new safety feature
and VG-2 Guard™*

**BEL 735i *Plus*** is the result of over 25 years of electronics expertise. In Radar. In Laser. In design innovation.

In fact, BEL's expertise has been well documented in leading industry publications. In 1994 alone, two major automotive magazines rated BEL-TRONICS' models their number-one choice. Today, the new BEL 735i *Plus* represents the next generation in integrated Radar/Laser detection from BEL-TRONICS – the industry leader.

BEL 735i *Plus* combines a unique, full-featured design with outstanding sensitivity to all Radar, including the complete Super Wideband Ka. New VG-2 Guard™ provides true invisibility to the Radar Detector Detector. And BEL's number-one rated Laser technology includes both front *and* rear Laser detection.

BEL 735i *Plus* also incorporates a new safety feature – an advanced road hazard alert. This alert warns to the presence of potential road hazards and emergency vehicles which employ safety radar transmitting devices, allowing you to take action and adjust your driving accordingly.

BEL 735i *Plus*, from the recognized industry leader, is available today for $229.95. To order or for a name of a dealer near you, call toll-free today:

*1-800-341-1401 USA*
*1-800-268-3994 Canada*

**⬭BEL⬭**

**BEL-TRONICS LIMITED**
Leadership through Innovation and Technology®

Defend your right to use a Radar/Laser detector. Contact RADAR, 4949 S. 25-A, Tipp City, OH, 45371 or call: 1-800-448-5170.

® registered trademark of BEL-TRONICS LIMITED. TM trademark of BEL-TRONICS LIMITED.
Protected under U.S. and foreign patents.

ber in an advertisement to mean that the advertised service is free of charge. This is because experience with virtually all existing 800 numbers and their ads tells consumers that the telephone call will indeed be free.

However, some telephone services have charged consumers for such seemingly free calls. An unintended loophole in a 1992 law allowed such pay services to use 800 numbers instead of the traditional 900 numbers that consumers know require payment. These services are required to ask for a credit card number or written approval to place charges on the consumer's local telephone bill. MCI billed consumers 75¢ every time they used its 1-800-CALL-INFO directory assistance service, as did others, such as telephone sex lines and psychic services, who hoped that consumers wouldn't notice the charges.

In response to complaints by AT&T to the Federal Communications Commission, MCI now bills through credit card numbers or by specific arrangements with the caller. Hotel management, university administrators, businesspeople, and parents of minors also complained when they were charged for the calls their patrons, students, employees, or children made on these 800 pay services. These institutions had blocked 900 number calls so that they would not have to pay for them, but they did not think to block 800 numbers since they assumed they were all free. In response to consumers' complaints, the Federal Trade Commission, the Federal Communications Commission, and the National Association of Attorneys General have introduced legislation that will require written approval from callers, an action intended to prevent unsuspecting consumers from being charged without their consent.

Do you think that consumers should expect that all 800 numbers are free so that they can rely on that perception when they view advertising? Once consumers saw their local phone bill with these 800 number charges and learned that their perception of these new pay services was incorrect, would it be realistic for them to expect that the charges be removed? Why or why not?

## ▼ LEARNING

**Learning is the process by which consumers organize knowledge and experience so that they can use them again in future activities.**

**Learning** is the process by which individuals organize knowledge so that it causes a permanent change in their behavior and can be used again in future consumer exchange activities.[19] This knowledge can be gained through a person's own experience or through information gathered from the environment. For example, you might buy *Stereo Review* to look for audio equipment advertisements, such as the one depicted in Figure 2.14, before you buy a compact disk player. In either case, learning requires that the individual organize these experiences and information into a useful framework to guide future activities.

Learning is an invaluable tool in increasing the efficiency and effectiveness of consumer behavior. If, as consumers, we were unable to organize knowledge from the past, we would have to complete every activity of the consumer exchange process every time we recognized a need. Instead, we are able to recall past situations and use accumulated learning to help us satisfy our needs. Furthermore, recalling past needs helps consumers recognize current ones. For example, you begin exercising furiously in March when you recall that every summer you are embarrassed to wear a bathing suit at the beach. Your search for alternatives—a new health club—begins with the products you considered the last time you made a similar purchase—last Spring. Finally, your evaluation of the purchase you made often involves a comparison to past purchases.

## ▼ ATTITUDE FORMATION

**Attitude formation is the process by which consumers evaluate an object, form a feeling or opinion about it, and develop a predisposition to act based on that opinion.**

**Attitude formation** is the process by which individuals form a feeling or opinion about objects in their environment. People's attitudes toward an object is based

■ FIGURE 2.14

Ads such as this one for a Technics compact disk player include a great deal of detailed information so that the consumer can gather knowledge about the product before making a purchase.

on a number of factors, including (1) *learned knowledge* from their own experiences with the object as well as information gathered from others; (2) an *evaluation* of the object based on their knowledge of it; and (3) a *predisposition to act* based on that evaluation. Simply stated, consumers form attitudes toward people, products, ideas, activities, and many other objects in their environment. They also form attitudes toward aspects of each product they have identified as important criteria in their purchase decision.[20] For example, most consumers think that BMWs are high-quality cars, but some also think that they are too expensive. Consumers use these attitudes in evaluating the alternatives before making a purchase and then again in evaluating the consumption experience after the purchase has been made. To form an attitude, individuals must first combine information they have gathered through perceptual processes with knowledge they recall from past experiences. Once this information has been gathered, it is evaluated in light of the person's needs and background characteristics to form an attitude.

## FACT OR FICTION REVISITED

⊛   Most consumer attitudes *do not* change very quickly; most are enduring structures that affect many kinds of behavior over extended periods of time.

| |
|---|
| **Decision making** is the tool consumers use to choose among alternative actions that are available to them. |

## ▼ DECISION MAKING

The last behavioral process, **decision making,** is the tool consumers use to choose among alternative actions available to them.[21] Decision making plays a key role in the search for alternatives, evaluation, and purchase of a product or service, as well as in providing feedback and ending the consumption process.

Psychologists and economists have studied decision making extensively and have provided a description of its key components. Indeed, our definition of the first steps of the consumer exchange process is rooted in the notion that consumer behavior is a decision making process. To choose among alternatives, a consumer must be able to identify what options exist, establish criteria for evaluating them, develop a method for combining these criteria into a simple rule, and then apply that rule in making a purchase.

To make a decision about which health club to join, for example, you would form an overall attitude toward each alternative, which would be based on a combination of your attitudes toward each individual aspect of the club. In doing this, you would need to develop a rule to combine your individual attitudes in a way that reflects your needs. If you are looking for a health club to satisfy your need for exercise, for example, you would emphasize your attitude toward the club's facilities and equipment and discount your attitudes about its social atmosphere.

## FACT OR FICTION REVISITED

⊛   When consumers choose among alternatives, they do indeed identify their options, establish criteria for evaluating these options, and apply those rules when they decide how to act.

# USING THE KEY COMPONENTS TO ANALYZE CONSUMER BEHAVIOR

Consider Carol Beutel and her purchase and use of her health club membership. Carol's background characteristics affected the way she used the behavioral processes to complete the activities necessary to join the gym. As a newly divorced single mother, she wanted the gym to offer her exercise and some social opportunities, for a moderate membership fee. Her personality, lifestyle, and psychographics caused her to consider the atmosphere of the health club. She visited the gym at which her friend exercised because she thought that a member of her reference group would have similar tastes.

Carol evaluated the costs, atmosphere, and cleanliness of various health clubs while making her decision about which one to join. She combined the information she gathered from her friend with her own observations of the clubs she visited to form her attitude about the gyms' abilities to satisfy her needs. After she joined one, however, she learned some interesting things about her own values and lifestyle. She found that she was so busy that getting to the gym for scheduled classes caused her more stress than it relieved, so she shifted her emphasis to individual exercise. She soon realized that riding her bike on her own time gave her exercise and satisfied her (and her son's) desire to act responsibly toward the environment. Carol never complained—it wasn't the management's fault that her needs had changed—with her busy lifestyle, she just stopped going to the gym.

In the next chapter, we will turn to a discussion of the marketer's role in consumer behavior. We will then begin our extensive discussion of consumers' background characteristics and behavioral processes in Chapter 4.

## SUMMARY

1. **Identify the activities consumers carry out during the consumer behavior process.** Consumers (1) recognize that they have a need; (2) search for alternative products that will satisfy that need; (3) evaluate and choose among the alternative products they have identified; (4) purchase and use the product; (5) evaluate their satisfaction with the product after they have used it and decide whether they would purchase the same product again; (6) offer feedback to the marketer from whom they bought the product as well as to other consumers; and (7) end the consumer behavior process by disposing of any leftover product and packaging.

2. **Distinguish among the activities carried out by diverse consumer segments during the purchase and use of a particular product and recognize the factors that cause the different patterns of activities.** Consumers differ in the ways they employ the consumer purchase activities because they vary in both background characteristics and in the ways they use behavioral processes to complete the activities. Background characteristics are the innate, stable parts of con-

sumers' lives, such as values, social factors, and psychological characteristics. Behavioral processes are the tools consumers use to interact with their environment and to gather knowledge they can use to choose the appropriate product to satisfy their needs.

3. **Determine which of the background characteristics distinguish among the diverse segments that complete the purchase activities in different ways.** Background characteristics include culture and values; demographics; personality, lifestyle, and psychographics; and reference groups. These characteristics are very difficult to change—for example, gender is unchangeable; age evolves slowly as consumers mature; and personality or lifestyle require a long-term, intensive effort to modify. As a result, consumer researchers identify those characteristics that result in different patterns of purchase activities. For example, health club marketers investigate whether men search for information about clubs differently than women, or whether daily swimmers look for different facilities than do once-a-week exercisers.

4. **Analyze how consumers use the behavioral processes to help them complete the activities involved in buying and using a product.** Motivation, perception, learning, attitude formation, and decision making are the processes that enable consumers to buy and use products. Consumers employ these processes as tools. For example, a consumer would use his or her perceptual and learning processes to search for the information needed in making a choice about which local health club to join. The individual would visit the club to look at the facilities and talk to members and then organize these observations and recollections of what members said in making a decision.

# KEY TERMS

Consumer purchase
  activities, *p. 37*
Involvement, *p. 44*
Consumer background
  characteristics, *p. 45*
Behavioral processes,
  *p. 46*

Culture, *p. 46*
Values, *p. 46*
Demographic characteristics, *p. 48*
Personality, lifestyle, and psychographics, *p. 50*
Reference group, *p. 52*

Motivation, *p. 53*
Perception, *p. 54*
Learning, *p. 56*
Attitude formation, *p. 56*
Decision making, *p. 58*

# SKILL-BUILDING ACTIVITIES

1. Assume that you are the manager of a local health club. List the steps in your customers' (and potential customers') purchase processes. How can you influence each?

2. Identify one high involvement and one low involvement product you have purchased within the past month. Considering the steps in the purchase process, in what ways was the purchase of the high involvement product similar to, and in what ways was it different from, the purchase of the low involvement product?

3. Interview someone who is very different from you in age, social class, or some other background characteristics. How do their background characteristics influ-

ence their purchases of inexpensive grocery and drug store items? Durable goods? Services? Which kinds of purchases are influenced most, and which kinds of purchases are influenced least?

4. Supposing, once again, that you are a manager of a local health club. What background characteristics of your customers and potential customers will you find to be most important in marketing the club? What characteristics will be most important in managing the club? Explain.

5. List the most important reference groups for the person you interviewed in activity (3). How have these groups influenced the person's consumer behavior?

6. Consider the high-involvment purchase you described in activity (2). How was that purchase influenced by
   a. perception     b. learning     c. attitudes     d. decision processes

---

▼ MULTIPLE CHOICE

# CHAPTER 2
# SELF-TEST

1. The first activity in any act of consumer behavior is
   a. search
   b. evaluation of alternatives
   c. recognizing needs
   d. purchase

2. Price, color, and a long-term warranty would be examples of evaluative _____ used to determine which alternative should be the one selected for purchase.
   a. judgments
   b. criteria
   c. standard
   d. benchmark

3. Ending the consumer purchase process may include which of the following techniques?
   a. leaving a concert when it is over
   b. deciding after you enter a store not to buy any products
   c. finding out that you do not have enough money to buy the product
   d. test driving a car but not purchasing the car

4. If a consumer places great importance on a purchase, that product would be considered a(n) _____ product.
   a. salient
   b. high involvement
   c. high-impact
   d. expensive

5. _____ are the things that people are, while behavioral processes are the tools people use in making decisions.
   a. Consumer background characteristics
   b. Consumer features
   c. Personality traits
   d. Reference characteristics

6. Beliefs about personal freedom, hard work, and individual rights are all considered American cultural _____.
   a. norms
   b. behaviors
   c. goals
   d. values

7. Friends, family, and co-workers would all be considered _____ groups, if they have a significant effect on consumer behavior.
   a. reference
   b. endorsement
   c. credential
   d. expertise

8. The processing of information and the interpretation of that information are components of the process called _____.
   a. memory
   b. perception
   c. impression
   d. insight

9. When consumers organize knowledge so that it causes a change in their behavior, they have experienced _____.
   a. learning
   b. comprehension
   c. realization
   d. evaluation

10. Your hobbies and membership in clubs and organizations are components of your _____.
   a. culture
   b. lifestyle
   c. motivation
   d. learned knowledge

▼ TRUE/FALSE

1. The search for alternatives is purely scanning your memory for information. T or F

2. The purchase process includes determining how you will pay for the product. T or F

3. Consumer feedback is always negative.   T or F

4. Consumers go through all of the consumer purchase activities for all their purchases.   T or F

5. A person's income, level of education, and gender are all considered demographic characteristics.   T or F

6. Personality is often used in marketing strategy formation because it is so easy to measure.   T or F

7. Motivation is based purely on consumer's biological needs.   T or F

8. Consumer attitudes are superficial and are relatively easy to change.   T or F

9. Consumers may share values but enact, or show, these values differently.   T or F

10. Postpurchase evaluation can be based not only on the actual performance of the product but also on the consumer's expectations.   T or F

▼ SHORT ANSWER

1. Describe the search process likely to be used when purchasing an automobile.

2. Describe how lifestyle and psychographics could play a role in your choice of a vacation spot.

3. What reference group(s) would be most influential to you in the following consumer behavior situations:  (a) the choice of a video rental  (b) choosing a restaurant for a first date  (c) buying a compact disk player. Explain your responses.

4. In what ways do consumers provide feedback about a purchase they have made?

▼ APPLICATION EXERCISE

Consumer behavior includes many different kinds of purchases. For example, you are presently consuming a business school education. Using the seven consumer purchase activities outlined in the text, describe the process you used in choosing your present college or university.

# 3

# MARKETERS AND CONSUMER BEHAVIOR

◉ Consumer Snapshot  *Lyn Welle is a 27-year-old credit representative for AT&T. She is single and lives in St. Paul, Minnesota.*

FACT OR FICTION?

◉ Instead of attempting to develop different products for different segments of the population, today's consumer marketers attempt to develop the one best product that will appeal to all of them.

◉ Product positioning signals a segment of the market for which the product is not intended to meet certain needs.

◉ Consumers can usually predict whether a new product will succeed.

- A market segment is a group of consumers who will respond relatively homogenously to a marketer's efforts.

- In a "customized" market, the segments are usually very large.

- Marketers who market to many small segments are more likely to benefit from economies of scale than are marketers who market to a small number of large segments.

- Marketers typically prefer to market to a small number of stable, accessible segments.

- The decision to target a segment is best made by balancing the expected sales from that segment against the expected cost of reaching that segment.

- Most automobile manufacturers adopt a concentrated marketing strategy.

- Product positioning is the complement of market segmentation.

- A product's actual price may include both money and time.

# EYE ON THE CONSUMER

Lyn Welle has always been physically fit—she was involved in several sports in high school, and she likes to play tennis, run, and ski cross-country. But the winters in Minnesota are harsh, and she's found that she can't always get out to do these things on a regular basis. So now that she is no longer in college and isn't working out in the school's gym, Lyn has decided to join a health club. Initially she used guest passes to try several of the clubs in her area, but she quickly rejected the big clubs like Bally's Jack LaLane because of the crowds and the atmosphere. With all those guys watching you work out, she said, it was like a meat market, and she wanted to be able to go and work out in a t-shirt and shorts and not have to worry about that kind of distraction.

Lyn joined the health club to which her friend Liz belonged. It was a small place that had all of the equipment she wanted, a wide variety of classes, and helpful instructors and staff. She takes three aerobic or step classes a week, does weight training twice a week, and is taking a boxing class. Sometimes she also works on the StairMaster, the exercise bicycle, and the treadmill. And she still runs outside of the gym, particularly some two- and five-kilometer runs for local charities. Lyn has made a lot of friends at the gym—people she can work out with and some who have become friends outside of the club. Lyn is even dating a man she met there. She is such a regular at the club that when she goes at a different time than usual other members will ask her later where she has been. She enjoys the attention because it helps to motivate her.

The ultimate goal of a marketer is to produce products and services that satisfy consumer needs. To do so, marketers must possess knowledge about consumers and their behavior. In Chapter 2, we discussed consumers' activities, their background characteristics, and the behavioral processes they use to complete their activities. In this chapter, we shift our focus to marketers and the activities they use to market products that satisfy consumers' needs. We will discuss why it is so important for marketers to understand consumer behavior and how they use their understanding to segment markets, position products, and develop the marketing mix.

After reading and thinking about this chapter, you should be able to:

❶ Understand the role that segmentation, positioning, and the marketing mix play in a firm's marketing strategy.

❷ Analyze the methods marketers use to segment markets and choose their segmentation strategy.

❸ Identify the positions of products and the strategies used by marketers to achieve those positions.

❹ Recognize the marketing mixes that marketers use to satisfy consumers.

# The Role of Consumer Behavior in Marketing Strategy

In today's diverse, complex, and rapidly changing consumer environment, marketers recognize that they cannot produce one product that will satisfy all consumers. Instead, they must develop a **marketing strategy**—a plan to guide their efforts to exchange specific products with specific consumer segments. The foundation of any marketing strategy and its resulting activities must be an analysis of consumer behavior. Table 3.1 shows some of the marketing activities that are necessary to develop a marketing strategy as well as areas of consumer behavior that must be understood to complete those activities.

> **A marketing strategy** is the plan marketers use to guide their efforts to exchange specific products with specific consumer segments.

## FACT OR FICTION REVISITED

◉ Consumer marketers *do not* typically attempt to develop the one best product that will appeal to all segments of the population. Even the largest mass marketers attempt to segment their markets.

## Table 3.1

### COMPONENTS OF MARKETING STRATEGY AND ASSOCIATED ACTIVITIES

| Components of Marketing Strategy and Associated Activities | Kinds of Necessary Consumer Behavior Knowledge |
|---|---|
| **Segmentation** | |
| Divide consumers into market segments | Bases of cultural, demographic, personality, lifestyle, and psychographic groups |
| Select the target market segment(s) | The behavioral processes used by consumer segments to complete purchase activities |
| **Positioning** | |
| Position the product in consumers' minds | Perception and learning to form attitudes about the product |
| **Marketing mix** | |
| Design the product and its features | Consumers' motivations to seek product benefits that will address and result in favor able attitudes and decision making |
| Set the price | Price perceptions, learning, and attitudes about price and its role in decision making |
| Design a promotion strategy | Role of perception and learning in searching for information about the product |
| Choose where the product will be sold | Perception and learning about where the product is sold |

**Marketing segmentation** involves dividing the total market into segments and then targeting specific products at selected segments.

**Product positioning** conveys to consumers in the selected target segment that a product is appropriate for them and signals to those in other segments that it will not meet their needs.

## ▼ COMPONENTS OF A MARKETING STRATEGY

The first component of a marketing strategy is **market segmentation**, which is the process of dividing the total market into segments based on consumer backgrounds, needs, and behavioral processes and then targeting specific products at selected segments. Choosing to target a product at a selected segment means that other segments are consciously excluded from the market for that product. For example, Gillette's Soft & Dri deodorant is targeted at women, while its Right Guard is aimed primarily at men, so advertising for these products include messages targeted at specific genders (Figure 3.1). Just think of the clothing stores at your local shopping mall; each offers a different mix of fashions that satisfies different kinds of consumers, from Gap for Kids for children's casual clothes, to Banana Republic for outdoor apparel, to Lane Bryant for women's larger sizes. Even shoe stores have begun to segment their products. You can buy men's sneakers at Foot Locker, women's sneakers at Lady Foot Locker, and sneakers for your children at Foot Locker for Kids.

The second component of the marketing strategy, **product positioning**, is a complementary process that indicates to consumers in the selected target segment that the product is appropriate for them and, at the same time, signals to those in other segments that it will not meet their needs. In other words, a prod-

■ FIGURE 3.1
Gillette targets its Soft &
Dri deodorant at women
and its Right Guard brand
at men.

uct's position is the "mental location" to which consumers assign the product in their minds; that is, their perceptions of the product relative to others that might satisfy the same needs. In advertisements for Ford's Mustang and Taurus, for example (Figure 3.2), both the information conveyed and the tone of the ads provide an overall image of each of the cars and indicate for whom each is appropriate.

Finally, marketers develop a product's **marketing mix**, which is often referred to as the "4 P's," for *product*, *price*, *promotion*, and *place*. The marketing mix consists of (1) the product's features, (2) its price, (3) its promotion to con-

> The **marketing mix** is
> the set of variables—
> product, price, promo-
> tion, and place—the
> marketer uses to facili-
> tate exchange with con-
> sumers.

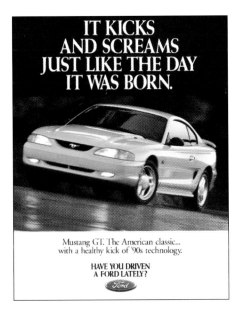

■ FIGURE 3.2
Mustang is positioned as a
sporty car for the younger
driver whereas Taurus is
positioned as a family automobile.

69

■ FIGURE 3.3

Waterman pens are aimed at an upscale target market whereas Papermate pens are targeted at a broader mass market.

sumers, and (4) the means by which it is delivered to the place where consumers can buy it. In other words, the marketing mix is the set of variables the marketer controls to facilitate exchange with consumers in order to satisfy their needs. Waterman fountain pens, for example, are designed, priced, advertised, and sold differently than are PaperMate pens (Figure 3.3).

## FACT OR FICTION REVISITED

◉   Product positioning does indeed signal a segment of the market for which the product is *not* intended.

## ▼ THE BENEFITS OF USING CONSUMER BEHAVIOR IN A MARKETING STRATEGY

Marketers want to identify those target market segments that will respond favorably to their products' positioning and marketing mix and, ultimately, purchase their products. As you will see in this chapter, segmenting, positioning, and developing an appealing marketing mix is a long, difficult process that takes a lot of work. Marketers cannot simply ask consumers what they want and then divide them into one segment that wants the product and one that doesn't; they need to *understand* consumer behavior.[1] Consumers, as marketers will attest, are not very good at forecasting what they want. Even when asked directly how appealing they find a product, consumers are often unable to answer the question accurately. Although there is some relationship between purchase intent, as reported by consumers themselves, and actual purchase in the future, consumers generally have difficulty expressing what they want, for the following reasons:

❶ They may not know what the products will do, and therefore ca`
   keters that they want them.

❷ They may want a product today, but there could be significa`
   their lives or in competitors' products in the future.

❸ They may be unable to imagine something different thar`
   products and express a reluctance to try anything new-
   start to buy the new product and then they will too.

❹ They may try to appease the marketers and tell them that u.
   ucts that they would never actually buy.

Thus, instead of relying solely on what consumers say they want, marketers musч
also analyze consumer needs based on their background and general behavior.

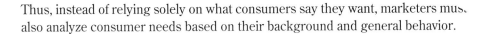

## FACT OR FICTION REVISITED

⊙    It is *not true* that consumers can usually predict whether a new product will
succeed. In fact, consumers are not very good at forecasting what they want.

# MARKET SEGMENTATION

Marketers cannot be all things to all consumers. A firm cannot satisfy every
consumer with the same product, no matter how effectively it designs the
product and its marketing mix. For example, consider what Lyn Welle
and Carol Beutel each wants from a health club. It would be difficult for one club
to meet the needs of an exerciser such as Lyn and someone like Carol. At the
same time, most firms cannot offer a customized product for every consumer in a
market at a cost that all the consumers could afford. As noted above, in order to
develop a successful marketing strategy, marketers must group consumers into
segments that can each be satisfied by a specific product.[2]

When a firm decides to design a new product, it makes decisions that it
knows will appeal to some consumers and not to others. Marketers such as Procter & Gamble offer many products in the same category, each of which is designed to appeal to a specific consumer segment, so that the company can profit
from sales to many diverse segments. Such multiple-product marketers must understand the arrangement of consumer segments and what appeals to each of
them so that they can configure their products to appeal to as many segments as
possible without duplication of effort. In doing so, marketers use segmentation as
part of every marketing decision they make. As discussed in the following Public
Policy box, marketers must also be careful that they do not use segmentation to
deny consumers the right to buy products and services that they need.

## PUBLIC POLICY

### When Does Segmentation Become Discrimination?[3]

Consumer behavior involves exchange between marketer and consumer segments. But when members of a consumer segment want to buy a product that a firm won't market to them, segmentation becomes a public policy issue.

A prominent example of recent discriminatory segmentation involves the issuance of home mortgages to African-American and Hispanic consumers. Two issues are of concern. First, the number of mortgage applications received from members of these two segments is lower than the proportion of African Americans and Hispanics in the population. And, second, African Americans and Hispanics are more likely to be denied home mortgages than are whites and Asians, even after accounting for differences in income. Banks and other mortgage providers maintain that they draw potential mortgage customers from the consumers in the areas they serve, and that they use economic, geographical, and housing criteria for awarding mortgages. Public policy actors, including civil rights and community groups and local, state, and federal policy makers, argue that mortgage providers use marketing strategies and programs that result in discrimination against those segments, even if it is not their intention to exclude African Americans and Hispanics from their target market.

Much of the issue is rooted in the historical relationship among race and ethnicity, income, and geography. The mortgage providers have historically located their offices and developed relationships with real estate agents in suburban and other upscale areas in the hopes of targeting home buyers who would seek bigger mortgages and have the finances to get them. Furthermore, mortgage products typically are awarded on strict financial criteria that home buyers in the upscale areas can meet but many African Americans and Hispanics cannot, even though there is little or no financial risk. For example, many mortgage providers won't lend money that includes housing rehabilitation expenses for properties that are currently unlivable. This creates a vicious cycle, in which buyers are unable to buy a house that they can afford because it needs some work but can't get the mortgage to finance the work to make it livable.

The implications for public policy issues of equity and economic and social welfare are great. Many African Americans and Hispanics cannot buy homes because mortgage lenders use a segmentation strategy and marketing mix that prevent members of those consumer segments from buying. The economic and social welfare of the larger communities are also affected because urban housing that could be rehabilitated is not. Federal policy makers have responded to these problems by issuing regulations that require lenders to revise their strategies and programs to demonstrate that they are addressing the issues. Federal oversight of the lenders' strategic plans for targeting previously underserved consumer segments is being enacted to help ensure that reform occurs.

Do you think that mortgage lenders should locate offices in areas of the city that they have previously avoided in order to equitably serve a segment of African-American and Hispanic consumers? Are the lenders acting equitably when they apply the same rules to consumer segments that face different housing opportunities? Should government policy makers use marketers' segmentation strategies as a tool to achieve social and economic welfare goals for a city?

## ▼ WHAT IS SEGMENTATION?

The goal of segmentation analysis is to divide a market composed of consumers with diverse characteristics and behaviors into homogeneous segments that contain persons who will all respond similarly to a firm's marketing efforts but who will respond differently from the consumers in the other segments that have been identified. These homogeneous segments will be composed of consumers with shared background characteristics, who will use their behavioral processes in the same way to complete their purchase activities.[4] For a health club operator, for example, avid exercisers such as Lyn Welle would be in a different segment than light exercisers such as Carol Beutel. As another example, high-income consumers would be likely to respond differently to a car priced at $50,000 than would low-income consumers. Consequently, luxury car makers, such as Mercedes Benz and BMW, target high-income consumers through their advertising and promotions. By contrast, income will have less of an impact on consumers' choices of such products as ground coffee or toilet paper.

Holiday Inn offers six different kinds of facilities to meet consumers' varying needs. Holiday Inn Express is a budget-oriented offering aimed at lower income travelers; Holiday Inn is a moderately priced product, targeted at the "average" traveler; Holiday Inn Select hotels are located in metropolitan areas and are aimed at business travelers; Crowne Plaza Hotels are more luxurious and expensive facilities aimed at the upscale business traveler. Holiday Inn SunSpree Resorts are designed to provide moderately priced family vacations, whereas Crowne Plaza Resorts are more luxurious facilities designed for vacationers who are willing to spend more money.

In determining how to target its efforts, the marketer wishes to identify those segments that will respond favorably to its efforts by actually purchasing its product. At the same time, the marketer would also like to identify segments that will *not* respond favorably to its marketing efforts so that it can avoid spending resources on attempts to influence unresponsive consumers. Thus, Mercedes Benz focuses its advertising on magazines read by wealthier consumers, whereas Holiday Inn would be unlikely to advertise its Crowne Plaza facilities in *Field and Stream* or *Hot Rod*. Marketers also want to identify segments whose consumers may be offended by its marketing efforts so that it can ensure they are not exposed to the ads. For example, alcohol and cigarette marketers don't display their products in *Weekly Reader*. Survey Sampling provides marketers with appropriate consumer samples to help them in their work, as shown in Figure 3.4. Given the wide variety of characteristics and behaviors that affect consumers' responses to marketing efforts, a comprehensive knowledge of consumer behavior concepts is necessary to segment a market effectively.

### FACT OR FICTION REVISITED

⊛   A market segment *is* a group of consumers who will respond relatively homogenously to a marketer's efforts.

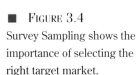

■ FIGURE 3.4
Survey Sampling shows the importance of selecting the right target market.

## ▼ THE RESULTS OF SEGMENTATION

It is important to recognize that the chosen number of segments rarely reflects some obvious or naturally occurring number. That is, it is the marketers and their analytic tool kits that determine the number of segments, once they decide how similar is "similar enough" for any set of consumers to belong to the same segment. The number of possible segments that will result from a segmentation analysis can be as few as one or as many as the number of consumers that are in the total market. The marketer's choice of segments should reflect actual similarities in consumer background characteristics and behaviors that will result in similar purchase decisions. Typically, three kinds of markets can result from a segmentation analysis:

❶ a **customized market**, in which each consumer has his or her own segment;

❷ a **segmented market**, in which meaningful differences among consumers result in a modest number of segments; and

❸ a **mass market**, in which consumers are indistinguishable and all are in one segment.

Figure 3.5 illustrates the difference between mass, segmented, and customized markets.

Successful marketers identify meaningful segments that are small enough so that the consumers that comprise them will be satisfied with the same positioning and marketing mix but large enough so that the products are affordable for the consumers and profitable for the firm. Procter & Gamble recently recognized that it didn't need to maintain two separate brands of toilet paper. Consequently, it moved its White Cloud toilet paper product to its Charmin brand and renamed it Charmin Ultra. In this way, the company found that it could still satisfy con-

> A **customized market** is one in which each consumer comprises his or her own segment.

> A **segmented market** is one in which meaningful differences among consumers result in a modest number of segments.

> A **mass market** encompasses all consumers.

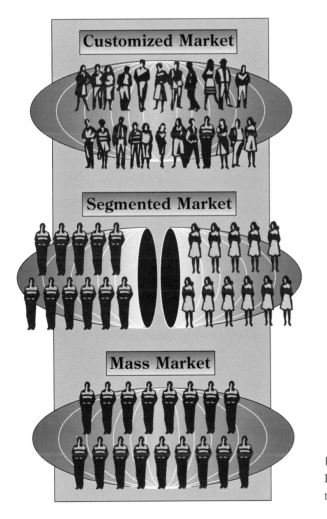

■ FIGURE 3.5
Possible results of segmentation.

sumers of White Cloud and increase its profits by merging the two brands into one product offered in several varieties.

**Customized Markets**   When a marketer detects as many segments as there are consumers, so that each segment is composed of only one consumer, it has identified a customized market. This results when the marketer believes that no two consumers will respond the same way to its marketing efforts. As a result, the marketer is forced to produce a customized product specifically designed and positioned for each consumer to whom it wants to market. Health and exercise marketers provide examples of customized marketing. They are the personal trainers who develop a customized exercise program for their clients and exercise with them on an individual basis. Although most of us can't afford such a luxury, the television and movie stars who do seem to get great results.

If a large number of segments results from a market segment analysis, each contains fewer consumers, and the consumers in a segment tend to be very similar to one another in background characteristics and behavior. Accordingly, the marketer can develop a marketing program that tailors the product and positioning specifically to satisfy each group's consumers in the hope that they will respond favorably to this personal attention. Car manufacturers offer special packages of options, and some home builders customize the design of their homes for each customer (Figure 3.6). Levi's recently implemented a computer-based program that offers custom-tailored jeans for women for just 10 dollars more than the cost of standard sizes.

## FACT OR FICTION REVISITED

⦿   It is *not true* that the segments in a customized market are usually very large. In fact, in a customized market, each consumer is his or her own segment.

**Mass Markets**   At the other extreme, a marketer may be unable to distinguish any differences in the response it expects from consumers to the firm's marketing efforts. In that case, it has identified a mass market. Mass marketing is very rare because consumers are so diverse that one product usually won't satisfy them all. Consumers want some variety even in a product such as toilet paper, which everyone needs. In this case, although consumers' basic needs are the same, differences in bathroom decor and available storage space encourage marketers to offer different colors and package sizes. Procter & Gamble, as we noted earlier, recently recognized that these subtly different needs required marketing only one brand of toilet paper in different varieties.

When fewer segments exist, each is larger and contains more consumers who are more diverse from one another. Consequently, the marketer must employ a more general marketing approach. This approach will likely be less effective, however, since the marketer cannot customize the marketing mix specifically to satisfy each consumer in the larger segment. For example, it is more efficient for you to buy a new business suit for your job interviews in your size off

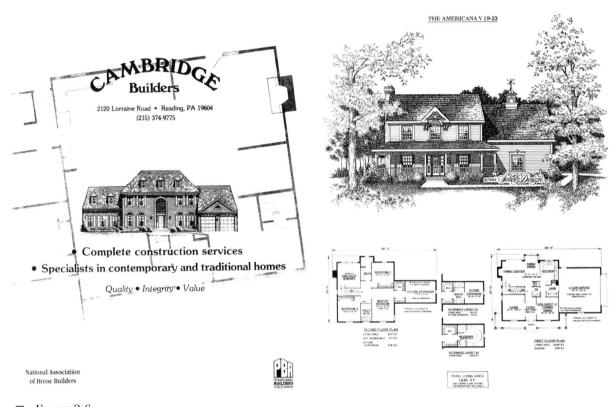

■ FIGURE 3.6

Cambridge Builders appeals to a customized market.

the rack from a local clothing store and have it altered than for you to pay for a tailor to make a custom suit. However, as a result, your suit may not fit as well as custom clothing would, and you will have to choose from the sizes, styles, and fabrics that are available at that store.

**Marketers Seek the Middle Ground: Segmented Markets**   Obviously, the firm has gained little from the segmentation process when either of these extreme outcomes—customized markets or mass markets—occurs. The art and science of market segmentation is to arrive at a segmented market with a *modest* number of segments. Ideally, marketers want to create enough segments so that they can recognize meaningful differences in consumer behavior but few enough so that they can understand the meaning of the differences among the segments and capitalize on them to develop a distinctive marketing mix that will appeal to each specific segment.

From the marketer's perspective, economies of scale make a large segment more efficient than many segments with only a few consumers in each. **Economies of scale** refer to the fact that it is cheaper to produce and market a single product to many consumers than it is to produce and market many differ-

**Economies of scale** are the efficiencies in production and marketing costs that come from producing many units of one product.

77

ent products to a few consumers. Production becomes more efficient as workers gain more experience with the same product; inventory costs are lower when there is a smaller variety of products to stock; and the costs of advertising and selling one product are cheaper than the costs of advertising and selling many products. Accordingly, Oldsmobile is selling some of its cars with a limited number of option packages rather than encouraging customers to custom order options. This is known as *value pricing*—paying a lower price for a "standard" set of features (Figure 3.7).

■ FIGURE 3.7
Oldsmobile attempts to appeal to a broad segment of consumers by emphasizing the economies it can offer through option packages instead of customized combinations of features.

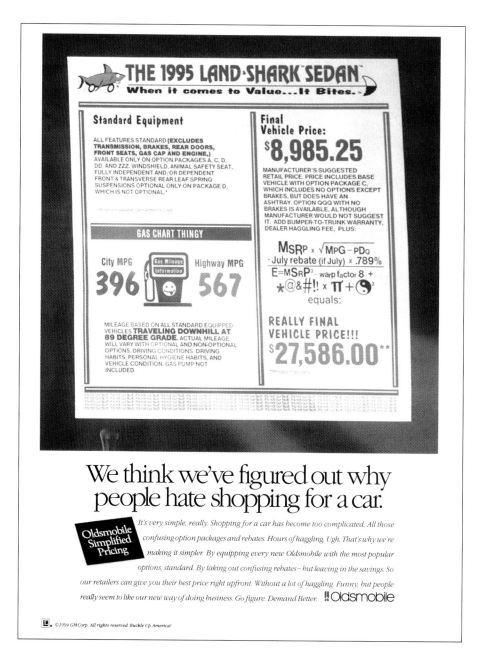

## FACT OR FICTION REVISITED

⦿ Marketers who market to many small segments *are not* more likely to benefit from economies of scale than are marketers who market to a small number of large segments. Economies of scale require a *small* number of *large* segments.

**An Example—Marketing a Health Club**  Consider the number of segments you could identify if you planned to use the knowledge you gained in Chapter 2 to open a health club in your area. You could assign each consumer to his or her own segment, in which case you would open a separate club for each consumer, with a customized exercise program and all of the exercise equipment that he or she would need. This would be a very *effective* marketing strategy because consumers would view this customized club as a great way to reach their exercise goals. But separate clubs for each consumer would not be very *efficient* because you would have to build many facilities that would stand idle much of the time, and the ensuing high membership fees would not appeal to most consumers.

At the other extreme, you could open one club for everyone. Because the needs of the mass of consumers are so diverse, you would have to construct a very large building with all kinds of facilities and exercise equipment. This would be very *efficient*, because you would divide the costs of one building among all of the consumers. However, it would not be a very *effective* marketing strategy since consumers may suspect that you are not able to provide what everyone wants in one place, and you may actually have difficulty putting all of the facilities in one accessible location.

Obviously, viable segmentation strategies would lie somewhere between the two extremes. You could segment by type of exercise and open a tennis or golf club that offers complete facilities for those who want to get their exercise through these sports activities, or open a club that offers exercise and physical therapy programs for senior citizens. If you wanted to satisfy Lyn Welle, you would have to provide a wide range of exercise equipment and ample support staff in an environment that encourages serious exercise. To satisfy Carol Beutel, you could offer a less "serious" environment that allowed members to exercise and mingle. Each of these alternatives would be focused enough to appeal effectively to the different groups of similar consumers.

### ▼ SELECTING TARGET MARKET SEGMENTS

Once marketers have identified specific segments, they must decide how many of the distinct segments to serve. This decision requires that marketers consider (1) the **size** of the market segment, measured by the expected total sales gained from the consumers in the segment; (2) the **stability** of the segment, or likelihood of the segment to maintain its size; and (3) the **accessibility** of the segment, or ease with which the firm's marketing mix programs can be used to reach the consumers in the segment. These three criteria for evaluating any segment's attractiveness concern the benefits the firm will gain from the segment's

The **size** of a market segment is the total sales a marketer expects to gain from the consumers in the segment.

The **stability** of a market segment refers to the likelihood that the segment will maintain its size.

The **accessibility** of a market segment includes the ease with which the marketer can reach the targeted segment and the costs of reaching those consumers.

favorable sales response to its marketing efforts and the costs the firm will shoulder in order to access the segment with its marketing efforts.

**Size and Stability**   Not surprisingly, marketers typically prefer large market segments over smaller ones and segments in which sales will either remain stable or increase, since size and stability provide the ongoing sales revenue that is required to maintain a profitable business. If a particular clothing style becomes popular quickly and then loses its appeal just as abruptly, the marketers who have based their strategy on that style will have a difficult time recouping their investments. To help prevent this from happening, marketers use **forecasting**—the process of predicting the sales level of a product *before* the product is introduced. As we discussed in the beginning of the chapter, predicting sales based on consumers' conjecture of their own future behavior is not an accurate method. Instead, consumers' background characteristics and behavioral processes all affect their product choices, so an accurate forecast of the segment size requires an understanding of these critical consumer behavior components.

> **Forecasting** is the process of estimating the size of a consumer market segment.

**Accessibility**   Marketers also prefer segments that are easily accessible to their marketing efforts. Accessibility includes two related components: (1) the ease with which the marketer can reach the consumers that comprise the targeted segment, and (2) the costs of reaching those consumers. The accessibility, and therefore the cost of access, of market segments varies widely. Some market segments may be readily identifiable and easily reached through mass media, such as middle-aged, middle-class golfers who can be reached through advertisements in televised golf tournaments or *Sports Illustrated* and *Golf* magazines (Figure 3.8). Some segments may be more difficult to reach, such as college students who do not consistently watch the same television programming, read the same magazines, or spend time reading newspapers. We will discuss specific ways of reaching consumers in detail in our discussion of communications in Chapters 15 and 16.

## FACT OR FICTION REVISITED

◉   It is true that marketers prefer to market to a small number of stable, accessible segments.

## ▼ HOW MARKETERS USE CONSUMER BEHAVIOR TO SEGMENT MARKETS

Because they are an innate part of the consumers' makeup, background characteristics are considered to be predetermined attributes that influence the behavioral processes of consumers. Therefore, the first step in segmenting target markets is to choose background characteristics that have the potential to allow meaningful segmentation of consumers. In doing so, marketers classify consumers into categories on the basis of culture and values, demographics, personality, lifestyle, psychographics, and reference groups. They then examine behav-

**■ FIGURE 3.8**
Marketers of specialized products, such as Rossignol skiis, can reach their markets by advertising in special interest magazines.

ioral processes within each of these categories. Table 3.2 lists the important factors considered by marketers for segmentation. A meaningful segmentation characteristic divides consumers into categories that exhibit similar behavioral processes and purchase activities.

The next step is to examine the behavioral processes of the members of each category that is being considered as a potential target segment. We noted previously that these psychological and social processes offer important opportunities for marketers to influence consumers. For consumers, the behavioral processes are the bridge between their background characteristics and their consumption of products. That is, consumers' motivations and needs are the expression of their culture and values, demographics and personality, lifestyle, and psychographics, and reference groups. Furthermore, consumers' perceptual processes, the way that they learn, the formation of their attitudes, and their decision making behavior are all affected by their background characteristics; in turn, these processes influence consumers' abilities to integrate new information from a marketer's program.

Indeed, marketers evaluate the accessibility of the consumers in a segment to their marketing efforts by examining how the consumers behave. They ex-

*Table 3.2*

## IMPORTANT FACTORS USED BY MARKETERS IN SEGMENTATION

| Consumer Behavior Factors | Examples of Categories |
| --- | --- |
| **Background Characteristics** | |
| **Culture and values** | |
| Nationality | American, British, Canadian, Chinese, French, German, Japanese, Kuwaiti, Mexican, Thai |
| Values held | Work ethic, materialism, patriotism, modernism |
| **Demographics** | |
| Age | Under 5, 5–12, 13–17, 18–24, 25–34, 35–44, 45–54, 55–64, 65–74, 75–84, over 84 |
| City size | Urban, suburban, small city, rural |
| Education | Didn't finish high school, high school graduate, attended college or other post-secondary school, graduated from college or other post-secondary school, attended advanced degree program, hold advanced degree |
| Employment | Employed full-time, employed part-time, unemployed |
| Ethnicity and race | African-American, English, Irish, Italian, Mexican, Puerto Rican |
| Family life cycle | Young single, single with children, married without children, married with children, divorced, separated,widowed with children, married with grown children, married and retired, widowed and retired |
| Gender | Female, male |
| Income | Under $10,000, $10,000–$19,999, $20,000–$29,999, $30,000–$49,999, $50,000 and over |
| Occupation | Agriculture, farming, and fishing; skilled crafts-people; clerical; homemakers; professional and technical; managers; proprietors; retired; students; unemployed |
| Region | New England, Middle Atlantic, South Atlantic, East North Central, West North Central, East South Central, West South Central, Mountain, Pacific |
| **Personality, lifestyle, and psychographics** | |
| Personality | Compulsive, authoritarian, innovative, introverted, extroverted |
| Lifestyle and psychographics | Yuppie, Generation X, strugglers, strivers, achievers |
| **Reference groups** | |
| | Family, friends, fraternal organizations, clubs, teams, gangs |
| **Behavioral Processes** | |
| Motivation | Benefits sought by consumers, level of involvement |
| Perception | Aware of product, unaware of product |
| Learning | Levels of knowledge about product |
| Attitude formation | Prefer product, prefer competitors |
| | Product loyal, use many products |
| Decision making | User of the product, tried it, tried it and no longer use it, never tried it |

plore what motivates consumers in a segment so that they can understand which needs consumers want the product to satisfy and, therefore, what benefits the product should offer. Marketers examine consumer motivations and needs so that they can identify how involved the consumer will be—products that are highly involving to the consumer will elicit different perceptual, learning, attitude formation, and decision making processes than will less involving products. For example, avid exercisers such as Lyn Welle would show high levels of involvement, pay more attention, and have more knowledge of exercise products than would light exercisers like Carol Beutel. High and low involvement decision making will be discussed in more detail in Chapter 13.

Finally, it is important for marketers to investigate the differences consumers are able to perceive among products, the means by which they learn about the products available to them, and the attitudes they form about what is important in choosing a certain type of product. In doing so, marketers look for similarities in these behaviors among the consumers in a chosen segment so that they can devise ways of reaching all the consumers in that segment through the same marketing method. The marketer must then determine whether there is a method that can be used to reach the segment at a reasonable cost. At the same time, the marketer examines each segment's decision making behavior in order to forecast purchase behavior and to understand consumers' views of products. This information is necessary to gauge the potential market size of the segment and to understand how consumers view the specific attributes of products in the category.

Of course, many of the potential categories of background characteristics do not suggest a clear method of access because the consumers are not similar enough to constitute an identifiable segment or they are not likely to be responsive to marketing efforts. For example, stock brokers and financial advisors seldom target low-income consumers because, to the extent that they need financial services, they rely on their banks and local accountants. Accordingly, each potential market segment is evaluated to check whether its members act similarly and, if so, to determine its accessibility and responsiveness. The attractive segments are then chosen as targets for the marketer's efforts.

## ▼ SEGMENTATION STRATEGY

As stated above, those segments whose consumers are unlikely to respond favorably to the product are discarded, but how many of the segments that respond favorably should the marketer choose? The decision to target a segment is best made by balancing the expected sales from that segment against the expected costs of reaching the segment. When there is more than one attractive segment, the marketer must consider the relationship among the segments, as shown in Figure 3.9. Are the segments similar enough to one another that they will all respond favorably to the same product and positioning? Or are they different enough from one another that they require separate products and positioning?

## FACT OR FICTION REVISITED

◉    The decision to target a segment is indeed best made by balancing the expected sales from that segment against the expected cost of reaching that segment.

■ FIGURE 3.9
Segmentation strategies.

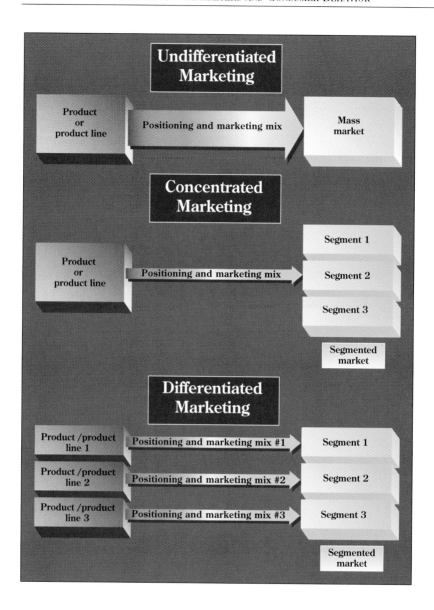

An **undifferentiated segmentation strategy** offers the same product or product line to the entire mass market.

A **product line** is a set of similar products that share a brand name which is offered to a single consumer segment composed of individuals who have some subtle variation in their shared needs.

A **concentrated segmentation strategy** identifies a segmented market but focuses efforts on positioning and producing one specifically tailored product or product line to one of those segments.

When choosing its segmentation strategy, the marketer has several alternatives. It can choose an **undifferentiated strategy** and market the same product or product line to the entire market. Or, if the marketer thinks that the market might contain consumers who have some subtle variation in their needs, it could introduce a **product line** with various products for the market, each of which addresses related "subsegments" within the segment. This is the strategy Nabisco has adopted to market its Oreo cookies. Nabisco offers low-fat Oreos for those consumers who want to eat a little healthier, and chocolate-covered Oreos for those who do not.

A marketer may recognize that distinct segments exist but choose to adopt a **concentrated strategy** and focus its efforts on only one of those segments, typi-

■ FIGURE 3.10

*Twins* magazine chose a concentrated segmentation strategy when it developed a magazine for the parents of twins.

cally the largest one that can be reached easily and at a reasonable cost. In this case, the firm produces and positions one specifically tailored product or product line with the maximum appeal to the consumers in that segment. Many firms have adopted a concentrated strategy, including shampoo marketer Ross Laboratories, which markets the Selsun Blue product line to consumers who require a dandruff shampoo; the publisher of *Twins* magazine, "the magazine for the parents of multiples" (Figure 3.10); and Rolls-Royce, which charges $149,000 for its *least* expensive model, the Silver Dawn.

Another option for marketers is to target multiple segments with a **differentiated** product or product line tailored for each segment. The Limited operates Abercrombie & Fitch, Henri Bendel, Lane Bryant, Cacique, Express, Lerner, Limited, Structure, and Victoria's Secret, each of which focuses on different kinds of clothing for a distinct segment of the population. And, as we noted, Procter & Gamble offers its six differentiated shampoo product lines (Pantene Pro-V, Vidal Sassoon, Pert Plus, Prell, Ivory, and Head & Shoulders) to satisfy the distinct consumer segments it has identified in its segmentation analysis.

> A **differentiated segmentation strategy** identifies a segmented market and targets multiple segments with a product or product line produced and positioned for each segment.

## FACT OR FICTION REVISITED

◉ Most automobile manufacturers *do not* adopt a concentrated marketing strategy; they adopt a *differentiated* marketing strategy.

**An Example—College Athletic Wear** Consider a marketer who wants to segment college students in your state to market athletic wear through a direct response catalog. Toward the one extreme, every fraternity, sorority, and club in each school is different, and our marketer could produce a separate catalog for each organization portraying members modeling clothing with the club logo on it. Seeing your friends donning the athletic wear you would actually purchase would be a very effective appeal, but the costs of producing small numbers of copies of such catalogs for each of the many campus organizations at each of the schools in the state would be very expensive.

Toward the other extreme, all the students in the state could be considered similar because they wear the same general fashions, although with different logos. In this case, the marketer could produce one catalog for all the students in the state, portraying models wearing clothing touting the name of the biggest school in the state. Although this would be much more efficient than producing specialized catalogs for each fraternity, sorority, and club, do you think the offer would be as attractive to you as would a catalog showing your friends modeling the clothes you would actually buy?

How would the athletic wear marketer arrive at the decision that individual schools were the appropriate characteristic to use as the basis for segmenting the students in your state? First, the marketer would choose specific consumer characteristics to examine. General demographic characteristics such as gender, age, and income are good candidates, as are some more college-specific characteristics such as the school attended, year in school, major, and campus organizations to which the student belongs. Our marketer might also employ a psychographic or lifestyle classification, perhaps a simple categorization of students into active campus-joiners, quiet campus-dwellers, and retiring commuters.

The marketer might then ask a sample of students at the colleges in the state to complete a marketing survey concerning general behavioral processes, such as their academic and social motivations and perceptions and general attitudes about fashion, education, their school and organizations on campus, and other schools and organizations in the state. The survey may also ask about the students' specific purchase activities, including their attitudes about athletic wear in general, what kinds and brands of athletic wear they have bought, and how, when, where, and why they purchased it.

Each survey respondent would be classified into categories on each of the consumer characteristics. The students in each category of each consumer characteristic would then be compared with the students in the other categories of that characteristic. Those characteristics that distinguished students on the basis of behavior and consumption would be used to segment the market, and particular categories of those characteristics would be chosen as the target segments. In our example, let's say that segmentation showed that the school the students attended was the most important background characteristic and that students from different schools would purchase only those products which contained their school logos; their motivation to purchase athletic wear is to demonstrate allegiance to their school in a fashionable way. Let's also suppose that the students found direct mail catalogs to be credible sources of information, particularly when they contained models from their own campus. Finally, let's assume that gender, age, income, class in school, and major *did not* distinguish students from one another, and that while there was some variation among members of different campus organizations, it was not as great as between schools. Accordingly, let's assume that the marketer recognizes that some segmentation and customization of the catalogs is necessary. In this case, perhaps the best segmentation is not a mass market of all college students or a catalog that is customized for each student organization, but one that is specific to each school.

Once our athletic wear firm has divided the market into segments, it must then choose which of these segments it will actually serve. When choosing its segmentation strategy, the firm has several alternatives. It can choose a concentrated strategy and focus its efforts on a single college, presumably the largest school in the state. The firm could then produce and position one product with the maximum appeal to the students in the selected school. Alternatively, the firm could introduce a product line composed of many products for that school, recognizing that each campus organization is distinct enough that its members would want to include both the school's logo and the symbol of their organization. Finally, the firm might choose to target multiple schools with differentiated products tailored for each school and try to satisfy students throughout the state.

# PRODUCT POSITIONING AND THE MARKETING MIX

Once the market has been segmented and attractive segments have been identified, the next task is to work within a targeted segment to position the product in the minds of the consumers and develop a marketing mix that will satisfy the consumer.

## ▼ PRODUCT POSITIONING

*Product positioning* is the creation of a clear image in the minds of consumers within the targeted segment about the nature of the product and the benefits to be gained from purchasing the product.[5] Positioning is the complement of segmentation. That is, segmentation identifies those segments of the population that will act similarly and develops products to meet each segment's needs, whereas positioning conveys information about the products back to the segments for which they are appropriate.

Product positioning is achieved through a wide variety of marketing mix programs in product design, pricing, distribution, and promotion. Consumer background characteristics are addressed primarily by creating advertising that features individuals who possess the characteristics of the target segment, but pricing must also be suitable for the economic attributes of the target market, and distribution must occur in the appropriate geographical areas. For example, Mercedes Benz advertises in magazines that reach upscale audiences and situates dealerships in areas frequented by high-income consumers.

Motivation and needs shape the product design by dictating the benefits the product must offer to its purchasers. The level of motivation, through its influence on the degree of involvement consumers feel for the product, will influence the effort consumers will exert in perceiving and learning about the product as well as the strength of the attitudes they hold about the product. The box below discusses the pleasures of consumption that come from sharing a purchase experience with others in a reference group who share common background characteristics.

 PLEASURES OF CONSUMPTION

**It's Fun to Have a Party With a Friend**

We all like to share fun experiences with friends and family—going to a party, a ball game, or a movie. Indeed, part of the fun of these experiences is that they are shared with friends or family you know will approve of the products you buy for the occasions. Soft drinks, beer, and snacks are part of the fun of a Super Bowl party. A cup of tea or coffee may be part of the ritual you share with your family when you return home for the holidays.

Marketers of these kinds of products study the background characteristics of consumers in an effort to identify the segments that will find their products appealing. They want to know what kinds of consumers prefer their products and what activities provide the occasions at which their products will be consumed. Pepsi and Coke both emphasize that their soft drinks are appropriate for a younger, "more hip" consumer than their competitor's and are perfect for a party atmosphere. Budweiser and Bud Light produce specific "Bud Bowl" advertising to encourage consumers to stock up for their Super Bowl parties. In contrast, General Foods International Coffees are targeted at small groups of friends or family who want to share an emotional moment. Some marketers use the party itself as a selling occasion—Tupperware and Mary Kay Cosmetics are sold at parties consumers arrange as an opportunity for their friends to meet the salespeople directly.

Do you think that the food and beverages consumers serve contribute to the success of a social occasion? Can a marketer such as Anheuser-Busch so tightly associate Budweiser with Super Bowl parties that consumers automatically think of them together? Are Tupperware parties so satisfying that people will buy the product just so that they can go to the party?

Consumers within a segment typically share an image of each of the products in the category as well as the important similarities and differences among them. In some cases, an equally important goal is the creation of a similarly clear image in the minds of consumers who are *not* in the target market so that they will know not to purchase the product and will therefore avoid an unpleasant consumption experience. Consumers with low or moderate incomes, for instance, would be disappointed if they visited a Mercedes dealer expecting to be able to buy a $12,000 car.

Creating this image of a product in consumers' minds relies on the wide variety of consumer behavior concepts we will discuss throughout the rest of this

■ FIGURE 3.11

Ford developed ads such as this one to help consumers understand the differences in positions among its various Mercury models.

book. These concepts are used in two broad types of positioning strategies: (1) *positioning by consumer characteristics and behaviors*, and (2) *positioning by competitor*.

There are numerous ways to position a product by consumer background characteristics and behavioral processes, each of which involves choosing a particular characteristic or behavioral process to associate directly with the product's image in consumers' minds. (Figure 3.11) An advertisement can address specific consumer characteristics or behavior directly, or it can illustrate them indirectly by portraying fictional people possessing these characteristics or behaviors. For example, Ford recently created an advertisement that highlighted the differences among the positioning of its different models. Behavioral processes can also be demonstrated by showing that the product offers benefits to satisfy the consumer's needs.[6] In contrast, positioning by competitor capitalizes on what consumers already know about competitive products. This is usually achieved through comparative advertising that makes explicit references to competitive

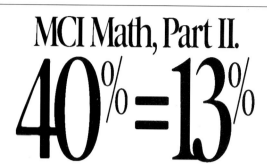

■ FIGURE 3.12

AT&T and MCI have each attempted to position their long-distance telephone services as less expensive and more rewarding than their competitor's.

products, as AT&T and MCI have done for years in the long-distance telephone wars (Figure 3.12).

## FACT OR FICTION REVISITED

◉   Product positioning is indeed the complement of market segmentation.

## ▼ THE MARKETING MIX

Marketers manage a set of variables that facilitate exchange with consumers in order to satisfy their needs. As previously mentioned, these variables, collectively called the *marketing mix*, include:

❶  the *product* itself and all of its related characteristics
❷  the *price* the consumer must pay for the product
❸  *promotion* of the product to consumers through a variety of communications media
❹  the organization of the delivery system to get the product to a *place* where consumers can use it

All of the activities related to designing, producing, and exchanging the product with consumers comprise the marketing mix. The four elements that make up the mix, or the 4 P's, each require its own strategy and implementation. The elements of the marketing mix are particularly important because they are the tools that marketers use to influence behavioral processes. Remember that consumers use the behavioral processes to complete the activities in the purchase process; a skillfully designed and implemented marketing mix helps consumers complete the activities necessary to satisfy their needs.

**Product**   The **product** component of the marketing mix encompasses all of the tangible and intangible attributes of the product itself; that is, everything related to the use and consumption of the product. It can include the actual exercise equipment at a health club, as well as the services of trainers, bookkeepers, and cleaning personnel. For car marketers, product attributes would include such commodities as safety, durability, comfort, and features (Figure 3.13). Volvo em-

> The **product** encompasses all of the tangible and intangible attributes of the product itself.

You're looking at a perfect Volvo. A Volvo that performed exactly as our safety engineers designed it to.

Its front and rear ends, for example, collapsed on impact. As a result, much of the crash energy was absorbed instead of being passed on to the passengers.

The car's middle section, however, didn't collapse. That's because the entire passenger compartment is surrounded by Volvo's unique "safety cage." Made of six box section steel pillars, this protective housing is strong enough to support the weight of six Volvos.

But the passengers of this car were also protected in ways you can't see. Because inside are such standard features as a driver's side Supplemental Restraint System, a collapsible steering column and, of course, 3-point seat belts, front and rear.

Every Volvo is designed to help protect its passengers in all these ways. And, as a result, will look remarkably similar to this one after being in the same type of accident.

If you're concerned about safety, you can't find a more beautiful car.

**VOLVO**
A car you can believe in.

CALL TOLL FREE FOR YOUR CATALOG OF 1991 VOLVOS. 1-800-221-9136.  © 1990 VOLVO NORTH AMERICA CORPORATION.

■ FIGURE 3.13
Volvo emphasizes the safety features of its cars in this ad.

phasizes safety in its advertising, for example, while Acura touts the luxury of its Legend.

During the purchase process, consumers evaluate alternative products by comparing them on a variety of criteria. The key task of marketers is to design the product so that it meets the evaluation criteria used by consumers in the chosen target segment. Marketers must ensure that the consumers they have targeted form favorable attitudes toward their product and that the product delivers those attributes that will satisfy consumers so that the postpurchase evaluation will be favorable as well.

**Price** is that which consumers exchange with the marketer in order to purchase a product.

**Price**   A product's **price** is that which consumers exchange with the marketer in order to purchase the product. Consumers consider price to be an important criterion in their evaluation of alternatives, both before and after making a purchase (Figure 3.14). Furthermore, if a product's design requires consumers to exchange both time and money, then the actual price includes more than just its monetary price. For example, the price of a home exercise machine that takes 12 hours to assemble must include the cost of the consumer's time invested to assemble it. Financing help for large purchases also affects the terms of the exchange. The monetary price of a new car, for example, would be a more important criterion for evaluation if long-term financing were not available.

## FACT OR FICTION REVISITED

◉   A product's actual price does indeed include both money and time. Assembling a product, or traveling to find a product, would be examples of investments of time.

**Promotion** involves the way the marketer communicates information the consumers use to ascertain a product's positioning.

**Promotion**   **Promotion** involves the way the marketer communicates information the consumers use to ascertain a product's positioning.[7] That is, consumers use the information provided by advertising, direct marketing, public relations, and salespeople to learn about the product's design, its price, where it's sold, and whether it is appropriate for them. This information is then used as input to all of the behavioral processes consumers use to complete the purchase activities. For example, advertising helps consumers learn about the product, form an attitude, and then reach a purchase decision. Furthermore, if the ad is confusing, the consumer's perceptions of the product may be incorrect.

**Place** is the means by which a marketer delivers a product to the location where consumers will use it.

**Place**   The means by which the marketer delivers the product to the location where consumers will use it is referred to as **place**. The path between consumer and marketer, called the *distribution channel*, can include many actors, including retailers, wholesalers, warehouses, and delivery services. The marketer manages the process of delivery by designing a system and selecting partners who will satisfy consumers.

Consumers' search for alternatives, evaluation, and actual purchase and use of a product will be affected by place decisions. For example, if there are no local

■ FIGURE 3.14

Suave claims that it offers the same benefits of other brands of shampoo at a lower price.

■ FIGURE 3.15

Baume & Mercier lists the locations of retailers that sell its watches so consumers know where to go to find them.

retailers available to exhibit a product, or the consumer doesn't know which retailers sell the product, the marketer must provide another method for consumers to learn about it (Figure 3.15). The distance consumers must travel to find a product also adds the cost of time to its monetary price.

# MARKETERS, CONSUMER BEHAVIOR, AND MARKETING STRATEGIES

Lyn Welle and Carol Beutel are both consumers who joined health clubs in the past several years. Although both women wanted to join a gym, they differed in many of their background characteristics. These discrepancies resulted in different uses of the behavioral processes—the two women had different needs, they formed varying perceptions and attitudes about the kinds of clubs they saw, and they used different criteria to make their purchase decisions. Lyn is single, she has long included exercise as an important part of her lifestyle, and she needs a serious place to exercise that won't offer any unnecessary distractions. By contrast, Carol is a divorced single parent who wants a health club that offers a stimulating social atmosphere as well as a place to exercise.

A health club marketer facing consumers such as Lyn and Carol would have to decide whether their differences indicate that they belong to different segments, decide whether the segments could be satisfied profitably, and then choose a segmentation strategy to satisfy one or both of the segments. The two women could share much of the equipment, but Lyn would use more of it than Carol and would demand more staff. But would Carol be willing to pay to support the equipment and staff that she doesn't use? And will the two women be satisfied by the same type of atmosphere? Lyn is looking for a smaller club with a more serious atmosphere, whereas Carol wants a larger club with more social opportunities. No marketer can develop a marketing mix to satisfy the distinctly different consumer purchase processes of the two women—undifferentiated marketing just will not work. Only through a thorough understanding of consumers' background characteristics and behavioral processes, which we will discuss in the remaining chapters, can marketers develop marketing strategies that will satisfy consumers.

# SUMMARY

1. **Understand the role that segmentation, positioning, and the marketing mix play in a firm's marketing strategy.** Consumers possess different background characteristics and use behavioral processes differently in order to satisfy their needs; some people want a dandruff shampoo, some want a shampoo that leaves their hair manageable, and others want the least expensive product they can find. Marketers must understand these differences in consumer behavior and offer distinct products to satisfy different consumers. To do this, marketers (1) divide consumers into segments that will respond the same way to a particular product; (2) position the product in consumers' minds to help them recognize whether it will satisfy their needs; and (3) develop a marketing mix—the set of variables that will create and deliver the product to the consumers who need it.

2. **Analyze the methods marketers use to segment markets and choose their segmentation strategy.** Marketers divide a market into segments composed of consumers who share background characteristics and use similar behavior to satisfy their needs. To segment the market, marketers must identify the characteristics that are relevant for their products—gender might be most relevant for choosing a deodorant, but income and family size might be more important for purchasing a car. Once marketers have distinguished the segments, they must decide how many of them to address. They can use an undifferentiated strategy to market the same product to the entire market, a concentrated strategy to market a product to one segment, or a differentiated strategy to market distinct products to each segment.

3. **Identify the position of products and the strategies used by marketers to achieve those positions.** A product's position is the image consumers have of it—the nature of the product, the consumers for whom it will be appropriate, and the needs it will satisfy. That image comes from the marketing mix, particularly from advertising

and other promotional tools that provide information about the product to consumers. Products are usually positioned either by portraying the characteristics and behaviors of the consumers for whom it is appropriate or by explicitly using other products to illustrate its position.

4. **Recognize the marketing mixes marketers use to satisfy consumers.** The marketing mix is the set of variables marketers control to produce satisfying products for consumers in their target market segments. The variables include (1) the product itself and the benefits it provides, (2) its price, (3) promotion of information that enables consumers to see that the product will meet their needs, and (4) the system that delivers the product to the consumer.

---

# KEY TERMS

Marketing strategy, *p. 67*

Market segmentation, *p. 68*

Product Positioning, *p. 68*

Marketing Mix, *p. 69*

Customized market, *p. 75*

Segmented market, *p. 75*

Mass market, *p. 75*

Economies of scale, *p. 77*

Size, *p. 79*

Stability, *p. 79*

Accessibility, *p. 79*

Forecasting, *p. 80*

Undifferentiated segmentation strategy, *p. 84*

Product line, *p. 84*

Concentrated segmentation strategy, *p. 84*

Differentiated segmentation strategy, *p. 85*

---

# SKILL-BUILDING ACTIVITIES

1. Assume that you are about to open a small company that will market t-shirts, coffee mugs, jackets, and other such items to your fellow students.
   a. How would you segment the market?
   b. How would you position your products?
   c. What decisions would go into your marketing mix?
   d. Who would be your principle competitors?
   e. How would those competitors influence your decisions?

2. Suppose that you decided not to segment this market but rather to regard it as a customized market or a mass market.
   a. How would you position your products?
   b. What decisions would go into the marketing mix?

3. How could this business benefit from economies of scale?

4. Suppose that your job required you to segment the compact disk market.
   a. How would go about it?
   b. How would you decide which segments to address?

5. In segmenting the compact disk market, what role would be played by:
   a. Demographics
   b. Culture
   c. Values
   d. Lifestyles
   e. Personality
   f. Reference groups
   g. Positioning by competitors

# CHAPTER 3 SELF-TEST

## ▼ MULTIPLE CHOICE

1. _____ _____ is the process of dividing the total market into segments and then targeting specific products at selected segments.
   a. Marketing division
   b. Population sampling
   c. Market segmentation
   d. Market channeling

2. The "mental location" to which a consumer assigns a product in his or her mind is called that product's _____.
   a. extension
   b. position
   c. image
   d. formula

3. Within a _____ _____, consumers are indistinguishable and are all in one segment.
   a. customized market
   b. mass market
   c. market system
   d. psychographic segment

4. When considering segmentation strategies, marketers must develop a strategy that is both effective and _____.
   a. efficient
   b. global
   c. extensive
   d. inclusive

5. The first step in segmenting target markets is to choose background characteristics relevant to your product, followed by an examination of the _____ processes of those within the background characteristic segments.
   a. thought
   b. behavioral
   c. physical
   d. decision making

6. The two types of product positioning strategies are positioning by consumer characteristics and behaviors, and positioning by _____.
   a. competitor
   b. price
   c. product life cycle stage
   d. product type

7. If a concentrated segmentation strategy is selected, the marketer positions and produces _____ product(s) or line(s) to _____ segments.
   a. one
   b. two
   c. five
   d. 10

8. A company that is experiencing lower inventory and advertising costs because it is producing and marketing a single product to many consumers is benefiting from _____.
   a. value pricing
   b. accountability
   c. economies of scale
   d. psychographic analysis

9. Age, family life cycle, gender, and income are all _____ consumer characteristics used in the process of segmenting a market.
   a. demographic
   b. psychographic
   c. cultural
   d. personality

10. When a market is segmented based on consumers' behavioral processes, consumer decision making and _____ may be used as bases of segmentation.
    a. demographics
    b. lifestyle
    c. perceptions
    d. value systems

## ▼ TRUE/FALSE

1. The ultimate goal of a marketer is to produce products and services that satisfy consumer needs.   T or F

2. Of the three kinds of markets discussed, a customized market would have the largest number of consumers per segment.   T or F

3. Product positioning is a strategy marketers may use in lieu of a segmentation strategy.   T or F
4. The marketing mix includes product, price, promotion, and politics.   T or F
5. The size of a market segment is determined by the expected total number of sales that a marketer forecasts for the segment.   T or F
6. Marketing strategy consists of market segmentation, product positioning, and the development of the marketing mix.   T or F
7. Simply asking consumers what they want is a good way of collecting information to develop marketing strategy.   T or F
8. There is no product that will satisfy every consumer.   T or F
9. Segmentation is purely a marketing concept and is not relevant to public policy.   T or F
10. During the segmentation process, marketers should be concerned only about identifying those segments that will actually purchase the product.   T or F

▼   SHORT ANSWER

1. Explain the outcome of an undifferentiated segmentation strategy versus a differentiated segmentation strategy.
2. Describe the three criteria used in evaluating whether a particular segment would be an acceptable target for a marketer.
3. Why is segmentation based on behavioral processes, purchase activities, and background characteristics more effective than a strategy that uses just one of those types of segmentation bases?
4. Describe how consumer behavior knowledge is used in the development of the four components of the marketing mix.

▼   APPLICATION EXERCISE

You have been promoted to the position of director of marketing for a company that produces fozen foods. The research and development department of your company is developing a new breakfast product—a frozen waffle that is low in fat and cholesterol. Your job is to develop a marketing strategy for that product. You have decided to use a concentrated marketing strategy, so you will be targeting one segment. Describe the segment you have chosen to target.

# 4

# CULTURE AND VALUES

⦿ Consumer Snapshot    *Eliot Spiegel is a 29-year-old manufacturer's representative in the seasonal and party supply industry. He lives in New Millford, New Jersey, with his wife, Fran.*

### FACT OR FICTION?

⦿    Each generation develops its own culture

⦿    Each subculture maintains its own distinct heritage.

⦿    David Letterman's Top Ten List would be considered part of American culture.

⦿    With international travel, mass communication, and the lifting of trade barriers, differences among cultures have almost disappeared.

⦿    In cross-cultural market analysis, one of the most important elements to consider is women's roles.

● Most multinational marketers rotate marketing personnel across markets.

## EYE ON THE CONSUMER

Eliot Spiegel bought his Harley-Davidson at the age of 24 so that he could feel the freedom of being on the open road, just riding his bike and feeling as if he were part of the scenery. He had wanted one since he was 15, the summer he had worked with a truck driver who constantly talked about Harleys. At the time he bought the bike, Eliot already owned a small sports car he had bought on the spur of the moment and a Chrysler station wagon he had once used for his job as a deliveryman. But Eliot still wanted that Harley, so he walked into the dealer one day, plopped down 5000 dollars, and ordered the bike. Before that day, he had never been on a Harley.

Eliot loves the feeling of being part of the Harley culture. No matter who you are, he says—whatever your job or your background, however thin or heavy you are, whatever you look like—other Harley riders accept you. They often wear clothes emblazoned with the Harley logo, particularly the classic black t-shirts, and the Harley Owner's Group (HOG) sponsors all kind of family get-togethers. Today, you're just as likely to see stock brokers, or *rubies*—rich, urban bikers, like Malcolm Forbes—riding Harleys as blue-collar guys. Eliot likes them all, except for the guys who think "Harleys are the BMWs of the '90s." But sometime soon the fashion will change, he says, and they'll move on to the next "in thing."

Eliot loves to get out on the open road on his Harley, where he can feel part of the world that he's watching go by. And don't try to argue with him about the need to wear a helmet—he's firmly against helmet laws because he feels the government is there to protect him from others, not from himself. For Eliot, riding his Harley is a continuation of the wild frontier—the lonely rider on the quintessential American bike. He used to ride quite a bit more than he does today, but riding through the New Jersey winters at 60 miles an hour began to give him a constant headache, and he got married a few years ago, so now he just rides a few thousand miles during the summer.

The purpose of this chapter is to discuss culture and values, the first of the four important areas of consumer background characteristics first presented in Chapter 2. Culture is the core of a society—the essential character of its people that distinguishes it from other societies—and the defining element of a culture is its values—the underlying beliefs that are shared by a society. These values dictate what is acceptable and not acceptable for a society's members—how they should think, feel, and act. Consumer behavior is strongly affected by the culture to which consumers belong through the values it teaches them.

In this chapter, we will discuss the importance of culture and values for consumers and the similarities and differences among cultures and subcultures in the modern global economy. Because of the increasing importance of the global economy, marketers who understand the nature of others' cultures and values can capitalize on opportunities to market their products in those cultures. Although we will touch on the nature of subcultures in this chapter, we will leave our presentation of the subcultures to which American consumers belong to the next two chapters.

After reading and thinking about this chapter, you should be able to:

❶ Examine the nature of culture and subculture and the roles they play in consumers' lives.
❷ Identify the components of culture.
❸ Analyze the differences in culture and values among societies in the global economy and the impact of those differences on international marketing strategies.
❹ Identify the ways that values have been used to discriminate consumer cultures and subcultures from one another.
❺ Recognize the core values that are shared by Americans.

# CULTURE ◀

**C**ulture is the unique pattern of shared meanings that characterize a society and distinguish it from other societies. It is passed down from generation to generation and has been described as a society's "personality." It is the constellation of ideas and objects that determines what is acceptable in a society and to which all of the members of a society subscribe.

> **Culture** is the unique pattern of shared meanings that characterize a society.

Before we turn to a detailed discussion of the nature of culture itself, we will preview some of the components of culture—values, language, myths, customs, rituals, laws, and material artifacts—that interact to provide a rich context for consumer behavior (see Table 4.1). *Values*, as mentioned earlier, are the underlying beliefs that are shared by a society about appropriate ways to live, whereas *language* is the tool the members of a culture use to communicate with one another. A *myth* is a story that illustrates the values that a society shares, such as the story of Santa Claus or Paul Bunyan. A *custom* is culturally acceptable routinized behavior that occurs in particular situations; brushing one's teeth before going to bed or tipping the staff in a restaurant are examples of customs. A *ritual* is a set of interrelated patterns of behavior that have a symbolic meaning, such as throwing a party and giving gifts at a baby shower. *Laws* are formal rules and regulations that have the sanction of a governmental body. Finally, *material artifacts* are goods that the culture has imbued with special meaning. A green pine has no cultural significance during most of the year, but it becomes a "Christmas tree" during December in many Christian homes.

## ▼ THE NATURE OF CULTURE

Culture is pervasive—it encompasses all the things consumers do without conscious choice because their culture's values, customs, and rituals are ingrained in their daily habits. A culture is made up of the assumptions about the way things

*Table 4.1*

## THE COMPONENTS OF CULTURE

| Component | Examples |
| --- | --- |
| Values | Success through hard work |
| | Materialism demonstrated through possession of consumer goods |
| | Personal freedom to control one's own time |
| Language | English |
| | Japanese |
| Myths | Santa Claus emphasizes the importance of material goods |
| | Benjamin Franklin is the example of success through hard work in a capitalist system |
| Customs | Bathing and washing hair daily |
| | Buying new clothes for children's first day of school |
| Rituals | Wedding ceremony and banquet |
| | Thanksgiving dinner |
| Laws | Legal safeguards for private property |
| | Equal access to education |
| Material artifacts | Diamond engagement ring |
| | Clothing styles |

are and the way they always should be. For example, the British assume that tea should be served hot. To introduce the cold iced teas that are popular in the United States and elsewhere, therefore, Unilever has introduced Liptonice, a carbonated soft drink that is available in cans. To combat the British assumption that iced tea is hot tea that has been left in the pot too long, the marketer chose to confront the custom explicitly by introducing the beverage with the slogan "Made with tea, surprisingly."

**Culture Is Functional**  Consumers depend on cultural prescriptions to guide their behavior, and they assume that others will behave in ways that are consistent with their culture. Culture unites a group of people in a unique way and supports the group's unity. It is essential to a society because it provides the framework within which the members operate. The functions of culture are so fundamental that every living group studied throughout history has possessed elements of culture. Even animals develop a system for communication, leadership, and perpetuation of the species.

As consumers, we expect that the marketers we deal with will operate according to the values, customs, laws, and rituals of our culture. For example, capitalist values indicate that marketers are in business to make a profit by meeting consumers' needs. Consequently, we would expect that the car we buy will perform as advertised, but we do not expect the marketer to give the car to us for free. More specifically, American business customs prescribe that consumer electronic stores, such as Circuit City, will be open for business during posted hours, will permit customers to pay for a Sony television with a credit card, and will replace the product if it does not work during a guaranteed period of time.

**Culture Is Learned**  Consumers are not biologically endowed with culture; instead, they learn from family and friends about what is acceptable and unacceptable. Consumers read, watch television, and experience aspects of their culture continually. For example, Americans communicate in the English language and celebrate July fourth as Independence Day, whereas the British speak a noticeably different version of English and are less sanguine about July fourth celebrations.

Children internalize the values that govern their behavior as they are taught them by their parents, teachers, and peers. American culture perpetuates itself through myths, customs, and rituals that are passed down from generation to generation. Simple gestures such as shaking hands to greet someone are elements of the American culture. American kids learn to eat hot dogs and apple pie and to wear blue jeans and sneakers. Adults come to value youth, appearance, materialism, capitalism, and success. All of this is learned through the process of *enculturation*, as the members of our society are steeped in American culture as they grow up. **Enculturation** is the process of learning one's native culture. By contrast, **acculturation** is the process of learning a new or foreign culture. Marketers who wish to introduce products in other countries need to understand the process of acculturation so that they can develop ways to help consumers accept new customs, as shown in the Liptonice example.

The choice of products consumers buy is ultimately determined by culture as well. Whereas tea is the most popular hot beverage in Britain, for example, coffee is more popular in America. Think of the kind of car that you drive and the brands of laundry detergent and toothpaste you use—many of us learn about these products in our parents' houses while growing up; the Spiegel family has traditionally owned Chrysler vehicles, so Eliot bought a Chrysler as a young adult. Additionally, the ways in which consumers search for information about products, buy and use them, and evaluate their product experience is largely cultural. You may have gone grocery shopping with your mother every Saturday morning, watched your parents as they bought Chevrolets, and listened to them complain to the dealer when the car broke down. Through experience, consumers learn about their culture so that they can buy products appropriately and effectively.

> **Enculturation** is the process of learning one's native cultural values, language, myths, customs, rituals, and laws.

> **Acculturation** is the process of learning the values, language, myths, customs, and rituals of a new or foreign culture.

## FACT OR FICTION REVISITED

⦿    Each generation *does not* develop its own culture. Rather, most aspects of culture are handed down from generation to generation.

**Culture Is Dynamic**  Culture changes and expands to reflect the dynamic environment. In part, such changes occur so that culture can remain functional. For example, women moved into the workforce in larger numbers during World War II to replace the working men who were overseas in the armed forces. During much of the early part of the 20th century it was inappropriate and sometimes illegal for women to run for political office, to teach while they were pregnant, or to vote. By contrast, today our society espouses women's rights and equal rights as basic values of our culture.

For marketers, changes in technology and fashion are among the most dynamic aspects of culture. Changes in computer technology helped spur the growth of the credit card, and credit, once thought to be undesirable, is now commonplace. Fashions have ranged from pill box hats to mini skirts to the "grunge look" and Doc Martens. Fashions even repeat themselves, as we see "retro" looks from the 1960s and 1970s becoming popular again in the 1990s. And new words such as "fax," "multimedia," and "rap" have been added to our collective consciousness and our formally accepted language.

Culture evolves continually to reflect society at any given point in time, but marketers attempt to initiate change as well. For example, breakfast in Latvia is typically a heavy meal that includes sausage, bacon, potatoes, macaroni, and eggs. In response, Kellogg has begun to implement an educational program to emphasize the nutritional value of breakfast cereal in its attempt to market Kellogg's Corn Flakes in that country.

## ▼ SUBCULTURES

A **subculture** is a group of consumers from a culture that share its values but exhibit them in different ways.

Despite the pervasive nature of culture, not all of the consumers *within* a society think, feel, and act the same way. Every society has **subcultures**—groups of consumers that share values but exhibit them in different ways.[1] Within a society such as the United States, individuals who share the core values of a culture may enact them differently because they have different demographic characteristics or lifestyles. For example, many college students show their faithfulness to the value of progress by listening to the latest music. But gender, race, geography, and lifestyle will result in disparate musical tastes. Some students will listen to alternative rock, some to hip-hop, others to rap, and still others to contemporary Christian rock.

Sociologists have long held that a subculture is simply a culture that is not dominant in its society. For example, Hispanic Americans comprise a subculture that has its own values, language, customs, and rituals, just as we have described for a cultural group. The term *subculture* is used to position cultural groups within the dominant culture of that society. Marketers have used the term to refer to a wide variety of situations. Some consider any group of consumers that has a passionate tie to the same product, such as Eliot and his fellow Harley enthusiasts, a subculture. Others label demographic groups, such as the elderly or Generation X, subcultures.

The most useful way to think of a subculture is in terms of a group that shares aspects of the common culture, such as its values, legal framework, and language, but that has its distinctive vocabulary, myths, customs, rituals, and material artifacts that reflect the shared values but are based on the history and lifestyle of the subculture. In other words, a single culture can be divided into consumer subcultures that exhibit shared values in different ways. Members of a society may choose disparate customs, rituals, or material artifacts to show their adherence to the shared values of their society. For example, a freelance writer may buy her own Compaq personal computer and Hewlett-Packard printer/copier/fax machine to achieve independence in her work life, whereas Eliot Spiegel gains independence and personal freedom from the mobility and solitude long rides on his Harley offer him. Both the freelance writer and Eliot achieve the goal of personal freedom, but in very different ways.

Some subcultures maintain communications in their native language and purchase products from members of their group. The Hispanic-American market is one example. As we will discuss in the next chapter on subcultures, the Hispanic market enjoys Spanish television, radio, and print media. In urban Hispanic neighborhoods, many purchases are made at small local stores, called "bodegas," that carry products from the native Hispanic culture. The Asian-American market is similar, with local television, magazines, and newspapers enjoying great popularity in areas heavily populated with Asian Americans, such as Los Angeles, San Francisco, and New York. Marketers advertising products and services to these subcultures must make adjustments. Advertisers must develop ads in other languages, using appropriate models, and they must be sensitive to the values and customs of the subculture.[2] In the United States, for example, marketers have begun to recognize the Hispanic celebration Cinco de Mayo and the Chinese New Year as occasions when Hispanic Americans and Asian Americans, respectively, seek native products to accompany their celebrations. Most grocery stores, particularly delis and bakery departments, stock special foods for Cinco de Mayo, such as jalapeño bread, churros, enchiladas, and burritos. Many decorate their departments with red, white, and green streamers. One local grocery store fried homemade tortilla chips, selling them warm at a special price. In 1991 McDonald's added chicken fajitas to its menu in recognition of this celebration. The approach to marketing for the Chinese New Year is similar, with grocers featuring items such as noodles and vegetables (bok choy, bamboo shoots, etc.). Store owners hope to attract non-Chinese customers with these specials as well. Some say they have seen a five percent increase in business on these days.

Unfortunately, much still needs to be learned about consumer behavior in subcultural groups. Some subcultures look to assimilate quickly into the dominant culture, while others seek to maintain virtually all aspects of their native culture in their new home.[3] It is obvious that American marketers have struggled with these issues and that marketing to these subcultures is not an easy task.

## FACT OR FICTION REVISITED

⊙    It is true that each subculture maintains its own distinct heritage. Without a distinct heritage, a group would not be considered a subculture.

## ▼ COMPONENTS OF CULTURE

Culture provides guidelines for consumers to use in deciding how to think, feel, and act. As noted above, values offer general guidelines about appropriate goals toward which the society's members should strive, yet they leave latitude for consumers in different subcultures to choose their own ways of thinking, feeling, and acting as they show their agreement with their society's goals. The remaining components of culture include the thoughts, feelings, and actions consumers use

■  FIGURE 4.1

The movement of meaning
in a consumer culture.

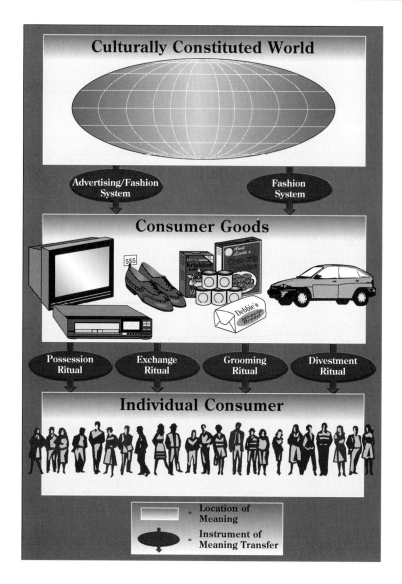

to achieve those goals. As Figure 4.1 illustrates, consumers use some of these components, particularly rituals and material artifacts, to demonstrate adherence to their society's cultural values. For example, most Americans speak English, but there are regional, ethnic, and age-related variations in the syntax and words that are used. Some consumers will exemplify the success they have achieved by working hard by driving a luxury car; some might choose to wear an expensive watch (Figure 4.2); still others will dress in the latest fashions (Figure 4.3).

Marketers must understand the components of culture so that they can (1) use advertising and product design to link their products to values in consumers' minds, and (2) identify the consumer subcultures for whom those links will be appropriate. That is, marketers must offer products to serve as material artifacts that will be consistent with consumers' values, myths, customs, and ritu-

■ FIGURE 4.2

Wearing an expensive watch, like a Gucci, is a sign of material success.

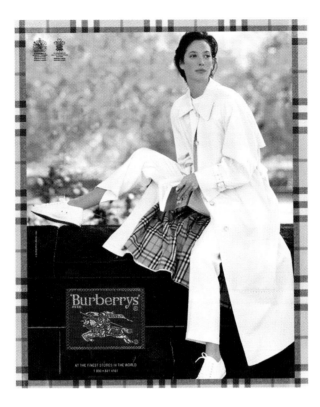

■ FIGURE 4.3

For some consumers, dressing in name-brand, high-quality fashions is a statement of personal success.

als—products that are consistent with the cultural assumptions made by consumers. For example, few consumers would give a Black & Decker drill or toaster oven to a lover for Valentine's Day or wear a polyester leisure suit today. As discussed in Chapter 3, segmentation and positioning are the tools marketers use to identify and communicate with the consumers for whom their particular products will be appropriate. For example, consider the growth of the contemporary Christian music market in the following box on the pleasures of consumption.

## PLEASURES OF CONSUMPTION

### Selling Christianity[4]

Sales of Christian-themed books and music are growing at a rapid pace, as are related videos and other novelty items, such as coffee mugs and t-shirts. Contemporary Christian music is a booming business, selling close to one billion dollars of recordings and concert tickets and projected to make up 10 percent of the music industry. A number of the major recording companies have started new Christian music labels, and others are distributing the records of existing labels, such as Benson, Sparrow, Star Song, and Word, to a wider audience. Several radio networks program Christian music, and Z Music, a 24-hour cable channel, plays only Christian music videos.

Christian items have traditionally been sold by specialty retailers located in a small portion of the country. Today, mass market retailers as diverse as Wal-Mart,

Sam's Club, Kmart, and Blockbuster are expanding their offerings from special holiday promotions to year-round sales of these products. It is expected that 30 percent of Christian music will have been sold through secular retailers as of the middle of the decade.

The music itself is much like the spectrum of non-Christian music—everything from the rap sounds of DC Talk, to the heavy-metal sound of Petra, to the gospel sound of BeBe and CeCe Winans, to the more mainstream styles of Amy Grant and Steven Curtis Chapman. The music is similar to non-Christian tunes, but the lyrics emphasize the more traditional Christian values of faith, hope, love, and celibacy.

Do you think that the rapidly growing popularity of Christian products reflects marketers' attempts to satisfy the needs of a segment of consumers who want their entertainment to reflect their values? Will the move into mass market retailers change the values of consumers who are currently not in that segment?

> **Values** are the underlying beliefs about the appropriate ways the members of a culture should act, think, and feel.

**Values**    The defining element of a culture is its **values**—the core views members of a culture hold about the goals toward which they should strive and the appropriate thoughts, feelings, and actions necessary to achieve those goals. The members within a society share similar values, but they may have different values than do the members of other cultures. For example, American culture emphasizes the importance of personal freedom and individual success, whereas Japanese culture stresses the relationship between the individual and the wider society.

As we noted in our discussion of the role of background characteristics in segmentation, marketing judgment must be applied to the examination of cultural differences. Marketers are ultimately interested in consumer behavior—if con-

■ FIGURE 4.4

Ford recognizes that consumers from different cultures typically use similar purchase processes in buying mid-sized cars.

sumers from two cultures show the same behavioral processes when they buy and use products, the marketer would be uninterested in their cultural differences. A global marketer such as Ford might recognize that disparate countries share few values, use different languages, and exhibit distinctly different myths, customs, and rituals; but those differences are irrelevant if consumers use similar purchase processes to buy midsize cars (see Figure 4.4).[5] We will discuss the measurement of values in more depth later in the chapter.

**Myths**   **Myths** are stories that illustrate the values shared by members of a society. These stories usually involve a person, event, or idea that represents certain values. For example, Santa Claus represents the value of materialism[6]—if you are a good girl or boy, you will be rewarded with material gifts—whereas the Marlboro Man represents rugged individualism and freedom (Figure 4.5), and the stories of Benjamin Franklin and Horatio Alger are often used to illustrate the rags-to-riches success that typifies the American Dream (Figure 4.6).

Myths are used to teach the values of the culture to the members of a society. Children are often told the stories in an entertaining manner to teach them the values their culture emphasizes. Myths also reinforce the values for those who already know them through novels, television programs, and movies, such as *For-*

> A **myth** is a story that illustrates one or more of the shared values of a culture by describing a person, event, or idea that symbolizes the values.

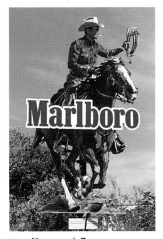

■ FIGURE 4.5
For decades, the Marlboro Man has been used to represent rugged individualism and the freedom of the Wild West.

■ FIGURE 4.6
The Franklin Templeton Group uses the image of Benjamin Franklin in its ads, representing financial success.

■ FIGURE 4.7

Movies such as *Forrest Gump* reinforce the American idea that anyone can succeed in America.

A **custom** is a culturally acceptable pattern of behavior that routinely occurs in a particular situation.

A **ritual** is a set of interrelated patterns of behavior that have a symbolic meaning.

**Laws** are formal rules and regulations that have the sanction of a governmental body to require or prohibit specific behavior.

*rest Gump*, which reminded us that anyone can succeed in America (Figure 4.7). Myths are also important for marketers because they provide symbols that can be used to illustrate the nature of a product—to help consumers position it in their minds. When consumers see the Marlboro Man, for instance, they know that the cigarettes advertised are different than, say, Virginia Slims.

**Customs**   A **custom** is a culturally acceptable behavior pattern that routinely occurs in a particular situation. Customs are functional in that they reduce the individual's fear that he or she will act inappropriately. The custom of giving a 15 percent tip to the staff in a restaurant reassures consumers that they are rewarding their waiter or waitress appropriately. Customs also function to make behavior more efficient, as when you wake up in the morning and brush your teeth and take a shower without having to think about those actions.

Marketers must be aware of people's customs of consumption. For example, Americans have traditionally consumed orange juice as a breakfast drink. But when the orange growers wanted to expand orange juice consumption, they introduced advertising that overtly addressed that custom, emphasizing that orange juice "isn't just for breakfast anymore." By contrast, in most other countries orange juice is not associated with breakfast. So in order to expand consumption to *include* breakfast time, Tropicana introduced its product in Japan with advertising that showed an American family drinking the juice to the tune of "Oh What A Beautiful Morning."

**Rituals**   A **ritual** is a set of interrelated patterns of behavior that have a symbolic meaning.[7] Like customs, rituals involve actual behavior, but they concern more involved sets of behavior that have a symbolic component. For example, many American families have a custom of eating dinner together, but Thanksgiving Day dinner involves a more specific set of preparations and is itself a symbol of gratitude for the year's successes.[8] Some consumers incorporate certain products as part of these rituals, such as a Butterball turkey, and many rituals involve the purchase of products for gift giving (Figure 4.8). Rituals are often a part of holidays and special events, such as the Super Bowl, and ceremonial occasions, such as weddings and births. But they are also part of many everyday occurrences, such as grooming rituals before a date or the ways in which consumers may indulge themselves after a difficult day. Table 4.2 lists examples of rituals that occur in consumers' lives as well as some of the customs and material artifacts associated with them.

**Laws**   **Laws** are values, customs, and rituals that have been codified into rules and regulations and are backed by the power of government. Laws govern virtu-

SOME BUNNY TO LOVE.

Nothing becomes a habit like a rabbit from Godiva. Except of course our chicks and eggs. So why not lavish someone with one of our luscious gifts? And make Easter simply the best thing about spring. Hop in or call 1-800-643-1579.

GODIVA
*Chocolatier*

■ FIGURE 4.8
Godiva turns an everyday product—chocolate—into a ritual on Easter by shaping it into an Easter bunny and wrapping it in gold foil.

*Table 4.2*

## RITUALS AND ASSOCIATED CUSTOMS AND MATERIAL ARTIFACTS

| Ritual | Customs | Material Artifacts |
|---|---|---|
| Wedding ceremony | Bride and groom dance the first dance | Wedding cake |
| | Decorate the couple's car | Bridal gown |
| Thanksgiving Day | Turkey cooks all day | Turkey |
| | Head of the house carves the turkey at the table | Stuffing |
| | | Cranberry sauce |
| Senior high school prom | Take pictures at home | Formal dress and tuxedo |
| | Drive to the dance in a limousine | Flowers |
| | Stay out all night | |

ally every kind of human activity, from jaywalking to murder, and represent the values of a culture as they have been formally applied to its members. Many marketing activities are governed by laws—advertising, copyrights, personal selling, packaging, pricing, product safety, retailing, trademarks, and warranties, to name a few (Figure 4.9).

Rules and regulations pertaining to marketing activities vary greatly from culture to culture. For example, bargaining over price is common in the United States and has even become a ritual for some new-car buyers. But in Germany, bargaining is eliminated by a complex web of laws that limits retailers to holding sales no more than twice a year, prohibits them from advertising the amount of price cuts, and forbids them from giving customers more than a three percent price break.[9]

**Material artifacts** are goods a culture has imbued with special meaning.

**Material Artifacts**   **Material artifacts** are goods that have a special meaning to the members of a culture. Many artifacts acquire their special meanings because of the role they play in myths, customs, and rituals. They can be everyday prod-

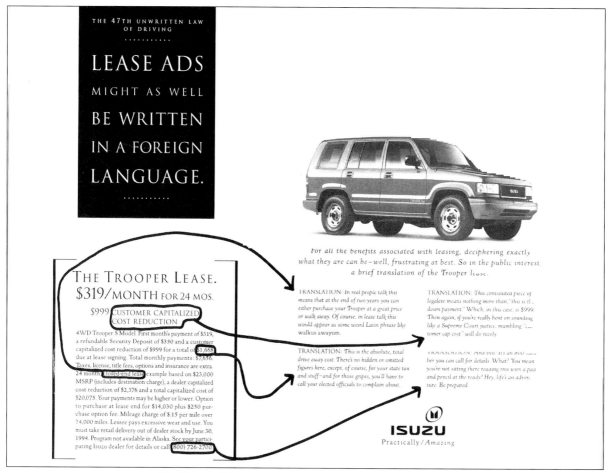

■ FIGURE 4.9

This Isuzu ad pokes fun at the legalese car makers are required to include in their advertising.

Padre Island.
Midnight.

"Yes."

Make
the diamond
as meaningful
as the
moment.

The Diamond Engagement Ring. How else could two months' salary last forever?

Call the Jewelers of America at 1-800-487-1480 for your free guide on "How to buy the perfect Diamond Engagement Ring."

De Beers                                                          A diamond is forever.

■ FIGURE 4.10
DeBeers has taken an every-day item—a ring—and turned it into a meaningful token of affection.

ucts that have symbolic meanings that give them special status in a culture, such as Easter eggs, which have a particular significance when painted and hidden for children to find but are no different than the eggs Americans eat every day. Or they can be special objects that have a significance in and of themselves—many consumers keep the dress they wore to their first formal, their first baseball glove, or a special fountain pen they were given as a child. DeBeers popularized the custom of diamond engagement rings in this country in the early part of this century, creating an artifact that now accompanies most engagements (Figure 4.10).

# INTERNATIONAL MARKETING STRATEGIES

As the global economy has increased in importance to marketers worldwide, a thorough understanding of the nature of consumers' cultural values, language, myths, customs, rituals, laws, and material artifacts is required for a marketer to be able to successfully market products internationally.[10] It is difficult enough to communicate and promote products to groups within our own country; it is even more difficult to move into foreign markets. The most difficult groups for American marketers are those who speak distinct languages or possess val-

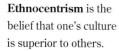

**Ethnocentrism** is the belief that one's culture is superior to others.

ues that differ from those of the American mass market. It is also difficult to overcome **ethnocentrism**—the belief that one's culture is superior to others and the rejection of products that reflect foreign cultures. For example, American brewers have had difficulty marketing their products in Germany and Belgium because consumers in those countries have a strong tradition of drinking local beers, which they feel are superior to any American beer.

## ▼ CULTURAL SIMILARITIES

All cultures ever known have created some type of system to address the issues of communication, housing, medicine, law, and marriage. What is surprising is that the list of cultural similarities does not end there. Anthropologists have discovered a range of other aspects of culture that appear to have been a part of human existence throughout the entire history of the world, including dancing, calendar making, gift giving, joke telling, magic tricks, and dream interpretation.

### FACT OR FICTION REVISITED

◉   David Letterman's Top Ten Lists would indeed be considered part of American culture. Even jokes are part of a culture if they are widely shared.

## ▼ CULTURAL DIFFERENCES

But even in light of these similarities and the accommodations of international travel, mass communication, and the lifting of trade barriers, significant differences remain among cultures, which leads to important variations in consumer behavior. It is important for marketers to be aware of those dimensions of another culture which are different so as to make important strategic decisions regarding market potential, product use patterns, and possible disposal problems. Major differences are usually found in the areas of economic conditions, technological advances, and government policies.

The *economy* of a region will certainly affect consumer behavior. At the time McDonald's opened its first restaurant in Moscow in January 1990, prices soared; a Big Mac, fries, and a drink cost about 10 rubles—20 percent of the average weekly salary.[11] And when Disney ventured outside of the United States and opened parks in France and Japan, it experienced very different reactions. Euro Disney opened during a European recession and failed to reflect Europeans' attitudes toward waiting in lines or their preferences for types of entertainment.[12] By contrast, attendance at the Tokyo theme park steadily increased; even after waiting several hours for the most popular rides, people returned. Amazingly, in its first 10 years, nearly 140 million people (17 million more that Japan's entire population) have moved through Tokyo Disneyland, making it the most profitable Disney theme park.[13] Unlike Euro Disney, the Tokyo park opened at a time when the Japanese economy was booming and consumers were looking for ways to spend unaccustomed spare cash and leisure time.

In addition to economic conditions, *technology* is another important consideration for marketers. The state of technology not only affects communications, it also often determines demand for certain products. Electricity may not be rea available, and the existence of refrigeration in homes and stores, electronic media, and mail service will all affect a marketing strategy.

Finally, the *government* plays an important role in encouraging or discouraging certain types of consumption behavior. Trade barriers, import–export quotas, protected species, and domestic commitments all play a role. Many governments control utilities, power plants, or railroads. Cigarettes or liquor may be heavily taxed to discourage their use, or their advertising may be prohibited, as in much of Europe.[14] Thus, a country's government can significantly influence the desirability of a certain consumer market. For example, the German town of Kassel placed a significant tax on disposable packaging, bottles, and utensils, prompting McDonald's to threaten to close its restaurants in the town in response to the financial burden.

## FACT OR FICTION REVISITED

◉ Despite the reality of international travel, mass communication, and the lifting of trade barriers, differences among cultures *have not* disappeared; many important differences among cultures remain.

## ▼ SEGMENTATION STRATEGIES IN THE INTERNATIONAL MARKET

The first decision a marketer must make in taking on an international market is whether to make its products available worldwide or only to certain countries in the international market.[15] As you recall, this decision is made on the basis of the size, stability, and accessibility of the countries involved. The marketer must then decide whether to use a localized marketing strategy for each individual culture or an identical global strategy for all cultures. These choices actually represent the ends of a continuum; some marketers customize every element of their marketing strategy for each country in which they operate, whereas others market their products identically in every country, as shown in Figure 4.11.

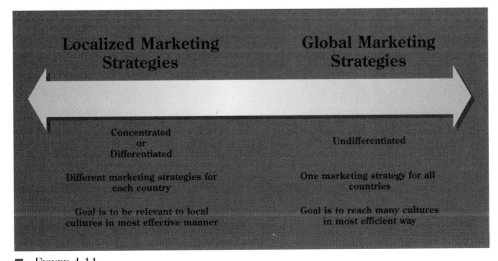

**■ FIGURE 4.11**

Segmentation strategies in the international market.

A **global marketing strategy** is one that maintains the marketing plan across all countries; that is, the product name, function, and ingredients remain the same in all markets. A global approach yields a consistent worldwide image and global name recognition. The company name and product names are not translated into many languages, and few, if any, adjustments in product attributes are made.[16] Examples of companies that use global approaches include Coca-Cola, Pepsi, IBM, Singer, Ford, and McDonald's (Figure 4.12).

By contrast, a **localized marketing strategy** takes into account the differences in consumer behavior, such as culture and behavioral processes, as well as the differences in the systems needed to market products, such as technology, law, the media, and transportation. This type of strategy requires in-depth research of the consumer behavior in the targeted population. Often the name of the product varies, and some American firms alter product characteristics for other cultures. Procter & Gamble manufactures many formulas of Tide detergent, for example—one for use in hard water, another for soft water, and still others for various types of mineral water. And Quaker Oats oatmeal isn't eaten as a breakfast cereal in certain cultures; instead, it is served as a dessert product in parts of Holland, Germany, and the Scandinavian countries (Figure 4.13). In all of these cases, using a local strategy requires that marketers be aware of cultural differences in terms of product preferences, product use, promotional communications, and product formulations.

> A **global marketing strategy** is one that maintains one marketing plan across all countries and yields global name recognition.

> A **localized marketing strategy** takes into account differences in consumer behavior and the systems needed to market products in different countries.

■ FIGURE 4.12

Coca-Cola is an example of a company that uses a global approach to market its products in different countries.

■ FIGURE 4.13

A Quaker Oats oatmeal advertisement is targeted at a Dutch market.

## ▼ CROSS-CULTURAL ANALYSIS

As new markets open up for American manufacturers, and other markets decline, it is important for marketers to pursue any appropriate opportunities available to them. Doing so entails conducting systematic comparisons of the similarities and differences in all aspects of the targeted cultures. This research is called **cross-cultural analysis**. To maximize opportunities in foreign markets, it is essential to learn about culture and values; how consumers see the world, what they buy, and how they evaluate products and services are all rooted in culture.[17] Every element of that culture has an impact on marketing strategies, as discussed next.

**Cross-cultural analysis** involves conducting systematic comparisons of the similarities and differences in all aspects of the targeted cultures.

**Language**   All languages include both a formal and informal vocabulary; the latter includes slang expressions that would not be meaningful to someone studying the formal version of the language. For example, the common American Pepsi slogan, "Come Alive," was interpreted differently all over the world. The Germans thought it meant "come back from the dead," and the Chinese understood it as "it brings your ancestors back from the grave." Needless to say, marketers need to make language a priority. Product names should be checked for double meanings, to see whether they can be pronounced in cultures lacking certain phonetic sounds, and to ensure that another product in another culture does not use the same name.

**Customs**   American marketers have had to make adjustments for certain local customs in their marketing strategy. For example, the Singer sewing machine company experienced severe declines in sales as American women moved into the labor force and had less time to sew, so the company turned to other markets, including Muslim countries. Singer quickly found out why no one came to its stores in these countries—Muslim women are often not allowed to go out and shop or to attend sewing lessons. More careful cross-cultural analysis might have prevented such a marketing blunder. Similarly, Gerber's advertised baby food in an African country using a full-page photo of a beautiful African baby with a small jar of baby food in the corner. The custom in that country was to depict the contents of any packaged product in its advertising, and the unpleasant implication was that Gerber was selling cut-up babies! Once again, more careful analysis could have prevented the embarrassing connotation.

**Color**   Colors have different connotations and traditional uses across cultures. In Southeast Asia, for example, light blue symbolizes death and mourning. In China, white is associated with death, and traditional brides dress in red. In Malaysia, green is used to designate jungle areas where there is danger or disease. When designing advertisements and packages, marketers must be careful to avoid using colors that will send the wrong message to the consumers of another culture.

**Time**   How consumers view and use their time differs greatly across cultures. In Ethiopia, for example, the time required to make a decision is directly proportional to the importance of that decision. As a result, Americans that connect time with money are viewed as minimizing the significance of their business decisions. In the Middle East time depends on relationships. American businesspeople may find they have to wait for hours to meet with an executive whose brother has stopped by to visit. Close relatives take absolute priority over any previous schedule of appointments. Many Middle Easterners resist fixed schedules, viewing them as rude and insulting to relatives who must wait while strangers are seen first. Marketers who use sales personnel to demonstrate their products in person must consider such customs when they try to schedule appointments.

**Space** The distance at which business is conducted varies across cultures. Cultural rules about physical contact and social distance are usually unwritten but are extremely important to the people of a culture. In America, for instance, most business discussions occur across a table or desk, usually at a distance of five to eight feet; more personal business might be carried out within two to three feet. By contrast, in the Middle East and Latin America people are more likely to touch or work very closely together. The opposite is true in Germany and the Scandinavian countries, where physical distance is maintained and the parties seldom touch. England also has a specific cultural dictate regarding the Queen: It is considered inappropriate for anyone to touch the queen. On a visit to the United States, then-President Ronald Reagan made the mistake of putting his arm around Queen Elizabeth in order to guide her to an exit. The British press criticized this "faux pas" the following day.

Cross-cultural analysis covers other aspects beyond those discussed above. Research should be conducted in the following areas before introducing a product or service.[18]

*(1)   Check the product's appeal to the consumers in the target market.* Kentucky Fried Chicken entered the Brazilian market only to find that charcoal-broiled chicken was made and sold on street corners everywhere and was both cheaper and tastier to Brazilian consumers than the Colonel's version.

*(2)   Learn the limits of the physical and environmental resources.* Nestle suffered negative publicity when it marketed instant baby formula in powdered form in developing Third World countries. Because the water necessary to mix the formula was often germ ridden, the formula put the health of babies at risk.

*(3)   Never assume success based on the home country's experience.* In Italy, women feel a house should be dusted and furniture polished at least three times a week. By contrast, American women set a low priority on dusting and polishing furniture. In the United States, canned soup is usually mixed with water and heated. Europeans find this kind of preparation distasteful and prefer larger cans of premixed soup ready to heat and eat (Figure 4.14).

*(4)   Watch for changing market conditions, such as economic, social, and political trends, as well as changes in product use.* Women's roles, in particular, are changing in many cultures.[19] The status of women, in turn, will determine their response to various promotional strategies. More generally,

■  FIGURE 4.14

Europeans prefer large cans of premixed soups that are ready to heat and eat to the canned soups that are to be mixed with water and heated that are popular in America.

countries suffering from difficult economic times have to be carefully examined to determine whether the consumers have the means to secure certain products. Furthermore, sometimes a product introduced for a specific purpose is adapted by a local culture for a different use. This happened to the Vicks Vapo-Rub creme, which is used in some countries to relieve the congestion associated with colds and flu but is also marketed and used as an effective mosquito repellent in tropical climates. Knowledge of these alternative uses offer opportunities to enter new markets or to reposition products in current markets.

## FACT OR FICTION REVISITED

◉   The role of women in society is indeed an important element to consider in cross-cultural market analysis since the status of women influences market response to many products.

*(5)   Study the laws of the targeted country as they apply to advertising, registration, copyrights, logos, and trademarks.* Countries such as Canada and Belgium require that advertisements be bilingual or that an equal number of ads in each required language are available. In many countries, trademark registration is much less formal than in the United States. Often the first to use a particular sign, symbol, or name has the rights to it.

*(6)   Avoid rotating marketing personnel in a foreign market.* It takes time

for marketers to learn the nuances of any culture and to develop insights into cultural practices and preferences. Marketers can make local connections and friendships that are helpful in marketing a product in the culture. Local marketing managers should be allowed to use their familiarity with their market to make localized decisions. After all, they may be in a better position to make decisions than the headquarters in their home culture.

## FACT OR FICTION REVISITED

◉   It is *not true* that most multinational marketers rotate marketing personnel across markets. In fact, this practice has many potential disadvantages.

## CORE VALUES AND THEIR MEASUREMENT

Values serve as the invisible outline for the development of many of the other components of culture—the ideas, customs, traditions, myths, rituals, laws, and material artifacts. In order to recognize the differences among consumers in different cultures and subcultures, marketers must be able to identify the values that define the culture and their impact on consumer behavior. Because values are relatively enduring beliefs about what is appropriate or important and are widely accepted by the members of a society, consumer researchers have tried to develop ways to define, categorize, and measure these values. Once the values have been measured, marketers can then identify cultures and subcultures that have values to which they can link their products.

The limitation of these methods is that consumers who share values may exhibit them in different ways because of other background characteristics. Thus, even though Americans may share core values, they may enact them in different ways that require different marketing strategies. Consider the value of success. Americans believe that personal success is desirable and can be shown through material goods. Consequently, most Americans want to own their own home. But the *kinds* of homes differ greatly, from multimillion-dollar apartments in Manhattan to small farm houses in Kansas. Custom and tradition dictate that most young couples buy a house before they start a family and then move to successively nicer houses as they become more successful and affluent. As the price of houses has grown over the last generation, however, customs have changed, and some young couples have been fortunate to have parents who can afford to help them make the necessary down payment.

Although such subcultural differences in the way values are expressed exist, it is nevertheless useful to be aware of ways that have been proposed to measure values.

## ▼ THE ROKEACH VALUE SURVEY

The Rokeach Value Survey is a self-administered inventory that measures two kinds of values: (1) **terminal values**, which represent the goals and objectives consumers seek, and (2) **instrumental values**, which measure the ways in which consumers can *achieve* the objectives they seek.[21] Table 4.3 lists the terminal and instrumental values consumers rank when they complete the survey. As noted above, while these items represent values that are important in many cultures and subcultures, it is the way in which they are expressed in day-to-day life that is interesting to consumer researchers.

## ▼ THE LIST OF VALUES (LOV) APPROACH

In an effort to address the practical needs of consumers researchers, Lynn Kahle and his colleagues developed a shorter list of values that are intended to reflect more closely consumers' actual behavior.[22] The list, shown in Table 4.4, contains nine terminal values. As we will see when we discuss lifestyle in Chapter 6, the *List of Values* approach tries to encompass different styles used in enacting the values that it presents. The shorter list attempts to make it easier for consumers to rank the values. However, although this approach moves closer to the styles in which consumers actually enact their values, it still addresses values which leave consumers with considerable latitude to use different customs, rituals, and material artifacts to achieve their objectives. For example, a consumer who seeks excitement, fun, and enjoyment may choose to ride a Harley, like Eliot does, and an-

**Terminal values** represent goals and objectives consumer seek to reach.

**Instrumental values** represent the means by which consumers can achieve the objectives they seek.

---

*Table 4.3*

### VALUES MEASURED BY THE ROKEACH VALUE SURVEY

| Terminal | Instrumental |
|---|---|
| A comfortable life | Ambitious |
| An exciting life | Broad minded |
| A sense of accomplishment | Capable |
| A world at peace | Cheerful |
| A world of beauty | Clean |
| Equality | Courageous |
| Family security | Forgiving |
| Freedom | Helpful |
| Happiness | Honest |
| Inner harmony | Imaginative |
| Mature love | Independent |
| National security | Intellectual |
| Pleasure | Logical |
| Salvation | Loving |
| Self-respect | Obedient |
| Social recognition | Polite |
| True friendship | Responsible |
| Wisdom | Self-controlled |

*Table 4.4*

### THE LIST OF VALUES APPROACH

A sense of belonging
Being well respected
Excitement
Fun and enjoyment
Security
Self-fulfillment
Self-respect
Sense of accomplishment
Warm relationships with others

other might choose to water ski. Harley-Davidson must determine whether such a consumer is part of the market segment that will respond positively to its marketing efforts or if he would prefer to spend his money on new skiis.

### ▼ AMERICAN CORE VALUES

Based on research conducted using Rokeach and Kahle's approaches and other views of American culture, it appears that there are several values so central to the American way of life that we can refer to them as core values. Most Americans would agree that these enduring beliefs help to define who Americans are and why they are motivated toward certain goals. Some of these core values include the following:

(1) *Success* — Americans admire hard work, enterpreneurship, achievement, and success. The culture celebrates success with rewards ranging from money to status and prestige.

(2) *Materialism* —Owning tangible goods is important to Americans. The society encourages consumption, ownership, and possession. It is not unusual for people to judge others based on the number of cars they own, the style of clothes they wear, or other tangible possessions.

(3) *Freedom* —The American culture was founded upon the concept of religious freedom. From this foundation, the Constitution and the Bill of Rights went on to assure American citizens the right to life, liberty, and the pursuit of happiness. These freedoms are fundamental to the legal system and the moral fiber of the American culture.

(4) *Progress* —Moving ahead technologically, making advances in medicine, science, and health, and improving available products and services are all important to Americans. The American culture enjoys innovation and advancement. Books, movies, and museums chronicle the progress in every aspect of the society.

(5) *Youth* —Americans are said to be obsessed with youth. They spend a good deal of time and money on products and procedures to make them look younger.[20] The popular media encourages this practice by using trim, young models to sell products. Americans flock to health and fitness centers, and they spend millions on health and beauty aids.

(6) *Capitalism*—Americans believe in a free enterprise system. Competition is valued, and monetary success is acclaimed. The society views capitalism as a means of creating choices, quality, and value. Consequently, Americans are governed by laws that prohibit monopolistic control of a market and legislation that regulates free trade. Small businesses are an important and growing segment of American capitalism; those that can compete effectively may follow other small businesses into national and international fame. Examples include Apple, which started in a garage by two college dropouts; McDonald's, which began with one hamburger restaurant purchased by Ray Kroc; and Wal-Mart, which began with a few small five-and-dime stores in Arkansas.[23] Wal-Mart's wide-scale expansion has resulted in a conflict over

the core values of success, freedom, progress, and capitalism, however, as discussed in the next Public Policy box.

## PUBLIC POLICY

### The Wal-Mart Story[24]

In 1950 Sam Walton opened Walton's five-and-dime store in Bentonville, Arkansas; by 1962 he was the owner of 15 stores selling products at discount prices. In the 1960s and 1970s Wal-Mart enjoyed considerable growth as Americans moved away from fancy department stores to the lower prices of the discount stores. Sam Walton concentrated his early stores in rural southern towns with populations of 5000 to 6000. This strategy allowed Wal-Mart to grow without going head to head with Kmart, which located primarily in urban areas. As its expansion continued at a ferocious pace, Wal-Mart produced revenues of $1.6 billion in 1980 and $26 billion in 1990. By then Wal-Mart had begun expanding its location strategy to include stores in larger metropolitan areas. This was most often done by opening stores in the suburbs surrounding major cities.

By 1991 Wal-Mart had surpassed Sears and Kmart to become America's premiere discount store. Today Wal-Mart boasts over 2000 stores in 49 states (Vermont has yet to allow Wal-Mart to build any stores there). Stores are even operating in Mexico, Puerto Rico, and the Virgin Islands.

It would be difficult to find a more striking example of the American success story than Wal-Mart. Sam Walton built a discount store empire from a modest beginning in those values so often associated with the American culture—success, achievement, competitive spirit, and wealth. All this was not without controversy, however, and some say Sam Walton may have actually violated other cultural values in his pursuit of success.

In 1993 Wal-Mart was found guilty of engaging in "predatory pricing" by an Arkansas judge. The judge found in favor of three independent Arkansas pharmacies who claimed that Wal-Mart intentionally sold some drugs and health and beauty aids below cost at its Conway store in an attempt to drive its competitors out of business. The judge ordered an end to the practice and awarded the plaintiffs nearly $300,000 in damages. Wal-Mart has appealed the decision.

Wal-Mart has also faced significant opposition in many of the small towns in which it has tried to open new stores. This opposition has been particularly strong in several New England states that maintain a long-time custom of supporting independent retailers in their own downtown areas. Although evidence seems to indicate that prices to consumers will be lower, the residents of these towns want to preserve the local stores they have always patronized. In some cases, long-time social activists have opposed Wal-Mart because they want to preserve the local and regional cultures of their towns in the face of the mass market similarity of retailers such as Wal-Mart.

Questions of culture and values emerge in this story as Wal-Mart collides with small towns and small businesses who represent local subcultures and independent success. How do you view the nationwide expansion of mass merchandisers who dominate the retailing environment of local areas? Are the values of success and individual freedom for existing local retailers more important than the economic progress of other consumers in these small towns?

123

# CULTURE, VALUES, AND SUBCULTURES

Eliot Spiegel is a Harley rider. He rides because he likes the feeling of independence he gets from the open road and because he feels that he's part of a culture that will accept him for who he is. Harley riders don't judge him, even though he's more successful than some and less successful than others, richer than some and poorer than others. Eliot is part of the Harley subculture, and, as such, he shares some basic values about freedom, independence, and personal responsibility with other Harley riders.

Riding Harleys is not something many of Eliot's "type" do. He is young, private-school educated, has a professional job, and is married to another professional. But his demographic background—his age, social class, and family status—his personality and professional lifestyle, and the opinions of his friends, both riders and nonriders, do not change his values of freedom, independence, and personal responsibility.

Clearly, Americans differ on their views of how values should be exhibited by the many different subcultures that exist together in the United States. Factors such as demographics, personality, lifestyle, and psychographics, and reference groups all interact with Eliot's culture to direct the way he expresses his values. In the next chapters we will turn to a discussion of other background characteristics that may be used to segment consumers into subcultures that exhibit varied consumer behavior. We will discuss demographic subcultures in Chapter 5, segments based on psychographics and lifestyle in Chapter 6, and the role played by reference groups in Chapter 7.

## SUMMARY

1. **Examine the nature of culture and subculture and the roles they play in consumers' lives.** Culture is the unique pattern of shared meanings that characterize a society—the society's personality. Its effects pervade everything that consumers think, feel, and do. Culture is (1) functional in providing guidelines for consumers' behavior; (2) learned by consumers from family and friends and reinforced by books, movies, television, and advertising; and (3) dynamic, as it evolves to reflect changes in the environment. Subcultures are composed of consumers who share their culture's values but show distinct ways of thinking, feeling, and acting.

2. **Identify the components of culture.** The components of culture are (1) values, (2) language, (3) myths, (4) customs, (5) rituals, (6) laws, and (7) material artifacts. Values are the underlying beliefs shared by the members of culture about appropriate ways to live; language is the tool members use to communicate with one another; myths are stories that illustrate the culture's values; customs are acceptable ways of acting; rituals are sets of customs that have a symbolic meaning; laws are the formal codification of the culture's values; and material artifacts are goods that have a symbolic meaning to the members of the culture.

3. **Analyze the differences in culture and values among societies in the global economy and the impact of those differences on firms' international marketing strategies.** There are important variations in cultures and values among societies and cultures in areas such as demographic, psychological, and social characteristics; economic systems; technological advances; and government policies. Most importantly, these factors affect consumers' behavioral processes through different customs concerning color, time, space, and language. As a result, marketers must decide whether consumer behavior in the countries to which they wish to market differs significantly enough that localized marketing strategies are necessary or whether there are enough similarities that one undifferentiated, global strategy can work for all countries.

4. **Identify the ways that values have been used to discriminate consumer cultures and subcultures from one another.** The Rokeach Value Survey and List of Values approaches are two methods commonly used to measure values so that cultures and subcultures can be discriminated from one another. Whereas values may differ among cultures, they can also be enacted through different customs and rituals within the subcultures in a culture. Therefore, these approaches are best used for identifying differences in values among cultures, not in the other components of culture.

5. **Recognize the core values that are shared by Americans.** We discussed six core values that help define American culture and provide the motivation for much of American consumers' behavior. They are (1) success, (2) materialism, (3) freedom, (4) progress, (5) youth, and (6) capitalism.

## KEY TERMS

Culture, *p. 101*
Subculture, *p. 104*
Values, *p. 108*
Myths, *p. 109*
Customs, *p. 110*
Rituals, *p. 110*
Enculturation, *p. 103*

Acculturation, *p. 103*
Laws, *p. 110*
Material artifacts, *p. 112*
Ethnocentrism, *p. 114*
Global marketing strategy, *p. 116*
Localized marketing strat-

egy, *p. 116*
Cross-cultural analysis, *p. 117*
Terminal values, *p. 121*
Instrumental values, *p. 121*

## SKILL-BUILDING ACTIVITIES

1. Remember the last birthday party you attended—a celebration of your own birthday or that of someone else. Describe the event briefly. What aspects of this event were influenced by culture? In what way?

2. Visit a local shopping mall. Identify 10 items imported from abroad. For each item, state whether that same item would be more attractive or less attractive if it were not imported and explain why.

3. Why was Tokyo Disneyland more successful than Euro Disney? This is a research assignment that will require some library work.

4. What are the principle subcultures in your local community? How were you able to identify them?

5.  List ten cross-cultural problems McDonald's would be likely to encounter when marketing in India. Explain why each would be a problem. This is another library research task.

6.  Imagine you are responsible for opening a Wal-Mart in a major metropolitan area in the United States. What aspects of Wal-Mart tradition must be preserved? What aspects must be changed?

# CHAPTER 4 SELF-TEST

## ▼ MULTIPLE CHOICE

1.  The unique patter of shared meaning that characterize a society and distinguish it from other societies is the definition of _____.
    a.  marketing
    b.  sociology
    c.  culture
    d.  subculture

2.  Which of the following would be considered a cultural myth in the United States?
    a.  the story of Cinderella
    b.  Thanksgiving
    c.  Easter eggs
    d.  the wedding ceremony

3.  Culture is _____ because it guides consumers' behavior and also _____ since it changes to reflect changes in the environment.
    a.  instinctive; transparent
    b.  functional; dynamic
    c.  instinctive; dynamic
    d.  functional; transparent

4.  Divisions of a culture based on such things as race, age, or religion are called
    a.  reference groups
    b.  equity groups
    c.  subcultures
    d.  cultural clusters

5.  If a company uses one marketing mix throughout the world, that company has chosen a _____ marketing strategy.
    a.  localized
    b.  global
    c.  differentiated
    d.  concentrated

6.  Goals and objectives consumers seek are called _____ values, whereas the ways consumers achieve the objectives they seek are called _____ values.
    a.  functional; terminal
    b.  material; instrumental
    c.  terminal; instrumental
    d.  material; functional

7.  Major differences in cultures are usually found in the areas of economic conditions, government policies, and _____.
    a.  technological advances
    b.  mass communication
    c.  law
    d.  housing

8.  The underlying beliefs regarding what is important and how people should live are called cultural _____.
    a.  norms
    b.  values
    c.  action rules
    d.  laws

9.  The marketing research that involves comparisons of various cultures is called _____.
    a.  intercultural research
    b.  multinational research
    c.  cross-cultural analysis
    d.  diversified marketing research

10. When conducting cross-cultural analysis, one of the most important areas of research involves determining the product's _____ to the targeted consumers.
    a.  price compatibility
    b.  appeal
    c.  name recognition
    d.  number of uses

▼  TRUE/FALSE

1.  There are some aspects of culture that are consistent throughout the world.
    T or F
2.  Culture is instinctive not learned.   T or F
3.  Marketers need not be concerned about cultural customs since customs will never change.   T or F
4.  When marketing to a new culture, all elements of that culture should be analyzed.
    T or F
5.  A product's success in one culture assures the same product's success in another culture.   T or F
6.  Success, materialism, and youthfulness are all core American values.   T or F
7.  Material artifacts can be everyday items.   T or F
8.  Consumers in different cultures often differ in how they search for information and how they evaluate alternatives.   T or F
9.  Understanding culture is not important in the development of advertising.   T or F
10. If the restaurant chain Pizza To You changes its menu and pricing policies in every culture within which it does business, it is using a global marketing strategy.
    T or F


▼  SHORT ANSWER

1.  Describe the differences and similarities of laws and customs.
2.  Discuss why marketers should study a culture's perspectives on time, space, and color.
3.  Discuss why moving marketing personnel from one culture to another is not advantageous to an organization.
4.  Describe some of the implications of a culture's language in the development of marketing strategy targeted to that culture.


▼  APPLICATION EXERCISE

You are the vice president of marketing for a sausage company based in the United States. You are exploring new markets for your product. Several of these new markets are located outside the United States. Describe what components of the culture, as related to your product, should be studied before you enter any of these new markets.

# 5

# DEMOGRAPHIC SUBCULTURES

◉ Consumer Snapshot    *Luis Hermoza is a 36-year-old Computer Support Systems Analyst. He was born in Peru and now lives in Bal Harbour, Florida, with his wife, Sherry, and their infant son, Nicholas.*

## FACT OR FICTION?

◉  Compared with female consumers, male consumers are more likely to write checks or use credit when making purchases.

◉  Children are a major factor in fast food purchasing, auto buying, and purchases of televisions and consumer electronics.

◉  On-site promotions are especially effective with college students.

◉  Baby boomers look for products that can either be recycled or reused.

⦿ Members of the elderly segment of the consumer market have more discretionary income than do baby boomers.

⦿ African-American households watch less television than does the average American household.

⦿ The Hispanic segment of the United States consumer population is older than other segments.

⦿ Compared with other American consumers, Asian Americans are more likely to prefer premium brands and technically oriented products.

⦿ Members of the working class are more likely to take risks and experiment with new products than are members of other classes.

⦿ Most American consumers go through the family life cycle in the same order.

## EYE ON THE CONSUMER

Luis Hermoza lives in the Miami, Florida area with his wife, Sherry. Luis and Sherry have moved a number of times in the last few years, from Luis's native country of Peru to Minnesota and then New Jersey before moving to Florida about six months ago. Luis and Sherry chose to rent an apartment in the only rental complex in the somewhat expensive and exclusive Bal Harbour area because they want to live someplace quiet and safe. Safety is important to Luis. He still can't believe the amount of violence in this country and the fact that the television news dwells on it so much.

The apartment Luis and Sherry rent is rather typical and modern; the kitchen is furnished with a built-in dishwasher and microwave, and washers and dryers are available on every floor. These appliances are important to the Hermozas because Luis and Sherry both work and they just don't have the time to do all of the household chores without all of these conveniences right on hand. The apartment is also close to the beach, where Luis and Sherry bicycle, swim, and snorkel.

The Hermozas want to start a family, but before they do so, they want to buy a house that has enough space for children, friends, and relatives. They are trying to save money by keeping to a strict budget, which they monitor with a program on their personal computer, and by running every purchase past their "budget committee," which is what they call the discussions they have before either of them makes a purchase. Luis is still adjusting to the different attitudes Americans have about money. America, he says, is a society of consumers who are willing to be in debt their entire lives. In Peru people are more cautious about their spending because wages are so much lower and personal credit is much tougher to get.

The goal of this chapter is to discuss demographic subcultures, as first introduced in Chapter 2. Marketers use demographic characteristics, along with culture, values, lifestyles, and reference groups, to divide consumers into segments that exhibit different behavior. We discuss some of the more important demographic characteristics marketers use to group and target consumers—specifically, gender, age, race and ethnicity, religion, social class, geography, and household characteristics. As we discussed in the previous chapter, demographic characteristics can be the basis for consumer subcultures. A subculture's members enact their shared values through customs and rituals that guide their behavioral processes. Here we introduce some relevant findings about specific demographic subcultures based on these characteristics and discuss their implications for consumer behavior. Finally, we examine the public policy implications of the ways in which marketers classify consumers into demographic segments and direct their marketing efforts toward some of those segments.

After reading and thinking about this chapter, you should be able to:

❶ Recognize demographic characteristics that can be used to divide consumers into meaningful segments.

❷ Judge the usefulness of gender, age, race and ethnicity, religion, social class, geography, and household characteristics as segmentation characteristics for a consumer behavior problem.

❸ Analyze the public policy implications of a segment that is based on demographic characteristics.

# THE BASES OF DEMOGRAPHIC DIFFERENCES ◀

As noted in Chapter 2, demographic characteristics are the innate physical, social, economic, and geographical attributes that comprise an individual and describe the location of that individual in his or her social environment. For example, we can describe Luis Hermoza as a married, middle-class man of Peruvian descent who lives in a suburban community in the Southeast United States. Demographic characteristics provide the impetus for both tangible and intangible variations among the ways consumers think, feel, and act. For example, elderly consumers may differ from teenagers in both tangible ways—such as physical changes in skin and hair—and intangible ways—such as different protocols concerning financial matters; the elderly are typically more conservative about spending money because they remember the financial hardships they suffered during the Depression.

Sensor For Women.
Feel Why It's The Razor Worth Holding Onto.

■ FIGURE 5.1

Gillette introduced the Sensor razor for women to address the unique shaving requirements of women.

## ▼ TANGIBLE ATTRIBUTES

Certain tangible attributes may be the result of actual demographic differences among consumers, such as physiological distinctions stemming from gender and ethnicity, developmental features that accompany aging, and physical attributes caused by geographical variations in climate. For example, women use different personal care products for health and beauty than men, such as razors, deodorants and antiperspirants, and feminine hygiene products. In response, Gillette introduced the Sensor for Women razor, specially designed for women's shaving needs (Figure 5.1). Furthermore, consumers' bodies change as they age; teenagers may use acne remedies, such as Clearasil or Oxy 10, whereas older consumers might apply Avon Anew Face Cream to soothe damaged skin caused by aging (Figure 5.2).

## ▼ INTANGIBLE ATTRIBUTES

Other, intangible attributes may be based on cultural, social, economic, and psychological distinctions. We considered cultural differences and the importance of subcultures in the last chapter when we discussed consumers who share the values of their culture but exhibit them through different customs, rituals, and material artifacts. Marketers respond to cultural differences by developing products for distinct demographic groups of consumers. For example, General Mills recently introduced to the Hispanic market Buñuelitos, a breakfast cereal designed to taste like the traditional Mexican buñuelo pastry (Figure 5.3). Social relationships and psychological outlooks may also vary with demograph-

■ FIGURE 5.2

A consumer's physical needs change as she ages. The same person who used Stridex to fight acne as a teenager may purchase Avon Anew Face Cream as an adult to fight the effects of aging.

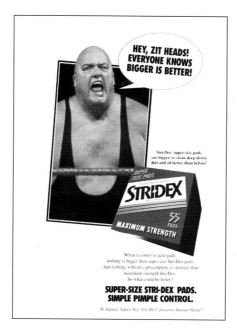

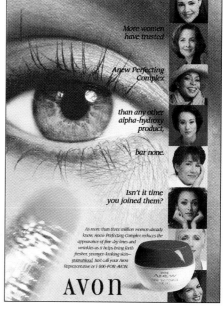

ics. Thus, Dewar's Scotch chose to advertise its product to young adults by addressing the social and psychological changes that occur as members of this demographic group establish themselves in their adult lives (Figure 5.4).

■ FIGURE 5.3
In segmenting racial and ethnic groups, General Mills introduced Buñuelitos cereal to the Hispanic market, hoping to imitate the taste of the traditional buñuelo pastry.

■ FIGURE 5.4
In this ad, Dewar's appeals to young adults by addressing the social and psychological changes they can expect to experience as they establish themselves in their adult lives.

Specific characteristics define demographic subcultures. In particular, gender, age, race, ethnicity, religion, social class, geography, and household composition often distinguish consumers from one another. For example, although both college students and their parents might value youth, the parents may have to rely quite a bit more on health clubs and health and beauty products to demonstrate the youthful appearance that comes naturally to their children.

# GENDER

Women and men differ on important tangible attributes, such as physiology, as well as intangible factors, such as social and economic status. As we mentioned earlier, physiological differences result in different needs for health and beauty aids in men and women. Equally important are the distinct cultural, social, and economic roles that women and men occupy and the effects these roles have on their behavioral processes.[1] For example, if men and women looked for the same features in an automobile, there would be no need to segment the car market based on gender. This is not the case, however. In fact, women buy over half of the cars and trucks sold in the United States today, spending about $65 billion dollars a year. More specifically, women who must shuttle kids around on a daily basis might prefer different features in a car than men would (Figure 5.5).[2] This insight has encouraged automobile manufacturers to implement different strategies when appealing to men and women. Since more than half of all minivans are purchased and driven by women, door handles and controls have been adjusted to accommodate women's smaller hands and longer fingernails; seats have been raised and placed forward; and the pedals have been positioned with consideration for high-heeled drivers.

At the same time, the traditional *Leave It to Beaver* stereotype that portrays men and women as completely different—men work outside the home among society whereas women stay at home and raise the children—is rapidly fading. For example, while 57 percent of all women kept house full time in 1962, only 26 percent did so in 1990.[3] Thus, it is the *interplay* of differences between the genders and converging gender roles that make gender an important demographic characteristic.

## ▼ THE FEMALE MARKET

The female market, which includes working women, homemakers, single mothers, and older women, is much more diverse today than it was a generation ago. Nearly 60 percent of all women over the age of 18 work outside the home today. This expansion of women's roles has resulted in a variety of new needs and diverse consumer behaviors.[4] Working mothers, for example, have created an enormous demand for child care, housekeeping, and other services and convenience products.

The Mazda MPV You've got schedules. Appointments. Lunch. Managing a household demands a lot of time in the field. So we designed the Mazda MPV minivan to be like a company car for family business. With comfortable car-like handling. Smooth V6 power, standard. Room for seven. And a swing-out side door that even your most junior partner can handle. Most important, the MPV comes with a driver's-side air bag, rear-wheel anti-lock brakes and the best basic warranty" in its class. So you have a little less to worry about. Which is really nice for someone who always takes their work home with them.

There's no such thing as a stay-at-home Mom.

mazda
IT JUST FEELS RIGHT

■ FIGURE 5.5
Mazda targets its MPV Minivan at busy mothers, appealing to their desire for safety features, smooth handling, and convenient door designs.

Studies show that women differ from men in the ways in which they use the behavioral processes to read and view media, respond to advertising, and evaluate products. For example, nearly 40 percent of women identify themselves as prime time TV viewers; more affluent women prefer cable stations like Cable News Network (CNN) and the Weather Channel. The growing numbers of working women also increasingly respond to radio advertising during commuter hours, making this medium an effective marketing tool for reaching this segment of the consumer market. At the same time, women tend to avoid ads that depict extremes like "superwoman" or the "happy homemaker," seeing both as unrealistic. Finally, female consumers typically spend more time browsing in stores and are more likely to comparison shop, use coupons, and write checks or use credit cards when making purchases than are men.

## FACT OR FICTION REVISITED

◉ Male consumers *are not* more likely to write checks or use credit when making purchases; these are behaviors more indicative of women, in general.

■ FIGURE 5.6
Tilex portrays a 1990s man, doing domestic household chores, in this ad for its Soap scum remover.

## ▼ THE MALE MARKET

The male market has also undergone significant changes in recent years. Faced with a less secure work environment and increased work demands on the women in their lives, many men are more active in domestic and child-rearing activities than in the past. As women entered the work force, men entered the supermarkets and began assuming responsibilities traditionally handled by women (Figure 5.6). In fact, men make up 40 percent of supermarket shoppers and 65 percent of convenience store shoppers, and many men say they don't mind grocery shopping.[5]

Although some men have assumed a larger share of the domestic chores, they are also the biggest consumers of beer, sporting goods, and many hardware products. In general, men tend to watch more commercial television and are less likely to read a daily newspaper than women. And with over 80 percent of men between the ages of 20 and 54 employed, much of the advertising during weekend sports programming is targeted at them.

# AGE

Consumers change as they age; consequently, their behavioral processes and purchase decisions change too. Table 5.1 shows the broad generational segments that comprise the United States population. Each segment represents a potential market for specific products and services, although sophisticated marketers will further divide them into more focused subcultures. For example, the youngest generation is composed of 68 million children and

## Table 5.1

### GENERATIONS IN PROFILE

**(U.S. generations by age, percent of total population, and size in 1995)**

| Generation | Ages | Percentage of Population | Size (in millions) |
|---|---|---|---|
| Kids and teens | Under 18 | 26% | 68 |
| Baby busters | 18 to 29 | 17 | 45 |
| Baby boomers | 30 to 49 | 31 | 81 |
| Mature market | 50 and older | 26 | 68 |

Source: American Demographics' calculations from Census Bureau surveys

teenagers. Approximately 45 million **baby busters,** also known as *"Generation X,"* were born after the baby boom, beginning in 1965. Some members of this subculture are college students, and others have begun their careers in the face of the unsettled economy that followed the boom years of the early 1980s. The **baby boomers,** the large generation born between 1946 and 1964, comprise a market of 81 million consumers. Beyond the baby boomers are the approximately 68 million **mature market** Americans over the age of 50.

The physiological and developmental differences that characterize different age groups are often accompanied by social and psychological contrasts. For example, the consumer purchase processes are very different for products like Huggies and Depends Undergarments, although both address the same biological need (Figure 5.7), and although consumers of all ages like to listen to music, so-

> **Baby busters** are the approximately 45 million Americans born between 1965 and 1976.

> **Baby boomers** are the 81 million Americans born between 1946 and 1964.

> The **mature market** contains approximately 68 million Americans over the age of 50.

■ FIGURE 5.7
Huggies UltraTrim diapers and Depends Undergarments both meet the same biological need, but the differences in age in the target markets for each product result in very different social and psychological tones in the advertisements.

A **cohort** is an age-based subculture whose members shares childhood and young adulthood experiences that influence their customs, rituals, and behavioral processes.

cial and cultural differences between young and old consumers result in different markets for Sheryl Crow and Frank Sinatra.

Once they have formed, age subcultures, or **cohorts,** tend to follow rather predictable paths. Marketers rely on the fact that the size of an age subculture can be accurately forecasted based on current population figures. For example, it is easy to forecast the growth of the mature market during the next 20 years because the size of the baby boomer segment that will move into maturity is known. It is also possible to monitor the life-long thoughts, feelings, and behaviors of an age subculture because they are affected by the experiences the members of that age group had as children and young adults. As we noted earlier, for example, the financial behavior of elderly consumers who came of age during the Depression tends to be rather conservative.

## ▼   CHILDREN

The United States is home today to approximately 18 million children between the ages of 5 and 10 and about the same number between 10 and 15 years of age. This number will continue to grow as the children of the baby boomers move through these age segments.

Children today have an extraordinary amount of money to spend. Some studies estimate that children receive, on average, approximately $5 per week, or $250 per year, from allowances, gifts, or earnings. Most of the money is spent on toys, collectibles, games, snacks, clothes, or movies. Many toys simulate reality— Mattel introduced a pregnant doll with a removable baby in its stomach, while Tyco markets crash dummies similar to those used to test automobile safety standards (Figure 5.8). Others reflect adult pastimes, such as the popular new children's collectibles "pogs" discussed in the Public Policy box below.

■  FIGURE 5.8

Many childhood toys simulate reality, such as Playskool's Magic Smoking Grill, complete with smoke, sizzling sounds, and cookout foods.

★  PUBLIC POLICY

### Kids and Their Pogs[6]

Pogs are just another in the long line of collectibles, including baseball cards and marbles, that have attracted kids for years. Pogs are modeled after the cardboard caps found on milk bottles. The current fashion began in Hawaii in 1991, where the game was played with the caps from a bottled *p*assionfruit, *o*range, and *g*rapefruit drink. It has since spread to the mainland United States, where the caps are manufactured specifically as collectibles for children and sold in toy stores. Children collect the caps, decorated with images of cartoon characters, sports heroes, and other celebrities, and trade them with their friends

So why are school officials, parents, and public policy actors around the country trying to prevent children from bringing the caps to school? For one thing, in addition to the cartoon characters and celebrities, some of the caps are adorned with

pornographic, occult, or drug symbols. More prevalent, however, are fears that kids are gambling for their classmates' pogs. Children play a game that involves throwing a heavy metal or plastic "slammer" at each others' pogs and then keeping whichever of their opponent's pogs they have flipped over. Many adults fear that playing pogs for keeps is a form of gambling that leaves the losers distraught and encourages children to engage in a competitive activity that could lead to future gambling obsessions.

In response, the leading marketer of the caps, the World Pog Federation, created posters to discourage kids from playing for keeps, distributing them to schools around the country. Many schools have implemented rules preventing kids from playing with the pogs at school; others have banned them completely from school grounds. Some parents favor such bans, while others see playing pogs as no different from shooting marbles or flipping baseball cards, which they did as kids.

What do you think of kids and their pogs? Should the product be blamed for the way some children use them? Should children be deprived of their version of an activity in which millions of adults engage at blackjack and roulette tables?

In addition to making their own purchases, children are also important to marketers because they influence family buying decisions and are learning consumer skills that they will use in later years.[7] In particular, children are a major factor in purchases of fast food, cars, children's clothing, consumer electronics, and televisions. Through their current decision making, they will come to know manufacturers and brand names that will influence their decisions for years to come.

### FACT OR FICTION REVISITED

⦿   Children are indeed a major factor in their family's fast food purchases, auto buying, and purchases of televisions and consumer electronics.

Advertising to children is a controversial topic for parents who face their children's purchase requests, as well as for marketers and public policy actors. Consequently, the Federal Communications Commission (FCC) regulates the number and nature of commercials that appear during children's television programming. Channel One, a news program sponsored by advertisements and delivered via satellite into some 12,000 subscribing schools at no charge, recently has been at the center of controversy because some parents, teachers, and policy makers feel that schools should not be commercialized in such a way.

## ▼ GENERATION X

"Generation X," "baby busters," "twenty-somethings," and "young adults" are all terms used to describe the age cohort born after 1964 and the baby boom.[8] Members of this subculture live in the shadow of the baby boom and have suffered from the effects of diminished economic opportunities; most have had great difficulty finding their first job, and many were forced to take jobs that don't require a college degree even though they possess one. It is likely that they were raised by either a single working parent or by two full-time working parents.

The members of Generation X are accustomed to technically sophisticated, wry, irreverent television, such as MTV and VH1. Combining their economic and social disillusionment with media polish, Generation Xers are more responsive to advertising that both expresses honesty and provides entertainment. The college market is a particularly important component of this subculture—they are among the last of their group to develop their thoughts, feelings, and attitudes as Generation X gives way to the next cohort.

**The College Market**   The college market is made up of over 7 million full-time undergraduate students whose discretionary income is spent on food, clothes, beer, books, and vacations. College students tend to experiment with products and brands, buying some that they remember from their childhood and teen years as well as trying other, new types. Consumers are likely to develop loyalties during their college years. Consequently, many credit card companies send representatives to campuses and use direct marketing efforts to promote their cards to the college market (Figure 5.9).

■  FIGURE 5.9
Since consumers are likely to develop brand loyalties in their college years, many credit card companies, such as MasterCard, advertise in on-campus magazines or use direct marketing efforts to promote their products to the college market.

■ FIGURE 5.10
Spring break vacation spots, such as Daytona Beach, offer special deals to college students.

Certain specialized media have proven to be particularly effective in reaching the college market.[9] For example, studies show that most college students regularly read their campus newspaper. On-site promotions at sports and social events and spring break vacation spots are also effective in reaching a college audience (Figure 5.10), as are late-night television programs, such as *The Late Show* with David Letterman, and youth-oriented radio programs. Soft drink marketers, such as Coca-Cola and Pepsi, sports equipment companies, such as Nike and Reebok, and car companies, such as Chevrolet, are the most popular major advertisers to the college market.

## FACT OR FICTION REVISITED

◉   It is true that on-site promotions are especially effective with college students. Marketers of soft drinks, sports equipment, and automobiles find this vehicle particularly effective.

## ▼ BABY BOOMERS

The baby boom generation, made up of individuals born between 1946 and 1964, includes approximately 81 million consumers, accounting for over 30 percent of the United States population. The baby boomers are particularly important to marketers, not only because they make up such a large segment, but because they are entering their highest earning years. Baby boomers are interested in financial products—insurance, securities, and real estate—as well as travel and leisure and products for their children. Members of this generation are older, better educated, and more socially aware than their predecessors. Their high levels

# To Most Moms It's A Bleach. To Mother Nature, It's Salt And Water.

### It's A Little Known Fact That After Use Clorox® Bleach Breaks Down To Little More Than Salt And Water.

The same Clorox Bleach you've relied on all these years is also an environmentally sound choice. That's because it breaks down naturally to simple elements after use, just as it always has. And if you didn't know that, then there are some terrific uses of Clorox Bleach you may be missing out on.

Did you know Clorox Bleach extends the life of freshly cut flowers? It's true. Just add 1/4 teaspoon (20 drops) of Clorox Bleach to each quart of water used in your vase.

And did you know pouring Clorox Bleach down your sink is an easy and environmentally sound way to get rid of odors in the disposal? That's because Clorox Bleach works quickly and always breaks down to little more than salt and water after use. That's the great thing about Clorox Bleach. No matter how or where you use it, it's always an environmentally sound choice, as the diagram shows. And that's something you and mother nature can both feel good about.

### The Simple Solution For A Healthy Home.

**■ FIGURE 5.11**

Clorox educates consumers about the environmental benefits of using its products around the house.

of education make them an attractive market for such high-tech products as personal computers, camcorders, home fax machines, and cellular phones.[10]

The baby boom generation can actually be divided into two somewhat different subsegments. The older baby boomers, those born between 1946 and 1954, account for the smaller half of the generation, but they have defined many of the stereotypes typical of baby boomers. They are the segment that opposed the Vietnam War and fought for political change and environmental concerns. They fought the "establishment" in the 1960s and 1970s and then moved into positions of power and wealth in the affluent economic climate of the '80s, earning the label "yuppies" (*young urban professionals*). To balance these two phases of their lives, many now exemplify a concern for the social, political, economic, and ecological environment in which they live by the products they buy and the organizations they support (Figure 5.11).

The younger baby boomers, those born between 1955 and 1964, were less involved in the political protests of the '60s and shared less of the affluence of the '80s. They tend to be more cynical about society and their own opportunities, in large part because they came of age after Vietnam, Watergate, and the economic boom that launched the older boomers' careers. Marketers must be sensitive to the two subcultures and develop distinct products and marketing communications that appeal to the more successful, politically oriented older boomers and to the less successful and less involved younger boomers.

## FACT OR FICTION REVISITED

◉   Baby boomers do indeed tend to look for products that can be recycled or reused in an effort to maintain their socially conscious identities.

Convenience is a major consideration to the baby boomer segment. Over 70 percent of female, married baby boomers are in the work force, leaving little time for other things, such as shopping. Thus, catalog shopping, home delivery, and computer access to products and services are in high demand among these consumers. House cleaning, child care, lawn care, and other services are also flourishing as baby boomers are more willing to pay for help and convenience. As this group moves toward middle age, however, they tend to become more concerned about aging, and physical fitness, cosmetics, and antiaging medications take precedence over other products and services. Marketers appealing to this group use nostalgia in their advertising to remind the aging baby boomers of their carefree youth as they long for a simpler time.

Baby boomers can be targeted through most mass media. Prime time situation comedies about successful 40 year olds like *Murphy Brown* and *Frazier* draw this audience (Figure 5.12), and news shows, print media, and commuter radio have all been found to be effective in communicating with the baby boom segment.

## ▼ THE MATURE MARKET

The demographic data on age show an aging American population.[11] There are approximately 68 million consumers over the age of 50 in the United States today, of whom about 33 million are age 65 and over, and nearly 4 million are age 85 and over.

■ FIGURE 5.12

Prime-time situation comedies about successful 40 year olds like Murphy Brown attract the baby boomer audience, making it an appropriate vehicle for advertisers targeting this market segment.

The number of Americans 65 and over is expected to grow nearly 20 percent between 1995 and 2010, even before the large group of baby boomers enters that age group. This growth is fueled by the increasing life expectancy of the consumers who are already in the mature market.

Contrary to popular belief, the mature market is predominantly in good health and debt free. Today's elderly consumers are socially active and are less likely to need long-term hospital care or nursing home facilities until they become the "old old," those 85 and older. The "young old" group, those between the ages of 65 and 85, have more discretionary income to spend because they are unlikely to have children at home and are done paying college tuition bills and mortgages. As a result, the mature consumer is an especially good prospect for luxury goods and travel. A survey of readers of *Modern Maturity* magazine found that 70 percent of this segment engage in outdoor activities such as gardening and bicycling; most dine out several times a month and travel frequently. In fact, nearly half reported traveling abroad in the past three years.

Service organizations typically have been more responsive to the mature market than have traditional product manufacturers. Banks, travel and health care services, and restaurants continue to introduce innovative and attractive services, including an array of financial services, bus trips, home care products, and "early bird" specials. In addition, mature consumers often express a desire for more flattering apparel, more comfortable footwear, and such amenities as com-

IT'S SURELY NO ACCIDENT THAT THE MOST UNIVERSAL TOAST IS, "TO LIFE."

WATERFORD
WORTHY OF THE WOMEN
FOR OVER TWO CENTURIES

■ FIGURE 5.13
The elderly are often depicted in positive, engaging ways in advertising, such as this ad for Waterford crystal.

fortable seating in stores or malls and accessible rest rooms. As a result of their financial condition and attitudes about money, these consumers are more likely to pay cash, use coupons, and comparison shop than their younger counterparts.

It is important to remember that chronological age and nonchronological age (or psychological age) differ greatly in this population. That is, not all 75-year-old consumers "feel" 75; they have carried many of their activities, interests, and opinions along with them from their middle-age years. Thus, market research that focuses on attitudes and opinions is important in segmenting this market. In response to such research findings, marketers are beginning to use older models in ads (Figure 5.13) and to introduce products more accustomed to the need of mature consumers. For instance, Ford Motor Company has appointed a Mature Consumer Advisory Board to provide input on the design of their cars in order to make them more comfortable and easier for mature drivers to handle.

### FACT OR FICTION REVISITED

◉   Contrary to popular belief, it is true that members of the mature market have more discretionary income than do baby boomers.

# RACE AND ETHNICITY

The United States is a tapestry of racial and ethnic groups, as illustrated in Table 5.2, which shows that minority groups have the highest growth rates as a result of higher birth rates and immigration. Consequently, minority subcultures have become increasingly important consumer segments for marketers to consider. Racial and ethnic groups in the United States represent subcultures that share the typical American values but enact different customs and rituals based on their individual cultural backgrounds.[12] For example, African Americans celebrate Kwanzaa, a seven-day celebration of African-American values that begins the day after Christmas.

A person's position in the social and economic structure of his or her country, as exemplified by such demographic variables as income and education, is also affected by race and ethnicity. For example, figures from the most recent United States Census in 1990 showed that the median household income for whites was $31,231; for African Americans it was $18,676; for Hispanics, $22,330; and for Asian and Pacific Islanders, $38,450.

**Table 5.2**

## MINORITY MARKETS

**(U.S. population by major racial and ethnic group, 1995; percent of total; median age in 1995; percent change 1990-95; and percent of 1990-95 growth for each group)**

| Race | Population in millions | Percentage of total | Median age | Percentage change 1990-1995 | Percentage of 1990-1995 growth |
|------|------------------------|---------------------|-----------|------------------------------|--------------------------------|
| All persons | 262 | 100.0% | 34 | 5.6% | 100% |
| White, non-Hispanic | 193 | 73.8 | 36 | 2.8 | 38 |
| Black, non-Hispanic | 31 | 12.0 | 29 | 7.8 | 16 |
| Asian, non-Hispanic | 9 | 3.4 | 30 | 24.8 | 15 |
| Hispanic* | 26 | 10.0 | 27 | 18.8 | 30 |
| American Indian, Eskimo and Aleut, non-Hispanic | 2 | 0.7 | 27 | 7.0 | 1 |

*Note: Hispanics may be of any race. Number may not add to total due to rounding.

Source: American Demographics' calculations from Census Bureau data

In the past, marketers traditionally targeted neighborhoods that were segregated by race or ethnicity only in local markets. Today racial and ethnic subcultures are targeted at the national level. However, although different racial and ethnic groups do exhibit distinct product preferences, marketers must be careful to guard against stereotyping any particular group; detailed research must be conducted to investigate the market potential of a subculture prior to beginning a marketing efforts. A brief look at the composition and buying behavior of some of these subcultures will demonstrate both the potential and the complexity of using race and ethnicity as a basis for segmenting consumers.

## ▼ THE AFRICAN-AMERICAN MARKET

African Americans make up 12 percent of the United States population. This 12 percent exhibits differences in its consumer behavior based on cultural, social, economic, and geographical factors. In general, African Americans are more likely to live in economically depressed urban areas, to have lower educational levels and incomes, and to hold less prestigious and secure jobs. They tend to spend proportionately more on baby products, cooking ingredients, cognac and other liqueurs, and toiletries and cosmetics than do other racial groups.[13] In fact, African American women spend three times more than white women on health and beauty products, prompting marketers such as Maybelline to introduce specific products for the black female market (Figure 5.14).

African-American consumers tend to be heavy users of media. African-American households watch more television and listen to more radio than does the average American household. Readership of local newspapers is 30 percent higher among African Americans than for the overall population, and African Americans are more likely to read classified ads and circulars. African Americans can be

■  FIGURE 5.14

Maybelline has introduced a line of cosmetics targeted at African-American females in response to the large consumption behavior of health and beauty products by this market segment.

reached through both mainstream media as well as media targeted specifically toward the market, such as *Jet, Ebony, Essence,* and *Black Enterprise* magazines. In recent years broadcasters, particularly the Fox Network, have offered programs with African-American casts and themes, such as *In Living Color, Martin, Roc,* and *South Central;* the Black Entertainment Network is a cable network that reaches many African Americans nationwide.

It is essential to remember that the African-American market is not homogeneous and can be further divided into important subsegments based on additional demographic factors, such as gender, age, and income. For example, radio stations targeting African-American consumers have segmented their market based on age and cultural preferences, offering a range of programming, from gospel stations, to rap and hip-hop, to urban adult contemporary stations that play the music of such artists as Anita Baker and Barry White.

## FACT OR FICTION REVISITED

◉    It is *not true* that African-American households watch less television than the average American household; in fact, the opposite is true.

## ▼ THE HISPANIC MARKET

The United States is home to a number of diverse groups of consumers who classify themselves as Hispanic—Mexicans, Puerto Ricans, Cubans, and others from Latin American countries, including Peruvians, such as Luis Hermoza.[14] Such self-identification illustrates the important role cultural factors play in Hispanic life—consumers identify themselves as Hispanic because they consider themselves to be part of the subculture and actively practice their culture's customs and rituals.

The diversity within this segment is extensive—Puerto Ricans in New York City exhibit substantially different buying behavior than do Cubans in Miami, for example—and marketers must examine these differences carefully to gain the business of these sizable and fastgrowing subcultures. These large variations within the Hispanic market are based on distinct customs, dialects, and consumer behavior. In response, Anheuser-Busch, for example, created one television commercial targeted at Cubans and Puerto Ricans living in America, which featured salsa music and a tropical environment, and another commercial targeted at Mexican consumers, which featured men donning cowboy hats in a bar playing ranchera music.

Although it is difficult to get an exact count of the Hispanic population in the United States because some Hispanics are in the country illegally, the Hispanic population is growing dramatically, showing an increase of nearly 19 percent since 1990. Furthermore, the Hispanic population in the United States is geographically concentrated—nearly two-thirds live in Florida, Texas, and California; more specifically, the cities of Los Angeles, New York, and Miami are home to the greatest number of Hispanics in the United States. The Hispanic population is also young, with a median age of 27 years in 1995, compared with the United States average of 34.

### FACT OR FICTION REVISITED

⦿  The Hispanic segment of the United States population *is not* older than other segments; in fact, the opposite is true.

Hispanics typically have a strong belief in family and adhere to traditional family values, which exhibit themselves in conventional gender roles and a commitment to the Spanish language and customs. For example, among Cubans living in Miami, families throw an expensive, elaborately choreographed party, called a *quince,* to celebrate a girl's fifteenth birthday. This willingness to spend money extends to attitudes about everyday consumption. The Hispanic homemaker is concerned with the end result rather than ease of use. Thus, product quality takes precedence over speed or convenience, and Hispanic consumers are brand loyal and seldom buy generic products.

Whereas most Hispanic Americans can speak English, many prefer to communicate in their native language. In fact, over 75 percent of the Hispanic market speaks Spanish at home, creating a dilemma for marketers: Which language

CRISTINA
with
*CRISTINA SARALEGUI*

TALK SHOW

*Controversial*

CRISTINA
with
*CRISTINA SARALEGUI*

■ FIGURE 5.15

Spanish-language television networks, such as Univision, broadcast soap operas, talk shows, and situation comedies to Spanish-speaking consumers.

should be used in advertising to the Hispanic consumer? A number of attempts at English-to-Spanish translations have caused public embarrassment for such companies as Perdue chicken and Coors Beer. Perdue's slogan "It takes a tough man to make a tender chicken" was translated in Spanish as "It takes a sexually active man to make a chick affectionate," and Coors' "Get loose with Coors" slogan was translated as "Get the runs with Coors." Even General Motors erroneously marketed its Chevrolet Nova in Puerto Rico without changing its name—"no va" literally means "it does not go" in Spanish. As you can see, marketers would be wise to avoid English–Spanish translations without first conducting significant research into the needs and opinions of Hispanic consumers. Once such research is conducted, an array of media is available to reach the Hispanic American market. Spanish language television networks Univision and Telemundo, along with local television stations, broadcast soap operas, talk shows, and situation comedies (Figure 5.15), and numerous Spanish radio stations, newspapers, and periodicals are available to marketers.

## ▼ THE ASIAN-AMERICAN MARKET

Asian Americans, including Asian and Pacific Islanders, represent approximately 3.4 percent of the United States population. Although their numbers are still relatively small, Asian Americans are the fastest growing minority group in the United States. Marketers find this segment of consumers particularly attractive because of their high income and education levels: The average household income of Asian Americans is more than $7000 greater than the average for whites, more than $16,000 greater than Hispanics, and nearly $20,000 greater than African Americans. Furthermore, nearly 40 percent of Asian Americans over the age of 25 have completed four years of college, while only 22 percent of whites hold a college degree.

The Asian market is comprised of over 20 different ethnic groups, Chinese, Filipino, and Japanese being the three largest. Languages spoken most frequently in this market are Mandarin Chinese, Korean, Japanese, and Vietnamese. Filipinos are the only Asians who predominantly speak English; the others prefer media in their native languages. Such variation complicates matters for marketers, who must study each segment in order to understand the significant cultural variations among the specific Asian groups.

Locating Asian consumers is a relatively easy task—56 percent live in California, New York, or Hawaii; most of California's 3 million Asians live in the Los Angeles or San Francisco areas.[15] Specialized media have emerged in these communities, providing daily newspapers, magazines, and radio programs that cater to the Asian-American market.

Asian Americans tend to value family, education, and personal achievement. They are more likely to own their own businesses or to work in professional or managerial occupations than are their non-Asian counterparts, and they typically save more of their earnings and spend less. When they do make purchases, they

■ FIGURE 5.16
Asian celebrities, such as champion ice skater Kristi Yamaguchi, have been very successful in advertising products and services to Asian-American consumers.

prefer premium brands and technically oriented products. Asian celebrities, such as Kristi Yamaguchi, the 1992 Olympic gold medal winner in ice skating, have been particularly effective in reaching this market through advertising (Figure 5.16).

### FACT OR FICTION REVISITED

◉   Asian Americans are indeed more likely to prefer premium brands and technically oriented products, compared with other American Consumers.

# RELIGION

Intangible differences exist among diverse religious groups and exhibit themselves in distinct religious customs, rituals, and material artifacts.[16] However, with some obvious exceptions, religion has not been used extensively by marketers as a characteristic for segmentation. Those exceptions are religious products, often marketed in local geographical areas, that reflect overt religious customs, rituals, or material artifacts, such as the decision to join a religious order, membership and attendance in a specific church or synagogue, a crucifix or Chanukah menorah, and kosher foods. We discussed one such effort in the Pleasures of Consumption box in Chapter 4, which discusses selling Christianity.

It is often difficult to obtain information about a consumer's religious background. Neither the United States Census nor most private marketing research sources ask about a person's religious background on the grounds of separation of Church and state. Although much is known about the significant differences in the customs and rituals and social and political attitudes among religious groups, very little research has been conducted on the purchase and consumption behavior of religious subcultures. Until recently, it was also difficult to reach specific religious groups on a national basis. The growth in national religious media, such as the Family Channel Christian cable network and the Christian music video network Z Music, has made this easier. Together, the widening appeal of such products as Christian music, the growth of new media outlets, and the ability of marketers to communicate with members of religious subcultures through direct marketing mean that religion may gain importance as a segmentation characteristic for some marketers in the next few years.

# SOCIAL CLASS

> **Social class** refers to one's position in the social and economic structures of a society.

**S**ocial class refers to one's position in the social and economic structures of a society. It is based on criteria such as income, education, and occupation. Classes are hierarchical—that is, high social classes have more social, economic, and political power than do lower social classes (Figure 5.17). Sociologists have proposed various measures of social class, but they have generally been difficult for marketers to apply in their efforts to segment consumers. Available measures vary in the emphasis they put on income, education, and occupational prestige, and it is not clear which of these factors will be relevant for a specific product. For example, income is more important to a luxury car maker such as Mercedes-Benz, but education may be more important to IBM in marketing its latest personal computer.

Sociologists also differ in their theories of how many social classes exist in the United States. Most designate upper, middle, and lower classes but differ in the ways they divide these segments into smaller subsegments, such as upper-middle class and lower-middle class. This obscurity is further complicated by the fact that membership in a social class is not fixed. Through marriage, employment, and other factors, individuals move up or down the social ladder. For these reasons, marketers often consider income, education, and occupation separately to determine which is the most relevant characteristic for potential consumers of a specific product.

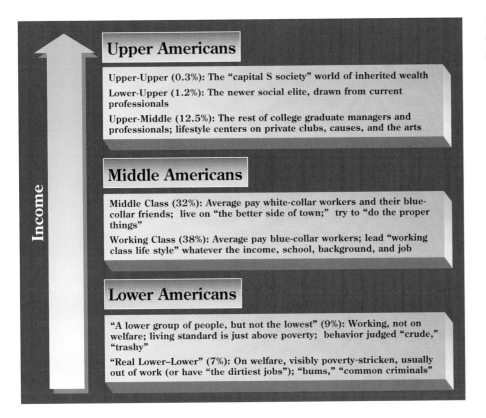

■ FIGURE 5.17
Coleman's American class structure.

Despite shortcomings in the use of social class measures, marketers have discovered substantial differences in buying behavior between classes.[17] For example, income affects the kinds of products consumers can afford as well as such intangible factors as the types and brands of products that are purchased. Education and occupation may affect the way consumers use the behavioral processes—the knowledge consumers have to evaluate and choose products, for example. These variables can also be combined with income to influence the definition of culturally and socially acceptable products. Working class consumers, for example, tend to evaluate products based on function, durability, or comfort rather than fashion or style; they are less likely to take risks or experiment with new products. The upper classes are more appearance conscious, fueling purchases relating to fitness, diet, and high fashion. Even those products virtually everyone uses are viewed differently by members of different classes. The American Express Gold Card is seen as a convenience and sometimes a status symbol to the upper classes. For lower social classes, credit is often a necessity to purchase products they could not otherwise afford; it is viewed as a means of installment buying.

Marketing appeals are constructed with these differences in mind. Advertising embodies images, celebrities, and copy that reflect the particular social class being targeted (Figure 5.18). Print media can be used to target affluent upper class consumers as well as lower class consumers. Magazines from *Architectural*

*Digest* to the *National Enquirer* appeal to certain groups. Television and radio
programming can also be utilized effectively by examining the social class of
viewers of particular shows, allowing marketers to segment and target consumers based on income, education, and occupation.

## FACT OR FICTION REVISITED

⊙    Members of the working class *are not* more likely to take risks and experiment with new products than are members of other classes; in fact, the opposite
is true.

▶

# GEOGRAPHY

Geography describes both tangible effects, rooted in climatic and topo-
graphical differences among areas, and intangible effects—the impacts of
local and regional cultures on their members.[18] The climate and physical
landscape of a geographical location dictate purchases of such items as clothing,
sports equipment, and house and garden supplies, and the topography of the land
itself often demands particular forms of transportation and recreation. Those who
have traveled or relocated from one part of the country to another know that each
area also has a stereotypical social and cultural "feel"—from the laid-back chic of
Southern California to the fast-paced frenzy of Manhattan. Cultural differences

*Table 5.3*

## REGIONAL SHIFTS

**(Population in millions for U.S. regions, percent of population, 1995; and percent change 1990-95)**

| Region | Population | Percentage | Percentage Change 1990–1995 |
|--------|-----------|------------|------------------------------|
| Northeast | 51.4 | 20% | 1.2% |
| Midwest | 61.8 | 23 | 3.7 |
| South | 91.1 | 35 | 7.0 |
| West | 57.8 | 22 | 9.9 |
| U.S. Total | 262.1 | 100% | 5.6% |

Source: American Demographics' calculations from Census Bureau data

are demonstrated in the consumption of food, music, entertainment, and other leisure activities. Accordingly, marketers would be more likely to sell snorkel gear in Florida and California to consumers like Luis Hermoza, and skis and four-wheel drive vehicles in the Colorado Rockies and Alaska.

Food preferences also vary geographically. In response to diverse geographical tastes, Campbell soup added nacho cheese soup to its line in the Southwestern market and sells its ranch type beans only in Texas. Some fast food chains offer Cajun food on their menus in Louisiana and biscuits in much of the South. McDonald's test marketed a lobster sandwich in the Providence–Boston market and plans to add it to the menu in some New England stores.

The geographic distribution of the United States population is changing as the South and West continue to grow more quickly than the Northeast and Midwest and urban areas grow more quickly than rural areas (see Table 5.3). In particular, Florida, Texas, and California have been the sites of a majority of the total population growth during the last 25 years. Much of that growth has been dependent on job opportunities and immigration, however, so that pattern may change as job opportunities decline and strict legislation against illegal immigration increases. Furthermore, because Americans are so mobile, often moving both within and between areas, local and regional cultures may lose some of their distinctive effects on consumer behavior.

## ▼ GEODEMOGRAPHICS

Geography is strongly related to the other demographic characteristics discussed throughout this chapter in that people of similar age, ethnicity, and social class often choose to live together. **Geodemographics** is the segmentation of a local geographical area based on an analysis of the demographic characteristics of its residents. Many parts of the country have similar kinds of neighborhoods—most big cities have an affluent downtown area inhabited by young, urban professionals, just as most rural areas have poor, isolated areas inhabited by older, blue-collar workers.

**Geodemographics** is the classification of geographical neighborhoods into segments that reflect the fact that people of similar demographic characteristics often choose to live together.

153

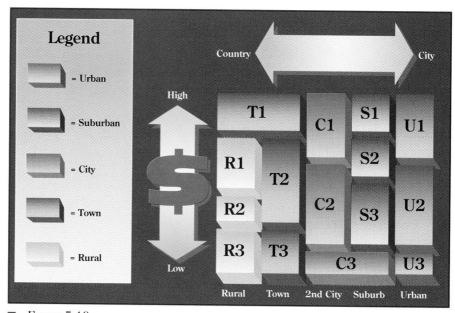

■ FIGURE 5.19

Standard PRIZM social groups.

One prominent system marketers use to analyze geodemographics is Claritas' PRIZM, which divides the United States into 62 types of geographic areas that can be further grouped into 15 broad types according to the characteristics of their residents (Figure 5.19). The system uses demographic characteristics such as age, family size, social class, type of housing, and ethnicity to classify census block groups—areas that contain between 300 and 400 households. Combined with additional information from sources such as consumer surveys, PRIZM can be used to provide insight into the purchase behavior and lifestyle characteristics of the residents of each type of area. Figure 5.20 shows the profiles of several of these areas, including lifestyle characteristics, which we will discuss in detail in Chapter 6. Figure 5.21 more specifically compares and contrasts the purchase of midsize imported cars among the areas. Other geodemographic segmentation systems include CACI Marketing Systems' ACORN, and Strategic Mapping's ClusterPLUS 2000.

# HOUSEHOLD CHARACTERISTICS

Household characteristics influence consumer behavior in both tangible and intangible ways. Tangible influences can stem from the number of consumers in the household and their gender distribution. For example, a single-person household will be likely to use smaller quantities of everything from

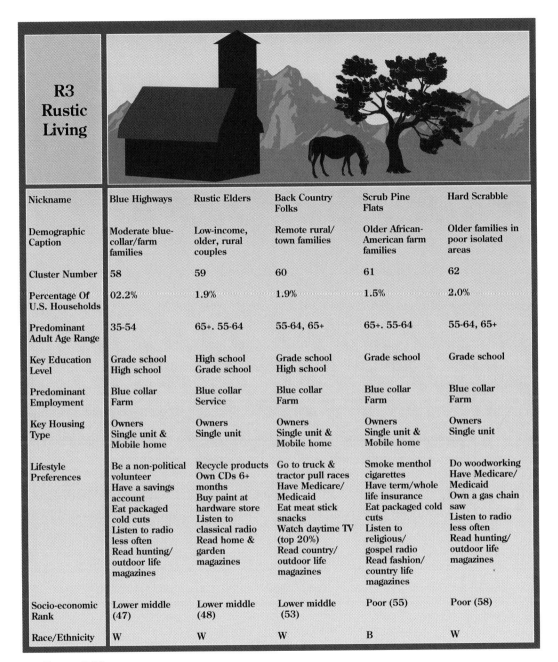

| | Blue Highways | Rustic Elders | Back Country Folks | Scrub Pine Flats | Hard Scrabble |
|---|---|---|---|---|---|
| **R3 Rustic Living** | | | | | |
| Nickname | Blue Highways | Rustic Elders | Back Country Folks | Scrub Pine Flats | Hard Scrabble |
| Demographic Caption | Moderate blue-collar/farm families | Low-income, older, rural couples | Remote rural/ town families | Older African-American farm families | Older families in poor isolated areas |
| Cluster Number | 58 | 59 | 60 | 61 | 62 |
| Percentage Of U.S. Households | 02.2% | 1.9% | 1.9% | 1.5% | 2.0% |
| Predominant Adult Age Range | 35-54 | 65+. 55-64 | 55-64, 65+ | 65+. 55-64 | 55-64, 65+ |
| Key Education Level | Grade school High school | High school Grade school | Grade school High school | Grade school | Grade school |
| Predominant Employment | Blue collar Farm | Blue collar Service | Blue collar Farm | Blue collar Farm | Blue collar Farm |
| Key Housing Type | Owners Single unit & Mobile home | Owners Single unit | Owners Single unit & Mobile home | Owners Single unit & Mobile home | Owners Single unit |
| Lifestyle Preferences | Be a non-political volunteer Have a savings account Eat packaged cold cuts Listen to radio less often Read hunting/ outdoor life magazines | Recycle products Own CDs 6+ months Buy paint at hardware store Listen to classical radio Read home & garden magazines | Go to truck & tractor pull races Have Medicare/ Medicaid Eat meat stick snacks Watch daytime TV (top 20%) Read country/ outdoor life magazines | Smoke menthol cigarettes Have term/whole life insurance Eat packaged cold cuts Listen to religious/ gospel radio Read fashion/ country life magazines | Do woodworking Have Medicare/ Medicaid Own a gas chain saw Listen to radio less often Read hunting/ outdoor life magazines |
| Socio-economic Rank | Lower middle (47) | Lower middle (48) | Lower middle (53) | Poor (55) | Poor (58) |
| Race/Ethnicity | W | W | W | B | W |

■ FIGURE 5.20

Detailed profiles of the clusters in three representative PRIZM social groups.

soap to electricity than would a household comprised of two parents and three children. If the three kids are teenage boys, they might use more Right Guard; if they are teenage girls, they might use more Suave Salon Formula Mousse. Parents of young children may buy Tylenol with a child-proof cap, while a childless couple probably won't consider the packaging of their headache remedy.

| S1 Elite Suburbs | | | | | |
|---|---|---|---|---|---|
| Nickname | Blue Blood Estates | Winner's Circle | Executive Suites | Pools & Patios | Kids & Cul-de-Sacs |
| Demographic Caption | Elite super-rich families | Executive suburban families | Upscale white-collar couples | Established empty nesters | Upscale suburban families |
| Cluster Number | 01 | 02 | 03 | 04 | 05 |
| Percentage Of U.S. Households | 0.8% | 1.9% | 1.2% | 1.9% | 2.8% |
| Predominant Adult Age Range | 35-54 | 35-54, 55-64 | 25-34, 35-54 | 55-64, 65+ | 35-54 |
| Key Education Level | College grads | College grads | College grads | College grads | College grads |
| Predominant Employment | Professional | Professional | Professional | Professional | White collar Professional |
| Key Housing Type | Owners Single unit | Owners Single unit | Owners Single unit | Owners Single unit | Owners Single unit |
| Lifestyle Preferences | Belong to a country club Own mutual funds $10,000+ Purchase a car phone Watch TV golf Read business magazines | Uses a maid/housekeeper Have a line of credit account Eat Brie cheese Listen to classical radio Read travel magazines | Play raquetball Use financial planning services Own a camcorder/video camera Listen to jazz radio Read business magazines | Attend live theatre Own investments $50,000+ Drink Scotch Listen to news radio Read epicurean/ leisure magazines | Buy trivia games Have 1st mortgage loan Own a piano Listen to soft contemporary radio Read infant /parenting magazines |
| Socio-economic Rank | Elite (1) | Wealthy (2) | Affluent (8) | Affluent (9) | Affluent (10) |
| Race/Ethnicity | W (A) | W (A) | W (A) | W (A) | W (A) |

■ FIGURE 5.20 (continued)

Intangible influences reflect cultural, social, and psychological characteristics. For example, in traditional nuclear families, the children are expected to do household chores, so there may be less of a need to pay for outside services such as lawn care. In households where both parents work, teenage children may be expected to do the grocery shopping for the family every week and to buy their own clothes. We will discuss the family decision making process in Chapter 7, but it is important to realize that household composition has implications that are independent of the actual interactions among family members.

| | U1 Urban Uptown | | | | |
|---|---|---|---|---|---|
| **Nickname** | Urban Gold Coast | Money & Brains | Young Literati | American Dreams | Bohemian Mix |
| **Demographic Caption** | Elite urban singles & couples | Sophisticated townhouse couples | Upscale urban singles & couples | Established urban immigrant families | Bohemian singles & couples |
| **Cluster Number** | 06 | 07 | 08 | 09 | 10 |
| **Percentage Of U.s. Households** | 0.5% | 1.1% | 1.1% | 1.4% | 1.7% |
| **Predominant Adult Age Range** | 25-34, 35-54 | 55-64, 65+ | 25-34, 35-54 | 35-54 | Under 24, 25-34 |
| **Key Education Level** | College grads | College grads | College grads | Some college | College grads |
| **Predominant Employment** | Professional | Professional | Professional | White collar | Professional |
| **Key Housing Type** | Renters, Multi unit 10+ | Owners Single unit | Owners & Renters Multi unit 10+ | Owners Single unit | Renters, Multi unit 10+ |
| **Lifestyle Preferences** | Go scuba diving, snorkling Make 3+ stock transactions/yr Spend $250+ on a sports jacket Watch late night television Read computer magazines | Go sailing Use stock rating service Drink cordials & liqueurs Watch news/business television Read travel magazines | Travel to Japan, Asia Own tax exempt funds Buy a Montblanc/ Waterman pen Listen to urban contemporary radio Read style/fashion magazines | Rent foreign videos Own a gold/premium credit card Drink domestic wine Listen to news/talk radio Read entertain- ment magazines | Do painting, drawing Have a Visa card Buy lots of film Listen to jazz radio Read fashion/ music magazines |
| **Socio-economic Rank** | Affluent (3) | Affluent (5) | Upper (6) | Upper middle (14) | Middle (17) |
| **Race/Ethnicity** | W (A) | W (A) | W (A) | Mix | Mix |

■ FIGURE 5.20 (continued)

## ▼ FAMILY LIFE CYCLE

Households change as people marry and have children and the children grow up, leave the house, and sometimes return later.[19] Single consumers move from living alone to sharing their living space with others; parents progress from caretakers of small children to managing households with young adults; consumers plan for careers, retirement, and, eventually, death. This progression from single to

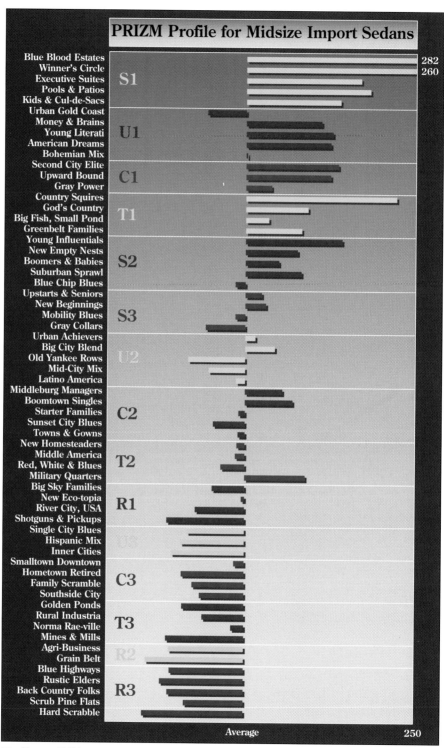

■  FIGURE 5.21

This PRIZM pofile shows that residents of elite suburbs are most likely to purchase midsize import sedans.

married to parenthood to retirement to death is known as the **traditional family life cycle** (see Table 5.4). The concept was developed to classify households according to the age, marital status, and number and ages of children present.

Over the years, the types and numbers of households have changed as fewer consumers have elected to follow the traditional progression through their lives (see Figure 5.22). The traditional family life cycle assumed that most consumers followed a certain path in a certain order. However, social attitudes toward marriage, divorce, childbearing, and child rearing have shifted over the years. Alternative paths have appeared, and new household forms, including single parents, same-gender couples, childless couples, and middle-aged parents with young children, have been added to the traditional family life cycle.[20] One early attempt to account for the alternatives to married couples is shown in Figure 5.23, but a complete picture would require us to include those consumers who never married as well.

> The **traditional family life cycle** is a concept used to classify households according to the age, marital status, and the number and ages of children that are present—it describes the traditional progression of steps in family life, from singlehood to marriage to parenthood to retirement to death.

*Table 5.4*

## THE TRADITIONAL FAMILY LIFE CYCLE

**Traditional Family Life Cycle Categories**

**1. Young Singles**
Single people under the age of 35. Incomes are low since they are starting a career, but they have few financial burdens and a high level of discretionary income.

**2. Newly Married**
Newly married couples without children. High level of discretionary income because the wife is usually working.

**3. Full Nest I**
Married couples with the youngest child under 6. Greater squeeze on income because of increased expenses for child care.

**4. Full Nest II**
Married couples with children from 6 to 12. Better financial position since parents' income is rising. Most children are "latchkey kids" because both parents are working.

**5. Full Nest III**
Married couples with teenage children living at home. Family's financial position continues to improve. Some children work part-time. Increasing educational costs.

**6. Empty Nest I**
Children have left home and are not dependent on parental support. Parents are still working. Reduced expenses result in greatest level of savings and highest discretionary income.

**7. Empty Nest II**
Household head has retired, so couple experiences sharp drop in income. Couple relies on fixed income from retirement plans.

**8. Solitary Survivor**
Widow or widower with lower income and increasing medical needs.

Source: William D. Wells and George Gubar, "Life Cycle Concept in Marketing Research," *Journal of Marketing Research,* 3 (November), 355–363 (1966).

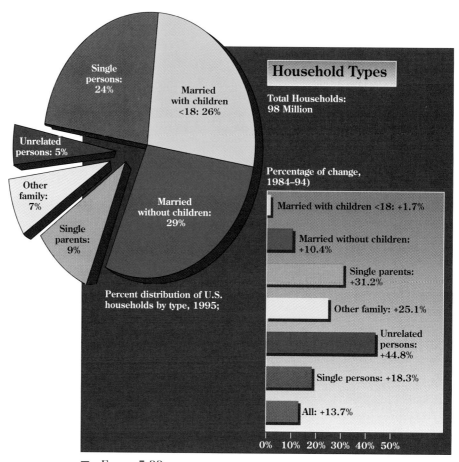

Household Types

Total Households:
98 Million

Percentage of change,
1984–94)

Married with children <18: +1.7%

Married without children:
+10.4%

Single parents:
+31.2%

Other family: +25.1%

Unrelated
persons:
+44.8%

Single persons: +18.3%

All: +13.7%

0%   10%  20%  30%  40%  50%

Single
persons:
24%

Married
with children
<18: 26%

Unrelated
persons: 5%

Other
family:
7%

Married
without children:
29%

Single
parents:
9%

Percent distribution of U.S.
households by type, 1995;

■ FIGURE 5.22
Household Types.

Marketers recognize that a family's makeup is a significant determinant of the products and services that household buys. Consequently, marketers targets segments that reflect characteristics appropriate to different products. For example, Procter & Gamble targets Pampers at families with very young children; Apple targets its personal computers at families with older children; and the travel industry, retirement communities, insurance companies, and health care services focus on retired couples whose children no longer live at home.

## FACT OR FICTION REVISITED

⦿   Most American consumers *do not* go through the family life cycle in the same order; in fact, fewer consumers have elected to follow the traditional progression over the years.

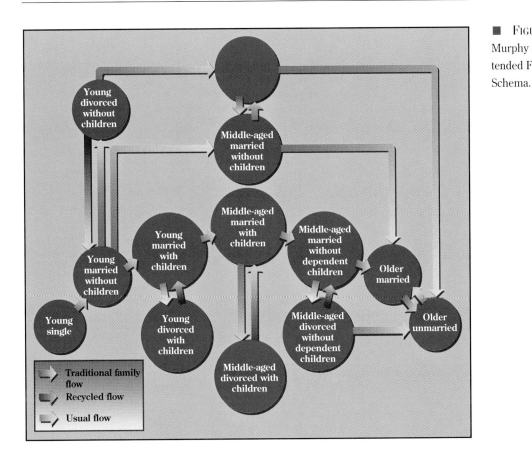

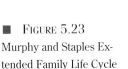

■ FIGURE 5.23
Murphy and Staples Extended Family Life Cycle Schema.

▼ THE GAY MARKET

Estimates of the percentage of the United States population that is gay or lesbian range from three to five percent, and the buying power of this segment has been estimated at about $500 billion.[21] Homosexuals have a higher than average income and educational level and are typically concentrated in major metropolitan areas, such as New York, San Francisco, and Los Angeles. Because the gay market is difficult to identify, there is some dispute over whether its members in fact have higher incomes and educational levels. Nevertheless, many marketers have come to realize that the subculture is an attractive consumer segment because most homosexual households do not include children, giving them higher amounts of discretionary income. More specifically, surveys done by the *Advocate,* a magazine targeted at the gay population, show that homosexuals tend to be heavy consumers of travel, books, real estate, home entertainment equipment, alcohol, physical fitness, and credit cards.

Many marketers have ignored this segment, however, fearing a backlash from other consumers; others have actively targeted the gay community, including American Express, AT&T, Campari, Ikea, MCI, and Miller Lite. Some of these efforts include advertising in gay publications, direct mail pieces, and sponsorships of special events, such as the Gay Games. Some local car dealers have targeted the gay population in the face of opposition from their parent car manufacturers. The furniture maker Ikea has chosen to broadcast mainstream television advertisements in its attempts to reach the gay market (Figure 5.24).

■  FIGURE 5.24
The furniture maker Ikea targets homosexual consumers in its advertising, which has proved to be quite controversial.

## PUBLIC POLICY AND DEMOGRAPHIC SUBCULTURES

As we have discussed throughout this chapter, marketers use demographic characteristics to divide consumers into meaningful subcultures. Inherent in this process is the risk that public policy concerns will ensue. Equity issues arise whenever marketers draw distinctions among consumers and choose to ignore some segments when developing their segmentation strategies. Because demographic characteristics are unchangeable, consumers and public policy actors alike tend to be very sensitive to marketers who treat demographic segments inequitably. Targeting demographic segments is justifiable only when the consumers in the excluded segments have access to products that will meet their needs. For example, we noted in Chapter 3 that policy makers are actively trying to change conditions whereby African-American and Hispanic consumers are deprived of mortgages because banks and mortgage providers avoid doing business in their neighborhoods.

Similarly, whereas marketers acknowledge the affluence of homosexuals, many have been reluctant to openly seek gay consumers; stereotypes and fear of a backlash from other consumers have kept marketers at bay. Virtually every state now has legislation addressing discrimination against homosexuals, and public policy is likely to move toward extension of those antidiscrimination laws. The gay community represents a formidable political force and will likely keep these issues at the forefront of American politics for years to come. Marketers and public policy actors must decide whether to ignore market segments for political reasons or to acknowledge their ethical responsibility to provide products to any viable consumer segment.

When marketers choose to market products to certain demographic groups, issues of fairness, safety, and economic and social welfare ensue. Marketers also face criticism when they treat consumers in some segments unfairly because of their demographic characteristics or offer unsafe or harmful products to those segments. For example, some public policy actors are critical of the *Mighty Morphin Power Rangers* television program and action figures because they feel that children should not be exposed to such violent content. In fact, the program has been banned in Canada and New Zealand. Similarly, R. J. Reynolds has been criticized for its use of Joe Camel in its advertising because of the cartoon character's potential appeal to kids. Finally, safety and economic and social welfare issues are at the root of the debate concerning drinking among college students, as discussed in the Dark Side of Consumption box that follows.

## DARK SIDE OF CONSUMPTION

### College Drinking[22]

Although strict enforcement of drunken driving laws, advertising campaigns advocating responsible drinking, and social and cultural trends that emphasize healthy habits have reduced the levels of public drinking among the general population, drinking appears to remain a problem among a significant portion of college students. Available evidence shows that the number of students who drink heavily, drink to get drunk, and who are binge drinkers has remained constant over the last 15 years. In fact, estimates show that consumers in the college market spend more money on alcohol than on nonalcoholic drinks and books combined. White males drink more than any other gender and ethnic group, and students in the Northeast tend to drink more than those in other parts of the country.

The effects of drinking are exhibited in many ways. Injuries and violent crime involving innocent bystanders are more likely to involve students who are drunk, and heavy drinkers are more likely to appear among students who have D or F grade point averages. The responsibilities of the students, college administrators, and wine, beer, and liquor marketers are unclear. Federal alcohol labeling requires manufacturers to post warnings about the effects of their products on pregnant women, driving, and health, but labels need not advise that excessive consumption can lead to death. In a recent case of a Texas college student who died after drinking large amounts of alcohol during a day-long binge, the courts ruled that marketers need not warn consumers about the short term effects of drinking too much. The decision stated that although it might be morally responsible to place such a warning on labels, there was no legal responsibility to do so.

Do you think there are some inherent characteristics in the college student demographic group that result in significant levels of heavy drinking? If so, are those tangible or intangible characteristics? What roles should students, alcohol marketers, college administrators, and other public policy actors play in resolving this consumer behavior problem? Do injuries and crimes that affect nondrinking students challenge the rights of students to drink?

# DEMOGRAPHIC SUBCULTURES

Luis Hermoza is a married, middle-class man of Peruvian descent who lives in a suburban community in the Southeast United States. He and his wife Sherry are in the early stages of creating a household and live in a rented apartment near the ocean. They intend to have children someday, but they first want to buy a big house in a nice neighborhood so that the kids will grow up in a safe environment. Their current incomes force Luis and Sherry to work hard to save money to buy that house, and since they both spend a lot of time working, they are willing to purchase some of the time-saving conveniences that reduce the time spent on household chores. Luis' cultural background has shaped the ways he and Sherry view their futures. He feels that they must be frugal in order to achieve their dreams and to avoid falling into what he views as a typically American trap that ensnares consumers of their social class—perpetually living on credit they will never be able to pay off.

Luis' age, ethnicity, social class, geographical location, and stage in the family life cycle influence the way he thinks, feels, and acts in buying the things he wants. Some of these effects are tangible, such as the geographical location that lets him enjoy swimming and snorkeling, and the budget limitations his age and income impose on him. Others are intangible, such as the way his ethnic background has shaped his personal financial customs. His stage in the family life cycle have both tangible effects, such as the need for a bigger house, and intangible influences, such as his attitude about financial security. All of these demographic characteristics interact with Luis' personal style to form the basis for his everyday life. We will now examine these personal factors and their everyday manifestations in our discussion of personality, lifestyle, and psychographics in Chapter 6.

1. **Recognize the demographic characteristics that can be used to divide consumers into meaningful segments.** Demographic characteristics include the physical, social, economic, and geographical attributes that describe the position of a consumer in his or her social environment. Demographic characteristics can be used to divide consumers into segments based on tangible effects, such as physical differences between the genders, as well as intangible effects, such as the distinct customs and economic standings of various ethnic groups in the United States.

2. **Judge the usefulness of gender, age, race and ethnicity, social class, geography, and household characteristics as segmentation characteristics for a consumer behavior problem.** These characteristics all provide useful bases for segmenting consumer markets; each is more or less appropriate for certain products. Gender distinguishes consumers on important physiological characteristics as well as distinct social roles assumed by each gender. Age reflects the physiological, developmental, and social and cultural characteristics that often motivate individual needs and tastes in products. Racial and ethnic groups often differ in their customs and rituals as well as their positions in the social and economic structure of their country. Social class is a direct measure of a consumer's position in the social and economic structure, whereas geography reflects physical, cultural, and social distinctions among the people who live in a specific area. Finally, household characteristics such as family life cycle and household composition reflect the number, age, and gender of the consumers in a household, the resources that are available, and the different roles family members play.

3. **Analyze the public policy implications of a segment that is based on demographic characteristics.** Demographic characteristics are innate parts of a consumer's background; accordingly, consumers and public policy actors alike are sensitive to marketers who treat demographic segments inequitably by denying some consumers access to products that will meet their needs. Marketers also face criticism if they treat consumers in some segments unfairly because of their demographic characteristics or offer unsafe or harmful products to certain segments.

Baby busters, *p. 137*

Baby boomers, *p. 137*

Mature market, *p. 137*

Cohort, *p. 138*

Social class, *p. 150*

Geodemographics, *p. 153*

Traditional family life cycle, *p. 159*

1. Divide the class into three kinds of two-person groups—male–male; female–female; and male–female. Assign each group to visit an automobile dealership and ask questions about the cars. Afterwards, compare how the three kinds of groups were treated by sales personnel.

2. Visit a supermarket and observe the influence of children on purchases made by adults. Aside from products purchased for consumption by the children themselves, in what product classes was the influence of children strongest? Why?

3. Purchase a copy of *Modern Maturity* magazine. What products are most heavily advertised? What kinds of appeals are used most often?

4.  Interview a person who is ethnically different from you concerning the purchase of an expensive product and an inexpensive product. In what way are your respondent's motives, perceptions, and preferences different from your own?

5.  Why are consumers who have the same zip code demographically so much alike? On what demographic characteristics would consumers who have the same zip code be most diverse?

6.  Mr. A and Mr. B have the same income but differ in social class. How will their consumer behavior differ?

# CHAPTER 5 SELF-TEST

## ▼ MULTIPLE CHOICE

1.  Women are more likely than men to:
    a.  spend less time browsing
    b.  use cash when making a purchase
    c.  comparison shop
    d.  positively evaluate advertisements that include superwomen or happy homemakers

2.  A(n) _____ is an age-based subculture whose members' childhood experiences influence their customs and behaviors.
    a.  cohort
    b.  affiliate
    c.  consort
    d.  syndicate

3.  Which subculture, based on age, includes college students and young adults experiencing diminishing economic opportunities?
    a.  baby boomers
    b.  Generation X
    c.  young achievers
    d.  junior adults

4.  Which of the following family purchases are often influenced by children?
    a.  housing
    b.  consumer electronics
    c.  adult clothing
    d.  newspaper subscriptions

5.  Which racial subculture households watch more television and listen to more radio than the average American household?
    a.  Asian American
    b.  African American
    c.  Hispanic
    d.  Eastern Europeans

6.  Which of the following is the fastest growing minority group in the United States?
    a.  Asian Americans
    b.  African Americans
    c.  Hispanics
    d.  Eastern Europeans

7.  Product quality is considered more important than speed or convenience to the _____ homemaker.
    a.  African-American
    b.  Asian-American
    c.  Hispanic
    d.  Filipino

8.  The _____ class predominately evaluates products based on a product's function, whereas the _____ class is more conscious of a product's appearance.
    a.  middle; working
    b.  middle; upper
    c.  working; upper
    d.  lower; middle

9.  The two geographical areas of the United States that are increasing most rapidly in population are:
    a.  midwest and east
    b.  south and west
    c.  south and northeast
    d.  midwest and south

10.  _____ is segmentation based on geography and demographics.
    a.  Demogeography
    b.  Double segmentation
    c.  Geodemographics
    d.  Multi-segmentation

▼ TRUE/FALSE

1. Demographics reflect only the tangible differences between consumers.   T or F
2. Nearly 60 percent of all women over the age of 18 work outside the home.
   T or F
3. Men are less likely than women to read a daily newspaper.   T or F
4. The baby boom generation consists of those people born between 1946 and
   1964.   T or F
5. The mature market is not a lucrative market because its members are predominately in poor health and have few resources.   T or F
6. African Americans spend more on toiletries and cosmetics than do other racial
   groups.   T or F
7. Social class is based solely on a person's income.   T or F
8. Claritas' PRIZM, CACI's ACORN, and ClusterPLUS 2000 are all geodemographic
   segmentation systems.   T or F
9. The traditional family life cycle is useful to today's marketers since all consumers
   follow that path through life.   T or F
10. Some marketers are now targeting the gay market since that segment has a greater
    amount of discretionary income than most segments.   T or F

▼ SHORT ANSWER

1. Describe the media preferences of the college market.
2. What types of products are now being consumed by the baby boomer generation?
   What types of products will this subculture be buying in the next decade?
3. Describe what types of purchases might be affected by a consumer's religion.
4. Discuss how household characteristics can have both a tangible and an intangible
   influence on consumer behavior.

▼ APPLICATION EXERCISE

You work for a company that manufacturers small kitchen appliances. A new product, a
machine that not only makes pasta but also cooks it, is under development; it is expected
to be priced at $300. As marketing manager, you must determine whether there is a seg-
ment of the population that may be interested in this product. First, you must examine
what age groups might consider buying this type of product. What cohort would you target for this product if in fact your organization chooses to market it? Explain your choice.

# 6

# PERSONALITY, LIFESTYLE, AND PSYCHOGRAPHICS

⊛ Consumer Snapshot   *Denise Walsh* * *is a 35-year-old homemaker who sells educational Discovery Toys during the Christmas season. She lives in Tuscon, Arizona, with her husband, Mark, and their two young children, Brandon eight, and Meghan, five.*

FACT OR FICTION

⊛ Most personality traits are transitory.

⊛ "Hero worship" is a form of identification

⊛ In Freudian theory, the id represents desire for immediate pleasure, regardless of costs or circumstances, whereas the ego has to do with thought or planning.

⊛ A short list of personality traits consistently segments consumers.

⊛ Consumers usually act in accordance with the actual self rather than the ideal self.

*Last name changed for privacy.

⊙ Personality is a poor predictor of consumer behavior.

⊙ Lifestyle and psychographic research focus on attitudes, interests, and opinions.

⊙ The VALS program, developed by the Stanford Research Institute, is the most widely used segmentation method.

## EYE ON THE CONSUMER

Denise Walsh is a mother of two who lives in Tucson, Arizona. She holds a degree in marketing and worked for five years in pharmaceutical sales before she and her husband, Mark, started their family. Denise wants to go back to full time work at some point, but right now her life is just too busy—caring for two children, serving on the school district's public relations and political lobbying committees, and working part time selling educational Discovery Toys to large corporations in the area during the Christmas season take up all of Denise's time.

The Walshes moved from California to Arizona when Mark changed jobs. They chose their house based on two criteria. The first was the reputation of the school district. Denise and Mark both support the public school system, but they wanted to be sure that their children would get a superior education, so they chose to live in an area renowned for the quality of its schools. The second criterion was the particular style of the house. Denise wanted a house where the kids' bedrooms were close to hers and Mark's so she could keep an eye on them. It was also important to her that the kitchen and family room were close together so the kids could play in the family room while she worked in the kitchen.

Denise furnished the house in a combination of southwestern and traditional styles. The southwestern style is appropriate for a house in Arizona, but it is important to Denise that the furniture be flexible enough to fit in in other parts of the country should they decide to move again. Her grandfather was a woodworker, so Denise prefers to buy high-quality furniture even if it is more expensive. At the same time, she and Mark are "deal shoppers"; they try to buy their furniture wholesale whenever possible, even if it means they have to order individual pieces and wait patiently for them to arrive.

One of Denise's favorite pieces is the table in the family room—it's modeled after the weathered door of an old Mission. Denise saw it in a store and hoped to find something like it for less money, but it was such a unique piece that she couldn't find it anywhere else. So she paid full price—$900. But because it looks weathered, Denise isn't worried about keeping it in the family room with the kids. She doesn't allow the children to play on it, but if they have a friend over who accidentally crashes a toy into the table, it will just look even more weathered. To accessorize the table, Denise brought home about 10 items from the store and tried them all on the table. She chose the three she liked best and just paid the $300 they cost. It wasn't typical for her to pay full price, but she had just sold a large toy order that Christmas, so she had the money to spend.

In the last two chapters we discussed the cultural and demographic characteristics used to divide consumers into market segments. There is more to consumers than just their cultural and demographic backgrounds, however. Consumers have a personal style of interacting with their environment. Denise's interaction style—her active life, her interest in home furnishings, and her opinions about child rearing—may differ from that of others who share the same cultural and demographic background. In this chapter, we discuss the effect of personality, lifestyle, and psychographics on the consumer purchase process.

After reading and thinking about this chapter, you should be able to:

❶ Recognize the role of personality in individual behavior and apply various perspectives to that role.
❷ Understand the relationships among a consumer's personality, lifestyle, and psychographics.
❸ Identify those attributes of a consumer's lifestyle and psychographics that affect his or her consumer behavior.

# PERSONALITY, LIFESTYLE, AND PSYCHOGRAPHICS ◀

Throughout the years researchers have adopted theories from psychology and sociology to describe the ways in which consumers interact with their environments. Some see consumers' interaction styles as the result of a predisposed way of approaching one's environment; this predisposition is referred to as one's *personality*. You may recognize such a predisposition in yourself, although most people are quicker to recognize it in others. For example, a consumer might be innovative and continually change the way she acts. She may even make a conscious effort to act differently than the people around her. Another consumer might be conservative and follow the same routines as those around him day after day. Personalities also affect the way people approach their consumer behavior. The innovative consumer will probably be willing to try new products, whereas the conservative consumer will tend to buy the same products again and again.

Consumers express their personalities in their daily activities, interests, and opinions. Consumer behavior specialists believe that such expressions of personality are easier to observe and are more relevant to consumer behavior than the personalities themselves. Consequently, they have developed lifestyle and psychographic research that focuses on the cultural and social context and psychological bases of personality as they are expressed in consumers' activities, interests, and opinions, as illustrated in Figure 6.1. For example, a consumer might

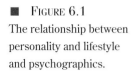

The relationship between
personality and lifestyle
and psychographics.

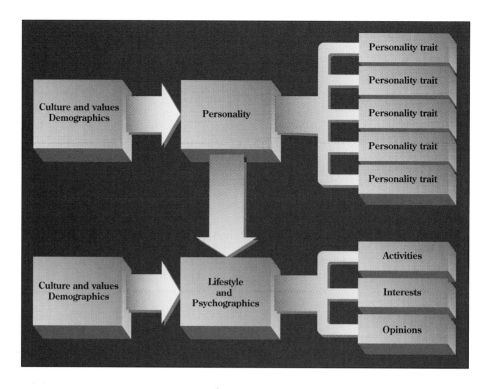

have a predisposition toward neatness and order. He expresses this personality
trait through the clothing he wears, the place he lives, and the opinions he holds
about environmental causes.

# PERSONALITY

Every consumer is innately predisposed to act in particular ways. When
asked why he acts a certain way, a consumer may reply that he has acted
that way for as long as he can remember. He may add that his behavior is a
result of the way his parents interacted with him during childhood; his parents
were very neat, and demanded that he be the same way growing up. Even though
he may have rebelled a bit during his teenage years, it still bothers him when
things around him are not orderly. This is **personality**–an individual's unique
psychological makeup that predisposes that person to behave in a particular way
in interacting with his or her environment.[1]

An individual's personality develops as a result of a lifetime of interactions. It
is important to recognize this *social dimension* of psychological makeup. A personality is not something a person is born with; rather, it is strongly linked to the
culture, values, and demographics of the environment in which he or she grew
up. For example, Denise's children's personalities will be shaped by the way their
parents raise them. Furthermore, an individual's personality cannot be changed

> **Personality** is a con-
> sumer's unique psycho-
> logical makeup that pre-
> disposes that person to
> behave in a particular
> way.

■ FIGURE 6.2
This ad for Birkenstocks is designed to appeal to consumers who share particular personality traits.

**Birkenstock**

quickly or easily; it represents the cumulative effects of past interactions, and even significant shifts in current circumstances have great inertia to overcome. The individual would have to expend a great deal of effort over an extended period of time to change the way she expresses her personality.

## ▼ PERSONALITY TRAITS AND TYPES

Although an individual's personality reflects his or her unique social interactions, there are common elements to all personalities that have allowed psychologists to develop theories that describe personality traits and types. A **personality trait** is a person's predisposition to behave in a particular way when interacting with his or her environment to achieve needs and desires *in a specific area of the person's life* (see Figure 6.2). In other words, personality traits are the specific predispositions that comprise the personality an individual exhibits. A **personality type** is a group of people that share common personality traits and can therefore be expected to act similarly. For example, consumers who share an innovative personality type may be of interest to computer manufacturers because they exhibit curiosity and a willingness to learn new skills—traits that may lend themselves to an interest in computers. Marketers must be able to identify groups that share a personality type that is relevant to a particular kind of consumer behavior if they want to use personality as a background characteristic for market segmentation.

> **Personality traits** are the underlying dimensions of the predisposition to behave in a particular way.

> A **personality type** is a group of people that share personality traits that result in a common predisposition to behave similarly.

### FACT OR FICTION REVISITED

◉ It is *not true* that personality traits are transitory; rather, they are enduring modes of interaction with the environment.

173

# THEORIES OF PERSONALITY

A number of personality theories attempt to provide insight into how an individual's personality develops and how it affects the person's current behavior. The theories are also used to identify the personality traits that distinguish one personality type from another (see Table 6.1). In this chapter we discuss several theories: (1) Freudian *psychoanalytic theory,* which focuses on the development of an individual's personality; (2) *trait theory,* which investigates current personality configurations to identify personality types; and (3) *self-concept theory,* which concentrates on those aspects of personality that reflect individuals' views of themselves. We have chosen to focus on these three theories because they represent a sample of the popular conceptions of personality that many consumers and marketers find to be sensible and credible. They also provide much of the foundation of the lifestyle and psychographic approaches we discuss later in the chapter.

**Psychoanalytic theory of personality** addresses the individual's interaction styles, rooted in the desire to satisfy both the individual's own needs and society's culture and values.

## ▼ FREUDIAN THEORY AND THE DEVELOPMENT OF PERSONALITY

Sigmund Freud developed his **psychoanalytic theory of personality** during a long career spent trying to understand how society socializes its members and the effects of socialization on individual behavior. Freud believed that an individual's personality grows out of the tension that exists between his or her needs and desires and the socialization process society uses to control its members. The way an individual resolves this conflict shapes his or her personality. At the

*Table 6.1*

**THEORIES OF PERSONALITY**

| Theory | Main Components |
|---|---|
| Freudian psychoanalytic theory | Conflict between an individual's needs and the socialization process |
| | Personality system comprises three styles of interaction with the environment: |
| |     id: do what you want |
| |     ego: plan to satisfy your needs within society's values and rules |
| |     superego: do what society says |
| | Mechanisms to resolve conflict |
| Trait theories | Trait is a predisposition to behave in a specific area |
| | Individuals segmented into personality types that share a configuration of traits |
| Self-concept theories | Individual's view of him- or herself and his or her personality |

heart of psychoanalytic theory is the belief that unconscious needs and drives, many of them sexual, are the basis of one's personality. The stereotypical view of a patient lying on a couch pouring her heart out to a psychoanalyst stems from the process Freud himself used to understand his patients' conflicts. Freud employed intensive, one-on-one analysis to understand the patient's personality. In doing so, he often uncovered memories of childhood experiences that had shaped the patient's personality at a very young age as he or she developed mechanisms to reconcile personal desires with society's rules.

**Personality Systems**   Freud proposed the existence of three psychological systems that comprise an individual's personality: (1) the id, (2) the ego, and (3) the superego (Figure 6.3). The **id** represents the desire for immediate pleasure, regardless of the costs or circumstances. It emphasizes the need to satisfy such primitive physiological drives as hunger, thirst, and sexual gratification. By contrast, the **superego** represents the individual's subconscious attempts to do what is right and moral as a society's culture and values define it. Mediating the impulsive desires of the id and the moral conscience of the superego is the job of the **ego,** which accommodates the social situation and tries to reconcile individual needs with the demands and circumstances of the environment. According to Freud, the ego develops in response to the recognition that, in a social environ-

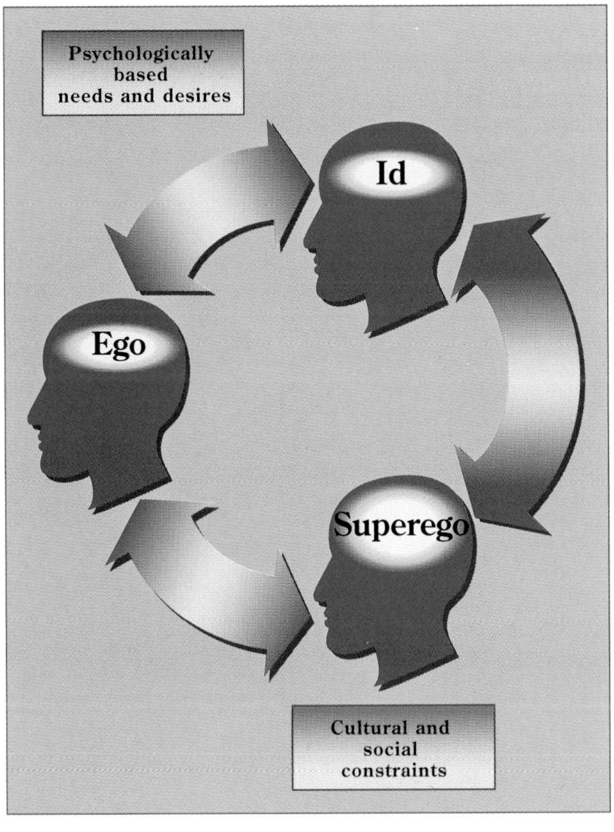

The **id** represents the desire for immediate pleasure.

The **superego** represents those interactions in which the individual attempts to do what is right and moral as defined by society.

The **ego** is the personality style that tries to reconcile individual needs with the demands and circumstances of the environment.

■   FIGURE 6.3
The relationship among id, ego, and supergo.

ment, an individual cannot always get what he wants when he wants it and without cost. When you were a baby and cried to be fed, sometimes you were fed and sometimes you had to wait. In response, you developed an interaction style that utilized thought, planning, and skills to get what you wanted.

The id, ego, and superego are inherently in conflict. The id says "do everything you want to now"; the ego tells you to "plan the best way to get people around you to help you satisfy your needs"; and the superego plants the unconscious suggestion that you should only do what those around you want you to do.

## FACT OR FICTION REVISITED

⊛    Both of these statements are true. The id represents the individual's desire for immediate pleasure, regardless of costs or circumstances, whereas the ego accommodates the social situation and involves rational thought and planning.

**Identification** is the process of adopting another person's proven method of integrating the id, ego, and superego.

**Repression** involves controlling a physiological, pleasurable id-based need by leaving it unsatisfied.

**Personality Mechanisms for Resolving Psychological Conflict**  Freudian theory goes on to identify the ways in which individuals deal with these conflicting styles of interaction (Table 6.2). According to Freud, the methods an individual chooses as a child shapes the development of the adult personality. As a child, the individual employed certain methods to reconcile the conflicts that arose from wanting to act immediately, plan, and act morally, all at the same time. As an adult, the individual relies on these same methods to balance conflicting demands. The methods Freud described include *identification, repression, displacement, projection,* and *rationalization.*[2]

❶  **Identification** is the process of adopting another person's proven method of integrating the three styles of interaction. A child may act like her parents, or an individual may identify with a celebrity as an adult.

❷  **Repression** involves controlling a physiological, pleasurable, id-based need by leaving it unsatisfied. A child may dream of his younger brother cruelly

*Table 6.2*

### MECHANISMS FOR RESOLVING PERSONALITY CONFLICT

| Mechanism | Example |
|---|---|
| Identification | Imitate an older sibling's behavior |
| | Buy the same clothes and dress the same way as a celebrity |
| Displacement and sublimation | Suck on a lollipop instead of one's thumb |
| | Buy a sports car instead of having an affair |
| Projection and rationalization | Claim to be too smart to enter a spelling bee when you're actually afraid to lose |
| | Continue smoking and claim that everyone will die sometime anyway |

but not act on it, just as a consumer may fantasize about striking an uncooperative sales clerk but complains to the manager instead.

❸ **Displacement** involves converting an id-based need into a more acceptable form. For example, a seven year old might chew on the end of a pencil to avoid sucking her thumb. That same child might take up smoking cigarettes as an adult for the same purpose.

❹ **Projection** occurs when an individual justifies actions that satisfy his or her needs by blaming someone else for them. For example, a child may hit a classmate because he believes that the classmate has intended to hit him first or because he wants to prevent him from hitting another playmate. An adult may throw away cans and bottles with the rest of the trash instead of recycling them because "everyone else does it too."

❺ **Rationalization** is the invention of a rationale to justify actions instead of admitting to the true reasons for them. A child may say that she doesn't want to play baseball when, in fact, her playmates refuse to play with her. An adult may claim that he bought a small Ford Escort because it is easy to park when, in fact, he couldn't afford the Mustang he really wanted.

> **Displacement** involves converting an id-based need into a more acceptable form.

> **Projection** is the process of justifying one's actions by blaming someone else for them.

> **Rationalization** is the invention of an excuse to justify actions.

## FACT OR FICTION REVISITED

⊙  Hero worship is indeed a form of identification. An individual may imitate the behavior of parents, peers, or celebrities in an attempt to balance the conflicting demands of the id and the ego.

**Freudian Theory and Consumer Behavior**   Freud's theories have had a significant impact on the study of psychology and human behavior, some of which have been quite controversial. The developmental perspective Freud adopted and the systems and conflict resolution methods he identified continue to be widely debated throughout the psychological community. However, marketers do need to understand the current background characteristics of the consumers they study. How can they use Freud's insights about psychological development to understand the effects of a consumer's background on the behavioral processes?

Freudian theory offers several useful insights that can be applied to segmentation. First, it may be useful to segment consumers on the basis of the personality system that drives their interaction style. That is, marketers can divide consumers into three segments on the basis of their dominant personality system; each segment would exhibit the behavioral processes differently during the purchase process. For example, superego-based consumers tend to be susceptible to the influence of family and friends and to incorporate their opinions into an elaborate learning, attitude formation, and decision-making process to ensure that they satisfy these external demands. At the same time, Freudian theory maintains that such consumers would employ a variety of mechanisms to reconcile the conflicting demands of their superego and their own id-based desires. For example, you might want to go to Cancun to party with your friends but you tell your parents that you are going to study Mexican culture for your international business course.

While this kind of insight is fascinating, and may be valid, it is difficult to use as the basis for practical segmentation analysis. Freudian theory requires in-depth exploration of the individual's psychological state by a trained analyst. Thus, using personality as a background characteristic is difficult at best. For example, even if a marketer of cleaning products could identify consumers who have strong predispositions for neatness and cleanliness, it would be difficult to determine whether those consumers would buy a cleanser to act on that predisposition or choose to ignore the dirt by rationalizing that their children would only dirty the house again anyway. Accordingly, Freudian theory has had its greatest impact in the area of research. We discuss two popular examples below—neo-Freudian personality theories, such as that of Karen Horney, and the study of purchase motivation.

**Neo-Freudian Personality Theory** Like Freud, Karen Horney was interested in the mechanisms individuals use to resolve the conflicts that make them anxious[3]. She examined the results of childhood relationships with parents and discovered that individuals could be divided into three personality types—(1) *compliant* individuals, who advance toward those around them; (2) *aggressives,* who move

■ FIGURE 6.4

Pontiac designed this ad for the Firebird to appeal to consumers who are motivated to buy a sporty car to reflect their "cool" personality.

against others; and (3) *detached* individuals, who remove themselves from others. Consumer researchers, in turn, developed various systems to classify consumers into these three personality types and examined differences in their consumer behavior. One prominent system is Cohen's CAD scale, named for the *compliant, aggressive,* and *detached* personality types.[4] This system could be used to show, for example, that compliant consumers would be more likely to use mouthwash and deodorant soaps to ease their path toward others.

**Purchase Motivation** The consumer motivation process is discussed in detail in Chapter 8. Here we restrict our discussion to a brief example of the way Freudian theory has been used on a practical level to explain purchase behavior. Motivational researchers conduct in-depth interviews with consumers to uncover the unconscious psychological factors that motivate them to make a purchase.[5] Specifically, they employ a Freudian perspective in investigating the personality system and conflict-resolution methods that motivate the consumer's purchase.

One of the most famous motivational researchers was Ernest Dichter, formerly a psychoanalyst in Vienna. The classic example of Dichter's application of Freudian theory was his notion that a man's purchase of a convertible represents his desire for a mistress. Valid or not, it is an insight based on the displacement of an id-based sexual fantasy onto the purchase of a car. On a greater level, once marketers understand such consumer motivations, they can create advertising that illustrates the relevant personality system or conflict-resolution method, as illustrated in Figure 6.4. Similarly, the Diet Coke ad depicted in Figure 6.5 turns the denial associated with a diet soda into a fulfilling experience.[6]

■ FIGURE 6.5

Coca-Cola has turned the denial associated with drinking diet soda into a fulfilling experience in this advertisement.

▼ TRAIT THEORIES AND PERSONALITY TYPES

Freudian theory was a great impetus in encouraging psychological research into simpler methods of identifying and measuring personality traits. Trait theorists recognize the importance of personality but focus on the specific personality traits that emerge from the individual's psychological development process. Whether or not that process occurs as Freud described it does not matter; it is the identification of the individual's personality traits that is important.

Trait theories explicitly seek to classify individuals into groups of people who share personality types. In doing so, they first identify certain personality traits

179

and then classify individuals on the basis of the configuration of the traits they possess.[7] The theories can be further divided into simple trait theories and general trait theories. *Simple trait theories* identify a limited number of traits that define personality and classify individuals based on their level of those traits. Such theories are used to explore a particular kind of behavior by identifying traits that are relevant to the behavior in question. For example, Hyundai might want to identify consumers who show little ethnocentrism to target for their Korean made cars.

By contrast, *general trait theories* measure a wide variety of traits. Statistical analysis is employed to determine the configuration of traits that best segments individuals into meaningful groups that represent broadly applicable personality types. On-line services such as Prodigy, for example, might want to identify curious, innovative consumers who would be open to learning the skills necessary to to use the service to shop interactively.

Trait theories make intuitive sense as a reasonable way of classifying individuals into groups. Every consumer thinks of himself or herself as a particular type of person and, in turn, intuitively labels friends and acquaintances as certain personality types. If consumers can identify personality types in their own interactions, it is reasonable to assume that a scientific measurement of personality traits would be a useful means of distinguishing individuals from one another. Psychologists have created many such scientific measurement tools which consumer behavior experts have used to classify consumers into distinct market segments that respond similarly to marketing efforts. These tools typically involve survey questionnaires that contain a variety of items. The responses are analyzed statistically to classify the respondent on the personality traits that have been measured. The **Edwards Personal Preference Schedule (EPPS)** is an example of a personality trait measurement instrument that has been widely used in consumer behavior. The EPPS uses a questionnaire to measure the 15 distinct personality traits described in Table 6.3.

> The **Edwards Personal Preference Scale (EPPS)** uses a questionnaire to measure 15 distinct personality traits.

**Trait Theory and Consumer Behavior** Trait theory seems to be a more practical approach than Freudian developmental theory for understanding consumer behavior, since it focuses on a consumer's *current* personality configuration to understand how it affects other aspects of his or her behavior. [8] Trait theories recognize that it is not necessary to understand the individual's historical personality development to be able to identify his or her current personality traits. If an individual possesses a trait for order that causes her to respond positively to environmentally safe packaging, for example, she would likely belong to a desirable target market segment for a variety of environmentally conscious products.

Unfortunately, such traits have proved to be elusive. Over the years, a number of personality theories and their associated measurement tools have been investigated. Some have been effective in studying certain products or behavioral processes but could not be generalized. Others worked once but did not produce the same results over repeated trials. Many showed a weak relationship between personality and consumer behavior, adding little to our understanding. In fact, there is little evidence that trait theories can be used effectively to analyze con-

**Table 6.3**

SUMMARY OF PERSONALITY TRAITS MEASURED BY THE EDWARDS
PERSONAL PREFERENCE SCHEDULE

1. *Achievement:* To do one's best, accomplish tasks of great significance, do things better than others, be successful, be a recognized authority.
2. *Deference:* To get suggestions, follow instructions, do what is expected, accept leadership of others, conform to custom, let others make decisions.
3. *Order:* To have work neat and organized, make plans before starting, keep files, have things arranged to run smoothly, have things organized.
4. *Exhibition:* To say clever things, tell amusing jokes and stories, talk about personal achievements, have others notice and comment on one's appearance, be the center of attention.
5. *Autonomy:* To be able to come and go as one pleases, say what one thinks, be independent in making decisions, feel free to do what one wants, avoid conformity, avoid responsibilities and obligations.
6. *Affiliation:* To be loyal to friends, do things for friends, form new friendships, make many friends, form strong attachments, participate in friendly groups.
7. *Intraception:* To analyze one's motives and feelings, observe and understand others, analyze the motives of others, predict their acts, put one's self in another's place.
8. *Succorance:* To be helped by others, seek encouragement, have others feel sorry when sick, have others be sympathetic about personal problems.
9. *Dominance:* To be a leader, argue for one's point of view, make group decisions, settle arguments, pursuade and influence others, supervise others.
10. *Abasement:* To feel guilty when wrong, accept blame, feel need for punishment, feel timid in presence of superiors, feel inferior, feel depressed about inability to handle situations.
11. *Nurturance:* To help friends in trouble, treat others with a kindness, forgive others, do small favors, be generous, show affection, receive confidence.
12. *Change:* To do new and different things, travel, meet new people, try new things, eat in new places, live in different places, try new fads and fashions.
13. *Endurance:* To keep at a job until finished, work hard at a task, keep at a problem until solved, finish one job before starting others, stay up late working to get a job done.
14. *Heterosexuality:* To go out with opposite sex, be in love, kiss, discuss sex, become sexually excited, read books about sex.
15. *Aggression:* To tell others what one thinks of them, criticize others publicly, make fun of others, tell others off, get revenge, blame others.

sumer behavior, because the tests are designed to be administered to a specific population in controlled surroundings in order to measure overall predisposition toward the environment.[9] In real life, however, consumer researchers use them in a very different context:

❶ Consumer surveys are often administered via telephone interviews or in shopping malls, usually as part of a larger questionnaire about purchase behavior. This is not the controlled atmosphere that was intended by the personality researchers who developed them.

❷ Consumer research studies often cover a broad range of people in order to identify segments. Many of the tests were developed to understand neuroses and mental illness in certain types of people, however, so expanding beyond this group will not yield responses indicative of the average consumer.

❸ Consumer behavior researchers want to be able to predict the appeal of a particular product category or brand. By contrast, personality trait tests were designed to identify broad personality traits, so the tests typically will not yield the kind of specific information marketers are looking for.

## FACT OR FICTION REVISITED

⦿ A short list of personality traits *does not* consistently segment consumers. In fact, research relating traits to consumption has not produced consistent results.

## ▼ THE SELF-CONCEPT

| |
|---|
| **Self-concept theory** explains those aspects of an individual's personality that are the expression of the individual's self. |

**Self-concept theories** focus on that aspect of personality that is the expression of the individual's image of him or herself. Consumer researchers turned to self-concept theories when they recognized that individuals hold views of their own personalities and that this view has more of an impact on their behavior than do any objective measurements of personality traits. In fact, the methodological problems associated with trait theories could be avoided simply by asking individuals to label those parts of their personality they think are important. For instance, Denise Walsh sees herself as frugal and consciously shops at wholesalers and warehouse stores to save money.

| |
|---|
| The **actual self** is an individual's view of who he or she is. |

The self-concept is comprised of two components—the actual self and the ideal self. The **actual self** is an individual's view of who he or she is, whereas the **ideal self** is one's image of who he or she *wants* to be. Self-concept theories explicitly recognize that individuals' interactions with others affect their self-concept. Furthermore, whereas both Freudian and trait theories recognize the role other people played in one's personality development in the past, self-concept theories emphasize the influence of the social setting on one's *current* personality configuration.

| |
|---|
| The **ideal self** is an individual's view of who he or she wants to be. |

Self-concept theory maintains that individuals can express their personality in one of two ways: Either they can act consistently with their actual view of themselves, or they can act in ways that move them closer to their ideal self and increase their self esteem. These two expressions come into conflict when one's actual and ideal self-images differ. In such situations, the individual must decide whether to act consistently with her actual image or to support her desired ideal image. The choice will depend on such situational factors as the visibility of the action, the particular audience who will view the action, and the importance of the action for the person's self-image. For example, you may want people to think of you as a sensitive and caring person even though you often don't have the time or resources to act that way. Consequently, you may attend a charity event when your boss asks you to, but you would turn down a telephone request for a donation to the same charity.

**Table 6.4**

## EXAMPLES OF METHODS USED TO MEASURE THE SELF-CONCEPT

**Direct rating scale**

Please rate the following adjectives on how well they describe you:

|  | **Describes me very well** |  |  |  | **Does not describe me at all** |
|---|---|---|---|---|---|
| Happy | 5 | 4 | 3 | 2 | 1 |
| Sensitive | 5 | 4 | 3 | 2 | 1 |
| Fashionable | 5 | 4 | 3 | 2 | 1 |

**Sorting task**

Please sort each of these cards into three piles based on how well the adjective on each describes you. Place the card into the pile labeled "describes me well" if the adjective is an accurate description of you, into the pile labeled "doesn't describe me at all" if the adjective is not at all an accurate description of you, or into the pile labeled "not an accurate nor inaccurate description of me" if it is not a pertinent description of you.

Cards containing adjectives are then sorted.

**Semantic differential scale**

For each pair of descriptions listed below, please check the point on the continuum that most accurately describes how you view yourself:

| | | | | | | |
|---|---|---|---|---|---|---|
| Happy | ____ | ____ | ____ | ____ | ____ | Sad |
| Fashionable | ____ | ____ | ____ | ____ | ____ | Conservative |

Self-concept can be measured by asking individuals to describe themselves. In order to simplify the measurement of large groups of people, quantitative survey methods are often used (Table 6.4). These surveys ask people to describe themselves using adjectives such as "happy," "sensitive," or "fashionable." Some ask respondents to rate themselves on each adjective on a numerical scale. Others ask them to sort the adjectives into groups that reflect how well each adjective describes them. Another commonly used method is the *semantic differential scale,* which asks respondents to choose one of two opposite adjectives that best describes them; the choices are given as bipolar adjectives at each extreme of the scale (e.g., happy/sad).

**Self-Concept and Consumer Behavior** Self-concept theories have been widely applied to the study of consumer behavior, particularly in terms of the congruence between self-concept and the brand image of products.[10] Self-concept theories maintain that consumers will buy and use products that have the same image as they do. Consumers who view themselves as rugged and active, for example, would will be more likely to buy a Jeep than a Volvo (Figure 6.6).

■ FIGURE 6.6
This ad for Jeep Cherokee is targeted to appeal to consumers who have a rugged, active self-concept.

**TO A JEEP ENGINEER, THIS IS A COBBLESTONE ROAD.**

When this is your idea of a cobblestone road, building an ordinary luxury vehicle is pretty much out of the question. Which explains why Jeep engineers built the extraordinary one you see here: Jeep Grand Cherokee Limited.

For exceptional control,

our engineers created Quadra-Trac*—an all-the-time four-wheel drive system so advanced, it actually senses each axle's need for traction and automatically distributes power accordingly.

Other amenities include automatic temperature control, anti-lock brakes, an optional 220 horsepower V8, and a 120-watt eight-speaker stereo.

For more information, call 1-800-925-JEEP. It will forever change your impression of luxury vehicles. Not to mention cobblestone roads.

**There's Only One Jeep®...**
A Division of the Chrysler Corporation.

Always wear your seat belt. Jeep is a registered trademark of Chrysler Corporation.

Many consumers view individual brands as having their own "brand personality."[11] By extension, consumers tend to buy and use products that send a message about themselves to others. If a student wants his classmates to think he is fashionable and contemporary, for example, he will be more likely to play Sheryl Crow than Barry Manilow on his stereo. This symbolic function of products is very important in helping consumers define their self-image. In fact, some consumers deem their possessions so important to their self-image that they actually consider them part of their extended self.[12] For example, you may have a favorite article of clothing you wear for luck; a club, fraternity, or sorority jacket that symbolizes your membership; or a pet you think of as a family member.

How useful is the self-concept in helping marketers segment consumers? Like Freudian and trait theories, self-concept theories have shown somewhat more promise than they have actually realized. Although self-concept theories provide useful insights into the motivation process, it is difficult to apply these insights to the segmentation task. Consumers have many selves, and it is sometimes difficult to know which one will operate in the case of a specific product. A person who wants to project a fashionable, trendy self-concept, for example, may drink Arizona or Snapple Iced Tea in the company of friends but stick with generic iced tea powder in the privacy of his or her home. And some products may not be relevant to a person's self-image at all. A consumer may not think of Nabisco Shredded Wheat or Cheerios as having a brand personality that should be consistent with his or her self image.

## FACT OR FICTION REVISITED

⊛   The statement that consumers usually act in accordance with the actual self rather than the ideal self is false; in actuality, consumers typically act in accordance with their *ideal* self.

# LIFESTYLE AND PSYCHOGRAPHICS

For it to be relevant to consumer behavior, personality must be considered in combination with the rest of a consumer's background. This insight was a significant impetus for the development of lifestyle and psychographics, which integrate insights from various personality theories and place them in their cultural and social context. As discussed above, researchers have largely been unsuccessful in their attempts to devise a practical method for segmenting large groups of consumers on the basis of their personalities alone. By contrast, lifestyle and psychographic analysis explicitly addresses the way consumers express their personalities in their social and cultural environment; it represents an attempt to characterize psychological characteristics, including personality, by examining outward expressions of that inner state.[13]

## FACT OR FICTION REVISITED

⊛   It is true that personality is a poor predictor of consumer behavior. This is because it works together with other background characteristics and cannot be isolated.

**Lifestyle analysis** emphasizes actions in a social and cultural context.

**Psychographic analysis** focuses on the psychological basis of a consumer's thoughts and feelings.

**Lifestyle and psychographics** describes the way a consumer expresses the psychological bases of his or her personality in the cultural and social context of day-to-day activities, interests, and opinions.

The terms "lifestyle" and "psychographics" are often used interchangeably, or, as we have done here, together, since most analyses of consumer behavior for the purpose of segmenting a market combine the two. It is possible to distinguish between **lifestyle analysis,** which emphasizes values and actions in their social and cultural context, and **psychographic analysis,** which focuses on the psychological basis of opinions and attitudes—that is, *lifestyle* is usually used to describe the way consumers live; *psychographics* describe the opinions they hold—but it is more useful to view them as a complimentary pair.

**Lifestyle and psychographics** is the study of the way consumers express their culture and values, demographics, and personality through the allocation of such resources as time and money. Lifestyle and psychographics reflect a variety of dimensions, as illustrated in Table 6.5 and listed as follows:

❶ *Cultural*—A consumer's lifestyle and psychographics reflects his or her cultural background and the values taught by that culture. For example, a "yuppie" lifestyle is much more likely to occur in the materialistic culture of urban America than in the agrarian culture of rural China.

❷ *Demographic*—The subcultures to which a consumer belongs—gender, age, race and ethnicity, geographic location, household status, and other social characteristics and relationships—present both opportunities and constraints on the consumer's ability to choose a lifestyle.

❸ *Economic*—The economic characteristics that reflect a consumer's social class—educational background, occupational surroundings, and available resources—influence the consumer's ability to choose a lifestyle.

❹ *Psychological*—The configuration of personality traits affects the consumer's motivation to exhibit a particular lifestyle and psychographics.

To summarize, consumers express themselves through their activities (work, hobbies), interests (sports, the arts), and opinions (about themselves and

### Table 6.5

#### FOUNDATIONS OF CONSUMER LIFESTYLE AND PSYCHOGRAPHICS

| Dimension | Sample characteristic | *Grace Under Fire* | *Frasier* |
|---|---|---|---|
| Cultural | Values | Family and survival | Materialism and the good life |
| Demographic | Gender | Working mother | Unattached male |
| | Geography | Suburban | Urban sophisticate |
| | Household status | Divorced parent | Divorced absentee parent |
| Economic | Educational level | High school graduate | Professional school |
| | Occupation | Factory worker | Psychiatrist |
| Psychological | Personality | Abrasive, angry | Pompous and self-absorbed |
| | Self-concept | Hard-working, cynical | Witty and erudite |

others). Lifestyle and psychographics is an appropriate measure of consumer behavior in that it encompasses the consumer's allocation of time and money, acknowledging the keystone of consumer behavior—the exchange of personal resources for products that will satisfy the consumer's needs.

You are aware of the lifestyles and psychographics of the people around you every day. You use more than just demographics and cultural backgrounds to identify the different types of students on your college campus, for instance. You may hang out with the "jocks," avoid the "artsy" types, or want to be one of the campus "biggies." The members of each of these groups may have very different background characteristics, but they each have an interaction style that incorporates their meeting places, social activities, and attitudes toward their schools, their futures, and other students (Figure 6.7).

■ FIGURE 6.7

Consumers use lifestyles and psychographics to identify themselves as members of certain groups, such as "jocks."

Lifestyle and psychographic segments also exist in the broader marketplace. Consider a well-known demographic subculture such as baby boomers. All baby boomers share an age group—they were born between 1946 and 1964. But even that age group is comprised of people at different stages of their lives—some are 30 years old and are still single or engaged; others are approaching 50 and becoming grandparents. This large group also encompasses many different lifestyles (Figure 6.8). Some baby boomers are working-class, conservative-minded people who are financially at risk and hope that their factory job lasts until retirement—the character of Grace Kelly in the sitcom *Grace Under Fire,* for

■ FIGURE 6.8

The situation comedy *Grace Under Fire* depicts a working-class, single mother who is financially at risk and working to make ends meet. This lifestyle is in sharp contrast to that of her cohort, *Frasier,* who represents the "yuppie" urban lifestyle of a well-off professional.

example. These consumers would be more likely to drive Fords and Chevrolets, wear flannel shirts, and drink Budweiser beer. Other baby boomers are urban professionals with liberal attitudes and some disposable income, who see a bright future for themselves—"yuppies," such as *Frasier*. These consumers would be more likely to drive BMWs, wear silk shirts and wool suits, and drink Glenfiddich scotch. The Graces and Frasiers of the 1990s belong to the same age subculture, but the combination of their different demographic subcultures, economic factors, and psychological characteristics render very different consumer behavior.

# LIFESTYLE AND PSYCHOGRAPHIC APPROACHES

Several approaches are available for measuring lifestyle and psychographics to segment consumer markets. The approaches all utilize survey questionnaires to gather the quantitative data necessary to divide consumers into meaningful segments.

## ▼ ACTIVITIES, INTERESTS, AND OPINIONS

The most common approach to measuring lifestyle and psychographics is a survey questionnaire that asks a large number of detailed questions about the *a*ctivities, *i*nterests, and *o*pinions (AIO) of consumers, as shown in Table 6.6. Based on their responses, consumers are classified into one of a set of consumer segments; each segment shares a common set of activities, opinions, and interests.[14] Some analysts supplement the general measures with items that are tailored to the specific product that is being studied. For example, a marketer who wants to segment the market for an environmentally friendly product or service, such as recyclable packaging for beverages, might include specific questions about packaging, government intervention in environmental issues, pollution, shopping habits,

*Table 6.6*

### EXAMPLES OF ACTIVITIES, INTERESTS, AND OPINIONS USED TO MEASURE LIFESTYLE AND PSYCHOGRAPHICS

I support pollution standards even if it means shutting down some factories.
I would be willing to accept a lower standard of living to conserve energy.
I worry a lot about the effects of environmental pollution on my family's health.
I recycled paper products at least once in the past year.
I use a lot of low-calorie and calorie-reduced products.
I like to visit places that are totally different from my home.
I am interested in the cultures of other countries.
I always use a seat belt, even for a short drive.

Source: *The DDB Needham Life Style Study.*

and product loyalty. When combined with the general AIOs, these items would give additional insight into the consumer's "environmental style," as discussed in the Pleasures of Consumption box that follows.

## PLEASURES OF CONSUMPTION

### Citizen Environmentalists[15]

Some consumers live an "environmentally friendly" lifestyle, and some do not. Bill Wells and Mike Swenson recently identified two segments in a representative national sample—citizen environmentalists, the 25 percent of the sample who exhibited the most environmentally friendly lifestyle, and nonenvironmentalists, the 25 percent of the sample who were least environmentally friendly. A comparison of the citizen environmentalists and the nonenvironmentalists illustrates the usefulness of lifestyle segmentation for marketers or public policy actors who wish to target consumers who would respond favorably to such products as recycling programs, government legislation of environmental practices, or membership in environmentally friendly social action organizations.

The study found that citizen environmentalists are obviously more likely to engage in environmentally friendly activities such as recycling metal, paper, glass, plastic, and oil. But this segment of consumers exhibits activities, interests, and opinions that differ from those of nonenvironmentalists in many other areas as well. For example, citizen environmentalists are more likely to buy food products that are low in calories, fortified with vitamins, minerals, protein, and calcium, and contain fiber. They are more likely to listen to National Public Radio and watch The Discovery Channel, PBS, *Northern Exposure,* and documentaries. Citizen environmentalists also tend to check ingredients labels, consult *Consumer Reports,* and request informational or educational brochures before making a purchase.

The study also found that citizen environmentalists provide information about products and brands to their friends and neighbors and seek similar advice from them in turn. They are interested in world, national, and sports news, and animal rights. The opinions they voice characterize them as more sensitive to risk than nonenvironmentalists—they worry more about crime, they always wear their seat belts, they tend to make out complete shopping lists, and they compare prices on small items while shopping. They oppose smoking in public places, favor clean air regulations, want their homes and their family's clothes to always be clean, and are sensitive to hidden dirt and germs in their house.

How do culture and values, demographics, and personality provide the context for the lifestyle citizen environmentalists enjoy? Can you think of specific products and legislative or regulatory programs that will appeal to citizen environmentalists? How should marketers and public policy actors position these products and programs?

## FACT OR FICTION REVISITED

⊛  Lifestyle and psychographic research does in fact focus on attitudes, interests, and opinions.

## ▼ VALS ™

The most widely known commercial approach to measuring lifestyle and psychographics is SRI International (SRI) *Values and Lifestyles* (VALS) Program.[16] The VALS Program divides consumers into eight segments based on two dimensions—a psychological and a resources dimension (Figure 6.9). The psychological dimension is based on the consumer's self-concept and classifies consumers into three categories: (1) *principle-oriented* consumers, who hold strong personal beliefs about what is and is not appropriate, (2) *status-oriented consumers,* who are easily influenced by the approval of others in their social environment, and (3) *action-oriented* consumers, who are motivated by their passion for activity, variety, and risk. The resource dimension reflects the consumer's demographic, social, and economic position and the resources these characteristics provide. Each of the three psychologically based categories is divided into two segments that differ in terms of level of resources. In addition to the six segments that result from these combinations, two others exist—*Strugglers,* who have such limited resources that their psychological characteristics do not matter, and *Actualizers,* who have such abundant resources that they can exhibit all of the psychological orientations.

This VALS segmentation is actually the second generation of the program. The first was more closely tied to a theory of motivation that we will discuss in Chapter 8. The previous version of VALS divided consumers into nine segments that reflected two psychological dimensions: (1) the *needs* that motivated consumers (physical, social, ego, and self-actualization), and (2) the consumer's *orientation* toward life (focused inward or outward). Each segment revealed a different lifestyle based on the type of needs that motivated its members and whether

■ FIGURE 6.9
Dimensions of the VALS 2
Program.

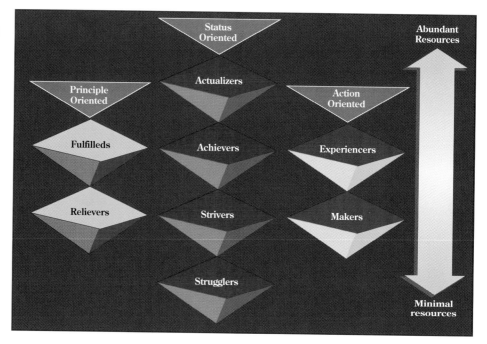

members focused internally or externally to achieve those needs. This scheme met with many of the same criticisms that plagued the personality theories noted earlier: It reflected personality differences among consumers but neglected their demographic and cultural characteristics in the process. The second generation of VALS explicitly addressed that criticism by adding the resource dimension.

## FACT OR FICTION REVISITED

⊙ The VALS program, developed by SRI International *is not* the most widely used psychographic segmentation system, because of its tendency to reflect personality differences among consumers but not their demographic and cultural characteristics.

A number of marketers have used VALS to identify attractive target market segments and to tailor their products' marketing mixes appropriately. For example, WISH-TV in Indianapolis classified its consumer audience using the VALS2 typology. As a result, the station was able to offer its advertisers insights about products that could be appropriately advertised on WISH. Other examples include a luxury car maker that targeted its new model at "actualizers," and a food company that positioned its family-style product for principle-oriented consumers with less access to resources—"believers."

# PUBLIC POLICY, LIFESTYLE, AND PSYCHOGRAPHICS ◄

How do you feel about marketers having access to information about your lifestyle—your leisure activities, your interests, the kinds of products you buy and use? Marketers are able to glean information about consumers' lifestyles from their hobbies, club memberships, magazine subscriptions, product purchases, and demographics. Access to such information enables marketers to identify target market segments and deliver direct marketing appeals to them, touching off public debate about whether the owners of this information have the right to provide it to others. Should states be allowed to provide voter-registration information to marketers? clubs their membership lists? magazines their subscriber lists? Is it ethical for credit card companies to supply information about the products you bought to other marketers? Those who sell such lists to marketers claim that doing so is beneficial to consumers because it gives them access to opportunities that are designed specifically for people like them. Opponents of the practice argue that a person's lifestyle is private and that it is an invasion of that privacy to reveal personal information without the person's consent. Many marketers have taken these concerns to heart, as discussed in the following Public Policy box.

## PUBLIC POLICY

### Is Your Lifestyle Private?[17]

Marketers spend a great deal of time, effort, and money accumulating the information they need to segment and target consumer markets. They want to know about culture, values, demographics, and lifestyle and psychographics so that they can effectively target responsive consumers. Modern information technology offers significant opportunities for marketers to gather some very specific—and often personal—information about individuals. The bank that holds your Visa or MasterCard knows what you bought using that card; Land's End, Spiegel, and L.L. Bean know what you bought from their catalogues; even your supermarket can use its checkout scanners and "shopper's cards" to catalog your grocery purchases. The Bureau of Motor Vehicles possesses information about the car you drive, your age, and gender, and if you have ever voted or owned a home, your state government knows your age and the value of your house.

Many of these sources are willing to offer their information to other marketers or specialists who combine the information for sale. For example, Metromail, a mailing list specialist, has been criticized for using voter information from Arizona and California. America Online, the interactive computer service, has been rebuked for providing its subscriber list to direct marketers. Lotus, the computer software firm, dropped its 1991 plans to market a CD-ROM database containing the demographics and shopping habits of 80 million American households after facing overwhelming criticism. Consumer surveys on privacy issues reveal that consumers are very concerned about the spread of such information at the same time that they want to receive the benefits that come from catalog shopping and credit card usage.

Consumers, marketers, and public policy actors are all concerned with protecting the privacy of consumer information. But it is not clear how to balance the sometimes conflicting needs of consumers to gain convenience from information technology and to maintain privacy on the one hand with the desire of marketers to use all of the information at their fingertips to develop effective and efficient marketing programs that will allow them to satisfy consumers on the other.

Do you think you "own" your lifestyle? Should marketers be able to use information about you to direct their marketing efforts? How much control do you want to maintain over information about you? What role should government policymakers play in regulating the use of such information?

# BACKGROUND CHARACTERISTICS, LIFESTYLE, AND PSYCHOGRAPHICS

Denise Walsh places a high priority on her role as a mother and devotes a great deal of time and effort to her children. She chose a neighborhood with a good school system, she supervises her kids closely, and she expects that they will be well behaved. At the same time, she is realistic and knows that sometimes kids will be rowdy and have accidents that may damage the furniture. Denise has a personal style that permeates her house. She treasures fine furniture and spends time, effort, and money to indulge her interest in her house even while seeking out economical ways to decorate.

Denise illustrates how lifestyle and psychographics express the aggregation of background characteristics—the culture and values in which she was raised, the demographic subcultures to which she belongs, the personality she exhibits—traits that she developed as she grew to adulthood. Denise values the importance of her role as a mother and the traditional craftsmanship her grandfather taught her. Her family's income allows her to live in an excellent school district; at the same time, it constrains her from buying every piece of furniture she wants. Maybe when the kids have grown a bit more she will be able to go back to work full time and indulge herself. Given her frugal personality, though, she'll probably always shop for a bargain!

Culture and values, demographic subcultures, and personality, lifestyle, and psychographics all influence the ways consumers like Denise think, feel, and act as they complete the steps in the purchase process. As a result, marketers must examine each of these consumer characteristics carefully to determine the best way to segment consumers. One other background characteristic is relevant for an understanding of consumer behavior and market segmentation—reference groups, the topic of the next chapter.

# SUMMARY

1. **Recognize the role of personality in individual behavior and apply various perspectives to that role.** Personality is a consumer's psychological predisposition to behave in a particular way as he or she interacts with the environment. Freudian theories of personality examine the conflicts between individual needs and desires and the socialization process, and the mechanisms individuals develop to resolve those conflicts. A personality trait is a consumer's predisposition to behave in a particular way in a specific area of his or her life and can be used to classify consumers into a personality type—a group of people that share personality traits and can therefore be expected to exhibit similar behavioral processes. A consumer's self-concept is the expression of his image of himself and his personality, which would allow him to label the parts of his personality he thinks are important.

2. **Understand the relationships among a consumer's personality, lifestyle, and psychographics.** Personality is important, but it is often not useful for segmenting consumers because it does not incorporate the cultural and social context in which consumers express their personalities. This insight was a significant impetus for the development of lifestyle and psychographic analysis, which explicitly addresses the way consumers express their personalities in their cultural and social environment; it represents an attempt to characterize psychological characteristics, including personality, by examining outward expressions of that inner state. Lifestyle analysis emphasizes actions in their social and cultural context, while psychographic analysis focuses on the psychological basis of a consumer's thoughts and feelings.

3. **Identify those attributes of a consumer's lifestyle and psychographics that affect his or her consumer behavior.** Lifestyle and psychographics is the study of the ways in which consumers express their culture and values, demographics, and personality through the allocation of their resources of time and money. Consumers express themselves through the activities and interests that comprise their day-to-day lives and the opinions they hold. These can include activities such as work or hobbies, interests such as sports or the arts, and opinions about themselves and appropriate behavior for others.

# KEY TERMS

| | | |
|---|---|---|
| Personality, *p. 172* | Identification, *p. 176* | Self-concept, *p. 182* |
| Personality traits, *p. 173* | Repression, *p. 176* | Actual self, *p. 182* |
| Personality type, *p. 173* | Displacement, *p. 177* | Ideal self, *p. 182* |
| Psychoanalytic theory of | Projection, *p. 177* | Lifestyle analysis, *p. 186* |
| personality, *p. 174* | Rationalization, *p. 177* | Psychographic |
| Id, *p. 175* | Edwards Personal Prefer- | analysis, *p. 186* |
| Ego, *p. 175* | ence Scale (EPPS), | Lifestyle and psycho- |
| Superego, *p. 175* | *p. 180* | graphics, *p. 186* |

# SKILL-BUILDING ACTIVITIES

1. Locate three magazine advertisements that seem to have been designed to appeal to the id; three that seem to have been designed to appeal to the ego; and three that seem to have been designed to appeal to the superego. How do these three groups of advertisements differ in:

   a. copy   b. illustration   c. format or layout

2. Within the realm of consumer behavior, describe an example of:

   a. identification   b. repression or displacement   c. projection or rationalization

3. Below is a list of adjectives that represents personality traits. Check the adjectives on this list that apply to (a) your actual self (the kind of person you really are), and (b) your ideal self (the kind of person who you would ideally like to be).

| | Not at all | | | | | to a "t" |
|---|---|---|---|---|---|---|
| 1. Assertive ...........1 | 2 | 3 | 4 | 5 | 6 |
| 2. Cold ...............1 | 2 | 3 | 4 | 5 | 6 |
| 3. Broad-minded .......1 | 2 | 3 | 4 | 5 | 6 |
| 4. Worried ............1 | 2 | 3 | 4 | 5 | 6 |
| 5. Self-confident .......1 | 2 | 3 | 4 | 5 | 6 |
| 6. Insecure ...........1 | 2 | 3 | 4 | 5 | 6 |
| 7. Steady .............1 | 2 | 3 | 4 | 5 | 6 |
| 8. Unpleasant .........1 | 2 | 3 | 4 | 5 | 6 |
| 9. Warm .............1 | 2 | 3 | 4 | 5 | 6 |
| 10. Irresponsible .......1 | 2 | 3 | 4 | 5 | 6 |
| 11. Cooperative ........1 | 2 | 3 | 4 | 5 | 6 |
| 12. Undependable ......1 | 2 | 3 | 4 | 5 | 6 |
| 13. Hard-working .......1 | 2 | 3 | 4 | 5 | 6 |
| 14. Emotional ..........1 | 2 | 3 | 4 | 5 | 6 |
| 15. Leader-like .........1 | 2 | 3 | 4 | 5 | 6 |

| | | | | | |
|---|---|---|---|---|---|
| 16. Cool . . . . . . . . . . . . . .1 | 2 | 3 | 4 | 5 | 6 |
| 17. Persevering . . . . . . . .1 | 2 | 3 | 4 | 5 | 6 |
| 18. Disagreeable . . . . . . .1 | 2 | 3 | 4 | 5 | 6 |
| 19. Good-natured . . . . . . .1 | 2 | 3 | 4 | 5 | 6 |
| 20. Withdrawn . . . . . . . . .1 | 2 | 3 | 4 | 5 | 6 |
| 21. Responsible . . . . . . . .1 | 2 | 3 | 4 | 5 | 6 |
| 22. Grumpy . . . . . . . . . . . .1 | 2 | 3 | 4 | 5 | 6 |
| 23. Impulsive . . . . . . . . . .1 | 2 | 3 | 4 | 5 | 6 |
| 24. Lazy . . . . . . . . . . . . . .1 | 2 | 3 | 4 | 5 | 6 |
| 25. Gregarious . . . . . . . . .1 | 2 | 3 | 4 | 5 | 6 |
| 26. Mannerly . . . . . . . . . .1 | 2 | 3 | 4 | 5 | 6 |
| 27. Organized . . . . . . . . . .1 | 2 | 3 | 4 | 5 | 6 |
| 28. Curious . . . . . . . . . . . .1 | 2 | 3 | 4 | 5 | 6 |
| 29.. Quiet . . . . . . . . . . . . .1 | 2 | 3 | 4 | 5 | 6 |

**4.** Divide the class into users and nonusers of cigarettes, beer, chewing gum, or some other consumer product that will cut the class into two groups of about the same size. Tabulate the actual self-ratings and the ideal self-ratings obtained in question 3 for the "user half of the class versus the "nonuser" half of the class. Are there any actual self differences between the user half of the class and the nonuser half of the class? If so, what explains the differences? If not, why did differences fail to appear?

**5.** Develop ten AIO items that might discriminate between the "user" half of the class and the "nonuser" half of the class. For each item, explain why you think a difference might appear.

▼ **MULTIPLE CHOICE**

# CHAPTER 6
# SELF-TEST

**1.** The predisposed way a person approaches his or her environment is referred to as _____ .

a. lifestyle
b. personality
c. motivation
d. psychographics

**2.** A _____ _____ is a group of people who share common personality traits.

a. personality type
b. personality tribe
c. personality segment
d. personality subgroup

**3.** _____ _____ is based on the belief that a person's personality is based on his or her unconscious needs and drives.

a. trait theory
b. self-concept theory
c. psychoanalytic theory
d. attribution theory

**4.** If using the symbols of an angel and a devil, the angel would represent the _____ portion of one's personality and the devil would represent the _____ portion.

a. superego; ego
b. id; ego
c. superego; id
d. id; superego

**5.** A person's self concept consists of his or her actual self and _____ self.

a. ideal
b. important
c. defined
d. consumer

6. Marketers can develop a profile of lifestyles and psychographics by asking AIO questions related to consumers' *activities*, _____ , and *opinions*.
   a. *information*
   b. *interests*
   c. *involvement*
   d. *image*

7. The _____ category of the most recent version of VALS includes individuals who are driven by what is right and wrong.
   a. action-oriented
   b. strugglers
   c. status-oriented
   d. principle-oriented

8. Wearing the same type of basketball shoe as your favorite professional basketball player is an example of the _____ mechanism for resolving personality conflict.
   a. identification
   b. displacement
   c. sublimation
   d. projection

9. Achievement, endurance, and aggression are all personality _____ measured by the Edwards Personal Preference Schedule.
   a. criteria
   b. traits
   c. ratings
   d. foundations

10. If a researcher asked you to describe yourself as either shy or outgoing, that researcher is using a _____ scale to measure your self-concept.
    a. numerical
    b. direct rating
    c. semantic differential
    d. sorting

▼ TRUE/FALSE

1. Marketers prefer to use personality in their segmentation strategies rather than psychographics and lifestyle because personality is easier to measure.   T or F
2. People are born with their personality.   T or F
3. It is difficult to change someone's personality.   T or F
4. Freudian theory can be used to analyze consumers' motivation for puchase.   T or F
5. Trait theory is based on the idea that individuals have specific personality characteristics that can be used to classify them into groups.   T or F
6. Consumers always buy products that are consistent with their actual self.   T or F
7. People's lifestyles include their opinions but not their values.   T or F
8. Catalog purchasing records, credit card holder lists, and voting records are all sources of lifestyle and psychographic data.   T or F
9. Lifestyle and psychographic analysis is often used in marketing since it addresses the way individuals express their personalities.   T or F
10. Projection is the process of rationalizing or offering excuses for one's actions.   T or F

▼ SHORT ANSWER

1. Explain the components of the CAD scale. If you were a marketer of a video game of which the objective is to "conquer a dreaded enemy," which of the personality types within the CAD scale would you target?

2. Describe the differences between the direct rating scale, sorting task, and semantic differential scale methods used to measure self-concept.

3.  Describe the public policy issues of a marketer selling customer data to another organization.
4.  Describe the differences between the "ideal self" and the "actual self."

## ▼ APPLICATION EXERCISE

You are a marketing research director of a company that manufactures electric mulching lawnmowers. You have been asked to develop a survey consisting of activities, interests, and opinion questions that will be administered to buyers of your mower. The buyers' responses to the survey will help you develop future marketing strategies by giving you a profile of who buys your product. Your boss has requested that before you develop the entire survey, you send her a sample of six questions (two "A" questions, two "I" question, and two "O" questions) for review. Develop those six questions.

# 7

# REFERENCE GROUPS, COMMUNITIES, AND FAMILIES

⦿ Consumer Snapshot   *Mark Walsh\* is a 40-year-old sales and marketing manager. He lives in Tuscon, Arizona, with his wife, Denise, and their two young children, Brandon, eight, and Meghan, five.*

### FACT OR FICTION

⦿ Much consumer behavior is influenced by the socialization people received as children.

⦿ As individuals pass through childhood and adolesence to adulthood, parental influences on consumer behavior increase.

⦿ Most reference groups have formal membership requirements.

⦿ The most influential reference groups generally lack both resources and power.

*Last name changed for privacy.

- Clubs, resource organizations, professional associations, schools, and companies can serve as either positive or negative reference groups.

- Separation from a reference group is a common development among children as they grow up.

## EYE ON THE CONSUMER

Mark Walsh and his wife, Denise, recently took a vacation to Club Med in the Dominican Republic. They'd heard all about Club Med from friends who had vacationed there three times and loved it. Mark and Denise thought it was a great idea because they could bring their kids with them and make it a family vacation, but there were also opportunities for the two of them to be alone together. Club Med offers a Kid's Club, which includes group activities and meals for children, so that parents can spend time by themselves.

Mark's idea of a vacation is constant motion; at Club Med he had the opportunity to wind surf, water ski, and snorkel. Denise has a different idea—she prefers to relax when she is on vacation, so she took the time to read books while relaxing on the beach. Their different approaches to free time carry over into the rest of their lives as well. As a child, Mark was raised in a very active family, and he continues to swim, play tennis, and hunt as an adult. By contrast, Denise was raised by parents who believed that ballet was the only appropriate sport for girls; today her most compelling motivation to get to the gym to exercise is peer pressure from her friends.

At home Mark and Denise divide their chores and their purchases along pretty traditional lines. Mark's "department" is the television and stereo—electronics equipment; Denise is responsible for home decorating and grocery shopping. In fact, Mark sometimes calls Denise the "food boss," even though he recognizes that it's probably a sexist allusion. Mark and Denise come together when it comes to the decisions they must make as parents of two young children. For example, they both agree that there is too much violence portrayed in many of the television programs and movies children watch today. Mark sees a difference between the kinds of cartoons he watched on Saturday mornings as a kid, such as the *Road Runner,* and the "robot figure" programs his kids watch today which show everyone blowing each other up. While Mark acknowledges that the coyote and the road runner hit each other, he maintains that the action was far less violent than what is currently depicted on television.

Mark and Denise also agree that it is important for their kids to eat healthy so they reduce the amount of sugary junk food and high-fat products they buy. They admit that the kids are always complaining about what their friends are allowed to eat and drink. For instance, Mark and Denise serve only Minute Maid 100% orange juice. Recently their daughter was at a friend's house, where she was offered Sunny Delight, a very sweet juice drink. She had already drank three glasses when she complained to her friend's mother that she wasn't allowed to have it at home, even as she asked for another glass!

Mark and Denise comprise a reference group for their children—the topic of this chapter. We begin this chapter by considering the processes involved in selecting a reference group. As part of this discussion, we discuss the roles of the family, community, and media in the selection process. We then describe the types of reference groups that are available for selection and examine the ways in which reference groups exert their influence on consumers. Finally we discuss the dynamics of a particularly prevalent reference group—the family.

After reading and thinking about this chapter, you should be able to:

❶ Identify the reasons that a consumer needs to select a reference group.
❷ Recognize the various reference groups available to consumers.
❸ Assess the influence reference groups have on a consumer's purchase process.

# WHY SELECT A REFERENCE GROUP?

A **reference group** is a person or group that a consumer uses as a standard of reference for his or her general or specific thoughts, feelings, and actions.[1] A consumer can have many different reference groups at any given time and may turn to one group for guidance in making some purchases and another group for other decisions. Family members, friends, work colleagues, members of the local community, or groups the consumer aspires to join all provide standards for consumer behavior, influencing the ways in which he or she uses the behavioral processes to select, purchase, use, evaluate, and dispose of products. This influence is revealed when the consumer adopts the standards of a reference group and models his or her behavior after that of the group's members.

In selecting a certain individual or group to serve as a reference standard, the consumer increases that group's potential to affect his or behavior and reduces the impact of other groups. In this way, reference groups provide the route through which the rest of the background characteristics—culture and values, demographic subcultures, lifestyle and psychographics—influence the consumer's behavioral processes (Figure 7.1). That is, reference groups provide models for the consumer's motivations, perceptions, learning, attitude formation, and decisions and influence the steps the consumer uses to complete the purchase process by supplying cues about how to apply the behavioral processes to these activities. For example, your friends' attitudes about parties—the wilder the better—may be the standard they use in evaluating alternative vacation spots. These attitudes are probably very different from those of Mark and Denise. If you select your friends as your reference group rather than a married couple with children, your travel plans for spring break would more likely be Fort Lauderdale, Florida than the Kid's Club at Club Med.

A **reference group** is a person or group a consumer uses as a standard of reference for his or her thoughts, feelings, and actions.

■ FIGURE 7.1

The relationship between reference groups and background characteristics and behavioral processes.

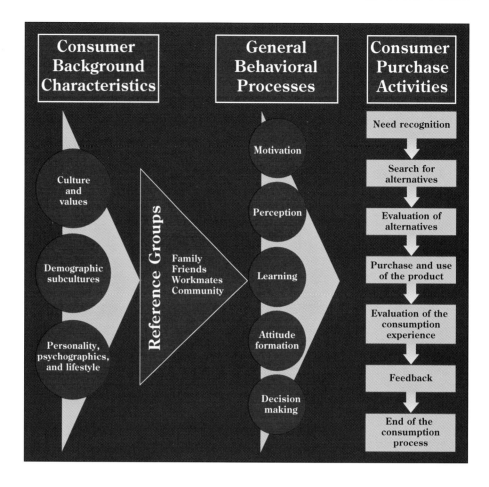

Consumers turn to reference groups for several reasons. First, the consumer purchase process can be a confusing and difficult one, and the consumer might need *information* from others to make his or her way through the steps in the purchase process. For example, Mark and Denise were able to rely on information from friends who had just taken a vacation at a Club Med. Their friends' travel experiences and knowledge enabled Mark and Denise to gather information, evaluate alternatives, and reach a purchase decision more quickly and effectively than they would have been able to do alone.

In other cases, a consumer might recognize the *power and resources* others possess. The consumer might need help to pay for a product or to carry it home. A college student might borrow money from his parents to go to Cancun with his fraternity brothers during spring break, for example, or he might ask a friend to help him carry his new mattress home from the warehouse. Reference groups exert their power intangibly as well. Consumers typically want to avoid the backlash they may experience if they buy a product their friends or family don't like, so they will model themselves after their reference groups to avoid criticism, ostracism, or even punishment.

Consumers might rely on reference groups because they use their purchases to make a statement about the *image* they want to project and to identify themselves as part of the group; by buying the same products as their friends, they indicate that they are like them. For example, you might wear sweatshirts or baseball caps emblazoned with the name of your college to demonstrate your identification with your school. On campus, you might wear clothing touting your class, department, fraternity, or sorority to show that you are a member of these specific groups (Figure 7.2).

Now that we understand *why* consumers select reference groups, the question remains: *How* do consumers choose among all the possible reference groups that are available to them? For example, what model will a college student follow when shopping for a business suit to wear on a job interview? He could seek advice from his family, neighbors, friends, teachers, or the professionals in the industry where he wants to work. He might choose to adopt his parents' fashion style because they are going to help him pay for the suit. He might buy a suit his friends will like so he can also wear it to the spring formal. Or he could consult with his faculty advisor or observe what kind of clothing his future coworkers are wearing and buy something similar.

Each potential reference group offers certain advantages to a consumer. In choosing among the groups, the individual must weigh the information, resources, and image to be obtained by buying the same products in the same way the group members do. In doing so, the consumer must have some knowledge of how the members of the group act and the values they hold. For example, a college student may be likely to model his business attire after that of professionals in the industry in which he will work—his prospective colleagues—because they can provide accurate information about the kind of image that will impress prospective employers and get him the job he wants.

■ FIGURE 7.2
Students often wear clothing touting the name of their school, fraternity, or sorority to demonstrate their identification with members of these groups.

## ▼ THE ROLE OF GROUPS IN CONSUMER SOCIALIZATION

Throughout our lives, we learn about consumer behavior from our family, friends, community, and the media. During childhood, we were typically surrounded by relatives, friends, and community members from the same subculture, with whom we shared common background characteristics, such as race and ethnicity, religion, social class, geography, and lifestyle. These values, customs, and rituals were continually reinforced throughout our childhood, and it would have been very difficult for us to adopt a new cultural background at will. As we've grown, however, we have been exposed to people from other subcultures with different backgrounds, both directly, through face-to-face interactions, and indirectly, through mass media vehicles such as television, movies, and magazines. This process, whereby people acquire the skills and knowledge relevant to consumer purchase behavior, is referred to as **consumer socialization** and involves various reference groups, from the family to mass media.

**Consumer socialization** is the process whereby people acquire the skills and knowledge relevant to purchase behavior.

**Role of the Family**   Much of an individual's behavior is influenced by the socialization that takes place during childhood.[2] Parents teach their children the

■ FIGURE 7.3

Parents act as direct influences on their children's behavior by teaching them about certain customs, rituals, and activities.

steps in the consumer purchase process and the behavioral processes through both direct and indirect means. Direct influences involve the overt efforts of parents to teach their children about certain customs, rituals, and activities (Figure 7.3). For example, Mark's family bolstered his interest in athletics, while Denise's family did not encourage her in the same way. Parents teach their children about specific products, invoking favorable attitudes about some and unfavorable attitudes about others. They also demonstrate the behavioral processes to be used in completing the purchase process. That is, parents may teach their children that certain needs should be satisfied and others ignored, or they may show them how to gather information about alternative products and evaluate them. For example, some kids learn that it's OK to drink Coke when they're thirsty; others are encouraged to drink Mott's Apple Juice; and still others are taught to drink only tap water.

## FACT OR FICTION REVISITED

◉   It is that a great deal of consumer behavior is influenced by socialization individuals receive as children.

Parents have indirect influences on their children as well. Children watch the way their parents purchase products and adopt their behavior as a model for their own. If a child's parents consulted *Consumer Reports* whenever they evaluated expensive products, for example, the child may grow up to do the same as an adult. In fact, as adults, many people still use the same products their parents purchased when they were kids; at the same time, they may consciously choose to avoid other products their parents used. For example, a person may continue to use Dial soap in her own home because her parents bought it when she was a child, but she may steadfastly avoid ever buying a car that's similar to the Buick station wagon her parents drove.

Finally, parents manage their children's exposure to alternative models of consumer behavior by exerting some influence over the people with whom they may spend time and the mass media they are allowed to view. For example, Mark and Denise only allow their children to watch the cartoons they approve of, and only on weekends; they chose their house because its layout allows Denise to keep an eye on the kids when they play with their friends.

**Communities of Reference and the Mass Media**   Family is just one part of a child's social environment—friends, schoolmates, and neighbors all increase in importance as children grow older and become more aware of their community and the world at large.[3] Although parents may mediate the effects of these other groups when children are young, friends and acquaintances become more powerful influences as the child begins to spend more time away from home. Mark and Denise, for example, try to monitor which cartoons their children watch, but the kids watch and talk about television programs with their friends outside of their parents' domain. Specifically, their son's friends provide alternative standards of reference by telling him about the Mighty Morphin Power Rangers and encouraging him to ask his parents for the toys his friends have. As children enter their teenage years, they began to shop with their friends instead of their parents (Figure 7.4), and the products they buy are the ones approved by their friends, not their parents.

■ FIGURE 7.4
As children enter their teenage years, they turn to the influence of their peers over their parents as references for the types of clothing they wear and the music they listen to.

As they grow, children are exposed to people from diverse backgrounds and geographical areas as they move from elementary school to junior high to high school. As young adults, this diversity increases in college or the work environment, increasing the exposure to people from different communities, demographic subcultures, and lifestyles. This progression into adulthood is accompanied by a shift in focus from the place people live to the place they work or study. Accordingly, the range of available reference groups widens beyond the family to include the residential community, classmates and club members, and, ultimately, the occupational community.

As children make these transitions through childhood and into adulthood, they are also exposed to potential reference groups through the mass media. As consumers watch television and movies, read magazines and newspapers, and listen to the radio, they become familiar with reference groups whose members they may have never met. By observing the behavior of members of these groups, people acquire new models for their own behavior. For example, clothing styles may be modeled after celebrities, from Madonna or Kris Kross for younger teenagers to Pearl Jam and Sheryl Crow for older ones (Figure 7.5). Although

■ FIGURE 7.5
Although most teenagers will never meet Madonna, many of them identify with her by imitating her appearance.

205

most consumers will never meet celebrities in real life, they are able to feel a solidarity with them by buying the same products they use and dressing the same way. Similarly, interactive communications media—such as discussion groups that communicate via interactive services, the Internet, or electronic bulletin boards—allow consumers to interact with people they never see face to face.

## FACT OR FICTION REVISITED

⊙   The idea that as consumers pass through childhood and adolescence into adulthood, parental influence on consumer behavior increases is *false*. In fact, alternative reference groups become increasingly important during these stages of life.

> A **consumption community** is a reference group based on common consumer purchase behavior.

The historian Daniel Boorstin uses the term **consumption community** to describe reference groups that are based on common consumption styles rather than culture, values, or demographic subcultures. Consumers often use products as a way of identifying the kinds of people they are—wearing clothes purchased from Kmart projects a very different image than wearing Calvin Klein's latest fashions, for example. The members of a consumption community receive their consumer socialization through interpersonal contacts in their traditional community—family, friends, neighbors, workmates—and through nontraditional ways that do not involve face-to-face contact, such as interactive discussion groups, mass media, and marketing efforts.[4] These nontraditional communities need not share common background characteristics because a consumer can learn about the members' consumption choices through electronic communication and mass media. Consumers often find great pleasure in identifying with others who have made the some product consumption choices as they do, as illustrated in the following Pleasures of Consumption box.

### PLEASURES OF CONSUMPTION

**Consumption Communities[5]**

It is natural for people to feel a kinship with others who like and use the same products they do. Some consumers identify with others who have the same hobbies and interests (e.g., golf, tennis, hunting) and belong to clubs where they can share those activities. "Deadheads," for example, are the countless fans of the Grateful Dead who have seen the band perform many times over and enjoy talking about their favorite concert experiences with one another. Product-specific forums on on-line interactive services such as American Online, Compuserve, and Prodigy, smaller services, such as Sonicnet, a provider in New York City that specializes in alternative rock, and sites on the Internet all offer consumers the opportunity to share experiences with others, from those who have bought Quicken personal finance software to those who are planning a scuba diving vacation. Consumers are able to gain information and resources from fellow "community" members, and their common consumption allows them to share a common bond. Mass media provide similar experiences. Some young consumers feel they are part of the "in crowd" when they wear the same kinds of clothes worn by the VJs on MTV or VH1.

Marketers have long recognized that consumers take pleasure from feeling that they are members of consumption communities and have actively begun to create opportunities for consumers to find such reference groups. Nearly 200,000 Harley-Davidson owners worldwide, including Eliot Spiegel, belong to the Harley Owners' Group (HOG), which holds weekend meetings and rides, publishes its own magazine, and offers products and services such as Harley clothing, roadside service, and an insurance program. Many other groups, including professional associations such as the American Sociological Association, the University of Pennsylvania Alumni Association, General Motors, and the Rolling Stones, offer affinity credit cards which contain the name of the sponsoring group in addition to that of the bank. Some of the cards offer rebates to the sponsoring organization, so the Sociological Association or the Alumni group earns revenue; others offer additional services to the credit card holder, such as reduced prices on merchandise or rebates on all purchases made with the card. McDonald's and Burger King each sponsor clubs for children that entitle members to gifts and magazines. Similarly, *Car and Driver* magazine offers membership in its Performance Club to its readers.

Are there certain products you use simply because you like the kinds of people that use them? Do you buy the same products as your friends because you want to demonstrate that you are part of the community? Do you avoid some brands because you don't want to be associated with the people who use them? Do you think marketers are exploiting consumers when they deliberately create groups of purchasers whose members will support one another's product choices?

# TYPES OF REFERENCE GROUPS ◀

Consumers are exposed to an array of reference groups throughout their lives. Some are groups to which the individual already belongs—family, close friends, a college marketing club, or a fraternity or sorority. Others are groups the individual would like to join—the employees at a firm he or she hopes to work for after graduation. Still other groups might provide a model of behavior the consumer wants to avoid. A high school freshman may not want to go on vacation with her parents or to a place where there will be many people like her parents because she is trying to establish herself among her peers.

▼ GROUP DIMENSIONS

Three dimensions are often used to classify reference groups (Table 7.1):

A **social category** is a group of people who share some characteristics that make them easy to classify as members even though they need not have any interaction, contact, or rules.

The third type of group structure is the **social category,** which describes a group of people who share certain characteristics that make them easy to classify as members of that category. Unlike members of formal and informal groups, however, members of a social category need not have any interaction or contact, and they are not bound by rules for membership and behavior. Demographic subcultures, consumption communities, and lifestyles are common social categories. For example, "Generation Xers," working mothers, and urban Hispanics are all social categories that can serve as reference groups (Figure 7.6).

■ FIGURE 7.6
Whirlpool promotes the simplicity and flexibility of its refrigerators to a specific demographic subculture—working mothers.

# Ever wish there were more of you to help put it all away?

## Introducing the most flexible refrigerator in America.

Need a hand with the groceries? Our new refrigerator adjusts to anything you bring home.

Our EZ-Trak™ shelf slides side-to-side to make plenty of room for tall items.

*EZ-Trak™ Shelf*

You won't juggle things in the door either. Our Flexi-Slide™ bin adjusts every which way.

*Flexi-Slide™ Bin*

Plus, our Flexi-Glide™ Freezer Floor slides out to put frozen food right under your nose. Now food's easier to find, easier to put away. Together, you and Whirlpool® can make a home run.

*Flexi-Glide™ Freezer Floor*

**Whirlpool**
Home & Appliances

How To Make A Home Run.™

Whirlpool can help make your home run. Call 1-800-253-1301. Any day. Anytime.
©1995 Whirlpool Corporation  ®Registered trademark/TM Trademark of Whirlpool Corp.

## FACT OR FICTION REVISITED

⦿  It is *not true* that most reference groups have formal membership requirements. Many reference groups do not even have face-to-face contact, let alone formal membership requirements.

# THE INFLUENCE OF REFERENCE GROUPS ◀

The influence a particular reference group has on an individual's behavior is related to the reason the group was selected in the first place. Earlier in the chapter we described three important outcomes of selecting a reference group; the consumer gains: (1) information to use in the purchase process, (2) power and resources, and (3) an image that is projected to members of the group as well as to outsiders. We will discuss the influence of reference groups here, but we defer our discussion of the dynamics of communication between consumers and their reference groups until we consider interpersonal communication and opinion leadership in Chapter 16.

## ▼ BASES OF INFLUENCE

In addition to providing information, reference groups reward individuals for exhibiting appropriate behavior and criticize them for behaving inappropriately. At the same time, a reference group portrays a certain image the individual wishes to emulate.[7] Reference groups differ in the degree to which they exert these bases of influence, however. Similarly, some consumers are more susceptible to certain types of influence than others.

■ FIGURE 7.7

The use of experts, such as golf pro Jim McLean, lends credibility to advertising by assuring the consumer that the information being portrayed is accurate.

**Information**  A group's capacity to exert influence through the information it possesses is based on the credibility of the members' knowledge of the products and the purchase process. **Credibility,** in turn, is the belief that a source of information is both accurate and unbiased. If the members of a group are experts in a particular area—say, home improvement—the information they provide about products in that area will likely be accurate (Figure 7.7); if they are honest and interested in conveying accurate information, the information will be unbiased. Consumers evaluate both the expertise and motivation of a reference group when judging the credibility of the information that group provides.

> **Credibility** is the belief that a source of information is accurate and unbiased.

> **Normative influence** is the ability of a reference group to use rewards or punishments to influence an individual to behave in a way its members find acceptable.

**Resources and Power**   The ability of a reference group to use its resources and power to influence a consumer, also called **normative influence,** is contingent on three factors: (1) the desirability of the resources to the consumer, (2) the effectiveness of the available rewards or punishments, and (3) the visibility of the consumer's behavior to the group. Resources that are desirable to an individual will increase the influence of the group that possesses them. For example, if you are relying on your parents to help you pay for a Florida vacation during your Spring break, they will have a great influence on your purchase process. If you have other sources of funds, however, such as your college roommate, your parents' influence is reduced.

The ability of a group to reward or punish a consumer will also affect the individual's choice. For example, parents typically choose the cereals their children eat, but their choice is often influenced by their children's likes or dislikes. Although nutrition experts criticize heavily sugared cereals, kids often prefer them. Whereas the experts are more credible sources of information, children have much greater power in the household—parents never have to face the experts, but their kids become quite vocal when they are deprived of their Fruit Loops. Reference groups also have more influence on behavior that is readily visible to them. For example, your parents are more influential about your vacation plans than your current choice of cereal because a trip is more visible to them than what you eat in your dorm room or apartment.

## FACT OR FICTION REVISITED

⊚   The most influential reference groups *do not* lack resources and power; rather, resources and power increase a reference group's influence

**Image**   The ability of a group to use image to influence a consumer is related to the visibility of the symbolic meaning of the image and the credibility with which the consumer can adopt that image (Figure 7.8). That is, if the image portrayed by a reference group is visible to others whom a consumer wants to impress, the group has influence. For example, when you buy clothes like the fashions worn by your favorite *Beverly Hills 90210* characters, you don't want to explain to your friends that you are wearing clothes just like Kelly's or Donna's; rather, you want your friends to recognize the clothes and what they symbolize. The credibility with which a consumer is able to adopt a certain image is also important. If a consumer wants to project a serious, professional image with his new Armani suit, his reference group must believe that he indeed is serious and professional and not just an impostor who has borrowed the suit from his cousin.

## ▼ INFLUENTIAL TYPES OF REFERENCE GROUP

Linking the three dimensions—membership, affinity, and structure—generates 12 distinct combinations. When considering the influence of reference groups, we will consider the first two dimensions—membership and affinity. The third dimension, structure, is necessary to identify types of groups, but it does not affect

■ FIGURE 7.8
This ad for Classic Gardenia perfume presents a certain image the marketer hopes consumers will want to posess by buying the product.

the nature of the influence as strongly as membership and affinity. By combining the membership and nonmembership dimensions with the positive and negative dimensions of affinity, four types of reference group influence are possible—identification, separation, aspiration, and discrimination (Figure 7.9). Within each of these four types, the group that is exerting influence can be either formal, informal, or a social category.

■ FIGURE 7.9

Types of reference groups and their influence

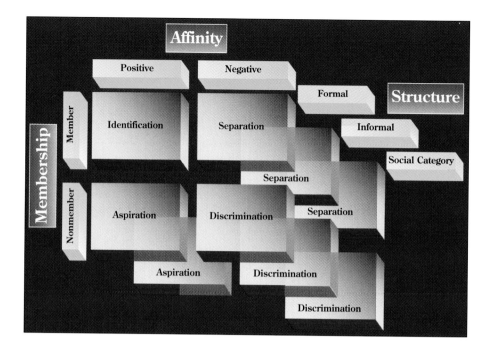

**Identification groups** are positive membership groups with which a consumer identifies strongly and whose values and behaviors the individual incorporates into his or her behavior.

**Identification With Positive Membership Groups**    **Identification groups** are *positive membership* groups with which a consumer identifies strongly and whose values and behaviors the individual endorses by incorporating them in his or her consumer behavior. Membership in a positive reference group gives the consumer the opportunity to learn how members of the group enact their values and behave in everyday situations. The consumer closely observes members of identification groups and responds to their rewards for acting appropriately and their criticisms for acting inappropriately. Contact with fellow group members can be face to face or indirect, through telephone calls, mail, or electronic mail.

Identification groups can have a powerful influence on consumer behavior. Because the consumer belongs to the group and feels positive about the other members, he or she finds their information to be credible and, consequently, wants to utilize their resources, gain their approval, and be considered part of the group. Frequent interactions with group members provide the consumer with opportunities to learn about their behavior processes and to model his or her behavior after theirs.

Informal identification groups, in particular, including family, friends, and colleagues, are the source of much of a child's consumer socialization, and they continue to be the major source of social interaction in a consumer's life. For example, when choosing a place to go for Spring break, your friends and family may be involved in the process from the need recognition stage to the conclusion of the purchase process. Your motivation to go on vacation might have been initiated by a discussion with your friends about the fun you would have going away together. You would subsequently share the information you gather about Cancun, Daytona Beach, Myrtle Beach, and other alternatives with your friends and agree on criteria to use to evaluate them. You might then create a description of a trip you think your parents would find acceptable. While on vacation, you would be sensitive to what your friends are doing so that you can do the same things, indicating that you are proud to be part of the group. When you return to campus, you might recount the same stories about your trip as your friends do to demonstrate how much fun you had together. The only exception to the storytelling might be your parents, who will get a tamer version of some of the events so that they won't protest the next time you want to go away with your friends.

Clubs, religious organizations, professional associations, schools, and companies constitute some of the formal groups with whom a consumer may choose to identify. Individuals or groups who share a consumer's cultural values, demographic subcultures, or lifestyle and psychographics comprise the social categories to which a consumer may belong. As noted previously, the kind of influence wielded by formal groups and social categories is the same as that exerted by informal groups. For example, you will be influenced to travel to the same Spring break destination as your friends (informal group), fellow fraternity, sorority, marketing club, or marching band members (formal group), and other college students (social category).

## FACT OR FICTION REVISITED

◉   Clubs, religious organizations, professional associations, schools, and companies all can serve as either positive or negative reference groups.

**Separation From Negative Membership Groups**   **Separation groups** are *negative membership groups* from which a consumer wants to separate himself or herself. Because the consumer is a member of the group, he or she has the opportunity to observe the members' behavior closely and to become familiar with the influence they exert. If the individual disapproves of the behavior of the group, he or she can exhibit this disapproval by purchasing and using a product that will create an image distinct from the rest of the group. For example, a suburban couple can conspicuously buy a Mazda Miata sportscar to distinguish themselves from their neighbors who drive Chrysler and Ford minivans. Separation groups typically do not have a stable, long-term influence on a consumer; the individual will eventually withdraw from the group or choose a more salient membership group on which to model his or her behavior.

> **Separation groups** are negative membership groups from which a consumer wants to separate himself or herself.

Separation from a membership group is a common occurrence among children as they grow older. For example, a teenage boy might pierce his ear in order to separate himself from his parents and others who don't think it's appropriate for men to wear earrings. Many teenagers and young adults, in particular, declare their independence from their family and other peer groups by the fashions they wear and the styles they embody.

## FACT OR FICTION REVISITED

◉   Separation from a reference group is indeed a common development among children as they grow up.

> **Aspiration groups** are positive nonmembership groups that have a powerful influence on an individual who aspires to be a member.

**Aspiring To Join Positive Nonmembership Groups**   **Aspiration groups** are *positive nonmembership groups* that have a powerful influence on a consumer who aspires to be a member of the group. Because the consumer does not belong to the group and does not share common experiences with its members, he or she must come to know the group by initiating personal contact or through direct observation or the mass media. For example, fashion and home magazines, such as *Vogue* and *Architectural Digest,* depict images of the clothing and homes of the upper class and celebrities many consumers aspire to be like.

Aspiration groups offer consumers the reward of future membership. A college student who wants to break into advertising after graduation, for example, might contact advertising executives for advice and then imitate their dress and style in the hopes of impressing them enough to warrant a job offer. This influence is largely image based—people adopt the behavior of a group to which they don't belong because they want to project the image of membership. This concept also applies to individuals. Celebrities, for example, often serve as an individual referent; many people imitate the dress and style of their favorite celebrities in the hopes that they will be seen as positively as the celebrities are.

> **A discrimination group** is a negative nonmembership group whose members an individual does not identify with and with whom the individual has little familiarity.

**Discrimination from Negative Nonmembership Groups**   A **discrimination group** is a *negative nonmembership group;* it is the least influential type of reference group because a consumer does not identify with its members and has little familiarity with their behavior. The group's information and resources are of little use to the consumer, and its ability to exercise power over the individual is limited. As in negative membership groups, any influence that is exerted is primarily image based. That is, a consumer can choose to discriminate himself or herself from a certain group by clearly exhibiting behavior that is different from members of the group. For example, if a particular group on campus frequents a local nightspot, an individual may label herself a nonmember of the group by avoiding that location.

▼ **DOES REFERENCE GROUP INFLUENCE VARY BY PRODUCT?**

Regardless of the type of group they turn to, consumers are more susceptible to the influence of reference groups in choosing certain products over others. Bearden and Etzel investigated this issue and found that influence varied by:

❶ the type of product—a luxury versus a necessity, and
❷ its visibility—whether it is used in public or private settings.[8]

Bearden and Etzel examined the effects of reference groups on both the decision to purchase the type of product and the choice of a specific brand (Figure 7.10). They found that reference groups most often affect product and brand decisions involving public luxuries, such as golf clubs and skis. Furthermore, reference groups influence both the consumer's need for the product in general as well as the choice of brand, because the consumer doesn't *need* to buy the product. By contrast, when a consumer buys a public necessity, such as a wristwatch or a car, the reference group affects only the brand choice but not the decision to make

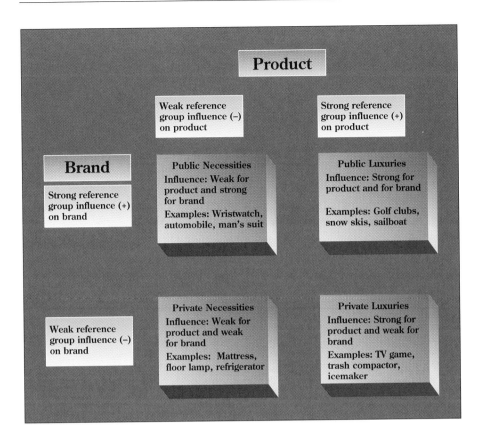

■ FIGURE 7.10

Effects of reference groups on product and brand purchase.

the purchase in the first place, since the consumer has deemed the product necessary and will purchase it regardless of input from the reference group. Reference groups also influence the consumer's decision to purchase a private luxury, such as fine furniture or stereo equipment, but the brand choice is unaffected because the product is not visible. Finally, private necessities, such as soap or a mattress, are not affected by reference groups at all.

# THE FAMILY AS REFERENCE GROUP

A person's family or household is a very important influence on his or her consumer behavior.[9] As such, the family is considered a significant reference group; in fact, the family is the first reference group to provide consumer socialization in a child's life.

A family is composed of individual members who buy products for themselves and for other members of the family and who provide a standard of reference for the consumer behavior of other family members. Within a family, decisions may be *consensual,* whereby family members reach a mutual agreement, or *accommodative,* whereby differences in opinion require that agreement be negotiated or that some members make the decision for other members. Consensual decisions may involve shared decision making, as when Mark and Denice decide together about the family's vacation, or it may involve appointing members to buy certain products the entire family will use—Mark makes choices about consumer electronics, for example, while Denice decides on the home furnishings. Accomodative decisions include those which certain family members make for others either without consulting them, as when Mark and Denice choose which television programs their kids can watch, or with input from them, as when Mark and Denice consider their kids' preferences when choosing their food and drinks.

A family is made up of multiple consumers who collaborate to complete the steps necessary to purchase and use a product. Table 7.2 illustrates the roles family members play in reaching family consumption decisions. Although families are informal membership groups, the affinity experienced is dependent on the nature of the family and the particular family member being considered. In an intact and happy family, for example, the parents will presumably provide positive models for each other's behavior and respond positively to their children's' opinions. Mark and Denice consider each other's opinions and try to give the kids what they want as long as the requests don't conflict with their principles.

As we noted in our discussion of consumer socialization, children's views of their parents change as they grow. Young children usually model their behavior after their parents', but teenagers often view their parents as negative models as

*Table 7.2*

### ROLES PLAYED BY FAMILY MEMBERS IN HOUSEHOLD CONSUMPTION DECISIONS

| Role | Description | Example |
| --- | --- | --- |
| Initiator | Recognizes need | Wife hears noise in Plymouth Voyager's gearbox |
| | | Child is thirsty |
| Influencer | Searches for alternatives and information to use in evaluation | Husband reads *Consumer Reports* annual car issue |
| | Provides input into decision making | Child tells mom about new juice drink |
| Decider | Responsible for the decision | Husband and wife jointly decide to buy a Ford Windstar |
| | | Mom chooses Tropicana orange juice |
| Purchaser | Purchases the product | Wife applies for bank loan and picks up Windstar at car dealer |
| | | Husband does grocery shopping |
| User | Uses the product | Wife drives the Windstar |
| | | Child drinks Tropicana orange juice |

they try to separate themselves from them in order to gain approval from their peers. As adults, many people gain new respect for their parents' views as they start families of their own. Many "thirty-somethings" remark that they are amazed at how smart their parents became after they moved out of the house!

Like other reference groups, families rely on the information, resources and power, and image their members possess to guide them during their consumer behavior interactions. In most families adults share the role of information provider, each partner having a greater influence in the areas about which they have greater credibility. Recall, for example, that Mark made decisions about consumer electronics and Denise about home furnishings. Resources, power, and image are often a function of the particular family. However, traditional roles grant more power to men than to women, particularly in families where the husband works and the wife is financially dependent on him. As we saw in our discussion of demographic subcultures in Chapter 5, gender roles are changing, however, and the traditional dominance of husbands over wives is diminishing as two-career couples become more prominent.

As children grow, they acquire greater knowledge and expertise of their own. They develop independent sources of resources and power through their own schooling and jobs and look increasingly to their peers for images they want to emulate. As a result, they assume more influence in household decisions and in their own consumer choices. For example, Mark and Denice's children use their out-of-home experiences with friends concerning the *Mighty Morphin Power Rangers* and Sunny Delight to bargain for what they want inside the household. As discussed in the Public Policy box that follows, advertising to children is a particularly sensitive issue for parents, marketers, and public policy actors alike.

## PUBLIC POLICY

### Television Advertising and Children[10]

According to a study conducted by the American Academy of Pediatrics, the average child is exposed to 20,000 television advertisements a year. In response, the Academy has launched a campaign to radically restrict the efforts of marketers to advertise to children younger than eight years of age, denouncing all television advertising aimed at such young children as deceptive because the audience cannot understand the intent of commercials. The Academy has united with other social action groups, including the National Parents–Teachers Association (PTA) and the American Association of School Administrators, to form the Campaign for Kids' TV in an effort to lobby Congress and the Federal Communications Commission to restrict advertising aimed at children and accessible to children on adult programs. Specifically, the groups want to ban all alcohol advertising, cut the number of ads run during children's programs by 50 percent, and strictly regulate all toy-based shows, such as *Mighty Morphin Power Rangers*. Marketers of these products and television broadcasters oppose such motions.

Parental responses to advertising aimed at their children is complex, to say the least. Children pressure their parents for the toys, food, and beverages they see advertised on television. Many want the same brands their friends have so they will fit in with the group. Some children assume that if a product isn't on TV it must not be very good.

Some parents are more optimistic about watching television with their kids so they can explain the products when they see them and provide some perspective about the products and their costs. Whereas they consider advertising troublesome, they admit that their children know a lot more about buying and using products than they did as children because of the constant exposure to advertisements.

Do you think that advertising directed at children should be blamed for the information children use to influence their parents' decisions? Should advertising of children's products be held to a stricter standard than that targeted at adults because of the children's inability to understand and evaluate the arguments? Should it be held to a stricter standard because it affects the balance of household decision making? What role should parents play in monitoring their children's television viewing?

# REFERENCE GROUPS

Mark Walsh relies on many reference groups to guide his day-to-day consumer behavior. The members of his household in particular have a significant influence on the products he buys and uses. Mark's eating habits are strongly influenced by his wife, for example; Denise cooks most of the time—even when Mark barbecues, she's the one who does the grocery shopping. His children pressure him to let them watch the programs their friends watch and to buy them the toys and food they see at their friends' houses. Mark's "old household"—the family in which he was raised—still has an influence on his behavior; his parents encouraged his interest in sports at an early age, and he still enjoys athletic endeavors as an adult. His friends and work colleagues influence the vacations he takes with his family and the clothes he wears on certain occasions—he took the family on a vacation to Club Med because friends of his recommended it, and he always wears his newest suits to business meetings even though he doesn't care much about clothes in general.

Reference groups, like the ones that influence Mark, are the last of the background characteristics that affect consumer behavior. They are composed of those people a consumer chooses to provide guidelines for his or her behavior; often, they are people with whom the consumer shares other background characteristics, such as cultural values, demographic subcultures, or lifestyles. Consumers choose those reference groups that provide them with the information, the power and resources, and the image they can use to complete the consumer purchase activities.

Now that we have completed our discussion of the background characteristics that affect a consumer's behavioral processes, we will turn to Section III and a discussion of the processes themselves.

SUMMARY

1. **Identify the reasons that a consumer needs to select a reference group.** Reference groups provide models for a person's motivations, perceptions, learning, attitude formation, and decision making. There are several reasons that consumers may allow other people to guide their consumer behavior. They might need information to help them search for alternatives, evaluate them, and reach a purchase decision. In other cases, they might recognize the power and resources that others possess that will help them buy and use the products they need. Finally, consumers can use their purchases to make a statement about the image they want to project. By following the model of a particular group for their consumer behavior, they identify themselves as part of the group.

2. **Recognize the different reference groups available to consumers.** Reference groups can vary by membership status, affinity, and structure. Consumers can choose from groups of which they are a member or groups of which they are not a member. They can adopt a group as a positive model by emulating its members' behavior, or as a negative model by behaving in an obviously different way. Finally, the group can have formally defined rules for membership and behavior or informal customs of behavior, or it can be a social category composed of people who share some characteristics but do not necessarily interact with one another. Consumers select those groups that offer them information, resources and power, and an image they can use to satisfy their needs.

3. **Assess the influence a reference group has on a consumer's purchase process.** Consumers identify with positive membership groups, aspire to be like the consumers in positive nonmembership groups, separate themselves from negative membership groups, and discriminate themselves from the consumers in a negative nonmembership group.

KEY TERMS

Reference group, *p. 201*
Consumer socialization, *p. 203*
Consumption community, *p. 206*
Membership reference group, *p. 208*
Nonmembership reference group, *p. 208*

Individual referent, *p. 209*
Affinity, *p. 209*
Positive reference group, *p. 209*
Negative reference group, *p. 209*
Formal group, *p. 209*
Informal group, *p. 209*
Social category, *p. 210*

Credibility, *p. 211*
Normative influence, *p. 212*
Identification group, *p. 214*
Separation group, *p. 215*
Aspiration group, *p. 216*
Discrimination group, *p. 216*

SKILL-BUILDING ACTIVITIES

1. List the five most important reference groups in your life. For each group, identify five products or services for which that group influences your behavior as a consumer.
2. For each of the reference groups you identified in activity 1 above, describe how the group provides:
   a. information   b. power resources   c. image models

3. What one product or service you now purchase is most influenced by the socialization you received as a child? Why is this influence so important in this particular case?

4. What one product or service you now purchase *least* influenced the socialization you received as a child? Why is the influence of socialization so minimal in this instance?

5. Name one consumption community to which you belong. Why would you call it a "community"?

6. Name a negative reference group that influences your behavior as a consumer. Name a negative reference group of which you yourself are a member. Other than being negative reference groups, what do these two groups have in common? Judging from these two examples, what kinds of products and services are most likely to be susceptible to negative reference group influences?

7. With your classmates, form a positive reference group and attempt to influence the consumer behavior of at least one other student.

# CHAPTER 7 SELF-TEST

## ▼ MULTIPLE CHOICE

1. A(n) _____ is a person or group that a consumer uses as a reference for his or her thoughts, feelings, and actions.
   a. endorsement group
   b. credential group
   c. recommendation group
   d. reference group

2. The process by which people acquire the skills and knowledge relevant to consumer behavior is called _____ .
   a. consumer socialization
   b. the family life cycle
   c. the cognitive decision process
   d. information processing

3. The three dimensions used to classify reference groups are structure, membership, and _____ .
   a. participation
   b. affinity
   c. similarity
   d. organization

4. If a young basketball player models his behavior after Michael Jordan, he is using Jordan as a(n) _____ .
   a. aversion referent
   b. formal referent
   c. individual referent
   d. negative referent

5. The American Marketing Association would be considered a(n) _____ reference group, while the friends you go to the movies with are considered a(n) _____ reference group.
   a. formal; negative
   b. formal; informal
   c. informal; formal
   d. individual referent; informal

6. The ability of a reference group to reward correct behavior is an example of the group's _____ influence on consumers.
   a. normative
   b. informational
   c. image creation
   d. cognitive

7. A group of college graduates would be a(n) _____ group for most college students, whereas a group of college dropouts would be a(n) _____ group.
   a. separation; discrimination
   b. aspirational; identification
   c. aspirational; separation
   d. discrimination; separation

8. When Chris supplies her family with information about possible winter vacation destinations, Chris is playing the role of _____ .
   a. initiator
   c. decider
   b. influencer
   d. user

9. Reference groups would have little influence on brand and product choice of which of the following products?
   a. milk
   c. big screen television
   b. wrist watch
   d. ski boat

10. Subcultures, consumption communities, and lifestyles are common types of what type of group structure?
    a. informal
    c. aspirational
    b. social category
    d. informational

▼ TRUE/FALSE

1. A consumer has only one reference group.   T or F
2. One advantage of using a reference group during the consumer behavior process is that the consumer can gain information about a perspective purchase from that group.   T or F
3. The family plays no role in the consumer socialization process.   T or F
4. The "consumption community" is a term used to describe the city within which a consumer makes a purchase.   T or F
5. A membership reference group does not always require its members to have face-to-face contact.   T or F
6. Negative reference groups are groups that consumers use as a reference to determine what behaviors should not be done.   T or F
7. Consumers evaluate a group's image when determining whether that group will be used as a reference.   T or F
8. When evaluating the information of a reference group, consumers determine the credibility of that information.   T or F
9. The person playing the role of initiator in a family's decision process must also play the role of purchaser.   T or F
10. Groups of which you are not presently a member cannot affect your consumer behavior patterns.   T or F

▼ SHORT ANSWER

1. What are the three main reasons that a consumer uses a reference group?
2. Discuss how the media might play a role in the consumer socialization process.
3. Discuss the role reference groups play in the purchase of "private luxury" products.
4. Differentiate an identification group from a discrimination group.

▼ APPLICATION EXERCISE

As the marketing director of a local nonprofit organization that grants wishes of terminally ill children, you are responsible for the fund-raising activities of the organization. Discuss which formal and informal groups may influence the decision of an individual to donate money to your organization.

# 8

# CONSUMER MOTIVATION AND NEEDS

◉ Consumer Snapshot    *Kate Borden is a 52-year-old freelance broadcast director. She lives in Denver, Colorado, with her husband, Bill, and is the mother of three children, Marie, 30, Lisa, 29, and Jeff, 27.*

## FACT OR FICTION

◉ Both a need and a goal are necessary to motivate a person to take action.

◉ Every purchase can be influenced by both innate and acquired needs.

◉ In most consumer purchases, the product is the goal.

◉ Most purchases satisfy needs at several different levels of Maslow's hierarchy.

◉ Consumers usually exert more effort when making high involvement decisions than when making low involvement decisions.

# EYE ON THE CONSUMER

Kate Borden had wanted a Honda for years. She only wanted to buy American, and now that Hondas are made in Ohio she felt comfortable getting one. She'd read about their dependability in *Consumer Reports* and their high quality ratings in the J. D. Power's surveys of owners' experiences with their cars. Kate was also impressed because the Honda was big enough for her husband Bill to get in and out comfortably and it retained a lot of its value. When it came time to buy the car, however, she couldn't get the dealer to sell it at a price she could afford. In fact, Kate had actually walked out of the showroom twice before the salesman took her seriously; even then she ended up paying a little more than she had wanted.

Kate's last big purchase was her La-Z-Boy recliner. She had wanted that for a long time, too, and when she saw that they were on sale, she ran out to buy one. She had tried out the La-Z-Boy in her friends' homes and knew they were comfortable and she wanted to have a big comfortable chair in the house for when her grandchildren came to visit.

Kate is a thrifty consumer. She uses coupons when she goes grocery shopping for the products she normally uses; at the same time, coupons will not influence her to buy something new. Kate is also conscientious about the types of products she buys. She tries to stick to low-fat foods, such as Nabisco Snackwell cookies, but she's not sure if they're an improvement because she just eats more of them! Kate has also started buying laundry detergents free of dyes and perfumes because her skin is more sensitive than it used to be. For a while, she was taking her plastic bottles and other recyclables to the grocery store when she went shopping, but it's become too much of a hassle. When the city starts to collect plastic, cans, and newspapers from her house during trash pickups, she says, then she'll recycle.

In this chapter we consider the needs that motivate consumers, like Kate, to purchase and use products as well as the benefits they seek from those products. We also note how consumer motivation affects the level of involvement—the importance or relevance the consumer purchase process for a particular product has for a consumer. Involvement is discussed in detail in Chapter 13. Finally, we examine a common public policy criticism that maintains that marketers and advertisers create unnecessary needs in consumers. In reality, it is very difficult for marketers to *identify* consumers' true needs, so creating them would be nearly impossible.

After reading and thinking about this chapter, you should be able to:

**❶** Describe the motivation process of consumers.

**❷** Recognize the needs that motivate consumers to begin the consumer purchase process and the benefits they seek from the process.

**❸** Identify those factors that influence an individual's selection of goals.

**❹** Recognize several common approaches used by marketers to understand the benefits sought by consumers.

**❺** Appreciate the debate over whether marketers and advertisers create consumer needs or reflect those needs that consumers already recognize.

# MOTIVATION

All consumer behavior begins with **motivation**—the process by which an individual recognizes a need and begins to take action to satisfy it, as illustrated in Figure 8.1. A **need,** in turn, is the discrepancy between an individual's current state and some ideal state that he or she desires, that ideal state being a **goal.** For example, a person may feel the need to be warm, to get some food to eat, or to go to a quiet, restful place. To satisfy those needs, the person's *goals* may be to buy an Eddie Bauer parka, a Big Mac, or a United Airlines ticket to Hawaii, respectively.

Needs and goals are both necessary to motivate an individual to take action: A person will not recognize a need for which there is no goal that can be achieved; similarly, a goal will not motivate action unless a person sees the need to achieve it. A product can satisfy a need because it offers the consumer a *benefit,* or outcome, from using the product. Kate Borden, for example, recognized that

**Motivation** is the process by which an individual recognizes a need and takes action to satisfy it.

A **need** is a drive to eliminate the discrepancy between one's current state and some ideal state.

A **goal** is the desired ideal state that will provide benefits to satisfy a need.

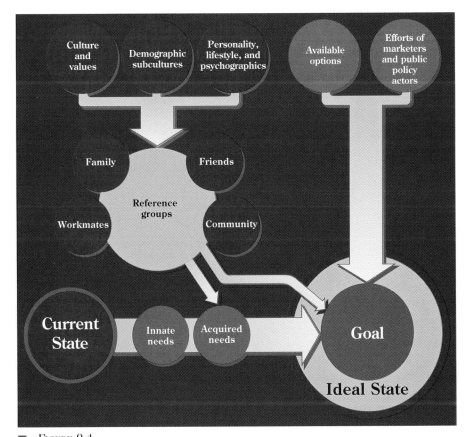

■ FIGURE 8.1

The relationship among motivation, needs, goals, and benefits.

she wanted a large, comfortable chair she and her grandchildren could sit in, so she set out to buy a La-Z-Boy recliner. Someone else might recognize the need for a swivel chair to use at a desk; this person would buy a very different kind of chair than Kate did.

As we noted in Chapter 2, motivation is the first behavioral process consumers use in buying a product. Once a person has used the motivation process to recognize a need, the other behavioral processes come into play: *perception* allows the individual to gather and interpret information about alternative products to satisfy the need; *learning* provides the means for organizing the information; *attitude formation* makes it possible for the individual to appraise the benefits offered by each product; and *decision making* enables the person to choose the product that will best satisfy the need. All of these processes operate in conjunction with the culture, values, demographic subcultures, and personality, lifestyle, and psychographics of the reference group with which the individual chooses to identify.

## FACT OR FICTION REVISITED

◉   It is true that both a need and a goal are necessary to motivate an individual to take action.

▼ NEEDS

> **Innate needs** are the biological needs a person must satisfy in order to stay alive.

> **Acquired needs** are social and psychological needs.

A person's needs can be divided into two types: (1) innate and (2) acquired. **Innate needs** are the biological or physiological needs an individual must satisfy in order to stay alive; they are sometimes called *primary* or *biogenic* needs because every human being must satisfy them in some way. Food, water, shelter and warmth, and sex are examples of innate needs. By contrast, **acquired needs** are the social and psychological needs that arise as a result of an individual's psychological state and his or her interactions with others; they are also called *secondary* or *psychogenic* needs because they can remain unsatisfied with no immediate danger to life. Examples of acquired needs are autonomy, prestige, or recognition from peers (Figure 8.2). We noted in our discussion of personality in Chapter 6 that an individual's psychological makeup is the cumulative effect of his or her past social interactions. Similarly, acquired needs can have a psychological basis, in addition to a social basis—that is, they may be rooted in an individual's cultural and social background in the form of his or her personality and psychographics. For example, you may feel the need to gain the recognition of your peers and feel that a sporty car can satisfy that need. The need for recognition may have psychological motivations—perhaps your personality has developed in a way that makes you sensitive to peer approval—as well as social ones—your friends make fun of the 1987 Chevrolet Caprice you currently drive.

People experience a variety of innate and acquired needs simultaneously. For example, you may be hungry, want to raise your grade-point average this semester, and need clean underwear to wear to a job interview tomorrow. You could satisfy each of these needs in many different ways. To satisfy your hunger, you could

**GET A LITTLE CLOSER WITH NEW ARRID XX® CLEAR ANTI-PERSPIRANT.**

A FRESHER, CLEANER WAY TO FIGHT WETNESS AND ODOR.

CLEAR

CLEAR GEL

SOLID AND GEL

■ FIGURE 8.2

Social acceptance is an acquired need consumers strive to satisfy through the use of certain products, such as antiperspirants and deodorants.

go to Taco Bell and order a seven-layer burrito, buy a Milky Way bar from a vending machine, or go home and make macaroni and cheese for dinner; you could raise your grade-point average by dropping your toughest course, studying harder, or hiring a tutor; and you could have clean underwear for tomorrow by buying new Jockey underwear, taking your laundry to a service, or washing it yourself.

## FACT OR FICTION REVISITED

◉　Every purchase can in fact be influenced by both innate and acquired needs; these concepts are so broad that they can be applied to all behavior.

## ▼ GOALS

As part of the motivation process, consumers identify a goal they think will satisfy their needs. Identifying a goal is not the same as choosing a particular product to satisfy a need, however. A goal is the ideal state that an individual thinks will satisfy a need; a product is a *tool* that provides the benefits consumers will use to achieve their goals.

A person's goals are affected by (1) the individual's background characteristics, (2) the available options and the individual's awareness of them, and (3) efforts on the part of marketers and public policy actors to influence the motivation process. These factors combine to influence a consumer's choice of goals as well as the *valence* a particular goal has for the person. **Valence** is a term used to describe the relationship between a consumer and a goal—some goals are *positive* ones that a consumer *approaches,* such as the appeal of good-tasting foods; others are *negative* goals that a consumer *avoids,* such as foods high in fat and cholesterol.

> **Valence** is a term used to describe the relationship between a consumer and a goal.

### FACT OR FICTION REVISITED

⦿    In most consumer purchases, the product *is not* the goal; rather, the product is merely a tool that provides the benefits that the consumer uses to achieve a goal.

**Background Characteristics**   Innate physiological needs are universal—we all need food and shelter to survive. But the goals individuals choose to satisfy these needs vary widely from person to person and culture to culture. Even a primary physiological need like hunger can have goals that are affected by a culture's values, customs, and rituals. For example, religious laws forbid Hindus to eat beef and Jews to eat pork.

Background characteristics, such as religion and personality, play a role in choosing goals to satisfy acquired needs as well. For example, the Amish do not consider cars to be an acceptable method of transportation; they prefer to ride in horse-drawn buggies to get them where they need to go. An outgoing, extroverted person might drive a sporty coupe, whereas a more conservative, cautious person might elect to drive a four-door sedan for the safety and dependability it offers (Figure 8.3).

**Available Options**   A particular option can be chosen as a goal only if it is available to the individual. If a consumer knows that certain options are not available, however, or if the consumer is *unaware* of the availability of certain options, they cannot select them as goals for satisfying their needs. For example, you would not make a warm-weather vacation your goal as a break from school if you know that you just don't have the money to pay for it. Similarly, if you want to raise your grade-point average, you won't think of looking for a tutor to help you if you are unaware that your school has a tutoring program.

**B**rewing beer has been a topic of conversation around my family's house since I can remember.

**SO BELIEVE ME,**

I know you might think about

*drinking before you're 21.* But do us AND **YOURSELF** A favor, *please don't.*

We'll wait for your business.

Pete Coors, Coors Brewing Company

For more information on Coors Alcohol Programs and Policies, call 1-800-328-6785.

■  FIGURE 8.3

Coors appeals to consumers who like to drink beer to do so in a responsible manner.

**Marketers and Public Policy Actors**  Marketers and public policy actors like to be able to influence a consumer's choice of goals. In the case of new products, marketers attempt to increase consumers' awareness of the availability of a certain product that offers a benefit that was previously unavailable. For example, pharmaceutical marketers often need to make consumers aware of new ideal states that are now attainable. For example, Upjohn (Figure 8.4) advertises Rogaine to people who are concerned about hair loss so that they know that there is now a treatment available for a previously incurable condition. Similarly, marketers of high-technology products and services advertise new advances in tech-

### Is thinning hair making every day a bad hair day?

Did you know that 20 million normal, healthy women start each morning the same way you do? Dealing with thinning hair.

In part, that's because female hair loss is *perfectly natural* and can be inherited from either side of the family. Fortunately, it's possible to regrow your hair with *Rogaine*® Topical Solution (minoxidil topical solution 2%).

You see, hair grows and rests in cycles. And while the exact mechanism by which minoxidil works to stimulate hair regrowth is unknown, many scientists believe that the prescription medication *Rogaine* works, in part, by prolonging the growth cycle of hair. With more hair growing longer and thicker at the same time, you may see improved scalp coverage. And that may mean more hair to work with. More styling options. More flexibility.

**When hair loss is at the root of the problem, no cosmetic solution will do. Fortunately, *Rogaine* has been proven to regrow hair.**

#### Will *Rogaine* work for you?

In 8-month clinical tests conducted by dermatologists, 59% of the women using *Rogaine* reported hair regrowth (40% had minimal regrowth and 19% had moderate regrowth). Those using a placebo (a similar solution without the active ingredient in *Rogaine*) reported 33% minimal regrowth and 7% moderate regrowth. No regrowth was reported by 60% of the group using a placebo and 41% of the group using *Rogaine*.

*Rogaine* should only be applied to a normal, healthy scalp (not sunburned or irritated). *Side effects:* About 7% of those who used *Rogaine* had

■ FIGURE 8.4
Upjohn advertises Rogaine to men and women who are concerned about hair loss or thinning hair to let them know that there is now a treatment for a previously incurable condition.

231

> **Primary demand** occurs when any product in a category can provide the benefits to satisfy a need; **selective demand** identifies a specific brand to satisfy a need.

nology to consumers. Telecommunications companies, like Nynex, promote caller identification, repeat dialing, and voice messaging as features consumers can use to enhance their daily communication.

Marketers may also try to influence consumers to purchase existing products by increasing their awareness of a product category. Consumers select products in two ways—**primary demand,** whereby consumers select a generic product category, such as milk or cheese, and **selective demand,** whereby consumers choose a particular brand from that product category, such as Borden or Kraft. Some advertising attempts to influence primary demand by making consumers aware that a product category would be an appropriate goal to choose to satisfy a need. Many commodities are advertised in this way. Examples include the beef and pork industries, which try to let consumers know that their products can satisfy both hunger and health concerns (Figure 8.5).

## ▼ CONFLICTING GOALS

A person's many needs and associated goals may conflict with one another at times. One simple example involves hunger and a healthy lifestyle. To satisfy hunger, a consumer's goal might be something filling and good tasting. To satisfy health needs, the goal might be to avoid sweet and high-fat foods. Unfortunately, these two goals are in conflict because good-tasting food is often sweet and high in fat.

Several types of conflicts are possible when it comes to choosing products to satisfy a person's many needs. The most common types are (1) approach–approach, (2) approach–avoidance, and (3) avoidance–avoidance, as illustrated in Figure 8.6.[1]

> An **approach–approach conflict** involves two needs, each of which motivates an attractive goal, that cannot be satisfied at the same time.

**Approach–Approach Conflicts**   When a person is presented with two needs, each of which motivates an attractive goal that cannot be satisfied at the same time, the conflict is referred to as an **approach–approach conflict.** For example, you may want to go on a vacation to Aruba during winter break and also buy a new suit for your job interviews. If you cannot afford to do both, you will have to resolve the conflict by pursuing one goal over the other. Because both goals are attractive, you will have to decide which need is more relevant and choose the goal that satisfies that need.

Marketers attempt to influence purchase behavior by increasing the salience of one conflicting goal over another. In this way, the consumer is motivated to seek products that will achieve one goal while ignoring products intended to realize another. For example, resort locations may advertise heavily in college newspapers during the month of September in order to reach students before they begin to think seriously about buying clothes for job interviews. Similarly, salespeople and in-store promotions that encourage consumers to make a purchase quickly attempt to increase the relevance of one goal while discounting others. For example, a salesperson at Ann Taylor may warn a shopper that the suit she is considering is due to increase in price next week to encourage her to buy it now.

Try stir-frying pork strips with some sesame oil and julienne veggies for an oriental-style dish.

# AFTER CHOPS AND ROASTS

**Peachy Pork Picante**
Cut one pound cubed boneless **pork loin** with **taco seasoning**; brown in a little **oil** in a skillet. Add an 8-ounce jar of **salsa** and 4 tablespoons **peach preserves** to skillet; stir to mix well, cover and lower heat. Simmer gently for 15 minutes. Preparation Time 25 minutes. Serves four.

Nutrient Information: Approximately, per Serving: Calories 263, Protein 24 gm., Fat 9 gm., Sodium 762 mg., Cholesterol 70 mg.

Nutrient analysis done by The Food Processor II Diet Analysis Software. Pork data from USDA Handbook 8-10 (1991).

*Pork is more than you remember.*
Cut up some boneless pork loin, and the options are endless. Slice strips for stir-fry or fajitas, cut cubes for kabobs or a quick stew. Go wild with fruits, vegetables, sauces and condiments. Pork will go as far as your imagination. *Boneless pork—chops, strips, cubes—absorbs flavor or a marinade in just 30 minutes.*

## TASTE WHAT'S NEXT™

pork®.The Other White Meat®

*Pork and fruit are a natural pair. Try simmering cutlets in your favorite jam, mixed with a little vinegar or water.*
For recipes, send a self-addressed, stamped, business-size envelope to: Recipes-Ad, Box 10383, Des Moines, IA 50306.

America's Pork Producers © 1996 National Pork Producers Council in cooperation with the National Pork Board.

**■ FIGURE 8.5**
The pork industry attempts to educate consumers about the good taste and nutrition of its products so that they will elect to eat pork to satisfy their needs for hunger and good health.

**Approach–Avoidance Conflicts**  When a person is presented with a goal that will meet one of his or her needs but prevent the satisfaction of another, the conflict is referred to as an **approach–avoidance conflict.** Approach–avoidance conflicts are typical of products that have both positive and negative characteristics. For example, Kate Borden faced an approach–avoidance conflict for years when she wanted to buy a Honda but also wanted to avoid foreign-made cars. Another example involves financing a car. Say you want to buy a car to meet your transportation needs, but the cost of the down payment and the monthly

> An **approach–avoidance conflict** involves a goal that will meet one need but prevent the satisfaction of another.

■  FIGURE 8.6
Approach–approach,
approach–avoidance,
and avoidance–avoidance
conflicts.

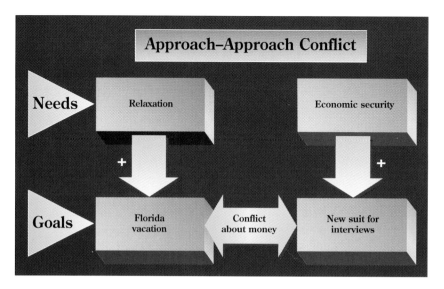

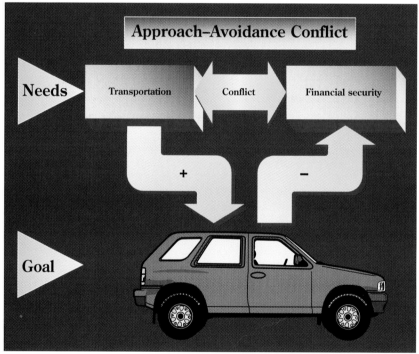

An **avoidance–avoid-
ance conflict** occurs
when an individual
must choose between
two unattractive goals,
which will satisfy a
need.

payments prevent from you achieving your financial goals. To help you resolve
this conflict, many car companies offer leasing options that allow you to forgo
ownership and reduce your costs.

**Avoidance–Avoidance Conflicts**   When a person is faced with two goals, each
of which he or she wants to avoid, the conflict is referred to as an
**avoidance–avoidance conflict.** In this case, the individual is forced to choose
between two unattractive activities—the "lesser of two evils." For example, when

■ FIGURE 8.6 (continued)

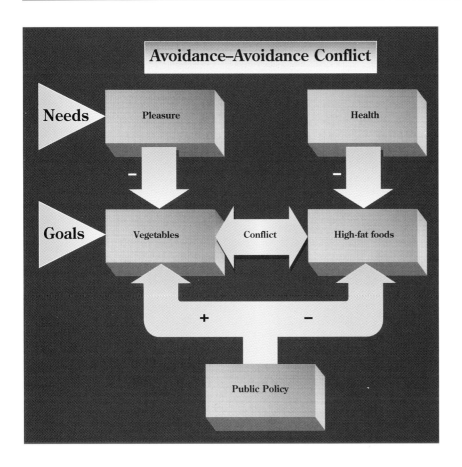

you are sick you may have to choose between waiting for help at the Student Health Service or paying for an appointment with your family doctor. The reason people consider choosing between two products they want to avoid is because doing so will satisfy another need.[2] In this case, you need to turn to either the Student Health Center or your family doctor to help you feel better.

Many avoidance–avoidance conflicts involve public policy issues. Public policy actors want consumers to avoid certain purchases; accordingly, they try to influence consumers to adopt a new goal that will be in conflict with the ones they already have. Many of these efforts target unhealthy, compulsive, or addictive behavior. For example, people tend to eat foods high in fat because they taste good and to avoid healthy vegetables because they don't. Public policy actors cannot affect the need for good-tasting food, so they use advertising or enlist doctors to counsel their patients about the negative aspects of fatty foods in order to create an avoidance–avoidance conflict with healthy foods. By doing so, both alternatives—high-fat foods and healthy foods—become unattractive, encouraging consumers to choose the *least* unattractive of the two, as illustrated in Figure 8.7.

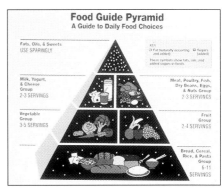

■ FIGURE 8.7

The USDA encourages consumers to eat healthily and emphasizes the need to avoid the negative aspects of foods high in fat and cholesterol, even though some may perceive healthy foods as poor tasting. This disparity is an example of an avoidance–avoidance conflict.

# APPROACHES TO CONSUMER MOTIVATION

A number of popular approaches to consumer motivation underlie our discussion of needs and goals. Some researchers have tried to understand motivation by developing lists of needs and using them to classify individuals into distinct categories. We considered several of these approaches when we discussed ways of segmenting consumers in Chapter 3. Others have considered values when analyzing a person's motivations. The list of values approach (LOV) we discussed in Chapter 4, for example, assumes that cultural values are significant determinants of consumer motivations. Still others focus on an individual's personality to explain motivation. Freud's theory of personality development, reviewed in Chapter 6, describes three personality systems, each of which emphasizes different types of needs and generates different consumer motivations. According to Freudian theory, id-based needs would be considered innate, and ego and superego needs are acquired. Another personality theory that can be used to analyze motivation is Henry Murray's list of acquired needs, such as affiliation, deference, and exhibition, that form the basis of the Edwards Personality Preference Test (EPPS).[3]

We will now introduce several other approaches that offer insights into consumer motivations. The first is a theoretical explication of motivation—Abraham Maslow's hierarchy of human needs. The others are empirical approaches researchers have used to identify the benefits consumers seek to satisfy their needs: (1) *motivational research,* which is rooted in Freudian personality theory and (2) *means–ends chains,* which examine values to understand consumer needs. These empirical approaches will be discussed in the next section on consumer benefits.

### ▼ MASLOW'S HIERARCHY OF NEEDS

One of the most popular theories of consumer motivation is Abraham Maslow's **hierarchy of needs.**[4] Maslow theorized five ordered levels of human needs: (1) physiological, (2) safety, (3) social, (4) ego, and (5) self-actualization (see Figure 8.8). The first two levels—all physiological needs and some safety needs—are innate; the higher level needs—social, ego, and self-actualization—are acquired. According to Maslow, the levels are hierarchical; that is, an individual will seek to satisfy lower order needs before he or she will recognize needs at a higher level. Therefore, individuals will not recognize social needs until they have satisfied their physiological and safety needs. This revelation is important for marketers as well. Yamaha, for example, must first convince consumers that its motorcycles are safe before it can appeal to their ego needs.

> **Maslow's hierarchy of needs** maintains that a person will satisfy lower order needs before attempting to satisfy higher order ones.

**Weaknesses of Maslow's Hierarchy**   Unfortunately, much of our discussion of needs and goals contradicts Maslow's notion of a hierarchy. Recall that we stated that consumers have many needs and goals and often act to satisfy them simultaneously. At any given moment, a consumer may be working to satisfy many needs and will not consider the relative levels of those needs. A person may be

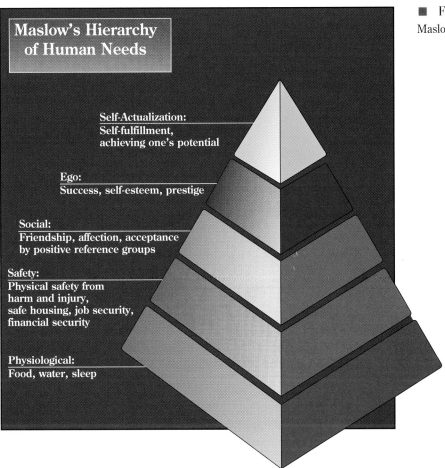

hungry, for example, but will choose to sit and talk with a friend for several hours first to satisfy social needs. That person may even satisfy both needs at the same time by sharing a meal with his or her friend. Furthermore, some products satisfy several needs that represent different levels of Maslow's hierarchy. Kate bought a Honda to satisfy her needs for comfort, affordability, and loyalty to American car makers. Another consumer might buy a Yamaha motorcycle to satisfy his or her ego needs even though it doesn't have certain safety features.

Maslow's theory also fails to acknowledge the strong influence of psychological and social factors on the goals people choose to satisfy their physiological needs. Religious dietary laws are a primary example. Observant Hindus and Jews elect to satisfy their self-actualization needs before their physiological needs.

Another important issue Maslow fails to address is whether the same needs exist in all cultures or even for all individuals in one culture. We must recognize that culture affects the motivation process; accordingly, we should expect the hierarchy of needs to vary as well. Individual differences in psychological makeup and choice of reference groups point to individual differences in needs. The dark side of consumer behavior, in particular, illustrates several important instances of individual variations in the hierarchy of needs. Some people skimp on food and other basic needs in order to meet social and ego needs—anorexics satisfy ego needs over physiological ones. Others smoke cigarettes or engage in unsafe sexual practices to satisfy physiological needs over safety needs (Figure 8.9).

## FACT OR FICTION REVISITED

⦿   Most purchases do in fact satisfy needs at several different levels of Maslow's hierarchy, often simultaneously.

■   FIGURE 8.9
This ad encouraging the use of LifeStyles condoms to help prevent the spread of AIDS is one attempt to appeal to individuals who emphasize physiological needs over safety needs.

# IDENTIFYING CONSUMER BENEFITS

The marketing concept asserts that products and services should satisfy consumer needs; that is, they should produce *benefits*—the outcome consumers obtain from their use of a product or service. Consumer researchers, in turn, attempt to identify the benefits consumers want to obtain so as to achieve their goals and satisfy their needs. For example, if your goal is clean clothes, you would search for a laundry detergent that offers the benefit of dirt removal; if your goal is soft clothes, you would look for a detergent that offers the benefit of a fabric softener.

Researchers have developed two popular empirical approaches to identify the benefits consumers seek. Used together, these approaches provide an effective array of tools for understanding how consumers use the motivation process to select the benefits they seek from a product purchase.

## ▼ MOTIVATIONAL RESEARCH

During the 1950s and 1960s **motivational research** was a prominent approach used to measure consumer needs and goals. Although its use as a formal method has waned in recent years, it still influences much of the research conducted by marketers and advertisers on consumer motivation.[5] As we mentioned in Chapter 6, motivational research was popularized by Ernest Dichter, a psychoanalyst who applied the insights of Freudian theory to consumer behavior. The basic assumption of motivational research is that the personality systems and conflict-resolution mechanisms Freud identified unconsciously motivate much of people's consumer behavior. Accordingly, Dichter maintained, by understanding a consumer's personality, researchers can discover his or her unconscious motivations for buying specific products. Table 8.1 shows some examples of Dichter's work, including products, their nominal, or stated, benefits, and the underlying, subconscious benefits they offer the consumer that uses them.

> **Motivational research** investigates the effects of personality systems and conflict-resolution mechanisms on a consumer's unconscious motivations for buying certain products.

### Table 8.1

**EXAMPLE OF NEEDS AND PRODUCTS IDENTIFIED BY DICHTER**

| Product | Nominal benefit | Unconscious benefit |
|---|---|---|
| Food wraps | Protect food | Concern for the family |
| Power tools | Home repairs | Show of skill and omnipotence |
| Ice cream | Nutrition, taste | Love and affection linked to childhood memories |
| Hats | Protection, warmth | Self-expression and individuality |
| Deodorant | Eliminates odor and wetness | Self-esteem and social benefits |

Source: Ernest Dichter, *Handbook of Consumer Motivations: The Psychology of the World of Objects,* New York: McGraw-Hill, 1964.

Motivational researchers primarily utilize qualitative techniques to explore motivation rather than quantitative methods.[6] The most common techniques are nondirective depth interviews with consumers and disguised projective tasks. These methods assume that purchase motivations are the cumulative result of a complicated long-term personality development process; such a complicated process, in turn, requires substantial effort to understand.

**Depth interviews,** as the name implies, are interviews that probe deeply into a person's psychological makeup to uncover the particular aspects of personality the person activates when buying a product. A trained analyst can then interpret the needs and motivations that drive that purchase. **Projective techniques** are disguised tasks that allow the analyst a glimpse past the individual's psychological defenses into the motivation process itself. The analyst may ask the subject to tell stories or draw pictures about an object, or may present ambiguous cues, such as inkblots, cartoons, or incomplete sentences, and interpret the subject's responses. Because the cues are ambiguous, the responses are taken to be a projection of the subject's motivation and not of the test itself. For example, the marketers of Combat roach killer found that their product, which consists of enclosed trays of poison, were not selling to some female consumers because the women wanted the action of spraying the roaches directly; as it turned out, the women were identifying the roaches with men they didn't like (see Figure 8.10).[7]

**Pros and Cons of Motivational Research** Motivational research has met with a certain amount of criticism for the assumptions it makes and the way it is conducted. Although many of the products consumers buy may have psychological significance to them, sometimes people buy a product simply because of the obvious function it performs for them. The criticism, therefore, is that motivational researchers tend to assign very sophisticated motivations to some very mundane purchases. For example, you might use a Craftsman power drill because it helps you get a tough chore done quickly and easily, not because it symbolizes the sexual prowess and potency you desire.

The methodology employed in motivational research has also come under fire because it relies on the subjective interpretations of the individual analyst. Many consumer researchers are uncomfortable with insights that rely on the idiosyncratic skill of a particular analyst. Instead, they prefer an objective tool that all researchers can understand and apply. Critics of the technique also object to the use of a small number of respondents who are assumed to be representative of an entire target market segment.

On the other hand, the insights that come from talking to consumers about their underlying motivations for buying a product can indeed be very powerful. Psychological and social factors can have a significant impact on a person's needs and goals, and researchers will have a better understanding of consumer behavior if they consider those factors. Motivational research plays an important role in the way many researchers analyze consumer motivations. That role, however, is clearly an exploratory part of the analysis process. That is, an in-depth analysis of psychological motivationsis just the first step in gaining a complete understanding of motivation. In the second step, researchers use the insights they have

**Depth interviews** probe deeply into an individual's psychological makeup to explain the needs that motivate a purchase.

**Projective techniques** allow a glimpse into an individual's psychological defenses and into the motivation process.

**The Mind of a Roach Killer**

The McCann-Ericson Ad Agency asked women to draw and describe how they felt about roaches. The agency concluded from the drawings that the women identified the roaches with men who had abandoned them and thus enjoyed watching the roaches/men squirm and die. That's why the agency figured, that women prefer spray roach killers to products that don't allow the user to see the roach die.

"I TIPTOED quietly into the kitchen. Perhaps he wasn't around. I stretched my arm up to the light. I hoped I'd be alone when the light went on. Perhaps he is running on the table, I thought. You think that's impossible! Nothing is impossible with that guy. He might not even be alone. He'll run when the light goes on, I thought. But what's worse is for him to

"ONE NIGHT I just couldn't take the horror of these bugs sneaking around in the dark. They are always crawling when you can't see them. I had to do something. I thought, 'Wouldn't it be wonderful if when I switched on the light, the roaches would shrink up and die like vampires to sunlight?' So I did, but they just all scattered.

"A MAN LIKES a free meal you cook for him as long as there is food he will stay."

■ FIGURE 8.10

An example of a projective technique.

gleaned from depth interviews and projective techniques as the basis for further quantitative research. We will discuss one of these quantitative approaches later in the chapter.

## FACT OR FICTION REVISITED

⦿ It is not true that motivational research leaves little room for interpretation by the research analyst. In fact, one of the major criticisms of motivational research is that it leaves *too much* room for interpretation by the research analyst.

## ▼ MEANS–END CHAINS AND LADDERING

A number of consumer researchers maintain that values are the key to understanding a person's motivation processes. As we discussed in the beginning of the chapter, cultural values—both the current social environment and their cumulative effect—have a significant influence on the choice of needs and goals a person faces. In keeping with this contention, *means–end chains* provide a model for the way consumers organize their knowledge about products.[8]

The name **means–end chain** reflects the assumption that a product is a person's means to achieve a desired end goal. According to the model, a consumer organizes his or her knowledge of products by classifying them according to the goals and values they help the consumer achieve. That is, the consumer uses a product's attributes, or characteristics, as an indicator of the benefits it will offer; these benefits, in turn, are a consequence of the consumer's use of the product and provide the means by which the consumer achieves his or her goals and values.

The means–end model suggests a clear method to help marketers explore consumer motivation: Begin with a product's attributes, explore what benefits the consumer will get from those attributes, and then identify the goals and values the consumer achieves by using the product. This process involves **laddering,** an in-depth interviewing technique that elicits the chain of associations among a product's attributes, the benefits that are a consequence of using the product, and the valued goals that are achieved. In laddering, a subject is first asked to list the attributes of a product; a chain of associations is then elicited through a series of "why" questions relating to the product's (1) concrete attributes, (2) abstract attributes, (3) functional consequences, (4) psychosocial consequences, (5) instrumental values, and (6) terminal values. Figure 8.11 shows a sample chain of associations for a sports car.

**Pros and Cons of Means–End Chains and Laddering**   Means–end chains and laddering can offer the same kinds of insights as motivational research. Although laddering has a very different theoretical basis, it can provide a comprehensive understanding of the underlying motivation for buying a product. It can

> A **means–end chain** assumes that a product means to achieve a desired goal.

> **Laddering** elicits a chain of associations among a product's attributes, benefits, achieved.

**■ FIGURE 8.11**
A sample chain of associations for a sports car.

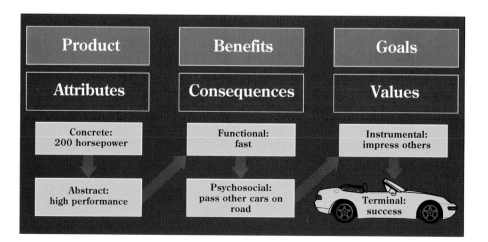

242

also provide useful input for further quantitative research on the benefits that motivate consumers. One advantage of laddering over motivational research is its methodology. The exploratory methods laddering entails can be used more easily by the many researchers who don't have psychoanalytic training. At the same time, however, laddering also requires in-depth interviews that are time consuming and limit its large-scale application.

## ▼ CONSUMER BENEFITS AND MARKETING

If marketers are able to identify the benefits consumers seek from products, they will be able to understand their underlying needs and goals. Indeed, some researchers feel that consumers view a product as a bundle of benefits.[9] This focus on benefits increases the marketer's understanding of consumer motivation and enables the marketer to apply that knowledge to segment markets, position products, and design an appropriate marketing mix. Americans, in general, belong to clubs and organizations that offer many benefits, as we discuss in the following Pleasures of Consumption box.

### PLEASURES OF CONSUMPTION

**Americans Love to Join**[10]

Americans love to join associations—from such clubs and organizations as the American Association of Aardvark Aficionados, the Delta Sigma Pi fraternity, the Jim Smith Society, the National Organization of Mall Walkers, the Sierra Club, and Smithsonian associates to countless local community-based bridge clubs, neighborhood associations, and sports clubs. The *Encyclopedia of Associations* lists over 22,000 national associations and reports that approximately 70 percent of all Americans belong to one organization and that 25 percent belong to four or more.

Clubs and organizations offer a variety of benefits to satisfy many different types of needs held by their members. Students of such associations classify the benefits into three kinds. *Normative benefits* are feelings of satisfaction that come from "doing the right thing," such as the gratification Sierra Club members feel when their association lobbies for government action that preserves the environment. *Affective benefits* are feelings that come from social interaction with other members. For example, many of the 1,700 Jim Smiths who belong to the Jim Smith Society meet annually for a three-day conference, and the National Organization of Mall Walkers offers partners to those who want to walk indoors to get their exercise. *Utilitarian benefits* are the goods and services members receive from an association, such as the *Smithsonian* magazine and accompanying merchandise discounts that Smithsonian associate members receive.

The men and women who manage such associations, many of whom belong to the American Society of Association Executives, must continually strive to understand the benefits their clubs must offer to satisfy members' needs. For example, social action organizations such as the Sierra Club ideally would like people to join simply because of the association's good works, but many consumers also (or only) want the magazines and merchandise that are additional benefits of membership. As many social action organization managers know, normative benefits must often be supplemented by affective and utilitarian ones.

Do you belong to any associations? Why did you join them? What benefits do you think are the most important motivation for Americans to join associations? Do you think it is fair and equitable for social action association managers to offer affective and utilitarian benefits to attract members?

Research into consumer motivation typically involves two major steps. The first is an in-depth analysis of consumer needs, goals, and desired benefits in the particular product area. The objective of this step is to understand the motivation process and to identify the benefits consumers seek from certain products. In order to gain this understanding, marketers explore the physiological, psychological, and social needs of consumers. They also investigate consumer goals in order to develop a comprehensive understanding of the benefits consumers seek to achieve those goals. This first step often involves detailed analysis of a limited number of individual consumers through intensive, qualitative research techniques. From this in-depth analysis, marketers are able to gain insights into the range of product benefits that are important to consumers. For example, a car manufacturer would like to know which benefits consumers seek from their cars. Whereas transportation is one obvious benefit, some buyers may also use their cars to make a statement about their lifestyle to the members of their reference groups.

The second step in understanding consumer motivation involves a broad-scale analysis of a large number of consumers. At this stage, marketers typically employ an efficient survey instrument to gather quantitative measurements of background characteristics and behavioral processes. Many such surveys ask consumers to answer questions about the benefits they seek from certain product categories. For example, consumers might be asked to rate the importance of a variety of a car's attributes. This step is usually less intensive than the in-depth analysis of motivation that preceded it, but it provides sufficient information about the benefits different consumers seek to allow marketers to identify target market segments that seek the same benefit from a product category. The marketer can then make the positioning and product mix decisions necessary to deliver the product to the consumers in each segment. For example, one group of consumers might want an Eagle Talon for the throaty roar and fast acceleration it offers to dazzle their friends, while another group might prefer the resounding "thunk" and luxurious interior of a Chrysler Concorde to impress their neighbors.

# MOTIVATION AND LEVELS OF INVOLVEMENT IN DECISION MAKING

Given the numerous product areas and buying decisions presented to consumers at any given time, just how do people decide which purchase processes will get their attention and which will not? For example, at this stage in your life, as a college student, you may find car insurance to be very important to you, but you may not care at all about life insurance. In contrast, your older brother, with two kids of his own, may find life insurance very important (Figure 8.12).

As we first mentioned in Chapter 2, consumer researchers use the term *involvement* to describe the importance or relevance a particular purchase has for a

■ FIGURE 8.12
A high involvement product, such as mutual funds, will be more important to consumers at certain stages of their lives than to others. This ad for Dreyfus is targeted at parents who wish to save for their children's college education.

consumer. The level of involvement in any purchase is influenced by the individual's background characteristics and needs. Cultural values and demographic subcultures make some needs more important to one person than to another, just as life insurance is more important to new parents than to college students. Similarly, an individual's personality, lifestyle, and psychographics will affect the relevance of certain needs and goals. For example, choosing a laundry detergent may be more involved for citizen environmentalists than for nonenvironmentalists because the former are concerned about chemical runoff from sewage and septic systems.

In turn, the involvement level generated by need has a significant impact on the way a person uses the other behavioral processes to complete the purchase steps. For a high involvement need, such as life insurance, people are generally more willing to exert more effort in searching for and evaluating alternatives before making a purchase. In doing so, subtle differences between products are likely to be perceived and considered—that is, a consumer is willing to spend a lot of mental effort to decide among alternatives and consider all of the options in detail. In contrast, when addressing a low involvement need, such as paper towels, a person may not engage in the process of searching out and evaluating alternatives at all, but will just buy whatever is available or least expensive or pick a favorite product and just keep buying that brand without any additional thought. We discuss the differences between high and low involvement decisions in greater detail in Chapter 13.

## FACT OR FICTION REVISITED

◉ Consumers do in fact exert more effort when making high involvement decisions than when making low involvement decisions.

# DO MARKETERS CREATE NEEDS?

Marketers are often criticized for creating needs—they are accused of developing products consumers don't really need and would not buy if it were not for the advertising that convinced them they needed the product.[11] Such criticism assumes that marketing and advertising have created a "consumer culture" that praises consumption and defines a person's identity by the things he or she consumes. The underlying assumption of this reproach is that marketers are able to manipulate consumers into believing that they need products they really don't. This argument maintains, for example, that any old pair of pants or skirt will keep consumers warm and clothed, but advertising encourages consumers to buy expensive Ralph Lauren fashions.

If the motivation process works the way we have described thoughout this chapter—that is, if consumers recognize needs and seek products that will provide the benefits they need to achieve their goals—it is doubtful, to say the least, that marketers can create needs. Although marketers do try to influence a person's choice of goals, a goal will not motivate someone to buy a product in the first place unless he or she believes that it will satisfy a need. Ads do "create" goals in the sense that they increase a consumer's awareness of the availability of certain products and demonstrate the goals the products will help the person achieve, but advertising itself cannot create a need without the consumer's cooperation in the motivation process and without a recognition on the part of the consumer that the goal is something he or she desires (Figure 8.13). For example,

**■ FIGURE 8.13**
Given the complexity of the motivation process, marketers maintain that it is quite unlikely that they can create needs for products for which consumers have no use.

247

the use of picture-perfect models in advertising does not create the need for dieting or exercise; rather it provides a "look" that serves as a goal to which some individuals aspire. The impact of advertising in encouraging consumers, particularly females, to diet compulsively is the subject of often heated debates, as we discuss in the following Public Policy box.

 PUBLIC POLICY

**Does Kate Moss Cause Anorexia?**[12]

The picture-perfect models we see portrayed in advertisements for everything from underwear to credit cards do not represent the typical American. Some advertisements are targeted at particular market segments, such as twenty-something females belonging to Generation X, and depict actors or models who are similar to the target market. Many show popular fashion models and entertainers consumers recognize and find appealing—supermodel Kate Moss advertises Calvin Klein's Obsession, while Kristin McMenamy promotes Diet Sprite. These ads reflect the popular "waif look" in fashion—young, thin models who do not in fact resemble the typical American woman. We all need to feel attractive, and American society has come to define attractive as trim and young. Fashion designers, in turn, portray such models in their advertising because they represent a mythical version of American beauty.

"Waif" advertisements have caused a great controversy, however. Many Americans feel that they need to lose weight in order to be attractive and successful and turn to a wide variety of methods of dieting. Some simply watch what they eat, some eat Healthy Choice or other special low-fat products, others join diet programs such as Weight Watchers or Jenny Craig. Medical authorities are concerned about those who take more extreme measures—individuals, mostly young women, suffering from eating disorders, such as anorexia and bulimia, who virtually starve themselves. A social action organization called Boycott Anorexic Marketing (BAM) has roundly attacked Calvin Klein and Coca-Cola, the maker of Sprite for using Kate Moss and Kristin McMenamy to glorify the goal of "ultrathinness," encouraging starvation diets and eating disorders in young women who strive to be like them. Many social scientists and medical experts who study anorexia and bulimia, however, believe that the disorders result from a *combination* of personality and social development issues that occur in an environment that values fitness and beauty—that is, personality and child and teenage experiences interact to cause an individual to focus obsessively on the shape of her own body.

Do American values create a beauty myth that prizes thinness? Is that myth shared by all demographic subcultures and lifestyles? Do you think that advertising helps support a beauty myth? Do you think marketers should be held responsible for causing eating disorders?

The **mirror controversy** argues that advertising is a mirror that reflects the products and lifestyles consumers want to see.

▼ **THE MIRROR CONTROVERSY**

The debate over the role of advertising in creating needs has been termed the **mirror controversy,** a phrase that refers to the metaphor defenders of advertising use to describe the way it works.[13] Proponents of advertising maintain that advertising is simply a mirror that reflects the products and lifestyles consumers want to see. This metaphor is consistent with the ideal of the marketing concept—marketers want to satisfy consumers' needs by developing marketing strategies and product positionings they will find attractive. In fact, several aspects of the marketing process support the notion that marketers and advertisers try to reflect consumer needs rather than create them.

❶ Marketers invest tremendous effort and resources in marketing research to investigate consumer needs and understand the dynamics of consumer behavior.
❷ As much effort as it takes to uncover consumer needs, it is still easier to satisfy existing consumer needs than to create new ones and then satisfy them.
❸ Advertising is a competitive environment replete with many marketers trying to market to the same consumers and public policy actors monitoring their efforts. Although this checks-and-balance system does not eliminate the potential for creating needs, it does provide a countervailing force that would expose such efforts.

# MOTIVATION

Like any consumer, Kate Borden has many needs; also like any other consumer, motivation is the behavioral process she uses to recognize those needs, to choose suitable goals, and to launch the purchase process that will provide her with the products that satisfy her needs. Kate has both innate needs, such as hunger and thirst, that she satisfies on a daily basis with the products she buys at the grocery store, and acquired needs that reflect her social situation, such as the need to provide a home her grandchildren will be comfortable visiting and a car both she and her husband will be comfortable driving. Sometimes Kate's needs conflict, as when she wants an effective laundry detergent but avoids any that contain perfumes, dyes, softeners, and other additives, or when she wants to be a good citizen and recycle but doesn't because of the inconvenience of carrying the recyclables back to the store.

Motivation is the starting point for all consumer behavior. It is also a very complex process. All of the products consumers like Kate buy begin with the recognition of a need and a choice of goals to satisfy that need. On the way to satisfying the need, there may be conflicts, and there will certainly be attempts on the part of marketers and public policy actors to influence the consumer's choice of goals. To influence the motivation process effectively, however, marketers must understand the underlying needs of consumers; techniques such as motivational research and means–end laddering analysis can help provide some insights. We now continue our presentation of the behavioral processes with a discussion of the way consumers *perceive* available products.

# SUMMARY

1. **Describe the motivation process of consumers.** Motivation—the starting point for all consumer behavior—is the process by which individuals recognize a need and begin to take action to satisfy it. A need, in turn, is the discrepancy between an individual's current state and a goal—the ideal state he or she desires. Both a need and a goal are necessary to motivate individuals to take action. Identifying a goal is not the same as choosing a particular product to satisfy a need. A product is not a goal; instead, it is a tool that provides the benefits consumers will use to achieve their goal.

2. **Identify the needs that motivate consumers to begin the consumer purchase process and the benefits they seek from the process.** We can divide needs into two broad types: (1) innate and (2) acquired. Innate needs, also called *primary* or *biogenic* needs, are the biological or physiological needs a person must satisfy in order to stay alive. Hunger, thirst, shelter, warmth, and sex are examples of innate needs. Acquired needs are the social and psychological needs that arise from a person's psychological state and social interactions with others. Autonomy, prestige, and recognition from peers are examples of acquired needs, which are also called *secondary* or *psychogenic* needs because they can remain unsatisfied with no immediate danger to life.

3. **Identify the influences on a consumer's goals.** The choice and valence of goals will be affected by (1) a consumer's background characteristics, (2) the options available to the consumer and his or her awareness of them, and (3) efforts on the part of marketers and public policy actors to influence the motivation process.

4. **Recognize several common approaches used to understand the benefits sought by consumers.** Maslow's hierarchy of human needs is a theoretical approach that maintains that consumers organize their needs into levels and aim to satisfy physiological, safety, social, ego, and self-actualization needs, in that order. Motivational research and means–ends laddering analysis are empirical approaches researchers have used to identify the benefits a consumer seeks to satisfy his or her needs. Motivational research tries to understand the unconscious motivations that are driven by a consumer's personality, whereas laddering research attempts to uncover the means–end chains that link a consumer's values with his or her needs.

5. **Appreciate the debate about whether marketers and advertisers create consumer needs or reflect the needs that consumers already recognize.** Critics of advertising claim that marketers try to create needs in consumers; marketers defend themselves by maintaining that their advertising reflects the needs consumers have already recognized. Given our discussion of the motivation process, it is very unlikely that marketers can create needs; instead, they try to understand consumers' needs and create and market products that will offer the benefits consumers seek. When consumers are exposed to advertising for products that offer such benefits, they will adopt the products as goals for needs they have already recognized.

# KEY TERMS

Motivation, *p. 227*

Need, *p. 227*

Goal, *p. 227*

Innate needs, *p. 228*

Acquired needs, *p. 228*

Valence, *p. 230*

Primary demand, *p. 232*

Selective demand, *p. 232*

Approach–approach conflict, *p. 232*

Approach–avoidance conflict, *p. 233*

Avoidance–avoidance
   Conflict, *p. 234*
Hierarchy of needs, *p. 236*
Motivational research,
   *p. 239*

Depth interview, *p. 240*
Projective technique,
   *p. 240*

Means–end chain, *p. 242*
Laddering, *p. 242*
Mirror controversy, *p. 248*

# SKILL-BUILDING ACTIVITIES

1. Purchase a copy of *Time* and a copy of *Ladies' Home Journal.* Select the five most interesting (to you) advertisements from each. For each advertisement, identify the:
   a. need(s) the advertisement appeals to
   b. goal(s) the advertised product or service can satisfy
   c. benefit(s) that will help the purchaser achieve that goal(s).

2. In activity 1, you selected 10 advertisements you found interesting. How do these ads differ from those you did not select in:
   a. needs appealed to
   b. goals satisfied
   c. benefits offered

3. Describe your most recent purchase of a product or service. What was the goal of that purchase? How was the choice of *goal* (not the choice of the product or service) influenced by:
   a. available options
   b. awareness of available options
   c. personal tastes
   d. social environment
   e. cultural values
   f. efforts to influence your motives
   Now answer the same questions for the choice of the product or service.

4. Of the 10 advertisements you selected in activity 1, which are intended to influence primary demand and which are intended to influence selective demand? How do these two sets of ads differ?

5. In the purchase described in activity 3, identify any potential
   a. approach–approach conflict
   b. approach–avoidance conflict
   c. avoidance–voidance conflict

6. Which of the 10 advertisements selected in activity 1 raise public policy issues based on avoidance–avoidance conflict? For each advertisement, briefly describe the issue raised.

7. How would a motivational research analyst go about studying the purchase described in activity 3? What are the assets of this approach to understanding consumer behavior? What are its liabilities? Now develop a means–end chain for the same purchase.

8. Was the purchase described in activity 3 a higher involvement purchase or a low involvement purchase? If the level of involvement had been low instead of high or high instead of low, how would the means–end chain have changed?

9. Choose the most interesting of the 10 advertisements you selected in activity 1. Does this ad mirror consumers' perceptions of the advertised product (or service) or does it (and others like it) cause those perceptions? Explain.

# CHAPTER 8
# SELF-TEST

▼ MULTIPLE CHOICE

1. _____ needs include the need for food and water.
   a. Acquired                          c. Basic
   b. Innate                            d. Secondary

2. A _____ is the ideal state that an individual thinks will satisfy a need.
   a. benefit                           c. goal
   b. motivation                        d. value state

3. A goal's _____ describes whether the goal is positive or negative.
   a. valence                           c. equanimity
   b. polarity                          d. relevance

4. When consumers must choose between two positive goals that cannot be satisfied at the same time, they experience a(n) _____ conflict.
   a. approach–avoidance                c. avoidance–avoidance
   b. avoidance–approach                d. approach–approach

5. A focus group can be considered a _____ method of motivational research since group members are interviewed at length about the actual processes they use when buying products.
   a. projective technique              c. conflict-resolution
   b. depth interview                   d. impact analysis

6. The three components of a means–ends chain model are attributes, benefits, and _____ .
   a. outcomes                          c. consequences
   b. virtues                           d. evaluative criteria

7. The _____ is based on the idea that advertising reflects the products and lifestyles consumers want to see.
   a. reflector controversy             c. laddering confrontation theory
   b. mirror controversy                d. laddering effect

8. If your goal is to attend medical school, you will seek an undergraduate institution that provides the _____ of a pre-med program.
   a. consequence                       c. niche
   b. objective                         d. benefit

9. Research by Ernest Dicter identified two types of benefits received from products—nominal benefits and _____ benefits.
   a. unconscious                       c. personality
   b. reasonable                        d. quantifiable

10. Maslow classified needs into a hierarchy that has physiological needs as its base and _____ needs as its peak.
    a. safety                           c. ego
    b. social                           d. self-actualization

▼ TRUE/FALSE

1. Motivation includes identifying needs and taking action to satisfy those needs. T or F

2. The need to be popular with your peers is an example of an acquired need.   T or F

3. Physiological needs are not affected by cultural values and customs.   T or F

4. When consumers ask for Lays Potato Chips, they are expressing primary demand.   T or F
5. Motivational research is usually reported in a quantitative form.   T or F
6. The outcome of a laddering interview is a means–end chain.   T or F
7. The first step of consumer motivation research is an in-depth analysis of needs, goals, and benefits of products.   T or F
8. Motivation is not related to a consumer's involvement with a product. T or F
9. Research has shown that marketers can create needs.   T or F
10. Marketers and advertisers find it easier to create needs than to satisfy existing needs.   T or F

## ▼ SHORT ANSWER

1. Describe the three factors that contribute to a person's choice of goals.
2. Describe the difference between an approach–avoidance goal conflict and an avoidance–avoidance goal conflict.
3. What are the weaknesses of the Maslow Hierarchy of Needs approach of consumer motivation?
4. Outline the argument that maintains that advertising does not *create* needs but *mirrors* the needs of consumers.

## ▼ APPLICATION EXERCISE

Before developing a print advertisement for a self-tanning lotion, you are asked to outline the needs that may be fulfilled by this product. Based on your knowledge that consumers have both innate and acquired needs, list the needs that may be fulfilled by using this product.

# 9

# PERCEPTION

◉ Consumer Snapshot *Dolly Banzon is a 55-year-old Fashion Consultant. She lives in Broomfield, Colorado, with her husband, Rick. She is the mother of two daughters, Regina Rosa, 32, and Pia Angela, 29.*

## FACT OR FICTION?

◉ All perception involves interpretation.

◉ Sensory thresholds for advertisements differ from person to person and from ad to ad.

◉ When stimuli are very intense, consumers tend to notice small changes in them.

◉ Colors with short wavelengths produce warm feelings.

◉ Most marketing imagery depends on subliminal perceptions.

◉ High expectations increase perceived quality.

◉ Consumers believe that price is usually a good indicator of quality.

# EYE ON THE CONSUMER

Dolly Banzon lives with her husband, Rick, in the house they bought 15 years ago in Broomfield, Colorado. Before making their purchase, the Banzons had been house sitting for a friend who had recently moved out of the area. But when their friend sold the house, the Banzons moved to the house they now live in because the price was right; in fact, the house was on sale—$59,000 down from $64,000. Dolly and Rick also liked the house because they felt safe in the neighborhood; the quiet, country area and presence of families in the development signaled a safe area to them.

Dolly and her husband own two cars, a Chevy and a Toyota, both of which they bought used from private owners because they feel that car salesmen put too much pressure on customers. Dolly prefers American cars because she likes the way they look—the slick lines and details—but Rick prefers Japanese cars because he perceives them as higher quality. Dolly disagrees. She feels that Japanese cars seem to rust too easily, a perception she formed from experience—her family and friends owned Japanese cars when she was a child in her native country, the Philippines.

When it comes to choosing beverages, Dolly prefers Diet Rite over any other cola. She maintains that she can tell the difference between Diet Rite and other brands because the Diet Rite tastes lighter and has a smoother feel in her mouth when she drinks it. Dolly also has definite opinions about coffee. She buys Yuban ground roast coffee because she feels it tastes and smells different from others she has tried. On those occassions when she drinks instant coffee, she prefers Taster's Choice over Nestle's other brand, Nescafe, because Nescafe tastes too bitter. When shopping for other products, Dolly usually looks for packaged goods that have recyclable packaging, but only if they are not more expensive. She also looks at the packaging itself because she doesn't like blue packages. She feels that blue is a "dead" color, and it just doesn't appeal to her.

In this chapter we focus on the ability of consumers to make sense of the world around them by selecting, organizing, and interpreting stimuli through their five senses. A discussion of thresholds and subliminal perception will help you better understand why consumers respond to certain stimuli, such as advertisements, store environment, packaging and labels, and how marketers use these stimuli to communicate successfully with consumers. We also discuss marketing imagery—the ways in which consumers use their perceptions of brands and their quality to reduce the risks they feel they are taking when purchasing products. Finally, we discuss public policy issues concerning two subjects of controversy—deception in advertising, and product packaging and labeling.

After reading and thinking about this chapter, you should be able to:

❶ Analyze the role perception plays in consumer behavior.
❷ Identify the ways in which consumers select and organize stimuli to construct a coherent picture of their environment.
❸ Recognize the role of perception in reducing the risks inherent in consumer behavior.
❹ Determine how consumers interpret a product's position and quality.
❺ Investigate public policy issues concerning consumers' perception of marketing stimuli.

# DEFINING PERCEPTION

**Perception** is the process by which an individual selects stimuli from his or her environment, organizes information about those stimuli, and interprets the information to form a coherent, meaningful view of the world (Figure 9.1). **Stimuli** are inputs into any one of the five senses—vision, hearing, smell, taste, and touch. An individual uses his or her perceptual processes to select from the many stimuli that exist in an environment, to organize the selected stimuli into a coherent picture, and to interpret that picture to make sense of what is happening. It is this subjective interpretation of the individual's environment that becomes the basis for the behavioral processes of learning, attitude formation, and decision making.

Perception has a physiological basis since it involves the use of the individual's five senses. At the same time, it has cultural, social, economic, and psychological bases since it requires the selection, organization, and interpretation of what the individual senses. The physiological basis of perception governs **sensation**—the direct and immediate response of an individual's sensory receptors to stimuli. Humans use their **sensory receptors**—their eyes, ears, nose, tongue, and skin—in physiological response to stimuli in their environment as the foundation of the perceptual process. For example, when looking for a house to buy, if Dolly heard sirens and saw flashing lights that illuminated otherwise dark streets, she would have sensed she was looking at a dangerous neighborhood and would probably elect not to buy a house in that area. The cover of the textbook you are currently reading illustrates a physiological principle in sensation—it pictures an autostereogram that demonstrates the human capacity to see three-dimensional depth in two-dimensional pictures. The following Pleasures of Consumption box describes the popularity of products that demonstrate this novel application of their sensory abilities to consumers.

**Perception** is the process by which an individual selects stimuli, organizes information about those stimuli, and interprets the information.

**Stimuli** are inputs from an object that are perceived by one of the five senses.

**Sensation** is the direct and immediate response of an individual's **sensory receptors**—their eyes, ears, nose, tongue, and skin—to stimuli in the environment.

■ FIGURE 9.1
The perceptual process.

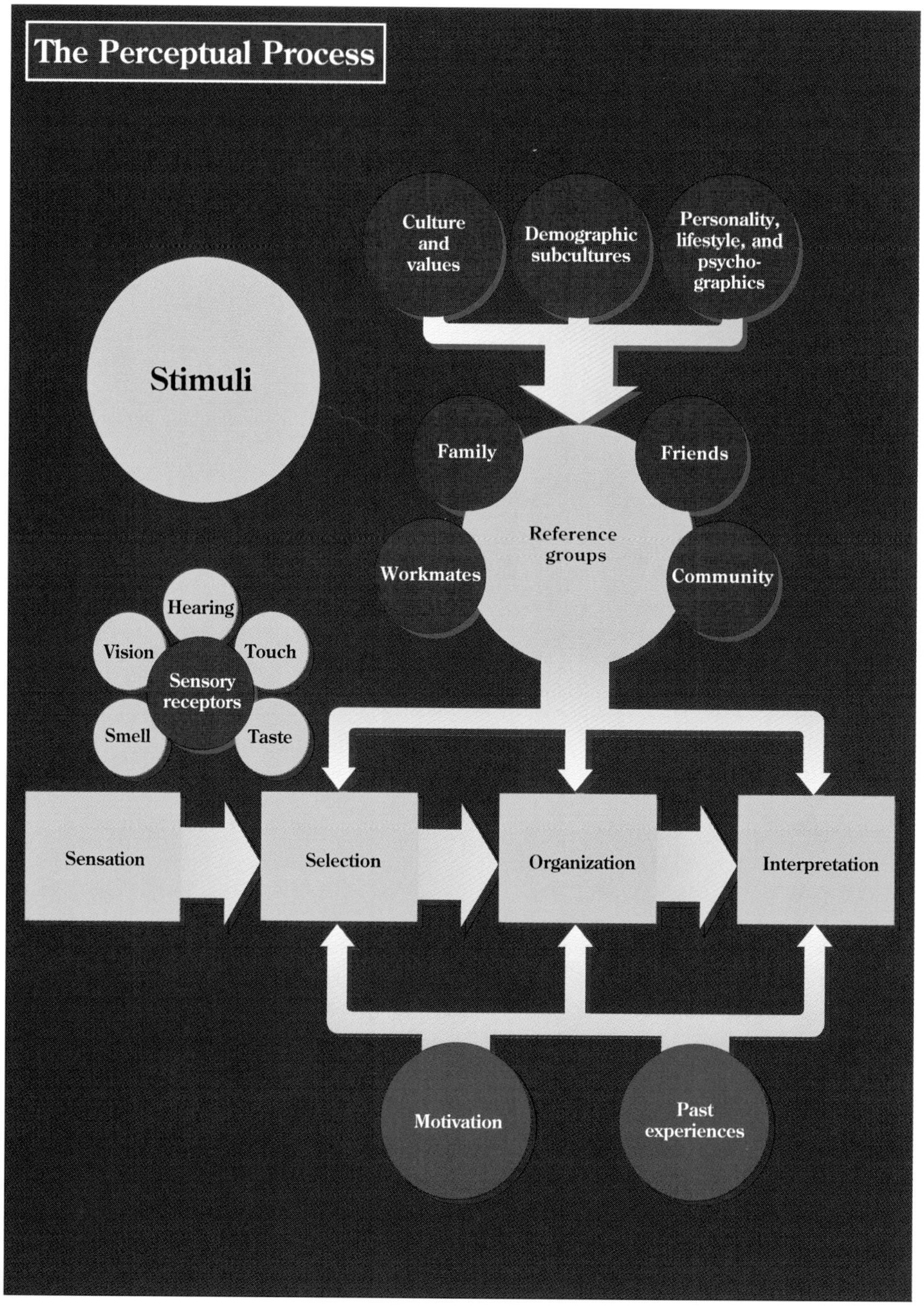


## PLEASURES OF CONSUMPTION

**The Magic Eye[1]**

"Magic Eye" books, posters, calendars, and other products comprise a multimillion dollar industry that delights adults and children throughout Japan, Europe, and the United States. These pictures contain wildly colorful repeating patterns that incorporate a hidden stimulus embedded within the patterns. Two versions of the stimulus' image are contained in the repeating patterns, but they can be detected only if the individual is able to ignore the obvious repeating pattern and focus on the embedded stimulus. Humans are able to detect three-dimensional depth in two-dimensional printed material because the brain combines the slightly different perspectives of the two eyes to sense the relative distances of the stimuli in a picture. In a Magic Eye, the mind combines the two slightly different versions of the stimulus and senses a single three-dimensional object.

Thomas Baccei's N.E. Thing Enterprises has capitalized on the enjoyment consumers receive trying to detect the embedded stimulus and their fascination with this perceptual novelty by marketing books, calendars, posters, and even a weekly image in Sunday newspaper comic sections. Other products, such as Cheerios and Pepsi in the United Kingdom, have printed autostereograms on their packages to increase consumers' interest in their products. And there is at least one computer program, I/O Software's Stereolusions for Windows, that allows consumers to create their own autostereograms.

Magic Eye images rely on physiological principles of vision and cognition to embed the stimuli into pictures. What do you think motivates consumers to purchase Magic Eye pictures? Do background characteristics and past experience with the pictures help an individual identify the embedded images? If you tell someone what image is embedded in a Magic Eye, will it help the individual organize and interpret the picture?

Our discussion in this chapter focuses on *subjective perception*—the individual's perception of what his or her senses have detected. *Objective perception* would reflect only the physiological sensations detected by an individual's sensory receptors before selection, organization, and interpretation occurs—as though the individual could record a "mental videotape" of a stimulus. The subjective selection of stimuli for organization and interpretation is strongly influenced by the individual's culture and values, demographic characteristics, personality, lifestyle, psychographics, and reference groups, as well as his or her past experiences and motives.

Perception is both unique to an individual and powerful in its implications for marketers. What an individual perceives determines how he or she behaves; no consumer purchase will take place unless the individual perceives that the product or service will offer the benefits he or she needs. Accordingly, marketers must understand how perception works in order to communicate successfully a product's benefits. Regardless of how innovative a product, service, or advertisement might be, it will fail if it is not perceived favorably by potential consumers.

At the end of the semester you may be asked to complete a teacher evaluation form for this course. Even though you and your classmates have sat through the same lectures with the same book and the same instructor, inevitably the evaluations will differ from student to student. To understand this disparity, we could look at the components of the perceptual process. Your Consumer Behavior professor may obtain higher teacher evaluations if he or she recognizes how you perceive lectures, reading, assignments, and grading. Similarly, you may obtain a higher grade in the class if you understand your professor's perception of your work in the class. For example, you may perceive attendance as voluntary, whereas your professor interprets it as an indication of your interest in the class.

## FACT OR FICTION REVISITED

⊛ It is true that all perception involves interpretation; it is unique to each individual.

# PERCEPTUAL SELECTION AND ORGANIZATION

Every time you go to the grocery store you are inundated with thousands of colors, sounds, and smells. But you manage to purchase certain products and leave the store without becoming overwhelmed. This is because your background characteristics, past experiences with grocery shopping, and motivations to satisfy your needs help you assign meanings to the stimuli and recognize products that will offer certain benefits to you. Accordingly, marketers design their packages so that consumers will be able to distinguish them from other stimuli in this hectic retail environment.

The perception process begins when incoming stimuli compete for detection by an individual's sensory receptors. Human physiology causes some stimuli to fall short of sensation; of those stimuli that are detected, some are selected, organized, and interpreted to make them meaningful to the individual. This perceptual process is facilitated by **schema**—the collection of knowledge and beliefs held by an individual.[2] A schema provides a filtering process for an individual, who pays attention to only a small percentage of the original stimuli he or she senses and organizes them into categories based on knowledge and beliefs. An individual's memories are organized in such a way that he or she can quickly perceive an incoming stimulus by assigning it to a familiar category of objects. As we discussed in Chapter 2, for example, consumers perceive 1-800 numbers to be toll-free calls. The restaurant chain Boston Chicken is in the process of attempting to overcome a popular consumer perception. To prevent consumers from continuing to assign it to the category of "chicken restaurants" as it introduces a wider menu, Boston Chicken is changing its name to Boston Market.

An individual's background characteristics, past experiences, and motives provide the bases for his or her schema. For example, as a college student, you might perceive subtle differences among Snapple, Fruitopia, and Lipton iced teas while barely noting Gerber and BeechNut baby foods. By contrast, a Generation X new parent would be likely to select baby foods and, accordingly, would have a quite detailed schema for organizing and interpreting the benefits offered by different brands and flavors (Figure 9.2). This schema would reflect cultural, sub-

A **schema** is a collection of knowledge and beliefs held by an individual.

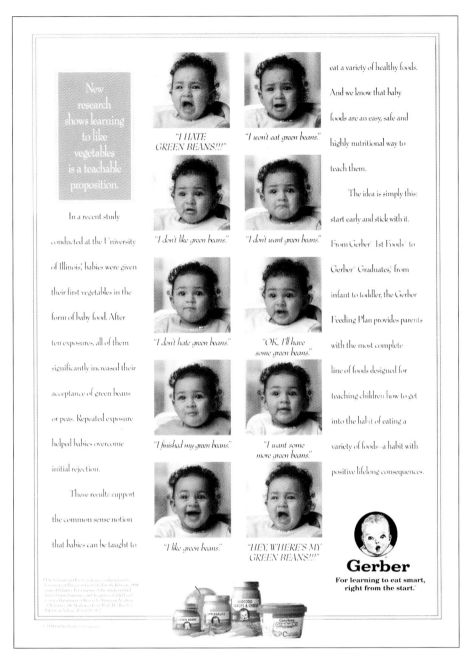

Gerber baby food products are targeted at parents of newborns, infants, and toddlers, who perceive a need for the product at this stage in their lives and are therefore able to organize and interpret the benefits offered by different brands and flavors.

cultural, lifestyle, and reference group influences about the appropriateness of prepared foods for babies as well as past experiences with the baby's preferences for different varieties and flavors. In other words, the individual's schema influences the way he or she selects, organizes, and interprets the stimuli that exist in the baby food aisle of the grocery store.

We now turn to a discussion of the important factors that influence an individual's selection and organization of stimuli from his or her environment.

### ▼ SELECTIVE PERCEPTION

**Selective perception** enables a person to screen out some stimuli while allowing others to be perceived.

**A sensory threshold** is the level of intensity a stimulus must exhibit for an individual to be able to perceive it.

**An absolute threshold** is the lowest possible amount of stimulation that can be detected by an individual's sensory receptors.

**A differential threshold** is the smallest possible change in a stimulus that an individual is able to perceive.

As you read this chapter, it is possible that the television is on, your roommate is talking on the phone, and the smell of a hot pizza is in the air. If individuals attempted to pay attention to all competing stimuli around them at the same time, they would be confused and immobilized. To protect them from this overload, the perceptual process includes a component called **selective perception**, which allows individuals to screen out some stimuli while allowing other stimuli to be perceived. **Sensory thresholds** are the levels of strength or intensity that stimuli must exhibit so that the individual is physiologically able to perceive them. For example, humans have **absolute thresholds** to their physiological abilities to sense small objects or hear faint sounds; consequently, advertisers do not use print that is too small or sounds that are too faint. Humans also experience **differential thresholds**—the minimal level of change in a stimulus that is necessary for a person to detect that something has changed. For example, the inability of most people to detect slight taste changes in products allows marketers to use any of a variety of different sweeteners in their soft drinks in order to respond to cost changes in the sweetening agents.

**Absolute Thresholds**   It is common for consumers to miss commercial messages if the volume is too low on their television sets or someone is talking during the commercial. Each of our five senses has an absolute threshold that determines the lowest possible amount of stimulation that can be detected. Absolute thresholds differ from person to person, and any stimuli below one's absolute threshold will go undetected. Examples include warning labels on cold remedy packaging that are too small to read, images that change too quickly on a television commercial, or audio that is too low to be heard.

Many marketers place perfume inserts in popular magazines that allow consumers to lift a flap and smell the perfume. Consumers with a low absolute threshold for smell complain that these inserts are so strong that they get headaches just reading the magazines even if they haven't opened the perfumed flaps. Others with higher thresholds may never notice the fragrances advertised. It is important for marketers to test their products and communications to assure that the majority of consumers can detect the incoming stimuli without being overwhelmed. Otherwise, even the best product or advertisement will go undetected.

## FACT OR FICTION REVISITED

◉   Sensory thresholds for advertisements do in fact differ from person to person and from ad to ad.

**Differential Thresholds**   As noted above, *differential threshold* refers to an individual's ability to perceive change in a stimulus. In other words, the differential threshold is the point at which an individual notices that something is different— the new Tide makes clothes softer and whiter than the old formula; the redesigned Scoop Away cat litter jug is easier to hold; Taster's Choice is less bitter than Nescafe. Consumers tend to see things generally and not with great specificity, so it is not unusual for small changes to go undetected. Most people would not perceive one less cough drop in a package or a few less chocolate chips in a cookie, for example.

There are times when marketers want consumers to notice differences and times when they prefer that differences go unnoticed. If Hershey planned to add more nuts to its almond chocolate bar, for example, the marketer would want to be sure consumers noticed the change. If the cost of almonds rose dramatically, however, and Hershey decided to reduce the number of nuts per bar, it would certainly hope that consumers did not notice the difference. Some marketers have made a number of subtle changes over the long history of a product, and although none of the individual changes exceeded differential thresholds, their cumulative effects was great (Figure 9.3). Changes in style and packaging and printing technology have enabled manufacturers such as Kellogg to change the packaging of their Corn Flakes, for example, but they have made subtle, individual changes so that consumers would not notice that the package has changed.

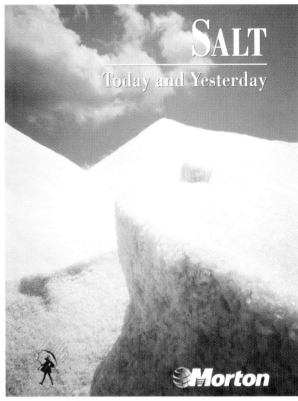

■ FIGURE 9.3

Morton Salt has made changes to its Morton Salt Girl symbol which fall below the differential threshold so that the cumulative effect is continued recognition in a brand name.

**The Just Noticeable Difference (JND)**    To help define the differential threshold for consumer products and services, marketers refer to Weber's law, or the *just noticeable difference (JND)*. Ernst Weber was a psychophysicist (a scientist who studies the physical foundations of psychological principles) who during the nineteenth century formulated a mathematical equation to determine the point at which a change could be detected. The most important aspect of Weber's law was his finding that the JND was not an absolute figure but depended on the intensity of the stimulus under study. To create a noticeable difference, Weber maintained, the amount of change must be larger for a large original stimulus than it is for a small one. For example, Dolly and Rick Banzon perceived the decrease in the price of their house (from $64,000 to $59,000) as a significant difference; by contrast, a wealthy business executive might not be spurred to action by a $5,000 decrease on a $2.2 million dollar Manhattan penthouse. To summarize, the greater the original stimulus (time, price, size, amount of an ingredient) the greater the change necessary for consumers to perceive it.

In those cases where positive changes are made but are below the differential, advertising can attempt to draw attention to them (see Figure 9.4). For example, Kellogg advertises that its Raisin Bran cereal contains more raisins than be-

■ FIGURE 9.4
Neutrogena informs con-
sumers about the new non-
stick advantage of its sun-
screen products in this ad,
a change consumers may
not notice without the help
of advertising.

fore, whereas AT&T claims clearer connections for long-distance telephone calls.
In these cases, consumers probably would not have noticed the changes in these
products or services without the help of advertising. AT&T even went so far as to
provide a toll-free 800 number consumers can call to hear a demonstration of the
improved service.

## FACT OR FICTION REVISITED

◉   When stimuli are very intense, consumers *do not* tend to notice small
changes in them; rather, the more intense the stimulus, the larger the
change needed to produce a just noticeable difference.

## ▼ ORGANIZING INPUT FROM THE SENSES

Once an individual has selected stimuli for attention, he or she must organize those stimuli into a coherent picture. Sensory cues, such as color, smell, and sound, affect the way an individual responds to stimuli.[3] Part of the impact is physiological, such as our eyes' response to the wavelength that is reflected by colors, or our taste buds' response to chemical compounds. But background characteristics and past experiences also play an important role. For example, most Americans tend to respond favorably to a combination of red, white, and blue because they associate these colors with the American flag; brides wear red in China; and white is the symbol of death in much of the Pacific Rim. Savvy marketers incorporate sensory cues such as color, smell, and sound in their marketing efforts to help consumers assign the products to favorable categories in their schema.[4]

**Color**  The effects of various colors on consumer perceptions have been widely studied. Table 9.1 lists a number of colors and their common perceptions as well as examples of marketing stimuli that have utilized these colors to elicit certain perceptions. At one end of the light spectrum, colors with long wavelengths—reds, oranges, and yellows—tend to elicit warm feelings in consumers. An example of a marketing application are the bright red seats typically found in fast food restaurants. These establishments want to move customers quickly through the eating process. The bright colors encourage faster movements; consumers perceive the seats as "warm" and tend not to linger. At the other end of the spectrum, short wavelength colors—blues and greens—are associated with coolness and encourage slower movements. The seats in an expensive restaurant are more likely

## *Table 9.1*

### COMMON PERCEPTIONS OF COLORS

| Color | Perceptions | Marketing Examples |
|---|---|---|
| Red | Powerful<br>Dangerous<br>Exciting<br>Hot<br>Passionate | First Alert fire extinguisher<br>Era laundry detergent—"The power tool for stains" |
| Green | Cool<br>Calm<br>Natural | Scope mouthwash<br>Healthy Choice food products |
| Blue | Cool–cold<br>Sad<br>Respectful<br>Authoritative | Phillips' Milk of Magnesia laxative and antacid<br>Aqua Velva cooling after shave |
| Black | Cold<br>Prestigious<br>Sophisticated | Mont Blanc pen<br>Johnnie Walker Black Label scotch |
| Clear | Clean<br>Pure | Palmolive Sensitive Skin dishwashing liquid<br>Clear Choice mouthwash<br>Crystal Pepsi |

to be blue or green—cool colors—to promote a more leisurely dining experience. Look around your classroom. Are the seats colored in such a way as to encourage you and your classmates to sit comfortably for an extended period of time?

## FACT OR FICTION REVISITED

⊚    Colors with short wavelengths *do not* produce warm feelings; rather, colors with *long* wavelengths, such as reds, oranges, and yellows, tend to produce these feelings.

**Smell**    Many people have strong memories of smells from their childhood—the smell of baby powder, the aroma of a special holiday dinner. Smells often serve as cues for current activities, as well—the aroma of your favorite food or drink, the fragrance worn by a loved one. As we mentioned in our discussion of thresholds, fragrance strips in advertisements for perfumes and colognes are a common promotion method. Because these products are designed to stimulate smell, an ad featuring the fragrance will be a more powerful influence on consumer behavior than even the most compelling description.

Creating new fragrances for marketers has become a booming industry. Often new perfume products contain a familiar base fragrance, such as rose or jasmine, to make consumers comfortable, and then add a distinctive scent to distinguish it from existing competitors. Similarly, in response to the familiar aroma of beer to drinkers, Samuel Adams has used its distinctive hops in a scent strip ad to entice beer drinkers to buy its product. Bath and body product retailers, such as Bath & Body Works and The Body Shop, rely on the appealing fragrances of their products on two levels—to offer a benefit to users and to create an appealing store environment.

**Sound**    Like sight and smell, sound provides cues to help individuals organize their perceptions—some products sound "tinny," others "deep and rich." Grocery shoppers thump cantaloupes to see if they are ripe and bang on the walls of a house to test its construction. Lincoln–Mercury engineers conducted extensive research into the sounds of closing car doors to determine what kind of "thunk" indicated quality to consumers. The results can be heard by shutting the door of a Lincoln Continental.

Music, in particular, is often used in television commercials to help viewers classify products. A rap or hip-hop beat, for example, may signal younger viewers that a product is appropriate for them, while big-band jazz tends to attract an older audience. Janis Joplin's voice singing the lyric "Oh Lord, won't you buy me a Mercedes-Benz" attracted the attention of a new audience to that carmaker's advertisements as it attempted to portray a more contemporary image to baby boomers.

**Gestalt psychology** maintains that the physical pattern of stimuli influences the way an individual organizes his or her perception of each distinct stimulus.

## ▼ PERCEPTUAL ORGANIZATION

The physical pattern or configuration of stimuli will influence the way individuals organize those stimuli so that they can interpret them. **Gestalt psychology**, de-

**Principle of Figure-Ground**   **Principle of Closure**   **Principle of Similarity**

■ FIGURE 9.5
Physical patterns derived from Gestalt psychology.

rived from the German phrase meaning *configuration* or *pattern*, is a school of thought that studies how an individual organizes a set of stimuli into a coherent picture. Gestalt theories maintain that the configuration of physical relationships among stimuli will influence the individual's perception of each stimulus in the configuration. In this section we discuss three common physical patterns considered by marketers in their advertising—figure and ground relationships, incomplete stimuli presentations, and similarity and proximity of stimuli (see Figure 9.5).

**Figure and Ground Relationships**   As an individual perceives a set of stimuli, he or she distinguishes the *figure*—the stimulus that is given greater prominence—from the *ground*—the remaining stimuli that assume background prominence. Thus, when we speak of figure and ground, we are referring to the relationship between an object and the background in which it is perceived. Marketers want to ensure that consumers correctly distinguish the message or image conveyed in an advertisement from the background elements in the ad. In an ambiguous picture, figure and ground can be reversed and the image will present a confusing stimulus to viewers. At the same time, marketers must be careful not to create ads that are so entertaining or visually appealing that the creative elements become the figure and the product recedes into the ground. In the retail environment, marketers try to ensure that consumers will view their package as the figure in a ground of competitors by creating packages that stand out on store shelves.

**Closure**   *Closure* occurs when an individual responds to an incomplete stimulus by filling in the missing elements. People prefer to perceive a coherent picture; when past experience indicates that a stimulus is not complete, perception fills in the gap. Marketers sometimes use the principle of closure to elicit better recall of a message by requiring that consumers participate in completing the message. Wendy's famous ad with "Where's the beef?" was eventually run with the charac-

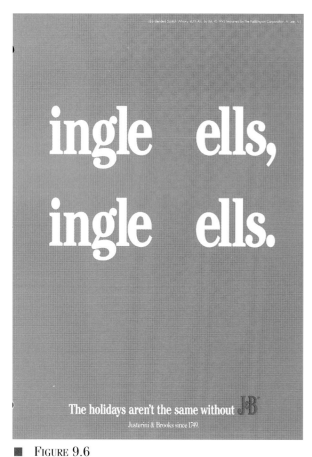

**ingle ells,**

**ingle ells.**

The holidays aren't the same without J&B

Justerini & Brooks since 1749.

■ **FIGURE 9.6**
J&B's advertising provides a classic example of closure. The consumer participates by mentally filling in the gaps.

ter saying only "Where's the . . ."; consumers were quick to finish the phrase. J & B runs a successful advertising campaign during the holiday season using closure—the two large words, "_ingle _ells" are centered above the message, "The holidays aren't the same without J & B." Consumers have to participate to complete the message (see Figure 9.6).

**Similarity and Proximity in Groups of Stimuli**
The principles of *similarity* and *proximity* refer to an individual's assumption that stimuli should be grouped together when they are perceived to be similar or are in close proximity to one another. For example, consumers assume that products that have similar appearance are related; accordingly, marketers incorporate such assumptions in their package designs. Proctor & Gamble designed its line of Pert Plus shampoo bottles with a common shape and graphic design so that consumers will identify the products as related; color is used to distinguish different formulas. Many marketers have taken legal steps to protect product stimuli that are unique to their products, as we discuss in the Public Policy box that follows.

 **PUBLIC POLICY**

**Don't Flatter These Marketers by Imitating Them**[5]
Some say that imitation is the sincerest form of flattery, but a number of American marketers disagree and have taken vigorous legal action against firms they feel are imitating their products too closely. To prevent mistaken consumer perceptions of similarity, Procter & Gamble files about a dozen lawsuits each year against manufacturers and retailers who market products the company fears will confuse customers and dilute the positive image enjoyed by its brands. The company has sued—and beaten—firms that have sold products with shapes, designs, and colors similar to its Head & Shoulders, Pantene Pro-V, and Pert Plus shampoos, Secret and Sure deodorants, and Noxzema cleansing cream. P&G also filed suit against a firm that markets Oil of Love skin care products in packages that imitate the P&G Oil of Olay skin care brand.

Computer companies have joined the fray of marketers fighting to keep its distinct characteristics just that—distinct. Microsoft forced a specialty software maker who produced a product called "The First Electronic Jewish Bookshelf" to rename the software because the firm feared the close similarity to its own Microsoft Bookshelf product. And products are not the only target of imitation. The Atlanta Olympic Committee has moved against a number of local restaurateurs and retailers, tour operators, and even church groups for using the Olympics name in their products and services. The

Olympic Restaurant, named in 1983 for the owner's native country, Greece, was forced to change its name; tour operators are forbidden from advertising "Olympic '96" trips; and local churches have been warned against holding "Christian Olympics."

The U.S. Patent and Trademark Office has gone so far as to allow colors to be trademarked, but court battles have been waged over the past dozen years concerning the legality of that position. Courts have long upheld the *pattern* of colors in a logo, such as the red and white scheme of Coca-Cola's logo, but the debate continues over whether a marketer can maintain sole use of a color in a product category. In 1985, Owens-Corning won the right to the exclusive use of pink in the insulation category and has since invested over $200 million in "pink" promotion, including ads that feature the Pink Panther cartoon character and a consumer hotline, 1-800-GET-PINK. More recently, however, Monsanto was denied the exclusive right to use the pastel blue of its Equal artificial sweetener. In March 1995 the Supreme Court addressed this contradiction when it ruled that Qualitex had exclusive rights to a green-gold color for ironing board pads. The Court maintained that when consumers come to recognize a color as the symbol of a particular brand over time, the marketer can trademark that color for the brand.

Consumers' perceptions of products are often organized according to the Gestalt principles and the similarity of shapes, colors, designs, and names. Do you think consumers would confuse Oil of Love with Oil of Olay, or First Electronic Jewish Bookshelf with Microsoft Bookshelf? Should a marketer be able to prevent competitors from capitalizing on the existing brand image of its product by imitating a package design and color? Should the owner of a restaurant that has been in business for 15 years be forced to change its name just because a particular city is chosen to host the Olympics?

Marketers often portray products in an appealing setting in advertisements because a product is typically perceived in the same way as other stimuli in its proximate surroundings. That is, the proximity of a product to its surroundings influences the consumer to assume some relationship between the use of the product and a similar outcome. For example, consumers who see an advertisement showing a couple drinking General Foods International Coffee in a romantic setting will likely perceive the product as appropriate for romantic situations. Similarly, beer advertisers depict fun and social settings, and clothing manufacturers drape their designs over beautiful models in interesting places.

## ▼ SUBLIMINAL PERCEPTION

Most marketers want their communications to be above consumers' thresholds so that they are easily recognized. However, marketers have been accused of intentionally creating messages that *cannot* consciously be perceived so that the consumers will not be able to defend against them.[6] **Subliminal perception**, as this phenomenon is called, occurs when stimuli are below the threshold of perception and, consequently, influence consumers subconsciously. Although there is no tangible evidence of this phenomenon, two events brought it to the attention of Americans in 1957. The first was the publication of Vance Packard's book, *The Hidden Persuaders*; the second was the widespread publicity of a subliminal perception experiment at a New Jersey drive-in theater. Packard's book criticized

> **Subliminal perception** is the selection, organization, and interpretation of stimuli that are intentionally designed to be below consumers' threshold of perception.

269

marketers and advertisers for what the author felt were "secretive" methods and attempts to manipulate consumers' motivations and perceptions. The reports of the drive-in experiment noted that the messages "eat popcorn" and "drink Coca-Cola" were inserted for 1/3000 of a second throughout the showing of the films. Although this rate was too fast for viewers to consciously see and read the messages, the theater manager reported a 20 percent increase in the sales of popcorn and a 60 percent increase in the sales of Coke at the concession stands. Ultimately, however, it was revealed that the findings had been fabricated by the researchers in an attempt to generate publicity.

Despite the denunciation of the New Jersey study, the idea of subliminal communication remains strong 40 years later. Studies of subliminal perception typically have focused on two areas—embedding in print media, and the use of auditory input messages. *Embedding* is a process by which figures, shapes, or letters are inserted into print advertising using high-speed photography or airbrushing. Popular examples are the faint outline of a nude body or suggestive words such as "sex" some people claim can be found in the ice cubes of a drink in a liquor ad or the use of suggestive phrases that have been attributed to musical records, tapes, and compact disks. Other examples of embedding are self-help tapes that contain advice that is spoken above the auditory threshold along with messages such as "I will eat less" or "I will act decisively" uttered below the threshold. Despite the popularity of such self-help tapes, there is no evidence that they are effective in changing one's behavior.

The use of low-level auditory stimulation shows more promise as a valid means of subliminal communication. Department stores that play music over their public address system sometimes include messages that are actually above the absolute threshold of customers but are barely audible, such as "I am honest" or "I won't steal." Some retailers have reported a subsequent decrease in levels of shoplifting. However, this low-level stimulation may only be effective in reinforcing the behavior of those individuals whose values make them responsive to the message; this would exclude the professional thief, who will steal despite any conscious or unconscious indication not to.

Despite the number of people who claim to see printed embeds or to hear subauditory messages, there is no evidence to indicate that such a technique is effective in influencing consumer behavior. The sensory and perceptual processes require that stimuli be sensed, selected, organized, and interpreted. Although a subliminal message may be sensed, the rest of the perceptual processes will not be triggered to help the consumer utilize the information. In short, a subliminal message would not be as powerful as a "conventional" message; accordingly, marketers have no incentive to use them in the place of more obvious communication.

## FACT OR FICTION REVISITED

◉ It is not tue that most marketing imagery depends on subliminal perceptions. In fact, most marketing imagery depends on ordinary supraliminal perceptions.

# Interpreting Marketing Imagery

O nce the selection and organization processes have been completed, the consumer must interpret the chosen stimuli; this interpretation, in turn, serves as a basis for completing the activities in the purchase process. Perceiving sensory cues through the five senses and from the perspective of one's schema, the individual gathers information about a product and the benefits it offers to use as input for his or her decision making. For example, if Generation X consumers interpret Hootie and the Blowfish as youthful and contemporary and opera as old fashioned and stuffy, they will likely assume that a store that plays opera music in the background is inappropriate for them.

At times consumers may feel uncertain about whether a product will offer the benefits they seek. For example, it may not be apparent whether a Plymouth Neon or a Chevrolet Cavalier is a more reliable vehicle, or which shade of Clairol Loving Care will provide the right hair color. Marketers want to help consumers overcome their fears and feel confident that the product they are considering will provide the benefits they need. To do so, marketers utilize color, smell, taste, feel, and sound in the marketing mix to help convey a product's benefits and to position the product in consumers' minds. Consumers, in turn, consider these cues as they compare different products and appraise the overall quality of each one.

We will now consider how consumers attempt to reduce their perception of the risk associated with a product's use and how they interpret a product's position, image, and quality. We will also discuss how marketers attempt to influence consumers' perceptions of products.

## ▼ Perceived Risk

Inherent in the consumer purchase process are numerous decisions to be made concerning which brands to purchase, what price to pay, and how, when, and where to make the purchase. Accordingly, the purchase process may result in uncertainty and evoke the fear of negative consequences if the wrong product is selected. Marketers call this belief **perceived risk**—it is the uncertainty people feel when they cannot clearly interpret stimuli to estimate the consequences of their purchase and use of a product.[7] Perceived risk can take many forms, depending on the product and consumer characteristics.

> **Perceived risk** is the uncertainty and fear of negative consequences consumers experience when they cannot clearly interpret stimuli.

**Types of Risk**   The perception of risk varies with each consumer, product, and situation. An individual's background characteristics will affect his or her perception of risk. For example, a recent college graduate will discern more risk in buying a new car than will a successful businessperson who is buying a second car for weekend trips. Some products, such as a formal dress or a tuxedo, will entail greater risk than others, such as bedroom slippers, since the former is a more expensive purchase. The situation in which the product will be used can also affect the level of risk. Choosing the right wine will be a more uncertain experience the

*Table 9.2*

TYPES OF PERCEIVED RISK

| Type of risk | Examples of uncertainty about negative consequences |
|---|---|
| Functional | Will this discount car battery last two years?<br>Will this stereo system be loud enough for house parties? |
| Physical | Will my drug prescription have harmful side effects?<br>Will the heater spew carbon monoxide fumes? |
| Financial | Am I paying too much for this used car?<br>Will this mutual fund make money? |
| Social | Will the home perm make my hair frizzy?<br>Will my friends like these new CDs? |
| Psychological | Will I feel stupid trying to understand my new computer?<br>Will I be embarrassed by these new eyeglasses? |

first time you invite your boss to dinner than when your buddies from college visit for the evening.

Researchers have indentified five major types of perceived risk:

❶ *Functional risk*—the risk that a product will not provide the expected benefits.

❷ *Physical risk*—the risk that the product will be physically dangerous or harmful to the consumer.

❸ *Financial risk*—the risk that the product will not be worth the money the consumer pays for it.

❹ *Social risk*—the risk that positive reference groups will not approve of the product choice.

❺ *Psychological risk*—the risk that the product will not be consistent with the consumer's self concept or will not satisfy self-esteem needs.

Examples of each of these five types of risk are shown in Table 9.2.

## ▼ RISK REDUCTION STRATEGIES

As we will discuss at greater length in Chapters 15 and 16 on marketing and interpersonal communications, consumers can minimize risk a number of ways. They can collect information from reliable sources, comparison shop, buy only well-known brands, or shop at stores where they feel comfortable. Marketers can help by providing information, offering money back guarantees and service contracts, and educating their sales staff.

**Seeking Information**    Consumers are exposed to two general sources of information about products, marketers, and brands. The first is marketing —advertising in the media; promotional communications, such as store brochures and direct marketing; and publicity about products. Most consumers can cite specific product attributes touted in commercials. Consumers know that Lysol kills germs (Figure 9.7), Burger King Whoppers are grilled, not fried, and Tab has just

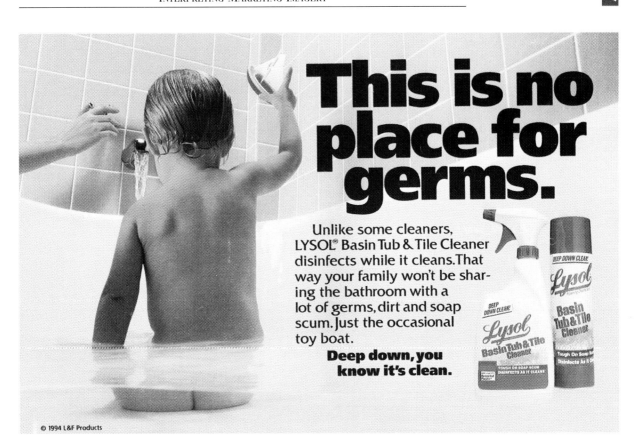

This is no place for germs.

Unlike some cleaners, LYSOL® Basin Tub & Tile Cleaner disinfects while it cleans. That way your family won't be sharing the bathroom with a lot of germs, dirt and soap scum. Just the occasional toy boat.

**Deep down, you know it's clean.**

© 1994 L&F Products

■ FIGURE 9.7

Lysol has been successful at using advertising to educate consumers about its germ-fighting capacity.

one calorie. When more detailed information is necessary, consumers often can obtain a brochure and videotape demonstrating the product's attributes. Ford and Soloflex provide such promotional materials about their cars and exercise equipment, respectively.

The second source of information is interpersonal communication. Friends, family members, and acquaintances often view themselves as credible sources of information and offer their opinions and knowledge to others. You probably consulted with your friends to gather information about certain professors and classes before you registered this semester, for example. The more information people collect, the more comfortable they feel making purchase decisions. A person's perception of risk is substantially reduced after learning about the product in question from those who have had experience with it.

**Brand Loyalty**   Consumers may reduce or avoid risk by remaining with a tried-and-true brand that provides a certain level of satisfaction. Purchasing the same brand over time eliminates the need to interpret new information and reduces the possibility of negative consequences. Marketers are aware that, for some consumers, switching brands is perceived as a risky proposition. Accordingly, they

273

try to simplify the process by providing free samples, money-back guarantees, testimonials, and factual information in an effort to reduce the level of risk in the mind of the consumer. For example, McNeil distributes complimentary samples of Tylenol Allergy and Sinus medication to consumers who are considering using the brand, and Lands' End allows consumers to return clothing they have purchased through the company's catalog if it does not meet their satisfaction.

**Brand Image**   In the absence of information, consumers often rely on *brand image*—their beliefs or impressions of a particular brand. Purchasing a brand that is considered reliable reduces risk in the mind of the consumer. Consumers form these judgments based on their exposure to marketing sources, their impressions of the store that sells the product, information from friends and acquaintances who use the product, and impartial reviews in magazines such as *Consumer Reports*.

**Store Image**   The atmosphere of a store can be reassuring to consumers. Stores that offer reliable service and generous return policies and that have a good reputation ease the risk inherent in the purchase process. For example, Nordstrom's department store has earned a reputation of excellent customer service, offering a no-questions-asked return policy and personal touches such as home delivery and followup thank you notes to customers. Store loyalty instills

■ FIGURE 9.8

A perceptual map using similarity data.

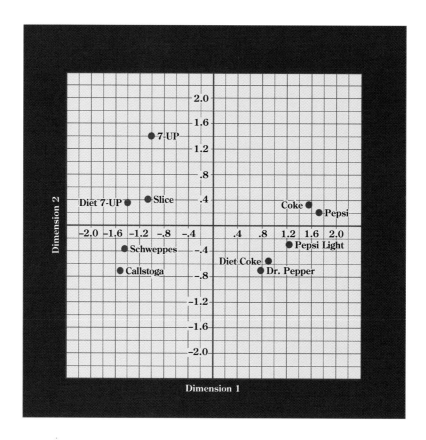

consumer confidence in the products they purchase because they know and trust the store and its policies.

**Price**   Consumers sometimes rely on price alone to reduce risk in selecting products and services. A high price implies high quality; accordingly, consumers assume that a more expensive product will provide more of the benefits they seek. This relationship between price and quality often fades as consumers glean additional information about the product, however. Accordingly, marketers often emphasize attributes other than price in an effort to assist consumer decision making. For lower priced products, communication must focus on performance attributes and benefits. The concept of value is addressed by Helene Curtis, for example—when the company assures customers in its advertising that although its Suave hair care products might cost less than other brands, they are just as high in quality.

## ▼ POSITIONING AND BRAND IMAGE

In real estate there is a saying: Only three things are important—location, location, location. The same can be said about products. Consumers use their perceptual processes to develop a clear image in their minds about the attributes of a product and the benefits to be gained by its purchase. Marketers call such an image of com-

peting products a *positioning* or *perceptual map* and use sophisticated statistical techniques to translate consumers' perceptions of products into such a map. When asked to describe products in a certain category, such as soft drinks, most consumers have a mental picture about how the products are related to one another (Figure 9.8). Some, such as Coca-Cola and Pepsi, may be perceived as close together because they share a carmel-brown color and a sweet taste. Others, such as 7-Up and Slice, are perceived as similar to each other because they have a clear color and sweet taste, whereas diet drinks, waters, and flavored juices are seen as distinct from clear sodas.

Marketers attempt to influence consumers' mental pictures through their product positioning efforts; as we discussed in Chapter 3, marketers emphasize product distinctions in their advertising and other elements of the marketing mix. The result of successful positioning is a distinctive brand image or mental picture of the product in consumers' minds. Coke and Pepsi have long recognized their similar perceptions in the minds of most consumers and have conducted taste tests and utilized direct comparisons in advertising to differentiate themselves from each other. Similarly, 7-Up capitalizes on its sensory differences from the colas by describing itself as the "Uncola" (Figure 9.9); Avis

■   FIGURE 9.9

7-Up capitalizes on its color and taste by describing itself as the "Uncola."

275

challenged Hertz by positioning itself as the number two rental car company and the one that tries harder to please its customers; and Easy Spirit developed the tag line "looks like a pump, feels like a sneaker" to distinguish its dress pumps from other, less comfortable brands.

## ▼ PERCEIVED QUALITY

When it comes to quality, every consumer interprets the word differently, depending on his or her expectations. A person may try a new pizza place because it is conveniently located but not expect the food to be great. Under those conditions, a "good tasting" pizza will be perceived as high in quality. If eaten at the person's favorite restaurant, that same pizza might be judged as lower quality than anticipated and "not as good as usual."

### FACT OR FICTION REVISITED

◉ High expectations *do not* increase perceived quality—*low* expectations encrease perceived quality.

In judging quality, consumers utilize many of the same cues they use to reduce risk—available information, past experience, brand name, price, packaging, and store image all contribute to the final perception.[8] Often consumers do not possess the expertise, knowledge, or information they need to make decisions on their own, particularly when it comes to electronic equipment, household and technical products, and cars. In those cases, other sensory cues become substitutes for one's quality judgments. One person might decide to buy a computer at a reliable store, like CompUSA, while another might opt for brand name, like IBM, to assure quality. Color, smell, sound, and texture can all be indicators of quality. Black or titanium finishes are typically used to present a "professional" image, making it a good color for audiovideo equipment, while a strong chemical odor is presumed to signal effective cleaning products.

As noted earlier, although price and quality are not necessarily related, price is often perceived as a good indicator of the quality of a product or service (Figure 9.10). L'Oréal informs women that even though its hair coloring products cost more, they're "worth it"; Mercedes-Benz notes that although its cars are expensive, skimping on quality could compromise passenger safety. The implication is that it is worthwhile to indulge oneself with these high-quality products. Supermarkets are full of brand name items as well as less expensive, generic or store brand products of the same quality. More often, however, consumers perceive the brand name products as higher quality.

### FACT OR FICTION REVISITED

◉ Consumers do tend to believe that price is a good indicator of quality.

■ FIGURE 9.10
Consumers perceive price as
an indicator of quality, a
perception Summer Infant
Product promotes in its
advertising.

Finally, the retailer who sells a product or the provider of a service is often used as an indicator of quality. A retailer's image may be based on the lighting, colors, and sounds of the store environment, the appearance and manner of the salespeople, and the range of customer services offered. For example, most consumers tend to perceive Kmart as a lower quality store than Bloomingdale's or Saks Fifth Avenue. For services that consumers cannot measure at the time of purchase, such as tax preparation or automotive maintenance, the appearance of the tax preparer or mechanic provide sensory cues. In some cases, as in H&R Block offices, the sparse surroundings signal an economical service.

## PUBLIC POLICY AND PERCEPTION

In 1962, President John F. Kennedy proposed a "consumers' bill of rights" to recognize the rights of consumers to buy and use safe products in an environment conducive to gathering information from and providing feedback to marketers. The proposition was developed in response to widespread consumer discontent with poor product quality, incomplete or inaccurate information, inadequate warranties, and fraudulent marketing. Since that time, a number of federal laws have been passed toward eliminating deception and fraud in marketing and increasing consumers' trust in their own perceptions of marketers' activities.[9]

### ▼ DECEPTIVE ADVERTISING

In 1914 Congress established the Federal Trade Commission (FTC) to address antitrust concerns and unfair business competition. The Wheeler Lea Amendments of 1938 expanded the FTC's power to include unfair or deceptive marketing practices; the FTC has even acted in cases where there was *potential* deception, regardless of intent. Deceptive advertising is primarily a public policy issue of fairness: Do consumers have access to unbiased information about products and services?

When it comes to advertising, deception often concerns fabrications, such as claiming that a cleaning product will remove dirt when it cannot. A striking example is Spray-U-Thin, a product that promises weight loss without diet or exercise. Its maker claims that the mouth spray, an appetite suppressant with the active ingredient phenylprophanolamine, is "proven safe and effective." The Food and Drug Administration disagreed and forwarded a complaint to the FTC. More often, however, deceptive advertising involves consumers' perceptions of a product's appearance and performance. Advertising stimuli must be presented so that the average consumer can reasonably organize and interpret them in a way that will allow the consumer to draw the "correct" conclusion.

The question of deception often arises when advertisers use props or mockups in advertisements. For example, the photos displayed on billboards advertising Dove Ice Cream Bars are actually pictures of mashed potatoes in a chocolate covered resin coating. Such mockups are necessary because real ice cream would melt under the hot lights necessary for high-quality photography. The FTC does not consider such instances deceptive because the intent is to reproduce what the product *would* look like if it *could* be photographed; therefore, the ad does not misrepresent the benefits offered by the product. The ad would be considered deceptive, however, if it showed the mashed potatoes and touted the creamy texture of the ice cream.

An example of an advertisement the FTC declared deceptive is Campbell's Chicken & Stars Soup. A print ad contained shards of glass that were put in the bowl of soup so that the tiny stars would be visible in the photograph. The intent of the ad was to reproduce the perception that a typical consumer would have while stirring the soup with his or her spoon. But because the ad implied that the soup contained enough stars to reach the surface of the soup, the FTC objected. Later ads showed soup (and stars) flowing from a ladle into the bowl.

### ▼ PRODUCT PACKAGING AND LABELING

A number of policy makers are involved in packaging and labeling regulations, including the U.S. Congress, the FTC, the Food and Drug Administration (FDA), and the Consumer Product Safety Commission. The Fair Packaging and Labeling Act, passed by Congress in 1966, mandates providing specific information on a

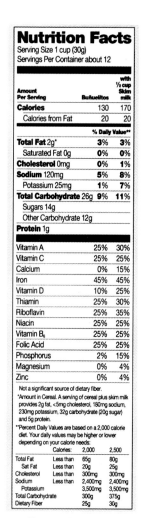

**■ FIGURE 9.11**

The Nutrition Labeling and Education Act requires all packaged food products to carry the uniform nutrition label pictured here.

product's label about the marketer, the product, and the quantity of product in a package. The act is intended to help consumers perceive differences among products and changes in quantity when package designs make such interpretations difficult. For example, consumers can refer to labels to identify a reduction in size that would not otherwise be noticeable simply by looking at the package. As of May 8, 1994, the Nutrition Labeling and Education Act requires all packaged food products to carry a uniform nutrition label (Figure 9.11). The label provides a consistent stimulus on all food packages, enabling consumers to compare products and their ingredients. For example, consumers are now able to discriminate the nutritional content of Ocean Spray grapefruit juice, which contains 100% juice, from its Mauna Lai Guava juice, which contains only 12% juice.

Efforts are currently underway to provide consumers with nutritional information that is easier to interpret and to develop more uniform "green" standards to help them determine which products are actually environmentally friendly (Figure 9.12). The FTC has issued guidelines for health and nutrition claims, defining specific criteria that must be met for a marketer to use a specific term. For example, a food must have 10 percent of the daily requirement of a nutrient and no more than 3 grams of fat or 1 gram of saturated fat, 20 milligrams of cholesterol, and 140 milligrams of sodium to be called "healthy." The FTC also monitors the use of environmental claims. A marketer must provide reliable scientific evidence for environmental claims such as "biodegradable" or "recyclable" before it can place these words on its package labels.

■ FIGURE 9.12

Jockey International promotes the environmental advantages of its Jockey Naturals, a product line of clothing free of dyes and biodegradable.

# SELECTING, ORGANIZING, AND INTERPRETING STIMULI

**D**olly Banzon utilizies her perceptual tools in her efforts to find, evaluate, and purchase products that will satisfy both her and her husband's needs. Her perceptions of Japanese and American cars, for example, are rooted in her childhood experiences in the Philippines. When she and her husband decided to buy a house, the sounds and sights of prospective neighborhoods were used to interpret the safety of the area, but, ultimately, price became an issue—a noticeable drop in price provided the immediate incentive for the Banzons to buy their house.

Dolly uses the colors, tastes, smells, and physical feelings of products as the basis to organize and interpret product information. Based on these cues, she utlimately decides that she prefers one brand of cola or coffee over another. The brands she likes best—Diet Rite, Yuban, and Taster's Choice—have a positive brand image in her mind, and she uses that brand image to reduce the risk of future purchases.

In this chapter we have discussed how consumers select, organize, and interpret stimuli from their environment. Perception has a physiological basis in the five senses—vision, hearing, smell, taste, and touch—and the thresholds of what can be sensed. It also has a subjective basis in the consumer's culture and values, demographic characteristics, personality, lifestyle, psychographics, reference groups, past experiences, and motives. Consumers use the cues they obtain from their senses to organize and interpret information about products and to reduce the feelings of risk they may experience when making uncertain decisions. In the next chapter we continue our presentation of consumer behavior processes with a discussion of the ways consumers use the information they perceive as the basis for learning about products.

# Summary

1.  **Analyze the role perception plays in consumer behavior.** Perception is the process by which an individual selects stimuli from his or her environment, organizes information about those stimuli, and interprets the information to form a coherent, meaningful view of the world. This perceptual process is facilitated by schema—an individual's knowledge and beliefs—that provide a filtering process based on background characteristics, past experiences, and motives. When consumers perceive that a product will offer the benefits they need, they begin the behavioral processes of learning, attitude formation, and decision making that result in the purchase of the product.

2.  **Identify the ways in which consumers select and organize stimuli to construct a coherent picture of their environment.** Consumers use the process of selective perception to select stimuli. Absolute thresholds prevent some stimuli from being detected, and differential thresholds prevent others from being sufficiently different to become noticeable. Consumers utilize sensory cues such as color, smell, and sound and the gestalt principles of figure and ground, closure, similarity, and proximity to organize input from their senses into coherent pictures of objects in their environment. Objects that are below the threshold of perception—subliminal stimuli—do not trigger the selection and organization processes.

3.  **Recognize the role of perception in reducing the risks inherent in consumer behavior.** Consumers often feel uncertain and perceive risk about whether a product will offer the benefits they seek. These perceived risks can be functional, physical, financial, social, or psychological. To reduce the risk, consumers may seek information from marketers and interpersonal communication sources; or they may use products that have images with which they are already familiar; or they may use store image and price as additional stimuli in interpreting the product's benefits.

4.  **Determine how consumers interpret a product's position and quality.** Consumers develop perceptions of a product's position relative to other similar products as well as its quality by considering stimuli that signal the product's attributes and the

benefits it can provide. Sensory stimuli, similarity and proximity to other products, store image, and price are all inputs into the interpretation of the product's position and quality. Marketers attempt to influence these interpretations by stressing distinctive attributes that will provide stimuli that can be easily differentiated.

5. **Investigate public policy issues in consumers' perception of marketing stimuli.** Advertising and packaging and labeling are two key marketing stimuli that consumers must organize and interpret in order to purchase and use products. A consumer's ability to perceive such stimuli is often compromised, however; accordingly, public policy makers have created a legal and regulatory structure to monitor marketers' efforts in those areas. Deceptive advertising is defined as that which contains stimuli that the average consumer would be unable to organize and interpret in order to reach an unbiased conclusion. Product packaging and labeling laws and regulations are intended to enable consumers to perceive both the true contents of a single product and to detect meaningful differences among competing products.

## KEY TERMS

Perception, *p. 257*

Stimuli, *p. 257*

Sensation, *p. 257*

Sensory receptors, *p. 257*

Schema, *p. 260*

Selective perception, *p. 262*

Sensory threshold, *p. 262*

Absolute threshold, *p. 262*

Differential threshold, *p. 262*

Gestalt psychology, *p. 266*

Subliminal perception, *p. 269*

Perceived risk, *p. 271*

## SKILL-BUILDING ACTIVITIES

1. Locate a term paper from another class for which you received a lower grade than you think you deserved. Considering this paper as a product, how might each of the following processes *on the part of the consumer* (the grader) have affected your grade?
   a. selection
   b. organization
   c. interpretation
   Note that this question refers to selection, organization, and interpretation on the part of the grader, not the characteristics of the paper itself.

2. How could the paper have been changed so that these three processes would have worked more in your favor?

3. Describe a recent purchase (or return to the purchase described in activities 4 and 5 in Chapter 8).
   a. What schema influences this purchase?
   b. How was this purchase influenced by sensory thresholds?
   c. by Weber's law?
   d. by color?
   e. by figure-ground relationships?
   f. by the principle of proximity?
   g. by imagery?

4. Select five advertisements from a recent issue of *Time* and five advertisements from a recent issue of *Ladies' Home Journal*. Identify the ad that makes the best use of:
   a. Weber's law
   b. the meanings of color

c. figure–ground relationships
d. the principle of proximity
e. multiple positioning
f. quality cues
g. perceived risk
Explain the reasons for your choices.

**5.** Identify the advertisement that makes the *poorest* use of each of the above. Explain your reasoning in each case.

**6.** Do any of these advertisements make use of subliminal perception? Explain.

---

# CHAPTER 9 SELF-TEST

▼ **MULTIPLE CHOICE**

**1.** Perception involves the selection of stimuli, organization of information about those stimuli, and _____ of that information.
   a. analysis                          c. monitoring
   b. interpretation                    d. direction

**2.** Which of the following would be considered a sensory receptor used during the perceptual process?
   a. eyes                              c. television
   b. brain                             d. radio

**3.** A collection of knowledge and beliefs held by an individual that provides a filtering process through which perception occurs is called a(n) _____ .
   a. database                          c. schema
   b. experience                        d. personality

**4.** A _____ threshold is the point at which a stimulus is detected by one of the five senses, whereas a _____ threshold is the point at which the consumer notices a change in a stimulus.
   a. differential; absolute            c. absolute; differential
   b. subliminal; absolute              d. differential; subliminal

**5.** If consumers notice the actor in a television advertisement but not the product, Gestalt theory would indicate that the product has become the _____ of the stimulus.
   a. figure                            c. platform
   b. peripheral component              d. ground

**6.** When consumers buy a product that is on the shelf near a brand-name product because they perceive the products to be the same, they have based their purchase on the Gestalt theory of _____ .
   a. proximity                         c. figure and ground
   b. closure                           d. subliminal messsages

**7.** _____ is the uncertainty consumers feel when they cannot determine the consequences of their purchase and use of a product.
   a. Cognitive dissonance              c. Perceptual cuing
   b. Perceived risk                    d. Selective perception

**8.** Which of the following is *not* an attempt on the part of consumers to reduce their perceived risk when buying a product?
   a. rely on brand image              c. purchase the least expensive product
   b. purchase the most expensive product   d. avoid store loyalty

9. Which U.S. President proposed the "consumers' bill of rights" which instigated many of the present consumer protection laws?
   a. Harry Truman
   b. Franklin D. Roosevelt
   c. Lyndon Johnson
   d. John F. Kennedy

10. Purchasing the same brand over and over again is called _____ .
   a. brand loyalty
   b. consumer consistency
   c. product adoption
   d. consumer experience

## ▼ TRUE/FALSE

1. Perception is based purely on physiology.   T or F
2. Subjective perception is a person's perception of what his or her senses have detected.   T or F
3. Colors with a short wavelength are perceived to be "warm."   T or F
4. Sound is not relevant during the perception process.   T or F
5. When marketers use the principle of closure, they are asking consumers to be more active in the communication process.   T or F
6. Subliminal perception means that a stimulus has reached a person's absolute threshold.   T or F
7. Being brand loyal is one way consumers try to reduce the risk of buying a new product.   T or F
8. The FTC is only commissioned to regulate advertising that is created by intent to be deceptive.   T or F
9. Similarity and proximity to other products, store image, and price are all used by consumers in determining a product's position and quality.   T or F
10. Since the information obtained is not considered credible, consumers never use marketing information to help reduce the risk involved in a purchase.   T or F

## ▼ SHORT ANSWER

1. Explain how consumers are selective during the perception process.
2. Describe how Weber's law could be used in pricing a product.
3. Describe the five major types of perceived risk.

## ▼ APPLICATION EXERCISE

Imagine you work for a company that sells camping equipment to consumers via a catalog. The company's budget does not allow for color photos within the catalog but the budget does give customers access to a toll-free telephone number to use to place orders. What can you and your organization do to help your customers reduce their risk of ordering products from your catalog?

# 10

# LEARNING

● Consumer Snapshot *Chris Madonna is the mother of an 11-year-old son and a 14-year-old daughter. She lives in Catalina, Arizona, with her husband, Steve, where they own their own business, Madonna Home and Window Cleaning.*

### FACT OR FICTION?

● When consumers learn they generally integrate past and present experiences.

● Perception provides the raw material for learning.

● Through classical conditioning consumers learn many responses without knowing they have learned them.

● Punishment is negative reinforcement.

● Short-term memories last 2 or 3 weeks.

⊙ Compared with verbal stimuli, visual stimuli are more likely to encourage elaborative processing.

⊙ Warning labels prevent misuse of about 90 percent of the products to which they are attached.

# EYE ON THE CONSUMER

Chris Madonna is the grocery shopper for herself, her husband Steve, and their two kids. She uses a "mental shopping list" when she goes to the supermarket, rather than a formal, written one. Her 14-year-old daughter is the biggest eater in the family and reminds Chris of the things they need. Chris then goes from aisle to aisle, trying to remember what she has at home and what she needs to replenish. Of course, she always forgets a few things, so it's back to the store a couple of days later to pick up the forgotten items.

Chris shops at two stores for groceries. Fry's is closest to home, and is convenient when she is carrying ice cream in the heat of a Tucson summer, but the Safeway offers more coupons and save her money. Chris typically restricts her grocery shopping to these two stores because they are both familiar to her. She knows the layout of each store so she can start at one end and work her way through the aisles, which helps jog her memory about the things she needs. It also makes it easier for her to run into the stores on her way home from work, get what she needs quickly, and leave.

Ingredients labels are very important to Chris, and she reads them carefully. She has developed an allergy to corn, and since many products contain corn syrup she must be careful in her selections. Reading every ingredients label takes a lot of time, however, so a shopping trip that used to take 30 minutes now takes over an hour. Chris also reads labels to check the fat content of food products—she will not buy any products that have more than 30 percent of their calories from fat. When it comes to specific brands, Chris prefers a number of brand name products over generic brands. For example, her son likes Kraft Macaroni and Cheese, her daughter puts Heinz Tomato Ketchup on everything she eats, and Chris herself is a Miracle Whip connoisseur and a proponent of Green Giant vegetables.

In this chapter we focus our attention on the learning process. We present the major theories concerning how learning occurs and discuss marketing applications of consumer learning. Marketing strategies based on learning theories attempt to educate consumers, like Chris, about their products and services. There are times, however, when public policy actors seek to ensure consumer safety by *unlearning* existing knowledge, such as preferences for fatty foods. A discussion of the effectiveness of warning labels later in this chapter describes the controversy that exists between marketers and public policy actors.

After reading and thinking about this chapter, you should be able to:

❶ Describe consumer learning and its characteristics.

❷ Recognize the types of behavioral learning processes.

❸ Determine the roles played by information processing and memory in cognitive learning processes.

❹ Identify marketing applications of consumer learning.

❺ Analyze public policy implications of the information provided on warning labels.

# LEARNING ◀

As illustrated in Figure 10.1, **learning** is the process by which individuals organize knowledge so that it causes a permanent change in their behavior and can be used again in future purchase activities. Individuals use their perceptual processes to gather information from stimuli in their environment, including products, advertisements, and other consumers; they then utilize the learning process to organize this knowledge for their use. Learning enables individuals continually to integrate their past experiences with information gained from current stimuli to create a useful framework to guide their activities.

When you register for next semester's classes, for example, you may consider taking another course with a professor from whom you received an "A" last semester. Your decision will integrate past knowledge—your previous experience with the professor, your academic strengths and weaknesses, and the list of courses you need to graduate—with up-to-date information—the days and times classes are offered, your friends' course selections. Understanding how consumers learn enables marketers to plan all of the elements of the marketing mix so that they can provide information through packaging, labeling, pricing, and advertising.

Experts have long disagreed about precisely how learning occurs. In this chapter we discuss two general approaches to understanding learning: (1) *behavioral learning theories,* which propose that learning is the result of behavioral responses to events in an individual's external environment, and (2) *cognitive learning theories,* which posit that learning results from an individual's conscious information processing activity to solve problems. These two approaches should not be viewed as theoretical competitors, however, since each offers insights about particular kinds of learning used by consumers. A behavioral approach may best explain how consumers associate the golden arches with satisfying their hunger at McDonald's, whereas a cognitive approach offers insight into the ways consumers learn about the performance differences among Aiwa, Panasonic, and Sony personal stereos.

> **Learning** is the process by which individuals organize knowledge so that it causes a permanent change in behavior.

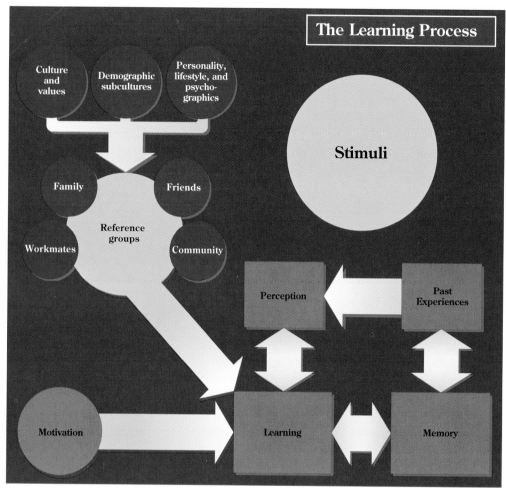

**■** FIGURE 10.1
The learning process.

## FACT OR FICTION REVISITED

◉    It is true that when consumers learn, they generally integrate past and present experiences.

## ▼ CHARACTERISTICS OF LEARNING

Learning is a process that evolves over time and cannot be directly observed. Each time an individual perceives new stimuli in the environment, he or she acquires new information, which is integrated with existing knowledge. Learning, therefore, reflects both current experiences and background characteristics. Current experiences include such factors as marketing efforts and interpersonal communications with reference groups. Consumers learn from advertisements, labels, promotions, and salespeople, and they tell other consumers about their experiences. You may have seen an ad for Ray-Ban sunglasses, for example, that provided you with information about their fashionableness and effectiveness. Background characteristics, such as culture, values, demographic subcultures, personality, lifestyle, and psychographics, affect the existing knowledge an individual possesses and that has been acquired over time. Your parents, for example, learned about music at a different time than you did, so they may purchase different kinds of music, as may other students who come from different backgrounds than you.

Because learning is a process, we cannot directly observe the learning process in individuals; we can only *infer* that someone has learned by observing behavior that *should* be affected by the knowledge the individual has acquired. For example, by reading your exams and papers, your professor may conclude that you have learned the material presented in this text. If research indicates that consumers are able to recall the "You've got the right one baby! Uh huh!" slogan from Diet Pepsi ads or recognize it when asked what product it advertises, the advertising manager could conclude that learning has taken place. In other words, it is only by observing behavioral evidence that we can infer that learning has occurred.

Consumers employ learned knowledge in all the behavioral processes they use to complete purchase activities. Learning allows consumers to store large quantities of information over time, which they use to form attitudes and make decisions about which products or brands to buy. Accordingly, learning and perception are tightly linked. Perception provides the raw material for learning—individuals select, organize, and interpret information from stimuli and then integrate that information with past knowledge. At the same time, consumers learn from past experiences, and that knowledge affects the organization and interpretation of new stimuli. Individuals will perceive stimuli differently if they have already learned to recognize cues that help them organize and interpret those stimuli. For example, if you have learned to expect to see artists that you like featured on MTV, you may have viewed Tony Bennett's appearance on *MTV Unplugged* differently than if you had simply learned about him from your grandparents.

Learning does not necessarily result in the behavior marketers want to encourage. Consumers may interpret stimuli inaccurately and then organize the resulting knowledge incorrectly. They sometimes mistake the sponsoring product of an advertisement, for example, associating, say, a Calvin Klein Obsession ad with another perfume. And even if the information gathered is correct, other purchase activities, such as product evaluation and decision making, may result in a different purchase. Consumers who remember the Nike slogan, for example, may purchase Reebok sneakers. That does not mean that they did not process and retain information; it simply means they chose not to act based on the acquisition of that knowledge. Similarly, a person may be aware of the disadvantages of eating hot dogs, yet choose to overlook that knowledge when walking by a hot dog vendor. This disparity between learning and behavior is frustrating for marketers. A marketer can provide the information necessary to encourage a desired behavior, but, as we will see in the next chapter on attitude formation, consumers use a wide variety of learned knowledge to evaluate products. And sometimes, as we discuss in the following Public Policy box, the marketer may be prevented from providing some information to consumers.

## FACT OR FICTION REVISITED

⦿  *Perception* indeed provides the raw material for *learning*; the two are tightly linked.

### PUBLIC POLICY

**How Much Alcohol is in That Beer?**[1]

In April 1995, after a 60-year ban that began shortly after Prohibition, the U.S. Supreme Court ruled that beer marketers could state the alcohol content on beer packaging. The ruling upheld an appeals court decision in a suit filed by the Coors Brewing Company against the federal government in 1987. Althought the federal government does not ban stating alcohol content in advertising, 18 individual states do. In its unanimous decision, the court noted several reasons for lifting the ban on labels: (1) it is in opposition to free speech; (2) it goes against government policies of greater disclosure of information to consumers; (3) it is inconsistent with the brewers' right to include alcohol content in those states that allow it; and (4) it is inconsistent with regulations that allow alcohol content to appear on wine and liquor labels.

In the period since the appeals court decision, Miller and Molson, both distributed in the United States by the Miller Brewing Company, have included the alcohol content on their ice beers. Miller ran afoul of the Bureau of Alcohol, Tobacco and Firearms (BATF) and antialcohol social action groups by prominently featuring the labels in its ads, but the brewer maintained that it is legal to show packaging and labels in advertising. The ice beers contain more alcohol than regular or light beers, and Miller has been criticized for touting the more potent alcohol content. Public policy actors fear that this kind of labeling freedom will result in a battle among brewers to market stronger beers to consumers. Only one brewer, Anheuser-Busch, has opposed content labeling; at the same time, it recently increased the alcohol content of its ice beer.

Do you think that alcohol content should appear on beer labels? Do beer drinkers want to know the percentage of alcohol in a beer? How will they use such knowledge? Is it something that beer drinkers will remember and use as a basis for comparing products?

# BEHAVIORAL LEARNING THEORY

> **Behavioral learning theories** define learning as the unconscious association between a *stimulus* and a *response*.

As we mentioned earlier, consumer researchers have developed a number of theories to explain how learning occurs. The first group of theories we examine can be classified as **behavioral learning theories.** They define learning as the association between a *stimulus*—an external event or object the individual perceives—and a *response*—an act of behavior the individual exhibits in reaction to the event. These theories view the individual as a "black box"—that is, they focus on the external *stimulus* and the individual's observable *response*

and are less concerned with the internal cognitive processes (Figure 10.2). The individual learns to associate the stimulus with a certain response so that whenever the stimulus occurs he or she will respond with the same kind of behavior. If a student raises his or her hand to answer a professor's question in class and the professor compliments the response given, it is likely that the student will volunteer again. Similarly, if a consumer receives a cash-back rebate for using the Discover charge card, he or she likely will continue to use it.

The two most widely known behavioral learning theorists are Ivan Pavlov and B.F. Skinner. Pavlov, a Russian physiologist, pioneered the theory of classical conditioning, and Skinner, an American psychologist, developed much of the theory that forms the foundation of instrumental, or operant, conditioning. A brief discussion of each theory will help explain consumers' responses to some basic marketing strategies.

## ▼ CLASSICAL CONDITIONING

**Classical conditioning** occurs when an individual learns to associate an *unrelated stimulus* with a particular *behavioral response* that was previously elicited by a *related stimulus* (Figure 10.3).[2] Through a series of repetitions in which the first and second stimulus occur together, the second stimulus becomes associated with the first and evokes the same response. Pavlov did much of his work with dogs, and the standard example of classical conditioning is the dog who learned to salivate when it heard a bell after many repetitions of the bell sounding as the dog was fed. In this case, the food is an *unconditioned stimulus* because it will elicit the response without any additional conditions, and the bell is a *conditioned stimulus* because the dog must be conditioned by many repetitions to learn its association with food. Over time, the ringing of the bell alone caused the dog to salivate as it exhibited its *conditioned response*.

Classical conditioning demonstrates that a consumer's choice of goals that can satisfy a need, such as hunger, fear, or social acceptance, can be influenced by connecting them to external stimuli. Consumers learn to associate unrelated stimuli, such as package shapes and corporate symbols, with products to satisfy their needs. L'Eggs hosiery was long associated with its plastic egg-shaped package and only recently changed to an egg-shaped cardboard container in response

**Classical conditioning** occurs when an individual learns to associate an unrelated stimulus with a particular behavioral response that has previously been elicited by a related stimulus.

291

■ FIGURE 10.3

Components of classical conditioning.

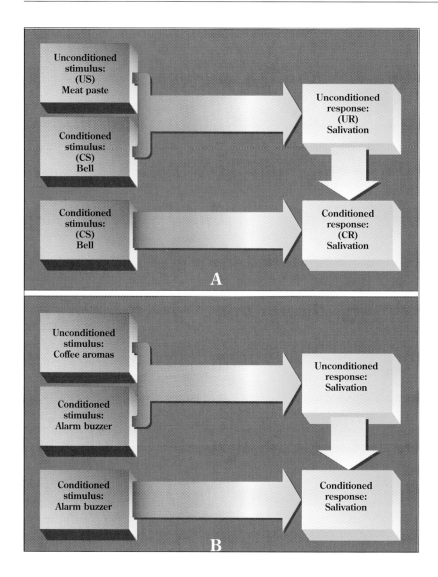

to recycling concerns. Coca-Cola plastic containers have returned to an hourglass contoured shape reminiscent of the shape of the glass bottle which was available for many years. Similarly, many companies have created widely recognized corporate symbols, such as the Prudential rock or the Nike "swoosh," that are readily recognized by many consumers.

Many marketers use advertising and promotional campaigns to associate their products with the positive feelings consumers experience when they satisfy their needs. For example, Kodak markets its film as an important part of loving family gatherings, enabling consumers to document the "times of their lives" in "true colors," and AT&T demonstrates how "you will" use its technological advances to make your life more satisfying.

## FACT OR FICTION REVISITED

◉ It is a fact that consumers learn many responses without knowing they have learned them through classical conditioning.

**Repetition**   An important aspect of classical conditioning is repetition. Pavlov noted that repetition increases the likelihood of a subject's responding to a conditioned stimulus. The more often the conditioned stimulus is paired with the unconditioned one, the stronger the association becomes and the more likely it will be remembered. Kraft used this technique in an early advertising campaign that attempted to influence consumers to associate Parkay margarine with butter. The ads consisted of persistent repetition of the product name, "Parkay," always followed by the word "butter." Similarly, Miller repeated the phrases "tastes great" and " less filling" throughout its long-running series of ads for Miller Lite beer so that consumers would learn to associate the lighter tasting product with the same enjoyment afforded by regular beers.

**Stimulus Generalization**   In his experiments, Pavlov also noted that the dogs salivated when they heard a sound similar to that of the bell that had initially triggered salivation. **Stimulus generalization** occurs when a new stimulus is sufficiently similar to an existing conditioned stimulus that it evokes the same response. In marketing, consumers generalize what they have learned about one product to other products they perceive to be similar. Marketers who want to encourage generalization use similar packaging for all the different products in a product line, such as the different varieties of Green Giant canned and frozen foods that Chris Madonna buys. Consumers recognize the Green Giant trademark and generalize that stimulus, making it easy to recognize other Green Giant products. Similarly, all Absolut vodka ads contain a similarly shaped object viewers recognize as an image of the bottle.

> **Stimulus generalization** occurs when a new stimulus is sufficiently similar to an existing one that it evokes the same response.

**Stimulus Discrimination**   The opposite of stimulus generalization is **stimulus discrimination**. In this case, the consumer is able to *discriminate* the new stimulus from the existing one and, subsequently, *does not* exhibit the same behavioral response. For example, consumers sometimes mistake the sponsoring product of an advertisement. A common misconception is that consumers think the Energizer bunny represents Duracell batteries instead of Eveready. In the Public Policy box on packaging imitations in Chapter 9, we noted that many marketers aggressively oppose copycat packaging because consumers may confuse the imitation and the real product. Because consumers are already familiar with the appearance of the real product, similar packaging may lead them to the erroneous conclusion that the copycat product is the same. Procter & Gamble, for example, wants competing shampoo packages to be different enough from one another that consumers can discriminate between the copycat shampoo and the real Head & Shoulders brand.

> **Stimulus discrimination** occurs when an individual is able to discriminate a new stimulus from an existing one.

### ▼ INSTRUMENTAL CONDITIONING

Another important element of behavioral learning is **instrumental conditioning**, also called **operant conditioning**, which maintains that individuals will only learn to associate a stimulus and response if they are rewarded for doing so.[3] Instrumental conditioning occurs when the subject learns to exhibit behaviors that are positively reinforced and to avoid those behaviors that yield negative reinforcement (Figure 10.4). Skinner noted that animals and humans act instrumentally—that is, they repeat behaviors that get them what they want and avoid acting in ways that will *not* get them what they want. According to Skinner, learning has three components: a *discriminative stimulus* evokes a *response* that is, in turn, followed by a *reinforcing stimulus*. Skinner developed his theory by training rats and pigeons to peck levers in order to receive food pellets. In more scientific terms, the levers are the discriminative stimuli, the pecking is the response, and the food is the reinforcing stimulus, or reinforcement.

**Kinds of Reinforcement**   There are several different kinds of reinforcements that can elicit learning in individuals. The first type is *positive reinforcement*, which involves rewarding the individual for a behavioral response, thereby encouraging repetition of the response. Many consumers repeat their purchase of a particular brand as long as it continues to provide benefits; they will switch brands only when the original one stops working. For example, a consumer who buys milk every week at the local 7-11 will continue to do so as long as the milk he or she buys is fresh.

The second type of reinforcement is *negative reinforcement*. This method also encourages the individual to take particular actions, but in this case they are

> **Instrumental** or **operant conditioning** occurs when a consumer learns to associate a stimulus with a response when given a reinforcement for responding to the stimulus.

■ FIGURE 10.4
A model of instrumental conditioning.

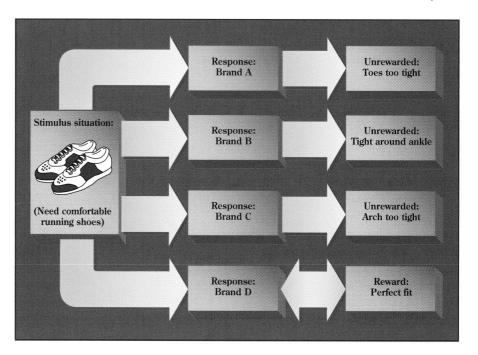

taken to *avoid* receiving the negative reinforcement. For example, a consumer who bought an unbranded sweatshirt at a local discount store, only to have it fall apart after only a few wearings, might be more likely to purchase a Champion sweatshirt the next time.

Consumers learn through negative reinforcement that an alternative behavior will provide rewards. Accordingly, marketers can successfully incorporate negative reinforcement in their advertisements if their product offers consumers a way to avoid the negative consequences. For example, consumers use Sure deodorant or Scope mouthwash to avoid being shunned by friends and acquaintances, while Zantac promises relief from ulcer and heartburn pain.

[The third type of reinforcement, *punishment*, discourages the individual from taking a particular action that will have negative consequences. Product marketers rarely incorporate punishment in their advertising because consumers are not likely to use a product or watch an advertisement that punishes them. A notable exception is the Aromapower Diet, a diet plan that relies on a device that emits a rotten-cheese odor. Dieters are instructed to sniff the offensive odor when they eat a fattening food they like. The intention is that, after several repetitions, the consumer will stop eating the food because he or she will have associated it with the punishing effects of the odor. Many medical authorities doubt the efficacy of this product because the dieter is left to apply the punishment to himself or herself. Public policy actors who want to discourage dangerous behavior, such as drug abuse, continue to create ads that exemplify the self-inflicted punishments that will occur as a result of taking drugs; these ads have proved to be effective in teaching some young people to avoid drug use.

## FACT OR FICTION REVISITED

◉   Punishment *is not* the same as negative reinforcement; they are two different types of reinforcement.

**The Reinforcement Schedule**   Skinner pointed out that the reinforcement schedule—the frequency with which reinforcement follows the behavior—has an important influence on the degree of learning. He favored *intermittent reinforcement,* which rewards consumers on an irregular schedule. According to Skinner, rewards should not automatically follow every desired behavior because the reward becomes expected and is no longer effective. Some marketers have tried to delay reinforcement by requiring consumers to make a certain number of purchases before they receive reinforcement. Frequent flyer programs, such as Continental Airlines' One Pass, require 25,000 miles of air travel before issuing a free ticket. Such rewards are designed to be frequent enough to attract some travelers but still rare enough that consumers will see it as a special reward for frequent patronage. In fact, many airlines created a furor when they increased the number of miles required because consumers objected to a change in the reinforcement schedule they had already learned.

# COGNITIVE LEARNING THEORY

**Cognitive learning theories** posit that learning occurs when an individual processes information using conscious mental processes.

Unlike behavioral learning theories, **cognitive learning theories** stress the importance of complex mental processes (Figure 10.5). These theories examine an individual's active use of creativity, insight, and information processing to solve problems. Cognitive learning theorists examine the "black box" in addition to the stimuli that enter it and the behavioral responses that leave it. Responses are neither automatic nor are they solely the result of conditioning; rather, the individual understands incoming stimuli and creates a set of expectations about outcomes. You may, for example, choose to take a sociology course because you think that it will teach you about human interactions in organizations and you anticipate needing that knowledge to succeed in your first job. At the same time, cognitive theorists concede that some behavior might be automatic and involve little or no mental processing. For example, consumers might move through the grocery store mindlessly throwing Coke, Tostitos, and Old El Paso Burritos in their shopping carts. This does not mean that they are unable to make critical decisions about the nutritional value of what they eat, however.

## ▼ INFORMATION PROCESSING AND MEMORY

**Information processing** is the storage, organization, and retrieval of information from one's memory.

Cognitive learning theories focus on **information processing**—the storage, organization, and retrieval of knowledge from an individual's memory.[4] Individuals store knowledge they have gathered and interpreted in their memories, recalling and using it when they need to solve problems. As they go about problem-solving tasks, individuals integrate new information they have gathered through their

■ FIGURE 10.5
Cognitive learning theory.

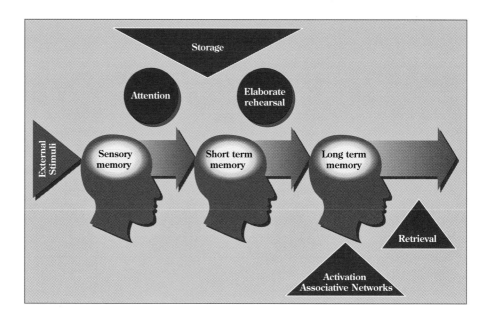

perceptual processes with the existing knowledge they have stored in their memories and use the newly integrated knowledge to solve the problem at hand. As we noted earlier, a decision such as which course to take next semester integrates what you already know about your needs, courses, requirements, and professors with new information available from the current registration guides.

## ▼ STORING AND ORGANIZING KNOWLEDGE

Memory can be thought of as the "location" in which individuals store the knowledge they will be able to recall and use for later problem solving. Individuals utilize different types of memory—sensory, short term, and long term—and cognitive processes—attention and elaborative rehearsal—that move information from one type of memory to another so that it can be stored and organized as knowledge for future use. It is helpful to think of these types as metaphors for the interdependent steps individuals use to process information rather than as distinct physical locations in the brain.

**Types of Memory**  The first type of memory, **sensory memory** temporarily stores information that is received from the senses during the perceptual process. Sensory memory is of very short duration; sensations last just long enough for perceptual interpretation to occur. An advertisement for Wendy's, for example, presents a set of images—sizzling hamburgers, the Wendy's logo, and Dave Thomas, the spokesperson and chairman of the company. If the images are recognizable to the consumer because of prior knowledge, he or she might pay attention to see what Dave is saying. If they are not recognizable, or if the consumer does not want to pay attention to a fast food message at the time, he or she may focus attention on some other stimulus or "zap" the ad by switching channels.

> **Sensory memory** temporarily stores information that is received during the perceptual process.

If an individual pays attention to the image, it will move into **short-term memory**, where it is briefly stored for processing. This is the individual's *working memory*. At this point, the stimuli are examined for their meaning. If the individual is hungry, for example, information about Wendy's new bacon double cheeseburger with ranch dressing may be a goal that will satisfy his or her hunger.

> **Short-term memory** briefly stores information to which attention has been paid.

There are limitations to the number of distinct pieces of information an individual can retain in short-term memory. Because the senses are constantly interpreting new stimuli, short-term memory could quickly become overloaded. At this stage, the individual evaluates whether the meaning of the information is sufficiently relevant to be remembered. The process of moving images into short-term memory and evaluating them for their meaning is quite brief. Most people can only remember four or five pieces of information simultaneously, and for a maximum duration of only 20 to 30 seconds. If the information has not been evaluated for its meaning within that time, it will be forgotten.

## FACT OR FICTION REVISITED

⊛  Short-term memories *do not* last 2 or 3 weeks; instead, they last less than a minute.

**Long-term memory** permanently stores knowledge after elaborative rehearsal has evaluated the information for meaning and stored it.

Some information is stored in **long-term memory** using *elaborative rehearsal*—the process of evaluating information for meaning and storing it in long-term memory according to the organizing principles the individual has developed based on his or her past experiences and background characteristics. Chris Madonna, for example, has elaborate memories of the Fry's and Safeway supermarkets in which she regularly shops. As another example, some women may store the beach party images of a Coors' Light advertisement differently than men because of their experiences of such parties and the perspective of their gender about beach parties. A female consumer's storage of such images may classify the Coors' ads as those that use scantily clad women to attract men and that do not provide useful information about the product itself.

**Associative Networks**    The process of integrating new information into existing, organized knowledge is called **activation;** the organized knowledge, in turn, is referred to as an **associative network**, or the structure of knowledge about a particular domain, such as college courses or fast food restaurants (Figure 10.6). Information that is seen as similar is linked together in chunks that represent a more general area of information; the individual then classifies or labels that chunk of knowledge. For example, the Wendy's chunk may link information about Frosty's, chili, biggie fries, Dave Thomas, made to order, and quick service. These associative networks form the knowledge base of *schema*—the collection of knowledge and beliefs held by the individual, as we noted in Chapter 9.  For example, you may have an associative network for restaurants, with separate chunks for ice cream, pizza, chicken, and hamburgers. The hamburger chunk includes product knowledge about hamburgers, such as nutrition, taste, toppings, and size, as well as knowledge about brands, such as Big Macs, Quarter Pounders, and Whoppers. When an individual uses the activation process to store the new information about the new bacon double cheeseburger with ranch dressing, that information is linked to the related concepts in the Wendy's chunk. On the other hand, if a local restaurant advertised a new soy burger, it might not be linked to hamburgers at all.

**Activation** is the process of integrating new information into existing **associative networks**— the structure of knowledge about a particular domain.

### ▼ RETRIEVING KNOWLEDGE

Individuals retrieve information from long-term memory to use in problem-solving activities. Recall that when consumers recognize a need, they begin their search for alternatives to satisfy that need. Much of the knowledge about alternatives can come from existing knowledge in their memories. Existing knowledge, in turn, affects new information because the new information is integrated into existing associative networks. Several factors can influence a consumer's ability to retrieve knowledge: (1) familiarity with the information; (2) the relevance of the information; (3) the form in which the information is provided; and (4) repetition of the information.

**Familiarity**    When consumers are already familiar with a product or service it is easier for them to remember information about it because they will have well-developed associative networks that contain a great deal of information linked to the

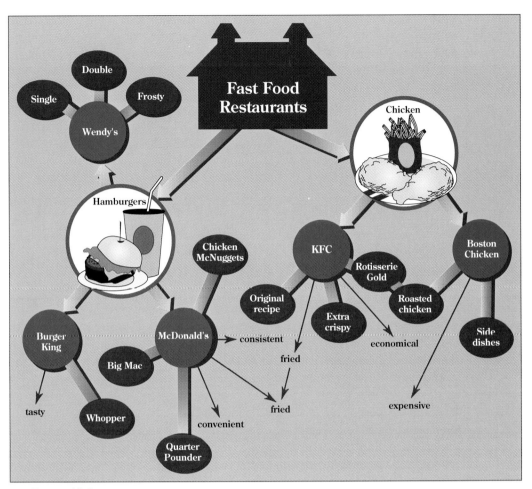

■ FIGURE 10.6

A sample associative network for fast-food restaurants.

product. New information can then be stored via appropriate links to existing knowledge and is, therefore, more easily remembered and retrieved. If a consumer eats frequently at fast food restaurants, for example, he or she will have more elaborate associative networks about fast food products, such as Wendy's hamburgers versus McDonald's Big Macs, than someone who does not eat such food.

**Relevance**  Similarly, when information is relevant to an individual, he or she will have both the motivation and the capacity to store that information in long-term memory through associative networks. For example, a business major would be more familiar with the business courses being offered than would an art history major and would find them more relevant; accordingly, the business major will have well-developed networks for such courses. When course registration occurs, he or she would be  more likely to be able to retrieve information about the business courses than would the art history major.

**Form**   The form in which information is initially perceived before storage also affects the ease with which it is retrieved. There appears to be a superiority of visual memory over verbal memory, and consumers spend more time examining a visual in an ad than reading the copy. Therefore, information that is conveyed through pictures is more likely to get attention during the storage phase of learning. Unfortunately, although recognition is high, comprehension of visual stimuli may be reduced because the consumer uses less processing to interpret a picture than to interpret words. Some ads attempt to connect words and pictures to link the visual to the copy.

## FACT OR FICTION REVISITED

⦿   Visual stimuli *are not* more likely than verbal stimuli to encourage elaborative processing; in fact, they are *less* likely to do so.

Music provides a second sensory channel to help consumers recall product information. Some marketers use familiar, popular music, such as the Nike ad that used the Beatles song "Instant Karma" to back up dramatic images of athletes competing wearing Nike sneakers  Others create their own jingles, such as the famous  "Like a good neighbor, State Farm is there" tune that closes every State Farm television commercial.

**Repetition**   Information is forgotten almost immediately after it is learned. Consumers generally do not store new information very effectively without repetition during elaborative rehearsal. When a friend tells you her address or telephone number, for example, you may repeat it a couple of times to help you remember it. Marketers help consumers remember their products by repeating their brand names and their slogans within ads and by running their ads over and over again. For example, ads for Wrigley's Doublemint chewing gum continually repeat the jingle "Double your pleasure, double your fun with Doublemint, Doublemint gum."

# MARKETING APPLICATIONS OF CONSUMER LEARNING

Both the behavioral and the cognitive approaches to learning have implications for how marketers and public policy actors attempt to provide information to consumers. Although the two approaches to understanding consumer learning differ, they offer complementary insights about how consumers use information provided by marketers and interpersonal communication to learn about products, brands, attributes, and benefits. For example, it doesn't matter whether we adopt a behavioral perspective—repetition increases the strength of the association between unconditioned and conditioned responses—or a cognitive perspective—repetition strengthens the links between new information and existing associative networks—the conclusion is the same: repetition helps consumers learn. With this understanding, we now turn to a discussion of some of the strategies marketers use to influence consumers through the learning process.

## ▼ REWARDS

Rewards increase the likelihood that a behavior will be repeated. Consumers must receive a continual reward—that is, the product must satisfy their needs—if they are to continue to buy the product. Only when they have learned, through the experience of consistent rewards, that a product will satisfy their needs, will they accept an occasional unsatisfying experience. This is why service marketers, such as American Express, go to great lengths to resolve customer problems. However, if the reward is given too often, over time, the consumer may come to expect the continual reward, in addition to the product benefit, and the reward will have lost any effect it originally may have had on the consumer's behavior. In response, some marketers have chosen to offer *occasional* rewards that complement their product, such as a toothpaste that offers a free toothbrush as a special promotion (Figure 10.7).

Many marketers have developed such intermittent reward schedules, including retailers who put merchandise on sale several times during a year and gambling casinos that program slot machines to pay off at irregular intervals. Obviously, this approach works only as long as the product consistently provides another benefit that meets the consumer's needs. Retailers sell products that consumers need even when they are not on sale, for example, and gambling provides other benefits even when the gambler is not winning. The box below discusses the rewards some consumers derive from gambling, an activity many observers define as an example of the "dark side" of consumer behavior.

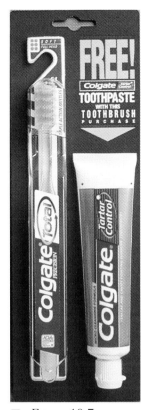

■ FIGURE 10.7

Some marketers offer occasional rewards for purchasing their product, such as a free toothbrush, hoping to increase the likelihood that the purchase behavior will be repeated.

## ● DARK SIDE OF CONSUMPTION

### The Rewards of Gambling[5]

Elaine Cohen spends three days a week playing blackjack at Bally's Grand Hotel in Atlantic City, losing an average $30,000 a year. Elaine is not a rich woman—she is in her seventies and is living on her savings, having retired several years ago from her job as the manager of a small electronics company. She figures that her savings will last another 5 years or so, and her daughter says she will support her, but not her gambling habit, after that. Gambling is the center of Elaine's life, but it is not the only thing she does—she also spends time with her daughter and volunteers two days a week at a local program for the mentally disabled near her home in New Jersey.

The amount of money spent by consumers on gambling is difficult to determine, but estimates of the revenue gained from gambling indicate about $30 billion from legal gambling activities, such as casinos, lotteries, and sporting events, and another $43 billion from illegal gambling in the United States alone. Gambling marketers are attempting to put gambling on commercial air flights, and the Internet Online Offshore Electronic Casino operates a gambling operation on the World Wide Web.

Elaine Cohen says she "lives for" the interaction with the casino employees and other gamblers. She is well known by everyone at Bally's and is so involved with them that she brings gifts every week and was even invited to the wedding of two of the dealers. As a "regular," Elaine receives perks, such as complimentary rooms and meals. Casino employees admit, however, that the free services and personal treatment will end when she can no longer afford to lose such large sums.

Casinos do much to reward gamblers who return and gamble as frequently as Elaine does. Harrah's in Las Vegas gives high-stakes gamblers cards they can place in slot machines as they play. The slot machines flash their names and notify management of their birthdays so that drinks, balloons, and a cake can be delivered to them. When a customer wins a large amount of money at a slot machine, the noise and lights attract other gamblers' attention and glitter is spread around the machine so that the others will be able to identify the hot area. The casino also trains employees to identify compulsive gamblers and publicizes a hotline, 1-800-GAMBLER, for such addicted persons to call for help.

All of these rewards play a large role in encouraging consumers to learn to gamble large amounts of money. How would you characterize the learning that gamblers exhibit? Are the gaming wins sufficient reward to reinforce their gambling behavior? Do memories of losing money have the same relevance as immediate losses? Can you think of any background characteristics that might affect how consumers learn from their gambling experiences?

## ▼ REPETITION

Repetition enhances learning in two ways—first, it helps consumers associate an unconditioned stimulus with a conditioned stimulus, and, second, it strengthens the links between the new information and associated nodes in long-term memory.[6] Marketers have long known the value of repetition—consumers need to hear new information several times before they learn it; each repetition increases the likelihood that the consumer will pay attention to the ad and learn the desired associations among the brand, its attributes, and its benefits. The Partnership for a Drug Free America, for example, publicizes the negative effects of drugs through a number of different sources, including television and magazine ads, brochures, and lectures and discussions. The hope is that repeated exposures to the information will educate children and teenagers about the dangers of drugs.

## ▼ STIMULUS GENERALIZATION AND DISCRIMINATION

Marketers utilize stimulus generalization when they want to provide information about product line extensions. In doing so, the marketer uses similar branding or packaging across products to capitalize on the positive associations with an existing product (Figure 10.8). Stimuli that can be generalized include company names, such as Arm and Hammer, or brand names, such as Ivory. Arm and Hammer introduced a number of diverse products, from deodorant to laundry detergent, each carrying the company name and the distinctive yellow packaging. Similarly, Proctor and Gamble's Ivory brand has extended from the original bar soap to include laundry detergent, liquid hand soap, and shampoo and conditioner, all using the same brand name and logo and similar color schemes. Stimulus generalization is carried even further when competitors use copycat packaging. As we discussed in the Public Policy box in Chapter 9, consumers may assume that a similar color or package is related to a specific brand simply because they have made the association in the past.

By contrast, stimulus discrimination occurs when consumers *differentiate* between similar products, regardless of how similar they might appear.[7] In this case, the marketer has succeeded in making its product distinct in the mind of the consumer. Even though the Food and Drug Administration has approved generic substitutions for many prescription medicines, for example, some doctors still insist on the brand name version for their patients. Similarly, many consumers are willing to spend more for brand name products than similar store brands because they believe that the products are significantly different. Advertising, in turn, plays an important role in stimulus discrimination by blatantly emphasizing product and packaging differences.

## ▼ EXPERIENCE

A fundamental insight of learning theories is that consumers learn from their experience with products.[8] Marketers apply this insight when they distribute free samples. In this type of promotion, consumers are allowed to try the product and experience its rewards without having to make a purchase. If the product experience is positive, it will likely encourage the consumer to purchase the product in the future. This is particularly appropriate for products for which actual use is the most effective learning tool. For example, Smartfoods popcorn uses sampling extensively because the taste of its product appeals to consumers. Similarly, analgesics and cold remedies are difficult to learn about simply by reading packages or comparing features. But if a consumer tries the product and it relieves his or her symptoms, that positive reinforcement will be an effective learning tool. Accordingly, many pharmaceutical companies, such as McNeil, distribute samples of their over-the-counter medications.

## ▼ SIGNS AND SYMBOLS

Signs and symbols facilitate consumer learning through the process of association.[9] Marketers have long used corporate logos to enhance consumer recognition—Texaco's red star, Merrill Lynch's bull, and Allstate's cupped hands are familiar to many consumers. Through advertising that is repeated over a period of time, consumers learn to connect signs, symbols, and even package shapes to products. Few consumers would struggle to link a Green Giant, Tony the Tiger, or Charlie the Tuna with their respective products. These links are the result of frequent, long-term advertising campaigns that repeatedly present the products and symbols together so that consumers have learned to associate the two.

Marketers use a variety of signs and symbols in an effort to communicate information. The "Good Housekeeping Seal" (Figure 10.9) is a concise statement of a limited warranty, while Mr.

■ FIGURE 10.8

Marketers, such as Land-O-Lakes, often use similar packaging or designs across product lines to capitalize on positive associations.

■ FIGURE 10.9

The Good Housekeeping Seal has become known as a symbol of limited warranty and customer satisfaction.

Yuk, a cartoon face with its tongue sticking out, is used to convey toxicity or poison. In recent years new symbols have been created to indicate food that has been irradiated and products that can be recycled.

# PUBLIC POLICY AND INFORMATION

Inherent in the ability to learn are important public policy issues of fairness and economic and social welfare.[10] Consumers must be able to gather and organize unbiased information if they are to have fair opportunities to satisfy their needs. This means that information must be both accessible to the consumer and presented in a fashion that allows the consumer to incorporate accurate and useful knowledge in purchase activities. Labels on food packages and car leasing terms, for example, should present information that the average consumer can comprehend and use as a basis for his or her buying decisions. Informed consumers, in turn, will be better prepared to act in ways that will advance the general welfare of society. For example, consumers should possess the knowledge that is necessary to assess the health risks of consuming products such as cigarettes and alcohol.

## ▼ UNLEARNING—THE EFFECTIVENESS OF WARNING LABELS

Whereas marketers concentrate their efforts on educating consumers about their products so that they will make a purchase, public policy officials often concern themselves with persuading consumers to "unlearn" old knowledge. Learning and unlearning can be seen as two divergent processes that require different approaches on the part of the marketer and the public policy actor. For example, whereas cigarette marketers encourage consumers to learn the social and taste benefits of smoking, antismoking policy makers and social action groups encourage smokers to unlearn the knowledge and positive memories that support that habit.

Warning labels are one attempt to help consumers learn the proper use of products that may pose danger to the user. For years warning labels were viewed by regulators as a means of informing consumers about unsafe products. Industry representatives initially fought the idea, but many now comply with the government regulations for warnings. In some cases, these hotly contested labels have proved to be a legal asset. For example, the tobacco industry maintains that labels on cigarette packages warn consumers of possible health risks and that is the extent of their responsibility. Local, state, and federal courts are not so quick to agree and are considering whether the health warnings required on cigarette packages since 1966 are enough to relieve the manufacturers from the responsibility of paying damages to consumers who allege that they developed cancer from smoking.

The issue is largely one of the effectiveness of warning labels. Suppose consumers do not respond to warning labels by changing their buying behavior.

Who is at fault? Who is liable for damages—the government, for requiring the in-effective label? the manufacturer, for heavily advertising the product? or the consumer, for ignoring the warning?

**Arguments Against Warning Labels**   Warning labels seem to be an effective device for providing information to consumers, but learning theories actually provide several arguments *against* them. Specifically, labels can: (1) present information in a confusing way; (2) be ignored by consumers; and (3) provide information consumers cannot integrate with their experiences and needs. Let's examine each of these concerns in more detail.

The first argument against warning labels is that they often present information in a format from which consumers cannot learn. In some cases, the words, terminology, or symbols that are used are unfamiliar to consumers. For example, whereas the international symbol for poison is a skull and crossbones, this image is often not recognized by American children. In response, poison control experts in the United States developed Mr.Yuk—a character with a bright green face poking out his tongue in disgust (Figure 10.10). Similarly, the pictogram used to show flammability—a small camp fire—was interpreted by some consumers to mean they should heat the product or dispose of it by burning. Often too much information is provided on a product and consumers cannot handle the information overload. A Werner three-foot step ladder, for example, has three separate warning labels: (1) a warning on the second step not to stand at that level, (2) a warning on the back of the ladder not to climb on that side, and (3) a list of *30* distinct safety instructions on the side rail of the ladder.

A second drawback of labels is that consumers can become immune to the impact of labels they see each time they use a product or on more and more of the products they use. In the case of a product that is used frequently, such as a household cleaner, the consumer recalls knowledge from his or her memory and does not reread the label each time. In such a situation, instructions on how to use the product are more likely to be rehearsed and remembered than would seemingly unnecessary warnings about harmful side effects. The consumer already knows that cleaning products are potentially toxic and will not be likely to pay attention to similar warning labels on any new products he or she begins to use.

A third consideration is that warning labels sometimes require impossible behavior. Cigarette lighters contain a warning label that advises consumers not to bring the product close to their faces, but this is the way that most smokers light their cigarettes; it would be very difficult for them to learn to accomplish this task in a different way. Some four-wheel drive vehicles carry a label warning the driver that the vehicle can tip during sharp turns that occur in emergency situations. Avoiding sharp turns in an emergency would also be difficult.

■ FIGURE 10.10
Poison control experts in the United States developed Mr. Yuk to warn children against playing with products that are poisonous.

### FACT OR FICTION REVISITED

◉ Warning labels *are not* very effective at preventing the misuse of even close to 90 percent of the products to which they are attached.

In the context of learning theories, a behavioral perspective would posit that consumers often do not associate the stimuli of warning labels with the desired response of eliminating unsafe behavior, whereas a cognitive perspective might state that consumers are not integrating the new information with existing knowledge about dangerous behavior. For example, sales of diet soft drinks continued to increase even after labels were added warning consumers about the link between saccharin and cancer in laboratory animals. Regardless of the perspective, consumers' existing perceptions and knowledge of the dangers involved and the difficulty of compliance with the warnings prevent them from learning about the dangers.

# LEARNING

Chris Madonna has learned how to shop for groceries in an efficient and effective way. She remembers much of what she needs to buy, and her daughter reminds her of other items they need. Chris usually shops at either of two stores because the way they are arranged matches her mental shopping list. The Safeway has an added benefit—it offers her the reward of price savings when she uses its coupons. She gathers useful information from package labels to help her avoid foods she is allergic to and to help her family avoid unnecessary fat. And, to Chris, some brand names are symbols of quality, saving her the trouble of having to learn new information to make her purchase decisions.

As we have discussed throughout this chapter, learning is the tool that consumers like Chris use to organize their knowledge so that they can make the most appropriate purchase decisions for themselves. Learning enables consumers to keep track of all of their past experiences and to integrate that existing knowledge with all of the new information they receive from marketers, public policy actors, and interpersonal relationships with friends and others in their reference groups. Consumers have elaborate storage facilities to incorporate new information as well as to retrieve existing knowledge. As we will see in the next chapter on attitude formation and change, this knowledge is the basis for many of the opinions consumers develop about the products they buy as well as those they choose not to buy.

## SUMMARY

1. **Describe consumer learning and its characteristics.** Learning is the process by which consumers organize knowledge so that it causes a permanent change in their behavior and can be used again in future purchase activities. Consumers use their perceptual processes to gather information from stimuli in their environment. Learning is a process that evolves over time as consumers remember knowledge they have accumulated from past experiences and integrate it with information from current stimuli to create a useful framework to guide their behavior. Learning cannot be directly observed; it can only be inferred by observing behavior that *should* be affected by the acquired

knowledge. Finally, learning and perception are tightly linked—perception provides the raw material for learning, and consumers use the knowledge they have learned from past experiences to organize and interpret their perceptions of new stimuli.

2. **Recognize the types of behavioral learning processes.** Classical conditioning occurs when a consumer learns to associate an unrelated stimulus with a particular behavioral response that has previously been elicited by a related stimulus. After repetition, the unrelated response elicits the same behavior as the related one. Consumers associate products' shapes, logos, and brand names with the benefits they receive from the product and generalize those benefits to other products with similar product attributes. Instrumental, or operant, conditioning occurs when a consumer learns to associate a stimulus with a response if he or she is rewarded for exhibiting the response. Positive reinforcements are rewards for exhibiting a particular response, whereas negative reinforcements teach consumers to take actions that will avoid such penalties, and punishments are penalties that teach the consumer to avoid exhibiting particular behavior.

3. **Determine the roles played by information processing and memory in cognitive learning processes.** Cognitive learning theories focus on a consumer's information processing—the storage, organization, and retrieval of knowledge from the individual's memory. A consumer uses the attention process to move sensory information stored by the perceptual process from sensory memory into short-term memory. The individual then uses elaborative rehearsal to evaluate the information for its meaning and store it in appropriate locations in his or her long-term memory. To integrate this new information, the consumer uses the activation process to link it with similar information in associative networks of existing knowledge. Factors that influence how efficiently and effectively the consumer can retrieve knowledge include the familiarity, relevance, and form of the information as well as how often the information is repeated during storage.

4. **Identify marketing applications of consumer learning.** The behavioral and cognitive approaches to understanding consumer learning offer complementary insights into how consumers use information provided by marketers and interpersonal communication to learn about products, brands, attributes, and benefits. Rewards increase the likelihood that a consumer will repeat a particular purchase activity; thus, marketers work to guarantee that a consumer is satisfied with the benefits a product offers as well as other aspects of the buying experience. Marketers also attempt to repeat the messages they send to consumers to help them learn, and they design packaging and advertising to present stimuli consumers can perceive and learn accurately. Signs and symbols are used in advertising to help consumers generalize their learning, such as transferring positive feelings to related products, and to discriminate, such as identifying and rejecting copycat products.

5. **Analyze public policy implications of the information provided in warning labels.** The ability to learn encompasses important public policy issues of fairness and economic and social welfare. Whereas most marketers want consumers to learn about products so that they ultimately make a purchase, public policy actors often concern themselves with persuading consumers to "unlearn" old knowledge about harmful products. For example, warning labels are often used as a means of informing consumers about unsafe products. However, there is some controversy about the effectiveness of warning labels because they are sometimes confusing and consumers may ignore them or be unable to integrate the information with their existing knowledge and practices.

# KEY TERMS

Learning, *p. 287*
Behavioral learning
  theories, *p. 290*
Classical conditioning,
  *p. 291*
Stimulus generalization,
  *p. 293*

Stimulus discrimination,
  *p. 293*
Instrumental (operant)
  conditioning, *p. 294*
Cognitive learning
  theories, *p. 296*

Information processing,
  *p. 296*
Sensory memory, *p. 297*
Short-term memory, *p. 297*
Long-term memory, *p. 298*
Activation, *p. 298*
Associative network, *p. 298*

# SKILL-BUILDING ACTIVITIES

1.  Visit a local supermarket and observe the environment and the activities of its customers. Locate and describe one example of each of the following processes:
    a. stimulus generalization
    b. stimulus discrimination
    c. instrumental conditioning
    d. positive reinforcement
    e. negative reinforcement
    f. intermittent reinforcement
    g. information processing
    h. sensory memory
    i. short-term memory
    j. activation
    k. occasional rewards
    l. effects of repetition
    m. effects of symbols
    n. unlearning

2.  Revisit the advertisements you collected for the skill-building activities in Chapter 9. In those ads, locate and describe one example of an attempt to induce each of the above processes.

3.  Assume that you are a government official interested in encouraging teenagers not to smoke. How would you use each of the processes listed in activity 1 above?

# CHAPTER 10 SELF-TEST

▼ MULTIPLE CHOICE

1.  Learning is the process by which consumers organize knowledge so that it causes a _____ in their behavior.
    a. temporary change
    b. permanent change
    c. purchase decision
    d. marketing change

2.  Behavioral learning is based on the association between a _____ and a _____ .
    a. consumer; marketer
    b. consumer; product
    c. stimulus; response
    d. stimulus; consumer

3.  _____ occurs when learning is the result of information processing.
    a. Behavioral learning
    b. Inference learning
    c. Response learning
    d. Cognitive learning

4.  Playing patriotic music during a product advertisement so that consumers associate the product with their country is an example of what type of learning theory?
    a. cognitive learning
    b. classical conditioning
    c. operant conditioning
    d. observational learning

5.  When a consumer purchases a product that is packaged similarly to a name brand product because the consumer assumes the two products to be of the same quality, _____ has occurred.
    a. stimulus generalization
    b. stimulus discrimination
    c. instrumental conditioning
    d. operant conditioning

6. Coupons, rebates, and free service after the sale are all examples of what type of reinforcement?
   a. negative
   b. helpful
   c. positive
   d. referral

7. Which type of reinforcement should rarely be used in a marketing context?
   a. punishment
   b. negative
   c. positive
   d. repetitive

8. Consumers place information into their _____ memory so that they can evaluate whether or not the information should be remembered.
   a. short-term
   b. long-term
   c. sensory
   d. acute

9. Included in a consumer's _____ for snack foods might be potato chips, crackers, popcorn, and pretzels.
   a. elaboration network
   b. associative network
   c. product diagram
   d. category map

10. If a restaurant provides two-for-one meals once every month, a(n) _____ reward schedule is being used.
   a. intermittent
   b. negative
   c. perceived
   d. discount

▼ TRUE/FALSE

1. Learning is relevant only to the promotion component of the marketing mix.   T or F
2. Learning cannot be directly observed.   T or F
3. If a consumer learns about a product, he or she will buy the product.   T or F
4. During classical conditioning, the stimulus occurs after the response.   T or F
5. Learning that is based on rewards and reinforcement is called instrumental conditioning.   T or F
6. Sensory memory is where information about a stimulus is permanently stored.   T or F
7. Activation occurs after information is placed into long-term memory.   T or F
8. Information about unusual or unfamiliar products is remembered more easily than information about a familiar product.   T or F
9. Free sampling enhances the learning process by providing the consumer with experience with the product.   T or F
10. The goal of some warning labels is for consumers to "unlearn" old knowledge.   T or F

▼ SHORT ANSWER

1. How does repetition enhance learning?
2. What are the four factors that affect a consumer's ability to retrieve knowledge?
3. Explain why marketers would want consumers to exhibit stimulus discrimination.

▼ APPLICATION EXERCISE

You have been asked to develop a promotion strategy for a new restaurant that serves low-calorie, low-fat Mexican food. Using the principles of operant conditioning, describe how you might promote this new restaurant.

# 11

# ATTITUDE FORMATION AND CHANGE

◉ Consumer Snapshot *Sarah Muckerman is a 26-year-old preschool teacher. She is single and lives in Atlanta, Georgia, where she rents a townhouse with a roommate.*

## FACT OR FICTION?

◉ Many of our most important attitudes are inherited.

◉ Consumers form attitudes because they make them effective and efficient in dealing with the environment.

◉ Beliefs generally have very little effect on attitudes.

◉ Marketers generally try to change consumers' needs, not their attitudes.

◉ Consumers seek consistency in their thoughts, feelings, and actions.

⊙ The fewer benefits a product offers, the more perceived value is generated in the minds of consumers.

⊙ Social marketing is generally conducted person to person rather than through mass media communication.

# EYE ON THE CONSUMER

Sarah Muckerman has strong attitudes toward some popular marketers, products, and brands. She is an advocate of Sony products—her small television is a Sony, so is her big 30-inch set, and she used to have a Sony Walkman because her friends thought that was the only brand to have when she was younger. But she has since replaced the Walkman with an inexpensive personal tape player she bought at a Sears in the mall where she worked; she dropped the Walkman the day before an airplane trip and needed to replace it quickly to listen to tapes on the flight. When it comes to soft drinks, Sarah also has very definite brand preferences. She likes Coke better than Pepsi because it's not as sweet tasting and because she lives in Atlanta, where Coca-Cola is located. "People will run you out of town on a rail if you don't drink Coke," she says.

Sarah also has strong social and environmental attitudes that influence what she buys. She will not buy any products manufactured by Nestle or Reebok because she believes these companies supported apartheid in South Africa. She was told about Nestle's political leanings by her mother when she was growing up, but she is not sure where she heard about Reebok. She does own a pair of Reebok sneakers, but only because they were given to her as a gift.

Sarah does not think it's right to kill an animal just to make a coat, so she won't wear fur. She rationalizes that it is okay to wear leather, though, because the cow is already slaughtered for its beef. Little baby harp seals are entirely different, though. She only buys dolphin-safe tuna because she feels that killing mammals that can communicate with humans is disgusting. Sarah is also sensitive to environmental issues. She buys pumps instead of aerosol sprays because she doesn't want to destroy the ozone layer and paper towels and napkins that are made from recycled paper even though they're more expensive. She doesn't currently recycle cans, however, because there are no collection bins where she lives and she doesn't know where to take them.

The focus of this chapter is attitudes—consumers' feelings and opinions about products, marketers, and other objects and their resulting predisposition to behave in particular ways toward those objects. We discuss how individuals form attitudes and explore the role marketers can play in changing consumers' attitudes toward their products. We also consider how marketers and consumer researchers study and measure attitudes and the techniques marketers use to try to change attitudes. Finally, we discuss the public policy implications of social marketing and its attempt to shape consumers' attitudes and behavior.

After reading and thinking about this chapter, you should be able to:

**1** Recognize how consumers form attitudes.
**2** Examine consumers' attitudes using relevant attitude models.
**3** Identify appropriate methods to measure consumer attitudes.
**4** Analyze the methods used by marketers to try to change consumer attitudes.
**5** Apply the principles of attitude formation and change to analyze the public policy implications of social marketing.

# ATTITUDE FORMATION

In the course of your day, you make hundreds of decisions about activities, such as what to wear, what to eat, where to study, and even whether or not to attend your Consumer Behavior class. Each of these decisions relies on your feelings and opinions about the alternatives you have for those activities. These feelings and opinions are called *attitudes*, and individuals use them in a variety of ways.[1] Attitudes simplify consumer decision making by providing a way for the individual to evaluate alternatives based on his or her knowledge of the attributes and benefits offered by each.

An **attitude** is a learned predisposition to act in a consistent way toward an object based on feelings and opinions that result from an evaluation of knowledge about the object. **Attitude formation**, in turn, is the process by which individuals form feelings or opinions toward other people, products, ideas, activities, and other objects in their environment. A person's attitude toward an object is composed of three factors: (1) *learned knowledge* from the individual's own experiences with the object, as well as information gathered from others; (2) an *evaluation* of the object based on the individual's knowledge of it; and (3) a *predisposition to act* based on that evaluation.

> An **attitude** is a predisposition to act in a consistent way toward an object.

> **Attitude formation** is the process by which an individual forms a feeling or opinion toward objects.

## ▼ ATTITUDES ARE LEARNED

Consumers form attitudes about products based on the needs they have recognized through the motivation process and the knowledge they have gathered through perception and organized through learning. That is, consumers use perception and learning to gather new information and integrate it with existing knowledge about a product's attributes and benefits. This integrated knowledge serves as the basis for evaluating the alternative products from which the consumer will make a purchase decision.

## FACT OR FICTION REVISITED

◉ It is *not true* that most of our important attitudes are inherited. Instead, all attitudes are learned.

For example, you may have learned about recycling through your own experiences in separating recyclable packaging from your trash, from lectures in your biology or political science courses, from television programs about the environment, or from friends or family members who belong to environmental groups. Based on that knowledge, you have evaluated recycling as an activity and formed your opinions about how important it is to recycle cans and bottles and whether it is more environmentally sensitive to buy reusable containers and large-size product refills. When faced with concrete situations, your attitudes guide the decisions you make, such as whether to buy Pepsi, Lipton Brisk iced tea, or Fruitopia. You use your attitudes about recycling, as well as your attitudes about other benefits offered by these products, such as taste and cost, to reach a purchase decision. You may decide to buy a Pepsi in a reusable beverage holder emblazoned with your school's logo, or a cup of Lipton Brisk iced tea from the fountain served in a paper cup you can discard in the trash, or a bottle of Fruitopia that will require you to walk an extra 30 yards to drop in the recycling bin.

Attitudes are important to marketers for one simple reason: A consumer with a positive attitude toward a product is more likely to buy that product. But because attitudes are the result of motivation, perception, and learning, they cannot be observed directly. The only way to uncover a person's attitudes is to ask him or her about them. For example, Sarah wears Reebok sneakers because she got them as a gift, not because she has a favorable attitude toward Reebok. Thus, marketers and consumer researchers must utilize a variety of direct techniques, such as interviews and surveys, which we discuss later in the chapter, to measure consumers' attitudes.

The fact that attitudes are learned means that they can be affected by new information and experience. There are some attitudes that remain very resistant to change, however, regardless of incoming information. Some individuals love the Frosted Flakes they ate as a child or continue to favor a manual typewriter over improved computer technology, for example, whereas others enjoy smoking, oppose seat belts and motorcycle helmets, or shun condoms despite growing awareness of the consequences of such activities.

It is easier to understand such lasting attitudes if we turn our attention to the question of why individuals form attitudes in the first place. The answer is simple: People form attitudes because attitudes make them more efficient and effective in dealing with their environment. It is important to recognize that attitudes are *functional* for consumers—that is, attitudes serve important functions in people's lives, as discussed below.

## FACT OR FICTION REVISITED

  ◉  Attitudes do indeed make consumers more effective and efficient in dealing with the environment.

## ▼ THE FUNCTIONS OF ATTITUDES

Attitudes provide a way for individuals to apply their knowledge to an evaluation of alternative products and, consequently, to make faster, easier, and less risky

## Table 11.1

### EXAMPLES OF ATTITUDE FUNCTIONS

| Function | Objects of the Attitude | Examples |
|---|---|---|
| Utilitarian | Products that provide utilitarian benefits | Fluoride prevents cavities<br>ACT Fluoride dental rinse will keep teeth strong |
| Value-expressive | Products that illustrate values, personality, lifestyle, and psychographics | American-made cars are good for the U. S. economy<br>Oldsmobile Aurora is a better choice than the Acura Legend |
| Ego-defensive | Products that support self-concept | Dandruff is an embarrassing problem<br>Head & Shoulders is an effective anti-dandruff shampoo |
| Knowledge | Products that structure knowledge and provide certainty | Acetaminophen is gentler on the stomach than aspirin<br>Tylenol is safer than Bayer |

purchase decisions to satisfy their needs. For example, if a consumer had a positive experience with Timberland boots because they were durable and attractive, this knowledge would result in a positive attitude toward that product. When the time comes to buy another pair of boots that will last a long time and look good, the consumer will likely recall the positive attitude that summarizes those experiences and purchase Timberlands again.

Attitudes help individuals in four primary ways, as illustrated in Table 11.1. Attitudes reflect an individual's motivation to: (1) gain utilitarian benefits; (2) express his or her values and lifestyle; (3) defend the ego or self-concept; and (4) organize knowledge about objects in his or her environment.[2]

**The Utilitarian Function**   An individual develops attitudes toward certain objects because they offer *utility*—a reward or punishment the individual has learned to associate with that object. For example, some consumers have had positive experiences with the Ford Escorts they drive and developed a positive attitude toward that brand of car. These consumers may even generalize that stimulus and develop a positive attitude toward all Ford cars. On the other hand, a consumer who had a bad experience buying pants through a mail-order catalog because they didn't fit might develop a negative attitude toward buying any product by mail. For marketers, influencing a consumer's utilitarian attitudes can be as simple as providing information about how their product will offer the utilitarian benefits that satisfy consumers' needs better than existing alternatives. For example, Tums advertises that its antacid provides calcium in addition to antacid relief (Figure 11.1). For those consumers for whom calcium is important, such as women susceptible to osteoporosis, this product has an additional utilitarian benefit other antacids do not have.

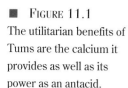

**FIGURE 11.1**

The utilitarian benefits of Tums are the calcium it provides as well as its power as an antacid.

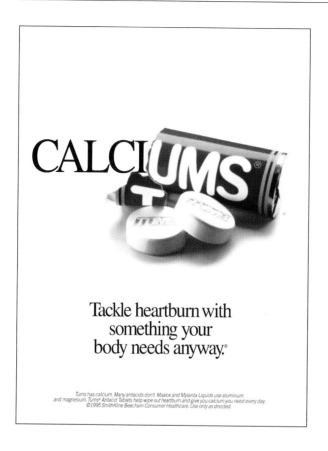

**The Value-Expressive Function** Consumers typically develop positive attitudes toward those objects that allow them to illustrate their values, personality, lifestyle, and psychographics—that is, products that express the basic cultural values and lifestyles enjoyed by consumers. For example, a consumer who wishes to express her Christian values would form more positive attitudes toward Amy Grant's music than toward Melissa Etheridge's. Many marketers try to encourage positive attitudes toward their products by positioning them in consumers' minds as suitable for a particular lifestyle. At the same time, some companies who market to many segments try to *avoid* becoming identified with individuals or small segments with distinct values and lifestyles. General Motors and Toyota both emphasize their contribution to keeping American workers employed, for example, to portray their products as representing core American values and broadly acceptable lifestyles.

**Ego-Defensive Function** Consumers form some attitudes to protect themselves from external threats or internal feelings. These *ego-defensive attitudes* are long lasting, deep rooted, and difficult to change because they go to the very heart of a person's self-concept. For example, when time-saving products such as instant cake mixes were first introduced in the United States and Italy, they were viewed as insulting and demeaning by homemakers. At the time, women's self-images were largely based on caring for their families, and using convenience products

THE SPECIALTY OF THE HOUSE
IS NOW AT YOUR HOUSE

*Cafe Classics*

Introducing Cafe Classics™ from Lean Cuisine.®
Nine delicious entrees inspired by restaurant cuisine. Each grilled or roasted with
innovative herbs, spices, glazes or sauces. Each low in fat and, amazingly, still under 300 calories.
Quite simply, you no longer have to go out for food that's out of this world.

©1995 Nestlé Frozen Food Company

■ FIGURE 11.2
Marketers of convenience
products, such as Stouffer's
Lean Cuisine, position their
products to appeal to the
ego-defensive function of
homemakers who prefer
products that allow them to
spend less time in the
kitchen and more time at-
tending to other family
needs.

conflicted with that image because it indicated that they favored their own time
over their families' welfare. Even today, many such convenience products are positioned to appeal to homemakers who have favorable attitudes toward products
that will give them more time to fulfill other family needs (Figure 11.2).

**The Knowledge Function** In some cases, consumers form attitudes to help
them organize and simplify knowledge of their environment into easily applied

evaluations that can be used to simplify decision making. Even attitudes based on imperfect generalizations from concrete information allow consumers to feel less risk when making purchase decisions. For example, since many consumers believe that chickens with yellow skin taste better than chickens with white skin, Frank Perdue advertises that his chickens are fed marigold petals to give them their yellow color. Similarly, public policy actors have long used advertising to

 FIGURE 11.3
Public policy actors use advertising to provide information about the importance of using seat belts.

provide information about the risks of cigarettes, drunk driving, drug use, and driving without seat belts to change consumers' attitudes about these risky activities (Figure 11.3).

**The Relationship Among Functions** The four functions noted above are not mutually exclusive. Rather, many consumer attitudes reflect a combination of the functions. An individual's values and lifestyles (value-expressive function) are often consistent with his or her self-concept (ego defensive). For example, people who live environmentally friendly lifestyles see themselves as environmentally conscious and hold attitudes about pollution that encourage them to commute by bicycle instead of car.

Similarly, utilitarian and knowledge functions often result in attitudes about a product's functional attributes and benefits that are based on the analysis of information. For example, you may gather a lot of information and talk to many friends and acquaintances about a high involvement product purchase such as a personal computer. Before you buy a Gateway 2000 computer, you would want to feel that you have significant knowledge about the benefits it will offer to you in completing your course assignments. Accordingly, Gateway offers detailed information through its ads and other promotional materials to help consumers form utilitarian and knowledge-based attitudes about its products.

Behavior may not always be a dependable indicator of a person's attitudes, however. A consumer may have a favorable attitude toward Gateway computers and still buy a Packard Bell model from a local store because of a fear that he or she will be unable to assemble the computer ordered by mail from Gateway (ego-defensive attitude). Similarly, Sarah Muckerman bought a Sears tape player because it was cheap and convenient, even though she has a more favorable opinion of Sony products. To understand how different attitudes are related to one another and to behavior, we will now consider several different attitude models that have been developed.

# ATTITUDE MODELS

There are three major types of attitude models: (1) *tricomponent models*, (2) *multiattribute models*, and (3) *attitude-toward-the-ad models*. Each type of model explores different components of an attitude and arranges them in different ways in an effort to describe how attitudes develop.

### ▼ TRICOMPONENT ATTITUDE MODELS

Tricomponent attitude models consider three components of an attitude: (1) cognitive beliefs, (2) affect, and (3) conative predisposition to act (Figure 11.4). The cognitive component of the model consists of consumers' knowledge about products, brands, and marketers. The knowledge usually takes the form of **beliefs**

> A **belief** is an individual's knowledge about a particular object, such as its attributes and benefits.

■  FIGURE 11.4
The tricomponent attitude
model.

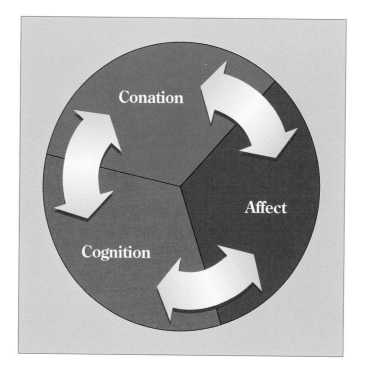

about an object's attributes and the benefits it offers, based on the consumer's
own experiences and information gathered from marketers and other consumers
of the product. Sarah's beliefs about killing animals for clothing and the value of
brand names play an important role in the attitudes she developed, for example.

The second component of the model—**affect**—encompasses the consumer's
feelings or emotions about an object, such as the evaluation of a product or brand.
This evaluation is based on cognitive beliefs that are evaluated in the context of
the consumer's needs. For example, users of Macintosh computers typically have
positive feelings about the brand based on their favorable evaluation of its convenient software in light of their needs for a product that offers ease of use (Figure 11.5). Finally, the **conative component** of the model involves a consumer's
intention to act in some way regarding an object—that is, the predisposition to
buy a particular product to satisfy a need. For example, a person might intend to
buy a Macintosh computer for his or her family for Christmas this year.

Tricomponent models explicitly recognize that behavior encompasses knowledge (cognition), feeling (affect), and action (conation). Our discussion at the beginning of this chapter emphasizes the affective component—the evaluation of
how well a product will meet the consumer's needs—as the key role of the attitude formation process.[3]  Cognitive beliefs are the product of perception and
learning, whereas the conative component focuses on the decision-making
process and purchase and usage behavior we will discuss in the next three chapters. Furthermore, although our presentation of the behavioral processes has so
far been rather linear—consumers learn about products, then form attitudes,
then make decisions—the three components may actually occur in different sequences, which we will discuss at length in our discussion of marketing commu-

**Affect** is an individual's
feeling or emotions
about an object.

The **conative compo-
nent** is an individual's
intention to act in a particular way or a predis-
position to take a spe-
cific action.

nications in Chapter 15. For now, however, remember that some marketers, such as the makers of Smartfood popcorn, distribute samples of their products because consumers will be more receptive to knowledge and form positive attitudes *after* they have taken the action of tasting the product.

## FACT OR FICTION REVISITED

◉ It is not true that beliefs have very little effect on attitudes; in fact, beliefs form the basis for most attitudes.

## ▼ MULTIATTRIBUTE MODELS

Unlike tricomponent models, multiattribute models focus on an object's multiple attributes and suggest that the individual's attitude toward the object is the result of the aggregation of his or her evaluations of each one. The most widely known multiattribute models were developed by Martin Fishbein and his colleagues and incorporate three components: (1) attributes on which the object is evaluated, (2) beliefs about whether an object possesses the attribute, and (3) an evaluation of the importance or relevance of each attribute in determining the individual's overall attitude toward the object.[4] Note that Fishbein's components have a different emphasis than the knowledge–feeling–action components we have discussed so far. He emphasizes that beliefs and evaluations both require evaluation of knowledge, as evident in the two models discussed below.

**Attitude-Toward-Object Model**   When evaluating a product, the consumer's overall attitude toward that product is the aggregation of his or her beliefs about each of its attributes as well as an evaluation of the importance or relevance of that attribute in providing the needed benefits (see Table 11.2). For example, a

*Table 11.2*

### EXAMPLE OF A MULTIATTRIBUTE ATTITUDE-TOWARD-OBJECT MODEL FOR LAUNDRY DETERGENTS

**Scales used to measure beliefs ($b_i$) about each attribute:**

For each pair of descriptions listed below, check the point on the continuum that most accurately describes your opinion of Wisk:

| | | | | | | | | |
|---|---|---|---|---|---|---|---|---|
| Wisk cleans effectively | +3 | +2 | +1 | 0 | -1 | -2 | -3 | Wisk does not clean effectively |
| Wisk is low priced | +3 | +2 | +1 | 0 | -1 | -2 | -3 | Wisk is high priced |
| Wisk leaves colors bright | +3 | +2 | +1 | 0 | -1 | -2 | -3 | Wisk fades colored clothing |
| Wisk's bottle can be recycled | +3 | +2 | +1 | 0 | -1 | -2 | -3 | Wisk's bottle cannot be recycled |
| Wisk is a brand name I trust | +3 | +2 | +1 | 0 | -1 | -2 | -3 | Wisk is not a brand name I trust |

**Scale used to measure the evaluative component ($e_i$):**

For each item below, check the point on the continuum that describes how important it is to you that a laundry detergent have these characteristics:

Cleans effectively

| | | | | | | |
|---|---|---|---|---|---|---|
| Important | 5 | 4 | 3 | 2 | 1 | Unimportant |

Low price

| | | | | | | |
|---|---|---|---|---|---|---|
| Important | 5 | 4 | 3 | 2 | 1 | Unimportant |

Leaves colors bright

| | | | | | | |
|---|---|---|---|---|---|---|
| Important | 5 | 4 | 3 | 2 | 1 | Unimportant |

Package is recyclable

| | | | | | | |
|---|---|---|---|---|---|---|
| Important | 5 | 4 | 3 | 2 | 1 | Unimportant |

Trustworthy brand name

| | | | | | | |
|---|---|---|---|---|---|---|
| Important | 5 | 4 | 3 | 2 | 1 | Unimportant |

**Sample calculation:**

| Attribute | Belief about Wisk | Evaluation of importance of attribute for laundry detergents | $b_i \times e_i$ |
|---|---|---|---|
| Cleans effectively | +3 | 5 | +15 |
| Low price | -2 | 1 | -2 |
| Leaves colors bright | +1 | 5 | +5 |
| Package is recyclable | +2 | 1 | +2 |
| Trustworthy brand name | +3 | 3 | +9 |
| Overall attitude | | | +29 |

consumer might evaluate Wisk laundry detergent on such attributes as its cleaning power, cost, color guard, recyclable packaging, and brand name. This model is usually depicted as an equation:

$$\text{Overall attitude} = \sum_{i\,=\,1}^{n} b_i e_i$$

For each of the $n$ attributes, the consumer evaluates the strength of his or her belief ($b_i$) that Wisk can deliver the attributes he or she is seeking. The consumer evaluates whether Wisk is a powerful cleaner, for example. Then, the consumer weights his or her beliefs when aggregating them—each attribute is evaluated ($e_i$) for its importance or relevance to the consumer in determining his or her overall attitude toward detergents. The consumer judges whether a detergent's cleaning power is more important than its price or brand name reputation, for example.

This formal equation implies that a consumer's attitude toward Wisk requires that he or she complete a mathematical computation to evaluate a product. Most consumers do not engage in such formal computations in their everyday lives. However, they do complete some kind of informal calculations in their own minds when they are forming attitudes about products, particularly for a high involvement purchase. When buying a car, for example, the consumer may even sit down with a pencil and paper and write out a list of benefits and drawbacks for each car under consideration in order to figure out how he or she feels about each. The consumer can then combine the different attributes to form an overall attitude; in doing so, some of the attributes will become more important than others. For example, a consumer who lives in Montana may consider four-wheel drive more important than a sun-roof because of the area's snowy climate, but the opposite would be true for a Floridian.

You might even engage in these calculations when buying laundry detergent. Say you needed to wash a sweatshirt that you borrowed from your roommate and accidentally stained with tomato sauce. In this case, you would probably develop an attitude about buying a laundry detergent that weighted cleaning power and fading effects as more important than cost and recyclability. Instead of just using any brand that you find in your laundry room, you might have to search for additional information from someone who is more knowledgeable about removing stains. Because you don't want your roommate to be angry, you would want to be able to demonstrate to him or her that you did everything you could to salvage the sweatshirt. These additional factors—the specific context of a purchase as well as social influences—are important extensions that Fishbein added to the attitude-toward-object model in his theory of reasoned action, as discussed below.

**Theory-of-Reasoned-Action Model** The theory-of-reasoned-action model explicitly examines the impact of (1) beliefs and attitudes about specific instances of behavior and (2) the subjective norm that exists in the specific social context (Figure 11.6).[5] In this theory, Ajzen and Fishbein focused their attention on specific instances of behavior, such as your purchase of a laundry detergent during the first week of April to remove the stain from your roommate's sweatshirt.

■ FIGURE 11.6
Theory-of-reasoned-action
model.

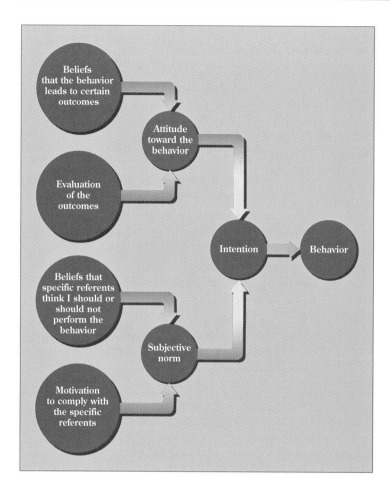

Ajzen and Fishbein posited that a specific purchase is a function of the consumer's intention to purchase the product. That intent, in turn, is affected by the consumer's attitude toward the particular purchase occasion rather than his or her general attitude toward the product. For example, you may not have a favorable attitude toward expensive detergents in general but you will look favorably on the purchase of one to remove a stain you have caused. Thus, the theory of reasoned action recognizes that overall attitudes toward a product may be modified in specific instances of purchase behavior.

The second influence on a specific purchase is the **subjective norm** that exists during the purchase process—the expectations of others in the consumer's reference groups. These norms are a function of the consumer's beliefs about the actions expected by the members of his or her reference groups and his or her motivation to comply with those persons. When you are deciding what to do about the stain on your roomate's sweatshirt, for example, you will consider both what your roommate and other friends expect you to do to compensate for your sloppiness and whether you care about their expectations. Consider another example: Suppose you are planning to buy a pair of jeans. Your purchase decision will include your own personal taste as well as impressions of what is considered

A **subjective norm**
represents the beliefs
about the behavior
expected by the members of one's reference
groups and the individual's motivation to
comply.

an "acceptable" kind of jeans in your social group (Figure 11.7).

The attitude toward a behavior and subjective norm are calculated using a formal method similar to that of the attitude toward an object—aggregating beliefs about the behavior weighted by evaluations of the outcome or motivations to comply.

### ▼ ATTITUDE-TOWARD-THE-AD MODELS

In an effort to understand how advertising influences consumer attitudes toward a particular product, researchers have developed models that investigate attitudes toward advertisements.[6] We will discuss advertising and other forms of marketing communication in detail in Chapter 15; for our purposes here, we will just note the relationship between an individual's attitudes toward advertisements and the product that is being advertised.

Attitude-toward-the-ad models conclude that consumers form feelings and judgments as the result of their exposure to an ad. In combination with the consumer's assessment of the product as it appears in the ad, these impressions form the resulting attitude. Variables in these models include where, when, and in what context the ad is seen as well as the effectiveness of the ad in generating feelings and dispelling negative beliefs. That is, an advertisement influences not only consumers' attitudes about the ad itself but also their view of the product. Furthermore, new products are more strongly influenced by consumers' attitudes toward their advertising than are familiar ones.

In order for marketers to use the various attitude models, they need to measure all of these beliefs and evaluative components. We now turn to a discussion of some of the techniques used to measure attitude components.

■ FIGURE 11.7
Jordache has successfully used attractive models in its advertising to appeal to the desire of young adults to fit in to a certain social group.

# MEASURING ATTITUDES

Researchers have developed three common methods of measuring attitudes: (1) observation of behavior, (2) qualitative investigations, and (3) attitude scales. Each has unique advantages, depending on the circumstances, and all are helpful in determining the strength and direction of a particular attitude. The resulting information allows marketers to plan the best strategy for connecting their product with the intended consumers.

### ▼ OBSERVATION

Observation allows researchers to infer attitudes from behavior. When consumers buy large quantities of a particular product, its marketer may conclude that consumers like that brand. When a Consumer Behavior class has an overenrollment of students, the school may infer that the professor is popular among the student body. It is obvious from these examples that observation alone may not be an accurate indicator of attitudes, however. The consumers stocking up on a product may simply be taking advantage of a special offer, whereas the overenrolled class might be the result of other course cancellations. Similarly, Sears and Reebok would be incorrect in assuming that Sarah Muckerman purchased their products because she prefered them over competing brands.  For this reason, observation is usually used to supplement other research methods and is seldom the sole method of attitude measurement.

### ▼ QUALITATIVE INVESTIGATIONS

Qualitative methods include *focus groups*, *depth interviews*, and *psychological tests*. The focus of each of these investigative techniques is on getting consumers to reveal their feelings and opinions through open discussion.

> A **focus group** is a small group of individuals who discuss their attitudes toward some object with the help of a moderator.

**Focus Groups**   A **focus group** is a small group of consumers—usually between 6 and 12 participants—who discuss a number of questions about a product, brand, or marketer, with the help of a moderator. The interaction among the group's members invites them to express feelings they might not remember or be comfortable expressing in another situation. Student focus groups have been held at many schools to assess student attitudes toward such issues as campus safety, and consumers are often brought together by marketing researchers to assess attitudes towards specific products.

Focus groups can be interesting and provide valuable insights, but a dozen people are seldom representative of an entire market segment. For that reason focus groups are most useful in providing insights into attitudes, but they must be used in conjunction with other methods to determine the attitudes held by all the members of a target market segment.

**Depth Interviews**   A depth interview, as we have noted in our discussion of motivation in Chapter 8, is a personal interview conducted one-on-one between a consumer and a trained interviewer; it often lasts for several hours. In such situations, consumers are encouraged to talk openly and in great depth about their feelings and opinions toward a product. Researchers encourage consumers to discuss their feelings and attempt to clarify their statements by asking probing questions such as "Why do you feel that way?" or "What do you mean by that?" The drawbacks of this method of investigation are that it is very time consuming and expensive to conduct and, like focus groups, is seldom representative of the entire target market segment.

**Psychological Tests**   The psychological tests consumer researchers employ include a range of projective techniques of the type we discussed in Chapter 8. Examples include asking a consumer to interpret a picture (the Thematic Apperception Test, or TAT), fill in the dialog in a cartoon situation, fill in a blank in a sentence about a product or brand, or offer the first word that comes to mind when a product is mentioned. In these cases, the freedom to respond to open-ended questions is intended to stimulate consumers to reveal their underlying feelings about a product.

## ▼ ATTITUDE SCALES

Researchers often use consumer survey questionnaires to measure attitudes on quantitative scales (Table 11.3). At the end of this course, for example, you will probably be asked to fill out a teacher evaluation questionnaire that contains numerical rating scales. The most common attitude scale is a Likert scale, which consists of a statement followed by degrees of agreement. For example, "The professor uses class time effectively" would by followed by "strongly agree . . . strongly disagree" with blanks in between. The consumer simply checks the blank indicating his or her degree of agreement with that attitude statement.

Semantic differential scales can also be used to measure attitudes. In this case, the scale is made up of opposite adjectives at each extreme. Scales of this type are often used to measure the components of multiattribute models. When administered to a representative sample of the target market, surveys containing these types of scales are fairly easy to execute and answer and offer reliable, valid ways to assess consumer attitudes.

### Table 11.3

#### EXAMPLES OF SCALES USED TO MEASURE ATTITUDES

**Likert scale items**

|  | Agree strongly | Agree somewhat | Neither agree nor disagree | Disagree somewhat | Disagree strongly |
|---|---|---|---|---|---|
| Wisk is effective at removing stains from my clothes | 5 | 4 | 3 | 2 | 1 |
| Wisk is worth the money that it costs | 5 | 4 | 3 | 2 | 1 |
| Wisk will not fade the colors from my clothes | 5 | 4 | 3 | 2 | 1 |

**Semantic differential scale**
For each pair of descriptions listed below, check the point on the continuum that most accurately describes your opinion of Wisk:

| Cleans effectively | ___ ___ ___ ___ ___ | Does not clean clothes |
|---|---|---|
| Low price | ___ ___ ___ ___ ___ | High price |
| Leaves colors bright | ___ ___ ___ ___ ___ | Fades colored clothing |

# CHANGING CONSUMER ATTITUDES

Since attitudes are comprised of three major components—knowledge, evaluation, and a predisposition to act—they can be changed by altering any of these components. Marketers cannot change consumers' needs, but they can attempt to influence their beliefs, affect, and conative intentions by providing information about the attributes and benefits consumers use to form attitudes as well as by influencing the social context in which consumers form those attitudes. Simply stated, consumers look to members of their reference groups for information and advice, and that information and advice can change their attitudes. In Chapter 15 we will discuss how marketers use communications tools to influence consumers; in Chapter 16 we will consider how interpersonal ties affect consumer behavior. But, first, we present some of the ways marketing and interpersonal communications influence consumers' attitudes specifically.

## FACT OR FICTION REVISITED

⦿ Marketers *do not* try to change consumers' needs; rather, they attempt to change their attitudes.

An individual is likely to change his or her attitudes to retain a consistent relationship with the changing environment. Marketing and interpersonal communications, in turn, influence the processes consumers use to interact with their environment—motivation, perception, and learning. As marketers communicate new facts about their products, and as members of reference groups provide new advice, consumers are motivated to recognize new goals, perceive new stimuli, and gain new knowledge. Accordingly, they constantly gain experiences and gather information that have the potential to change their feelings and opinions.

## ▼ ATTITUDE CONSISTENCY

An important principle underlies many of the forces that influence consumers to change attitudes: Consumers will, in general, seek consistency in their thoughts, feelings, and actions.[7] People want their attitudes to be consistent with their knowledge. They also want their attitudes about objects in their environment to be consistent, and they want their actions to be consistent with their knowledge and attitudes. We now consider two theories that address consistency among behavioral processes—cognitive dissonance theory and attribution theory.

## FACT OR FICTION REVISITED

⦿ Consumers do indeed seek consistency in their thoughts, feelings, and actions.

**Cognitive Dissonance Theory**   A person will experience feelings of discomfort, known as **cognitive dissonance,** when he or she has knowledge, holds attitudes, or takes actions that conflict with one another.[8] When dissonance occurs, the individual will seek to reduce it by changing the inconsistent cognitive elements. For instance, a person who knows that airbags reduce the risk of injury in a head-on car accident will have a positive attitude toward a vehicle that comes with airbags and will want to buy one that is equipped with them. If this person buys a Chevrolet Suburban, with the knowledge that it doesn't have a passenger airbag, however, he or she has a number of options for reducing the cognitive dissonance. The individual may seek to justify the purchase by discounting the role of the manufacturer in supplying airbags and, instead, emphasizing the responsibility of the consumer to wear a seat belt. Another approach is to gather additional information that will enable the individual to modify his or her beliefs about vehicle safety, such as additional accident statistics about the likelihood of damage in large trucks. Or, the individual may choose to  highlight different attributes of the product, such as the cargo carrying capacity or stylish looks, or  justify the purchase by emphasizing the specific situation or social context in which it has occurred, such as the role played by family members or the salesperson in the purchase decision.

> **Cognitive dissonance** is a person's discomfort when he or she has knowledge, holds attitudes, or takes actions that conflict with one another.

**Attribution Theory**   Individuals often make an **attribution** about the reasons for occurrences they observe.[9] These attributions may concern their own behavior, the behavior of others, or a product and the benefits it delivers. Consumers generally make attributions that are consistent with their existing beliefs, evaluations, and actions. For example, you may try to decipher the reasons you buy a donut and coffee every morning from Dunkin Donuts, or why Michael Jordan promotes Nike products on television advertisements, or why the Hyndai Excel your friend bought is giving her trouble. These attributions of causality—you like the quick service at Dunkin Donuts; Michael Jordan really believes that Nike makes high-performance athletic shoes; Hyundai's early products had quality problems—will be consistent with your current behavior.

> An **attribution** is an inference an individual makes about the reasons for occurrences.

Those attributions a consumer makes about his or her own behavior—his or her *self-perceptions*—may result in subsequent attitude changes. An example is the *foot-in-the-door technique,* whereby a marketer provides a substantial incentive for a small purchase. Consumers, in turn, see their own behavior as indicating that they "must have a positive attitude" about the product and are then predisposed to buy again. Requests for small initial donations to a charitable cause or cents-off coupons are examples of this technique.

## ▼ INFLUENCING CONSUMERS' ATTITUDES

All marketers attempt to demonstrate that their product offers benefits—specifically, that their product will satisfy consumers' needs better than the competitors' or better than they themselves have done in the past. In doing so, the marketer changes the consumers' beliefs or evaluation of the product.[10] The strategies marketers employ to influence and promote attitude change include (1) adding benefits, (2) changing the product or package, (3) changing the criteria for evaluation, and (4) linking products to existing favorable attitudes.

**Adding Benefits**  The value of a product is enhanced if it offers the consumer multiple benefits. Johnson's Baby Oil, for example, claims to soften a baby's skin, condition adults' skin, remove makeup, and promote tanning. Jell-O portrays its product as a dessert, a snack food for kids in the form of Jigglers, and a side dish in the form of a salad mold. As more car makers have begun offering passenger airbags in addition to the standard driver-side bag, Volvo has gone one step further and added side-impact air bags to maintain its image as the safest car available, and a number of car companies have added daytime running lights to influence consumers' attitudes about their products' safety. In general, consumer's attitudes become more positive as a product's perceived value increases; the more benefits a product offers, the more perceived value it generates in the mind of the consumer.

## FACT OR FICTION REVISITED

⦿  It is *not true* that the fewer benefits a product offers the more perceived value is generated in the consumer's mind. The opposite is true: More benefits generate higher value.

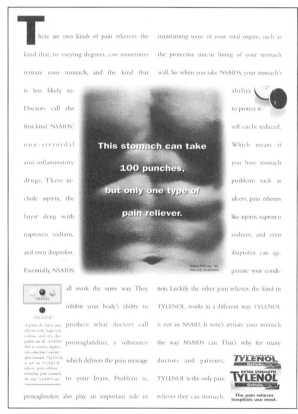

**Changing the Product or Package**  Consumers often form attitudes in response to changes that improve a product's ability to deliver benefits. Softsoap, for example, introduced liquid hand soap and, in turn, favorably influenced consumers' attitudes about the convenience of the product. Similarly, Gillette introduced a clear antiperspirant gel in response to consumers' negative attitudes toward the tendency of solids to leave white stains on clothing, and McNeil has continually introduced new forms of Tylenol—capsules, liquids, caplets, geltabs—to influence consumer attitudes about the ease with which the product can be swallowed (Figure 11.8). Although changing the physical form of a product is an expensive strategy, often requiring new manufacturing equipment as well as appropriate packaging and promotion, it does appear to impact consumers' attitudes toward a product by changing the consumers' beliefs.

An alternative to changing the product itself is changing its packaging. Tropicana orange juice that pours from a plastic spout with a screw-on cap; Jif peanut butter available in a plastic container; and safety seals on over-the-counter medicines are all examples of packaging changes. Consumers' attitudes are formed in part by evaluating packaging features that offer convenience, ease of use, and environmental benefits.

■  FIGURE 11.8

The various forms of Tylenol products have been designed to increase the brand's appeal to consumers.

**Changing the Criteria for Evaluation**  In developing an attitude toward a product, a consumer aggregates his or her many beliefs about the product's attributes and benefits. Because each attribute has a different importance (the $e_i$ in Fishbein's attitude-toward-object model) in determining a consumer's overall attitude, a change in the importance of any one attribute will influence the consumer's overall attitude toward the product. For example, the attributes by which the typical American consumer evaluates cars have changed over time. Cars were often judged by how large and ornate they were in the 1950s. These attributes were replaced by an emphasis on economical gas mileage in the 1970s. Today, safety and quality issues predominate.

Marketers are often able to influence consumers' attitudes toward specific products by changing the criteria consumers use to determine their overall evaluation—that is, by persuading consumers to emphasize different attributes from those they had previously considered. Marketers advertise and promote those attributes on which their product performs best and downplay the importance of attributes on which they do not perform as well. For example, Procter & Gamble emphasizes the fact that its new Aleve analgesic lasts 12 hours, which makes it more convenient and less costly for consumers than products from existing competitors. Waterman Pen emphasizes the fashionability and prestige of its expensive fountain pens to distinguish them from the affordable cost and convenience of disposable pens. As we discuss in the Dark Side of Consumption box that follows, social action groups sometimes try to encourage consumers to adopt a new criterion for evaluating a product, which results in negative attitudes toward consumption of that product.

### DARK SIDE OF CONSUMPTION

#### Don't Kill the Dolphins for a Tuna Sandwich[11]

For years many consumers had positive attitudes toward tuna—it was viewed as an inexpensive, convenient food served in sandwiches, casseroles, and salads. Few consumers felt it was important to learn about the fishing and canning process used to get tuna from ocean to table; instead, they felt that its taste, cost, and convenience were more important. But all that changed in March 1988, when an 11-minute videotape on tuna fishing was aired on the television networks. Sam LaBudde, an environmental activist, had taken a job on a Panamanian tuna boat that used a net fishing technique that had been regulated for American boats since passage of the Marine Mammal Protection Act in 1972. The video publicized the fact that dolphins swim above the yellowfin tuna used in light-meat canned tuna and were being swept into the nets and killed by the foreign fishing boats.

Publicizing the toll to the dolphin population, groups such as Earth Island Institute, Greenpeace, the Sea Shepherd Conservation Society, and the Sierra Club attempted to turn consumers' attention to the dark side of their consumption of tuna. Until that time, many consumers had been wholly unaware that the tuna they ate resulted in the death of dolphins. Once that fact was publicized, however, consumers responded to the environmentalists' calls for a boycott of canned tuna. Coupled with the highly visible lobbying efforts of Jerry Ross, the chairman of A & M Records, and a "green-teen" movement led by 17-year-old Joel Rubin, Heinz announced in April

**FIGURE 11.9**
The dolphin-safe logo on a can of tuna.

1990 that it would no longer buy tuna caught by foreign boats using nets for its Star-Kist brand. Chicken of the Sea and Bumble Bee quickly followed suit and added a "dolphin-safe" logo to their packaging (Figure 11.9). Responding to the same pressure from American consumers, the federal government then forbade the import of tuna that had been caught in nets, sparking a trade dispute with foreign fisherman who continue to use the nets. To increase falling sales that resulted from the boycott and the cost increases that accompanied new fishing methods, tuna marketers introduced such new products as soy-based tuna extenders, flavored tuna products, and a lunch kit that contains a single serving of tuna, mayonnaise, and relish.

Do you think the killing of animals for food shows a dark side of consumption? What attributes were emphasized by the environmentalists who organized the boycott of tuna? Are these attributes still important today in swaying consumers' attitudes toward tuna? Do you consider the source of the foods you eat as an important attribute in forming attitudes toward food products?

> **Cause-related marketing** is the linking of a product with cause in an attempt to influence consumers to change their attitudes toward the product.

**Linking Products to Existing Favorable Attitudes** Consumers seek to maintain consistent attitudes. Accordingly, many marketers employ **cause-related marketing**—an attempt to influence consumers' attitudes toward their products by linking them to existing favorable attitudes toward a cause. For example, Avon encourages its salespersons to talk to their largely female target market about breast cancer and to distribute brochures and pink ribbons that symbolize the breast cancer awareness movement. By promoting their link to an issue of concern to their consumers, marketers hope to promote the issues and, at the same time, influence attitudes toward their own products. Often, the marketer contributes to a cause when consumers purchase their products. Such efforts include Proctor & Gamble's link to the Special Olympics, American Express's Charge Against Hunger campaign, and numerous companies that are involved with Jerry Lewis's Muscular Dystrophy Telethon.

# PUBLIC POLICY AND ATTITUDE CHANGE

> **Social marketing** is the marketing of ideas or causes that will advance the economic and social welfare of a society.

The marketing of ideas or causes that will advance the economic and social welfare of the members of a society is called **social marketing** (Figure 11.10). Public policy actors—including consumers, marketers, policy makers, and social action groups—often attempt to influence consumers' attitudes toward the economic and social issues that contribute to the welfare of their broader society. Marketers and public policy actors often consider it their responsibility to influence attitudes toward dark side behavior that may be dangerous to the consumer or to others in society. Therefore, knowledge of attitude formation, attitude measurement, and attitude change has important public policy implications. For the remainder of this chapter, we will discuss several areas in which public policy debates have spurred social marketing efforts to influence consumers' attitudes.

Some areas of social marketing are widely supported. For example, beer, wine, and liquor marketers promote the idea of the designated driver, and car

■ FIGURE 11.10
ABC Canada's national literacy program is an example of social marketing.

marketers demonstrate the importance of wearing seat belts, using crash test dummies as props. Similarly, attitude change strategies have been used considerably in the area of drug education targeted at children and teenagers. Literature and advertisements in this area have been carefully crafted to influence the beliefs and feelings of those who are at risk. Policy makers and social action organizations provide information—describing the results of illegal drugs—and attempt to influence the evaluations of such behavior—portraying it as risky behavior that will not make individuals happy or popular.

## FACT OR FICTION REVISITED

⊙   Social marketing *is not* generally conducted person to person; rather, it utilizes all the common media.

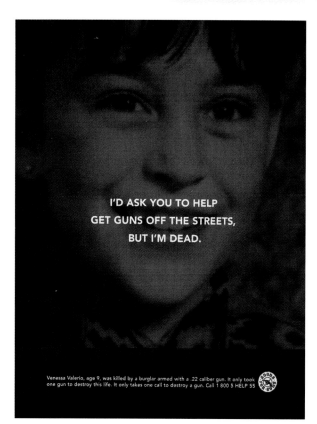

I'D ASK YOU TO HELP
GET GUNS OFF THE STREETS,
BUT I'M DEAD.

Venessa Valerio, age 9, was killed by a burglar armed with a .22 caliber gun. It only took
one gun to destroy this life. It only takes one call to destroy a gun. Call 1 800 5 HELP 55

■ FIGURE 11.11

Toys Я Us's toys for guns program is a powerful example of social marketing.

Not all areas of social marketing are as widely supported, however. As we have noted in our initial discussion of the dark side of consumer behavior, social ideas often ignite significant controversy. Gun control and environmental issues are just two topics of great debate, for example. Public policy actors on both sides of the gun control debate recognize that underlying attitudes are formed at a young age, and, as a result, children are often the target of influence. Accordingly, in 1993, New York businessman Fernando Mateo implemented a program, Toys for Guns, whereby Toys Я Us gift certificates were exchanged for illegal handguns (Figure 11.11). The next year, after two young teens were killed by police after brandishing toy guns, Toys Я Us stopped selling realistic toy guns altogether. In fact, the marketer was joined by KayBee Toys and Bradlee's, and the three stores continue to sell only water guns and other brightly colored toy guns.

Similarly, the issue of environmental protection has provided both concern for public policy officials and opportunities for marketers. As we noted in Chapter 9, the Federal Trade Commission regulates the use of environmental claims, mandating standards for the use of terms such as "biodegradable," "recyclable," and "refillable." At the same time, marketers use environmental claims on packaging and in advertising in an attempt to influence consumer attitudes toward their products. They may even go so far as to change their products to influence consumers' beliefs about their products' performance or attempt to change the criteria by which consumers evaluate their products. For example, consider marketers' attempts to influence consumers' attitudes toward diapers, as discussed in the following Public Policy box.

### PUBLIC POLICY

**Cloth or Disposable Diapers?**[12]

In 1990, environmental concerns about disposable diapers became quite prominent. Compared to reusable cloth diapers, the disposable paper products were viewed as environmentally irresponsible—a waste of resources that resulted in clogged landfills filled with soiled diapers that would be around longer than the children who used them. Of course, those parents who chose to use them were happy with the convenience and usability of the disposables. Public opinion was shifting against disposable diapers, and several states were considering taxing or banning disposables, when Procter & Gamble, the maker of Pampers and Luvs, decided to conduct research that would provide information about the environmental effects of the two competing types of diapers. Procter & Gamble was seeking to counter the effects of a 1988 study sponsored by the cloth diaper industry that highlighted the amount of solid waste produced by disposable diapers.

Conducted by Arthur D. Little, the P&G study found that the environmental effect of disposables was no worse than that of cloth diapers when the impact of producing, washing, delivering, and picking up cloth diapers was also considered. Both the 1988 study and the P&G study, along with later studies conducted by each side that also reached contradictory conclusions, made assumptions about the way consumers used the products and the costs of production, use, and disposal. Whereas both studies were criticized for various reasons, the new report successfully shifted the focus to the environmental effects of cloth diapers, and within two years public opposition and regulatory threats against disposable diapers had greatly subsided.

What effects do disposable diapers have on the economic and social welfare of our society? What attributes are most important to the parents and babies who use the disposables? What strategy did P&G use to shift consumers' attitudes toward disposable diapers? Do you think that either the cloth diaper industry or P&G should be considered reliable sources of knowledge about diapers?

# ATTITUDES

◀

Sarah Muckerman has some very definite attitudes about brands, products, marketers, and broader social and environmental issues. She likes Coke, pump spray products, and Sony, and she dislikes Nestle products and fur coats. Using her perceptual and learning processes, she has accumulated knowledge from her own experiences, her mother's influence, friends and acquaintances, advertisements, and salespersons. Her attitudes reflect the needs that motivate her—her tastes for sweet-tasting drinks and music, her desire to fit into her adopted hometown of Atlanta, and her distaste for unnecessary violence against animals. The knowledge and evaluations she uses to form attitudes affect many of her purchases, but not all. She bought a tape player she did not prefer, for example, because of circumstances at the time of her purchase.

Sarah's attitudes illustrate much about the way consumers form attitudes and the role those attitudes play in consumer behavior. To form an attitude, consumers combine their knowledge, evaluation, and predisposition concerning a product into an easily expressed opinion about the benefits they can expect to gain by purchasing the product. Attitudes help consumers simplify the purchase process by providing an efficient and effective way of summarizing their knowledge in the context of their needs. Attitudes are a significant input into the final behavioral process—decision making—the subject of the next chapter.

# SUMMARY

1. **Recognize how consumers form attitudes.** A consumer's attitude toward a product is composed of knowledge learned from his or her own experiences as well as that gathered from others, an evaluation of the product, and a predisposition to act based on the evaluation. Attitudes serve a variety of functions for a consumer, including utilitarian, value-expressive, ego-defensive, and knowledge functions. Attitude formation serves to help consumers make decisions by providing a way for them to evaluate alternatives based on the attributes and benefits of each.

2. **Examine consumers' attitudes using relevant attitude models.** Three types of attitude models—tricomponent models, multiattribute models, and attitude-toward-the-ad models—offer different perspectives on the components of an attitude. Tricomponent attitude models explicitly recognize that behavior encompasses knowledge, feeling, and action by focusing on the (1) cognitive beliefs, (2) affect, and (3) conative predisposition that form an attitude. Multiattribute models suggest that a consumer's attitude toward the purchase of a product is the result of the aggregation of his or her evaluations of the relevant attributes of the product in the context of the specific circumstances of the purchase and the subjective evaluations of the members of the consumer's reference groups. Attitude-toward-the-ad models investigate the attitudes formed by consumers toward a product as the result of exposure to advertising messages as well as the individual's assessment of the product as it appears in the ad.

3. **Identify appropriate methods used to measure consumer attitudes.** Three methods of measuring attitudes are commonly employed by consumer behavior researchers: (1) observation of behavior, (2) qualitative investigations, and (3) attitude scales. Observation is usually used to supplement other methods because it cannot fully consider unobservable factors. Qualitative methods, including focus groups, depth interviews, and psychological tests, provide insights into a consumer's feelings and opinions. Because qualitative methods require intensive analysis, they are more useful for exploring underlying components of attitudes than for determining representative attitudes of a target market segment. Consumer survey questionnaires are often used to measure attitudes on quantitative scales. When administered to a representative sample of the target market, these scales offer an efficient and effective way of measuring consumer attitudes in a reliable and valid way.

4. **Analyze the methods marketers utilize in an attempt to change consumer attitudes.** Marketers may change consumer attitudes by influencing any of their three major components—knowledge, evaluation, and predisposition to act. As researchers have discovered in cognitive dissonance and attribution theories, consumers typically try to keep these components consistent with one another; when they are inconsistent, consumers will gather additional information that enables them to modify their beliefs or evaluations to restore some measure of consistency. Marketers can aid in that process by adding additional benefits to a product, changing the product, persuading consumers to change the criteria they use for their evaluation, or linking the product to existing favorable attitudes.

5. **Apply the principles of attitude formation and change to analyze the public policy implications of social marketing.** Public policy actors often engage in social marketing—that is, they attempt to influence consumers' attitudes toward the economic and social issues that will contribute to the welfare of the broader society. Sometimes this involves attitudes toward dark side consumption. In their attempts to influence such attitudes, public policy actors provide information to add to consumers' existing knowledge and attempt to influence consumers' evaluations of such behavior.

Attitude, *p. 313*

Attitude formation, *p. 313*

Beliefs, *p. 319*

Affect, *p. 320*

Conative component, *p. 320*

Subjective norm, *p. 324*

Focus group, *p. 326*

Cognitive dissonance, *p. 329*

Attribution, *p. 329*

Cause-related marketing, *p. 332*

Social marketing, *p. 332*

# KEY TERMS

# SKILL-BUILDING ACTIVITIES

1. Below is an attitude scale that measures environmental concerns (from the DDB Needham Life Style survey). Use the scale to measure how concerned you are about the environment.

   5 = agree strongly
   4 = agree somewhat
   3 = neither agree nor disagree
   2 = disagree somewhat
   1 = disagree strongly

   _____ I make a special effort to buy products in packages made out of recycled materials.

   _____ I support pollution standards even if it means shutting down some factories.

   _____ I would switch from my usual brands and buy environmentally safe cleaning products, even I have to give up some cleaning effectiveness.

   _____ I would be willing to accept a lower standard of living to conserve energy.

   _____ I worry a lot about the effects of environmental pollution on my family's health.

   _____ The government isn't spending enough to clean up the environment.

   Give yourself an "environmental concern" score by adding up your answers. The highest possible score is 30. The lowest possible score is 6.

2. Below is a list of environmental activities. Check those you have engaged in at least once in the past six months.

   _____ Commute on foot or bicycle instead of by car.

   _____ Recycle newspaper.

   _____ Contribute money to an environmental organization.

   _____ Contribute time to an environmental organization.

   _____ Recycle glass.

   _____ Recycle cans.

   _____ Volunteer to clean up outdoor trash.

   _____ Write to a government official concerning the environment.

   _____ Use washable plates or cups instead of disposable plates or cups.

   _____ Boycott a product or service because of the company's record on environmental issues.

   Give yourself an "environmental behavior" score by adding up the check marks. The highest possible score is 10. The lowest possible score is zero.

3. Does your "environmental concern" score agree with your "environmental behavior" score? Why or why not?

4. Class project: Divide the class into quarters on the basis of their "environmental concern" scores. Does the top quarter of the class differ from the bottom quarter of the class in environmental behavior? What accounts for the cases where those with

high concerns do not show the appropriate behavior? What accounts for the cases where those with low concerns have unexpectedly high behavior scores?

5. If you were a government official, what measures could you take to increase environmental concern (as measured by the scale above) among the general public?

6. If you were a government official, what measures could you take to close the gap between environmental concerns and proenvironmental behavior?

# CHAPTER 11 SELF-TEST

▼ MULTIPLE CHOICE

1. An _____ is a learned predisposition to act in a consistent way toward an object.
   a. evaluation
   b. intuition
   c. attitude
   d. ancillary

2. If Ruth has a positive attitude toward Oakwood University since it is located near her home and is the only school she can afford, that attitude has served what type of function for Ruth?
   a. value-expressive
   b. utilitarian
   c. ego-defensive
   d. knowledge

3. A marketer who emphasizes how a product fits the lifestyle of a consumer is promoting the _____ function of an attitude.
   a. ego-defensive
   b. knowledge
   c. value-expressive
   d utilitarian

4. Attitudes can be measured via observation, qualitative investigations, and/or _____ .
   a. attitude scales
   b. bar code data
   c. past purchase behavior
   d. physical examination

5. During a _____ , a small group of consumers is asked to discuss their attitudes and beliefs about products or services.
   a. focus group
   b. semantic differentiation group
   c. personal interview
   d observation group

6. Which of the following forms of attitude measurement uses a series of opposite adjectives, such as "sweet/sour" or "love/hate"?
   a. Likert scale
   b. semantic differential scale
   c. dual polar scale
   d. positive/negative scale

7. The three components of a multiattribute model are the attributes, the beliefs about whether the product posseses the attributes, and the _____ .
   a. price of the product
   b. sex of the consumer
   c. availability of the product
   d. evaluation of importance of each attribute

8. A consumer who feels discomfort because of conflicting attitudes is experiencing _____ .
   a. attribution
   b. cognitive dissonance
   c. attitude consistency
   d. consumption conflict

9. A marketer who sponsors a children's immunization drive is attempting to influence attitudes through _____ .
   a. community marketing
   b. causality marketing
   c. cause-related social marketing
   d. consumer protection marketing

10. Attitudes help consumers simplify the _____ process by providing an efficient way of _____ their knowledge.
    a. search; excluding
    b. purchase; excluding
    c. evaluation; combining
    d. purchase; summarizing

## ▼ TRUE/FALSE

1. Attitudes are instinctive, not learned.   T or F
2. Attitudes are purely feelings and are not related to actual knowledge about a product.   T or F
3. The only way to determine people's attitudes is to ask them.   T or F
4. An attitude can fulfill only one function for a consumer.   T or F
5. Cognitive beliefs about a product are always formed before the consumer develops feelings about the product.   T or F
6. The theory-of-reasoned-action model includes consumers' attitudes toward a product but not their intention to purchase the product.   T or F
7. One way to reduce cognitive dissonance is to gather more information about a purchased product.   T or F
8. Consumers make attributions about a purchase so that their attitudes will be consistent and balanced.   T or F
9. Public service announcements warning about the dangers of drug abuse are a form of social marketing.   T or F
10. Knowledge of how attitudes are formed is not important in the development of public policy.   T or F

## ▼ SHORT ANSWER

1. Describe the three components of the tricomponent model of attitudes.
2. Describe the importance of attitude-toward-the-ad models to successful promotion of products.
3. Describe the four ways marketers attempt to influence consumers' attitudes.

## ▼ APPLICATION EXERCISE

You are planning a spring break trip. Your choice of destination is either South Padre Island, Texas, or Copper Mountain Ski Area of Colorado. Develop your own attitude-toward-an-object model by first describing the attributes you would use in evaluating a vacation destination. Then, rank in importance each of those attributes and determine which of the two destinations you have the most positive overall attitude toward.

# 12

# CONSUMER DECISION MAKING

◉ Consumer Snapshot *Trupti Niak is a 19-year-old single college student at the University of Minnesota. She was born in India and moved to the United States when she was four. She currently lives in Minneapolis at the university.*

## FACT OR FICTION

◉ The more experience a person has with a product category, the more effort he or she is likely to exert when making purchasing decisions within that category.

◉ Need recognition is one of the first steps in consumer decision making.

◉ Information used in making purchase decisions usually comes from both internal and external sources.

◉ Rational consumers gather as much information as possible before making any purchasing decision.

- ◉ In most consumer decisions, benefits are the most important evaluative criteria.

- ◉ Marketers make great efforts to ensure that their products are included in the consumer's evoked set.

- ◉ Marketers are usually successful in influencing consumers' decision rules.

# EYE ON THE CONSUMER

Trupti Niak is a freshman majoring in mechanical engineering at the University of Minnesota. When she was deciding where to go to college, Trupti read about her alternatives through college catalogs and brochures and consulted with people who could help her—her parents, high school counselors, students, and program advisors. Ultimately, she chose the U of M for a number of reasons. First, the tuition was lower than some other schools she was considering, and it offered a better value for the money than Ivy League schools. Location was another factor. Trupti wanted to be within a reasonable distance of her parents in South Dakota so she could visit them easily during the school year and her summer internships, and going to school in Minnesota gave her this freedom. Perhaps the most important factor in Trupti's decision was the feeling of comfort she experienced when visiting the U of M. During her campus visit she was very impressed with the surroundings—the people were nice; the campus reminded her of her high school; and she liked the fact that the school puts an emphasis on undergraduate education.

Once she decided where to go to school, Trupti was faced with the tough decision of choosing a major. Trupti has always been interested in design and construction. As a child she played with Lego building blocks and worked on small building projects around the house; as a teenager she took architecture courses in high school. Perhaps her interest stemmed from her upbringing—her father was a civil engineer who took pride in his profession. When choosing her major, Trupti weighed several factors. First, she decided that a degree in mechanical engineering would have more to offer her than one in architecture since it would afford her the opportunity to work in construction as well as design. Second, some of the same financial concerns that influenced her choice of school influenced her choice of major—the job market for mechanical engineers is stronger than that for architects, and the brochure for the engineering programs at Minnesota touted a high placement rate for its graduates. Trupti realized that if she graduated with a degree in architecture, she would be lucky to get a job as a draftsperson. By contrast, she already has four opportunities for engineering internships, and she's only a freshman! A third consideration was the flexibility of the engineering curriculum—Trupti is taking math and science courses that she can apply to another degree if she chooses to switch majors. Overall, Trupti believes that she has made a good compromise between her desire to work in design and construction and the need to have a marketable degree.

Decision making is the behavioral process people employ when choosing which products and services to consume; it is the tool consumers use to evaluate and choose among alternative products that might satisfy their needs. By the time consumers reach the purchase decision, they have already utilized the other behavioral processes—motivation to identify a need; perception and learning to gather and organize information about available products; and attitude formation to evaluate these products—the subjects of the previous four chapters. In this chapter we discuss how consumers use decision making in their search and evaluation activities.

After reading and thinking about this chapter, you should be able to:

❶ Categorize the levels of effort involved in decision making.
❷ Identify the sources of information and search activities used by consumers in the search for alternatives.
❸ Recognize the evaluative criteria and decision rules consumers employ in choosing a product.
❹ Analyze the methods marketers employ to influence consumers' decision making.

# LEVELS OF DECISION MAKING ◀

A useful way to categorize consumer decision making is by the level of effort devoted to making a product choice—that is, the time and cognitive resources the consumer expends in completing the purchase process (Figure 12.1). This cognitive effort enables the individual to search for alternative products, organize information about them, develop criteria to use in evaluating products, and choose which product to buy. The level of effort, as illustrated in Table 12.1, can be seen as a continuum that is typically divided into three categories: (1) extensive, (2) limited, and (3) routine decision making.[1]

*Table 12.1*

## LEVELS OF CONSUMER DECISION MAKING

|  | Extensive | Limited | Routine |
| --- | --- | --- | --- |
| Search for alternatives | Significant amount of search activity | Limited search | No search |
| Gather information | Yes | Yes | No |
| Develop specific evaluative criteria | Yes | No | No |
| Integrate criteria into decision rule | Yes | No | No |
| Apply decision rule | Yes | Yes | No |

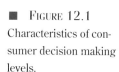

■ FIGURE 12.1
Characteristics of consumer decision making levels.

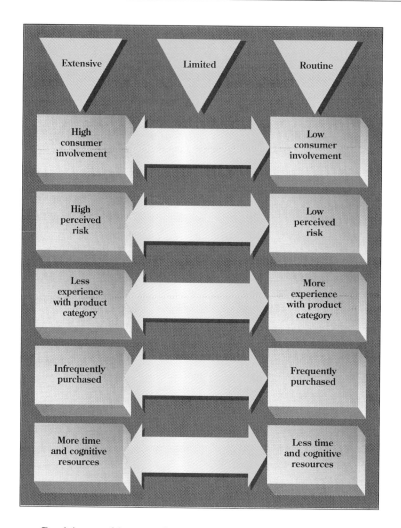

Decision making can be an *extensive* process that involves gathering large amounts of information, evaluating it painstakingly, and establishing elaborate criteria. For example, an individual may exert a great deal of effort in choosing among alternative makes of cars before deciding to buy an Acura Integra. When choosing a beverage to quench her thirst, however, that same individual may simply follow a *routine* that involves going to the convenience store and buying a Diet Coke. She may expend a *limited* amount of effort—less than that exerted in buying a car and more than that involved in buying a soda—to buy the new Stone Temple Pilots compact disk.

▼ INFLUENCES ON THE LEVEL OF DECISION MAKING

The level of involvement a consumer feels toward the need he or she is attempting to satisfy has a significant impact on the level of effort the individual will expend. Generally speaking, people are more willing to exert effort to satisfy a high involvement need than a low involvement one. For example, a person for whom fashion and clothing are highly involving will spend more time considering the purchase of a new outfit than, say, furnishings for her or his apartment.

If a consumer perceives a significant risk in choosing the wrong product, he or she will exert more effort during the purchase process. Consider the purchase of a home hair coloring or permanent kit, for example. While these kits are not very expensive—which is why some people choose them over going to a beauty salon—consumers have a high level of involvement with these products because they affect their appearance; a bad dye job or permanent can be very embarrassing indeed. Therefore, consumers typically exert a great deal of effort learning about them. The marketers of these products, in turn, attempt to simplify the effort for consumers by providing easily understood descriptions of their products to help consumers distinguish among them. For example, Clairol developed the Clairol Color Choice System, a sophisticated in-store display system, to provide detailed information to consumers at the point of purchase.

A consumer's experience with a product category will also affect the level of effort he or she expends. Once people have had experience with a product category, they may not expend as much effort in decision making as they did the first time they bought a product to satisfy a newly recognized need. At this stage, the consumer is more involved in routine decision making—choices consumers have made with enough frequency that they have become habit. For example, you frequently buy milk and soft drinks, so you probably don't think very much about such purchases. When you notice that you are out of milk, you automatically stop at the local convenience store on the way home. By contrast, a new product would elicit more effort because the consumer will not have had any experience with it. You probably put a little more thought into trying a "new age" beverage before you bought your first bottle of Mistic or Clearly Canadian (Figure 12.2).

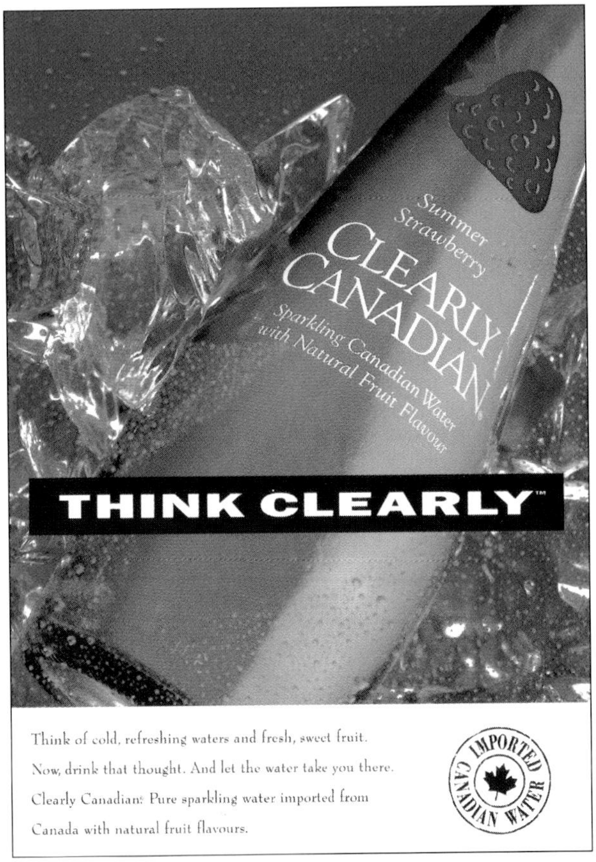
Summer Strawberry
CLEARLY CANADIAN
Sparkling Canadian Water with Natural Fruit Flavour
THINK CLEARLY™
Think of cold, refreshing waters and fresh, sweet fruit.
Now, drink that thought. And let the water take you there.
Clearly Canadian: Pure sparkling water imported from Canada with natural fruit flavours.
IMPORTED CANADIAN WATER

■ FIGURE 12.2
Buying a new product, such as Clearly Canadian, will require more effort on the part of the consumer than will buying products that have been around for a while, such as Coke and Pepsi.

## FACT OR FICTION REVISITED

◉ It is not true that the more experience a person has with a product category, the more effort he or she will exert when making purchase decisions within that category.

**Extensive decision making** involves significant effort in identifying criteria and choosing how to apply them to the purchase process.

### ▼ EXTENSIVE DECISION MAKING

As noted above, **extensive decision making** involves significant effort in identifying criteria and choosing how to apply them to the purchase process. Because consumers are highly involved with the need at this level, they put a lot of effort into gathering information about available alternatives. In the case of a long-time involvement, such as a hobby or intense interest, consumers constantly revise the way they make decisions. For example, if you are a computer fanatic, you probably read *PC Magazine* and *PC World* regularly to keep abreast of technological changes. As new models "push the performance envelope," your criteria tend to change to reflect the changing computer market. When you are ready to buy a new computer, you will apply complex decision criteria to reach your decision.

In the case of a highly involving purchase decision that consumers do not make frequently, such as replacing a washer or dryer, the consumer will need to identify new criteria and apply them to the decision. Because most consumers do not regularly keep up with the attributes of these products and may not even know which qualities are most relevant, they must spend time and energy to ensure that the Maytag they purchase is the right choice. Similarly, in the case of some low-cost products, such as hair coloring, the risk of damage to one's hair is probably enough to encourage the consumer to exert considerable effort in choosing just the right brand.

■ FIGURE 12.3
Marshalls advertises its casual, inexpensive clothes to consumers who value quality clothing but do not want to spend a lot of money. This ad lets interested consumers know that they have even more of a reason to come in to Marshalls—a 50% off sale.

## ▼ LIMITED DECISION MAKING

In the case of **limited decision making,** the consumer applies existing criteria to a recurring purchase decision. Here, the consumer's effort is limited to gathering new information with which to apply the existing decision making process. Buying clothes is one example. A woman may have a personal "clothing style," for example, which she is able to maintain by shopping regularly at Marshalls. She has developed certain criteria she uses to choose new clothes that are consistent with her style, and she uses these criteria to select specific articles of clothing that reflect that style (Figure 12.3).

> **Limited decision making** involves applying existing criteria to a recurring purchase decision.

## ▼ ROUTINE DECISION MAKING

**Routine decision making** involves the direct repetition of a prior decision making process—evaluative criteria, decision rules, or information about the alternatives—to recurring purchase decisions. Consumers tend to make the same brand decisions they have made in the past. This level of decision making involves very little effort because the consumer simply recalls the results of prior decision making processes and makes the same choice again. This level of decision making applies to frequently purchased packaged goods, such as soft drinks, toothpaste, or laundry detergent. At some point in the past you might have chosen to buy Purex laundry detergent. Unless something changes—you spill tomato sauce on your roommate's sweatshirt and need a more powerful brand to get out the stain, for example—you routinely buy Purex whenever the need occurs again.

> **Routine decision making** involves the repetition of a prior decision-making process to recurring purchase decisions.

# THE DECISION MAKING PROCESS

Decision making plays a significant role in the broader context of consumer behavior (Figure 12.4). Before making a decision, a person must be motivated to recognize a need and its attendant goals. As part of the motivation process, the consumer identifies the benefits—the outcomes sought from buying and using the product—that will help him or her meet those goals. Once the desired benefits have been identified, the consumer begins to search for alternative sources that will provide them.

### FACT OR FICTION REVISITED

⊛ Need recognition is in fact one of the first steps in the decision making process.

Consider what happens during the process of choosing a major. Like all consumers, college students have goals: to enjoy the content of their courses, find a job, and graduate with a high grade point average, to name a few. Their needs, in

The context of the decision making process.

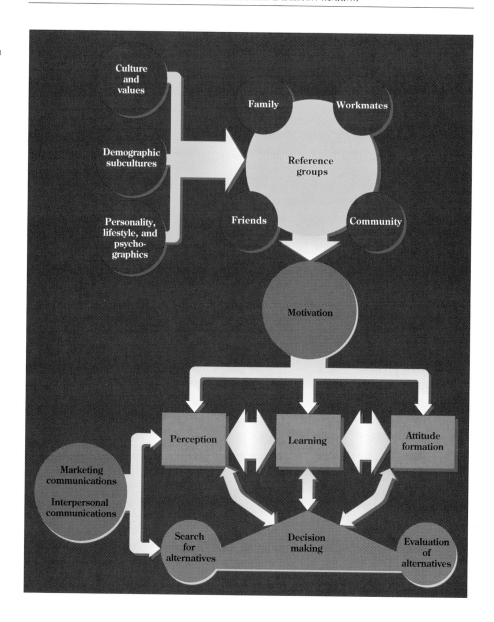

turn, reflect one or more of these goals. Trupti Niak loves architecture, for example, but she was reluctant to elect it as her major because she needs to find a job after graduation. If she thinks she might not be able to get a job as an architect, deciding not to major in architecture might conflict with her goal of choosing interesting courses (an approach–avoidance conflict).

It is important to recall that people don't necessarily progress through the steps in the purchase process in a rigid order. There are obvious exceptions, particularly for routine products, where consumers may skip the search and evaluation steps altogether. Likewise, they may cycle through the search, evaluation, and decision steps a number of times, even in an extensive decision making process. They may get to the decision step, for example, and realize that they need additional information or want more alternatives. Consumers sometimes anticipate the nature of their decisions and, consequently, are able to structure their searches. For example, Trupti knew that she would factor job opportunities into her choice of major. Accordingly, she collected information on job placement rates for each major she was considering.

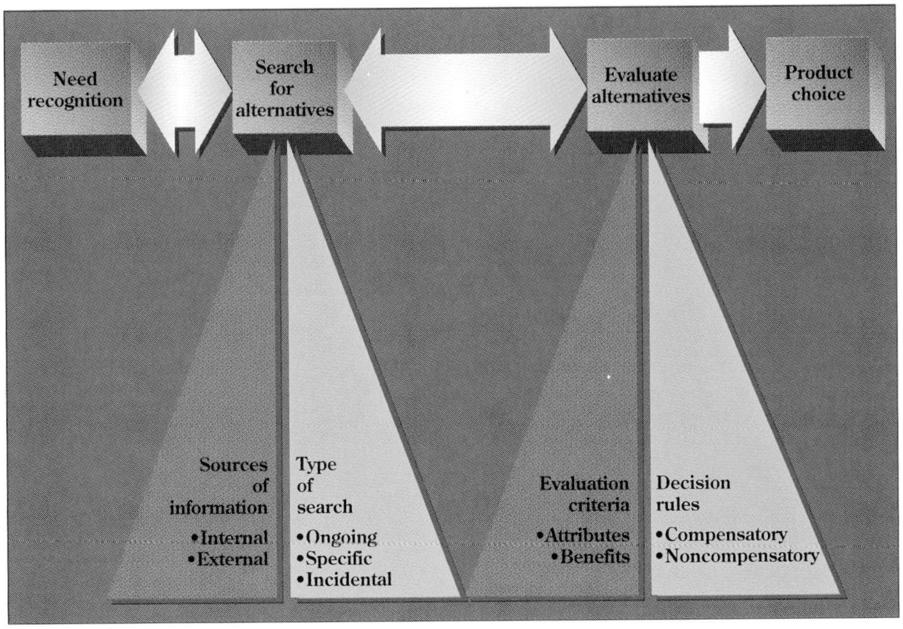

We turn now to a discussion of the steps involved in consumer decision making. First, we consider how consumers *search for alternatives* and organize the information. We then examine the ways consumers *evaluate alternatives* and integrate the criteria into a rule they can apply in choosing a product (Figure 12.5).

# SEARCH FOR ALTERNATIVES

The first step in decision making is the search for alternatives (Figure 12.6). The purpose here is for the consumer to identify any alternative products that have the potential to satisfy his or her needs and to gather information to evaluate them. In doing so, the consumer gathers both general information about the product category and specific information about particular alternatives. This information is available from a number of sources, as discussed below.[2]

## ▼ SOURCES OF INFORMATION

In searching for alternatives, consumers have access to two general sources of information: internal and external sources. *Internal sources* include the consumer's

■   FIGURE 12.6
The search for alternatives.

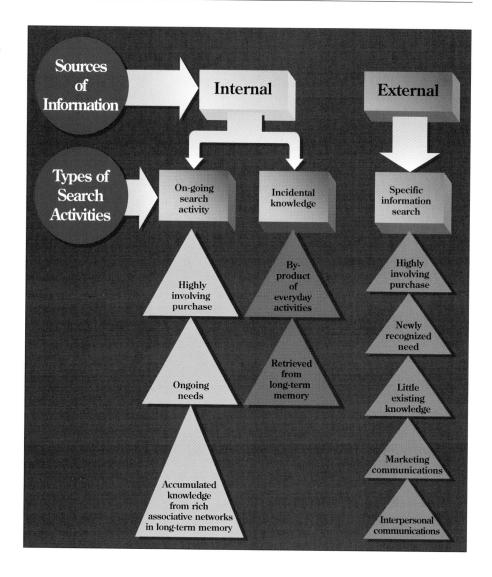

memories of experiences and accumulated knowledge that have been learned over the years. When choosing a college major, for example, students have previous experiences on which to draw. They have already taken courses in a number of different subjects in high school and college that may have sparked their interest; they can talk to their friends and family about the courses they took in college and their knowledge of certain subject areas; or they may peruse reading materials that discuss the kinds of training necessary for success in various careers. Students can also draw upon information stored away in their long-term memory.

Consumers can also consult a wide variety of *external sources* of information, including marketing communications (advertising, salespeople, the retail environment, and public relations), editorial sources (magazines and books), and interpersonal communications (with friends, family, acquaintances, and experts). Many of these sources are the same ones that have provided the information the consumer has retrieved from internal memory. Prior information retrieved from memory is considered an internal source, whereas new information gathered from the environment is considered an external source. For example, Trupti could have consulted a number of people for advice in choosing her major. She might have consulted her father, who worked in a field she was considering, or other experts, including faculty members, career counselors, and prospective employers; she could have talked to friends and classmates to gain their insights; or she might have conferred with recent graduates who could tell her whether they are satisfied with their decisions. At the same time, Trupti might have turned to other external sources of information, including books about potential majors, job hunting, or forecasted employment trends in the twenty-first century, as well as departmental promotional literature, such as catalog descriptions, brochures, and course syllabi.

## FACT OR FICTION REVISITED

◉ Information used in making purchasing decisions does in fact come from both internal and external sources.

### ▼ TYPES OF SEARCH ACTIVITIES

Consumers may engage in a number of different types of search activities, depending on the information they need to make a decision. Consumers may gather information through (1) ongoing attempts to keep abreast of a product category, (2) specific efforts spurred by a specific need, or (3) incidental knowledge gathered as a byproduct of other activities.

Consumers purposely engage in *ongoing search activities* when they are highly involved in using a product to satisfy a need. The learning process plays an important role in organizing information into rich associative networks so that it will be accessible when the consumer wants it. For some college students, for example, choosing a major is a highly involving decision. Accordingly, they may begin to gather information about potential majors from their first semester in college and continue to do so over the next couple of years. They may even consider every course they take a starting point for a potential major. Similarly, hobbyists are always looking for new information about their areas of interest—they may talk with others who share their interests, read magazines and books about their hobby, visit specialty stores, or collect sales brochures (Figure 12.7).

When consumers have little existing knowledge about a product, they will employ *specific infor-*

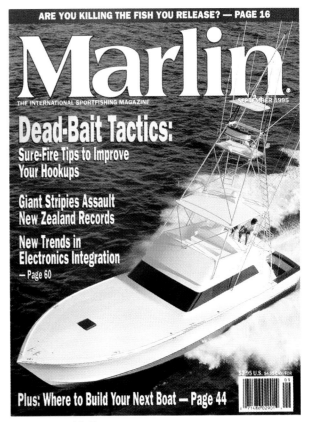

■ FIGURE 12.7

Hobbyists often subscribe to speciality magazines about their hobby, such as sportfishing, in an effort to engage in ongoing search activities about the sport.

*mation search* activities to learn about it. Consumers may recognize a new need that is highly involving for them, but they have not been searching for information on an ongoing basis because the need has not arisen until now. Once they recognize the need, they will exert extensive effort to gather specific information from external sources to help them satisfy it. When your advisor tells you that you must choose a major by the end of the semester, for example, it suddenly becomes a very involving need. Similarly, few consumers see personal relevance in buying a large appliance, like a washer or dryer, until the one they own breaks. Then, they become very involved because of the tremendous inconvenience and financial risk of making the wrong choice. As we discuss in the following Public Policy box, information must be available to consumers if they want to search for it.

### PUBLIC POLICY

**Campus Crime**[3]

After Connie and Howard Clery's daughter Jeanne was murdered in her college dorm room, they began an effort to force colleges and universities to make information about campus crime available to students, staff, and prospective students. The result of their efforts is the Crime Awareness and Campus Security Act of 1990, which requires all institutions of higher education that receive federal funding to distribute an annual security report to students and staff and to make the data available to prospective students and staff. The act was not received well by everyone, however. Some colleges expressed concern that the information could be misinterpreted and sensationalized, and critics complained that the lack of reporting guidelines made comparisons difficult.

Was crime an important consideration in your choice of a college or university? Did you receive a copy of your school's annual report this year? Did you know how to get a copy of your school's report when you were making your decision about where to enroll? Did you learn anything from the report?

Consumers combine any newly gathered information received from external sources with *incidental knowledge* retrieved from memory—the consumer's internal source of information. Perception and learning play an important role in influencing a consumer's ability to retain incidental knowledge. Consumers accumulate incidental knowledge as the byproduct of everyday activities, such as watching television, reading magazines, and talking with friends and acquaintances. In the past, for example, a consumer might have learned something about appliances from an ad in the paper or a conversation with a relative who complained about spending too much for a dryer. When it comes time to buy a new dryer, the consumer will use that stored information to help him or her make a purchase decision.

**The Rationality of Consumers**   To satisfy a low involvement need, incidental knowledge would likely provide enough information for the consumer to skip over the search step and make a decision directly. Because the need has little relevance, the consumer sees little reason to expend much effort to satisfy it. Assuming that this is not the way anyone chooses a major, let's consider what happens when a small appliance breaks. When most people recognize that they need a new toaster, they are usually able to make the quickest choice possible without searching for a lot of information or evaluating many alternatives. Because the decision is not highly involving, people typically use whatever incidental knowledge they already possess to seek out the easiest alternative possible.

This example raises an interesting question concerning consumer behavior and the search for information. Researchers debate the **rationality of consumers**—the assumption that people gather as much information as possible about all of the alternatives they possibly can, carefully evaluate all of the information, and choose the alternative that will maximize their satisfaction.[4] Does this process in fact reflect the way you make your product choices? When consumers buy toasters in the way just described, they are not really engaging in decision making at all—they do not gather any additional information, nor do they invoke a long dormant routine. Instead, they simply go to the closest mass merchandiser and buy a toaster in the quickest and easiest way possible. Certainly consumers make many decisions rationally, but even the majority of extensive decision making does not consider *all* the information about *all* of the alternatives available. For example, you just knew you had no interest in majoring in Classics, even though you may never have taken a Classics course and don't really know much about the field. It is important to recognize that some consumers, when purchasing some products, do not retrieve the necessary information from memory or gather new information to use in the decision making process we are discussing here.

> The **rationality of consumers** assumes that consumers gather as much information as possible about all of the alternatives they can, evaluate the information, and decide to purchase the alternative that will maximize their satisfaction.

## FACT OR FICTION REVISITED

◉ Rational consumers *do not* always gather as much information as possible before making any purchasing decision; sometimes extensive search is not worth the effort.

> The **evoked** or **consideration set** is the alternatives a consumer retrieves from memory or identifies during search activities.

## ▼ THE RESULTS OF SEARCH

The set of alternatives the consumer actively considers during the decision making process is called the **evoked** or **consideration set** (Figure 12.8). Consumers construct their evoked set from two sources: the alternatives they already know and retrieve from their internal memory, and those they identify from external sources. Of these alternatives, consumers exclude some and place them either in their **inept set**—the brands they will not consider buying—or their **inert set**—those toward which they are indifferent. To summarize, consumers use perception and learning to gather and organize the information they acquire and store in memory about alternatives. They form attitudes about the alternatives of which they are aware and then make decisions about whether or not to include them in their evoked sets.[5]

> The **inept set** is composed of the alternatives a consumer will not consider buying.

> The **inert set** is the set of alternatives toward which a consumer is indifferent.

■ FIGURE 12.8
Evoked, inept, and inert sets.

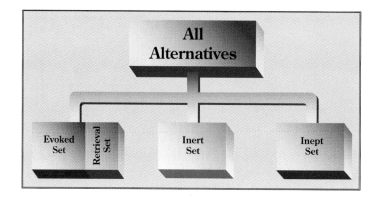

# EVALUATION OF ALTERNATIVES

O nce the consumer has identified alternatives and gathered information about them, one must be selected.[6] Consumers may choose among various products in a number of ways, depending on the level of effort they expend. In some situations, consumers make very simple choices for routine purchases—they buy Diet Coke because it's the same brand they have always bought. In other cases, such as choosing between an Acura Legend and a Mazda 626, those same consumers might utilize a rather sophisticated evaluation scheme and weigh a number of factors to determine their preferred brand in an extensive decision making effort.

The evaluation of different brands that make it into the consumer's evoked set occurs in two stages (1) the consumer selects certain *evaluative criteria*, and (2) the consumer establishes a *decision rule* to integrate those criteria into a choice.

▼ EVALUATIVE CRITERIA

**Evaluative criteria** are
the attributes a con-
sumer uses to discrimi-
nate among the benefits
offered by alternative
products in his or her
evoked set.

**Evaluative criteria** are the attributes consumers use to discriminate among the competing products in their evoked set. Often, consumers use many criteria to evaluate a set of alternatives either because the product may help them satisfy more than one need or because one product may have many benefits that will help them satisfy a single need. Returning to our running example, a student's choice of a major might meet two needs: (1) it allows the student to enjoy his or her college experience, and (2) it may help the student get a job after graduation. These needs may be in conflict if the subject area the student enjoys is one in which employment opportunities are scarce or difficult to come by, such as Theater Arts. On the other hand, if the student's only need is to get a job, he or she might look for more than one benefit from a major. The student may want a major that will provide him or her with both marketable skills and contact with supportive faculty members who will help the student in his or her job search.

**FIGURE 12.9**
Kaplan's testing services offer a specific benefit to consumers—strategies for improving their scores on standardized exams.

Individuals buy and consume products for the benefits they offer; in turn, the ability of products to deliver those benefits is the most important criterion consumers have for discriminating among them (Figure 12.9). Furthermore, consumers look for different benefits from different products—some benefits may be functional, others psychological, and still others social—and the benefits sought by one consumer will often be different from those sought by another. In choosing among products, consumers apply the evaluative criteria to each product's attributes, since these attributes indicate the benefits a product offers. Consider, for example, two benefits a student might seek from a major: marketable skills and faculty assistance. To determine whether a major provides marketable skills, the student might examine such attributes as the percentage of graduating seniors who get jobs in their major field of study and the availability of internships in area businesses. To measure faculty assistance, the student might inspect class size and the availability of faculty office hours.

## FACT OR FICTION REVISITED

⊛ Benefits are in fact the most important evaluative criteria used in most consumer decisions.

## ▼ DECISION RULES

Consumers are faced with a constant challenge: to consider all of the evaluative criteria they have identified and to make appropriate product decisions. If many attributes and associated benefits are important to an individual, that can become a daunting task indeed. To simplify the process, consumers implement a **decision rule**—a method of integrating multiple criteria into a single ordering of all the alternatives in an evoked set. That is, the decision rule helps consumers combine all of the evaluative criteria into one choice. When choosing a major, for example, a student may be faced with some alternatives that are stronger on certain attributes, and other alternatives that are stronger on other attributes. The student can then rate each major on each attribute. Say a student has identified eight attributes that are important; each attribute can then produce a different ranking of alternative majors. For example, an advertising major may rate highest on the attribute that measures student's interest in the course content, whereas accounting may receive the highest rating on job placement for graduating seniors, and so on for each attribute. The decision rule provides a way for the student to integrate these different rankings to arrive at one overall ranking and then choose the major that ranks first on that overall ranking.

Many different decision rules are available to consumers to help them distill the myriad choices they encounter. Psychologists and economists have studied and described these rules in very formal terms; more formally, in fact, than consumers actually apply them. As we noted in our discussion of multiattribute models in the previous chapter, most consumers do not apply the rules in the way they have been described. The average consumer does not sit down with pencil, paper, and calculator and complete the mathematical calculations the decision rules say they do. Rather, they apply **heuristics**—the "rules of thumb" consumers actually use to make choices among alternative products; instead of elaborate calculations, they do the reasoning in their minds. The decision rules are still useful, as we will see, because their formal descriptions correspond to the spirit of the heuristics consumers actually use to compare alternatives.

The two primary categories of decision rules are *noncompensatory* and *compensatory rules*. When consumers use a **noncompensatory rule,** they consider each attribute by itself; that is, they don't use a high rating on one attribute to compensate for a low rating on another. If interesting courses are the most important criteria to a

---

A **decision rule** is a method used to integrate multiple evaluative criteria into a single ordering of alternative products.

**Heuristics** are the "rules of thumb" consumers apply to choose among alternative products.

**Noncompensatory decision rules** consider each attribute separately in deterring a product choice.

student in choosing a major, for example, and he or she finds advertising courses the most interesting, the student would choose to major in advertising even though marketing might be nearly as interesting and offers better job prospects.

By contrast, when consumers use a **compensatory rule,** they consider all attributes simultaneously and use a high rating on one attribute to compensate for a low rating on another; that is, compensatory rules average an alternative's rating on many attributes. If the student in the above example considers all of the evaluative criteria, marketing would probably score the "highest" and would be chosen.

Plugging our example of choosing a major into the stages of the decision making process, we would make the following assumptions: Students consider the needs, goals, and benefits they seek from their majors; they identify the evaluative criteria and the attributes they will use to rank the majors in their evoked sets; they determine the relative importance of each criterion and rank them in order of their importance; and they rate each alternative on all of the criteria. As you know, most students do not actually go through these formal calculations. But they do know that majors differ from one another, and they identify the ways in which they differ. They do acknowledge which criteria matter to them and which do not. And they do know how the majors perform on each criterion. Let's examine a hypothetical student, named Shirley, and her choice of a college major under each of these decision rules. Table 12.2 shows the evaluative criteria Shirley has identified and the results of decision rules she may apply.

> **Compensatory decision rules** consider all attributes simultaneously to calculate an integrated, multiattribute rank ordering.

*Table 12.2*

## AN EXAMPLE OF CONSUMER DECISION MAKING

|  | Importance | Accounting | Astronomy | English | Marketing | Advertising |
|---|---|---|---|---|---|---|
| Interesting course content | 5 | 1 | 2 | 3 | 4 | 5 |
| Percentage of graduating seniors who get jobs in field | 4 | 5 | 1 | 1 | 4 | 2 |
| Availability of internships in local businesses | 4 | 4 | 1 | 2 | 4 | 1 |
| Average class size | 3 | 2 | 2 | 3 | 4 | 3 |
| Number of faculty office hours | 3 | 2 | 2 | 4 | 4 | 3 |
| Number of quantitative courses required | 2 | 1 | 1 | 5 | 3 | 3 |
| Workload required in courses | 2 | 2 | 1 | 4 | 3 | 4 |
| Number of credits required for graduation | 1 | 2 | 2 | 3 | 3 | 3 |
| **Multiattribute Compensatory Rule:** |  |  |  |  |  |  |
| Marketing has the highest sum |  | 61 | 36 | 69 | 91 | 72 |

**Noncompensatory Rules**
Lexicographic: Interesting course content is most important. Advertising is highest rated major for this attribute.
Elimination by aspects: With a score of four required on interesting course content, accounting, astronomy, and English are eliminated. The next most important attribute, seniors who get jobs, eliminated advertising, leaving only marketing.
Conjunctive: Using a score of 4, all majors are eliminated. Using a score of 3, only marketing remains.
Disjunctive: Using a minimum score of 3, 4, or 5, only astronomy is eliminated.

**A lexicographic decision rule** considers the one attribute that is most important and chooses the alternative that is rated highest on that attribute.

**The Lexicographic Rule**  One simple noncompensatory rule is the **lexicographic rule,** whereby the consumer selects one attribute as the most important and then chooses the alternative that is rated highest on that attribute. In our example, Shirley has selected course content as the most important criterion; she is therefore likely to choose advertising as her major. If two majors had the same rating, Shirley would use her next most important rating—say, accessibility to jobs after graduation—to distinguish between them. This is an example of a simple noncompensatory rule—the student chooses the major that rates highest on the most important attribute and ignores all other attributes. Shirley considers course content to be the most important attribute and gives no weight to the others.

**Elimination by aspects** eliminates alternatives that don't meet a minimum cutoff level on each attribute.

**The Elimination by Aspects Rule**  A more complex noncompensatory rule is the **elimination by aspects** rule, whereby the consumer considers the most important attribute and eliminates any alternatives that don't meet a minimum cutoff level on that attribute. This rule uses the attributes, one after the other, to discard alternatives that are not rated highly on important attributes. The consumer continues to use attributes to eliminate alternatives until only one remains. In this case, Shirley has decided that instead of trying to choose the alternative she likes most, she will eliminate those she likes least, one by one, and choose whichever major remains. Say Shirley chose to eliminate any major that didn't have a rating of 4 or better on the "interesting course content" attribute. According to Table 12.2, accounting, astronomy, and English would be eliminated on this basis. Shirley would then turn to the next most important attribute—the percentage of graduating students who get jobs—and eliminate advertising because of its score on that attribute. Marketing would then be the choice of major, even though it doesn't have the highest score on either of these criteria.

**The conjunctive rule** eliminates an alternative if any of its attribute ratings do not meet a minimum cutoff level.

**The Conjunctive Rule**  A noncompensatory rule that uses the same approach as elimination by aspects but applies the elimination procedure to each alternative rather than each attribute is the **conjunctive rule.** Using this rule, the consumer eliminates an alternative if any of its attribute ratings do not meet the minimum cutoff level—that is, an alternative must be acceptable on all attributes in order to be chosen. In our example, Shirley has decided that she wants her major to offer a minimum level of 4 for all benefits and will reject any alternative that can't offer all of those benefits at a rating of 4 or better. Using this rule, however, Shirley would be unable to choose a major because none of the alternatives has a score of 4 or higher on *all* the attributes. Faced with this outcome, she might lower the cutoff to 3 and choose marketing as her major.

**The disjunctive rule** sets a cutoff point for each attribute and retains any alternatives that exceed the cutoff on any of the attributes.

**The Disjunctive Rule**  Unlike the conjunctive rule, the **disjunctive rule** is a noncompensatory rule that sets a cutoff point for each attribute and retains those alternatives that exceed the cutoff on *any* of the attributes. Using this rule, the consumer will consider an alternative as long as it delivers any of the benefits he or she seeks. If Shirley decides to consider any major that has a minimum rating of 3 on any attribute, she will retain all majors except astronomy; only at the relaxed cutoff of 2 would she consider that major.

**A Multiattribute Compensatory Rule**   Turning to compensatory rules, a **multiattribute compensatory rule** employs a method similar to the multiattribute attitude models we discussed in Chapter 11. Whereas the noncompensatory rules use only one of the evaluative criteria at a time, the multiattribute compensatory rule considers all of the criteria and takes their relative importance into account. In our example, Shirley wants to try to balance all of the benefits potential majors have to offer and choose the one that has the best combination of the benefits she seeks. In doing so, Shirley would need to calculate a weighted sum for each major based on all of its attributes and the importance of each one. Using this process, she would choose marketing as her preferred alternative. Even though marketing does not rate highest on any of the attributes, its overall rating is the highest when the relative importance of the attributes is used to weight the calculations.

> A **multiattribute compensatory rule** calculates a rank ordering based on all attributes weighted by their relative importance.

**Selecting Decision Rules**   A consumer's level of involvement and effort will affect his or her choice of a noncompensatory versus a compensatory rule. If the consumer has little involvement in the decision and wants to avoid exerting effort in making a choice, he or she is more likely to use a simple, noncompensatory rule. These rules provide simple heuristics that are quite simple to apply. In some product decisions, price is used as the criterion in a lexicographic rule (Figure 12.10). Consumers may choose to buy the cheapest gas they can find for their cars, for example. Brand names are also often used as the attribute in this rule. Think of some of the long trips you have taken. When you realized you were hungry, you might have stopped at the first McDonald's you found. Because the search and evaluation process for unfamiliar restaurants is risky and complex, you focused on one criterion you could easily use to distinguish among the alternatives.

Similarly, elimination rules help consumers discard a number of alternatives quickly and easily. If Shirley really doesn't care about her choice of major, eliminating alternatives because they are uninteresting or they won't help her get a job after graduation will simplify her decision making. Consider the process of choosing among laundry detergents. Say you consider the cleaning power, size of the container, and price important attributes. Once you have eliminated any products that don't remove stains, are too large to carry to the laundromat, and cost too much, whatever brand is left will be okay with you. You're not concerned about getting the best; you'll use any reasonable product.

Disjunctive rules help consumers satisfy their needs when there are a number of attractive options—that is, they help them resolve approach–approach conflicts. For example, suppose you need to kill some time on a Sunday night and you have a number of attractive alternatives, none of which you have a particularly strong preference for. You could rent a video at Blockbuster (Figure 12.11) or work an extra shift at your restaurant job for overtime, or go to the library and get some work done. As long as an alternative offers some fun, or money, or a chance to improve your grades, you'll consider it.

■ FIGURE 12.10

Price is often used as the single criterion on which to judge a product, as featured in this ad for Aire Royale ceiling fans.

The rules change if the consumer is very involved and willing to expend extensive effort in making a decision. In this case, the consumer has both the motivation and the knowledge to consider many attributes and to balance the relative strengths and weaknesses of the alternatives. Accordingly, the individual may apply a sophisticated multiattribute rule and extensively evaluate the alternatives to make sure that the best alternative is selected. Choosing a major, buying a car, or picking an insurance plan are examples of such decisions. It helps to think of multiattribute models as a metaphor for one of the ways consumers may make a decision—by weighing many attributes in an attempt to use as much information as possible in coming to a decision. The consumer doesn't actually calculate the complicated weighted averages for each brand; instead, he or she weighs the different attributes and makes complex comparisons. When choosing a major, Shirley might have balanced her interest in the subject, the likelihood of getting a job, and the difficulty of each major in coming to her decision.

The selection of a decision rule is not quite as black and white as it appears. In some cases, even noncompensatory rules can play a role in a very involving decision. Consumers may use elimination rules to narrow down a large set of alternatives to a manageable set of choices. They can then focus on the remaining set and apply a more complex compensatory rule. For Shirley to balance her interests, job prospects, and the difficulty of each potential major, she needs to narrow down the possibilities to just a few. She can eliminate some majors quite quickly because they hold no interest for her.

■ FIGURE 12.11

Blockbuster markets its videos as an attractive option for staying home on a Sunday night. Often, it is one of many attractive options among which a consumer must choose.

# MARKETERS' INFLUENCE ON THE DECISION MAKING PROCESS

So far we have discussed the ways consumers search for alternatives and evaluate them in order to choose the product that will best satisfy their needs. We now turn to a discussion of the marketers' view and their efforts to influence the decision making processes. Different marketers adopt different strategies to influence consumers' choices, depending on their products and the characteristics of their target market segments. For example, the University of Minnesota would use a different strategy to attract high school seniors to attend its college than Farmland Dairy uses to influence consumers to choose their low-fat chocolate milk.

## ▼ SEARCH FOR ALTERNATIVES

Marketers want consumers to include their products in their evoked sets. Therefore, they must ensure that consumers are aware of their products and the needs they can satisfy. To do so, they employ a number of different strategies:

❶ To be included in the evoked set of involved consumers who gather information through *ongoing search activities,* marketers provide detailed background information about their products. They place information-rich advertisements in specialized media targeted at fans; use public relations to gain mentions in editorials; and distribute detailed promotional information. Consider sports equipment, such as skis. Ski manufacturers, such as Nordica, advertise extensively in skiing magazines, seek to be mentioned in articles and reviews about skis and skiing events, and offer brochures that detail the features of their products.

❷ Marketers adopt a different strategy to influence highly involved consumers who have begun a *specific information search* to satisfy a new need they have recognized for the first time. Recall the example of a consumer's new interest in major appliances when a washer or dryer breaks down. Appliance marketers place advertisements that emphasize their brand names and attributes in widely targeted media to convey background information they hope consumers will store as incidental knowledge in their memories. The consumer, in turn, will retrieve his or her knowledge of the product when the search process begins and seek out specific information about that product from specialized home magazines and retailers. General Electric's "We bring good things to life" is an example of an attempt on the part of a marketer to create background awareness (Figure 12.12).

❸ To gain awareness among uninvolved consumers who have only *incidental knowledge,* marketers can adopt two methods. Most marketers of frequently purchased routine products seek widespread distribution because consumers learn of the product through its presence in retail outlets. Products such as Ruffles potato chips, for example, are sold in a number of different outlets to ensure that consumers will see the product when they are ready to purchase it. Some marketers also advertise heavily to their target market so that incidental knowledge will be as common as possible. Beer and soft drinks are prominently advertised to increase *top-of-mind* awareness—easily retrieved incidental memories—of these products.

## FACT OR FICTION REVISITED

⦿ It is true that marketers make great efforts to ensure that their products are included in the consumer's evoked set.

## ▼ EVALUATION OF ALTERNATIVES

Obviously, marketers want consumers to choose their brands over their competitors' when they evaluate alternative products. To accomplish that goal, marketers attempt to influence evaluative criteria and decision rules in a number of ways.

## TO ORDINARY DISHWASHERS, THESE DISHES LOOK THE SAME. (IF THEY ONLY HAD A BRAIN.)

Introducing the new GE Profile™ Dishwasher with the amazing electronic brain. No other full-size dishwasher made in America saves you more energy– because the new GE Profile actually analyzes the soil content of each wash load and programs the perfect cycle.*

Shorter, for lighter loads. Longer, for dirtier ones. That means no more of the overwashing and underwashing so common with ordinary machines.

And that saves you money.

The new Profile also comes with an entire system of noise reduction features, making it the quietest dishwasher we've ever made. Add GE's innovative SmartRack design, with over 20 loading options–and there's no better, more efficient way to get your dishes brilliantly clean.

Call us at the GE Answer Center,® 800.626.2000, and we'll tell you more about the smart, new GE Profile Dishwasher. The kind of dishwasher ordinary machines would like to be. If they only had a brain.

*Profile*™

We bring good things to life

*Actual energy usage may be higher depending on use.

■ FIGURE 12.12
GE's long-running campaign "We Bring Good Things to Life" is an example of advertising that creates background awareness for consumers who have already begun a specific information search.

❶ Marketers try to influence consumers to consider the evaluative criteria on which they perform well. We noted in our discussion of motivation that marketers cannot create needs. However, marketers can try to influence the choice of goals consumers select to satisfy a need and the attributes they use as evaluative criteria. For example, marketers of sport–utility vehicles, such as the Range Rover and the Isuzu Rodeo, foster off-road performance as the goal that will meet the consumer's need for a rugged vehicle. Similarly, Wisk laundry detergent popularized its ability to remove "ring around the collar" as the attribute that represents cleaning power.

❷ Marketers also attempt to influence the decision rules consumers choose. If a product has an attribute that differentiates it from the competition, the marketer would want consumers to use that attribute as a lexicographic rule. If a product possesses a certain attribute that its competitors do not, the marketer of that product would encourage consumers to apply a disjunctive rule. For example, Volvo was the first car model of its class to include daytime running lights, so it emphasized that feature and tried to position the lights as mandatory for any sensible car owner.

❸ The marketers of powerful, well-known brands want to encourage *brand loyalty* by influencing consumers to adopt a routine purchase process. Once consumers have engaged in search and decision making activities and chosen their product, marketers want them to make the results of those activities their routine purchase behavior. The marketer will attempt to reinforce consumers' perceptions that they have made the right choice so that they will not engage in another decision making process that might result in a different outcome. For example, Excedrin attempts to combat the appeal of new analgesic products such as Aleve, Nuprin, and Advil by reinforcing its power to relieve headaches. Of course, Excedrin's competitors want consumers to reopen the decision making process by emphasizing different benefits.

## FACT OR FICTION REVISITED

◉ It is *not true* that marketers are usually unsuccessful in influencing consumers' decision rules; in fact, they often succeed in doing so.

# PUBLIC POLICY AND DECISION MAKING

All decision making requires information. Consumers must understand the relationship between attributes and benefits in order to develop evaluative criteria that will help them meet their needs. If they do not recognize, for example, which fat in a food product is "bad fat" and which is less harmful, they cannot correctly assess the health benefits of that product. The consumer must also be able to gather information about the attributes of each alternative. How much fat, and what kinds, does a particular product contain?

Both advertising and packaging have been criticized for the lack of information they provide to help consumers recognize and apply important evaluative criteria. At the same time, marketers and public policy actors are taking on increased responsibility to ensure that consumers have the necessary information to make decisions as they would like. In our discussion of perception in Chapter 9 we noted that the Nutrition Labeling and Education Act requires that all packaged food products carry a uniform nutrition label. Now, let's consider the implication of these labels for consumers' decision making.[7]

## PUBLIC POLICY

### Do You Know What You're Eating?[8]

New nutrition labels, required by law since May 1994, provide detailed dietary information for consumers to use in their decision making. To publicize the new labels, the Food and Drug Administration turned to such diverse channels as televised public service announcements, the Times Square electronic billboard, the Goodyear blimp, and scoreboards in baseball stadiums around the country. Trade associations and marketers helped promote the labels as well. The National Food Processors Association produced pamphlets and brochures that were distributed by the Food Marketing Institute to supermarkets for their customers. Food marketers, such as Kellogg's, promoted the brochures on their packages, offering to send complimentary copies to consumers free of charge upon request (Figure 12.13).

After only 6 months, there was already evidence that the labels provide useful information for consumers attempting to evaluate the nutritional content of what they eat. According to a study conducted in January 1995 for *Prevention* magazine and the Food Marketing Institute, 78 percent of consumers are aware of the label changes. Of those consumers, 53 percent claimed to always read the labels, and an additional 31 percent said they read them sometimes. One-third of consumers reported that they didn't buy a particular food product because of negative information they read on the label, whereas 22 percent stated that label information had encouraged them to try a new product.

Consumers and nutrition experts alike have some concerns about the new labels, however. Two-thirds of consumers feel that the recommended serving sizes—on which all of the nutritional information is based—do not represent the amount the average consumer actually eats. Some nutritional experts fear that consumers are looking exclusively at the fat content of food products and ignoring information about sugar, salt, cholesterol, and vitamins. The consumers, in turn, acknowledged that fat was in fact the key factor influencing their purchases; 78 percent of those who changed their purchases did so because of fat content.

Do you read nutritional labels when you shop for food? Are the labels arranged in a way to emphasize some kinds of information more than others? Do you think consumers can accurately utilize the information provided by labels to make comparisons among products? What kinds of decision rules would consumers use to make these comparisons? Can consumers use the labels to decide whether a single product's nutritional content is acceptable? What kinds of decision rules would they use to make that decision?

**Are You Ready for New Food Labels?**
Kellogg's

**Nutrition Facts**
Serving Size 1 cup (30g/1.1 oz.)
Servings Per Container 16

| Amount Per Serving | Cereal | Cereal with ½ Cup Vitamins A & D Skim Milk |
|---|---|---|
| **Calories** | 100 | 140 |
| Calories from Fat | 5 | 5 |

| | % Daily Value** | |
|---|---|---|
| **Total Fat** 0.5g* | 1 % | 1 % |
| Saturated Fat 0g | 0 % | 0 % |
| Polyunsaturated Fat 0g | | |
| Monounsaturated Fat 0g | | |
| **Cholesterol** 0mg | 0 % | 0 % |
| **Sodium** 230mg | 10 % | 12 % |
| **Potassium** 180mg | 5 % | 11 % |
| **Total Carbohydrate** 25g | 8 % | 10 % |
| Dietary Fiber 5g | 20 % | 20 % |
| Soluble Fiber 1g | | |
| Insoluble Fiber 4g | | |
| Sugars 6g | | |
| Other Carbohydrate 14g | | |
| **Protein** 3g | | |
| Vitamin A (20% as beta carotene) | 35 % | 40 % |
| Vitamin C | 25 % | 25 % |
| Calcium | 0 % | 15 % |
| Iron | 45 % | 45 % |

■ FIGURE 12.13

# CONSUMER DECISION MAKING

Trupti Niak used her decision making skills to choose her school and her major. She gathered specific information about her alternatives from marketing brochures provided by the colleges she was considering and from family members, students, and counselors during her senior year in high school. In addition, she retrieved information about engineering and architecture that she had accumulated through life experience. Trupti applied criteria such as cost, distance from home, and educational atmosphere to choose among schools, and she considered her interests and job prospects in picking her major. Having weighed all of these factors, she decided to major in mechanical engineering at the University of Minnesota. In doing so, she recognizes that she compromised some of her needs in order to satisfy others.

Trupti's choices of school and major illustrate how decision making can be an extensive process that involves both the search for information and careful synthesis of that information to arrive at a choice. Not all decisions elicit similar effort, however; some can be made in a very quick, routine way. Regardless of the effort exerted, consumers implement the behavioral processes of motivation, perception, learning, attitude formation, and decision making to complete the activities in the purchase process.

Now that we have completed our discussion of the behavioral processes, we will review them in Chapter 13 by looking at the different ways they are used to complete the activities for different kinds of purchases. We will look specifically at a high involvement purchase—buying a car—and a low involvement purchase—choosing a soft drink.

## SUMMARY

1. **Categorize the consumer's level of effort involved in decision making.** Decision making can be categorized by the amount of time and the level of effort the consumer spends in completing the purchase process. This level of effort is influenced by the consumer's involvement, perceived risk, product experience, and frequency of purchase. Extensive decision making involves a complete search for alternatives and development of evaluative criteria and decision rules. By contrast, limited decision making is less involving; the consumer applies existing criteria and rules to newly gathered information about alternatives. Routine decision making is even less involving; the consumer repeats previous purchase behavior by applying existing criteria and rules without gathering new information.

2. **Identify the sources of information and search activities used by consumers in the search for alternatives.** Consumers gather information from both internal and external sources through ongoing search activities, specific information gathering activities, and incidental knowledge. Information that is either gathered purposely through ongoing search activities or accumulated incidentally is stored and retrieved from the consumer's internal source of knowledge—long-term memory. Consumers

gather additional information for a specific instance of decision making from external sources, such as marketing and interpersonal communications.

3. **Recognize the evaluative criteria and decision rules consumers employ in choosing a product.** Evaluative criteria consist of the attributes of the available alternatives in the consumer's evoked set. These attributes, in turn, serve as indicators that the product will offer the benefits the consumers is seeking. Decision rules provide a means of integrating the multiple criteria into one ordered ranking of alternatives. Noncompensatory decision rules consider each attribute separately, whereas compensatory decision rules consider all attributes simultaneously. Although decision rules provide sophisticated methods for choosing among alternatives, many consumers use heuristics—rules of thumb that provide a more practical way of implementing the decision rules.

4. **Analyze the methods marketers employ to influence consumer decision making.** Marketers want consumers to include their products in their evoked sets and to evaluate them favorably so that they will be purchased. Marketers may adopt different strategies to achieve these goals. To influence the search for alternatives, they may provide detailed background information to consumers engaged in ongoing search activities; promote their general reputation for quality so that consumers will store incidental favorable attitudes and seek detailed knowledge when they begin the purchase process; and provide continual reminders to keep the incidental knowledge active. To influence the evaluation of alternatives, marketers may attempt to convince consumers to emphasize evaluative criteria on which their products perform well, influence consumers to use decision rules that will favor their products, or encourage existing users to consider their products as a routine purchase that should not be reevaluated.

---

# KEY TERMS

Extensive decision making, *p. 345*

Limited decision making, *p. 347*

Routine decision making, *p. 347*

Rationality of consumers, *p. 353*

Evoked (consideration) set, *p. 353*

Inept set, *p. 353*

Inert set, *p. 353*

Evaluative criteria, *p. 354*

Decision rule, *p. 356*

Heuristics, *p. 356*

Noncompensatory decision rule, *p. 356*

Compensatory decision rule, *p. 357*

Lexicographic decision rule, *p. 358*

Elimination by aspects rule, *p. 358*

Conjunctive rule, *p. 358*

Disjunctive rule, *p. 358*

Multiattribute compensatory rule, *p. 359*

---

# SKILL-BUILDING ACTIVITIES

1. Construct an interview guide (a set of questions to be asked in an interview) that will cover the following aspects of decision making:
   a. level of involvement
   b. type of search
   c. evoked and consideration set
   d. evaluative criteria
   e. decision rule(s) used
   f. outcome

2. Using this guide, interview a classmate about a recent purchase he or she has made. Write a description of the purchase, following the outline in activity 1, (a) through (f).

3. Which aspects of this decision were influenced by marketers? In what way?

4. In which aspect of this decision could government officials or public policy advocates be expected to intervene? How might these interventions occur?

---

# CHAPTER 12 SELF-TEST

▼ MULTIPLE CHOICE

1. Consumers will exert more effort during a purchase that satisfies a high _____ need, and when the purchase or product is perceived to be _____ .
   a. price; risky
   b. status; difficult to use
   c. involvement; risky
   d. involvement; difficult to use

2. Purchases such as cars, boats, houses, and wedding gowns usually involve _____ decision making.
   a. extensive
   b. limited
   c. costly
   d. routine

3. The first stage of the decision making process is _____ .
   a. evaluation of alternatives
   b. specific search for alternatives
   c. need recognition
   d. development of evaluative criteria

4. If a consumer attends a car race where a motel chain's name is predominately displayed on the winning vehicle but the consumer doesn't have a need to stay in a motel in the near future, the information obtained from seeing the ad would be considered _____ .
   a. ongoing search activity information
   b. incidental knowledge
   c. need driven search information
   d. problem recognition information

5. If a consumer will only purchase either Nike or Adidas athletic shoes, Reebok and Converse would be in either that consumer's _____ or _____ sets.
   a. evoked; consideration
   b. inept; evoked
   c. inept; inert
   d. inert; consideration

6. Price, color, size, and availability are often used as _____ when a consumer is evaluating alternatives.
   a. classification rules
   b. measurements
   c. consumer ratings
   d. evaluative criteria

7. When Christy is evaluating cars, she is willing to consider a higher priced car only if it has a keyless entry system. Christy is using a _____ decision rule.
   a. noncompensatory rule
   b. resolution rule
   c. survival of the fittest rule
   d. compensatory rule

8. When a consumer identifies one attribute as important and then selects an alternative that rates the highest on that attribute, a _____ rule is being used.
   a. disjunctive
   b. lexicographic
   c. elimination by aspects
   d. conjunctive

9. _____ rules are useful to consumers who have no strong preference for any of the alternatives being evaluated.
   a. Disjunctive
   b. Lexicographic
   c. Conjunctive
   d. Elimination by aspects

10. The last stage of the decision making process is _____ .
    a. determination of decision rules
    c. product choice
    b. applying a decision rule
    d. comparison of evoked set alternatives

## ▼ TRUE/FALSE

1. High involvement products are always high priced.   T or F
2. Most product purchases involve extensive decision making.   T or F
3. Consumers do not always include search and evaluation during their decision making process.   T or F
4. The search for alternatives occurs only when the consumer is actively seeking to fulfill a need.   T or F
5. Consumers use decision rules to combine their evaluative criteria into one choice.   T or F
6. Always buying the cheapest product is an example of a consumer heuristic.   T or F
7. Using a conjunctive rule during the evaluation of alternatives, a consumer would eliminate any alternative that does not meet a minimum cutoff level assigned to an attribute.   T or F
8. Consumers who are highly involved in a purchase will probably use a simple, non-compensatory rule.   T or F
9. One way marketers try to influence a consumer's decision making process is by emphasizing how the product being marketed performs on an important evaluative criterion.   T or F
10. Brand loyalty can be an outcome of routine decision making.   T or F

## ▼ SHORT ANSWER

1. Explain the difference between limited decision making and routine decision making.
2. Describe some external information sources that might be used by a consumer during the decision making process of purchasing a car.
3. Describe how a consumer might use the elimination by aspects rule when selecting an apartment to rent.

## ▼ APPLICATION EXERCISE

You are the marketing director of a new cut-rate airline offering service between your city and New York City. Since the airline is new, few leisure travelers currently include your airline in their evoked set of airlines offering service to New York City. Develop at least two strategies to help move your airline into the evoked set of leisure travelers.

# 13

# HIGH AND LOW INVOLVEMENT DECISION MAKING

◉ Consumer Snapshot *Kim Bannister is a 37-year-old Administration Associate. She is single and lives in Tucson, Arizona, where she grew up.*

FACT OR FICTION

◉ Consumers usually exert more effort when making high involvement purchases than when making low involvement purchases.

◉ Most high involvement purchases include relatively high levels of perceived risk.

◉ Anticipated purchase and usage situations play important roles in determining level of involvement when making a purchase.

⦿  Consumers usually search for more information when making low involvment purchases than when making high involvement purchases.

⦿  Consumers complain more about defects in high involvement products than they do about defects in low involvement products.

⦿  In low involvement purchases, habit often replaces search for alternatives.

# EYE ON THE CONSUMER

Kim Bannister drives an 11-year-old Mazda, a car that has been reliable since the day she bought it. When Kim decided to buy a car, she knew she wanted something new and reliable; she didn't look at used cars that would come with somebody else's problems. Kim doesn't read car magazines, and she can't tell one model from another. "A V-8 to me is a juice, you know," she jokes. To help her in her car search, she referred to *Consumer Reports* to find out about reliability and fuel economy, and she took her father along with her to visit car dealerships.

Kim's family has always favored Japanese cars for their dependability and reliability. Kim has been satisfied with the Mazda she ended up buying because it is small and maneuverable but still has a hatchback to hold all of her gardening supplies. She knows the car won't last forever and when she needs a new car she'll have to read *Consumer Reports* again and consult with friends to see what they can tell her about more current models. Maybe next time she'll try to avoid the hassle she experienced at the car dealer by using a buying service—the credit union provides the services of a car broker who will do all the negotiating once she picks the kind of car she wants.

Kim does her grocery shopping quite a bit more frequently than she buys cars, usually at one of the two Safeway supermarkets close to home. She typically makes a short list of the things she knows she needs and takes along a coupon or two she has clipped for frequently purchased products. Kim skips over the aisles containing products she knows she won't buy—cereal, which she doesn't eat, and shampoo and beauty aids, which she buys at the discount Drug Emporium. She's not particularly loyal to any specific brands, with the exception of Whiskas and Friskies canned food for her cats; they won't eat any other brands. She doesn't have a preference for certain soft drinks, but some of her friends do, so she buys Diet Pepsi rather than Diet Coke or the generics.

This chapter reviews what you have learned so far about behavioral processes by applying two specific examples of consumer behavior—buying a car and choosing a soft drink. Cars are complex, carefully evaluated, and risky purchases, whereas soft drinks are simple purchases with little risk. What distinguishes a consumer's behavior in buying the two products is his or her *involvement.* We first introduced involvement in our discussion of motivation and needs in Chapter 8. To review, involvement is the importance or relevance a particular purchase has for a consumer.[1] In this chapter we distinguish between high and low involvement purchases. For each type of product, we highlight the consumer's application of the behavioral processes, the marketer's efforts to influence those processes, and subsequent public policy concerns.

After reading and thinking about this chapter, you should be able to:

❶ Determine the level of involvement a consumer exhibits during the purchase process.

❷ Recognize the extensive purchase activities that accompany high involvement purchases.

❸ Identify the routine purchase activities that accompany low involvement purchases.

# MOTIVATION AND INVOLVEMENT ◀

The driving force in recognizing needs and choosing goals to satisfy them is motivation. Once a consumer recognizes a need, he or she begins the activities that will result in the purchase of a product to satisfy that need. Because consumers typically have many needs at the same time, they must prioritize the effort they devote to each of the resulting purchase processes. In general, consumers devote more effort to satisfying those needs that have higher costs and benefits and that are more important, interesting, and relevant to them.

A person's level of involvement reflects the benefits and costs the consumer expects to receive from buying a product to satisfy a need that occurs in a specific situation. The benefits come from satisfying the need; the costs come both from the price that must be paid for the product as well as the risk of any losses that might accompany use of the product (Figure 13.1). For example, if a consumer buys an expensive video camera and it does not take work correctly, he or she may be unable to record family celebrations and be inconvenienced by repeated visits to the repair shop. As we noted in the previous chapter, some inexpensive products may also be high involvement because they carry the risk of costly side effects. Although the cost of the meal that you eat on a first date is relatively inexpensive, for example, the possibility that your date will not like the food or become sick makes it a high involvement purchase.

■ FIGURE 13.1

The costs of a high involvement product often include a high price.

Some purchases hold little or no interest for the consumers in a particular market segment; although they recognize a need, they don't care which specific product they buy to satisfy it. Most college students don't care which brand of laundry detergent they buy as long as their clothes come out reasonably clean. By contrast, other purchases may have great interest for those same consumers. College students tend to be very involved with the clothes they wear. Thus, there may be a time when the student becomes interested in laundry detergent—when his or her favorite college sweatshirt is stained at a party, for example.

For most consumers, buying a car invokes a high involvement purchase process, whereas buying a soft drink involves a low involvement purchase process. First, consumers deliberate about each of their infrequent purchases of a car, whereas they may buy several soft drinks in a day without giving much thought to any of them. Second, most consumers can remember every car they have ever owned, whereas they may have trouble remembering the soft drinks they have bought so far today, let alone all of the soft drinks they bought this week. Third, if your car doesn't work as you expect it to, you may face a great deal of inconvenience, significant repair costs, and possible physical danger; if you don't like a soft drink you bought, you may just throw it away and get another.

## FACT OR FICTION REVISITED

◉   Consumers do in fact exert more effort when making high involvement purchases than when making low involvement purchases.

## ▼ FACTORS THAT AFFECT INVOLVEMENT

As Table 13.1 indicates, three types of factors influence involvement, in conjunction with the expected costs and benefits of the purchase: (1) the *background characteristics* of the consumer making the purchase, such as culture and values, demographics, personality, lifestyle, psychographics; (2) *product characteristics*, such as its attributes, benefits, cost, and the perceived risk of buying and using the product; and (3) *situational effects* that accompany a particular purchase or usage occasion or any competing needs that may arise at the same time.

Because a consumer's background characteristics affect involvement, the purchase of a particular product may be highly involving for one consumer and not as involving for another. For example, homemakers tend to be more involved with furniture polish than are college students. Involvement can also vary by product—the "average" level of involvement among all consumers is greater for some products (e.g., cars) than others (e.g., soft drinks). Finally, the same consumer may be more involved

### Table 13.1

## FACTORS THAT AFFECT INVOLVEMENT

**Background Characteristics**
Culture and values
Demographics and demographic subcultures
Personality, self-concept, lifestyle, and psychographics
Reference groups

**Product characteristics**
Attributes and benefits
Costs
Perceived risks

**Situational effects**
Purchase occasion
Usage occasion
Competing needs

with a particular product in some situations and less involved in others. For example, you may be more involved in choosing a case of soft drinks to take to your boss's picnic than in choosing one to drink for lunch. Scales such as the one depicted in Figure 13.2 are often used to measure a consumer's involvement with a purchase process.[2]

The following examples illustrate just some of the factors that influence involvement: [3]

❶ A person's lifestyle makes some purchase processes more involving than others. For example, even though cars are higher involvement purchases than many others, lifestyle affects the degree of involvement. The purchase process will be more involving for a person who watches car racing, does his or her own car repairs, and regularly reads car magazines than for the typical consumer.

❷ Consumers tend to be more involved with purchases that are consistent with their self-concept. A person who views herself as trendy and fashionable, for example, might be more involved than the average consumer with her beverage purchases because she wants to ensure that she is always drinking the latest new beverage instead of the usual drinks that other people buy. This

| (Insert name of object to be judged) | | |
|---|---|---|
| Important | ❏❏❏❏❏❏❏ | Unimportant* |
| Of no concern | ❏❏❏❏❏❏❏ | Of concern to me |
| Irrelevant | ❏❏❏❏❏❏❏ | Relevant |
| Means a lot to me | ❏❏❏❏❏❏❏ | Means nothing to me* |
| Useless | ❏❏❏❏❏❏❏ | Useful |
| Valuable | ❏❏❏❏❏❏❏ | Worthless* |
| Trivial | ❏❏❏❏❏❏❏ | Fundamental |
| Beneficial | ❏❏❏❏❏❏❏ | Not beneficial* |
| Matters to me | ❏❏❏❏❏❏❏ | Doesn't matter |
| Uninterested | ❏❏❏❏❏❏❏ | Interested |
| Significant | ❏❏❏❏❏❏❏ | Insignificant* |
| Vital | ❏❏❏❏❏❏❏ | Superfluous |
| Boring | ❏❏❏❏❏❏❏ | Interesting |
| Unexciting | ❏❏❏❏❏❏❏ | Exciting |
| Appealing | ❏❏❏❏❏❏❏ | Unappealing* |
| Mundane | ❏❏❏❏❏❏❏ | Fascinating |
| Essential | ❏❏❏❏❏❏❏ | Nonessential* |
| Undesirable | ❏❏❏❏❏❏❏ | Desirable |
| Wanted | ❏❏❏❏❏❏❏ | Unwanted* |
| Not needed | ❏❏❏❏❏❏❏ | Needed |

■ FIGURE 13.2
A scale used to measure product involvement.

*Indicates item is reverse scored.

Items on the left are scored (1) low involvement to (7) high involvement on the right.

Totaling the 20 items gives a score from a low of 20 to a high of 140.

Source: Judith Lynne Zaichowsky (1985), "Measuring the Involvement Construct," *Journal of Consumer Research,* 12 (December), (350). Reprinted with permission of The University of Chicago Press.

consumer would have been among the first to buy such products as Miller Lite Ice or Zima (Figure 13.3).

**❸** A person's perception of the risk involved in purchasing a particular product—that is, the uncertainty of making the "wrong" purchase decision and suffering the costs—will increase his or her involvement. As we have noted in Chapter 9, the perception of risk stems from a feeling of uncertainty about the functional, physical, financial, social, or psychological costs of the purchase decision. For example, cars are highly involving products because

■  FIGURE 13.3
A consumer with a trendy self-concept would likely have been one of the first to try the new Zima alcoholic beverage.

**Some people hanging<sup>·</sup> around rinsing mud from their teeth.<sup>··</sup>**

* That moment in time between the last thing you did and what you're about to do next; it's only loitering if there's a sign. ** Zima is no substitute for brushing regularly, but it is refreshing when served cold. Oh yeah, and it comes in cans. ©1995 Zima Beverage Co. Memphis, Tennessee. Clear malt beverage with natural flavors. Adult humans only. refresh@zima.com

they carry significant costs. Buying the wrong car carries functional risks (you may be stranded if the car breaks down) as well as physical risks (design or manufacturing flaws that can cause accidents).

❹ Consumers are typically more involved with their purchases when they are faced with many widely different alternatives from which to choose. When the products are very different from one another, the consumer must devote more effort to learn about each product and to make a purchase decision. For example, some consumers view athletic shoes as a high involvement purchase because they want to ensure that they choose a pair that will meet their specific needs from the many choices available. A person who takes a lot of high-impact step aerobics classes, for instance, will want to be sure he or she chooses just the right pair of athletic shoes for that particular activity.

❺ Situational factors, particular purchase or usage occasions, tend to increase the level of consumer involvement. This is particularly true of the in-store games and sweepstakes sponsored by fast food restaurants, such as McDonald's and Burger King. Similarly, as we noted earlier, a consumer who is buying a case of soft drinks for her boss will be more involved in the purchase process than when she is purchasing one can to have with lunch. These situation-specific purchases are distinct from **enduring involvement**, whereby the consumer experiences ongoing high involvement with a product category as a result of personal factors that generate greater interest on his or her part.[4] For example, car aficionados have enduring involvement with cars; by contrast, the average consumer becomes highly involved with cars only during the time of a specific purchase but is less involved during the years in between.

> **Enduring involvement** is a person's ongoing, high involvement with a product category.

## FACT OR FICTION REVISITED

⊙ Most high involvement purchases do include relatively high levels of perceived risk.

## ▼ THE EFFECTS OF INVOLVEMENT

Involvement matters: consumers who are highly involved with a purchase process complete the purchase activities differently than do consumers who are less involved with a purchase. Even the same consumer will act differently during a high involvement process than during a low involvement one. As we have discussed, consumers typically are willing to exert more effort in searching for alternative products and evaluating them for a high involvement purchase. Because they are involved, they are also able to perceive subtle differences among products. By contrast, when faced with a low involvement purchase, consumers may skip the search and evaluation activities altogether—they will simply buy whatever is available or decide on a favorite product and keep buying that without giving it any additional thought. Such low involvement purchases invoke only a routine level of decision making effort.

The activities involved in the decision making process—search, evaluation, purchase, postpurchase evaluation, feedback, and disposal—all elicit more extensive cognitive effort for a high involvment purchase. When consumers are more highly involved with a purchase, they are more receptive to information from others in their environment, and communication from marketers and public policy actors plays a larger role. For example, car advertisements tend to be more informational than soft drink ads because consumers are willing to exert the effort to understand them. However, as we note in our discussion of the effects of advertising in Chapter 15, the *noninformational cues* in marketing communications—the attractiveness of the setting or the models used in ads, for example—may have an influence on consumers for low involvement purchases as well. Similarly, the interpersonal influence of positive reference groups exists for both high and low involvement purchases. Few people want their friends to laugh at their choice of cars or beverages, but most will value their friends' opinions about the cars they drive more highly than their choice of soft drinks.

## FACT OR FICTION REVISITED

⊙   Anticipated purchase and usage situations do in fact play important roles in determining the level of involvement when making a purchase.

# HIGH INVOLVEMENT PURCHASES

Buying a car is a high involvement purchase for most consumers. People use their cars to satisfy many needs. Cars offer many different functional, psychological, and social benefits—transportation, pleasure, and a statement of personality, to name a few. They are also expensive products that carry significant risks for their consumers, who are exposed to many different models, each available with options that further lengthen the list of alternatives.

Consumers talk frequently about cars and driving, if only to complain that their cars are not working or to admire other cars they see on the road. Car advertising appears regularly on television and radio and in magazines, newspapers, and direct mail efforts; some magazines and television and radio programs are devoted solely to cars. Stories about car makers appear in news, consumer, lifestyle, and sports articles and programs. We will now review the consumer activities that comprise this high involvement consumer purchase process.

## ▼ RECOGNIZE NEEDS

It is important to recognize that a high involvement purchase process does not mean that the need for that product is greater than another need or that the product will be purchased before a lower involvement purchase. Rather, the high involvement product will require more effort and time to choose the best alternative, whereas the low involvement product may be a biological need that can be satisfied quickly with little effort. For example, a person may need both a car and a soft drink but will have to choose which need is greater at the moment. In fact, car dealerships often provide refreshments and other amenities to divert consumers from the distractions of less involving but innate biological needs.

A consumer may not actually purchase a car even though he or she recognizes it as a high involvement purchase. Many people are very involved in the purchase process and would like to buy a new car more frequently than they actually do. They recognize the need but decide that it is not great enough to require a purchase. Instead, they may repair the car they currently own to satisfy a functional need for transportation, or they may buy new accessories or repaint the car to satisfy a psychological or social need. Marketers attempt to influence this process by emphasizing psychological and social benefits as well as functional ones (Figure 13.4). Some people choose not to buy a car if it conflicts with competing goals. A person who needs both a new car and a vacation may decide that the vacation is a more attractive goal at the moment and that the new car can wait another 6 months.

## ▼ SEARCH FOR ALTERNATIVES

The search for alternatives in a high involvement purchase process is an extensive information-gathering activity. Using their perceptual and learning tools, consumers gather general information about cars and specific information about alternative models. Some consumers engage in ongoing search activities—they read articles about new cars and look at the cars their friends drive, for example. When it comes time to buy a new car, they can then supplement this information with specific information-gathering efforts—they may peruse car advertisements, read car magazines or *Consumer Reports*, visit car dealerships for product news, or ask acquaintances for advice or personal experiences.

Other consumers for whom the car purchase is a new and sudden need—they have had an accident or an unexpected breakdown—will typically search for specific information before making a decision. Most consumers do not rely solely on their own memories for a high involvement purchase; instead, they turn to interpersonal and marketing communications as sources of information.

Many consumers, even those who have maintained an ongoing interest in a high involvement product, need to gather specific information about rapidly changing attributes, such as price. However, as we discuss in the Public Policy box that

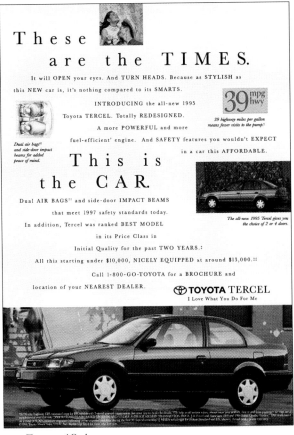

**■ FIGURE 13.4**

This ad for the Toyota Tercel appeals to consumers' social need to fit in with the "in crowd" by owning a "cool" car.

follows, consumers are sometimes unable to interpret information about car pricing effectively because they do not have access to the necessary information.

## PUBLIC POLICY

### What Does a Car Cost?[5]

With the average price of a new car surpassing $20,000, prospective car buyers are increasingly interested in reducing the prices they pay. Some consumers have turned to two new options that offer reduced prices: leasing and car-buying services. Nearly 30 percent of new cars and over 20 percent of new trucks have been leased in recent years. Many consumers prefer leasing to buying because they are able to make a monthly lease payment that is lower than the loan payment would be for the same car. Lease payments are lower, in part, because consumers pay only for the time they lease the car. At the end of the lease, the consumer has the option of either paying a lump sum to buy the car or returning it to the leasing company.

The down side is that most consumers have little idea about whether they are actually paying less to lease the car than they would to buy it—comparing total lease to purchase costs is very difficult, at best. A sophisticated financial analysis is required to calculate a leased car's total cost from the monthly payment, any required down payment, any capital-cost reduction or processing fees that are required, and the interest rate. Thus, even though the monthly lease payment may be lower, the total cost may be much higher. To combat this kind of criticism from consumer groups, state attorneys general, and the Federal Reserve, the American Financial Services Association—the auto leasing industry's trade group— has adopted a voluntary standard that encourages its members to disclose the actual cost of the cars they are leasing.

The second option, car-buying services, provides information about the *actual* cost of the cars consumers buy from local dealers—that is, the dealers' costs before their profit is added, not the suggested retail price. Some of the services have running agreements with dealers to sell cars to their members at a fixed amount over the dealer cost, eliminating the negotiations many consumers find frustrating. Providers of these services include such diverse organizations as local American Automobile Association (AAA) clubs; Wal-Mart, which offers a program through its Sam's Club discount warehouses; and the nonprofit CarBargains program of the Center for the Study of Services in Washington.

Do you think consumers are able to gather information about the total cost of a car lease from the typical car lease advertisements you have seen? Would the standardized method of calculating bank loan costs—the annual percentage rate (APR)— help consumers to better understand costs? Do you think the information provided by car-buying services helps consumers gather information more effectively than the stereotypical visit to a car showroom? Why or why not?

## FACT OR FICTION REVISITED

⦿   It is *not true* that consumers search for more information when making low involvement purchases; rather, they search for more information for high involvement purchases.

### ▼ EVALUATE ALTERNATIVES

Consumers are typically willing to exert great effort to evaluate the alternative products in a high involvement category such as cars. One way of doing so is to use the advice and product experiences they have gathered from members of their positive reference groups to develop strongly held, well-defined attitudes about cars. These attitudes, in turn, are incorporated in the extensive decision making process. Recall that extensive decision making means that consumers are continually refining their evaluative criteria and decision making rules. For example, even consumers who haven't bought a new car in several years are aware of safety advances such as air bags and antilock braking systems.

Consumers are likely to use compensatory decision rules for highly involving products; that is, they are willing to exert the additional cognitive effort to consider all of the relevant attributes simultaneously. Car purchasers for whom safety is most important, for example, will still try to balance safety, styling, luxury, and cost rather than simply choose the safest car.

### ▼ PURCHASE AND USE THE PRODUCT

Most consumers dread the experience of purchasing a car and would prefer the purchase environment be free of those factors that might prevent them from purchasing the product they have chosen, such as aggressive salespersons and crowded showrooms. The physical and social surroundings of a car showroom are often unpleasant to consumers; they fear that they won't be able to find a car with the features they want, at the price they can afford, and that salespeople will aggressively pursue them with a barrage of high-pressure sales techniques. A car is an expensive purchase, and the financial risks of overpaying during the price negotiation are daunting.

In response, some car dealerships have changed their purchase environment to address many of these concerns. Saturn has taken a rather determined approach by training its salespeople to function as low-key sources of information rather than aggressive persuaders. Price negotiation does not exist at Saturn; all cars are sold at the sticker price. Similarly, many car dealers have adopted a "value-pricing" approach that sets the price and doesn't allow the traditional price haggling, while others market their cars through shopping services that prenegotiate discount prices. Currently, about 40 percent of new cars are purchased without the negotiation that many consumers find distasteful. Even used car sales are changing. CarMax is a fixed-price, no-haggle used car retail location being tested in Richmond, Virginia, by Circuit City, a large appliance retailer.

Consumers and marketers are not the only ones affecting change in this high involvement industry. Public policy actors have also sought to change the purchase environment through regulations that require full disclosure of information such as fuel economy and foreign content.

### ▼ EVALUATE THE CONSUMPTION EXPERIENCE

Once the purchase is made, the consumer will perform some kind of postpurchase evaluation to determine his or her level of satisfaction with the product. Because the purchase involved an extensive decision making process, the postpur-

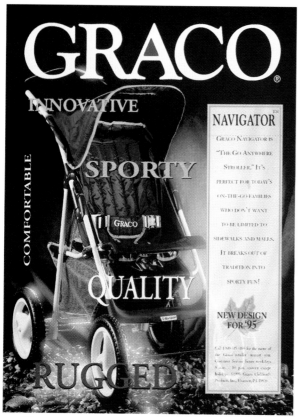

**FIGURE 13.5**

Graco touts its quality features loud and clear in this ad for the Navigator stroller.

chase evaluation will typically involve several criteria as well. The consumer might carefully examine his or her experience with the car so far, look at the fit and finish of the body and interior, listen for "suspicious" noises, watch the gasoline mileage, and show it to friends to gauge their reactions. This postpurchase evaluation considers both the car's actual performance and its performance relative to the consumer's expectations. The consumer may then revise his or her attitude toward the product on the basis of this evaluation.

To ensure that consumers have realistic expectations for the postpurchase evaluation, car marketers try to provide an accurate picture for consumers *before* the purchase. Many dealers show consumers how to use the features of their cars before they drive them away and encourage them to test drive the model before making a purchase. Marketers design product advertising, showroom signs and displays, and owners' manuals to give accurate, but favorable, expectations of the car during the decision making process. They also attempt to influence postpurchase evaluations by influencing the criteria consumers use and the attitudes they develop. Ford's "Quality is Job #1" advertising campaign, for example, has two goals: (1) to persuade prospective buyers that Ford builds quality cars, and (2) to convince Ford owners that any problems they may have with their cars are isolated events that don't reflect the inherent quality of Ford products. Like all car makers, Ford wants consumers to believe that its manufacturing quality is high and to attribute any problems to incidental factors, such as hard use or bad luck (Figure 13.5).

## ▼ PROVIDE FEEDBACK

The satisfaction consumers get—or do not get—from their purchase drives their future communication with the dealer and the car manufacturer as well as interpersonal communication with friends and acquaintances and complaints to third parties. Because they have exerted significant effort to make this risky purchase, most consumers have a strong incentive to complain when they are not satisfied. Dissatisfied consumers may write letters to car magazines, respond to requests about their personal experiences from car magazines or *Consumer Reports*, or complain to the local Better Business Bureau or consumer affairs office (Figure 13.6). Many states have "lemon laws"—formal arbitration mechanisms consumers can use to solve problems with their car purchase. Dealers and manufacturers, in turn, engage in ongoing efforts to solicit feedback about their products. They may use customer satisfaction surveys to gather information to improve

■ FIGURE 13.6
Consumers who are dissatisfied with the purchase of a high involvement product sometimes relate their experiences in such magazines as *Consumer Reports*.

their own operations or to convey concern to buyers in the hopes of garnering a more favorable evaluation. For example, Chrysler distributes a quarterly magazine containing service tips and coverage of new models to all its customers.

## FACT OR FICTION REVISITED

⊚   Consumers do tend to complain more about defects in high involvement products than in low involvement products.

### ▼ END THE CONSUMPTION PROCESS

Most car buyers end the consumption process by recycling the car at a junk yard or passing it along to another buyer—either trading it in at the dealer for a new one or selling it to another consumer. Although they may keep the car in a garage or some other location, most consumers do not accumulate cars the way they may clothes or tools. The reasons are obvious: Cars require space; they are costly to maintain and insure; and many consumers do not need more than one at a time.

As we noted earlier in the chapter, some consumers may wish to end the consumption process for a car they own but instead choose to repair or refurbish it.

■ FIGURE 13.7

Jaguar's Select Edition program enables consumers to buy its luxury cars used by previous consumers and maintained in mint condition.

Introducing *Select Edition* Pre-Owned Jaguars

Just as the gardens were tended, the marble polished and the pools filtered, these Jaguars have been pampered, groomed and coddled.

Superb condition, however, is merely the starting point. To be eligible for sale as a *Select Edition* vehicle, a Jaguar must pass our rigorous 120-point inspection and meet strict age and mileage criteria.

| Certification | Factory Warranty | Value |
|---|---|---|
| 120-point mechanical and cosmetic inspection. | 6 years/75,000 miles from original purchase.* | Recent model years with low mileage.** |

The *Select Edition* program offers exceptional values on exceptional Jaguars. Which means that for a reasonable price, you can drive away in a fully certified Jaguar with the added assurances of a factory warranty and free 24-hour Roadside Assistance.*

Have you ever imagined a Jaguar parked in front of your home? Well, now you can put it there for real.

For more information, call 1-800-4-JAGUAR.

They come from good homes.

JAGUAR
SELECT EDITION
PRE-OWNED AUTOMOBILES

For those who don't keep their old car, trading it to the dealer is often the easiest option. Car dealers commonly accept cars in trade and then pass them along to other consumers who want to purchase used cars. Current car leasing programs have shifted the responsibility for product disposal from the consumer to the dealer. The consumer pays for the use of the car for a fixed time period, usually two or three years, and then returns it to the dealer. The dealer then leases the car again or sells it to another consumer (Figure 13.7).

# LOW INVOLVEMENT PURCHASES ◀

Low involvement purchases tend to be less important and relevant to consumers because both the costs and benefits are lower than those associated with a car or other high involvement purchase. Soft drinks are a low involvement purchase for most consumers. People need to satisfy their innate biological need of thirst, and soft drinks offer benefits to do that. Few consumers have a lifestyle that revolves around their soft drinks, however, even though some may be in the habit of drinking one product or another. Most consumers perceive little significance in the physical characteristics or functional benefits offered by different soft drinks; accordingly, soft drink marketers develop advertising to try to differentiate their products in the minds of consumers. Furthermore, there is little risk involved in buying a soft drink—if it doesn't meet the consumer's expectations, it can simply be thrown away and replaced. There are situations where the choice of a particular soft drink does matter, however, such as when a consumer is buying soft drinks to serve to friends at a party, most of whom prefer Pepsi. One situational factor that does affect the purchase of soft drinks is availability. Vending machines sell only one marketer's products, and, in many restaurants, only one major brand is available—often Coca-Cola or Pepsi products.

## ▼ RECOGNIZE NEEDS

Consumers easily recognize thirst. They can then choose a number of goals to satisfy that need and quench their thirst—water, milk, coffee, juice, soft drinks, or alcoholic beverages. A person's culture and values, demographics, and lifestyle all influence his or her choice of beverage (Figure 13.8). Consumption of soft drinks varies widely from country to country, for example, because of the different cul-

**■ FIGURE 13.8**

Miller appeals to the youthful, sociable lifestyle of its audience in its "The Night is Young" advertising campaign.

tures and values of its citizens—colas are the most popular soft drink in the United States, but they are less popular than iced coffees, teas, and fruit flavored beverages in many Pacific Rim countries. A demographic characteristic such as age may also influence the choice of beverage. Babies drink milk, and children may be allowed a wider range of beverages, but only adults can turn to alcohol to satisfy their thirst.

A consumer's recognition of the need for a soft drink may not involve thirst at all. Many people keep a supply of soft drinks in their homes so that they are available whenever they become thirsty. In such cases, need recognition may be triggered in other ways. It may occur when the consumer notices that the supply is below an acceptable threshold (e.g., the last can or six-pack remains). Likewise, it may occur when the consumer sees the product in the store or views an advertisement. In this case, the marketer's efforts have not *created* the need but have reminded the consumer of a preexisting need and a way of satisfying it.

## ▼ SEARCH FOR ALTERNATIVES

Consumers do not engage in an extensive search for new alternatives each time they want to buy a soft drink; instead, they form habits that restrict their search for alternatives in this routine decision making process. Consumers have an evoked set of soft drinks with which they are familiar from their own experiences, and they usually do not supplement these brands with advice from friends or acquaintances. In order to get a new product into a consumer's evoked set, it is up to the marketer to communicate the distinctive benefits it has to offer. Often, the most effective way to do this is to target the purchase situation with in-store advertising and promotion; sampling programs, such as Coke's distribution of 25,000 samples of its new 16-ounce contoured glass bottles in just one weekend in New York; or special events, such as Pepsi's participation at Woodstock's 25th Anniversary celebration in 1994.

## ▼ EVALUATE ALTERNATIVES

In choosing a soft drink, most consumers use a routine decision making process that requires little new cognitive effort; it often reflects habitual purchase or the application of a simple noncompensatory decision rule to a limited set of evaluative criteria. Some consumers simply pick the soft drink they like best and continue to purchase that same brand each time they are thirsty. They perceive little difference among brands and see the financial cost of the product as the only potential risk from a bad choice. Until they have a dissatisfying experience, they will continue to purchase the same product. Other people may apply a noncompensatory rule to the alternatives in their evoked set; they may select whichever brand of cola is on sale at the supermarket this week, or choose caffeinated cola before dinner and caffeine-free cola after dinner.

Soft drink marketers utilize a variety of communications tools to attempt to disrupt the routine purchase process that results in this kind of habitual purchasing. As we mentioned previously, marketers must get their new products into the consumer's evoked set for it to be considered. To do so, and to induce consumers to use more extensive decision making, marketers tend to emphasize new attributes or superior performance that will discriminate their brands from others (Fig-

**SUBWAY** **SUBWAY** **SUBWAY** **SUBWAY** **SUBWAY** **SUBWAY** **SUBWAY** **SUBWAY** **SUBWAY** **SUBWAY** **SUBWAY** **SUBWAY** **SUBWAY** **SUBWAY**

# WORLD'S GREATEST SANDWICH!

Only one chain is gaining popularity so quickly that it has surpassed most others.

■ FIGURE 13.9
Marketers often compare the superior performance of their products to competing brands to encourage consumers to consider their product among the alternatives.

ure 13.9). Some marketers try to create relevance for a new attribute. Lipton, for example, advertises that its iced teas are brewed before bottling, unlike the powdered tea used by its competitor Snapple. Others may use comparative advertising. For example, Pepsi uses taste comparisons in its "Pepsi Challenge" campaign to convince consumers that its product is different from Coca-Cola. Soft drink marketers with large market shares typically use repetitive advertising to reinforce the habitual purchasing of their regular customers.

## FACT OR FICTION REVISITED

◉ It is true that habit often replaces the search for alternatives in low involvement purchases.

## ▼ PURCHASE AND USE THE PRODUCT

Because a soft drink is a low involvement purchase, situational influences will have a significant impact on the consumer in the purchase environment. Consumers don't typically have strongly held attitudes about soft drinks, so they can be easily swayed to buy another brand if their preferred choice is not available. Accordingly, marketers employ intensive distribution so that their products are available in as many locations as possible, including supermarkets, convenience stores, mass merchandisers, restaurants, and vending machines.

In addition to intensive distribution, soft drink marketers are able to enhance the purchase situation for the consumer in a number of ways:

**1** By selling their products in vending machines that simplify the transaction by accepting coins or dollar bills

**2** Through packaging innovations, such as three-liter bottles, that make the product more visible and the purchase more convenient

**3** Through the extensive use of special displays in grocery stores to increase the product's visibility

Marketers often are able to influence consumers to move away from their routine purchases and differentiate among competing products during specific usage situations, thereby increasing their level of involvement. As we noted earlier, parties, the holiday season, and atypical usage occasions may disrupt the consumer's routine purchasing processes. Marketers often promote special products and packaging for holidays and commemorative events to influence consumers to earmark some purchases for special occasions (Figure 13.10). They have also recognized the increasing interest of some people in consuming soft drinks with higher levels of caffeine, often at breakfast, and have introduced a number of differentiated products to increase the level of involvement of those

■ FIGURE 13.10
Hersheys packages its chocolate kisses in colored foil for the Easter holiday.

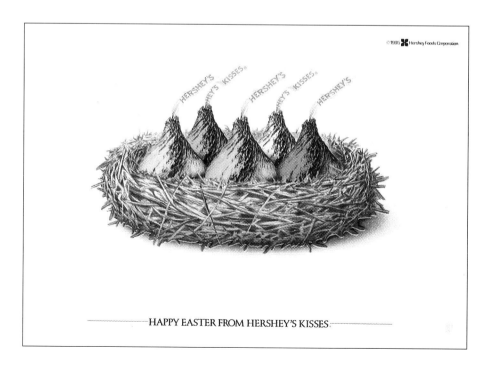

HAPPY EASTER FROM HERSHEY'S KISSES

consumers. For example, as we discuss in the following Pleasures of Consumption box, Pepsi introduced Pepsi A.M. to capture this segment of the market; unfortunately, the product has not been successful.

## PLEASURES OF CONSUMPTION

**Trade in Your Coffee for a Soft Drink at Breakfast[6]**

Marketers have responded to the estimated 10 percent of Americans who consume soft drinks at breakfast by introducing new colas, iced teas and coffees, and energy drinks in an effort to encourage even more consumers to replace or supplement their traditional coffee and orange juice. In the 1950s, hot Dr. Pepper was served as a breakfast drink in parts of Texas, but the fad only lasted a short time. In the late 1980s, Coca-Cola sponsored a "Coke in the Morning" radio campaign, and Pepsi made several unsuccessful attempts to market its Pepsi A.M., containing nearly 35 percent more caffeine than regular cola, in Fort Wayne, Indiana and Waterloo, Iowa. Jolt Cola, which contains more caffeine than either Coke or Pepsi A.M., was introduced at about the same time and continues to be marketed today.

The latest effort at increasing soft drink consumption is SunBolt, a product introduced by Gatorade in 1994. SunBolt is marketed as a soft drink that offers an extra boost of energy to help people start off their day. It contains a blend of carbohydrates, vitamin C, and caffeine that is similar to that of popular breakfast energy drinks in Japan. The product actually contains more caffeine than Pepsi and Coke, but less than Jolt, and much less than coffee.

Do you drink soft drinks in the morning? Do you think there is a consumer segment that would respond to a specially tailored morning soft drink? What benefits should this product offer, and how should its marketer position it? Do you think that SunBolt, with its additional benefits of carbohydrates and vitamins, is more likely to succeed than previous entries?

## ▼ EVALUATE THE CONSUMPTION EXPERIENCE

The postconsumption evaluation of a low involvement product is a simple procedure that reflects the routine decision making that went into choosing the product. Because it was a routine purchase based on simple, noncompensatory criteria, the consumer can quickly decide whether it has been a satisfying experience. Was it enjoyed by the guests at a party? Was it the cheapest option available? Did it quench the person's thirst? Expectations are modest: The product should simply perform as it has in the past. In the case of mass-produced soft drinks that are remarkably consistent from occasion to occasion, this is an easily met expectation.

## ▼ PROVIDE FEEDBACK

The feedback provided about a low involvement product is direct—satisfied buyers continue to purchase the product, and dissatisfied buyers do nothing. If consumers can attribute their dissatisfaction to the product itself, they will disrupt their own routine purchase process and choose a different product the next time. If they can attribute it to random circumstances, such as leaving the product out in the sun too long, they may continue to buy it. In either case, they are unlikely

**Brooklyn Recycles!**

**Starting June 1**

Plastic Bottles & Jugs    Glass Bottles & Jars    Metal Cans    Aluminum Foil Wrap & Trays

Newspapers    Magazines & Catalogs    Phone Books    Corrugated Cardboard

**(212) 219-8090**

NYC Department of Sanitation

City of New York, David N. Dinkins, Mayor
Department of Sanitation, Emily Lloyd, Commissioner

Help Reduce New York's Waste. Please Recycle.

■ FIGURE 13.11

Recycling is the means of disposing of a low involvement product.

to go so far as to seek other consumers or third parties to whom they will express their dissatisfaction.

Accordingly, marketers of low involvement products typically limit their attempts to create satisfaction to quality control, ensuring that the product is indeed consistent with consumers' past experiences. This is why many product changes in low involvement products are so subtle that consumers will not detect them. Many marketers of such products also provide toll-free numbers consumers can call to voice their complaints. In this way, the marketer is able to explain or correct any problems so that consumers will not reopen their search and evaluation activities and consider other products.

▼ END THE CONSUMPTION PROCESS

Consumers end their consumption of a soft drink by disposing of the packaging. The usual options are to throw the container away or recycle it. Most consumers prefer to do the easiest thing and just throw their empty soft drink containers away. In response, public policy actors have sought to influence the disposal process for such products. Years ago, soda bottles were recycled through the retailer from which the consumer bought them and returned to the bottlers, who refilled them. Consumers had an incentive to recycle the bottles because they paid a minimal deposit upon making the purchase that was refunded to them when they returned the empty bottles. Reusable bottles and cans are rare today. Some states continue to require a deposit, and the retailer recycles the bottles for the consumer. Other states have legislated mandatory recycling—consumers must separate cans and bottles from other trash so that they can be collected and recycled (Figure 13.11).

## INVOLVEMENT AND DECISION MAKING

Kim Bannister has made both high involvement and low involvement purchases in recent years. Her car was a high involvement purchase. It was very important for Kim to find a car that she wouldn't have to think about replacing for a long time, so she devoted a great deal of effort to finding just the right one to suit her needs. She read magazines, consulted with family and friends, examined the alternatives, and chose a car that has been very satisfying for her. Kim acknowledges that she'll probably have to do it again sometime in the future, and she says she'd be willing to exert the same effort again to ensure that she's happy with the results.

Kim's purchases of cat food and soda are quite different. She has figured out what her cats like to eat and her friends like to drink, and she buys those products on a routine basis. She doesn't have to think about either purchase, and she knows that the results will be just as satisfying as her choice of a car.

This chapter illustrates the activities consumers employ to complete two different kinds of purchase processes. Some purchases are particularly important and relevant for a consumer; others are not. In completing all of the purchases to satisfy their many needs, people set priorities about how much cognitive effort to devote to each one—high involvement purchases receive more effort than low involvement ones. Although the behavioral processes used to complete the purchases are the same, the processes are applied in different ways commensurate with the cognitive effort each purchase elicits. Now that we have fully reviewed the purchase activities and behavioral processes, we turn our attention to actual purchase occasions and their aftermath in Chapter 14.

# SUMMARY

1. **Determine the level of involvement a consumer exhibits during his or her purchase process.** The level of involvement—the importance or relevance the purchase of a particular product has for a consumer—reflects the benefits and costs the consumer expects from buying that product to satisfy a need that occurs in a specific situation. Three types of factors influence involvement: (1) the background characteristics of the consumer; (2) characteristics of the product; and (3) situational effects that accompany a particular purchase or usage occasion.

2. **Recognize the extensive purchase activities that accompany high involvement purchases.** Consumers typically are willing to exert more effort searching for and evaluating high involvement products. They perceive subtle differences among such products and are willing to exert considerable effort to learn about them. They also exert more effort to complete specific search activities by gathering information through marketing and interpersonal communication. Finally, they exert great effort to evaluate their level of satisfaction with the purchase and provide feedback to marketers, public policy actors, and other consumers.

3. **Identify the routine purchase activities that accompany low involvement purchases.** Consumers typically do not devote significant effort to search and evaluation activities for a low involvement product. Instead, low involvement purchases invoke a routine level of decision making effort; consumers employ existing evaluative criteria and noncompensatory decision rules, or they simply repeat past decisions. They are likely to buy whatever alternative is readily available or to pick a favorite product they will continue to buy without giving it any additional thought. Only if they do not get the benefits they expect from the product will consumers consider other products in a limited decision making process. Even then, they will rarely exert serious effort to express their dissatisfaction to the marketer.

# KEY TERMS

Enduring involvement, *p. 377*

# SKILL-BUILDING ACTIVITIES

1. Consider the following products: automobiles, stereos, laundry detergents, soft drinks. Apply Zaichowsky's Involvement Scale (Figure 13.2) to each.

2. How do the high involvement products differ from the low involvement products in:
   a. decision rules most likely to be used
   b. decision rules least likely to be used
   c. postpurchase evaluation
   d. end of the consumption process

3. How do the marketing strategies and tactics commonly used to promote the high involvement products differ from the marketing strategies and tactics commonly used to promote the low involvement products?

4. How do the activities of government officials and consumer advocates interested in protecting the consumer differ for high involvement and low involvement products?

5. In the entire realm of consumer behavior, are high involvement products more or less important than low involvement products? Why?

6. The Federal Trade Commission has instructed its staff to concentrate deceptive advertising cases on advertisements for high involvement products rather than on advertisements for low involvement products. Do you think this is a good idea? Why?

# CHAPTER 13 SELF-TEST

▼ **MULTIPLE CHOICE**

1. _____ is the importance of a particular purchase process to a consumer.
   a. Dissonance                    c. Motivation
   b. Involvement                   d. Cognition

2. Consumers are more involved in purchases that are consistent with their lifestyle and _____ .
   a. family                        c. bank account
   b. self-concept                  d. attitude

3. Which of the following is not likely to be a high involvement purchase?
   a. umbrella                      c. house
   b. boat                          d. prom dress

4. If a consumer is buying a high involvement product, such as a home, he or she would most likely use a _____ decision rule to evaluate alternatives.
   a. noncompensatory               c. elimination by aspects
   b. conjunctive                   d. compensatory

5. Marketers should provide information _____ a high involvement purchase so that consumers have realistic _____ for the postpurchase evaluation.
   a. during; expectations          c. before; goals
   b. after; goals                  d. before; expectations

6. Dissatisfied consumers of high involvement purchases are more likely to provide feedback during postpurchase by _____ .
   a. doing nothing                 c. wishing they had not purchased the product
   b. complaining                   
                                    d. using the product anyway

7. _____ would most likely be a low involvement product.
   a. A stereo                      c. Paper towels
   b. A vacation                    d. Diamonds

8. Consumers of low involvement products are not likely to engage in _____ search; rather they form _____ that dictate their future purchases.
   a. internal; complex evaluative criteria    c. external; complex evaluative criteria
   b. external; expectations                    d. external; habits

9. The most effective ways for a marketer to get its low involvement product into the evoked set of a consumer is through in-store advertising and promotion, sampling, or _____ .
   a. personal selling
   b. telemarketing
   c. sponsorship of special events
   d. lowering the price

10. When marketers use innovative, eye catching packaging they are attempting to influence the _____ stage of a low involvement purchase decision process.
   a. need recognition
   b. postconsumption
   c. internal search
   d. purchase

## ▼ TRUE/FALSE

1. Consumers devote more effort to satisfying needs that have higher costs and benefits.   T or F
2. Involvement with a product does not change when the situation changes.   T or F
3. A purchase that is inexpensive is always a low involvement purchase.   T or F
4. Products that could cause some physical harm to a consumer are usually considered high involvement.   T or F
5. Reference groups can influence both high and low involvement purchases.   T or F
6. Consumers who make high involvement purchases always engage in ongoing search activities.   T or F
7. Consumers of low involvement products often use a noncompensatory rule when evaluating alternatives.   T or F
8. The distribution strategies of low involvement purchases are the same as for high involvement purchases.   T or F
9. Consumers quickly decide whether they are satisfied with a low involvement product.   T or F
10. Consumers of low involvement products are unlikely to communicate their dissatisfaction with a product.   T or F

## ▼ SHORT ANSWER

1. What are the three types of factors (excluding costs and benefits) that influence involvement?
2. Describe how the search process differs for a low involvement and a high involvement purchase.
3. Why do marketers promote their low involvement products as useful for holidays and special occasions?

## ▼ APPLICATION EXERCISE

As the advertising and marketing director for a local swimming pool construction company, you have begun planning your advertising campaign for the spring. During this campaign, you must encourage prospective home owners to call your company for an estimate on pool construction. Since this purchase is a high involvement purchase, describe some of the key ideas or concepts that should be included in the message.

# 14

# PURCHASE AND USAGE BEHAVIOR

◉ Consumer Snapshot *Dorothy Sinclair is a 28-year-old Manufacturing Coordinator for a publishing firm. She lives in New York with her husband and two daughters, Ayanna, three, and Maakeda, seven months.*

## FACT OR FICTION

◉  Credit and debit cards and automatic teller machines are examples of enabling conditions that have radically changed consumers' ability to purchase the products they want.

◉  Situational influences often cause consumers to buy irrationally.

◉  Many of the recent changes in retailing are intended to make the puchasing environment more hospitable for consumers.

◉   Home shopping eliminates most of the situational influences on purchasing.

◉   In consumer behavior, commitment generally precedes trial.

◉   Satisfaction is the key element in most repeat purchase decisions.

◉   Most marketers try to create unrealistic expectations.

# EYE ON THE CONSUMER

As a college student, Dorothy Sinclair owned four credit cards—an American Express card, two Visa cards, and a Sears card—and they all caused her trouble. Years later, she still describes her college experiences with credit cards as her "worst nightmare." Dorothy was lured into the world of credit through on-campus promotions for students and appealing television advertising. At the time, her only source of income was a part-time job through her school's work–study program, but she applied for the cards even though she knew she couldn't afford to use them.

At first, the fear that she she would spend her entire work–study paycheck paying off credit card bills prevented Dorothy from using the cards. After a while, she started using the American Express card—just for little things—but she couldn't afford to pay the whole balance when the bills came in. Before she knew it, she was in debt and had to use her Visa cards to pay off the balance on her American Express card. This kind of borrowing continued until she graduated, at which time Dorothy decided that being an adult meant taking responsibility for her finances, and she started paying off her credit card bills as she should have in the beginning. Ultimately, she was able to pay off her debts—which had amounted to nearly double what she had actually charged—and she gave up the cards altogether. Today she pays for everything with cash.

Dorothy has taken some other financial leaps into the adult world. She bought a used car from a neighbor (with cash!) and a life insurance policy to protect her young daughter. The insurance agent contacted Dorothy through a referral from a friend of hers. She found him to be quite persistent—he called Dorothy ten times before she finally agreed to meet with him! Dorothy didn't agree to buy insurance the first time they met, but she did agree to a second meeting with him; this time, her fiancee was also present. At the second meeting, the agent pointed out that the insurance policy offered a way for Dorothy to accumulate savings as well as a means of security to her daughter if anything should happen to her. The agent even had a conversation with Dorothy's daughter about college, albeit one sided since she was only 6 months old! The technique worked: Dorothy felt guilty about the need to protect her daughter should something happen to her, and she bought the life insurance policy.

In this chapter we turn our attention to the activities that define consumer behavior—the purchase and use of products to satisfy consumer needs. In the preceding sections of the book we discussed the background characteristics and behavioral processes that are the key components of consumer behavior. These characteristics and processes comprise *all* kinds of human behavior; they are part of *consumer behavior* only when they are used in the purchase of a product.

In the next four chapters we will apply the knowledge of the background characteristics and behavioral processes presented in Chapters 4 through 13 to a variety of consumer behavior issues. In this chapter we discuss the factors that affect the way consumers actually purchase and use products and what they do *after* they have made a purchase.

After reading and thinking about this chapter, you should be able to:

❶ Identify the situational influences that affect specific purchase activities.
❷ Recognize the characteristics of usage occasions that affect the activities necessary to complete a purchase.
❸ Analyze consumers' evaluations of their consumption experiences.
❹ Identify the options available to end the purchase process.

# ACTIVITIES IN PURCHASE AND USAGE BEHAVIOR

The purchase and use of a product encompass a variety of the purchase activities we outlined in Chapter 2, including (1) the actual purchase and use of the product; (2) evaluating the consumption experience; (3) providing feedback about the experience; and (4) ending the purchase process (Figure 14.1).

Most purchases are not isolated, one-time events that occur automatically once a consumer chooses a product. The consumer may end up buying a different product than the one he or she really prefers because it is not readily available or because the logistics of delivery or financing cannot be arranged. You may decide you want to buy a college sweatshirt, for example, but the bookstore is out of your size. Or, you may be unable to get a bank loan to buy the used car you want. Sometimes people buy a particular product because of the situation in which they intend to use it. For example, some consumers prefer Coke or Pepsi products and buy them for themselves when they are thirsty, but they may buy less expensive brands, such as Shasta or store brands, when their relatives are around to guzzle large quantities during a summer picnic. In some cases, consumers may change their minds as a result of salespeople or other marketing influences. For example, research has shown that people are more likely to buy products from special displays at the ends of aisles in the grocery store than from their typical locations on the shelves.

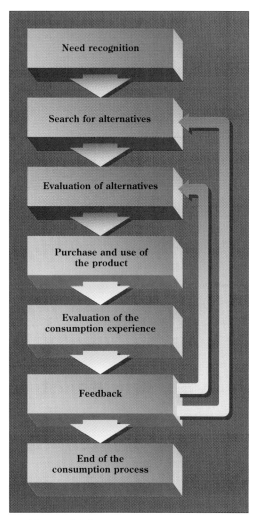

**■ FIGURE 14.1**
Activities in purchase and use.

Purchase and usage activities continue past the time the consumer buys the product. Consumers continually evaluate their experiences with the products they use for two reasons: (1) to provide information for their future attitude formation and decision making, and (2) to provide information to pass along to others. For more extensive, high involvement products, such as cars or computers, consumers continually evaluate their satisfaction with the product. If the product stops working, the consumer complains. As we discussed in Chapter 13, in some cases, consumers devote effort to evaluating the quality of even low involvement, routinely purchased products, such as milk. If the milk purchased at a local convenience store tasted sour twice in one week, most people would reevaluate their milk purchasing habits. People continue to purchase a low involvement product only as long as it continues to satisfy them. And most people, particularly if they are unhappy with a product, tell others about their dissatisfying consumption experiences.

The final activity—product disposal—has become increasingly important in today's social environment. Public policy demands respect for the environment, and consumers must dispose of any remaining product and packaging appropriately. This means that consumers must deal with cans, bottles, newspapers, corrugated packaging, and the shock-absorbing material in which many products are shipped. People who change the oil in their cars themselves must dispose of the cans the new oil came in as well as the old oil itself. Appliances, consumer electronics, and computers that are replaced with newer models must be kept, sold, scrapped, or recycled.

# ▶ INFLUENCES ON PURCHASE AND USAGE ACTIVITIES

Consumers begin the purchase and usage activities by forming attitudes toward alternative products and arriving at preferences as a result of communication with members of their reference groups as well as the motivation, perception, learning, attitude formation, and decision making processes. Without the following influences, people would simply purchase and use the alternative they prefer. This is not typically the case, however. Rather, a variety of *situational influences* arise during the purchase and usage process that may affect the choice of product.

## ▼ SITUATIONAL INFLUENCES

**Situational influences** are specific factors that affect the purchase activities by altering the product choices the consumer may have otherwise made on the basis of his or her background characteristics and behavioral processes and the product's attributes.[1] These influences affect the specific purchase situation and "short-circuit" the application of the purchase decision that may have resulted from the previous search and evaluation activities. A consumer might have evaluated all of the kinds of portable computers that were advertised and have chosen an IBM model that best suited his or her needs; upon discovering that the IBM computer would be unavailable for months, however, the consumer might choose another brand instead (Figure 14.2). Although the consumer's search and evaluation activities resulted in a preference for a particular product, the actual purchase situation resulted in a different purchase.

> **Situational influences** are specific factors that affect purchase activities by altering the product choices consumers make.

Situational influences may affect purchase activities in two ways: (1) they prevent consumers from purchasing the product they selected during their search and evaluation activities; or (2) they present information about additional alternatives that encourage the consumer to make a purchase without conducting search and evaluation activities. Examples of situational influences that may occur during the purchase situation are illustrated in Table 14.1. They include (1) physical characteristics of the purchase situation, (2) enabling conditions, (3) social interactions that occur during the purchase activity, and (4) the consumer's mood.

**Physical Characteristics** The physical attributes of a selling situation—the store's layout, lighting, noise level, or product displays—tend to evoke consumer reactions. For example, harsh lighting in a clothing store's dressing rooms tend to affect consumers' perceptions of how they look in the clothes they are considering.

Some physical attributes may prevent consumers from making a purchase they prefer. For example, consumers may not buy a product they want if they are confronted with a confusing retail environment. They may be unable to find the product or to examine it closely enough to confirm their previous evaluation. This is one reason why hypermarts—huge grocery and mass merchandisers, such as Carrefours, that are two to three times the size of such large warehouse clubs as Sam's or Price Club—have been unsuccessful in the United States; consumers find their size too daunting.

Some physical features influence consumers to buy products they had not evaluated before they entered the purchase situation. Retailers commonly place matching neckties and shirts alongside displays of men's suits to remind consumers of previously unrecognized needs. Grocery stores display items at the

■ FIGURE 14.2
Before the new IBM models were available, a consumer who wanted to buy one might have had to settle for another brand that was not her or his first choice.

### Table 14.1

**INFLUENCES ON PURCHASE SITUATIONS**

| Types of influence | Examples |
|---|---|
| Physical characteristics | Layout |
| | Lighting |
| | Music and noise level |
| | In-store advertising and displays |
| Enabling conditions | Credit cards |
| | Debit cards |
| | Automatic teller machines (ATM) |
| | Electronic funds transfer (EFT) |
| | Air express delivery |
| | Electronic ordering systems |
| Social interactions | Salesperson's background characterstics, knowledge, and attitude |
| | Background characteristics of other shoppers |
| Consumer's mood | Hunger and thirst |
| | Joy, anger, disappointment |

end of aisles to bring new alternatives to consumers' attention. "Impulse" items, such as candy, gum, magazines, and newspapers, are typically displayed alongside checkout lines to remind consumers about them before they leave the store.

**Enabling Conditions**    *Enabling conditions* are logistical factors that facilitate the consumer's ability to complete a purchase. Consumers require **access to funds**—the ability to pay for the products they have selected—and **access to products**—the capacity to acquire the product and transport it to the location where it will be used. If these enabling conditions do not exist, consumers cannot purchase the products they prefer.

The consumer's access to funds is his or her ability to complete the generalized exchange of money for a product at the time of purchase; it is distinct from the consumer's evaluation of the price or value of the product. The use of credit and debit cards and automatic teller machines has radically altered the ability of consumers to purchase the products they want. People don't need to carry cash to pay for their purchases anymore—they can provide payment without cash or they can acquire cash at the time of the transaction. However, such easy access to funds has a dark side too, as we discuss in the following box.

> **Access to funds** is the consumer's ability to pay for a product at the time of purchase.

> **Access to products** is the consumer's capacity to acquire and transport a product to where it will be used.

DARK SIDE OF CONSUMPTION

**What's My Credit Line?**[2]
Credit cards enable students to make a number of purchases—books, clothes, meals, CDs—in a convenient fashion. According to estimates, more than half of all college students have at least one credit card, and over 80 percent will have one before they

graduate. Nearly 25 percent of high school students have their own credit cards or share one on their parents' accounts.

Despite the high statistics of ownership, because college students typically earn low incomes and spend less, they account for less than three percent of the total credit card business in the United States. But each card issuer has a significant interest in getting students to choose its card because they are likely to keep it for years—75 percent of consumers keep their first card for 15 years; 60 percent never give it up. Accordingly, marketers such as Citbank, American Express, and Discover send applications to students in the mail, set up displays on college campuses, offer gifts to students who submit applications, and stuff applications in book bags. Some schools even have exclusive arrangements with card issuers to offer students affinity cards branded with the college's name.

But when a student's credit card balance starts to rise as a result of day-to-day purchases, airline tickets, or hotel bills from a spring break vacation, the debt can become overwhelming. Credit card counselors are seeing increasing numbers of college students, such as Dorothy Sinclair, who have amassed large debts they are unable to pay back. The credit card marketers have responded by producing and distributing personal finance programs to high school students to help them learn about potential problems before they occur. At the same time, the marketers have not stopped promoting the cards to students, in large part because they know that students will either seek help from credit counselors to consolidate their loans at lower interest rates, or their parents will help them pay their bills.

Do you think the dark side of accumulating debt on credit cards can be balanced against its usefulness in providing access to funds? How can consumers prevent the convenient access to cash provided by credit cards from turning into overwhelming debt? Should credit card companies modify their marketing efforts toward lower income consumers, such as students?

## FACT OR FICTION REVISITED

◉   Credit and debit cards and ATM machines have indeed changed consumers' ability to purchase the products they want; they have made it easier.

Just as credit cards and automatic teller machines provide easy access to funds, modern distribution technologies, such as air express delivery, provide ready access to products. Consumers today can easily overcome physical constraints and have greater access to the products they want. In addition, the effects of stock problems are lessened when retailers use efficient and effective physical distribution technologies (Figure 14.3). For example, opticians are able to keep a sample of eyeglass styles in their stores and use air express services to offer consumers overnight access to the product in their size. Similarly, Levi Strauss has implemented a new program in its Original Levi's Stores, which offers women the ability to buy a Personal Pair of jeans—one of roughly 400 possible combinations of waist, hip, inseam, and rise measurements. After a woman is measured, her personalized pattern and choice of style and color are transmitted electronically to the factory in Tennessee, where the jeans are manufactured and returned by air express to the store.

■ FIGURE 14.3
Effective physical distribution technologies, such as overnight delivery, provide ready, efficient access to products.

**Social Interactions**   Social interactions with store personnel and other consumers can have a significant effect on the purchase of a product. The attitude of salespeople and cashiers can certainly affect a purchase. At the extreme, a consumer might walk out of a store without purchasing a product because of intolerable service. At the same time, a pleasing interaction with a salesperson may encourage a consumer to make a purchase. The salesperson's knowledge, personality, interaction style, and demographic characteristics all affect the consumer's perception of that person and the retailer for whom he or she works. Saturn dealerships have successfully distinguished themselves from other car retailers by training their salespeople to avoid the traditional aggressive sales techniques of many car lines. Saturn salespeople provide information about the cars and their fixed prices and allow shoppers to browse unattended. Similarly, Dorothy Lane, a supermarket company in Ohio, calls customers who spend more than $100 dollars in a day to thank them for their patronage, while Borders Bookstores tests prospective employees on their knowledge of literature to ensure that they will be able to help shoppers.

Other consumers may also affect purchase activities by making the shopping experience more pleasant. Many fast food restaurants, such as McDonald's, have increased their patronage among the elderly by accomodating them with free coffee refills and opportunities to socialize while eating during the less occupied hours between breakfast and lunch. Similarly, many consumers consider interacting with other shoppers at the mall, a flea market, or a swap meet to be an entertaining experience. Some retailers, such as Ikea, remove social impediments to purchase by providing child care facilities (Figure 14.4). Parents can shop without the distraction of watching their own children, and other patrons are not subjected to the noise and hubbub of other people's children.

A consumer's perception of a retailer's positioning in the market often is affected by the types of customers seen patronizing the store—that is, the shoppers serve as an indicator of the kinds of people for whom the store is appropriate. Most people want to shop at a store that attracts customers like them. At the same time, many people are wary of stores devoid of shoppers because they fear the store satisfies no one.

■ FIGURE 14.4

Ikea eliminates a social impediment—watching after young children—by providing a supervised play area, enabling consumers to focus on their purchase activities.

**The Consumer's Mood**  A consumer's mood—her or his *physiological* or *psychological* state—may sway purchase behavior. At one time or another, many people have purchased more groceries than they intended because they went to the store when they were hungry, or they have left a store without purchasing a product they needed because they were in a grumpy mood and didn't feel like taking the time to search for it.

Physical characteristics and social interactions may combine to affect a consumer's mood. Physical distractions or annoying shoppers may spoil a consumer's mood and make the purchase experience an unpleasant one. By contrast, the presence of shoppers who are in a consumer's own positive reference group may make the consumer more comfortable. Shopping for personal health care products may be embarrassing to some consumers, who prefer an environment that allows privacy. Accordingly, some pharmacies, such as CVS, have installed private discussion areas that allow the consumer to consult discretely with the pharmacist (Figure 14.5).

■ FIGURE 14.5

CVS pharmacies have installed private discussion areas to enable consumers to conduct their business in private.

### ▼ How Marketers Influence the Situation

So far we have discussed instances in which the purchase situation itself alters the consumer's purchase. Marketers must be able to identify those situational influences that may alter purchase activities so as to promote their products effectively.

This is not to say that consumers are acting irrationally when they change their minds about a purchase; they do not simply toss away their reasoning power and buy randomly. At the same time, marketers are not trying to induce consumers to buy unneeded products with special displays. Rather, the consumer purchase process is a flexible and open one. Consumers integrate new information they gather at the time of purchase and use the purchase environment to help them recognize needs they may not have previously recognized. Sometimes the new information is that their preferred product is unavailable, in which case they will have to leave some of their needs unsatisfied. Other times, the information may be that a new product is available that better meets their needs.

### FACT OR FICTION REVISITED

⦿   Situational influences *do not* cause consumers to buy irrationally; even when situational influences intervene, consumers usually manage to meet their needs.

Marketers recognize that the purchase environment offers a powerful setting for their efforts to help consumers complete the purchase process. They can eliminate any physical features and social interactions that may obstruct consumers and facilitate enabling conditions that help them complete their purchase activities. Many nonstore forms of retailing are intended to make the purchasing environment more hospitable for consumers, including *direct selling organizations,* such as Tupperware and Avon, which we will discuss in Chapter 16, *direct catalog sales*, and *interactive electronic communications*—infomercials, cable-based shopping networks, and on-line shopping. Catalog sales in particular have grown rapidly in recent years—over 100 catalogs are delivered to every American household each year.

### FACT OR FICTION REVISITED

⦿   It is true that many of the recent changes in retailing are intended to make the purchasing environment more hospitable for consumers.

Home shopping through infomercials and cable television networks, such as the Home Shopping Network, has become quite popular among some consumers. This approach combines the distribution of products with promotion by using television programming both to communicate with consumers and to transform their own homes into the purchase environment. The very nature of home shopping directly addresses some of the situational influences we discussed earlier. The programs allow consumers to see products displayed and demonstrated.

The consumers, in turn, create their own comfortable, personalized shopping environment and can structure favorable social interactions by inviting friends over to share in the process. Credit card payments and air express shipping enable consumers to purchase products from marketers they never meet face to face.

## FACT OR FICTION REVISITED

⊙ Home shopping *does not* eliminate most of the situational influences on purchasing; instead, it creates its own situational influences.

On-line shopping, through the Internet's World Wide Web and such commercial services as America Online and Prodigy, offers many of the same benefits as televised home shopping. Consumers are able to search for information and make purchases directly through these channels, and the products are delivered via mail or air express. Some products can even be transmitted electronically, such as computer software and financial information. Profound, an on-line information service, for example, transmits business and financial information directly to customers.

## ▼ USAGE INFLUENCES

When consumers recognize a need, they often recognize a particular situation as well. McDonald's will satisfy your hunger, for example, but you probably wouldn't suggest it as a place to celebrate your parents' twenty-fifth wedding anniversary. Thus, the situation in which the consumer will actually use the product influences the purchase activities as well.[3]

During much of our discussion throughout the first 12 chapters, we talked about segmenting consumers on the basis of their background characteristics and behavioral processes. It is also important to note that the particular situation in which a consumer expects to use a product will influence his or her use of the behavioral processes to complete the activities. Usage situations may be categorized by where the product will be used, the time it will be used, and whether the user and the purchaser are the same person. For example, college students buy different clothes for different usage situations. They may wear business attire to a job interview, formal wear to parties and dances, and stylish clothes on campus. When choosing a suit to wear on a job interview, the student may consult with people in his or her aspirational reference group—friends who are now in the industry or others who can give them accurate information on the way professionals in their chosen field dress. When it comes to selecting fashions to wear on campus, however, fellow students will likely be the group of reference.

Using the behavioral processes in ways that are appropriate for the particular situation will mean that students will complete the various purchase activities for different types of clothes in different ways—from recognizing needs to ending the consumption processes. For each type of clothing purchase, they will search for different alternatives for the usage occasion, apply different evaluative criteria, evaluate the experience differently after the purchase, and end the purchase process in a different way. When buying a suit for an interview, the student may look for conservative clothes that will last a long time; price will be less important (Figure 14.6). When shopping for clothes to wear on campus everyday, however, the student may look for cheaper, stylish clothes that can easily be replaced when styles change next year.

■  FIGURE 14.6
The choice of a name-brand suit, such as Zanetti, will be affected by the use occasion for which it is intended.

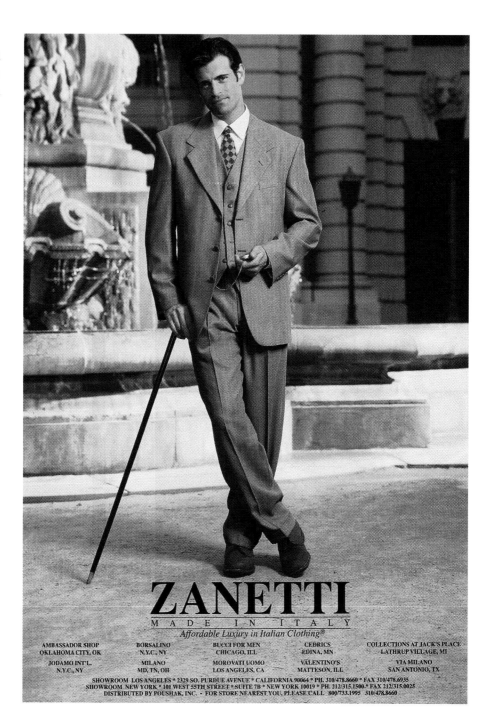

406

The effects of usage situations on purchase behavior require that when they are identifying target market segments, marketers understand just how consumers will use a product. In essence, a target market segment is composed of consumers who act similarly in a particular situation. For example, a clothing manufacturer may not normally identify students as part of the target market for business suits because they buy far fewer of them than do middle-aged professionals. Once the marketer recognizes that graduating seniors will need to buy suits for upcoming job interviews, however, it would be wise to target students as a viable segment as well. Gift giving is another common setting for usage-based marketing efforts. Along with obvious gift-situation purchases, such as cards and flowers for birthdays or anniversaries, many people purchase different pens, perfumes, and liquors as gifts for someone else from the ones they would buy for themselves.

To identify person–situation segments, the marketer must identify each potential member of the target market segment along with his or her usage occasions, as shown in Peter Dickson's analysis of suntan lotions in Figure 14.7. This analysis requires that consumer segments—on the basis of traditional background characteristics—and usage situations be identified first. Then the behavioral processes and purchase activities for each person–situation segment are examined and the attractive segments identified. Sometimes public policy actors direct their efforts toward the use of a product by particular person–situation segments, as we discuss in the Public Policy box that follows.

## PUBLIC POLICY

### Don't Drink and Drive![4]

Many Americans agree that moderate alcohol consumption is acceptable for consumers over the age of 21. Of course, there are exceptions, such as pregnant women, but, overall, drinking in moderation is generally accepted. However, public opinion is strongly opposed to alcohol consumption in any situation that also involves driving. Accordingly, marketers such as Anheuser-Busch, Bacardi, Coors, and Seagrams, and groups such as Mothers Against Drunk Driving and the Harvard Alcohol Project have targeted their efforts to encouraging responsible consumption of alcohol.

In particular, the alcohol marketers have attempted to discourage inappropriate drinking situations, primarily targeting younger males, among whom drunk driving after social gatherings is a severe problem. Coors, for example, created advertising contrasting appropriate situations for drinking Coors Light—"the right beer now"— with inappropriate ones—"but not now." Many of the campaigns focus on the idea of appointing a designated driver. Similarly, Seagrams developed a campaign focused around significant events—New Year's Eve, graduations, weddings—advocating selecting a designated driver. The tag line read, "Sometimes drinking responsibly means not drinking at all." Anheuser-Busch has developed a broader program that encourages parents to talk with their children before they reach driving age to instill in them proper attitudes about drinking. The "Family Talk About Drinking" program provides guidelines for talking about the effects of peer presure, recognizing teenage drinking problems, and discouraging drinking and driving.

## A PERSON–SITUATION–SEGMENTATION MATRIX FOR SUNTAN LOTION

| Situations | Young Children — Fair Skin | Young Children — Dark Skin | Teenagers — Fair Skin | Teenagers — Dark Skin | Adult Women — Fair Skin | Adult Women — Dark Skin | Adult Men — Fair Skin | Adult Men — Dark Skin | Situation Benefits/Features |
|---|---|---|---|---|---|---|---|---|---|
| Beach/boat sunbathing | Combined insect repellent | | | | Summer perfume | | | | a. Windburn protection b. Formula and container can stand heat c. Container floats and is distinctive (not easily lost) |
| Home-poolside sunbathing | | | | | Combined moisturizer | | | | a. Large pump dispenser b. Won't stain wood, concrete, furnishings |
| Sunlamp bathing | | | | | Combined moisturizer and massage oil | | | | a. Designed specifically for type lamp b. Artificial tanning ingredient |
| Snow skiing | | | | | Winter perfume | | | | a. Special protection from special light rays and weather b. Antifreeze formula |
| Person benefit/features | Special protection | | Special protection | | Special protection | | Special protection | | |
| | a. Protection critical b. Non-poisonous | | a. Fit in jean pocket b. Used by opinion leaders | | Female perfume | | Male perfume | | |

Source: Peter R. Dickson (1982). "Person–Situation: Segmentation's Missing Link," *Journal of Marketing*, 46 (Fall), 62. By permission of American Marketing Association.

■ FIGURE 14.7

Dickinson person–situation matrix.

Do you think that programs that target drinking and driving are effective in persuading young adults to change their alcohol consumption habits? Would they be more effective if they criticized *all* drinking by young adults? Why or why not? How might programs that target children affect their drinking behavior as young adults?

# POSTPURCHASE ACTIVITIES

After the purchase and usage activities have been completed, consumers typically evaluate their consumption experiences to determine whether they have been fulfilling. They adjust their attitudes toward the products on the basis of those experiences and provide feedback to marketers and others in their reference groups. They then end the process by disposing of anything that is left over from the purchase, such as packaging or an unused portion of the product. In completing these postpurchase activities, consumers make choices about whether they will continue to use the products they have bought in the future.

## ▼ PREPARING TO BUY AGAIN

Consumers constantly evaluate their consumption experiences with the products they use to decide whether they want to buy the product again. This evaluation is done for both products they have bought and used themselves as well as those they have used but have not purchased themselves—computers they use at work or school, rental cars, or clothes they have borrowed from friends.

**Trial**  A consumer's first consumption or usage experience with a product is a **trial** experience; it usually occurs without any commitment on the part of the consumer. The trial stage varies for different kinds of products. For an inexpensive packaged good, such as a new soft drink, trial is typically the first purchase. A consumer may have heard about an appealing new flavored iced tea and consequently buys a single can from a vending machine or snack bar. For less frequently purchased, high involvement products, such as computers, the consumer may spend a couple of hours testing out the product at the store or at a friend's house to gain trial experience. Many consumers drive a car before purchasing it by arranging a test drive with the dealer, driving a friend's car, or renting the model for a couple of days. In this case, trial commonly occurs after the consumer has evaluated alternative products and developed a preference for one. Other times consumers do not have an opportunity to try a high involvement product and must move directly from the evaluation stage to a purchase. In this case, the trial is also a commitment. Purchasing and using a home permanent is an example.

Sometimes the consumer's preference for a product may not be enough to stimulate trial. For some new products, as we will discuss in Chapter 17, con-

> **Trial** is the consumer's first consumption or usage experience with a product.

sumers may be so fearful of the negative aspects of the product that they will not act on their preference. For example, an individual may think that a new fashion will look good on her but is afraid her friends will dislike it and ridicule her. To overcome this obstacle, the consumer could take a friend to the store with her, try on the outfit, and see what her friend says. In some cases, situational influences may prevent consumers from trying out a product they want; these same situations may provide a trial opportunity for a product they haven't considered before, however. For example, an individual may not be able to buy a new pair of Doc Martens because the store doesn't have any in his size. But he may try on a new pair of Timberlands and decide to buy them instead.

## FACT OR FICTION REVISITED

⊛    Commitment *does not* precede trial in consumer behavior; in fact, the term *trial* implies lack of commitment.

> **Repeat** is the ongoing purchase of a product as a result of a favorable evaluation of the consumer's experience.

**Repeat**    Once the consumer has tried a product and evaluated the consumption experience, she or he must decide if it is worth making a commitment to the product and becoming a regular user. Consumers show commitment to a product by repeating the purchase the next time they have a similar need. Thus, **repeat** is the continuing purchase of a product as a result of the consumer's evaluation of the consumption experience and a consequent decision to use it regularly. Repeat of infrequently purchased, high involvement products, such as computers or cars, occurs when the consumer purchases the same product again. Since it may be years between purchases, however, consumers maintain their attitudes toward these products during these long periods. For example, during the several years between car purchases, consumers hold attitudes about their preference for their next car purchase. Their level of preference indicates their commitment to repurchasing the product. However, marketers can never be sure whether consumers will repeat their purchase until the next time they make an actual purchase decision.

How many times must a consumer repeat the purchase of a low involvement, frequently purchased product to be considered a "regular user"? The consumer who tried the new flavored iced tea may continue to buy other soft drinks in addition to frequent purchases of the new tea. If the consumer drinks a dozen canned soft drinks each week, does one iced tea per week constitute regular usage? Is a half-dozen a week enough? Or must the consumer purchase all 12 cans of the iced tea?

Packaged goods are rarely used exclusively, even by committed consumers. Different usage situations generate different needs. Many consumers regularly drink several different beverages—orange juice in the morning, a couple of different soft drinks during the day, one brand of beer at home, and another when they are out with friends. As we mentioned earlier, many marketers design distinct products for different target market segments and usage occasions. An individual might use a dandruff shampoo once every week, a cleaning shampoo another

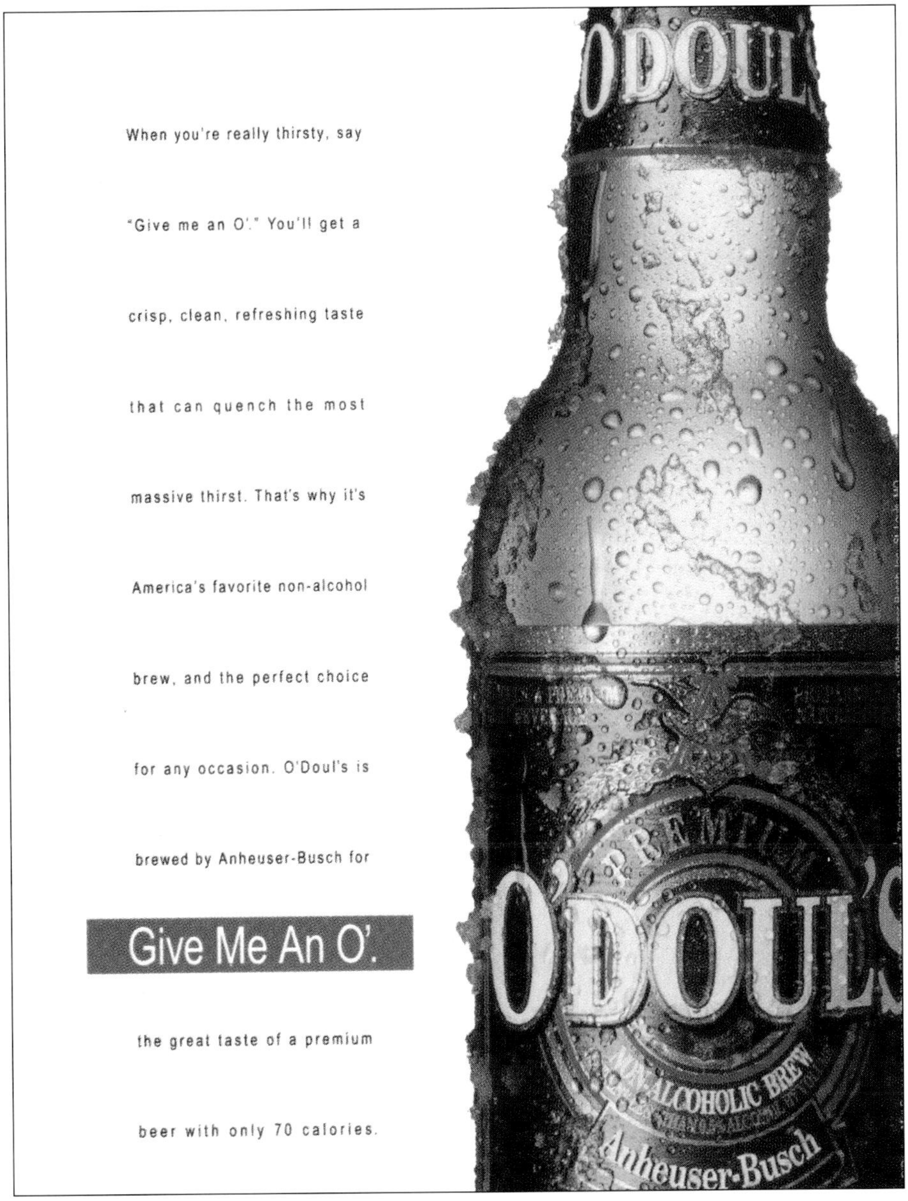
When you're really thirsty, say
"Give me an O'." You'll get a
crisp, clean, refreshing taste
that can quench the most
massive thirst. That's why it's
America's favorite non-alcohol
brew, and the perfect choice
for any occasion. O'Doul's is
brewed by Anheuser-Busch for
Give Me An O'.
the great taste of a premium
beer with only 70 calories.
O'DOUL'S
PREMIUM
O'DOUL'S
NON-ALCOHOLIC BREW
Anheuser-Busch

■ Figure 14.8
O'Doul's positions its nonalcoholic beer as appropriate for those occasions when the consumer wants the taste of beer without the alcohol.

time each week, and a combination shampoo and conditioner the rest of the time. Neutrogena positions its shampoo as a product to be used once a week to remove the buildup left by other brands. Similarly, nonalcoholic beers, such as Sharp's and O'Doul's, are positioned as appropriate for times when the consumer wants the taste of beer without the alcohol (Figure 14.8).

## ▼ Consumer Satisfaction or Dissatisfaction

The attitude a consumer develops as a result of his or her evaluation of the consumption experience with a certain product is known as **consumer satisfaction or dissatisfaction (CS/D)**. Consumer satisfaction is a key component of many,

**Consumer satisfaction or dissatisfaction (CS/D)** is the attitude toward a product that results from the consumer's evaluation of the usage experience.

if not most, repeat purchase decisions. After their first purchase of a product, consumers evaluate their own trial and repeat experiences and determine their level of satisfaction, which they store as knowledge to be retrieved from long-term memory and used to evaluate alternatives the next time they consider a purchase. Consumers communicate these experiences and evaluations to others in their reference groups and, in turn, incorporate the experiences of others into their own decision making. They also provide feedback to marketers about their satisfaction, or dissatisfaction, with products.

## FACT OR FICTION REVISITED

◉    Satisfaction is in fact the key element in most purchase decisions.

**Consumers Determine Their Satisfaction**    As Figure 14.9 illustrates, consumers typically adopt two perspectives in evaluating their experience with a product: (1) did the consumption experience satisfy their needs? and (2) how did the experience compare with their prepurchase expectations about how the product would perform?[5] The first perspective is an *absolute measure*—a measure of how the product has performed on the basis of the consumer's level of satisfaction or dissatisfaction. The second is a *relative measure*—a measure of how the product has performed *relative to what the consumer expected.*

According to the decision making model we laid out in Chapter 12, consumers evaluate the alternative products available to them on the basis of attributes that represent the benefits that satisfy their needs. Few products offer all the benefits consumers want. Even if the product delivers everything they expect, their postpurchase evaluation will likely include some positive and some negative

■  FIGURE 14.9
Consumer satisfaction or dissatisfaction.

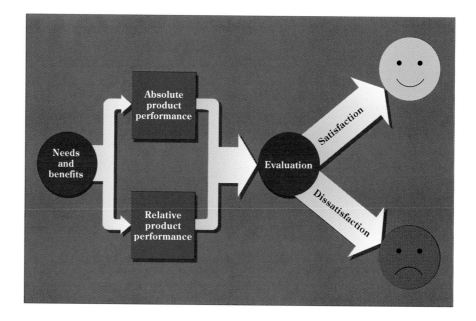

evaluations. For example, consumers know that some fashions that look good on them will require dry cleaning. Accordingly, they will feel happy about how they look in the clothes but annoyed about the inconvenience and cost of dry cleaning.

As consumers evaluate the absolute levels of the product's performance, they typically can't help but compare that performance to what they have expected. Three outcomes are possible from such a comparison:

❶ *Positive disconfirmation* results when the product performs better than expected.

❷ *Simple confirmation* results when the product delivers just what the consumer expected.

❸ *Negative disconfirmation* results when the product performs worse than expected.

Even when a product performs well, the consumer may be dissatisfied if it doesn't perform *as well as expected*. You may have had that experience going to the movies, for example. Perhaps you enjoyed *Forrest Gump* but felt that it wasn't as great as the reviews led you to expect it to be.

**Consumers Respond to Dissatisfaction**   Naturally, consumers who are satisfied with a product after they complete their postpurchase evaluation are more likely to maintain their commitment to that product and repeat the purchase the next time they recognize the same need. By contrast, consumers who are dissatisfied with their consumption experience have a number of different options:[6]

❶ They can *voice their dissatisfaction to the marketer* from whom they have purchased the product. Consumers often complain to marketers about a product's poor performance; some even offer suggestions for improvement. Often, the consumer requests some kind of response in the form of a refund or other means of compensation or additional service to increase the product's performance.

❷ They can communicate their dissatisfaction to others in their reference groups *on a private basis*. We will discuss negative word-of-mouth communication in more detail in Chapter 16.

❸ They can enlist the *support of a third party* by writing letters of complaint to newspapers, magazines, or television consumer advocates or by complaining to better business bureaus, trade associations, or government bodies. A more drastic approach is to hire legal counsel and file suit against the marketer.

Many consumers do not take any of these actions—they simply do not repeat their purchase of the dissatisfying product. A consumer's willingness to take any, or all, of these actions depends on a number of factors, including his or her background characteristics (e.g., education, lifestyle, personality) and level of involvement with the product. Consumers also measure the costs and benefits of taking action. Complaining, either verbally or in writing, costs the consumer time, effort, and perhaps even money; in return, any additional benefit offered by a new or modified product must compensate for those costs. Obviously, the level of dissatisfaction will influence the likelihood of acting—some dissatisfaction may be annoying but is not bothersome enough to warrant the time and effort to complain. Furthermore, if the consumer does not expect to get a favorable response from the marketer or third party, she or he will be less likely to act. Finally, situational influences may restrict the consumer's opportunity to act—you would be more likely to complain about a defective shirt you bought in a store around the corner than one you bought a thousand miles away while on vacation.

**Marketers Attempt to Create Satisfaction**   It is obviously in the best interest of marketers to ensure customer satisfaction. Accordingly, they employ a number of strategies to do so. Marketers (1) design products to be satisfying to the consumers who buy them, (2) structure consumers' expectations so that they do not experience negative disconfirmation, and (3) respond to consumers who voice their dissatisfaction in order to minimize private and third-party complaints.[7]

To design satisfying products and manage consumer expectations, marketers must understand the consumer purchase activities. That is, they must understand consumers' needs and the benefits they expect from products, and they must analyze the evaluative criteria consumers use to decide among alternative products so that they know what product attributes are important to them. For example, car manufacturers know that a consumer's perception of quality is greatly influenced by a car's level of fit and finish—how tightly the doors, hood, and trunk meet, for example. Thus, a car that delivers reliable service for an extended period of time would still be dissatisfying to a consumer if it has uneven gaps between the parts of the body (Figure 14.10).

To gain such complex understanding, marketers conduct extensive consumer research, often beginning before the product is designed. They investigate the product attributes consumers list as important evaluative criteria and examine how consumers rate the alternatives on those criteria. They also study how consumers make their purchase decisions and how they learn about products and develop their expectations. This kind of extensive research continues even after the product has been purchased. Many retailers, such as Neiman Marcus, use mystery shoppers—researchers employed by firms such as Feedback Plus who pose as shoppers—to evaluate the service provided by their store employees. Most marketers conduct extensive customer satisfaction surveys to gauge consumers' levels of satisfaction. Marketers of infrequently purchased products, such as cars and household appliances, survey consumers on a regular basis so that they can monitor consumer perceptions during the long time period between purchases.

In keeping with the "total quality management" movement that attempts to build products free of defects, marketers use the information they gather through research to address product design issues and consumer expectations. According to this philosophy, marketers design products to deliver the benefits consumers need and redesign products that fail to satisfy customers. For example, computer software firms continually develop new versions of software in response to consumers' complaints about the performance of current products.

If the beautiful lines of the new Monte Carlo seem somehow familiar, they should.

**■ FIGURE 14.10**
This ad for Chevrolet's Monte Carlo emphasizes the fit and finish of its product, important criteria for some consumers.

These decisions are not made randomly; instead, marketers want to ensure that consumers' expectations are realistic so that they will not be dissatisfied with the product as it actually exists. To achieve this goal, they create advertising and other marketing communications that provide a realistic view of how the product

415

will perform. They also offer consumers the opportunity to try a product with no obligation.

## FACT OR FICTION REVISITED

◉ Marketers *do not* try to create unrealistic expectations; instead, they try to create realistic expectations so that consumers will not be disappointed.

Finally, marketers develop programs to respond to dissatisfied consumers. Marketers prefer that consumers bring their complaints to them rather than buy another brand or complain to other consumers or third parties. In fact, they encourage this kind of direct feedback so that they can address the complaint before other consumers or public policy actors hear about it. In doing so, the marketer benefits as well by gaining insight into problems it may not otherwise have known about.

Marketing programs to address consumer dissatisfaction consider both the costs and benefits consumers face when they complain, in two ways: (1) by making it easy for consumers to complain, and (2) by responding to the complaint in a way that satisfies the consumer. When a customer's questions or complaints are addressed quickly, the customer is less likely to remain dissatisfied. Accordingly, such programs emphasize the following:

❶ *Easy access to customer service representatives.* Many marketers provide toll-free numbers customers can call to contact them directly. General Electric (GE) is well known in the appliance industry for its GE Answer Center, an extensive customer service operation that is open 24 hours a day, 365 days a year. Many computer and software marketers provide helpful on-line forums on services such as Compuserve and America On-line.

❷ *Ease of repair.* Many marketers provide at-home service for defective products. For example, Gateway 2000 includes diagnostic software with all its computers that allows technicians to work from their home base in South Dakota to diagnose problems in the user's home using a modem and a telephone. Luxury car marketers, such as Acura, offer their customers free loaner cars to eliminate the inconvenience of repairs. Similarly, Saturn replaced approximately 2000 cars that were found to have defective coolant and picked up and delivered other cars that had been recalled for other defects.

❸ *Concern on the part of the marketer.* Consumers want to purchase products from marketers who care about their needs. Marketers must therefore emphasize customer satisfaction and communicate that emphasis to consumers by exhibiting a willingness to analyze complaints and address the underlying causes. In 1994 Intel enraged users of its new Pentium microprocessor when the company failed to disclose a flaw in the product. It wasn't until Intel publicly apologized for the problem and offered free replacements that consumers were satisfied. Once marketers recognize their poor past performance, the best approach is to communicate with consumers about the subsequent improvements they have made. For example, 7-Eleven developed television advertisements featuring comedians Louie Anderson, Brett Butler, and Gilbert Gottfried joking about the store's poor reputation and noting the improvements that have been made recently.

## ▼ PRODUCT DISPOSAL

Product disposal may occur just minutes after the purchase has been made or years later.[8] Consumers typically dispose of a soda can shortly after buying it. By contrast, they may keep a refrigerator for 10 or 15 years before replacing it with a new one. Some wealthy consumers sell a piece of formal wear to a resale shop after they have worn it just once, whereas other consumers keep a favorite piece of clothing for years and years.

Consumers have three options for product disposal, as shown in Figure 14.11. They can: (1) keep it, (2) throw it away or recycle it, or (3) give it to another consumer. The decision depends on the nature of the product and its packaging, the consumer's background characteristics, and situational influences.

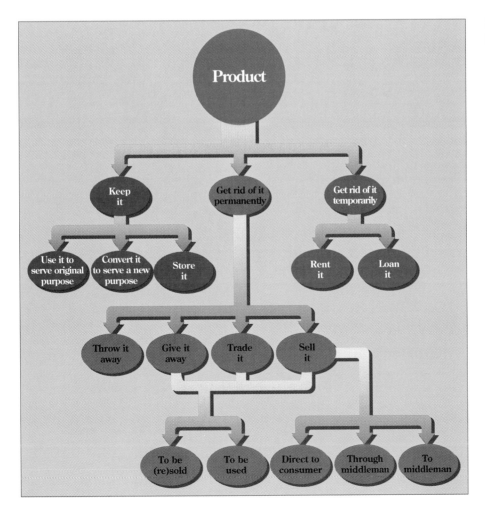

■ FIGURE 14.11
Disposal options.

417

People are more likely to hold onto products that may have another use some other time or that take up little space. Many people keep old newspapers, for example, because they can be used in a fireplace or for wrapping packages. Similarly, many people hold onto watches they no longer wear because they require little space and are a memory of past occasions. Many consumers keep the packaging products come in because it can be useful in transporting the product; stereo and computer equipment boxes are prime examples. There are other consumers who have a personal predisposition to hold onto products long after they

■ FIGURE 14.12
Many marketers, such as Hewlett Packard, offer trade ins or upgrades of products as a means of disposal.

You've got some tired old laser printers. We've got some brand new HP LaserJets. Want to trade?

If you've been wanting to upgrade to new HP LaserJet printers, now's your chance. HP's Cash In & Trade Up program means you can turn in your old laser printers—any brand—and get credit towards any new printer in the LaserJet family. You can even trade in select color printers.

You'll be surprised how much those old printers are worth. Of course, the amount of credit you get depends on what you turn in. For example, trade in an old LaserJet III and get a new LaserJet 4 Plus for under $1,000. Just remember, the printer—or

printers—you trade in have to work. You can be sure that HP has made the whole process easy. All of the shipping will be taken care of for you. And your users will never be without a printer.

You get a return on your original investment and your users get the latest laser technology. Whatever your business is looking for—more speed, more graphics capabilities, savings on consumables or precise 600-dpi print quality—you'll find a personal or network HP LaserJet that meets your needs.

Call your participating authorized HP dealer for all the details. Or call 1-800-TRADE-ME, Ext. 9472 for the current value of all your old printers. This offer expires October 31, 1995. So you'll want to trade up soon.

HP LaserJet Printers
Just what you had in mind.

 HEWLETT® PACKARD

In Canada, call 1-800-387-3867, Dept. 9472. See us at http://www.hp.com/info/9472 on the World Wide Web. ©1995 Hewlett-Packard Company  PE12556

have stopped using them. These consumers are reluctant to throw anything away. In some cases, the situation prevents the consumer from disposing of certain products. For example, some homeowners have old car batteries or flammable liquids, such as paints, lying around the garage or basement because they can't just trash or recycle them.

The second option—disposing of a product by placing it in the trash or recycling it—is one worthy of consideration by consumers, marketers, and public policy actors alike. In some cases, this is the *only* option because the consumer cannot keep the product and no one will accept it as a pass along. This is true of many packaged goods, such as diapers, detergent, and beverages, as well as for some cars and appliances.

As the options for trash disposal decrease, however, recycling has become much more important. Many local governments require consumers to recycle cans, bottles, plastic containers, and newspapers to reduce the nearly five pounds of trash the Environmental Protection Agency estimates each American produces daily. Increasing numbers of products are being recycled, such as re-refined engine oil that is sold at Wal-Mart and certified by Green Seal, an environmental social action organization. Government regulations have changed the nature of many other products as well. The detergent industry has shifted to concentrated forms that require less packaging and new forms of packaging that are easier to recycle, and car manufacturers have begun to pay attention to the ease with which components can be recycled.

The third option—passing along products—is a common alternative for a product that is still useful but is no longer wanted by its original purchaser.[9] Consumers return products to marketers for a refund or exchange; sell them at flea markets, garage sales, or resale shops; or give them to friends, family members, or charitable organizations. In some cases, the product simply may no longer be appropriate for the consumer—children outgrow their clothes and pass them on to younger siblings, and women often pass on their maternity clothes to friends or relatives. Other times, a consumer's needs change, and a product that was once satisfying may no longer be. For example, a person's golf skills may improve, requiring a better set of clubs. In response, many marketers buy or exchange old models for new ones. Play It Again Sports is a sporting goods franchise that specializes in buying, selling, and trading used sporting goods equipment, and car and stereo equipment dealers commonly provide this service for customers who want to replace or upgrade their old products (Figure 14.12).

# PURCHASE AND USAGE BEHAVIOR

Like most consumers, Dorothy Sinclair buys and uses a number of different products. Her background characteristics influence the ways she thinks about both her own and her daughter's needs. But sometimes other factors influence her as well. In particular, credit card marketers appealed to her desire to delay payment for products she couldn't afford at the time of purchase, and they made it easy for Dorothy to apply for them by appearing on her college campus. The cards made Dorothy's day-to-day life more convenient during college, but once she graduated she couldn't buy much at all as she paid off her credit card debts over the next few years.

Dorothy also wants to provide some financial security for her daughter. A persuasive insurance agent latched onto this concern and persuaded her to buy a life insurance policy to satisfy that need. He very astutely used her daughter as a reminder of her interests during the sales calls, and ultimately made the purchase.

Dorothy's experiences illustrate many of the important aspects of purchase and usage behavior. Once all of the activities that led up to a purchase have been completed, consumers are still subject to situational influences based on the physical characteristics of the purchase situation, social interactions, and their mood during the purchase situation, as well as their ability to pay for and transport the products they want to buy. Consumers must then decide if they have been satisfied with the purchase, and they will often comunicate their satisfaction or dissatisfaction to those around them and to the marketers who have sold them the products. Finally, the consumer must dispose of the product and its packaging.

Many of these influences on purchase and usage behavior stem from two sources—marketers and interpersonal communication with others in the consumer's environment. We will discuss the influences of marketing communications in the next chapter and interpersonal communications in Chapter 16.

# SUMMARY

1. **Identify the situational influences that affect specific purchase activities.** Situational influences may prevent consumers from purchasing their preferred alternative, or they may introduce new alternatives that are purchased without conducting prior search and evaluation activities. The four major types of situational influences are: (1) physical characteristics of the purchase situation, (2) enabling conditions, (3) social interactions, and (4) the consumer's mood. Physical characteristics include the physical attributes of the selling situation, such as the store's layout, lighting, noise level, or product displays. Enabling conditions include the consumer's access to funds—the ability to pay for the product—and access to products—the capacity to transport the product to where it will be used. Social interactions with store personnel and other shoppers affect the nature of the purchase situation as well as the consumer's perception of the store and the products it sells. The consumer's mood includes both physiological and psychological states, such as hunger and embarrassment, which may affect the immediate purchase situation.

2. **Recognize the characteristics of usage occasions that affect the activities necessary to complete a purchase.** Different usage situations require different benefits and therefore influence the consumer purchase activities and behavioral processes. Characteristics of usage situations include where the product will be used, the time it will be used, and whether the user and the purchaser are the same person.

3. **Analyze consumers' evaluations of their consumption experiences.** Consumers evaluate their experiences with products to decide whether they want to buy them

again. The consumer's level of satisfaction (or dissatisfaction) with a product is based on an absolute measure of whether it has satisfied the consumer's needs as well as a relative measure of how well it has met the expectations the consumer had before the purchase. Positive disconfirmation occurs when the product performs better than expected; simple confirmation takes place when the product delivers what the consumer has expected; and negative disconfirmation occurs when the product performs worse than expected. Naturally, satisfied consumers are more likely to repeat their purchase than are dissatisfied ones. Dissatisfied users, in turn, tend to voice their dissatisfaction to the marketer, members of their reference groups, and third parties, such as the media, consumer advocates, and public policy actors. To prevent consumer dissatisfaction, marketers try to design products that will satisfy consumers, to structure consumer expectations, and to develop programs that respond to dissatisfied consumers.

4. **Identify consumers' options to end the purchase process.** Consumers have three options for disposing of products and their packaging and ending the purchase process: they can keep the product, throw it away or recycle it, or pass it along for use by another consumer. Ecological and environmental concerns have increased the prevalence and appeal of recycling products rather than throwing them away. When consumers pass along products, they return them to marketers in exchange for new ones; sell them at flea markets, garage sales, or resale shops; or give them to friends, family members, or charitable organizations.

## KEY TERMS

Situational influences, *p. 399*

Access to funds, *p. 400*

Access to products, *p. 400*

Trial, *p. 409*

Repeat, *p. 410*

Consumer satisfaction or dissatisfaction (CS/D), *p. 411*

## SKILL-BUILDING ACTIVITIES

1. Think of a favorite high involvement product you own—a stereo, a musical instrument, or an automobile, perhaps. Trace your experiences with this item through each of the following steps. For each step, describe the factors that influenced your attitude toward the product and/or the brand:
   a. physical characteristics of the environment in which you acquired the product
   b. enabling conditions
   c. social interactions in the acquisition situation
   d. effects of your mood or other psychological state
   e. usage situation
   f. trial
   g. positive disconfirmation
   h. negative disconfirmation
   i. repeat, or intention to repeat
   j. other reactions to satisfaction or dissatisfaction
2. How will you dispose of this item? What attitudes will influence this decision?
3. How did marketers influence steps (a) through (j) in activity 1?
4. How did activities of government officials interested in consumer protection influence steps (a) through (j) in activity 1?

# CHAPTER 14
# SELF-TEST

▼    MULTIPLE CHOICE

1.  A store's layout, lighting and music are all components of a(n)_____ situational influence.
    a. enabling condition
    b. physical characteristics
    c. social interactions
    d. mood

2.  Enabling conditions include access to funds and access to _____ .
    a. promotional strategies
    b. marketing information
    c. products
    d. sales people

3.  If Max normally eats high-fat, high-calorie foods but on a date he eats only low-calorie, low-fat foods, the situational influence of _____ is effecting his purchase and consumption behaviors.
    a. consumer mood
    b. enabling condition
    c. access to products
    d. social interactions

4.  Hunger, depression, and boredom are examples of the situational influence of
    _____ .
    a. consumer mood
    b. consumer characteristics
    c. atmospherics
    d. sociology

5.  Usage situations include where the product can be used, the time at which it will be used, and whether _____ .
    a. the product is expensive
    b. it is a high involvement product
    c. the consumer will recycle the product
    d. the user and purchaser are the same person

6.  After Ruth evaluates and then decides to buy Diet Pepsi on a regular basis, her next purchase of Diet Pepsi will be called _____ .
    a. routine
    b. repeat
    c. rehearsal
    d. reintroduction

7.  If Leonard purchases a new shampoo after seeing an advertisement stating that the product adds shine to hair and after using the product his hair looks dull, he has experienced _____ .
    a. positive disconfirmation of expectations
    b. simple confirmation of expectations
    c. negative disconfirmation of expectations
    d. high cognitive dissonance

8.  When most consumers are dissatisfied with a purchase they _____ .
    a. hire legal counsel
    b. enlist the support of a third party
    c. voice their dissatisfaction to the marketer
    d. do not buy the product again

9.  When a customer's questions or complaints are _____ , the customer is less likely to remain _____ .
    a. answered quickly; dissatisfied
    b. insignificant; brand loyal
    c. complex; in the target market
    d. insignificant; dissatisfied

10. If a store offers a discount for each old pair of shoes brought into the store, that store is using a sales promotion strategy based on the _____ component of consumer purchase and usage behavior.
    a. consumer satisfaction/dissatisfaction
    b. product disposal
    c. product usage
    d. evaluation of alternatives

## ▼ TRUE/FALSE

1. After a consumer chooses a product, purchase of that product automatically occurs.   T or F
2. Other customers can affect a consumer's decision to make a purchase.   T or F
3. Marketers have no influence on consumer moods.   T or F
4. Consumers may consider how they are going to use a product when deciding which product to purchase.   T or F
5. The trial stage of consumption behavior occurs only if a commitment to purchase is made.   T or F
6. Packaged goods such as snack foods are rarely used exclusively.   T or F
7. The key component of repeat purchase decisions is consumer satisfaction/dissatisfaction.   T or F
8. If a product fulfills a consumer's expectations, the consumer will be satisfied with the purchase.   T or F
9. Consumers are more likely to act on their dissatisfaction if they believe their actions will have some result.   T or F
10. Consumers continually evaluate the products they have purchased.   T or F

## ▼ SHORT ANSWER

1. Describe the four components of the purchase and usage stage of the decision making process.
2. Describe the two ways that consumers evaluate their experience with a product.
3. List the three ways in which marketers attempt to ensure customer satisfaction.

## ▼ APPLICATION EXERCISE

You have been hired as the manager of a soon-to-be-built sporting goods store. You are presently involved in planning the construction and policies of the store. Describe some specific physical characteristics and enabling conditions that should be included in the store to encourage consumers to shop there.

# 15

# MARKETING
# COMMUNICATION

◉ Consumer Snapshot  *Bill Baker is a 67-year-old retired Director of Public Affairs for an insurance company. He lives in Denver, Colorado, with his wife, Kate. They have two grown children, Diane, 45, and Reginald, 44.*

## FACT OR FICTION

◉   In the marketing communication process, focus on one medium is generally more effective than use of several media.

◉   In the marketing communication process, feedback can be either positive or negative.

◉   Direct marketing is a one-way channel of communication

◉   Messages received through direct marketing generally have more personal relevance than messages received through advertising or publicity.

◉ Marketers have more control over what is said about their products in publicity than in advertising.

◉ Advertising can change the experience of using the advertised brand.

◉ The key difference between fair and unfair marketing communication is deception.

## EYE ON THE CONSUMER

Bill Baker admits that he is easily influenced by advertising. In fact, he has bought a number of products after seeing them advertised on television—which he calls it "the idiot box"—or in magazines and newspapers. He believes that ads entice people to buy things, even if they are only referring to the ads for information. Bill was particularly impressed with an ad for a Honda motorcycle that showed a guy riding his bike in the mountains under wide-open, sunny skies. He went out and bought one. After watching an ad for Ginsu knives that demontrated the product slicing a tomato, cutting a tin can, and sawing a piece of wood, Bill ordered the knives. At the time, he was having trouble cutting a piece of meat with his old knives, so he wrote out a check for $19.95 and purchased the Ginsu knives. Bill even ordered a set of golf clubs from a commercial he saw during a program he was watching at 2:00 in the morning. The spokesperson made Bill feel as if he could go on tour with Jack Nicklaus if he had those clubs; he called that night and received the golf clubs two days later. He's been happy with them ever since.

Bill is no pushover, however. He strongly dislikes shady or incompetent salespeople and the piles of "junk mail" he and his wife, Kate, receive regularly. On one ocassion, the Bakers were planning to buy a microwave oven that was on sale at Sears, but the salesperson told them the sale was over and tried to charge them $60 over the advertised price. Bill and Kate walked out of the store and haven't been back since. Similarly, when Bill was ready to sign the papers to buy a Ford van, the salesman let him sit and wait for an hour. Bill walked away from the sale. On the other hand, a good salesperson can make all the difference to Bill. He bought all of his stereo equipment at the Sound Track, for instance, because he was impressed with the store's knowledgeable and friendly sales staff.

Bill didn't receive much direct mail when he lived in a lower income section of Denver, but now that he and Kate live in a zip code "where the middle class white people live, with the money," they get quite a bit. In fact, Bill feels they get entirely *too much* of it, so he automatically throws away everything but first class mail.

This chapter begins with a discussion of the communication process—the foundation of marketers' efforts to promote their products. In this process, marketers are the source and consumers are the receivers of information. The marketer packages information in the form of a message and transmits it to the consumer through communication media. The consumer, in turn, interprets the message and provides feedback through purchase decisions.

After reading and thinking about this chapter, you should be able to:

❶ Understand the communication process.
❷ Analyze the effects of marketing communication on consumers.
❸ Recognize the methods marketers employ to communicate information about their products to consumers.
❹ Identify the strategies that guide marketing communications efforts.
❺ Appreciate the public policy implications of marketing communication.

# THE COMMUNICATION PROCESS

**M**arketing communication is a term used to describe the flow of information about products from marketers to consumers. Marketers use advertising, direct marketing, publicity, sales promotion, and direct selling to provide information they hope will influence consumer purchase decisions. Consumers, in turn, utilize marketing communication during the purchase process to gather information about the attributes and benefits of products. It is in the marketer's best interest to make its advertising as clear as possible; if advertising is confusing, the consumer's perceptions of the product may be incorrect. For example, consumers use the information provided in automotive advertising to learn about a car's features, to evaluate the relative merits of different models, and to reach a purchase decision.

> **Marketing communication** is the flow of information about products from marketers to consumers.

At the heart of the process is **communication**—the transmission of a message from a source through a medium to a receiver. Figure 15.1 illustrates the key components of the communication process:

> **Communication** is the transmission of a message from a source through a medium to a receiver.

❶ The *source* is the sender of the communication; the source *encodes* the desired information into a message that can be transmitted to the receiver.

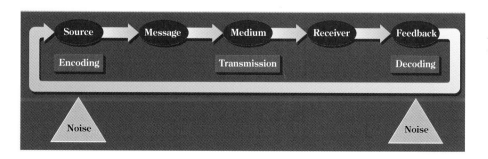

■ FIGURE 15.1
A model of the communication process.

❷ The *message* is the information content that is transmitted, as well as the creative form it takes.

❸ The *medium* is the communication channel the source uses to deliver the message to the receiver.

❹ The *receiver* is the target of the communication; the receiver *decodes* the message and extracts the information it contains.

❺ *Feedback* is the return of information from the receiver to the source.

## ▼ SOURCE

> A **source** is the sender of communication.

In the communication process, the **source** is the originator of information. In the case of marketing communication, the source is the marketer, and the intention is to provide information to persuade consumers to buy the marketer's product. Marketers have many specific *communications objectives,* depending on the circumstances: they may want to make consumers aware of their product so that they will include it in their evoked set; or they may want to provide information for consumers to use in their decision making process; or they may want to influence consumers' postpurchase evaluation of the product. The marketer will set these objectives to suit the target market and the product and to determine the message and medium it will use to communicate the information. For example, a toy manufacturer typically uses television advertising to let children know that a new action figure is available. Car manufacturers also advertise their new products, and they supplement their advertising with salespeople, who provide detailed information for consumers to use in the evaluation process.

**Encoding**   In order to communicate the information so that it is accessible, the source *encodes* the desired information into a message for transmission to the receiver. Marketers employ a variety of sophisticated techniques to encode messages so that consumers receive the desired information.[1] The goal is to create messages that accurately and easily convey the information the marketer wants to transmit. Consider a television commercial for a movie, such as *Batman Forever* (Figure 15.2). The marketer might encode information about the kind of target audience for whom the movie is appropriate by using a narrator to describe who would like the movie or an industry rating. The marketer could also show interviews with "typical" audience members as they leave the theater. The assumption is that the consumers featured in the commercial represent the target market segment for the film.

■ FIGURE 15.2

Movie marketers often encode information about the kind of target audience for whom their film is appropriate in their advertising.

**Source Credibility**   Consumers interpret the information they receive in the context of its source.[2] That is, the consumer's knowledge and attitudes about the source of the information—the marketer who creates an advertisement, the individuals who appear in the ad, or the salesperson who delivers a sales pitch—affect his or her attitudes and preferences for the product.

**Source credibility** is a consumer's belief that a communication source provides accurate and unbiased information based on objectivity and expertise. As we mentioned above, consumers tend to evaluate a film more favorably if they have a favorable view of the audience members who praise it. The consumer's opinion might be different if the audience members were paid to praise the film. Similarly, celebrities who appear in ads tend to be more credible if they have actual knowledge of the product—Cindy Crawford is more credible promoting Revlon cosmetics than she would be selling long-distance telephone service.

> **Source credibility** is the belief that a source provides accurate and unbiased information based on objectivity and expertise.

## ▼ MESSAGE

The **message** encompasses more than just the information content being transmitted; it also embodies the physical form the information takes. A message may introduce facts about a product's features, for example, as well as symbols designed to transmit attitudes, emotion, and imagery. Some messages are verbal, and some are visual; some rely on factual presentation, and others rest on emotional appeals. A newspaper ad that describes the sale items at a local retailer; a magazine ad that conveys the satisfaction consumers will feel if they decorate their homes with luxurious furniture; the telephone sales pitch of a volunteer asking for contributions to a local charity drive—all are examples of messages.

> A **message** is the information content communicated and the creative form it takes.

Sometimes the message the marketer conveys and the one the consumer receives may diverge sharply, for a number of reasons. The consumer may not pay attention to the message and misinterpret the content. Or the credibility of the marketer may be poor. Consumers recognize that marketers are not necessarily objective, and their skepticism may lead to disparate interpretations of the marketer's message.

Information is commonly encoded into messages in the form of *verbal* communications—spoken and written words—or *visual* communications—pictures and images. The advantage of verbal communications is that they can convey more factual information about a product's attributes. Words, in the form of ads that contain a great deal of information or a salesperson's appeals, are often more effective for high involvement purchases, where the consumer has the desire to seek and process extensive amounts of information. The advantage of visual images is that they usually have a more immediate impact and are easier for consumers to process, retrieve, and associate with a particular product. Accordingly, marketers often create visual logos to symbolize their brands, as we noted in Chapter 10.

## ▼ MEDIUM

In order for the message to be transmitted from the sender to the receiver, it must have a medium. The **medium** is the communications channel between the source and the receiver. It might be a television or magazine ad, a piece of direct mail, a publicity effort, an infomercial, an in-store display, or a salesperson. The choice of medium must be appropriate for the communications objectives, the

> A **medium** is the communications channel between a source and a receiver.

target market, and the product; each varies in its effectiveness at reaching different consumer targets and its ability to deliver messages about various products. For example, people who like to cook can gather detailed information through specialty cooking magazines, such as *Gourmet* magazine and *Fine Cooking*. Because these magazines are typically read by experienced cooks, marketers can assume that the target audience understands detailed, advanced descriptions. An infomercial may be effective for conveying the actual experience of using a piece of exercise equipment, such as a Soloflex or Proform Fitness machine, because consumers can see how the machine works (Figure 15.3). A 30-minute infomercial may demonstrate an average consumer using the equipment for a variety of

■ FIGURE 15.3
Thirty-minute infomericals are often used to demonstrate exercise equipment, such as the Soloflex machine.

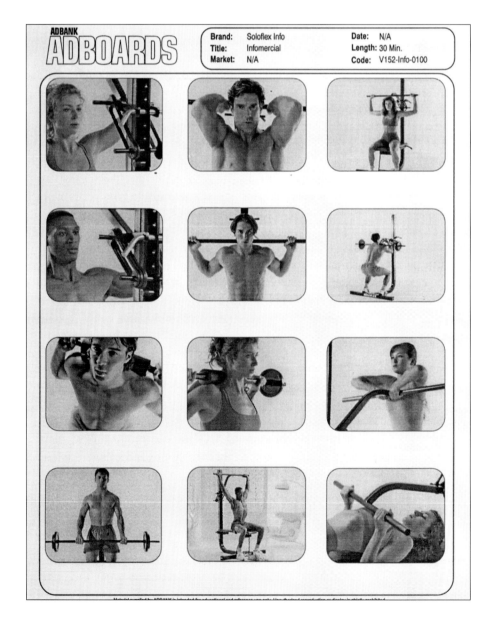

exercises in an everyday setting so that viewers can visualize how easily the product will work for them.

In recent years, marketers have come to realize that a *combination* of media, each with an appropriately tailored message, is more effective than any one medium used alone. We will discuss the use of several media—referred to as *integrated marketing communications*—in more detail later in the chapter.

## FACT OR FICTION REVISITED

◉  It is *not true* that focus on one medium is generally more effective than the use of several media in the marketing communication process; use of several media typically is more effective and is a growing trend.

## ▼ RECEIVER

As we noted above, the **receiver** is the target of the message—the consumer to whom the marketer wants to provide information and exposure. Consumers are the targets of advertisements, direct marketing solicitations, publicity efforts, infomercials, sales promotions, and personal selling. Often, they rely on the messages provided by marketing communications to help them complete the activities in the purchase process. In some cases the receiver may not be the end user of the product but someone who is indirectly involved in the purchase process. For example, a cereal marketer may advertise separately to children, who will ultimately consume the product; to parents, who purchase the product; and to pediatricians, who advise parents on their children's diets.

> A **receiver** is the target of a message.

**Decoding**  Once the message has been received by the consumer, it must be interpreted. *Decoding* is the interpretation process consumers employ to extract the information contained in the message. Consumers decode advertisements and other marketing communications and use the content to recognize needs, search for and evaluate alternatives, and, ultimately, make a purchase decision.

Researchers continue to debate just how consumers decode the content of marketing communications—that is, how consumers consume. We have noted in Chapter 1 that watching television is an example of consumer behavior. Similarly, consumers use the behavioral processes to consume marketing communications—they apply motivation, perception, learning, and attitude formation to decode the messages that are transmitted to them; ultimately, their evaluation of the message itself will affect their evaluation of the information being communicated. For example, as we noted in Chapter 11, at one time or another you have probably seen an ad you disliked so much that you vowed never to buy the advertised product.

## ▼ FEEDBACK

Once the consumer has decoded the marketing communication, he or she has the opportunity to respond to the source of the message. **Feedback** is a term used to describe the return of information from the receiver to the source. Typi-

> **Feedback** is the return of information from the receiver to the source.

cally, this exchange concerns the receiver's reaction to the message. Consumers can provide feedback to marketers in a number of ways—through their purchase decisions, by asking the marketer for additional information, or by complaining about the message, to name a few. In addition, marketers may solicit feedback from consumers by conducting research about their reactions to the message. Some forms of marketing communication provide routine channels for feedback. Direct mail and infomercials often provide a toll-free number to call for additional information, for example, and salespeople attempt to draw out a consumers' attitudes and feelings so that they can customize their presentation appropriately.

## FACT OR FICTION REVISITED

⦿ It is true that feedback can be either positive or negative in the marketing communication process.

# TWO PERSPECTIVES ON CONSUMERS

The information consumers gain from marketing communications provides much of the raw material for the behavioral processes we have discussed in Part 3 of this book. Consumers are motivated to examine marketing messages, and they apply perception and learning to gather and interpret the information they contain. They then use that information to form attitudes and make decisions about which products to purchase.

Two perspectives that characterize the effect of marketing communications on consumer behavior are the *hierarchy of effects* model and the *brand experience* perspective.

### ▼ THE HIERARCHY OF EFFECTS MODEL

Robert Lavidge and Gary Steiner developed the **hierarchy of effects model** to describe the steps consumers complete before they purchase a product.[3] The purpose of the model was to understand how consumers use advertising in their purchase processes. To achieve this purpose, Lavidge and Steiner broke down the purchase process into its component steps. By identifying the steps, they did a great service for advertising and consumer behavior researchers. Indeed, the hierarchy model provides the intellectual foundation for the consumer purchase activities introduced in Chapter 2 and developed throughout this book (Figure 15.4).

The hierarchy model describes seven steps in the purchase process: (1) unawareness, (2) awareness, (3) knowledge, (4) liking, (5) preference, (6) conviction, and (7) purchase. These steps can be grouped into three general processes: (1) gaining awareness and knowledge about a product, (2) developing an attitude toward the product, and (3) making a purchase decision. Awareness and knowl-

The **hierarchy of effects model** describes the seven steps consumers use to reach a purchase decision.

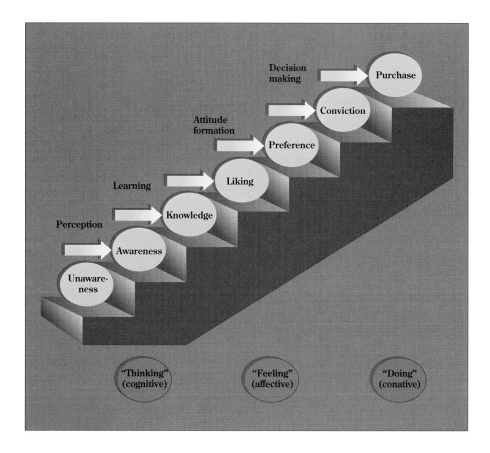

■ FIGURE 15.4
Stages in the hierarchy of effects model.

edge make up the *cognitive* or *thinking* component of purchase behavior; attitudes make up the *affective* or *feeling* component; and purchase is the *conative* or *action* component.

According to Lavidge and Steiner, all consumers proceed through the steps in the same order, but the speed with which they complete the steps may differ from person to person. Furthermore, individual differences among consumers mean that some people will never pass through all seven steps. For example, some people may never become aware that they can take a tour around the world on the QE2; others may be aware and knowledgeable about the opportunity and develop a positive attitude toward the cruise but not have the time or financial means to take it.

The hierarcy of effects model has been criticized by some researchers for assuming that consumers move in a linear fashion from thinking to feeling to action. In response, researchers have developed other models of the consumer purchase process which build on the same steps but arrange them in a different order or describe the transitions between steps in a different way.[4] For example, consumers may purchase some products without ever thinking much about them, such as a baseball cap or a T-shirt. A consumer may make such a low involvement purchase solely on the basis of reference group influences. Similarly, a consumer may initially buy a new soft drink because he or she likes its advertising. As we have dis-

■ FIGURE 15.5
Alternative hierarchies of
effects.

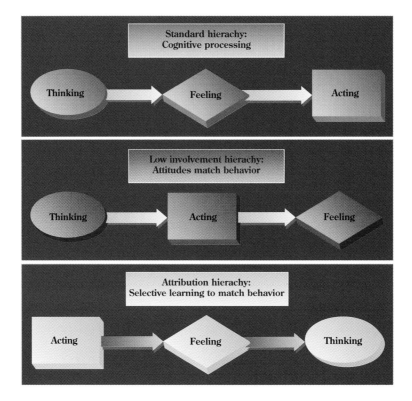

cussed in the comparison of high and low involvement purchase behavior in Chapter 13, consumers are more likely to think before feeling and acting in a high involvement purchase process, but they might first act and then evaluate their feelings when buying a low involvement product (Figure 15.5).

Regardless of the existence of different paths through the components of the purchase process, researchers agree that thought, feeling, and action do occur in consumer behavior. It follows that consumers have distinct communication needs and styles for each of these components, and marketers must match their messages and choice of media to these needs. For example, consumers may be more receptive to informative advertising when they are in the knowledge stage than when they are unaware. During this stage, consumers will actively seek additional information to use in developing attitudes to help make a purchase decision. By contrast, when they are unaware of a product—and perhaps even inattentive to their need for a product—they will be less observant of advertising and direct sales efforts. Most consumers may ignore a product like cold medications until they are not feeling well, at which time they tend to notice the overwhelming number of ads for cold and flu remedies. Of course, there are no more ads for these products than there were before; the consumer has just become more aware and attentive to the ads that do exist.

> The **brand experience perspective** acknowledges the complexity of the purchase process and the increasing volume of marketing communications targeted at consumers.

## ▼ THE BRAND EXPERIENCE PERSPECTIVE

The **brand experience perspective** acknowledges the complexity of the consumer purchase process and the increasing volume of marketing communications targeted at consumers today.[5] It also recognizes that consumers move back and forth among the component steps in the process. Therefore, consumers' thoughts and attitudes toward products and their purchase behavior are affected simultaneously by all different kinds of marketing communications (Figure 15.6).

Unlike the hierarchy of effects model, the brand experience perspective recognizes that the purchase process is not an orderly progression from cognition to affect to action. It also emphasizes the fact that consumers receive a flood of disarrayed information in many messages delivered through a variety of media, including advertisements, direct mail pieces, articles encouraged by publicity efforts, coupons, rebates, and displays, and sales presentations. These messages do not arrive in an orderly fashion, either. Instead, consumers receive the messages when the marketer transmits them, not when they

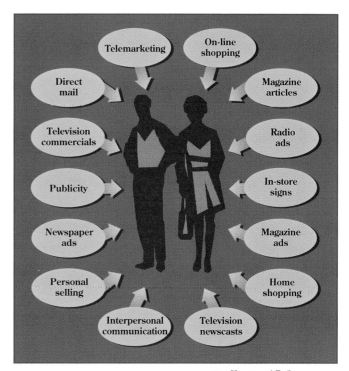

■ Figure 15.6
The brand experience perspective.

choose to receive them. As a result of the large influx of messages, some may provide conflicting information about a product. A consumer may see a print ad for a Cadillac which makes the driving experience seem luxurious and sophisticated on the same day that a newspaper ad announces new low lease rates on the same car. Or the consumer may receive detailed information at a time when he or she is just looking to identify alternatives. Later, when the consumer is ready to evaluate the alternatives seriously, he or she may struggle to retrieve the detailed information from long-term memory.

The brand experience perspective has been particularly well received by marketing and communications professionals developing integrated marketing communications programs. These programs seek to coordinate the different messages and media for a product so that the consumer will receive a coherent, consistent stream of information at the most appropriate time. Marketers who adopt the brand experience perspective make two key assumptions:

❶ Messages and media must be integrated so that consumers see a consistent set of marketing communications.
❷ Communications must afford feedback so that consumers can request information to use at the appropriate time in their own purchase process.

The combined insights of these two perspectives provide a realistic picture of how consumers receive marketing messages. The hierarchy of effects model correctly notes that consumers exhibit cognitive, affective, and conative behaviors. Its limitation is the assumption that these behaviors occur in strictly ordered steps during the purchase process. The brand experience perspective recognizes that consumers gather information, form attitudes, and make purchase decisions in varied sequences. It also acknowledges that consumers receive marketing messages through a disordered jumble of ads, editorial pieces, sales promotions, infomercials, and personal sales contacts, which do not necessarily correspond to a certain stage in the purchase process.

# INTEGRATED MARKETING COMMUNICATIONS

> **Integrated marketing communications** is used to coordinate the different messages and media for a product to provide a coherent, consistent stream of information.

As we mentioned earlier, **integrated marketing communications** is a more recent popular approach used by marketing and communications professionals to coordinate the many disparate experiences consumers have with the marketing communications for a particular brand.[6] Traditionally, organizational issues prevented such coordination. Marketers tended to use different communications specialists for each communications tool, and often coordination among these varied message encoders was lacking—advertising agencies create advertising; public relations firms secure editorial coverage of their products; and sales promotion agencies and the marketer's own personnel deliver promotional messages.

Today, many marketers recognize that consumer contacts with their communications efforts occur in a jumble. In response, integrated marketing communications programs seek to coordinate the different messages and media for a product so that consumers will receive a coherent, consistent stream of messages. It is important that each message arrive at the appropriate time—that is, when the consumer is ready to decode it for use in the purchase process. The use of multiple channels of communication is also advantageous for the consumer, who is able to learn from the medium with which he or she is most comfortable and to see and hear a variety of messages to prevent boredom. For example, Ragu promotes its pasta sauces in magazines and television ads; distributes coupons in free standing inserts (the glossy coupon circulars that are distributed in Sunday newspapers) and magazines; and operates a site on the World Wide Web.

The effects of integrated marketing communications are already prevalent, and the distinctions among media have been blurred. For example, an ad may provide information about a piece of direct mail consumers can expect to receive, or a coupon may be accompanied by a copy of the ad appearing in magazines. Furthermore, the idea of integrated marketing communications is not brand new; many traditional marketing communication tools mixed channels of communication, to a degree. Some early magazine advertisements included coupons that gave the consumer the opportunity to ask for more information, and salespeople have long known that telephone calls and notes are an effective follow-up to personal selling (Figure 15.7).

The four primary communications media marketers use to send messages are: (1) advertising, (2) direct response, (3) publicity, and (4) personal selling. The discussion below focuses on the role each medium plays in the purchase process.

■ FIGURE 15.7
Early magazine advertisements, dating back to the 1920s and 1930s, included coupons, giving the consumer an opportunity to ask for more product information, paving the way for today's integrated marketing communications.

## ▼ ADVERTISING

Consumers receive many advertising messages every day—in newspapers, magazines, radio, television, and place-based media. **Advertising** is defined as paid marketing communication delivered through mass media from marketers to consumers. The fact that marketers pay for this delivery often affects the credibility of the information in the minds of consumers.

> **Advertising** is paid marketing communication delivered through mass media from marketers to consumers.

■ FIGURE 15.8
This ad for Neutrogena HeatSafe incorporates positive impressions of satisfied customers.

Consumers use the information they gather from advertising in many of the steps in the purchase process. Specifically, consumers use advertising to learn about the alternatives available to them and to gather information to use in their evaluation. Some marketers try to affect the postpurchase evaluation of the consumption experience as well. For example, marketers often create advertising showing satisfied customers so that consumers will ascribe any potential problems that may occur to external causes rather than to the product itself (Figure 15.8).

The mass media component of advertising has its drawbacks, however. Because a mass media message must be general enough to be decoded and used by all of the consumers who make up the audience, the information may not address an individual's personal concerns. Furthermore, mass media are one-way channels of communication; accordingly, there is no opportunity for the consumer to provide immediate, direct feedback to the marketer.

▼ DIRECT RESPONSE

The **direct response** medium has two advantages—it delivers a message directly to the consumer, and it provides a method for the consumer to respond to that message. Many marketers use direct response media, such as direct mail, catalogs, telemarketing, direct selling, home shopping, and on-line shopping, to circumvent the limitations of mass media advertising noted above.

**Direct response** delivers a message directly from the marketer to the consumer and provides a method for the consumer to respond to the message.

## FACT OR FICTION REVISITED

⊛   Direct marketing *is not* a one-way channel of communication; it provides opportunities for feedback from customer to marketer as well as communication from marketer to consumer.

Direct response media allow the marketer to tailor the message to small segments or, in some cases, to each receiver. For example, the mailorder catalogs many people receive are often targeted at a focused segment of consumers defined by past purchases. These consumers can order from the direct marketing catalogs by returning a form or calling a toll-free number. Effective direct marketers use database management technology to record purchases; the data, in turn, are used to target consumers for additional catalogs appropriate to their purchase activities.

The feedback and tailored messages direct response affords mean that direct marketers can send specific messages to consumers at the appropriate point in the purchase process and that consumers can interact with the marketer and gain personalized information. Furthermore, the messages the consumer receives and the interaction he or she has with the marketer are more personally relevant because they reflect the consumer's purchase history. This personal relevance makes it easier for the consumer to use the perceptual and learning processes to decode the message, and it makes the incoming messages more motivating.

## FACT OR FICTION REVISITED

⊛   Messages received through direct marketing do in fact tend to have more personal relevance for consumers.

Two recent additions to direct response media, which we have discussed in the previous chapter, are interactive on-line shopping and home shopping, both of which allow two-way communication between the marketer and precisely defined consumer segments. Interactive on-line shopping, through commercial services or the Internet World Wide Web, enables consumers to provide immediate feedback to marketers and to search on-line for useful information. And, as we discuss in the following Pleasures of Consumption box, many consumers enjoy learning about products from infomercials, which have become quite prominent in the last several years.

### PLEASURES OF CONSUMPTION

#### 30-Second Ads Bore, 30-Minute Infomercials Entertain[7]

Infomercials are nothing more than long advertisements that run as programs on broadcast and cable television stations—most last 30 minutes, although some are even longer. These programs demonstrate a product and offer a toll-free 800-number consumers can call for additional information or to purchase the product. Just a few years ago, infomercials were predominantly produced by unknown marketers touting nontraditional products unavailable through any other distribution channel. However, the diet aids, baldness remedies, and miracle cleaners have given way to Fortune 500 companies that are using the extended time frame to provide detailed information about products that require high involvement and extensive decision making from consumers. General Motors produced an infomercial for its Saturn car line; Procter & Gamble used infomercials to advertise its denture adhesive Fixodent; and Apple used the medium to promote Performa, its low-cost Macintosh, to families contemplating buying their first home computer.

By 1994, infomercials accounted for about 25 percent of the programming on cable systems and produced nearly $1 billion dollars in direct sales. As their popularity has grown, new marketers have jumped on the bandwagon, producing shows that entertain as well as promote products. Kodak, for example, developed a movie preview infomercial promoting its products, and the Florida Citrus Commission sponsored an infomercial that combined elements of talk and cooking shows to tout the benefits of oranges and grapefruits. SmithKline Beecham broadcast *The Cable Snooze Network's Gooodnight Show,* containing a half-hour of comedy sketches airing at 3 A.M. to promote its Sominex sleep aid to the insomniacs likely to be watching at that hour.

Television broadcast and cable companies see a bright future in infomercials—so much so that they are creating new ways to expand the medium. One innovation is the Consumer Resource Network, a 24-hour infomercial network that began broadcasting in December 1994. Another is CBS Spot Plus+, a system developed by CBS and Gemstar Development, the creator of VCR+ technology. The system was created for marketers who broadcast their infomercials in the late night and early morning time slots. Marketers in the CBS Spot Plus+ program sponsor conventional 30-second commercials that advertise their infomercials followed by a 15-second spot that tells viewers the VCR+ code to use to program their VCRs to record the infomercial. The consumer can then watch the taped infomercial at a more convenient time.

Do you watch infomercials? Are infomercials more suitable for high involvement purchases than for low involvement ones? Why? Will consumers be able to gather information from infomercials that is not available through other media?

## ▼ PUBLICITY

A marketer's attempts to influence public opinion about its products through unpaid editorial settings is known as **publicity**. Press releases and stories and reviews about products that appear in magazines and newspapers and on television news programs are all forms of publicity. Examples include newspaper articles about personal finance that feature a writeup about the benefits offered by Quicken, a financial management program (Figure 15.9).

**Publicity** is unpaid communication about a product that appears within the editorial content of media.

Since publicity articles and reviews are unpaid, the marketer has little control over what is said about its product. Marketers will attempt to garner a favorable mention of their products, though, by providing the writers with information and opportunities to try the product. Good publicity can go a long way. Consumers recognize that the marketer has little control over the message and therefore view the information as more credible than paid marketing communications. Ac-

cordingly, a positive product review may increase a consumer's likelihood of buying the product. For example, a favorable airline article in a travel magazine or *Consumers' Report* may result in increased sales for top-rated airlines such as Midwest Express, Alaska Airlines, or Kiwi.

## FACT OR FICTION REVISITED

◉ Marketers *do not* have more control over what is said about their products in publicity; they have more control over the content of advertising.

**Personal selling** is interpersonal, two-way marketing communication between a paid salesperson and a consumer.

## ▼ PERSONAL SELLING

A particularly effective direct response medium is **personal selling**—interpersonal, two-way marketing communication between a paid salesperson and a consumer. Like all direct response media, personal selling is delivered to narrow consumer segments, often one customer at a time, and offers opportunities for consumer feedback. The retail shopping environment is the most prominent location for personal selling. Consumers encounter salespeople when they enter a Sears department store, a car dealership, or a specialty retailer, such as Circuit City or the Gap. Direct response marketers, such as Avon, rely on personal selling to deliver their marketing messages to consumers. Others rely on telemarketing—personal selling conducted over the phone—to communicate with those consumers who have responded to the initial direct marketing message.

The interpersonal nature of personal selling offers several benefits to the consumer. It enables the consumer to: (1) gather information about a product's attributes and benefits; (2) observe a demonstration of a product by a knowledgeable salesperson; and (3) interact with the salesperson to ensure that the sales presentation is tailored to the individual's needs. At the same time, consumers often question the credibility of the customized information they receive from a salesperson. Recall that the credibility of interpersonal communication is based on both the expertise and the objectivity of the source. Some salespeople possess expertise, but few are completely objective; after all, they represent the marketer.

# STRATEGIES FOR EFFECTIVE MARKETING COMMUNICATION

As the source of the marketing communications consumers use in the purchase process, marketers have one primary communications objective: to transmit messages consumers can decode when they need information. Obviously, the content of these messages is intended to be favorable to the marketer and its product.

Marketers employ two major strategies to achieve communication objectives—a *message strategy* and a *media strategy* (Figure 15.10). The message strategy addresses the content and form of the communication:

❶ The *communication content* is the information the marketer wants consumers to decode from the message.
❷ The *creative* strategy is the form the message takes.

The *media strategy* addresses the issue of which medium is to be used to deliver the message to the consumer:

❶ The *medium* is the channel used to deliver the message.

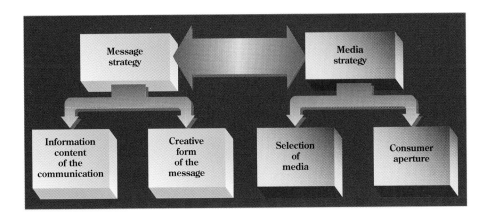

■ FIGURE 15.10
Components of a communication strategy.

❷ The *aperture* is the time and location the message is delivered to achieve its maximum impact.

## ▼ MESSAGE STRATEGY

Before the content and form of a message can be designed, the target market segment must be selected. As we discussed in Chapter 3, a target market is chosen because its members share background characteristics that result in the same behavioral processes and consumption behavior. Accordingly, the target market must be accessible to the communications efforts of the marketer. The marketer, in turn, creates and delivers a message that will elicit purchase and consumption behavior on the part of the members of the target market. For example, a perfume marketer may create a sexy advertisement that stimulates a particular target to recall the name of the fragrance. Members of this target segment are then more receptive to the personal selling efforts of the salespeople in stores that sell the product. That same ad may confuse or even offend some other target segments.

**Communication Content**   Marketers can have many communications objectives, each of which requires a different medium to deliver a certain message. Each objective addresses the needs of particular consumers who are at the same step in the purchase process and who therefore are likely to use information in the same way. For example, Coca-Cola may air a television commerical during Saturday morning cartoons to deliver a message to kids about the taste of Hi-C fruit drinks. That same marketer might run a print ad in *Good Housekeeping* magazine to inform parents about the product's nutritional value so that they will be receptive to their children's plea to buy it (Figure 15.11). At the same time, Coca-Cola may provide a coupon in the Sunday newspaper free standing insert (FSI) to give parents an added incentive to buy the product.

Obviously, communication content must be tailored to the consumer's information needs. When consumers are searching for alternatives, the marketer will want to make them aware of its product so they will include it in their evoked set; when they are evaluating alternatives, the marketer will want to provide informa-

■ FIGURE 15.11
Coca-Cola supplements this magazine ad for Hi-C fruit drinks with additional messages in different media, such as television advertisements during children's programming and coupons for the product in Sunday newspapers.

tion about the attributes and benefits of its product. The nature of the communication content will also depend on the type of product. A high involvement product that elicits extensive decision making effort, such as a Packard Bell multimedia computer, will require more technical information than a low involvement product that invokes routine decision making, such as a Snickers bar. People are more willing to exert the effort necessary to absorb technical information about a computer than involved nutritional information about a candy bar; accordingly, communication about the candy bar will emphasize simple benefits—it tastes good and provides a burst of energy.

**Creative Strategy**  Once the marketer has identified its target market and developed its communications objectives, it must create a message members of the target market will find appealing so that they will be motivated to decode and assimilate its content.[8] Marketers traditionally use two types of messages to appeal to consumers: (1) informational, or rational, and (2) emotional, or transformational.

*Informational appeals* attempt to transmit information about a product to the consumer to use in a rational purchase process. Print advertisements that contain detailed information about product features and attributes; publicity efforts that result in magazine articles containing facts and figures; and elaborate product presentations by salespeople are all used to convey rational appeals.

By contrast, *emotional,* or *transformational, appeals* attempt to evoke the emotions the consumer will experience using the product. Evocative television commercials and powerful salespersons are particularly effective at creating an emotional bond with a product, helping to transform the individual's consumption experience. For example, the United States Army tells young people "Be all that you can be," as it touts the self-actualization and patriotic benefits enlistment offers. The Army hopes that when the young recruit begins the enlistment process, he or she will recall the emotional response that was encoded in the ads and experience the same emotional response again.

Within these two broad categories of appeals are a number of different types of messages that employ creative strategies to deliver communications content:

**❶**  A *factual message* is a straightforward presentation about a product. The message presents the information consumers can use to form attitudes, choose evaluative criteria, and select a product. An ad for Rogaine describing the benefits of monoxidil in treating hair loss is an example of a factual message.

**❷**  *Comparative advertising* contains an explicit comparison among alternatives to demonstrate that the advertised product is superior. The message may offer an informal comparison—"New Kleenex Ultra. Three layers make it the softest"—or a more formal comparison of the attributes of each alternative.

**❸**  *Celebrity advertising* features a recognizable celebrity to attract consumer attention or to endorse a product. When celebrities, such as Michael Jordan, Charles Barkley, and Larry Bird, appear in a McDonald's ad, the message is more likely to rise above the consumer's perceptual thresholds than if the ad contained unknown actors. If a celebrity actually endorses a product's performance, he or she must have source credibility—that is, consumers must perceive the celebrity as objective and possessing some expertise that makes his or her opinion credible.

**❹**  *Fear appeals* portray a negative situation that can be solved by the advertised product. To be effective, the message must portray the situation in such a way that consumers recognize that the problem is solvable *and* perceive themselves as capable of using the product to solve it. In other words, the problem cannot be too negative, and the product's benefits must be clearly linked to its solution. Social marketers often employ fear appeals, such as the many drug abuse advertisements that portray the negative consequences of

**■ FIGURE 15.12**

Sex appeal is a popular form of advertising for many different types of products.

drug use and offer positive steps the consumer can take to avoid the situation.

❺ *Sex appeals* are often used in advertising because of their power to draw the attention of consumers to the message (Figure 15.12). Traditionally, such ads have featured women in order to appeal to men, but ads such as the Diet Coke campaign featuring the shirtless male construction worker have grown in popularity. To be successful, however, the sexual imagery in these ads must not distract the consumer's attention away from the content of the message.

❻ *Humor* is often used in conjunction with other types of creative executions to attract attention or increase a positive attitude-toward-the-ad so that the consumer will develop a more favorable attitude toward the product. Humor is subjective, however, varying significantly across cultures; if consumers do not recognize the humor, the ad will not be successful. Also, whereas successful humor is likely to draw a lot of attention, the marketer runs the risk of the humor's distracting consumers from focusing on the communication content and inhibiting their learning.

## FACT OR FICTION REVISITED

◉    Advertising can in fact change the experience of using the advertised brand; this is precisely what transformation advertising does.

**Is Content or Creativity Most Important?**    As you can see, consumers are influenced by both the information content and the creative form of the messages they receive. The question is, which has the greatest impact on the behavioral processes consumers use to complete the purchase activities? The **elaboration likelihood model (ELM)** is one attempt to answer this question.[9] The model asserts that a marketer has two possible routes to persuasion, and the choice depends on the consumer's level of involvement with the purchase process:

❶    Advertising will invoke a *central route to persuasion* when consumers are highly involved and devote significant effort to perceive and learn the available information. In this case, consumers are motivated to integrate the new information with existing knowledge stored in their long-term memories and will use this integrated knowledge to develop new attitudes or strengthen existing attitudes. In this case, the marketer would be wise to emphasize the

---

The **elaboration likelihood model (ELM)** asserts that consumers change attitudes through two distinct routes: (1) a central route, or (2) a peripheral route.

content of the messages because consumers will exert the cognitive effort necessary to process the information.

❷ Advertising will elicit the *peripheral route to persuasion* if the product elicits a low level of involvement from consumers. In this case, consumers are not stimulated to devote significant effort to perceive and learn product information and are more likely to permit the creative form of the ad—the type of appeal, the music, visuals, and tone of the ad—to influence their attitudes toward the product. These attitudes are not strongly held, however, because the consumer has not processed the information necessary to change the knowledge embedded in his or her long-term memory. When choosing the peripheral route, the marketer emphasizes the creative elements of an ad over information, as we saw in our discussion of soft drinks in Chapter 13.

### ▼ MEDIA STRATEGY

When planning a media strategy, the marketer must consider two factors: (1) the medium used to deliver the message, and (2) the time and location the message will be delivered to have maximum impact. We considered the first factor—various types of media—in our discussion of integrated marketing communications earlier in the chapter. Obviously, the choice of media depends on their ability to deliver messages at particular times and locations.

**The Aperture** The **aperture** is a term used to describe the time and location at which the consumer requires access to product information.[10] Earlier we mentioned the frustration consumers feel when they cannot find the information they want or when they are inundated with unwanted messages. Because consumers move back and forth among the steps in the purchase process and proceed through them at different paces, marketers face a daunting task: They want consumers to have the information they want, when they want it, but customized marketing communications are a difficult and expensive option. Instead, marketers use three complimentary approaches to provide information to consumers when they want it:

> **Aperture** is the time and location at which a message will be delivered for maximum impact.

❶ Marketers attempt to maximize the effectiveness of their mass media efforts to reach consumers during the aperture by conducting extensive consumer research to understand the purchase process and then delivering messages at the time when consumers can best use it. For example, many movie companies advertise their films on Thursday nights to reach consumers before they make their weekend plans. The most obvious examples are the seasonal patterns of advertising. Kingsford advertises charcoal primarily during the summer barbecue season, for instance.

❷ Marketers are increasingly utilizing integrated marketing communications to provide consumers with many kinds of messages, each at the appropriate point in the purchase processes. The idea is to build on the effective use of mass media to reach consumers in as many ways as possible. For example, marketers who use sports celebrities in advertising also plan publicity efforts to encourage sportscasters to mention the ads during the nightly news or the coverage of sporting events.

❸ Marketers use direct marketing tools to individualize their communications efforts and tailor their message to address consumers' needs. Direct marketing also enables consumers to provide feedback to marketers so they can further refine the information they disseminate. For example, Schering promotes its Claritin prescription allergy medication through direct mail pieces that are delivered shortly before the peak allergy season in each consumer's geographical area.

# PUBLIC POLICY AND MARKETING COMMUNICATIONS

Public policy actors have expressed concern about the *fairness* of the messages that are transmitted through marketing communications and the *equity* with which marketers transmit marketing communications. The issue of fairness concerns whether the content of a message accurately conveys information to consumers; equity addresses the choices marketers make regarding the targets of their marketing communications.

## ▼ FAIRNESS

Public policy actors rightfully expect marketing communications to be fair to consumers and to provide unbiased, truthful information. Many feel that marketers

### FACT OR FICTION REVISITED

⦿ The key difference between fair and unfair marketing communication is in fact deception.

have failed to meet those criteria, however, and list *deception* as the key offense. Objective claims made in an ad or a salesperson's pitch must be true—an ad cannot say that a car gets 50 miles to the gallon when it really only gets 20.

The content of the message is not the only issue—the creative form of the message should not be deceptive either. Consumers must decode the messages transmitted to them, and sometimes a message is constructed in such a way that it can be easily misinterpreted. Sometimes misinterpretations occur as a result of the consumer's background characteristics or perceptual and learning processes. A small child might mistakenly perceive that a toy is powered to be able to fly if it is shown flying through the air in an advertisement, but an adult would correctly recognize the creative setting of the ad. The Public Policy box that follows examines some marketing communications that could deceive even reasonable adults.

## PUBLIC POLICY

### Was That an Ad?[11]

Marketers often come under fire for skirting the line that separates marketing communications from editorial content. Consumers typically use the source of a message as a cue to help them interpret the information they gather from their environment. Most consumers are able to distinguish between television newscasts and magazine columns and the ads that appear in those media, but it is becoming more difficult to do so. Many local newscasts broadcast video press releases produced by advertisers without telling viewers that the station's own reporters had nothing to do with the segment. For example, Frito-Lay produced a video showing an ad for Dorito Tortilla Thins, an interview with its star Chevy Chase, and a description of how the ad was made. The interview segment was edited so that the local stations' own newscasters could read the questions Chase answered. Similarly, L.A. Gear produced a video release of a reenactment of a nighttime search for a lost child who was found by rescuers who followed the glow of her L.A. Twilights sneakers. The reenactment was broadcast nationally as a news story.

Walt Disney Studios has developed *Movie News*, a series of advertisements featuring an anchor "reporting" on several Disney films. The ads look like traditional newscast movie reviews and are broadcast during the last segments of local news shows. In the last 5 seconds of the 60-second spots a tiny credit line appears noting that the segment is a paid ad. Similarly, Mirage Resorts created a *Treasure Island: The Adventure Begins . . .* series chronicling a boy's vacation at the Treasure Island Casino and Resort in Las Vegas. Mirage purchased an hour of evening prime time on NBC to broadcast the show, which also features ads for Coca-Cola and the Las Vegas Visitor and Convention Authority but does not identify Mirage as the sponsor.

The blurring of marketing communications and content occurs in other contexts as well. Magazines, such as *Sun,* sponsored by Ray-Ban sunglasses, *Know How,* a women's magazine sponsored by General Motors, and *Your Body & Your Health,* produced by Jenny Craig, are all sold nationally at newsstands. Some video games include product placements, such as the Adidas logo that appears throughout *FIFA International Soccer* and the 7-Up signs that are prominent in the *Formula One Grand Prix* game.

Do you consider these examples of deceptive marketing communications? What cues could a reasonable consumer use to interpret the credibility of the source of such messages? Should these kinds of communications be regulated? Why or why not?

## ▼ EQUITY

*Equity* refers to both the selection of target markets for an "undesirable" product and the exclusion of some consumers from the target market for a "desirable" product. For example, marketers of cigarettes and alcohol have been criticized for the messages they deliver to some demographic groups. As a result, Anheuser-Busch stopped using Spuds MacKenzie, the "party animal," in Bud Light advertising in response to criticism that the dog was attractive to children. And, as we have noted in Chapter 3, banks and other financial institutions are often criticized for denying certain groups access to mortgages.

The public policy debate about most equity decisions juxtaposes the marketer's use of profit as its primary criterion for selecting target market segments with the larger societal concern about equal access to marketing communications and product offerings. The debate can be compared to the mirror controversy we discussed in Chapter 8: Marketers maintain that they target segments that will be satisfied by the products they produce and that they neither create needs among consumers nor exclude any segment that would allow them to make a profit. Many public policy actors argue that there should be a higher standard—*no* segment should be vulnerable to exploitation, through either selection (as a target for products that have clear risks) or exclusion (from information about products that provide benefits). Balancing the broad social needs of those who are exploited by such marketing practices as well as the larger society with the narrower concerns of marketers is a tough public policy and ethical dilemma indeed.

# MARKETING COMMUNICATION

Bill Baker is the target of many marketing communications efforts. He reads magazine and newspaper ads, watches television commercials, interacts with salespeople, and receives direct mail. Bill has strong opinions about which media he likes best—ads are fine, but he's pretty suspicious of most salespeople and does not like "junk mail" at all. He is particularly receptive to good television commercials and bought his motorcycle and golf clubs after seeing them advertised on TV.

Bill's experiences illustrate many of the key issues in marketing communications. Consumers receive countless messages from many marketing sources through different media. Some are welcomed because they are relevant to the consumer's concerns; others are ignored or rejected because they are unrelated to the consumer's activities. Furthermore, consumers make judgments about the messages, the retailers, and the products being advertised. Marketers, in turn, devise message and media strategies that enable effective communication with the consumers in their target markets. Interpersonal communications with friends and acquaintances are also an important source of marketing information, as we noted in Bill's description of his initial contact with the Sound Track stereo store. We consider interpersonal communication in more detail in the next chapter.

# SUMMARY

1. **Understand the communication process.** Communication is the transmission of a message from a source through a medium to a receiver. In the case of marketing communications, the source is the marketer, who encodes information into a message designed to persuade consumers to buy its product. The message—which consists of both the content of the information and its physical form—is delivered via a communications medium. The consumer is the receiver, who decodes the message to extract its

information content. Finally, the consumer may use feedback to relay to the marketer information about his or her reaction to the message.

2. **Analyze the effects of marketing communications on consumers.** Two perspectives characterize how consumers receive marketing messages and use them in the purchase process. The hierarchy of effects model provides a description of the seven steps consumers employ to reach a purchase decision: (1) unawareness, (2) awareness, (3) knowledge, (4) liking, (5) preference, (6) conviction, and (7) purchase. The steps reflect the presence of thought, feeling, and action in all consumer behavior. The brand experience perspective recognizes that consumers move back and forth among the steps and that their attitudes toward products are affected simultaneously by many different kinds of marketing communications. Because consumers must integrate the numerous messages they receive, marketers need to coordinate their communications efforts through an integrated marketing communications strategy.

3. **Recognize the methods marketers employ to communicate information about their products to consumers.** Integrated marketing communications programs seek to coordinate the various messages and media for a product so that consumers receive a coherent, consistent stream of messages at the time that they are ready to decode and use it. The major communications media marketers use to send messages are: (1) advertising, (2) direct response, (3) publicity, and (4) personal selling.

4. **Identify the strategies that guide a marketer's communications efforts.** Marketers have developed two strategies to achieve communication objectives—the message strategy and the media strategy. The message strategy addresses the information content and the creative form of the communication, both of which must be appropriate to the consumer's level of involvement with the purchase. More information and a central route to persuasion are appropriate for high involvement purchases, whereas less detailed information and a peripheral route to persuasion are appropriate for low involvement purchases. The media strategy addresses which media are to be used to deliver the message to the consumer as well as the aperture of the message—when and where the message can be delivered for maximum impact.

5. **Appreciate the concerns public policy actors have about marketing communications.** Public policy actors have expressed concern about the fairness of the messages that are transmitted and the equity with which marketers transmit marketing communications. Marketing communication should be both fair to consumers—it should provide unbiased, truthful information—and equitable—it should provide equal access for all consumer segments.

---

# KEY TERMS

Marketing communication, *p. 427*

Communication, *p. 427*

Source, *p. 428*

Source credibility, *p. 429*

Message, *p. 429*

Medium, *p. 429*

Receiver, *p. 431*

Feedback, *p. 431*

Hierarchy of effects model, *p. 432*

Brand experience perspective, *p. 434*

Integrated marketing communications, *p. 436*

Advertising, *p. 437*

Direct response, *p. 438*

Publicity, *p. 440*

Personal selling, *p. 442*

Elaboration likelihood model (ELM), *p. 446*

Aperture, *p. 447*

# SKILL-BUILDING ACTIVITIES

Locate a print ad for a product that you use or may consider purchasing. With respect to that specific ad:

1. Who is the source of the ad?
2. What is the message?
3. How is the message encoded?
4. What is the medium? Be specific.
5. Who are the intended receivers?
6. Can these receivers decode the message incorrectly? If so, how? Is the incorrect decoding intended or unintended?
7. How can the receivers of this advertisement provide feedback?
8. Where does this message fit into the hierarchy of effects?
9. What other brand contacts will receivers of this message receive?
10. Assume that this message is part of an integrated marketing communication program. What are the other elements of that program?
11. What is the creative strategy of the advertisement?
12. What is the brand's media strategy?
13. Is the advertisement informational or transformational or both? Explain.
14. What fairness issues might this advertisement create?
15. What equity issues might it create?
16. How might these issues be resolved in the best interest of consumers?

# CHAPTER 15 SELF-TEST

## ▼ MULTIPLE CHOICE

1. When a marketer translates advertisement copy into a foreign language so that the ad can be run in another country, _____ is taking place.
   a. decoding
   b. encoding
   c. message development
   d. media selection

2. Spoken and written words are forms of _____ communication, while pictures and images are forms of _____ communication.
   a. marketing; promotional
   b. verbal; visual
   c. modified; basic
   d. basic; promotional

3. Magazines, television, and in-store displays are all forms of communication _____ .
   a. media
   b. sources
   c. feedback
   d. decoding mechanisms

4. The three components of the hierarchy of effects model are the cognitive/thinking components, the action/conative component, and the _____ component.
   a. purchase/payment
   b. search
   c. evaluation
   d. feeling/affect

5. _____ programs seek to coordinate the different messages and media for a product so that the consumer receives a consistent stream of messages.
   a. Integrated marketing communication
   b. All marketing mix
   c. Consolidated marketing
   d. New product advertising

6. The four types of marketing communication media are advertising, direct response, publicity, and _____ .
   a. price
   b. marketing channels
   c. television
   d. personal selling

7. Paid marketing communication delivered through mass media from marketers to consumers is called _____ .
   a. promotion
   b. advertising
   c. publicity
   d. public relations

8. Marketers have the least control over _____ marketing communication media.
   a. advertising
   c. publicity
   b. direct response
   d. telemarketing
9. A/n _____ includes the time and location at which the consumer requires product information.
   a. aperture
   c. media address
   b. transmission
   d. target address
10. _____ would be most conducive to the use of a central route of persuasion.
   a. Mascara
   c. Hershey's chocolate
   b. Medical care
   d. Greeting cards

▼ TRUE/FALSE

1. An objective of marketing communication might be to influence a consumer's post-purchase evaluation of a product.   T or F
2. A disadvantage of visual communication is that it does not have an immediate impact.   T or F
3. The receiver of marketing communication is always the end user of the product.   T or F
4. Consumers are more likely to follow the hierarchy of cognition, affect, and then action when purchasing a high involvement product.   T or F
5. The brand experience perspective reflects the fact that marketing communication is often provided to consumers in many forms, and that information may or may not be applicable to the consumer's decision making stage.   T or F
6. Consumers only utilize information collected from advertising during the search stage of the decision making process.   T or F
7. Before a message is created, the marketer must select a target segment.   T or F
8. Marketers use a peripheral route to persuasion when marketing a high involvement product.   T or F
9. Advertising deceptiveness only occurs within the content component of a message.   T or F
10. Equity within marketing communication refers to both the selection of a target market for an "undesirable product" and the exclusion of some consumers from the target of a "desirable product."   T or F

▼ SHORT ANSWER

1. Describe how consumers utilize marketing communication during the purchase process.
2. Outline the communication process.
3. Describe the ways consumers provide feedback to marketers.

▼ APPLICATION EXERCISE

You are responsible for developing a new advertising campaign for a company that markets backpacks used by college students. The president and the vice presidents are unsure whether a factual, fear, or sex appeal should be used. Your job is to recommend one of those appeals as the basis of the new campaign.

# INTERPERSONAL COMMUNICATION AND OPINION LEADERSHIP

◉ Consumer Snapshot  *Fran Spiegel is a 26-year-old Senior Development Officer for the Newark Public Library. She lives in New Milford, New Jersey, with her husband, Eliot.*

## FACT OR FICTION

◉   In interpersonal communication, credibility results from expertise and objectivity.

◉   People are more likely to seek advice from members of their aspiration groups than members of their positive reference groups.

◉   Consumers use interpersonal communication to reduce perceived risk.

    ◉   Opinion leaders usually gather their information from the mass media rather than from other consumers.

    ◉   A person who is an opinion leader about one product is likely to be an opinion leader about many other products as well.

    ◉   Marketers can do little to influence word-of-mouth communication and reduce unfavorable communication.

# EYE ON THE CONSUMER

Fran Spiegel loves music—all kinds of music: rock and roll, hard rock, southern rock, Neil Young, Led Zeppelin, folk music, the acoustical, singer–songwriter stuff, classical, new age, even movie sound tracks. Her stereo and her CD collection are Fran's most prized possessions. She says she could do without her television, her VCR, even her car—but she needs her music. Fran listens to her favorites on CD and only plays the radio when she's driving in the car and has no other choice. Even then, she flips through all six of the preset buttons to see what each station is playing before going back to the one she likes best.

Fran and her husband, Eliot, own a CD player that allows them to play five disks at once, but Fran is the one who chooses what they play. Even her friends have no influence on what she listens to—instead, she tends to influence her friends' musical tastes. Fran recommends songs and artists she thinks her friends will like; sometimes she makes tapes and gives them to her friends so that they can listen to the artists she recommends. She admits that her musical creativity lies solely in her selection of music for herself, her husband, and her friends. She has tried to play a number of musical instruments over the years but has never been very good at any of them.

Whereas Fran is very opinionated about her music, she is happy to take advice from her family and friends in other areas of her life. For instance, a few years ago, she felt she was being too sedentary, and she was gaining weight, so she joined the gym her friend recommended and has been working out regularly ever since. When Fran has to make a large purchase she asks other people what they have bought and checks *Consumer Reports*. She doesn't think advertising influences her large purchases, but sometimes it does affect smaller ones. She bought a new liquid Comet cleanser after Eliot saw an appealing ad for it, for example.

Interpersonal communication is indeed a powerful force in consumer behavior. Like Fran, you probably talk with your friends, family, acquaintances, and strangers about the products you buy and use. You ask the people around you about their experiences with products when you are searching for alternatives and evaluating them. You talk with people both in and out of your reference groups about satisfying experiences, and you complain about the unsatisfying ones. You talk with the people you know, and some of them may refer you to people that *they* know. You talk with experts experienced with the kind of products you intend to buy, and you talk with people who are *not* experts because their needs might be more like yours. All of these forms of interpersonal communication play a vital role in your purchase behavior, and you, in turn, provide the same resource to others.

After reading and thinking about this chapter, you should be able to:

1. Determine the role interpersonal communication plays in the consumer purchase processes.
2. Analyze the characteristics of word-of-mouth communication.
3. Examine opinion leaders who provide information to consumers for a particular purchase.
4. Identify the ways in which marketers capitalize on interpersonal communication in their marketing efforts.

# INTERPERSONAL COMMUNICATION

From the time a person recognizes a need until the end of the consumption process, consumer behavior operates within an interpersonal network of friends, family, acquaintances, and strangers. Consumers are able to identify a set of people who will know something about the alternatives they should consider for any given need. You may have friends like Fran who know a lot about music, or others who know about cars or where to go in Florida for spring break. You may even know someone who can get a new winter coat for you "at a good price."

Consumers rely on two primary forms of communication to help them complete the purchase process. The first is *marketing communication,* which we addressed in the previous chapter. The second, and the topic of this chapter, is **interpersonal communication**—the informal, two-way exchange of information and influence among individuals. We ascribe the same components to interpersonal communication as apply to marketing communication—source, message, medium, receiver, and feedback. The difference is the context: Interpersonal communication occurs among individual consumers rather than between marketers and consumers.

> **Interpersonal communication** is the informal two-way exchange of information and influence among individuals.

# WORD-OF-MOUTH COMMUNICATION

> **Word-of-mouth communication** is informal communication among consumers about products.

Any informal communication among consumers about products that will satisfy their needs is known as **word-of-mouth communication**.[1] It is important to recognize that word-of-mouth communication is a *relational* concept—that is, it involves an *informal* relationship among two or more consumers. Word-of-mouth communication may differ from situation to situation, depending on the following circumstances: (1) the information content of the communication, (2) the receiver's purpose in gathering information, (3) the source's purpose in providing information, (4) the source's credibility, (5) the source's evaluation of the product, (6) the type of communication partner, and (7) the type of product.

## ▼ INFORMATION CONTENT

The information content of interpersonal communication can be classified into three broad types: (1) product news, (2) advice, and (3) personal experience. *Product news* is any information about products and their attributes that consumers gather during their search for information. Consumers solicit product news when they recognize a need and attempt to identify alternatives that may satisfy it. They then use this information to select their own evaluative criteria, which they apply in the form of decision rules. When you ask a friend whether she knows of any local health clubs that offer short-term memberships so that you can join for the school year you are gathering product news.

Advice and personal experience reflect the attitudes and decision making processes of the communication source. Consumers incorporate into their own purchase processes the attitudes, evaluative criteria, and decision rules of the sources they turn to for information. When people give *advice,* they are offering a statement of their personal attitudes toward the alternatives and their attributes. For example, your friend may tell you that the university health club has the best trainers of any club in town because that is her personal preference.

*Personal experience* reflects the product usage experiences of communications partners. People may supplement their decision processes with the personal experiences of their communication sources, or they may rely on the personal experiences of others as the only experiential input for products they have never used before. For example, recall our discussion in Chapter 12 of the extensive decision making process involved in buying a new, high involvement product, such as a washing machine. A person who has never had to buy a new washing machine before will have recent personal experience with just one alternative—the machine that broke down. Therefore, the experiences of other consumers will be a useful supplement to his or her own.

## ▼ THE RECEIVER'S PURPOSE

The receiver's *purpose* in word-of-mouth communication is to collect the information necessary to make a purchase decision. Gathering product news, advice, and personal experiences from others has two advantages. First, it helps *reduce the level of cognitive effort* the consumer must expend to gather and evaluate information. Information is often impacted—that is, it is distributed unevenly among consumers in a social environment. Some consumers are more involved with a particular product category than others and, consequently, have greater levels of knowledge and recent experience with the category. Less involved consumers can reduce the effort necessary to make their product choice by obtaining information from the more involved consumers. For example, when Fran's friends want to buy CDs, they talk with her rather than trying to listen to a variety of potential artists and reading hundreds of record reviews.

The second advantage of referring to others for knowledge, advice, or experience, is that it *reduces the uncertainty* of making the right choice. Most people prefer to have enough information to feel certain that they have chosen the right product to satisfy their needs. This is particularly true for high involvement products. Consumers are particularly likely to turn to experts and members of their positive reference groups for this purpose. Experts are able to apply their product knowledge to help the consumer feel more certain about the decision, and reference groups boost the consumer's confidence about making a socially appropriate choice.

## ▼ THE SOURCE'S PURPOSE

Different people provide information to their friends and acquaintances for different reasons. People who are very involved in a product category may simply enjoy talking about it; interpersonal communication gives them the opportunity to discuss their interests, provide product news, express their opinions, or talk about their experiences. Fran loves to talk about music, for example, and she enjoys making tapes for her friends so they can hear new artists she recommends. Others may experience a feeling of altruism by providing assistance, or they may feel powerful or competent when other people come to them for advice. Still others may have their own reasons for recommending a particular purchase. They may want to try a new product only after someone else buys it first, or they may be seeking to confirm their own purchase decision by enlisting others as users. Some people may give their opinion about a product with which they are dissatisfied in order to seize the opportunity to complain about it.

## ▼ SOURCE CREDIBILITY

As we mentioned in the previous chapter, *source credibility* is the belief that a communication source provides accurate and unbiased information. Credibility results from expertise and objectivity. People gain *expertise* in a product area through knowledge, training, and experience. For example, you probably think of your auto mechanic as a more credible source of information about cars than your uncle who lives in New York City and hasn't owned a car in 20 years. *Objectivity* is an equally important component of credibility. People want the sources they turn to to provide information for their benefit, not for the source's own profit. For example, if you think your brother only referred you to the Columbia House of Music to collect the six free CDs he gets for a referral, his credibility will probably decrease. That is why many consumers are skeptical of salespersons or celebrities who appear in advertisements—these individuals are paid to provide information to consumers (Figure 16.1); consumers therefore consider the information they provide marketing communication, not interpersonal communication.

### FACT OR FICTION REVISITED

⦿ Credibility in interpersonal communication does in fact result from expertise and objectivity.

■  FIGURE 16.1
Many consumers are skeptical of spokespersons, like Pat Riley, who are paid to promote products about which they are not experts.

▼  SOURCE EVALUATION: COMPLAINT VERSUS PRAISE
Word-of-mouth communication can be either positive or negative. Consider the number of times you asked others for their opinions about a product or service, and they complained that it didn't satisfy their needs.[2] People are more likely to complain about a product when it is highly involving—the product has great relevance for them—or when they are still not satisfied after voicing a direct complaint to the marketer—they are seeking another outlet for their dissatisfaction.

Complaints tend to be more influential than positive word-of-mouth. As we discussed in Chapter 14, marketers recognize that complaints are a significant problem and have instituted procedures such as toll-free telephone lines and customer surveys to give consumers an opportunity to complain directly to them. Sometimes, as we see in the Pleasures of Consumption box that follows, marketers are able to combat negative word-of-mouth by creating pleasant experiences.

## PLEASURES OF CONSUMPTION

### Saturn Dealers Treat Customers Right[3]

In designing and introducing the Saturn car line, General Motors made a radical break with traditional car manufacturing and marketing. The cars were designed with high-quality goals in mind and are built in a new factory by extensively trained workers who have the freedom to stop the assembly line any time to fix defects. Saturn cars are sold at listed prices, with no room for negotiation, and salespeople are trained to use a subdued, information-based approach when talking to customers. As a result, Saturn hopes to supplement its extensive advertising program with favorable publicity and word-of-mouth about the cars' benefits.

Shortly after Saturn introduced its line of cars in late 1990, the marketer faced two potential public relations disasters. Nearly 25 percent of the first 4000 cars the automaker produced had a faulty seat recliner mechanism. Acting immediately, Saturn sent overnight air express letters to *all* Saturn owners. Those whose cars had the defect were advised to return them for repair; the other 3000 were reassured that they did not have to worry. In addition, Saturn's advertising agency produced a television commercial featuring a repairman delivering and installing a replacement seat for an owner in a remote Alaskan location. About 3 months later, another 2000 Saturns were found to have defective radiator coolant. Saturn immediately *replaced the cars* to reassure owners that they would have no further problems.

In August 1993 another recall was announced; this time all 380,000 Saturns were recalled for potentially dangerous electrical problems that had caused about 30 car fires. Saturn dealers extended business hours and hired extra personnel to accommodate all the owners who returned their cars. To minimize any inconvenience, some Saturn dealers served food and beverages during the 25-minute repair and provided free car washes; others arranged door-to-door pickups at their customers' homes or workplaces. Some dealers even held day-long barbecues for their customers while their cars were being fixed; still others offered to take their customers to movies or sporting events as repairs were completed.

What do you think the typical owner thought of Saturn's efforts to deal with these problems? Were owners likely to blame the carmaker for the defects? Would the treatment they received from the company and its dealers discourage negative word-of-mouth? Might it encourage the owners to praise the treatment they received when talking with friends and acquaintances?

## ▼ TYPE OF COMMUNICATION PARTNER

Communication partners can come from a wide variety of settings. Consumers may seek information from members of *positive reference groups* because they

■  FIGURE 16.2

College students often seek advice about music from their friends, who comprise a positive membership group.

want to choose the same products as the members in order to gain approval. Following the advice of these members helps ensure that the consumer continues to be a part of a positive membership group; in some cases, it helps the consumer gain entry into a positive aspirational group to which he or she *wants* to belong (Figure 16.2).

Consumers may also gather information from people who are *not* in their positive reference groups. Sometimes the information a consumer needs is not available from friends; only other individuals who are *different* from them can provide the necessary information. This is likely for products that do not typically elicit high involvement from the members of a consumer's own reference groups. If you are looking for a CD of Broadway show tunes to give your grandmother for her birthday, for example, you might ask your friends to ask their grandparents for advice. The advantage of this type of link between distinct social groups is known as the *strength of weak ties*.[4] That is, weak ties link two distinct social groups that do not have significant overlap among their members.

### FACT OR FICTION REVISITED

◉ People *are not* more likely to seek advice from members of their aspiration groups because they have little in-person contact with them.

### ▼ TYPE OF PRODUCT

Word-of-mouth communication is affected by the nature of the consumer's needs as well as the types of products that will satisfy those needs (Table 16.1):

❶ Consumers need information and advice from credible sources when they are considering the purchase of a product that is *new* to them. The consumer is unlikely to have the necessary knowledge or experience with the product and will likely turn to highly involved consumers with whom he or she has direct contact. The consumer may identify people who always seem to know the latest musical groups or who are up on the latest computer technology or electronics equipment. Often the experts in one area are not experts in another, however.

❷ People are more likely to seek word-of-mouth communication about a *technically complex* product. In this case, the consumer is seeking explanatory information, advice about the product's attributes and their associated benefits, or

**Table 16.1**

## RELATIONSHIP BETWEEN TYPE OF PRODUCT AND OTHER WORD-OF-MOUTH COMMUNICATION CHARACTERISTICS

|  | New | Technically Complex | Risky | Visible Consumption Setting |
|---|---|---|---|---|
| Examples | Any product that is new to the receiver | Computers High-tech products | Personal care and appearance products Course selections Job opportunities Financial decisions | Clothing and fashion Entertainment |
| Most important types of communication content | Experiences Product news | Product news Advice | Advice Experiences | Experiences |
| Receiver's purpose | Reduce cognitive effort | Reduce cognitive effort and uncertainty | Reduce uncertainty | Reduce uncertainty |
| Type of partner | Highly involved sources from positive membership groups | Personal link or weak ties to any highly involved expert source of information | Members of positive membership or aspirational groups | Members of positive membership or aspirational groups |

any experiences others have had with the product. For example, before buying a computer, you may ask friends and acquaintances who are highly knowledgeable about computers about the features they find most useful.

❸ People are more likely to seek information when they *perceive risk* from using a product. People look for experts who can help them estimate the risks involved in making a certain purchase, and they consult with others like them who can reassure them that their product experience has been successful. For example, when debating between buying or leasing a new Saturn, you may ask your financially savvy friends about which option is better.

❹ People are more likely to seek information from members of their positive reference groups about products they use in *visible settings*. For example, you may want to make sure that you wear the same style of clothing as your friends or the members of a fraternity or sorority you hope to join.

### FACT OR FICTION REVISITED

◉ Consumers do in fact use interpersonal communication to reduce perceived risk.

# THEORIES OF THE FLOW OF COMMUNICATION

Sociologists who first studied word-of-mouth communication sought to understand the relative importance of *opinion leaders*, first described as the elite individuals in a community who provide guidance to the rest of the members. This view of opinion leaders supported a **two-step flow of communication**, the first step being the flow of information from the mass media to the opinion leaders, and the second step being the flow of information from the opinion leaders to the masses.[5]

> The **two-step flow of communication** theory posits that communication from mass media to consumers is mediated by opinion leaders who interpret the information.

## ▼ THE TWO-STEP THEORY OF COMMUNICATION

The most attractive contribution of the two-step theory was its assertion that word-of-mouth communication blunts the impact of mass media on the consumers who comprise the mass market. At the time, people feared that mass media would create an authoritarian society in which political figures and marketers would take advantage of its powerful influence to dominate public opinion. The two-step model helped alleviate these fears by maintaining that opinion leaders gather and interpret information from the mass media and forward it to other consumers; that is, opinion leaders stand between the media and the average consumer (Figure 16.3).

Over time, however, it became evident that the two-step theory is not an accurate description of the way consumers actually acquire information to use in their purchase activities, for the following reasons:

❶ *Opinion leaders are not a permanent elite.* Opinion leaders vary from product to product. An expert in one product area may not have the knowledge, training, and experience required to be an expert in another area. You may look to one of your friends for information about computers, but you may refer to your brother for advice about cars. Furthermore, different social groups have different opinion leaders. In your reference group, there may be certain people who set the fashion trends you follow, but other students on your campus may look to different people for advice about clothing.

■ FIGURE 16.3
The two-step theory of communication.

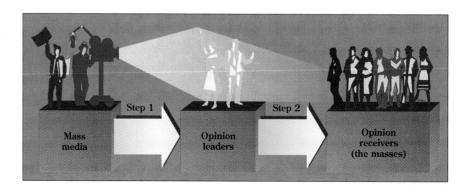

Mass media — Step 1 → Opinion leaders — Step 2 → Opinion receivers (the masses)

❷ *Information does not flow one way between opinion leaders and receivers.* Instead, both parties exchange information. Furthermore, opinion leaders are not the sole source of product information. Opinion leaders accumulate information from others. They may gather information more actively than other people; they may have greater expertise or accumulate more experience—but they are not the only sources of information. In addition, opinion leaders serve as weak ties to distant sources of information, locating information they do not themselves possess when others request it from them. For example, Fran may not be an expert on opera recordings but she knows who to turn to for such information when her friend needs advice about opera music to buy for her uncle.

❸ *Mass media and advertising influence everyone.* Although the original studies on opinion leadership were done before the advent of television, newspapers, magazines, and radio were accessible to much of the population, these sources influenced consumers as well as opinion leaders. The studies correctly recognized that advertising and mass media do not create consumer needs, as we argued in our discussion of the mirror controversy in Chapter 8, but consumers do *gather information* directly from these sources in addition to listening to the opinions of their "leaders."

## FACT OR FICTION REVISITED

⊙ It is *not true* that opinion leaders usually gather their information from the mass media rather than from other consumers; instead, opinion leaders often exchange information with other consumers.

## ▼ THE MULTISTEP THEORY OF COMMUNICATION

A more realistic theory of interpersonal communication recognizes the multiple steps and directions of the flows of information through word-of-mouth communication (Figure 16.4). Known as the **multistep flow of communication**, this theory maintains that individuals receive information both directly, through mass media, and indirectly, through opinion leaders. Unlike the two-step theory, the multistep theory of interpersonal communication recognizes the following:

> The **multistep flow of communication** theory posits that individuals receive information from mass media and marketing communications and exchange information with opinion leaders.

❶ *Mass media and marketing communications affect all consumers directly.* Opinion leaders play a role by interpreting information from these sources and forwarding it to other consumers. Thus, consumers receive information in two ways—they gather their own information directly from mass media and marketing sources, and they receive "processed" versions of the same information from others. The most obvious example occurs when you ask a friend to shop with you and then ask his or her opinion of what the two of you have seen.

❷ *The distinction between opinion leaders and receivers is fluid.* An individual may serve as an opinion leader for some products and social groups and a receiver for others. The individual's expertise, objectivity, and level of involvement determine her or his role in a particular purchase process.

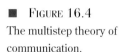
■  FIGURE 16.4
The multistep theory of
communication.

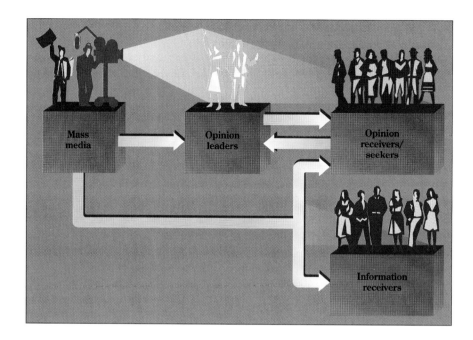

❸ *Opinion leaders and receivers interact during the communication process.*
Opinion leaders provide others with information, advice, and personal experiences. In return, they gather information, perceive attitudes, and receive
personal product experience from the consumers they counsel. They serve
as brokers of information, gathering it from some consumers and transmitting it to other consumers.

❹ *Opinion leaders can fill two roles.* Opinion leaders may provide product information, or they may influence other consumers' decision making by offering
advice and analysis of their own product experiences. The difference is
whether the individual is providing factual information or giving subjective
advice.

# OPINION LEADERSHIP

An **opinion leader**
uses his or her knowl-
edge and experience to
play a dominant role in
word-of-mouth commu-
nication.

By now it should be clear that an **opinion leader** is an individual who plays a
dominant role in a specific instance of word-of-mouth communication by
providing product news, advice, or personal experience to others. An opinion leader may play a number of different roles, depending on the occasion. For
some purchase activities, such as a doctor referral, a consumer might look to one
opinion leader; for others, such as a recommendation for a restaurant for a first
date, that same consumer might look to another leader. The three key roles
played by opinion leaders are (1) authority figure, (2) trend setter, and (3) local
opinion leader, as shown in Table 16.2.

*Table 16.2*

**RELATIONSHIP BETWEEN OPINION LEADERSHIP ROLES AND WORD-OF-MOUTH COMMUNICATION CHARACTERISTICS**

| | Authorities | Trend Setters | Local Opinion Leaders |
|---|---|---|---|
| Most important types of communication content | Product news<br>Advice<br>Experiences | Experiences | Advice<br>Experiences |
| Credibility | Expertise<br>Objectivity | Expertise | Expertise<br>Objectivity |
| Receiver's purpose | Reduce cognitive effort and uncertainty | Imitate trend setters to reduce uncertainty | Reduce cognitive effort and uncertainty |
| Source's purpose | Pleasure<br>Professional involvement<br>Little or no personal gain | Power<br>Prestige<br>Ego gratification | Pleasure<br>Power<br>Prestige<br>Personal involvement, personal gain |
| Type of product | Technically complex<br>New<br>Risky | Visible consumption settings<br>New | New<br>Visible consumption settings |
| Type of partner | Personal ties or weak ties to any highly involved expert source of information | Members of positive membership or aspirational groups | Members of positive membership or aspirational groups |

## ▼ AUTHORITIES

Opinion leaders who provide news, advice, or personal experience to help consumers satisfy their needs are considered **authorities**. Authorities use their knowledge, training, and experience to provide objective information, evaluative criteria, and decision rules to help others complete the purchase process without expending great effort or experiencing great risk. Consumers may seek out authorities in their reference groups or through weak ties to other groups whose members have interests and expertise different from their own.

To be an authority on a subject, a person must be highly involved with the product category. Many are professionals who work in the area; others are hobbyists with an active interest in the subject. Authorities enjoy talking about the subject and relish the prestige that results from acting the expert's role. They are able to provide information about complex, risky, or new products, which they gather through conversations with other authorities, by attending conferences and trade shows, or by reading the latest magazines and journals on the subject.

> An **authority** is an opinion leader who provides news, advise, or personal experience to help consumers satisfy their needs.

467

Consumers often turn to authorities to help guide them through their purchase activities. Before buying a computer, a car, or some other expensive, complex product, for example, a consumer may look for an authority who can provide the "inside information" on the best selection. This authority may be a family member, a friend, or an acquaintance. Likewise, the consumer may ask people they know whether they can recommend an expert in the area. Fran's friends may ask her whether she knows anyone who can advise them about opera music.

It is rare to find an opinion leader who is an authority in many different product areas. The expertise required to be an authority is significant, and an individual would have to exert a tremendous amount of ongoing effort to maintain expertise in more than a few areas. Some consumers are authorities who specialize in consumer behavior, however; they possess a wealth of knowledge about the kinds of products that are available, where they are available, and many other aspects of the consumer purchase process. Known as **market mavens**, these opinion leaders are authorities not on the products themselves but on the general process of buying products.[6]

> A **market maven** is an authority on the process of buying products.

## FACT OR FICTION REVISITED

⊙   People who are opinion leaders about one product *are not* likely to be opinion leaders about many other products as well; instead, opinion leadership tends to be specialized by product category.

> **Trend setters** are opinion leaders whose personal experiences are emulated by other consumers.

## ▼ TREND SETTERS

Unlike authorities, who possess objective product information, **trend setters** offer their personal experiences as examples of behavior for others to emulate. The source of their credibility is their experience—trend setters possess the skills to live an attractive lifestyle, but they don't really care whether others adopt the same way of living. Because trend setters have learned to buy and use products that support their lifestyle, consumers imitate their buying habits; the purchase process is less important than the outcome—the consumer simply wants to use the same products as the trend setter.

The people consumers label as trend setters are often individuals they respect and aspire to imitate. Trend setters may belong to positive nonmembership reference groups; although the consumer does not belong to groups in which the trend setters are active, he or she gains access to their experience and advice through chance interactions with these opinion leaders. When you were a freshman, for example, you may have admired certain seniors for their overall style. You might have seized any opportunity to talk with them about their fashions, interests, and activities so that you could emulate their behavior. Perhaps you stopped them in the hall before classes or spoke to them on the steps of the library.

## ▼ LOCAL OPINION LEADERS

People want the respect and approval of the members of the groups to which they belong or aspire to belong. Individuals in a consumer's positive reference groups who provide information that enables the consumer to make purchases to satisfy her or his needs and that are consistent with the values of the group are called **local opinion leaders**. Local opinion leaders provide advice and personal experiences about which products the consumer should choose. Their credibility is based on the fact that they know which choices are appropriate to be a "good" member of the group. For example, students who want to join a fraternity or sorority tend to dress like the group's members, listen to the same music, and participate in the same leisure activities, and they learn about these product choices by talking to the members themselves.

> A **local opinion leader** is an individual in a consumer's positive reference groups who provides advise and personal experience regarding purchase choices.

# MEASURING OPINION LEADERSHIP

Measuring opinion leadership involves identifying the opinion leaders on a given subject. Marketers commonly employ three methods to do so: (1) they ask consumers directly whether they are opinion leaders; (2) they ask a knowledgeable expert to identify the opinion leaders; or (3) they analyze the flows of communication among consumers and identify the leaders.[7] These methods enable marketers to identify the general characteristics of opinion leaders for a type of product; they can then target their marketing communications at all consumers who possess those characteristics, giving them product information to discuss with their communications partners. On some occasions, marketers are able to identify specific opinion leaders by name and deliver information to them through direct response media. For example, consumers who respond to an Alligator Records advertisement offering a newsletter about that blues label tend to pass the information on to friends who share their interest in blues music.

Consider how you and your friends decide which CDs to buy. A marketer measuring opinion leadership among your friends, family, and acquaintances may discover that campus musicians are the dominant influence—they serve as both authorities and local opinion leaders on music. The marketer can then target these musicians by name. Blues labels can deliver information about new bands to blues musicians, grunge labels to grunge bands, and so on. Students who consult with these musicians are then exposed to the marketer's information twice: They receive advertising through mass media as well as recommendations from the opinion leaders who communicate with them.

### ▼ THE SELF-DESIGNATING METHOD

The first method mentioned above—asking consumers directly whether they play the role of opinion leader in their communication with others—is the simplest and most commonly employed means of identifying opinion leaders. Known as the **self-designating method**, this approach typically involves asking a set of questions in a marketing survey about a specific product category (Figure 16.5). The

> The **self-designating method** asks consumers to indicate whether they play the role of opinion leader in their communication with others.

■ FIGURE 16.5
Self-designated opinion
leadership scales.

1. In general, do you like to talk about _____ with your friends?
   Yes _____ –1                    No _____ –2

2. Would you say you give very little information, an average amount of information, or a
   great deal of information about _____ to your friends?
   You give very little information                    _____ –1
   You give an average amount of information           _____ –2
   You give a great deal of information                _____ –3

3. During the past six months, have you told anyone about _____?
   Yes _____ –1                    No _____ –2

4. Compared with your cicle of friends, are you less likely, about as likely or more likely
   to be asked for advice about _____?
   Less likely to be asked                             _____ –1
   About as likely to be asked                         _____ –2
   More likely to be asked                             _____ –3

5. If you and your friends were to discuss _____, what part would you be most
   likely to play? Would you mainly listen to your friends' ideas or would you try to convince them of your ideas?
   You mainly listen to your friends' ideas            _____ –1
   You try to convince them of your ideas              _____ –2

6. Which of these happens more often? Do you tell your friends about _____, or
   do they tell you about _____?
   You tell them about _____                     _____ –1
   They tell you about _____                     _____ –2

7. Do you have the feeling that you are generally regarded by your friends and neigh
   bors as a good source of advice about _____?
   Yes _____ –1        No _____ –2

strengths of this method are that it is straightforward and easy to apply. To find out about opinion leaders who influence CD buying behavior, for example, the marketer would simply ask consumers in the target market about the characteristics of their word-of-mouth communication about CDs to identify the type of consumer that plays the opinion leader's role. The survey might address the following issues:

❶ Frequency of conversations about CDs with members of the reference group.

❷ Whether the consumer is more likely to give or receive information and advice.

❸ Whether the consumer's conversation partners consider him or her an expert on CDs.

The openness and ease of measurement of the self-designating method can also be its weakness, however. Marketers assume that people are able to report objectively about the nature of their word-of-mouth communications patterns, but this is not always the case. People want to believe that their friends and acquaintances look to them for help and advice; accordingly, they may report that they are more important than they really are. It is also difficult to measure the outcome of communications. Some people report that they provide information, but the receivers may not use it. You may know someone who tells everyone you know about his favorite musical groups, for example, but no one takes his opinions seriously. Finally, marketers must understand how receivers weigh the information they receive from the many sources they consult in order to get a clear picture of which ones are opinion leaders and which are not.

## ▼ THE KEY INFORMANT METHOD

The second method—asking a knowledgeable expert to identify the opinion leaders in a group—addresses the weaknesses of the self-designating method. Known as the **key informant method**, this approach relies on using an individual who knows about the communication patterns in a social environment to provide an objective picture of these patterns. That individual may either be a member of the group or an outside observer. For example, if you wanted to identify the opinion leaders in a fraternity or sorority, you might ask one of the officers or question the group's faculty advisor.

> The **key informant method** relies on a knowledgeable individual to indicate which consumers in a group are opinion leaders.

The strength of the key informant method is its ease of use. Since the marketer interviews just one person—the key informant—the method is easy to implement. At the same time, this simplicity is also quite limiting. One informant is required to "read the minds" of all the consumers in the group. Accordingly, this technique should be limited to products that are discussed in a small and self-contained social environment. The officers of a fraternity may know which members provide information about CDs to other members, for example, but they won't necessarily know all of the outside sources the members consult for information about other products and services, such as car repair. It would be even more difficult to find a key informant who knows all of the opinion leaders the members of a large target market, such as the sophomore class, might consult for information about CDs.

## ▼ THE SOCIOMETRIC METHOD

The third method—analyzing the flows of communication among consumers to identify those who stand out as leaders—is known as the **sociometric method**. This approach involves examining a complete outline of the pattern of information flows among the consumers in a target market for a particular product; opinion leaders stand out as those consumers who provide information to many others. This method can also be used to identify the leaders' sources of information to uncover the multistep flows we have noted earlier.

> The **sociometric method** identifies opinion leaders through the analysis of the flows of communication.

Marketers using the sociometric method develop survey research questionnaires that ask each consumer in the target market to list the people with whom they communicate and to describe the content of that communication (Figure 16.6). A CD marketer, for example, might interview students about their conversations about music, clubs, radio stations, and CDs. For each of these music-related topics, the marketer would ask the students where they get their

■ FIGURE 16.6

The sociometric method.

---

**Communicate Information to Others**

1. Did you talk to any other student here at Trenton State College about the new Alanis Morissette CD within the past month?
   _____ Yes → Please continue with question 2.      _____ No → Please continue with question 2.

2. Which student did you first tell about the Alanis Morissette CD?
   Name: _____      Major: _____

3. Which other students at Trenton State College have you talked to about the Alanis Morissette CD?
   Name: _____      Major: _____
   Name: _____      Major: _____
   Name: _____      Major: _____

4. Did you recommend that the students buy the Alanis Morissette CD?
   _____ Recommended      _____ Did not recommend purchase

**Receive Information from Others**

5. When did you first hear about the Alanis Morissette CD? (record date)
   _____

6. Who first told you about the Alanis Morissette CD?
   Name: _____      Major: _____

7. Is he or she a student here at Trenton State College?
   _____ Yes      _____ No

8. Did he or she recommend that you buy the Alanis Morissette CD?
   _____ Recommended      _____ Did not recommend purchase

9. Are there any other students who told you about the Alanis Morissette CD?
   _____ Yes → Please answer question 10.      _____ No → Thanks for your time.

10. What are the names of the other students at Trenton State College who have told you about the Alanis Morissette CD?
    Name: _____      Major: _____
    Name: _____      Major: _____
    Name: _____      Major: _____

---

product information: Who tells them about new releases? Who gives them advice about which releases are good? Who relays their experiences of listening to new groups? The marketer would then analyze this objective data to identify the opinion leaders of the group.

The advantage of the sociometric method is the control the marketer has over the information. Since the marketer gathers the data from consumers and uses its own analysis to identify the leaders, there is less chance of inaccuracy or bias. The weakness of the method is its large scale: Since information is needed on all of the consumers' communication to complete the analysis, the amount of data can become overwhelming, even for small groups of consumers. For example, you probably have numerous conversations with your friends about the products you buy. To complete a sociometric analysis, the marketer would have to gather information from all of your communication partners. This can quickly mushroom into a large number of people, particularly when weak ties link consumers to members of many other distinct groups. Thus, the data collection task often is too unwieldy to apply to most products that are discussed outside of a small, self-contained social environment.

# HOW MARKETERS USE INTERPERSONAL COMMUNICATION

The most obvious way marketers incorporate word-of-mouth communication and opinion leadership into their marketing efforts is by providing consumers with product information they can discuss with their families, friends, and acquaintances—that is, by providing some of the raw material for word-of-mouth discussions. At the same time, marketers aim some of their efforts directly at the opinion leaders, who will spread the word for them, and they simulate word-of-mouth communication and the actions of opinion leaders in their promotion efforts.

Before the marketer can use interpersonal communication to its benefit, it must first identify the general characteristics of the opinion leaders for its product category. The marketer can then target all consumers who possess those characteristics because they are likely to act as opinion leaders. For example, Canadian company Make-up Art Cosmetics (MAC) targets the makeup artists who work on models and actresses by offering them a 40 percent discount on its products (Figure 16.7). MAC understands that models and actresses will wear the products the makeup artists favor. Celebrity endorsements, in turn, can be used to encourage everyday consumers to talk about and purchase that product as well. Some marketers target authorities, who provide expert advice to other consumers, as we discuss in the following Public Policy box.

■ FIGURE 16.7

MAC cosmetics targets makeup artists who work on models and actresses as opinion leaders in this product category.

473

★ PUBLIC POLICY

**Why Did You Recommend That?**[8]

Most people assume that product recommendations made by doctors, pharmacists, and other health care professionals are the result of expert knowledge, training, and experience. What is little known is that these authorities are subject to the marketing efforts of drug marketers who provide information, free samples, and sometimes even direct payments to get them to recommend their products. Most drug marketers maintain large sales forces, composed of *detailers*, who regularly visit hospitals, pharmacies, and doctor's offices to distribute brochures and product samples and answer questions about the efficacy of their products.

Two recent cases involving prescription drugs brought such marketing practices into the limelight. In April 1994 the pharmaceutical firm Miles, Inc. agreed with 11 state attorneys general to end its program of paying $35 to pharmacists for every customer who switched to its Adalat CC blood pressure drug from another medication. The practice had been for pharmacists to counsel patients who used competing drugs about Adalat's benefits and encourage them to ask their doctors to change their prescription to Adalat. Even though it stopped providing the monetary rewards, Miles denied any wrongdoing, stating that it was merely compensating the pharmacists for providing information to consumers, not for persuading them to change brands.

The Upjohn Company signed a similar agreement. The company had been providing payments to pharmacists for every patient who switched from one of its diabetes drugs, Micronase, to another, Glynase. The reason was that Micronase was no longer patented, so it had lower priced generic competitors, whereas Glynase still had patent protection. The danger was that although both drugs contained the same active ingredients, they were not chemically identical, so patients ran the risk of adversely affecting their diabetes by switching drugs.

Do you think the typical consumer knows that drug marketers have programs that compensate pharmacists for using their products? Is it ethical for pharmacists to accept payments from drug companies to counsel consumers about their prescriptions? Does this practice undermine the credibility of pharmacists?

## ▼ CREATING WORD-OF-MOUTH AND OPINION LEADERS

Marketers have devised a number of methods to create opinion leaders who will actively support their marketing efforts through word-of-mouth communication. Some marketers have simply relied on a version of key informants to identify consumers who will play the role of "opinion leader for a day." Direct selling organizations, such as Tupperware and Mary Kay Cosmetics, for example, use word-of-mouth and opinion leaders extensively to market their products. Distributors from these organizations identify certain consumers, who invite their friends to home parties where the products are demonstrated. The guests are then offered the opportunity to purchase the products.[9] These direct selling firms rely on the identification of party hosts who can inspire their friends as well as the concentrated conversations about the products that take place in the party setting.

Some marketers identify consumers by name and deliver information to them through direct response media, encouraging them to act as opinion leaders.

For example, the Kentucky Bourbon Circle uses advertising to gather names of interested consumers, who then receive a quarterly newsletter containing information about new products and events. Similarly, MCI's Friends and Family calling circle programs offer discounts for long distance calls among a predefined group of consumers. Because all the group members must be MCI customers, each consumer who joins the program must influence his or her friends and family to become customers too. The incentive of increased savings encourages consumers to adopt the role of opinion leader in order to influence their communication partners to use MCI.

## ▼ SIMULATING WORD-OF-MOUTH AND OPINION LEADERSHIP

Marketers often simulate word-of-mouth communication and opinion leadership in their communications (Figure 16.8).[10] The example we discussed in Chapter

■ FIGURE 16.8
Marketers often use authority figures as spokespersons in their advertising.

15 is advertising in which celebrities play the role of authorities or trend setters. Nike and other athletic shoe marketers often use professional athletes to promote their products, and cosmetics marketers typically use models and actresses. Other marketers create advertisements that portray professionals playing the role of local opinion leaders. Marketers of household products may use plumbers or carpenters, whereas food marketers may feature chefs. Still other

■ FIGURE 16.9
A "slice-of-life" ad.

marketers attempt to recreate the word-of-mouth communication process by portraying consumers talking about the product in "slice of life" settings that are intended to simulate reality (Figure 16.9). Some consumers question the credibility of such ads, as do a number of advertising executives, such as Keith Reinhard, who criticizes the artificial nature of the conversations as "slice of bologna."

## FACT OR FICTION REVISITED

⦿ It is false that marketers can do little to influence word-of-mouth communication about their products; they can—and do—encourage favorable communication and reduce unfavorable communication.

# CONSUMERS GATHER INFORMATION FROM ONE ANOTHER

Fran Spiegel is an opinion leader in the area of music. She is a highly involved expert in many kinds of music, and she provides information, advice, and tales of her own listening experiences to her family and friends. She recommends artists and even provides sample tapes so her friends and family can listen to a song or two of the artists she likes. At the same time, Fran is influenced in other areas of her life by the same people whose musical tastes she sways. She seeks advice about clothes, health, and exercise purchases from family and friends. These interpersonal influences work in concert with the marketing communication efforts that affect her attitudes and purchases.

In this chapter we have described the seven major characteristics of consumers and products that shape the nature of the interpersonal communication. We have also discussed the roles played by opinion leaders, like Fran, in communication of specific products, and we have considered how marketers attempt to create and simulate interpersonal communications as part of their marketing communications efforts. In the final chapter we turn our attention to consumers' adoption of new products.

## SUMMARY

1. **Determine the role interpersonal communication plays in the consumer purchase processes.** Consumer behavior occurs within an interpersonal network of friends, family, acquaintances, and strangers. Consumers often identify a set of people who know something about the alternatives products they are considering. Interpersonal communication is the informal two-way exchange of this information and influence among individuals.

2. **Analyze the characteristics of word-of-mouth communication.** Word-of-mouth communication is informal communication among consumers regarding information,

advice, and personal experiences with products that will satisfy their needs. The most important characteristics of word-of-mouth communication are: (1) the information content of the communication, (2) the receiver's purpose in gathering information, (3) the source's purpose in providing information, (4) the source's credibility, (5) the source's evaluation of the product, (6) the type of communication partner, and (7) the type of product.

3. **Examine opinion leaders who provide information to consumers for a particular purchase.** An opinion leader is a consumer who uses her or his knowledge and experience to play a dominant role in a specific instance of word-of-mouth communication by providing product news, advice, or personal experiences to other consumers. The three key roles an opinion leader may play are: (1) authority, (2) trend setter, or (3) local opinion leader. Authorities use their knowledge, training, and experience to provide objective information to help consumers reduce the cognitive effort and uncertainty involved in choosing a product. Trend setters are individuals in positive non-membership reference groups whom consumers strive to emulate. Local opinion leaders are individuals in a consumer's positive reference groups whose respect and approval the consumer seeks.

4. **Identify the ways in which marketers capitalize on interpersonal communication in their marketing efforts.** Marketers wish to provide favorable information for consumers to transmit through word-of-mouth communication. In particular, they want to identify the opinion leaders to whom others turn for product information, advice, or stories of their own experiences. Marketers commonly employ three methods to measure opinion leadership: (1) allow consumers to designate themselves as opinion leaders; (2) ask a knowledgeable expert to identify the opinion leaders; or (3) analyze the flows of communication among consumers. The marketer can then target its communications efforts toward those consumers who meet the profile of opinion leaders, or it can target direct response efforts at specific consumers who act as opinion leaders. Marketers also simulate word-of-mouth communication and opinion leadership when they direct slice-of-life and celebrity testimonials at the consumers in their target markets.

# KEY TERMS

Interpersonal communication, *p. 457*

Word-of-mouth communication, *p. 457*

Two-step flow of communication, *p. 464*

Multistep flow of communication, *p. 465*

Opinion leader, *p. 466*

Authority, *p. 467*

Market maven, *p. 468*

Trend setter, *p. 468*

Local opinion leader, *p. 469*

Self-designating method, *p. 469*

Key informant method, *p. 471*

Sociometric method, *p. 471*

# SKILL-BUILDING ACTIVITIES

1. For one day, keep a word-of-mouth communication diary. List and describe all of the cases in which you communicate with someone else about a consumer product or a consumer service.

   a. Classify these incidents into product news, advice giving, and personal experience. Which type of information was most persuasive? Why?

   b. For which products or services was credibility most important? Why?

c. Which of these incidents depended upon the "strength of weak ties"?

d. Which involved a two-step flow of communication? What were the sources and what were the steps?

e. Which involved a multistep flow of communication? What were the sources and what were the steps?

f. In which cases were authorities involved? Explain.

g. In which cases were trend setters involved? Explain.

h. In which cases were local opinion leaders involved? Explain.

2. Within a group to which you belong, assess opinion leadership by the self-designated method and by the key informant method. What accounts for the differences in the findings these two methods yield?

3. Describe a case in which a marketer changed word-of-mouth communication within a group to which you belong.

4. Describe a case in which a marketer tried to change word-of-mouth communication and failed.

5. Aside from success and failure, what distinguishes Activity 4 above from Activity 5?

---

# CHAPTER 16 SELF-TEST

▼ MULTIPLE CHOICE

1. The two types of communication consumers use when making a purchase are marketing communication and _____ .

   a. advertising

   b. publicity

   c. interpersonal communication

   d. unbiased communication

2. When friends tell you about a movie they think you should see, _____ communication has occurred.

   a. consumer

   b. word-of-mouth

   c. segmented

   d. peer

3. Consumers use word-of-mouth communication to reduce the _____ and the _____ of making a purchase.

   a. cost; time required

   b. cognitive effort; uncertainty

   c. cognitive effort; cost

   d. displeasure; cost

4. If a mother asks her daughter's scout troop what type of doll she should buy her daughter for a birthday gift, the link between the mother and the scout troop members is called _____ .

   a. strength of weak ties

   b. referral

   c. dynamic continuum

   d. dyad

5. George's fraternity brothers ask George for information about cars. George would be considered a(n) _____ for the product category of automobiles.

   a. director

   b. category promoter

   c. opinion leader

   d. consumer helper

6. All of the following explain why the two-step theory of communication is not an accurate description of the way consumers actually acquire information except _____ .

   a. opinion leaders vary from product to product

   b. opinion leaders are not the only information source used by consumers

   c. opinion leaders are not susceptible to the influences of mass media

   d. different social groups have different opinion leaders

7. The _____ theory of interpersonal comunication maintains that consumers receive information from both the mass media and opinion leaders.
   a. single-step
   b. two-step
   c. bipolar
   d. multistep

8. Whenever anyone in Rachel's group of friends needs to buy gifts, they ask Rachel for her ideas on what they should buy and where they can get the best priced items. Rachel would be considered a _____ opinion leader.
   a. market maven
   b. trend setter
   c. multicategory
   d. product category

9. A consumer who needs to purchase camping equipment for the first time would rely on _____ communication content.
   a. advice
   b. experiences
   c. product news and experiences
   d. product news

10. What type(s) of opinion leaders gain their credibility from both expertise with the product category and objectivity?
    a. trend setters
    b. authorities and local opinion leaders
    c. trend setters and local opinion leaders
    d. trend setters and authorities

▼ TRUE/FALSE

1. The components of marketing communication are the same as those of interpersonal communication, with the exception of the context of the communication. T or F

2. All sources of interpersonal communication provide information in order to assist the receiver.   T or F

3. A communication source that is credible has both expertise and objectivity. T or F

4. Word-of-mouth communication is always positive.   T or F

5. Negative information about a product is more influential during the communication process than is positive word-of-mouth.   T or F

6. People gather information only from members of their reference group.   T or F

7. An opinion leader in one product category is probably an authority in several other product categories.   T or F

8. Trend setters don't really care whether others accept their lifestyle.   T or F

9. Local opinion leaders provide information on what is acceptable or not acceptable for the members of a reference group.   T or F

10. Marketers have no effect on who is an opinion leader for their product.   T or F

▼ SHORT ANSWER

1. Describe the three types of information conveyed through interpersonal communication.

2. The purchase of what types of products is likely to be affected by word-of-mouth communication?

3. Describe the three methods used to identify opinion leaders.

▼   APPLICATION EXERCISE

You are the marketing director at a local health club. You have discovered that one of the most effective communication strategies to promote your club is word-of-mouth. Specifically, your members are your best salespeople since they promote the benefits of the club to their friends. Discuss how your could create opinion leaders among your members to increase word-of-mouth communication.

# 17

# NEW PRODUCT PLANNING

◉ Consumer Snapshot *Ann Martin\* is a 59-year-old retired homemaker. She lives in St. Petersburg, Florida, with her husband, Gordon Lewis,\* a 77-year-old retired minister. This is Ann and Gordon's second marriage, both having been widowed. Ann has two children from her marriage, Marie, 35, and Wynn, 28. Gordon has three children from his first marriage, Francis, 49, Robert, 45, and Carlton, 39.*

## FACT OR FICTION

◉ Continuous innovations usually require radical changes in consumers' behavior.

◉ When a product is first introduced, it is purchased primarily by innovators.

◉ The behavioral processes consumers use when purchasing new products are substantially different from the processes they use when purchasing established products.

\*Last names changed for privacy.

- ◉ Trial is the key action in the adoption of a new product.

- ◉ In managing a new product introduction, the best way to overcome the usage barrier is to provide more information.

- ◉ When a new product is being introduced, its price is usually more apparent than its benefits.

# EYE ON THE CONSUMER

Ann Martin and her husband, Gordon Lewis, have experienced many changes in their lives. Both widowed, they met through their kids—Ann's daughter is married to Gordon's son—and married recently. Ann had been living in St. Petersburg, Florida, and Gordon left Minnesota and moved to be with her when they married.

Ann tries to keep up with environmental and health concerns. She's very careful about what she and Gordon eat, especially since Gordon had a heart attack and bypass surgery in 1993. Ann has learned to read labels to look for hydrogenated oils and fat content. As a child, her mother taught her that butter was better than margarine, but as an adult, she began listening to the medical experts, who advised that margarine was healthier than butter. Today those same experts now say that margarine coats the arteries more than butter, so Ann has gone back to buying her favorite butter. She has also started buying organic vegetables, and she hopes that they are indeed healthier, as the experts say, because they are more expensive than regular vegetables.

Recently, Ann began using a new toothpaste—Mentadent—that contains baking soda and hydrogen peroxide. The two ingredients are stored separately in an expensive plastic dispenser and then come together as the paste is squeezed onto the brush. Ann received a direct mail advertisement containing a sample of the product. Knowing that dentists recommend both hydrogen peroxide and baking soda because they are good for the gums, she and Gordon were intrigued enough to try the sample, and since they both liked it they went out and purchased the product.

Ann and Gordon own two cars—a Cadillac, which Ann drives, and a Mercury station wagon, which Gordon drives. The transmission in the Cadillac had to be replaced for the second time about a month ago, so Ann doesn't think they will buy another one when it comes time to replace it. Ann likes big cars—she feels safer in them, and she believes that an eight-cylinder engine is necessary to get good pickup and power. When the time comes, she and Gordon will look at *Consumer Reports* and visit the Cadillac and Mercury dealers who currently service their cars. Gordon also wants to look at the new Chryslers that were just introduced. He likes them because they look streamlined and stylish, unlike the typical big, boxy cars.

Marketers consider new products the lifeblood of their businesses. To maintain the growth in sales and profits that are demanded by their stockholders, marketers are constantly looking to create new products that will satisfy the consumers in their target markets. The new product planning process is of great importance to marketers and consumers alike. Accordingly, researchers have adopted two complimentary perspectives to understand consumers' new product behavior. The first perspective adopts a bird's eye view and examines the *diffusion process*—that is, how a new product spreads through a target market. The second perspective focuses more specifically on the behavioral processes consumers employ when deciding whether or not to adopt a new product.

After reading and thinking about this chapter, you should be able to:

❶ Identify types of new product innovations.
❷ Understand how new products diffuse through a consumer market.
❸ Analyze the factors that influence consumers' adoption of a new product.
❹ Recognize the barriers that impede consumers' adoption of a new product.

# TYPES OF NEW PRODUCT INNOVATIONS ◀

Some new products are only slightly different than the current alternatives; others are radically different than what is currently available. Wherever they fall on the continuum between slight modification and radical innovation, all new products are intended to meet changing consumer needs.

In deciding to develop a new product, marketers must understand how consumers will react to it. In some cases, a marketer will monitor consumers' evolving needs and introduce a new product to keep up with the changes. Only after analyzing the needs, motivations, knowledge, and attitudes consumers have about existing products can the marketer understand how they fall short of consumer needs and introduce modified new products to address those shortcomings. For example, manufacturers of portable computers know that consumers would like computers to have longer battery life, so they continue to introduce new models that use power more efficiently.

At other times, the marketer may recognize that a significantly different product can more effectively satisfy consumer needs. A radically different technology might satisfy an existing need in a more effective or efficient way, for example, so a computer manufacturer might introduce an entirely new technology to address the need for longer battery life. Sometimes an innovative product may satisfy a need consumers haven't even known could be solved. Computer users wanted access to vast amounts of data, for example, but they didn't know their needs could be met until CD-ROM technology was introduced.

## ▼ DIMENSIONS OF INNOVATION

New products can be classified according to their degree of innovation—from modifications of existing products and concepts, on the one hand, to significantly new products that differ radically from any existing products, on the other. Innovation, in turn, can be measured on two dimensions: (1) the *technological changes* in the product itself, and (2) the *behavioral changes* that are required of consumers to complete the purchase process and use the product. The first dimension focuses on the product itself and any new benefits it may offer, and the second emphasizes consumer behavior issues, including the symbolic nature of the new product.[1] For example, the introduction of handguns for women required that the purchaser be comfortable with a traditionally male symbol (Figure 17.1).

Some new products embody technological change in the construction of the product. For example, the progression from records and cassettes to compact discs involved a significant change in the technological basis of the product and the quality of sound offered, but the listening behaviors of consumers stayed the same. Other new products are physically quite similar to existing products but result in changes in the consumer's behavior. The home computers that are widely available in discount and appliance stores today aren't very different from the models that have been available in offices for the last several years, but they require very different behavior on the part of consumers who purchase them for home use and allow their users to do things they could not do without their home computers. Still other new products combine technological and behavioral changes. The introduction of cellular phones was based on a new technology that also involved a significant behavioral change—consumers can now make telephone calls from any location, but they pay significantly higher prices to do so.

A common way to classify new product innovations is to divide them into (1) *continuous innovations*, (2) *dynamically continuous innovations*, and (3) *discontinuous innovations*. Developed by Thomas S. Robertson, these three categories are defined by the two dimensions discussed above—that is, the degree to which they embody technological and behavioral changes (Figure 17.2). It is important to understand that the degree of technological change embodied in the product can differ from the degree of behavioral change required of consumers. Consumers may be less likely to adopt a new product that requires them to change their behavior than one that only involves technological change. For example, many people don't care if their computers are powered by an Intel or a Motorola chip, but they may be unwilling to buy a new

■ FIGURE 17.1

Marketing handguns to women required women to change their behavior and adopt a traditionally male symbol.

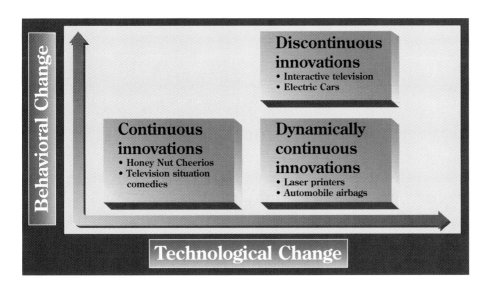

computer that requires them to abandon their favorite word-processing software.

## ▼ CONTINUOUS INNOVATIONS

A new product that involves the modification of an existing product with little
technological innovation and little behavioral change required of the consumer is
called a **continuous innovation**. Line extensions of existing consumer packaged
goods are common examples of continuous innovations. A **line extension** is a
new product that extends an existing product by introducing it in a new flavor,
size, or form. For example, Frosted Honey Nut, Apple Cinnamon, and Multi-Grain
Cheerios are line extensions of the original Cheerios brand of cereal. The technology used to produce these different flavors is not different from that used to
produce the original product, and the consumer does not have to adopt a new
purchase or consumption process to use them.

### FACT OR FICTION REVISITED

◉ Continous innovations *do not* usually require radical changes in consumers'
behavior; they typically require only gradual changes.

## ▼ DYNAMICALLY CONTINUOUS INNOVATIONS

Further down the continuum, **dynamically continuous innovations** are new
products that include some technological changes or new benefits but still require little or no behavioral change on the part of consumers. These types of innovations are often designed to address consumers' desires for a more efficient,
effective, or convenient means of satisfying an ongoing need. For example, Ann
Martin bought Mentadent because she thought its mixture of baking soda and
hydrogen peroxide would be more effective at keeping her gums healthy. Mar-

A **continuous innova-
tion** is the modification
of an existing product
which involves little
technological innova-
tion and little behav-
ioral change.

A **line extension** is a
continuous innovation
that extends an existing
product by introducing
a new flavor, size, or
form.

A **dynamically contin-
uous innovation** is a
new product that pro-
vides some technologi-
cal change or new ben-
efit but requires little or
no behavioral change.

487

■ FIGURE 17.3

Technologically advanced computer printers are an example of a dynamically continuous innovation—the technology is new and improved, but consumers don't have to change their behavior to use them.

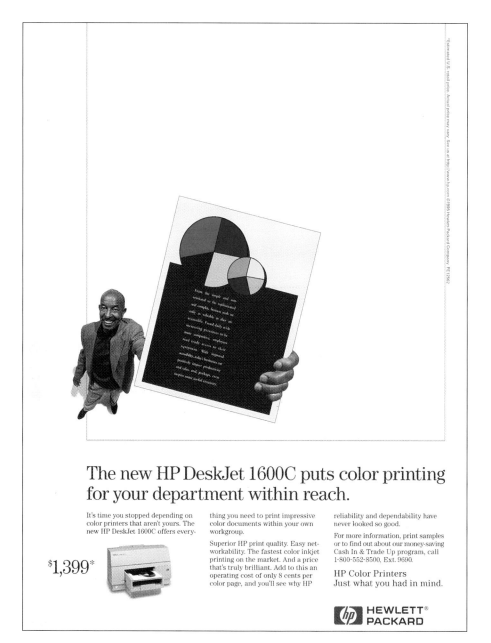

keters often use innovative technology to develop a new product that will better satisfy an existing need without disrupting the consumer's purchase and usage behaviors. For example, computer users are always looking for cheaper, faster, and higher quality printing. Printer manufacturers continue to respond with new technologies, such as ink-jet printers and enhanced laser technologies. The technologies are often new and improved, but consumers can still purchase the new printers in the same way as the old and they don't have to change their work behaviors—they can keep using their favorite software and achieve even better results (Figure 17.3).

## ▼ DISCONTINUOUS INNOVATIONS

At the other end of the continuum are **discontinuous innovations**—major technological innovations that require new consumer purchase and usage behaviors. For example, new technology has made it possible to recycle waste products such as cans, plastic bottles, and newspapers. As a result, many communities ask or demand that their residents separate those products from their trash and recycle them, as Ann Martin and Gordon Lewis do.

Many of the innovative products that comprise the "information superhighway" are discontinuous innovations. In the near future digital communications and video technology will be joined to computer innovations to bring new services to consumers in their homes. But that technology will require people to behave very differently. Consumers will need to become proficient at evaluating many competing entertainment alternatives to complete the purchase process and watch a "television" program. The consumption experience will also be different—people will be able to control the timing and pace of the program and interact with it to customize their viewing experiences.

> A **discontinuous innovation** is a new product that provides some technological change or new benefit and requires new consumer purchase and usage behaviors.

# THE DIFFUSION OF AN INNOVATION IN A MARKET

**D**iffusion of an innovation is a phrase used to describe the process by which a new product, service, or idea spreads among the consumers in a market.[2] Having examined a large number of diffusion studies, a researcher named Everett Rogers noticed a common pattern in the timing of the diffusion process based on when consumers joined the process. His method provides a way of thinking about the differences that exist among the consumers in any target market. If you look at the students at your school, for example, you might notice that some tend to adopt a new fashion trend or go to a new night spot faster than others. Much of Rogers' work is based on the interpersonal communication patterns we discussed in the previous chapter.

> The **diffusion of an innovation** is the process by which a new product spreads through a market.

## ▼ CATEGORIES OF ADOPTERS

According to Rogers, in studying diffusion of innovations, consumers can be divided into categories ordered by their time of adoption.[3] To simplify matters, Rogers created five distinct categories, although he acknowledged that the lines between the categories will depend on the particular innovation being studied.[4] The categories are based on a classic bell-shaped normal distribution that divides the target market into groups that reflect the order in which consumers adopt the innovation (Figure 17.4). You will notice that Rogers's scheme includes only those people who adopt the innovation, but virtually no new product diffuses throughout the entire target market. So, in actuality, there is a sixth category composed of consumers who never adopt the product. These nonadopters may

■  FIGURE 17.4
Normal distribution of
adopter categories.

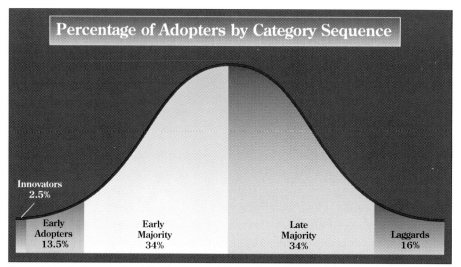

Source: Adapted with permission of The Free Press, a Division of Macmillan, Inc., from *Diffusion of Innovations,*
Third Edition, by Everett M. Rogers.  Copyright © 1962, 1971, 1983 by The Free Press.

be a small percentage of the population, such as people who never adopted basic
telephones or refrigerators, or they may represent the larger percentage of a market that has not yet adopted a product, such as videodisk players.

**Innovators**   *Innovators* make up the first 2.5 percent of the target market
adopters. They are the people who eagerly seek new ideas and innovative products. Innovators want to be the first to adopt any new product; they are likely to
have both the education to understand new products and the income to indulge
their wishes. Innovator are often exposed to new products earlier than others in
their community because they tend to have stronger ties to outsiders who transmit new information to them.

## FACT OR FICTION REVISITED

◉   It is true that innovators are primarily the first to purchase a new product.

**Early Adopters**   The next 13.5 percent of the target market adopters are *early
adopters*. These are people who will adopt an innovation because it meets their
needs, not because they are the type to adopt any innovation. Early adopters are
the opinion leaders in the target market segment—they have strong ties to the
group and make their purchase decisions on the basis of the product rather than
the desire to adopt every innovation. As a result of their credibility, early adopters
are often a key target for marketing communications.

**The Early Majority**   The *early majority* make up the next 34 percent of
adopters. Like early adopters, these individuals adopt the new product because it

meets their needs, but they tend to take longer to complete the purchase process. Because they are less interested in the product category, the early majority have not engaged in ongoing search activities. Therefore, they must gather more specific information than the early adopters and evaluate the information more fully.

**The Late Majority**  The next 34 percent of adopters are the *late majority.* Many people in this group adopt the innovation only once others in their positive reference groups have already done so. The late majority adopt an innovative product once they have evaluated it favorably on their own, but they are also responsive to the social influence of other members of their reference groups. Therefore, interpersonal communication is an important source of information for the late majority.

**Laggards**  *Laggards* make up the last 16 percent to adopt the product. Laggards are slow to adopt innovations because they are uninvolved with the product category; accordingly, they exert little effort to gather new information for use in their decision making and rely on a routine purchase process. In addition, their ties to others in the community tend to be weak, so they do not receive much interpersonal communication about new products.

## ▼ MARKETERS' VIEW OF DIFFUSION

The distribution of adopters is consistent with the life cycle many products exhibit. The **product life cycle** is the distribution of a product's sales during its history. When a product is first introduced, it is purchased primarily by innovators. Because they make up such a small percentage of the target market, however, sales often begin slowly. Once the rest of the target market begins the purchase process, sales will begin to grow rapidly. Early adopters will be the next to purchase the product, followed by the early majority. After the late majority purchases the product, sales will stop growing because the majority of those who will ever purchase the product have already done so. The product is now said to be in its *maturity stage*—sales levels will remain stable because only the laggards will provide additional sales here and there. For some products, the maturity stage is followed by a decline as the innovators, early adopters, and early majority change their purchase decisions and adopt a new product.

> The **product life cycle** is the distribution of a product's sales during its history.

Most marketers do not draw the fine distinctions that Rogers did. Instead, they divide adopters into early and late segments; they also add a category for nonadopters because they want to know the relative appeal of a product to various potential market segments. After all, the most important measure of a market segment is the overall sales level.

Under this abbreviated classification scheme, innovators and early adopters are grouped together because they both represent the opinion leaders in the target market segment. Furthermore, most marketers feel that while the innovators are too small a segment to warrant any special marketing effort, the two groups together comprise a segment of sufficient size. The early and late majority and the laggards are then grouped together with the late adopters because they represent those individuals who require additional time to complete the purchase process.

# The Adoption Process

A consumer's perspective of a new product may be quite different than the marketer's—a product that is new to a consumer may in fact have been available for years; it is only new to the consumer because he or she was unaware of it before. The general framework we have used so far in this book applies to the adoption of new products as well as existing ones. When consumers recognize a need, they search for alternatives, and some of the alternatives they find may be new products. A consumer may stumble upon an innovative product as a result of gathering information on an ongoing basis about product categories with which they are highly involved. What may differ is the *way* the consumer completes the activities.

## FACT OR FICTION REVISITED

●    The behavioral processes consumers use when purchasing new products *are not* substantially different from those used when purchasing established products; in fact, they are much the same.

## ▼ Traditional Models of the Adoption Process

Consumer researchers have developed a number of models to describe the steps in the adoption process, as illustrated in Figure 17.5.[5] As you can see, these models are similar to one another in many ways. They all postulate that consumers are motivated to use their perceptual and learning skills to gather the necessary information to form attitudes and make purchase decisions about new products. The models differ primarily in the labels ascribed to the various processes. Each of the models also divides the steps in the adoption process into three main functions—thinking, feeling, and acting—but they differ in their description of the actual steps through which consumers proceed. The traditional model of the adoption process, as well as Robertson's model, which we have discussed earlier, describes a purchase process similar to the hierarchy of effects model introduced in Chapter 15; that is, consumers become aware of a product, think about it, decide how they feel about it, and make a purchase decision. The difference is that these models explicitly include trial as a key action in the adoption of a new product.

As we discussed in Chapter 14, *trial* is the consumer's opportunity to evaluate a consumption experience without making a commitment to the product. The trial stage has different meanings for different kinds of products. For an inexpensive consumer packaged good, such as a new candy bar, trial is often the first purchase. You might have heard about a new chocolate bar you think you would like, so you buy one from a vending machine or candy stand. If you like the product, you may become a "regular" user and purchase it frequently. For a more expensive, one-time purchase, such as a computer, you might spend a couple of hours playing around with one in the computer lab at school or at a friend's house.

*Adoption* means that the consumer has already evaluated his or her own experience with a product and either uses the product or has rejected it and no longer thinks about purchasing it.

## ▼ ROGERS' MODEL OF THE ADOPTION PROCESS

As we noted earlier in the chapter, Rogers' model provides a popular perspective on the consumer purchase activities involved in the adoption of a new product (Figure 17.6). According to Rogers, the adoption of a new product occurs in

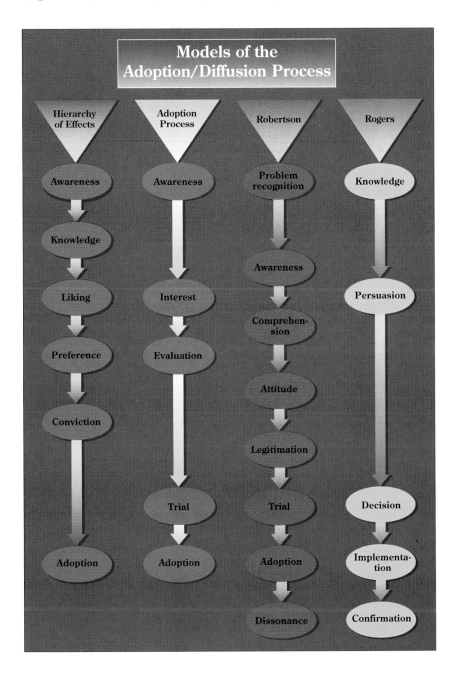

■ FIGURE 17.5

Antil diagram of adoption models.

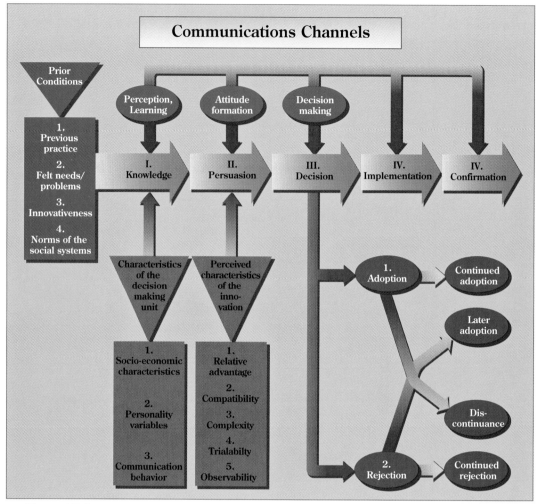

■ FIGURE 17.6

A model of the adoption process. Adapted from Everett Rogers, *Diffusion of Innovations,* 3rd Edition, New York: Free Press, 1983.

five stages: (1) knowledge, (2) persuasion, (3) decision, (4), implementation, and (5) confirmation:[6]

❶ During the *knowledge* stage the consumer uses perception and learning to gather information about alternative products.

❷ In the *persuasion* stage, the consumer forms attitudes, which are used to evaluate the alternative products.

❸ The *decision* stage is the point at which the consumer makes the mental choice to purchase and use the product, to choose another alternative, or not to purchase a product at all.

❹ *Implementation* involves trial and use of the chosen product. This is a particularly important stage to marketers because they must ensure that the marketing mix is structured to deliver the product easily and at a reasonable price.

■ FIGURE 17.7

In this ad, Cadillac touts the relative advantage of its car's ability to drive 100,000 miles before needing a tune-up.

⑤ The consumer moves from trial to adoption during the *confirmation* stage. At this point, the consumer either becomes a regular user of a frequently purchased product or commits to the purchase of an infrequently purchased product.

## ▼ FACTORS THAT AFFECT ADOPTION

A consumer's perception of the attributes of a new product may affect his or her willingness to adopt the innovation. Interpersonal and marketing communications play a vital role in this sense since they are the sources of many consumer perceptions of new products. The five factors believed to increase the rate of adoption of a new product are:[7] (1) the relative advantage of the product over existing products; (2) the product's compatibility with the existing backgrounds and behavior of consumers; (3) the ease with which the product can be understood and used; (4) the ease with which the product can be tried; and (5) the ease with which the product can be observed.

**Relative Advantage**   The degree to which consumers perceive that a new product offers them greater benefits than existing alternatives is its **relative advantage**. The innovation might be technologically superior to existing products; it might be easier to locate and buy; its price might be lower; or its benefits might be conveyed more effectively through marketing communications ( Figure 17.7).

**Relative advantage** is the degree to which consumers perceive that a product offers them greater benefits than alternative.

Product-based advantages tend to be very attractive to consumers. For example, advances in technology—both significant changes and incremental modifications—have increased adoptions of personal computers, both in the workplace and at home. As we noted earlier, advances in CD-ROM players, printers, and monitors have increased the relative advantage of personal computers compared to other types of computers, typewriters, and word processors.

Other components of the marketing mix have also provided the basis for the relative advantage of products. When Domino's pizza first opened its doors, it offered a product similar to those already available, but the company's speedy home delivery offered a distinct advantage over its competitors' distribution systems. Similarly, direct computer software vendors offer a distribution advantage to their customers by using air express services to allow next-day delivery. MCI radically changed the nature of long-distance telephone service by offering its product at a sizable price advantage, and Absolut vodka created a relative advantage by capitalizing on the distinctive shape of its bottle in witty and entertaining advertising.

> **Compatibility** is the degree to which a new product is consistent with the background and behavioral patterns of consumers.

**Compatibility**   The degree to which a new product is consistent with the background and behavioral patterns of the consumer is its **compatibility**. In general, continuous and dynamically continuous innovations are more compatible than discontinuous innovations because they do not require consumers to make significant changes in their purchase or usage behavior. For example, products targeted at men, such as shaving cream and men's fashions, tend to be compatible with their masculine self-image—depilatories for shaving and fashions traditionally worn by women, such as frills and ruffles and pastel colors, have not been widely adopted.

A new product will diffuse more quickly if it does not require consumers to change their values, lifestyles, attitudes, or behaviors. The use of automatic teller machines (ATMs) is a prime example: Usage of ATM machines spread more quickly among younger consumers, who typically have a higher level of familiarity and comfort with interactive computer technology. Older consumers tend to favor the more familiar personal interaction with bank tellers.

> **Complexity** is the ease with which consumers can understand and use a new product.

**Complexity**   The degree to which a product can be understood and used by consumers is its **complexity**. Products that require complex learning tasks in order for the consumer to evaluate and use them diffuse more slowly than those that can be easily learned. For example, computers diffused more quickly into homes for personal use once graphical user interfaces (GUIs) were added, eliminating the need for consumers to learn complex commands to use their computers. Many personal computer marketers also provide toll-free telephone assistance consumers can reach from their own homes. Similarly, VCRs that come with on-screen programming or the VCR+ system simplify the process of prerecording television shows (Figure 17.8).

> **Trialability** is the ease with which consumers gain experience with a new product without making a purchase commitment.

**Trialability**   The ease with which consumers are able to gain personal experience with a product without making a purchase commitment is its **trialability**. Sampling programs and return guarantees are the two primary methods mar-

Sophisticated. Simple. Sony.

America's most popular stereo VHS VCR has a
simple new Plus: VCR Plus+!™ It's as easy to program as dialing a phone.
Yet its sophisticated performance is pure Sony.
Which makes replacing your old VCR a simple decision.

■ FIGURE 17.8
VCRs with on-screen pro-
gramming or the VCR+
system help reduce the
complexity of the product.

keters use to increase the trialability of their products. Many marketers of packaged goods distribute trial-size samples through the mail or in grocery stores, or
offer special reduced size packages at a low price. Marketers of larger, more expensive products also create trial opportunities: Oldsmobile offers a money-back
guarantee on its cars in some parts of the country; direct marketers of computers
offer 30-day return privileges; and software marketers distribute sample versions
of their products that omit some functions but give consumers real experience
with the product. Even the on-line interactive services have jumped on the band-
wagon, as we discuss in the Pleasures of Consumption box that follows.

## FACT OR FICTION REVISITED

⊛　Trial is in fact the key action in adoption of a new product.

### PLEASURES OF CONSUMPTION

**Window Shop Before Buying**[8]
Approximately 30 million households currently own personal computers, and this
number continues to increase dramatically—by 3 to 4 million per year during the last

several years, according to estimates. On-line interactive computer services, such as America Online, Compuserve, and Prodigy, are also growing at a rapid pace, although not as quickly as computer ownership. Some 7 million households subscribe to on-line services, and the number continues to grow by 1 to 2 million households per year. On-line services provide consumers with access to information and news, shopping, recreation, conversation, the Internet's World Wide Web, and countless other sources.

On-line marketers would like more computer owners to subscribe to their services, and they have implemented a variety of marketing tools to encourage them to do so. One approach is to provide free trial software packages to computer makers, who distribute them to new customers. Another way is to advertise in magazines and on television, showing the benefits of the on-line services and offering trial software. Just by running the software, the consumer receives free access to the service, usually for a specified number of hours of basic service. The consumer is charged for any additional hours over the free trial period and for optional services.

Do you currently have access to on-line services? Do you think they offer benefits you could use? Is 10 free hours of on-line access an effective tool to encourage consumers to try the services? Will a free trial in the comfort of one's own home increase or reduce the complexity of learning how to use the services? Are there any risks associated with the free trials? If so, what are they?

> **Observability** is the ease with which a new product can be viewed in use.

**Observability**    The ease with which a new product can be viewed in use is its **observability**. Seeing a product in use enables consumers who haven't yet adopted it to see the benefits it will afford them. In general, tangible products are easier to observe than intangible services, such as nutrition and health practices. It is also more difficult to observe products whose benefits accrue over long periods of time, such as energy efficiency and durability in appliances. For this reason, marketers of furniture and home furnishings display their products in showrooms that resemble the rooms of a house so that consumers can see how they will look in their own homes. Car manufacturers often distribute large numbers of their new models to rental car fleets so that consumers are able to see them on the road as quickly as possible.

# BARRIERS TO ADOPTION

Just as increasing a new product's relative advantage, compatibility, simplicity, trialability, and observability will increase the rate of adoption, there are certain factors that can create barriers to the adoption of a new product (Table 17.1).[9] For many new products, even a positive attitude is not enough to stimulate a purchase. In some cases, consumers may be so fearful of the negative aspects of the product that they will not act on their positive attitudes. For example, you may think that the new spike heels are a great new fashion, but you might be afraid that your friends will dislike them and ridicule you if you wear them.

*Table 17.1*

## BARRIERS TO INNOVATION

| Barrier | Examples |
|---|---|
| Use | Electric vehicles must be recharged |
| | Recyclable products must be separated from trash |
| Value | Cable television is more costly than broadcast television |
| | Per-minute usage charges for cellular telephone are too costly |
| Perceived risk | An electric vehicle will strand me if it runs out of power |
| | I'm responsible for mistakes if I use tax software instead of my tax accountant |
| Psychological | Shampoo is for hair, not bathing, so I won't use a body shampoo |
| | A man shouldn't have a pierced ear |

The four primary barriers to the adoption of a new product are (1) usage, (2) value, (3) risk, and (4) psychological factors.

## ▼ USAGE

A product faces a *usage barrier* when consumers refuse to adopt a new product because it is incompatible with their existing behaviors. This barrier is difficult to overcome because it is rooted in actual behavior and cannot simply be changed by additional information. For instance, if people are resistant to using electronic mail to communicate because they are accustomed to using the telephone and writing memos, more knowledge about how the e-mail system works will not change their *preferences* for phones and written communication.

Marketers who face a usage barrier often appeal to innovative opinion leaders who can motivate others to adopt the innovation. A marketer of an electronic mail program might offer consumers the opportunity to communicate electronically with a celebrity who would otherwise be unreachable, or it might enlist the managers of a company to use electronic mail so that everyone else has to respond to them the same way. Once people use the new product—regardless of how they have been propelled to do so—their old usage habits are likely to be less compelling to them.

### FACT OR FICTION REVISITED

⊙ The best way to overcome the usage barrier to a new product innovation *is not* to provide more information; information seldom helps in this situation.

## ▼ VALUE

Consumers tend to resist adopting new products that do not offer better value than their existing alternatives. This resistance is known as the *value barrier*, and

**■** FIGURE 17.9

Pipeline USA used a penetration pricing strategy to encourage consumers to adopt their service.

the perceived lack of value may be the result of high prices or benefits that don't seem to be worth the price. Ideally, for example, you may want a new computer at home so that you can do your course work on your own schedule, but you don't see the added value of buying your own computer compared to using the ones in the computer lab. The computer lab doesn't charge you, so the additional benefit of having access to a computer any time you want it is not enough to justify spending several thousand dollars.

Price is often more apparent to consumers than are the benefits of a new product. People learn the price of a product quickly—through advertisements or articles or by visiting the store—but discovering the benefits of a product may require interpersonal communication or product experience. Accordingly, marketing communication is often used to demonstrate the benefits of a product.

Some price barriers are insurmountable—the benefits that come from driving a Lexus or a Mercedes are obvious, but many people just can't afford to buy one. Marketers often utilize the economies of scale that come from manufacturing large quantities of a product to overcome price issues. A marketer can price a product more cheaply if more units can be sold; and pricing the product more cheaply will *allow* more units to be sold. *Penetration pricing* involves pricing a new product at a lower price compared to the alternatives to induce consumers to adopt it. When enough consumers adopt the product, economies of scale result in a profit. The Pipeline USA on-line computer service took advantage of penetration pricing. The service was introduced at a low monthly price for unlimited usage to attract consumers (Figure 17.9). Many computer software marketers employ similar practices.

An alternative strategy is *skim pricing*, which involves pricing the product at a premium that will attract only early adopters for whom the product is particularly attractive. These early adopters, in turn, communicate the benefits to others, who adopt the product later on. Once the early adopters have purchased the product, the marketer will often lower the price of the product to overcome the value barrier among late adopters. Computers and many consumer electronics products, such as VCRs, CD players, and cellular phones were introduced using skimming pricing strategies.

## FACT OR FICTION REVISITED

⊙    When a new product is being introduced, its price is in fact usually more apparent than its benefits.

## ▼ RISK

Consumers may be reluctant to adopt a product if they feel uncertain about their purchase and usage of the product. This *perceived risk barrier* is a greater obstacle to the purchase of new products than an existing one—people may continue to buy and use an existing alternative rather than adopt a superior new product in order to avoid the risk of making a bad decision. Personal experience with a product and interpersonal communication of other people's experiences can help reduce this uncertainty.

Perceived risk and trialability are often related—trial provides the opportunity for consumers to gain their own product experience, which reduces their perception of its riskiness. Accordingly, many marketers offer low-cost or free trial opportunities. For example, if you are not sure that a new computer software package is worth the cost—the monetary cost as well as the time required to learn a new program—a trial version that demonstrates the benefits may change your attitude. America Online vastly increased its subscriber base by offering consumers a 10-hour trial membership. Many people who initially had been unwilling to buy the service joined after their free trial.

## ▼ PSYCHOLOGICAL BARRIERS

Consumers may hesitate to adopt a new product as a result of *psychological barriers* that stem from their prior attitudes and beliefs. The two most common sources of psychological resistance are tradition and image. The *tradition barrier* is a response to the consumer's attitudes about what kinds of behaviors are considered appropriate, whereas the *image barrier* reflects the consumer's attitudes about the attributes of a product's origins, such as its manufacturer, marketer, and country of origin.

Food products often face psychological barriers resulting from traditional attitudes. For example, many Americans feel that hamburgers and hot dogs should be made from beef or pork, so they have resisted trying hamburgers and hot dogs made from soy, chicken, or turkey. This is an ingrained tradition that is difficult to change. As we note in Chapter 13, attempts to introduce specific breakfast sodas, such as Pepsi AM, have largely not been successful.

Image barriers may restrict a marketer from using an existing brand name to market a new product that is significantly different than those for which the marketers is known. For example, Japanese car manufacturers Honda, Toyota, and Nissan feared that their image as producers of low- and moderately priced cars would make it difficult for them to introduce high-priced luxury models, so they created new divisions and brand names to circumvent these image barriers: Honda founded its Acura division for upscale cars; Toyota introduced its models under the Lexus name; and Nissan introduced the Infiniti line. Car makers will face a new challenge in 1998, as we discuss in the following Public Policy box.

## ★ PUBLIC POLICY

### Fill . . . I Mean Charge It Up[10]

In 1990 the state of California mandated that by 1998, two percent of each major automaker's sales in that state must be zero-emission vehicles (ZEVs); that figure increases to 10 percent by 2003. Because electric cars are the only existing form of emission-free vehicle, this regulation has forced automakers to develop electric vehicles and to design marketing strategies that will generate the required sales levels. Meeting the second of these requirements may be quite difficult, however. Current prototypes of ZEVs run on lead–acid batteries—technological improvements of those currently in cars—that can run about 100 miles in stop-and-go traffic on a single charge. But it takes approximately 30 minutes to recharge the batteries with special recharging equipment at "utility stations"; it can take three or more hours using regular household current. Furthermore, the acceleration of ZEVs is not quite as fast as the average gasoline-powered auto, and the vehicles will be more costly to produce, at least for the first year or two, until larger sales result in manufacturing efficiencies.

Existing feedback indicates that a majority of consumers would consider purchasing electrical vehicles and would even be willing to pay a slight premium if they offered quality and performance comparable to gasoline-powered cars. Unfortunately, the ability of automakers to deliver the desired performance at that cost is questionable. Automakers are aggressively lobbying California legislators to rescind the regulations, but they have also begun making plans to introduce electric cars on a small scale. Chrysler plans to offer electric versions of its popular minivans, and Ford is focusing on light trucks and vans. General Motors has ambitious plans to build a two-seat sport coupe, the Impact, which it is already testing across the country through its PrEView Drive program, which loans Impacts to consumers for several weeks at a time. So far, the response of the test drivers has been positive, and GM executives indicate that the Saturn division will probably market the car when it is introduced.

How have public policy actors influenced product innovation in the ZEV market? Would you be willing to buy and drive an electric car? What are the barriers to adoption of electric vehicles? Which of the factors to speed adoption should automakers emphasize, and with what kinds of marketing programs?

# CONSUMERS AND NEW PRODUCTS

Ann Martin is faced with new product choices every day. New cars, toothpastes, and organic vegetables, and new ideas about health and nutrition and environmental practices are just some of the goods, services, and ideas she must consider. Ann's own experiences as a Cadillac owner and her husband Gordon's interest in new car models will influence her decision when it comes time to replace the Caddy. But her long-time affection for big cars with big engines will limit her consideration of nontraditional cars—we won't see Ann driving a two-seat electric Impact!

Ann buys new products that reflect her and Gordon's changing circumstances. As they have grown older, nutrition and health concerns have become important, and organic vegetables and toothpaste that meet their changing needs have found their way into the house. At the same, changing environmental conditions have resulted in new habits to deal with the trash they produce. What once left the house in a single trash can is now separated into trash and recyclable streams of cans, plastic, and newspapers.

Consumers adopt new products because they often provide more effective and efficient ways of meeting existing needs and help satisfy the changing needs that are part of every person's life. Some new products are only slight variations on existing products; others are radical innovations that incorporate new technology and require significantly different behavior on the part of the consumer.

Different patterns of diffusion reflect the fact that some consumers adopt a new product earlier than others; some consumers will never use it. New products that offer a significant advantage over existing alternatives, that don't require major behavioral changes, and that can be easily observed, understood, and tested are perceived most favorably by consumers. Even these products will face resistance from some consumers, however, if they are risky or represent departures from traditional habits. It is incumbent on the marketer to identify a receptive target market and to show the consumers in that target that a new product will satisfy them. Given the breadth of consumers' background characteristics and the sophistication of the behavioral processes they use to purchase products that will satisfy their needs, some consumers will find the new product appealing. That is the essence of consumer behavior.

1. **Identify types of new product innovations.** New product innovations fall on a continuum, ranging from slightly different than the current alternatives to radical innovations that are significantly different from what is currently available. Products vary on two dimensions of innovation: (1) technological changes in the product itself and new benefits it may offer, and (2) behavioral changes that are required of consumers to complete the purchase process and use the product. Combining technological and behavioral changes yields three types of innovations: Continuous innovations are new products that involve a modification of existing products with little technological innovation and little behavioral change required of the consumer; dynamically continuous innovations are new products that involve some technological changes or new benefits but require little or no behavioral change on the part of consumers; and discontinuous innovations are major product innovations that require new consumer purchase and usage behaviors.

2. **Understand how new products diffuse through a consumer market.** The diffusion of an innovation is the process by which a new product spreads among the consumers in a market. A common method used to describe the diffusion of an innovation through a target market is to divide consumers into five categories, based on a classic bell-shaped normal distribution: innovators, early adopters, the early majority, the late majority, and laggards. Most marketers do not draw such fine distinctions, however, and simply divide the market into early adopters, late adopters, and nonadopters—those consumers who never buy the new product.

3. **Analyze the factors that influence consumers' adoption of a new product.** Consumers use the behavioral processes to complete the purchase activities for a new

# SUMMARY

product just as they do for existing products; that is, they become aware of a product, think about it, decide how they feel about it, and make a purchase decision. Because it is a new product, consumers use trial to evaluate the consumption experience without making a commitment to the product. If they are satisfied with their trial experience, they will likely make a commitment and adopt the product. The characteristics of a product that tend to affect consumers' perceptions of the innovation and their willingness to adopt it are (1) the relative advantage of the product over existing products, (2) its compatibility with the existing background and behavior of consumers, (3) a lack of complexity so that the product can be understood and used, (4) the ease with which the product can be tested, and (5) the ease with which consumers can observe the product in use before buying it.

4. **Recognize the barriers that impede consumers' adoption of a new product.** Even a positive attitude is not enough to stimulate some consumers to purchase and use a new product. Some people may be so fearful of the negative aspects of the product that they will not act on their positive attitudes. Usage that requires behavioral change, the product's value, the perceived risk of using the product, and psychological factors such as tradition and image are all barriers that may deter a consumer from purchasing a new product.

# KEY TERMS

Continuous innovation, p. 487

Line extension, p. 487

Dynamically continuous innovation, p. 487

Discontinuous innovation, p. 489

Diffusion of an innovation, p. 489

Product life cycle, p. 491

Relative advantage, p. 495

Compatibility, p. 496

Complexity, p. 496

Trialability, p. 496

Observability, p. 498

# SKILL-BUILDING ACTIVITIES

Invent a new product that you think will be successful—a realistic product, not a fantasy product.

1. Is this product a continuous, dynamically continuous, or discontinous innovation? How will that affect is likelihood of success?
2. Who will be the innovators? The early adopters? In each case, why?
3. As a marketer, what would you need to do in the knowledge stage? the persuasion stage? the decision stage? the implementation stage? the confirmation stage?
4. What is this product's relative advantage?
5. What is its degree of compatability? complexity? trialability? observability?
6. How will the characteristics described in activities 4 and 5 affect the likelihood of success?
7. How will you overcome the usage barrier? the value barrier? the risk barrier? the trial barrier? psychological barriers?
8. Are you sure you want to go ahead with the introduction? Suppose a failure could cost you your job. Are you still sure? Why or why not?

## ▼ MULTIPLE CHOICE

CHAPTER 17
SELF-TEST

1. Innovation is measured by both the technological changes made to the product it-self and the _____ that are required of consumers to purchase and use the product.
   a. resources
   b. behavioral changes
   c. time commitments
   d. personality changes

2. New flavors of Kool-Aid are considered a _____ product innovation.
   a. dynamically continuous
   b. discontinuous
   c. dichotomy
   d. continuous

3. _____ would *not* be considered a discontinuous innovation.
   a. Television
   b. The telephone
   c. The automobile
   d. Cable television

4. _____ is the process by which a new product spreads among the con-sumers in a market.
   a. Diffusion of an innovation
   b. Product life cycle
   c. New product introduction
   d. Product growth continuum

5. Opinion leaders are a part of the _____ category of product adopters.
   a. late majority
   b. early majority
   c. innovators
   d. early adopters

6. If Sarah waits to buy a product until she sees that all of her friends have purchased the product, she would be considered a part of the _____ category of new product adopters.
   a. late majority
   b. laggards
   c. early majority
   d. early adopters

7. When a product enters the _____ stage of the product life cycle, the late majority and laggards are the primary purchasers of the product.
   a. introduction
   b. growth
   c. maturity
   d. decline

8. If Ben installs solar outdoor lighting at his home and only then did his neighbors do the same, the _____ of the new product has encouraged product diffusion.
   a. complexity
   b. observability
   c. compatibility
   d. relative advantage

9. When a marketer introduces a new product at a very low price, a _____ pricing strategy has been used.
   a. skim
   b. introductory
   c. penetration
   d. experience curve

10. _____ may cause Kraft Foods to have slow sales of a paper towel product.
    a. tradition
    b. image
    c. trialability
    d. observableness

## ▼ TRUE/FALSE

1. New products are only classified as such if a new product category is created by their introduction.   T or F

2. Consumers are more likely to adopt a product that requires them to change their behavior than one that only involves technological change.   T or F

3. A brand extension is an example of a dynamically continuous innovation.   T or F
4. Remote control for television would be considered a continuous innovation.   T or F
5. Innovators are the smallest category of product adopters.   T or F
6. Laggards are highly involved in the decision process of buying a new product.
   T or F
7. Products that consumers find complex are slow to diffuse through the buying population.   T or F
8. Marketers should always offer a new product at a very high price so that all research and development costs will be recovered.   T or F
9. Marketers sometimes develop new products for problems that consumers have thought unsolvable.   T or F
10. A positive attitude toward a new product is enough to stimulate consumers to purchase a product.   T or F

▼  SHORT ANSWER

1. Describe the five stages of the new product adoption process.
2. Describe how marketers of larger, more expensive products could create opportunities for consumers to "try out" their products before purchase.
3. What are the four primary barriers to the adoption of a new product?

▼  APPLICATION EXERCISE

You have been asked by the Research and Development Department to evaluate a new product idea. The product is a cooking pot that has holes in the bottom that, when opened, allow liquids to escape from the pan. Using the five factors believed to increase the rate of adoption of a new product, describe how quickly you think this product will diffuse through the buying population.

# ANSWERS TO SELF-TESTS

## CHAPTER 1

### ▼ MULTIPLE CHOICE

| | |
|---|---|
| 1. C | 6. A |
| 2. C | 7. B |
| 3. A | 8. D |
| 4. D | 9. A |
| 5. C | 10. C |

### ▼ TRUE/FALSE

| | |
|---|---|
| 1. F | 6. F |
| 2. T | 7. T |
| 3. F | 8. T |
| 4. T | 9. F |
| 5. T | 10. T |

### ▼ SHORT ANSWER

**1.** The four major areas of consumer behavior affected by public policy are as follows: *fairness* (consumers should have the opportunity to satisfy their needs in an acceptable manner); *equity* (all consumers should have equal access to products and should be treated in a nondiscriminatory manner); *safety* (product safety requirements); and *economic and social welfare issues* (the ways in which consumer behavior affects a society's social and economic wellbeing).

**2.** Whereas consumers buy products for their personal use, organizational buying fulfills the needs of a business, nonprofit organization, or government body. Examples of consumer purchases include selecting a birthday gift, buying a car, and purchasing an airline ticket for a Caribbean vacation. Examples of organizational purchases include purchasing factory machinery, buying pens for a nonprofit counseling office, and purchasing coffee for the break room.

**3.** The mission of nonprofit organizations is usually not based on making a profit. Instead, these organizations strive to provide a needed service to the public. Though still required to market their services and products, nonprofits must do so on a very limited budget.

**4.** Psychology—the study of the ways in which individuals interact with their surroundings—is reflected in consumers' motivations, perceptions, and attitudes. Sociology—the study of the ways in which social environments affect people—is important to con-

sumer behavior because of the important roles that groups and societal trends play in consumer decision making.

### ▼ APPLICATION EXERCISE

Children's products are often purchased by adults. Therefore, both adults (including parents) and children would be considered consumer actors in this situation. Since the products may be considered violent in nature or possibly dangerous to small children, parents or other adults may also play a public policy role by protesting against the product and the manufacturer. Other public policy actors may include social action organizations such as the Consumer Product Safety Commission.

## CHAPTER 2

### ▼ MULTIPLE CHOICE

| | |
|---|---|
| 1. C | 6. D |
| 2. B | 7. A |
| 3. A | 8. B |
| 4. B | 9. A |
| 5. A | 10. B |

### ▼ TRUE/FALSE

| | |
|---|---|
| 1. F | 6. F |
| 2. T | 7. F |
| 3. F | 8. F |
| 4. F | 9. T |
| 5. T | 10. T |

### ▼ SHORT ANSWER

**1.** Most individuals consider the purchase of an automobile a high involvement purchase. Therefore, they complete both internal and external searches before they make the purchase. The external search process may include asking friends and family for their opinions and experiences, contacting local car dealerships for information, reading car magazines and/or such magazines as *Consumer Report,* or test driving vehicles.

**2.** Determining how you spend your time (lifestyle) and your activities, interests, and opinions (psychographics) would be critical in the selection of a vacation spot. If you are very active and enjoy physical challenges, you may want a vacation spot that offers many sports and outdoor activities. If you prefer to be sedate and take a vacation as a time to reflect, you would probably choose an alternative destination.

**3.** Individuals differ on what reference groups they utilize during consumer behavior. Possible answers to the question include:

| Purchase | Reference Groups Influencing |
|---|---|
| a. Video rental | Friends, movie reviewers, others in the video store |
| b. Restaurant | Friends, family members, coworkers, friends of your date |
| c. Compact disk player | Friends who have electronic equipment, salespeople, family members |

**4.** Consumers provide feedback to marketers in several ways. Feedback is provided via complaints, compliments, telling others about their experiences with the product, and/or writing letters to the mass media.

## ▼ APPLICATION EXERCISE

The steps utilized during the process of choosing a college or university might look like this:

| Purchase Activity | Example |
|---|---|
| Recognize needs | Want a good job<br>Economy makes finding a job difficult<br>No real work experience<br>Want to meet new friends |
| Search | College recruiters<br>Books and articles<br>Ask friends and family |
| Evaluate alternatives | Develop criteria that include low price, placement status, location, clubs/sports, scholarships available |
| Purchase product | Complete admissions application<br>File for financial aid<br>Begin classes |
| Evaluation of consumption | Does school meet my expectations?<br>Have I made new friends?<br>Should I be able to get a job after I graduate? |
| Feedback | Enroll in courses every semester<br>Tell friends about your experiences<br>Complete course evaluations |

## ▼ SHORT ANSWER

**1.** A company that uses an undifferentiated segmentation strategy develops one product or product line for the entire market. A company that uses a differentiated segmentation strategy develops several products to fulfill the needs of several segments of the market.

**2.** The three criteria used in determining how many distinct segments to serve are the (1) size of the segment, (2) the stability of the segment, and (3) the accessiblity of the segment.

**3.** Segmentation based on several criteria allows a marketer to better understand the needs and wants of a specific segment of the market. Understanding personal characteristics in addition to behavior patterns and purchase activities gives a marketer a more precise profile of the possible consumers of their product. This profile is then used to develop a marketing mix strategy consistent with the characteristics of the segment.

**4.** All activities related to the design, production, pricing, promotion, and distribution of a consumer product should be based on the characteristics and behavior patterns of the target market. For example, markcters must design products so that the product's attributes are consistent with those required to satisfy consumers. The price of a product must be consistent with the consumers' expectations of quality and durability. Understanding consumers is also important for effective communication, the goal of marketing promotions. Finally, delivering the product to the location where consumers will use it (the place component of the marketing mix) can only be done if the marketer understands the purchase patterns its target market exhibits.

## ▼ APPLICATION EXERCISE

There are several viable segments to which this product may be targeted. One segment may include those consumers with the following characteristics:

18 to 65 years of age

Employed at least part time

Above average income

Female

Interested in physical fitness and nutrition

The above profile is just one example of a possible target market for a low-fat and low-cholesterol frozen waffle product. Marketing research data ultimately dictate the characteristics of the segment of the frozen waffle market that will be interested in purchasing this product.

## CHAPTER 3

### ▼ MULTIPLE CHOICE

| | |
|---|---|
| 1. C | 6. A |
| 2. B | 7. A |
| 3. B | 8. C |
| 4. A | 9. A |
| 5. B | 10. C |

### ▼ TRUE/FALSE

| | |
|---|---|
| 1. T | 6. T |
| 2. F | 7. F |
| 3. F | 8. T |
| 4. F | 9. F |
| 5. T | 10. F |

## CHAPTER 4

### ▼ MULTIPLE CHOICE

| | |
|---|---|
| 1. C | 6. C |
| 2. A | 7. A |
| 3. B | 8. B |
| 4. C | 9. C |
| 5. B | 10. B |

### ▼ TRUE/FALSE

| | |
|---|---|
| 1. T | 6. T |
| 2. F | 7. T |
| 3. F | 8. T |
| 4. T | 9. F |
| 5. F | 10. F |

## ▼ SHORT ANSWER

**1.** *Customs* are culturally acceptable behaviors that are expected in certain situations. Examples are shaking hands when greeting someone or expecting people to bathe everyday. *Laws* are expected behaviors that are formalized and regulated by the government. Examples are prohibiting anyone under the age of 21 from drinking or prohibiting marketers from charging different prices to different consumers based on those consumers' ethnic backgrounds. Failure to follow laws results in penalties from the government.

**2.** Understanding how consumers spend their time, what type of personal space is required, and what colors mean to members of a different culture contributes to a more effective marketing strategy. These things reflect the culture and whether a product, its advertising, packaging, price, and use is compatible to that culture.

**3.** Marketing personnel become "acculturated" to a culture after they spend a period of time in that culture. In other words, they learn the culture and better understand the consumers within that culture. Therefore, it is usually the best business decision to leave personnel that are comfortable and successful there in that culture instead of requiring them to learn new cultures constantly.

**4.** Many aspects of marketing are based on communication. Language is the tool members of a culture use to communicate. Thus, the development of product and brand names, advertising, public relations, and publicity should be based on the language of each culture targeted.

## ▼ APPLICATION EXERCISE

For a product such as sausage, its appeal to a culture would certainly need to be evaluated. Additional research would also be required in the following areas: compatibility with the eating patterns of that culture; the technology available to store and maintain the product's freshness; and food product marketing laws. This list is not inclusive but a preliminary review of some of the things that could affect the success of a new sausage product in a culture. A complete analysis of any targeted culture would include a review of all aspects of that culture.

## CHAPTER 5

### ▼ MULTIPLE CHOICE

| | |
|---|---|
| 1. C | 6. A |
| 2. A | 7. C |
| 3. B | 8. C |
| 4. B | 9. B |
| 5. B | 10. C |

### ▼ TRUE/FALSE

| | |
|---|---|
| 1. F | 6. T |
| 2. T | 7. F |
| 3. T | 8. T |
| 4. T | 9. F |
| 5. F | 10. T |

### ▼ SHORT ANSWER

**1.** The college student market can be targeted via several specific media, including college newspapers, late–night television, and youth-oriented radio.

**2.** Baby boomers are presently buying products related to busy lifestyles. They are major purchasers of services such as child care, lawn care, and housecleaning. They are also beginning to buy products such as anti-aging medications, cosmetics, and fit-

ness products. In 10 years, the older portion of the baby boomers will be nearing retirement. Therefore, the boomer will begin purchasing products presently being purchased by the mature market, such as travel and other luxury items.

**3.** Researchers are beginning to explore the extent to which religion plays a role in consumer behavior. Some basic trends indicate that the religion of some consumers affects purchases such as restaurant and grocery store food products, videos and movies, liquor, and clothing, in particular.

**4.** The number and ages of people in a household have tangible effects on consumer behavior since each would determine both the quantity of purchases and the choice of brand names made. The household composition also affects consumer behavior on an intangible level because of cultural, subcultural, and psychological differences that characterize individual households.

## ▼ APPLICATION EXERCISE

The cohort that would most likely be the target for this type of product would be the baby boomers. This is due to this subculture's interest in products that both are convenient to use and offer some time savings. This group is also entering their highest earning years, so many can afford a product priced like the pasta maker. The other cohorts are less interested in expensive products that predominately offer the consumer some type of convenience.

## CHAPTER 6

### ▼ MULTIPLE CHOICE

| | |
|---|---|
| 1. B | 6. B |
| 2. A | 7. D |
| 3. C | 8. A |
| 4. C | 9. B |
| 5. A | 10. C |

### ▼ TRUE/FALSE

| | |
|---|---|
| 1. F | 6. F |
| 2. F | 7. F |
| 3. T | 8. T |
| 4. T | 9. T |
| 5. T | 10. F |

### ▼ SHORT ANSWER

**1.** The three components of the CAD scale are the personality traits compliant, aggressive, and detached. Consumers that are compliant or detached are not interested in volatile interactions with others. The aggressive personality type would be the target for a video game that is based on fighting.

**2.** A direct rating scale asks respondents to describe themselves in terms of how strongly a particular adjective describes them. A sorting task methodology requires respondents to sort adjectives into categories or piles based on whether those adjectives reflect who they are. A semantic differential scale uses a bipolar approach and asks respondents to choose which one of the two opposite adjectives best describes them.

**3.** With the advances in technology, marketers are collecting more and more information from their customers. Some marketers choose to sell that information to other companies. Opponents of this practice claim that the information is private and should not be given to second parties without approval by the customer. These concerns are now being addressed by marketers so that a balance can be found between using consumer data for marketing strategy development on the one hand, and maintaining the privacy of the individual consumer on the other.

**4.** The ideal self is the portion of a consumer's self concept that includes what that person wishes he or she to be. By contrast, a person's actual self is a realistic portrayal of the person. Consumers buy products to fulfill *both* of these selves.

▼ APPLICATION EXERCISE

Many types of AIO questions might be asked of the customers. Some examples are as follows:

*Activity Questions*
- Do you prefer to spend time inside or outside?
- Do you like to work in your yard?
- Do you like camping?

*Interest Questions*
- Would you rather spend time working in the yard or reading?
- How important to you is getting tasks done quickly?
- Do you like to use products that conserve fossil fuel?

*Opinion Questions*
- Electricity is less harmful to the environment than gasoline.

*Agree/Disagree*
- Recycling should be done by everyone. Agree/Disagree
- High-technology products are always the best. Agree/Disagree

The answers to these and other AIO questions can be used to develop a profile of the customers of the lawn mower. This profile can then be used to develop promotion, new products, pricing, and distribution strategies to increase the customer base.

## CHAPTER 7

▼ MULTIPLE CHOICE   ▼ TRUE/FALSE

| 1. D | 6. A | 1. F | 6. T |
|------|------|------|------|
| 2. A | 7. C | 2. T | 7. T |
| 3. B | 8. B | 3. F | 8. T |
| 4. C | 9. A | 4. F | 9. F |
| 5. B | 10. B | 5. T | 10. F |

▼ SHORT ANSWER

**1.** First, a reference group can provide needed information about products and purchasing. Second, the group may provide the power and resources needed to make a purchase. Third, consumers may adopt a certain image from a reference group that is consistent with how the consumer wants to be perceived by the public.

**2.** The media can play a role in the process of learning relevant consumer skills and knowledge. Children are exposed to many images and behaviors while watching television, communicating via interactive media, and reading print media. These images are combined with the information they have learned from their families and friends during the socialization process.

**3.** As outlined in Figure 7.14, reference groups may or may not effect the purchase of certain products. Since private luxury goods are often used in the home, just having that product is an indicator of a certain status within a group. Thus, the brand of the private luxury good is not influenced by a reference group; rather, the purchase of the product itself is influenced by the group.

**4.** An identification group is a positive membership group with which a consumer identifes strongly and whose behaviors and values are endorsed by the consumers. This differs from a discrimination group, which is a group to which the consumer not only does not belong but also does not identify with its members.

▼ APPLICATION EXERCISE

Potential donors may be influenced by several different formal and informal reference groups. Several examples are as follows:

*Formal Groups*

A church might ask its members to donate to this nonprofit organization.

Your employer might choose to give to this or another charity. This would effect whether the employee would want to give additional funds.

A sorority or fraternity may target this charity for funds so that its members may or may not want to give additional funds.

Certain professional clubs and/or organizations might require members to participate in some type of service project. The nonprofit might be discussed during one of the club's meetings, and the members might be influenced to choose this organization for its service project.

*Informal*

Friends may have given to this charity before and therefore influence others to give.

Individuals may be influenced by their family as to whether they should donate money. For example, if someone in your family had a terminal disease, you might be more likely to give.

Coworkers might discuss family members or friends they know who need this type of service. This might influence you to give to the charity.

## CHAPTER 8

▼ MULTIPLE CHOICE   ▼ TRUE/FALSE

| 1. B | 6. C | 1. T | 6. T |
|------|------|------|------|
| 2. C | 7. B | 2. T | 7. T |
| 3. A | 8. D | 3. F | 8. F |
| 4. D | 9. A | 4. F | 9. F |
| 5. B | 10. D | 5. F | 10. F |

▼ SHORT ANSWER

**1.** The three factors that effect the choice of goals are the individual's background characteristics, the available options and the individual's knowledge of those options, and the efforts of marketers and public policy actors to influence the motivation process.

**2.** When an approach–avoidance goal conflict occurs, the fulfillment of a goal that meets one need prevents the fulfillment of another need. An avoidance–avoidance conflict occurs when a consumer must fulfill a goal that is not pleasurable but will fulfill a need.

**3.** Maslow's theory is based on a hierarchy that can only be completed one step at a time. For example, people must satisfy their needs for safety before they can address their need for friends. In actuality, however, consumers can satisfy more than one type of need simultaneously. They do not need to wait to fulfill one need before addressing another.

**4.** The marketing concept states that marketers strive to satisfy consumers' needs by developing strategies and products that consumers find attractive. Based on the fact that marketers expend significant amounts of time and money researching needs, and that marketers have found that it is more difficult to create a need than to satisfy existing needs, it seems that advertising is not trying to create needs—it is merely trying to communicate to consumers options to fulfill their needs.

▼ APPLICATION EXERCISE

This type of product fulfills acquired needs because having a suntan is not a physiological need that a person must satisfy to stay alive. The goal of having a tan can evolve from many different needs. For example, a consumer may want to attract members of the opposite sex and believe that being tan can contribute to that result. Other needs that may be fulfilled include social acceptance in a group that may spend a lot of time outdoors or the need for prestige, since many believe that only the "rich and famous" can maintain a tan year round.

## CHAPTER 9

▼ MULTIPLE CHOICE    ▼ TRUE/FALSE

| | | | |
|---|---|---|---|
| 1. B | 6. A | 1. F | 6. F |
| 2. A | 7. B | 2. T | 7. T |
| 3. C | 8. D | 3. F | 8. F |
| 4. C | 9. D | 4. F | 9. T |
| 5. D | 10. A | 5. T | 10. F |

▼ SHORT ANSWER

**1.** Since consumers are constantly bombarded with stimuli, they must be selective in what they choose to process. Therefore, consumers select stimuli that they are interested in or that catch their attention. Consumers complete the perception process on only those stimuli that are important to them.

**2.** When marketers change the price of the product, Weber's Law and consumers' differential thresholds should be considered. Often marketers need to raise a price to cover increased production costs. When this occurs, a marketer should determine how much the price could be raised before consumers actually notice the change. Also, if a marketer wants to lower the price, it must determine how low the price must go for consumers to notice that the product is now cheaper and therefore might be considered for purchase.

**3.** There are five major types of perceived risk. *Functional risk* is

the risk that the product might not perform as well as the consumer wishes. *Physical risk* is the risk that the product might physically harm the consumer. *Financial risk* is the risk that the product will not be worth the money required for its purchase. *Social risk* is the risk that the product will be socially unacceptable. *Psychological risk* is the risk that the product will not be consistent with who the consumer perceives himself or herself to be.

▼ APPLICATION EXERCISE

Several types of perceived risk are relevant to the purchase of products from a catalog. For example, since the consumers cannot "try out" the products before purchase, the catalog might offer a money-back guarantee so that the consumers will not incur financial or functional risk from the purchase. Also, since the products are not shown in color, specific information on the colors available should be provided both within the copy of the catalog and also by the customer service representative taking the order. That would reduce both the psychological and social risks that might occur if a product's color is unacceptable to the consumer. The toll-free number included in the catalog is also a good strategy to reduce consumer risk, particularly financial risk. The catalog and all product packaging should also provide information on exactly how to use the products so that any physical risk can be reduced.

## CHAPTER 10

▼ MULTIPLE CHOICE    ▼ TRUE/FALSE

| | | | |
|---|---|---|---|
| 1. B | 6. C | 1. F | 6. F |
| 2. C | 7. A | 2. T | 7. T |
| 3. D | 8. A | 3. F | 8. F |
| 4. B | 9. B | 4. F | 9. T |
| 5. A | 10. A | 5. T | 10. T |

▼ SHORT ANSWER

**1.** Repetition enhances learning in two ways. When behavioral learning occurs, repetition of the stimulus increases the likelihood of a sought response. From a cognitive learning standpoint, repetition encourages consumers to pay attention to a stimulus and to associate new information with information already stored in long-term memory.

**2.** The four factors that influence a consumer's ability to retrieve stored information are familiarity, relevance, form, and repetition.

**3.** When stimulus discrimination occurs, a consumer responds only to a specific stimulus or brand. Thus, when some consumers exhibit stimulus discrimination they are being brand or product loyal. This is advantageous to the marketer of the product causing the stimulus discrimination since the consumer will not consider buying any competing brand.

▼ APPLICATION EXERCISE

Operant conditioning is based on reinforcement. Positive reinforcement encourages consumers to continue buying a particular product or service. Examples of how a new restaurant can "reward" or reinforce patronage include: discounts on food purchased during the first visit; free appetizers during the first month the restaurant is open; gift certificates to be used at local health clubs or sporting goods stores; free prizes for diners.

# CHAPTER 11

## ▼ MULTIPLE CHOICE

1. C    6. B
2. B    7. D
3. C    8. B
4. A    9. C
5. A    10. D

## ▼ TRUE/FALSE

1. F    6. F
2. F    7. T
3. T    8. T
4. F    9. T
5. F    10. F

## ▼ SHORT ANSWER

**1.** The three components of the tricomponent model of attitudes are (1) cognitive beliefs about an object; (2) affect, or feelings, about the object; and (3) conative predisposition to purchase the object to fulfill a need.

**2.** Attitude-toward-the-ad models investigate how attitudes toward a particular advertisement affect a consumer's decision to purchase the product being advertised. The models conclude that consumers form feelings toward an advertisement, which are then transferred to the product. In the development of advertisements, a marketer must determine whether consumers will have positive attitudes toward the ad in hopes that those feelings will contribute to the ultimate purchase of the product.

**3.** The four ways marketers attempt to influence attitudes include: (1) adding benefits to a product; (2) changing the product or its packaging; (3) encouraging consumers to change their evaluation of the product; (4) or linking products to favorable attitudes already held by the consumer.

## ▼ APPLICATION EXERCISE

An attitude-toward-the-object model (using a scale of 1 as "poor or unimportant" to 10 as "excellent or very important") for the choice of a spring break trip might look like the following:

Belief That Destination Has Attribute

| Attribute | Importance of Attribute | So. Padre | Copper Mountain |
|---|---|---|---|
| College kids welcome | 8 | 9 | 7 |
| Affordable | 10 | 7 | 5 |
| Other friends going there | 6 | 10 | 5 |
| Can get a tan | 5 | 9 | 5 |

If the importance is multiplied by the belief and then totaled, South Padre Island would score a total of 247. Copper Mountain would score a 161. Thus the person completing this attitude-toward-the-object would have a more favorable attitude toward South Padre Island.

# CHAPTER 12

## ▼ MULTIPLE CHOICE

1. C    6. D
2. A    7. D
3. C    8. B
4. B    9. A
5. C    10. C

## ▼ TRUE/FALSE

1. F    6. T
2. F    7. T
3. T    8. F
4. F    9. T
5. T    10. T

## ▼ SHORT ANSWER

**1.** Limited decision making occurs when a consumer is involved in a decision that has been made before, but some additional information may be needed to make a good decision. Therefore, some effort is needed to determine what product will best fulfill the imminent need. Routine decision making occurs when a consumer needs to make a decision to fulfill a low involvement need and the consumer is not willing to exert any extra effort in the decision process.

**2.** External sources of search information might include brochures, advertisements, car magazines, car salespeople, friends and family, the Internet, and television shows.

**3.** Assuming the consumer uses the evaluative criteria of rent, number of bedrooms, appliances, and location, the elimination by aspects rule would work as follows:

| Attributes (in order of importance) | Cutoff Level | Alternative 1 | Alternative 2 |
|---|---|---|---|
| Rent | $450 | $430 | $430 |
| Number of bedrooms | 2 | 2 | 2 |
| Appliances | Range, dishwasher | Yes | No |

The consumer would then select Alternative 1 since the lack of appliances in Alternative 2 cannot be compensated by its ratings on other attributes.

## ▼ APPLICATION EXERCISE

There are several ways to encourage consumers to consider your airline when making travel plans. You could advertise in the travel section of the local newspaper. You might send brochures about your airlines to travel agents so that they can help "sell" the airline to their clients. Several forms of sales promotion might be considered, including offering two-for-one tickets or giving prospective customers a small gift just for calling the airline and asking about rates or flight information. All of these strategies should increase the airline's awareness level in the community and could help move the airline from the status of an inert alternative to an alternative within the evoked set of the target market.

# CHAPTER 13

▼ MULTIPLE CHOICE       ▼ TRUE/FALSE

| 1. B | 6. B | 1. T | 6. F |
|------|------|------|------|
| 2. B | 7. C | 2. F | 7. T |
| 3. A | 8. D | 3. F | 8. F |
| 4. D | 9. C | 4. T | 9. T |
| 5. D | 10. D | 5. T | 10. T |

▼ SHORT ANSWER

**1.** The three types of factors that influence involvement are background characteristics of the consumer, characteristics of the product, and situational effects that accompany a particular purchase or usage occasion.

**2.** Consumers purchasing low involvement products have been known to skip the search process all together. If they do conduct any search activity, it is most likely in the form of internal search. Consumers of high involvement products not only conduct a search, but often that search is quite extensive. They would not only conduct an internal search but would also conduct an external search.

**3.** Associating a product with a special occasion may serve as a method to move low involvement consumers out of their routine. Thus, it is an attempt to make consumers think more about the purchase and to become more involved in choosing the product that will best meet the needs incurred during a holiday or special occasion purchase process.

▼ APPLICATION EXERCISE

Advertising for high involvement products should include substantial information not only about the product itself but also about how that product will fulfill a need. The following information might be included in an advertisement for swimming pool construction: prices, services offered by the company, information on how long the company has been in business, information about warranties and guaranties, and testimonials from pool owners.

# CHAPTER 14

▼ MULTIPLE CHOICE       ▼ TRUE/FALSE

| 1. B | 6. B | 1. F | 6. T |
|------|------|------|------|
| 2. C | 7. C | 2. T | 7. T |
| 3. D | 8. D | 3. F | 8. F |
| 4. A | 9. A | 4. T | 9. T |
| 5. D | 10. B | 5. F | 10. T |

▼ SHORT ANSWER

**1.** The four activities involved in the actual purchase and use of a product are: purchasing and using the product; evaluating the consumption experience; providing feedback about the consumption experience; and ending the purchase process.

**2.** Consumers use both absolute and relative measures to evaluate their product experiences. Absolute measurement involves determining whether the product fulfilled their needs, whereas relative measures concern a consumer's prepurchase expectations and how well the product has fulfilled those expectations.

**3.** Marketers attempt to create and ensure consumer satisfaction by designing products that meet consumers' needs, developing realistic expectations within the consumers, and responding to consumers who voice their satisfaction or dissatisfaction.

▼ APPLICATION EXERCISE

A sporting goods store might contain the following physical characteristics: bright lighting, up-beat music, spacious surroundings that allow consumers to "try" the products, displays that show the products being used, video monitors showing athletic events and activities, and vivid colors. Enabling conditions that might be included in the store include layaway programs, acceptance of several credit and debit cards, free delivery of large items, assistance in transporting products from the store to the customers' vehicles, and free "sizing" of products that can be tailored to a certain body type.

# CHAPTER 15

▼ MULTIPLE CHOICE       ▼ TRUE/FALSE

| 1. B | 6. D | 1. T | 6. F |
|------|------|------|------|
| 2. B | 7. B | 2. F | 7. T |
| 3. A | 8. C | 3. F | 8. F |
| 4. D | 9. A | 4. T | 9. F |
| 5. A | 10. B | 5. T | 10. T |

▼ SHORT ANSWER

**1.** Consumers utilize marketing communication to gather information about the attributes and benefits of products. Specifically, information is used throughout the decision making purchase and beyond.

**2.** A source encodes desired information into a message that is transmitted through a medium to a receiver, who then decodes that message and provides feedback to the source.

**3.** Consumers provide feedback to a message by purchasing or not purchasing a product, by asking the marketer for additional information, by complaining to the marketer about the message, and/or by responding to requests for feedback.

▼ APPLICATION EXERCISE

Any of the three types of appeals could be used to promote backpacks. For example, the marketer could develop a message that contains information on how the product was made and how it is used and feedback from past buyers. Thus, the marketer would be using a factual appeal. Using a fear appeal, the marketer could illustrate how a student would be "lost" without a backpack and how the student would not fit in with his or her peer group without this particular brand of backpack. Finally, a sex appeal approach might feature an attractive male or female pictured with the product, and the message could include the implication that using the backpack makes you more attractive to the opposite sex. The choice of appeal would be based on the positioning and segmentation objectives and strategies of the marketer.

## CHAPTER 16

### ▼ MULTIPLE CHOICE

| | |
|---|---|
| 1. C | 6. C |
| 2. B | 7. D |
| 3. B | 8. A |
| 4. A | 9. C |
| 5. C | 10. B |

### ▼ TRUE/FALSE

| | |
|---|---|
| 1. T | 6. F |
| 2. F | 7. F |
| 3. T | 8. T |
| 4. F | 9. T |
| 5. T | 10. F |

### ▼ SHORT ANSWER

**1.** Information conveyed through interpersonal communication can be classified as product news, advice, or personal experience.

**2.** Consumers use word-of-mouth communication when purchasing new products, technically complex products, risky products, or products that will be used in a visible setting.

**3.** Marketers identify opinion leaders through one of the following measurement techniques: self-designating method, key informant method, or sociometric method.

### ▼ APPLICATION EXERCISE

To create opinion leaders, a marketer needs to identify individuals who may be effective in opinion leadership. You may notice who attends the club on a regular basis and also observe which members seem to indicate leadership characteristics. These individuals would most likely have the credibility needed to be effective opinion leaders. You could then approach the identified members and ask for their assistance. You may have to consider providing those individuals some type of incentive such as use of the club free for a month when asking them to solicit their friends for possible club membership.

## CHAPTER 17

### ▼ MULTIPLE CHOICE

| | |
|---|---|
| 1. B | 6. A |
| 2. D | 7. C |
| 3. D | 8. B |
| 4. A | 9. C |
| 5. D | 10. B |

### ▼ TRUE/FALSE

| | |
|---|---|
| 1. F | 6. F |
| 2. F | 7. T |
| 3. F | 8. F |
| 4. F | 9. T |
| 5. T | 10. F |

### ▼ SHORT ANSWER

**1.** The five stages of the adoption process are as follows: knowledge (consumers gather information about the products); persuasion (evaluation of alternative products); decision (mental choice of the product to purchase); implementation (trial and use of the chosen product); and adoption (evaluation of the product after usage).

**2.** Marketers can promote "trial" of large or expensive products by way of liberal return policies, guarantees, samples, or by offering smaller or condensed versions of their products as a means for consumers to see how the product meets their needs before an actual purchase is made.

**3.** The four primary barriers to adopting a product are usage, value, risk, and psychological factors, such as tradition barriers and image barriers.

### ▼ APPLICATION EXERCISE

The product proposed would be considered a continuous innovation. When evaluating the pot on the four factors believed to increase the rate of adoption, the product seems to have characteristics that would encourage diffusion throughout the buying population. The product might offer a relative advantage to cooks since, presently, a separate colander or at the least the use of the pan top is required when draining liquid from a pot or pan. Since most people have pots and pans at their home, the product would most likely be compatible with how they presently use those products, although there may be some concern as to whether the pot could be used on gas versus electric stoves. Unless the process of exposing the holes is complex, the product itself does not seem to be difficult to use. Thus, complexity would probably not be an issue. The two factors that may hurt diffusion of the product are trialability and observability. The marketer may consider providing the product to local food "celebrities"; in turn, those celebrities will report on the product to others. Likewise, the marketer may choose to develop a demonstration program at local retailers so that consumers can see the product in use. Of course, marketing research will need to be conducted before a real determination is made as to whether the product should be introduced.

# GLOSSARY

**Absolute threshold** the lowest possible amount of stimulation that can be detected by an individual's sensory receptors.

**Access to funds** the consumer's ability to pay for a product at the time of purchase.

**Access to products** the consumer's capacity to acquire and transport a product to where it will be used.

**Acculturation** the process of learning the values, language, myths, customs, and rituals of a new or foreign culture.

**Acquired needs** social and psychological needs.

**Activation** the process of integrating new information into existing associative networks—the structure of knowledge about a particular domain.

**Actor** an individual or organization that plays the role of consumer, marketer, or public policy interest in a specific instance of consumer behavior.

**Actual self** an individual's view of who he or she is.

**Advertising** paid marketing communication delivered through mass media from marketers to consumers.

**Affect** an individual's feelings or emotions about an object.

**Affinity** the attractiveness or appeal that a reference group has for an individual.

**Aperture** the time and location at which a message will be delivered for maximum impact.

**Approach–approach conflict** a situation that occurs when two needs, each of which motivates an attractive goal, cannot be satisfied at the same time.

**Approach–avoidance conflict** a situation that occurs when a goal will meet one need but prevent the satisfaction of another.

**Aspiration groups** positive nonmembership groups that have a powerful influence on an individual who aspires to be a member.

**Attitude** a predisposition to act in a consistent way toward an object.

**Attitude formation** the process by which consumers evaluate an object, form a feeling or opinion about it, and develop a predisposition to act based on that opinion.

**Attribution** an inference that an individual makes about the reasons for occurrences.

**Authority** an opinion leader who provides news, advice, or personal experience to help consumers satisfy their needs.

**Avoidance–avoidance conflict** a situation that occurs when an individual must choose between two unattractive goals that will satisfy a need.

**Baby boomers** the 81 million Americans born between 1946 and 1964.

**Baby busters** the approximately 45 million Americans born between 1965 and 1976.

**Behavioral learning theories** hypotheses that define learning as the unconscious association between a stimulus and a response.

**Behavioral processes** the motivational, perceptual, learning, attitude formation, and decision making tools that consumers use to complete the activities that satisfy their needs.

**Belief** an individual's knowledge about a particular object, such as its attributes and benefits.

**Brand experience perspective** acknowledgment of the complexity of the purchase process and the increasing volume of marketing communication targeted at consumers.

**Cause-related marketing** the linking of a product with a cause in an attempt to influence consumers to change their attitudes toward the product.

**Classical conditioning** the result of an individual's learning to associate an unrelated stimulus with a particular behavioral response that has previously been elicited by a related stimulus.

**Cognitive dissonance** a person's discomfort when he or she has knowledge, holds attitudes, or takes actions that conflict with one another.

**Cognitive learning theories** hypotheses that posit that learning occurs when an individual processes information using conscious mental processes.

**Cohort** an age-based subculture whose members share childhood and young adulthood experiences that influence their customs, rituals, and behavioral processes.

**Communication** the transmission of a message from a source through a medium to a receiver.

**Compatibility** the degree to which a new product is consistent with the background and behavioral patterns of consumers.

**Compensatory decision roles** rules that consider all attributes simultaneously to calculate an integrated, multiattribute rank ordering.

**Complexity** the ease with which consumers can understand and use a new product.

**Conative component** the individual's intention to act in a particular way or a predisposition to take a specific action.

**Concentrated segmentation strategy** a strategy that identifies a segmented market but focuses efforts on positioning and producing one specifically tailored product or product line to one of those segments.

**Conjunctive rule** rule that eliminates an alternative if any of its attribute ratings do not meet a minimum cutoff level.

**Consumer background characteristics** the innate, stable characteristics of a consumer's life that are based on the consumer's cultural background and values and demographic, psychological, and social attributes.

**Consumer behavior** the study of consumers as they exchange something of value for a product or service that satisfies their needs through a process that involves searching for, purchasing, using, evaluating, and disposing of the product or service.

**Consumer satisfaction or dissatisfaction (CS/D)** the attitude toward a product that results from the consumer's evaluation of the usage experience.

**Consumer socialization** the process by which people acquire the skills and knowledge relevant to purchase behavior.

**Consumers** individuals who identify a need, buy and consume products or services to satisfy their need, and then dispose of the product or terminate the service when they are through with it.

**Consumption community** a reference group based on common consumer purchase behavior.

**Continuous innovation** the modification of an existing product that involves little technological innovation and little behavioral change.

**Credibility** the believe that a source of information is accurate and unbiased.

**Cross-cultural analysis** the conducting of systematic comparisons of the similarities and differences in all aspects of the targeted cultures.

**Culture** the essential character of a society that distinguishes it from other cultures; the unique pattern of shared meanings that characterize a society.

**Custom** a culturally acceptable pattern of behavior that routinely occurs in a particular situation.

**Customized market** a market in which each consumer constitutes his or her own segment.

**Decision making** the tool that consumers use to choose among alternative actions that are available to them.

**Decision rule** a method used to integrate multiple evaluative criteria into a single ordering of alternative products.

**Demographic characteristics** the physical, geographical, social, and economic attributes of consumers that are innate components of their day-to-day lives.

**Depth interviews** interviews that probe deeply into an individual's psychological makeup to explain the needs that motivate a purchase.

**Differential threshold** the smallest possible change in a stimulus that an individual is able to perceive.

**Differentiated segmentation strategy** a strategy that identifies a segmented market and targets multiple segments with a product or product line produced and positioned for each segment.

**Diffusion of an innovation** the process by which a new product spreads through a market.

**Direct response** the delivery of a message directly from the marketer to the consumer, providing a method for the consumer to respond to the message.

**Discontinuous innovation** a new product that provides some technological change or new benefit and requires new consumer purchase and usage behaviors.

**Discrimination group** a negative nonmembership group whose members an individual does not identify with and with whom the individual has little familiarity.

**Disjunctive rule** rule that sets a cutoff point for each attribute and retains any alternatives that exceed the cutoff on any of the attributes.

**Displacement** the conversion of an id-based need to a more acceptable form.

**Dynamically continuous innovation** a new product

that provides some technological change or new benefit but requires little or no behavioral change.

**Economies of scale**   the efficiencies in production and marketing costs that come from producing many units of one product.

**Edwards Personal Preference Scale (EPPS)**   a measure that uses a questionnaire to measure 15 distinct personality traits.

**Ego**   the personality style that tries to reconcile individual needs with the demands and circumstances of the environment.

**Elaboration likelihood model (ELM)**   model that asserts that consumers change attitudes through two distinct routes: a central route or a peripheral route.

**Elimination by aspects**   a technique used to eliminate alternatives that do not meet a minimum cutoff level on each attribute.

**Enculturation**   the process of learning one's native cultural values, language, myths, customs, rituals, and laws.

**Enduring involvement**   a person's ongoing high involvement with a product category.

**Ethnocentrism**   the belief that one's culture is superior to others.

**Evaluative criteria**   the attributes that a consumer uses to discriminate among the benefits offered by alternative products in his or her evoked set.

**Evoked (or consideration) set**   the set of alternatives that a consumer retrieves from memory or identifies during search activities.

**Extensive decision making**   the significant effort involved in identifying criteria and choosing how to apply them to the purchase process.

**Feedback**   the return of information from the receiver to the source.

**Focus group**   a small group of individuals who discuss their attitudes toward some object with the help of a moderator.

**Forecasting**   the process of estimating the size of a consumer market segment.

**Formal groups**   groups that have clearly defined rules for membership and frequent, organized patterns of interaction.

**Generic competitors**   independent firms that satisfy the same consumer need.

**Geodemographics**   the classification of geographical neighborhoods into segments that reflect the fact that people of similar demographic characteristics often choose to live together.

**Gestalt psychology**   a school of thought that maintains that the physical pattern of stimuli influences the way in which an individual organizes his or her perception of each distinct stimulus.

**Global marketing strategy**   a strategy that maintains one marketing plan across all countries and yields global name recognition.

**Goal**   the desired ideal state that will provide benefits to satisfy a need.

**Heuristics**   the "rules of thumb" that consumers apply to choose from among alternative products.

**Hierarchy of effects model**   the seven steps that consumers use to reach a purchase decision.

**Id**   the desire for immediate pleasure.

**Ideal self**   an individual's view of who he or she wants to be.

**Identification**   the process of adopting another person's proven method of integrating the id, ego, and superego.

**Identification groups**   positive membership groups with which a consumer identifies strongly and whose values and behaviors the individual incorporates into his or her behavior.

**Individual referent**   an individual to whom a consumer looks to provide examples of behavior to emulate.

**Inept set**   the set of alternatives that a consumer will not consider buying.

**Inert set**   the set of alternatives toward which a consumer is indifferent.

**Informal groups**   groups that have significant levels of interaction among members but no formal rules for membership.

**Information processing**   the storage, organization, and retrieval of information from one's memory.

**Innate needs**   the biological needs that a person must satisfy in order to stay alive.

**Instrumental (or operant) conditioning**   the result of a consumer's learning to associate a stimulus with a response when given reinforcement for responding to the stimulus.

**Instrumental values**   the means by which consumers can achieve the objectives they seek.

**Integrated marketing communications**   an approach used to coordinate the different messages and media for a product to provide a coherent, consistent stream of information.

**Interpersonal communication**   the informal two-way exchange of information and influence among individuals.

**Involvement**   the importance or relevance that the purchase process for a particular product has for a consumer.

**Key informant method** technique that relies on a knowledgeable individual to indicate which consumers in a group are opinion leaders.

**Laddering** a technique that elicits a chain of associations among a product's attributes, benefits, and goals that are achieved.

**Laws** formal rules and regulations that have the sanction of a governmental body to require or prohibit specific behavior.

**Learning** the process by which consumers organize knowledge and experience so that they can use them again in future activities.

**Lexographic decision rule** rule that considers the one attribute that is most important and chooses the alternative that is rated highest on that attribute.

**Lifestyle analysis** studies that emphasize activities and interests in a social and cultural context.

**Lifestyle and psychographics** descriptions of the ways in which a consumer expresses the psychological bases of his or her personality in the cultural and social context of day-to-day activities, interests, and opinions.

**Limited decision making** the application of existing criteria to a recurring purchase decision.

**Line extension** a continuous innovation that extends an existing product by introducing a new flavor, size, or form.

**Local opinion leader** an individual in a consumer's positive reference group who provides advice and personal experience regarding purchase choices.

**Localized marketing strategy** a strategy that takes into account differences in consumer behavior and the systems needed to market products in different geographic areas.

**Long-term memory** memory that permanently stores knowledge after elaborative rehearsal has evaluated the information for meaning and stored it.

**Market maven** an authority on the process of buying products.

**Market segment accessibility** the ease with which the marketer can reach the targeted segment and the costs of reaching those consumers.

**Market segment size** the total sales that a marketer expects to gain from the consumers in the segment.

**Market segment stability** the extent to which the segment is likely to maintain its size.

**Marketers** individuals or organizations that satisfy consumer needs in exchange for money.

**Marketing communication** the flow of information about products from marketers to consumers.

**Marketing concept** the view that a marketer must satisfy its consumers' needs in order to gain a long-term profit from its exchanges with those consumers.

**Marketing mix** the set of variables—product, price, promotion, and place—that the marketer uses to facilitate exchange with consumers.

**Marketing segmentation** dividing the total market into segments and then targeting specific products at selected segments.

**Marketing strategy** the plan that marketers use to guide their efforts to exchange specific products with specific consumer segments.

**Maslow's hierarchy of needs** a theory that maintains that a person will satisfy lower-order needs before attempting to satisfy higher-order ones.

**Mass market** a market that encompasses all consumers.

**Material artifacts** goods that a culture has imbued with special meaning.

**Mature market** the 68 million Americans over the age of 50.

**Means–end chain** the assumption that a product offers a means to achieve a desired goal.

**Medium** the communications channel between a source and a receiver.

**Membership reference group** a group of individuals who model their behavior after others in the group.

**Message** the information content communicated and the creative form it takes.

**Mirror controversy** the argument that advertising is a mirror that reflects the products and lifestyles consumers want to see.

**Motivation** the process by which consumers recognize their innate or acquired needs and initiate action to satisfy those needs.

**Motivational research** an approach that investigates the effects of personality systems and conflict-resolution mechanisms on a consumer's unconscious motivations for buying certain products.

**Multiattribute compensatory rule** rule that calculates a rank ordering based on all attributes weighted by their relative importance.

**Multistep flow of communication** theory that posits that individuals receive information from mass media and marketing communications and exchange information with opinion leaders.

**Myth** a story that illustrates one or more of the shared values of a culture by describing a person, event, or idea that symbolizes the values.

**Need** a drive to eliminate the discrepancy between one's current state and some ideal state.

**Negative reference groups** groups whose members

are viewed negatively and whose behavior serves as a model of what not to do.

**Noncompensatory decision rules**   rules that consider each attribute separately in determining a product choice.

**Nonmembership reference group**   a group to which a consumer does not belong but that provides a standard of reference for his or her behavior.

**Nonprofit organizations**   organizations that meet the needs of consumers but do not do so for a profit.

**Normative influence**   the ability of a reference group to use rewards or punishments to influence an individual to behave in a way that its members find acceptable.

**Observability**   the ease with which a new product can be viewed in use.

**Opinion leader**   person who uses his or her knowledge and experience to play a dominant role in word-of-mouth communication.

**Organizational buying**   the consumer behavior that occurs in businesses, nonprofit organizations, or government bodies.

**Perceived risk**   the uncertainty and fear of negative consequences that consumers experience when they cannot clearly interpret stimuli.

**Perception**   the process that consumers use to select stimuli or objects in their environment, gather information about them, and interpret the meaning of the information.

**Personal selling**   interpersonal, two-way marketing communication between a paid salesperson and a consumer.

**Personality**   a consumer's unique psychological makeup that predisposes that person to behave in a particular way.

**Personality, lifestyle, and psychographics**   the essential psychological characteristics that affect a person's behavior. *Personality* measures underlying psychological characteristics, whereas *lifestyle* and *psychographics* use consumers' current activities, interests, and opinions as indicators of the underlying characteristics.

**Personality traits**   the underlying dimensions of the predisposition to behave in a particular way.

**Personality type**   a group of people who share personality traits that result in a common predisposition to behave similarly.

**Place**   the means by which a marketer delivers a product to the location where consumers will use it.

**Policy makers**   government officials who have the authority to create and enforce legislation and regulations.

**Positive reference groups**   groups whose members'

behaviors and values are attractive and who provide a model for behavior.

**Price**   that which consumers exchange with the marketer to purchase a product.

**Primary demand**   demand that is satisfied by any product in a category.

**Product**   any object—whether a tangible, physical product, such as a car or a soft drink, or an intangible object, such as a concert or a tax preparation service—that satisfies a consumer need.

**Product life cycle**   the distribution of a product's sales during its history.

**Product line**   a set of similar products that share a brand name that is offered to a single consumer segment composed of individuals who have some subtle variation in their shared needs.

**Product positioning**   a means of conveying to consumers in the selected target segment that a product is appropriate for them and signals to those in other segments that it will not meet their needs.

**Projection**   the process of justifying one's actions by blaming someone else for them.

**Projective techniques**   disguised tasks that allow a glimpse into an individual's psychological defenses and into the motivation process.

**Promotion**   the way in which the marketer communicates information that consumers use to ascertain a product's positioning.

**Psychoanalytic theory of personality**   a theory that addresses the individual's interaction styles, rooted in the desire to satisfy both the individual's own needs and society's culture and values.

**Publicity**   unpaid communication about a product that appears within the editorial content of media.

**Public policy actors**   individuals or organizations that have an interest in the consequences and implications of the exchange of products or services between consumers and marketers.

**Rationality of consumers**   the view that assumes that consumers gather as much information as possible about all the alternatives they can, evaluate the information, and decide to purchase the alternative that will maximize their satisfaction.

**Rationalization**   the invention of an excuse to justify actions.

**Receiver**   the target of a message.

**Recurrent decision making**   the repetition of a prior decision making process in recurring purchase decisions.

**Reference group**   a set of people a consumer uses as the standard of reference for his or her thoughts, feelings, and actions.

**Relative advantage** the degree to which consumers perceive that a product offers them greater benefits than an alternative.

**Repeat** the ongoing purchase of a product as a result of a favorable evaluation of the consumer's experience.

**Repression** the practice of controlling a psychological, pleasurable id-based need by leaving it unsatisfied.

**Ritual** a set of interrelated patterns of behavior that have a symbolic meaning.

**Schema** a collection of knowledge and beliefs held by an individual.

**Segmented market** a market in which meaningful differences among consumers result in a modest number of segments.

**Selective demand** demand that identifies a specific brand to satisfy a need.

**Selective perception** a component of the perceptual process that enables a person to screen out some stimuli while allowing others to be perceived.

**Self-concept theory** a theory that explains those aspects of an individual's personality that are the expression of the individual's self-image.

**Self-designating method** an approach that asks consumers to indicate whether they play the role of opinion leader in their communication with others.

**Sensation** the direct and immediate response of an individual's sensory receptors—their eyes, ears, nose, tongue, and skin—to stimuli in the environment.

**Sensory memory** a memory function that temporarily stores information that is received during the perceptual process.

**Sensory threshold** the level of intensity that a stimulus must exhibit for an individual to be able to perceive it.

**Separation groups** negative membership groups from which a consumer wants to separate himself or herself.

**Short-term memory** memory that briefly stores information to which attention has been paid.

**Situational influences** specific factors that affect purchase activities by altering the product choices that consumers make.

**Social action organizations** groups that form to influence public policies, consumers' actions, and marketers' strategies in areas that interest their members.

**Social category** a group of people who share some characteristics that make them easy to classify as members even though they need not have any interaction, contact, or rules.

**Social class** one's position in the social and economic structures of a society.

**Social marketing** the marketing of ideas or causes that will advance the economic and social welfare of a society.

**Sociometric method** technique that identifies opinion leaders through the analysis of the flows of communication.

**Source** the sender of a communication.

**Source credibility** the belief that a source provides accurate and unbiased information based on objectivity and expertise.

**Stimuli** inputs from an object that are perceived by one of the five senses.

**Stimulus discrimination** a situation that occurs when an individual is able to discriminate a new stimulus from an old or existing one.

**Stimulus generalization** a situation that occurs when a new stimulus is sufficiently similar to an existing one that it evokes the same response.

**Strategic business unit (SBU)** a part of a large marketing firm that markets a set of homogeneous products to a set of homogeneous market segments.

**Subculture** a group of consumers from a culture that share its values but exhibit them in different ways.

**Subjective norm** representation of beliefs about the behavior expected by the members of one's reference groups and the individual's motivation to comply.

**Subliminal perception** the selection, organization, and interpretation of stimuli that are intentionally designed to be below consumers' threshold of perception.

**Superego** the personality style by which the individual attempts to do what is right and moral as defined by society.

**Terminal values** the goals and objectives that consumers seek to reach.

**Trade association** a social action organization formed by marketers in an attempt to influence legislation or public opinion.

**Traditional family life cycle** a concept used to classify households according to the age, marital status, and number and ages of children who are present; it describes the traditional progression of steps in family life from singlehood to marriage to parenthood to retirement to death.

**Trend setter** opinion leaders whose personal experiences are emulated by other consumers.

**Trial** the consumer's first consumption or usage experience with a product.

**Trialability** the ease with which consumers gain experience with a new product without making a purchase commitment.

**Two-step flow of communication** a theory that posits that communication from mass media to consumers is mediated by opinion leaders who interpret the information.

**Undifferentiated segmentation strategy** a strategy in which the marketer offers the same product or product line to the entire mass market.

**Valence** a term used to describe the relationship between a consumer and a goal.

**Values** the underlying beliefs that are shared by the members of a society and that indicate how they should act, think, and feel.

**Word-of-mouth communication** informal communication among consumers about products.

# FOOTNOTES

## Chapter 1

**1** Classic statements of marketing as exchange are in Wroe Alderson (1957), *Marketing Behavior and Executive Action,* Homewood, IL: Irwin and Richard P. Bagozzi (1975), "Marketing as Exchange," *Journal of Marketing,* 39 (October), 32–39. Recent treatments include Franklin S. Houston and Jule B. Gassenheimer (1987), "Marketing and Exchange," *Journal of Marketing,* 51 (October), 3–18 and Franklin S. Houston, Jule B. Gassenheimer, and James M. Maskulka (1992), *Marketing Exchange Transactions and Relationships,* Westport, CT: Quorum.

**2** Elizabeth C. Hirschman and Morris B. Holbrook (1982), "Hedonic Consumption: Emerging Concepts, Methods, and Propositions," *Journal of Marketing,* 46 (Summer), 92–101; Morris B. Holbrook and Elizabeth C. Hirschman (1982), "The Experiential Aspects of Consumption: Consumer Fantasies, Feelings, and Fun," *Journal of Consumer Research*, 9 (September), 132–140.

**3** Elizabeth C. Hirschman (1992), "The Consciousness of Addiction: Toward a General Theory of Compulsive Consumption," *Journal of Consumer Research*, 19 (September), 155–179; Thomas C. O'Guinn and Ronald J. Faber (1989), "Compulsive Buying: A Phenomenological Explanation," *Journal of Consumer Research*, 16 (September), 147–157.

**4** Michael deCourcy Hinds, *"The Program," New York Times*, October 20, 1993; "Disney Plans to Omit Film Scene after Teenager Dies Imitating It," *New York Times*, October 20, 1993; Caryn James, *"The Program," New York Times*, October 24, 1993; Kevin Goldman, *"Beavis and Butthead* Stirs Advertisers," *Wall Street Journal*, October 28, 1993; David Van Biema, *"The Program," Time*, November 1, 1993.

**5** Franklin S. Houston, (1986) "The Marketing Concept: What It Is and What It Is Not," *Journal of Marketing* 50 (April), 81–87. Frederick E. Webster, Jr. (1988), "Rediscovering the Marketing Concept," *Business Horizons*, 31 (May-June), 29–39.

**6** These sources discuss the intellectual roots of consumer behavior and research: Robert Bartels (1976), *The History of Marketing Thought,* 2nd Edition. Columbus: Grid; James R. Beniger (1986), *The Control Revolution: Technological and Economic Origins of the Information Society,* Boston: Harvard University Press; Jean M. Converse (1987), *Survey Research in the United States: Roots and Emergence 1890–1960,* Berkeley: California; and Christine Wright-Isak and David Prensky (1993), "A Brief Sociol-

ogy of Early Marketing Research: Science and Application," *Marketing Research: A Magazine of Management and Applications,* 5 (Fall) 16–23.

**7** Ajay K. Kohli and Bernard J. Jaworski (1990), "Market Orientation: The Construct, Research Propositions, and Managerial Implications," *Journal of Marketing*, 54 (April), 1–18; John C. Narver and Stanley F. Slater (1990), "The Effect of a Market Orientation on Business Profitability," *Journal of Marketing*, 54 (October), 20–35, and Bernard J. Jaworski and Ajay K. Kohli (1993), "Market Orientation: Antecedents and Consequences," *Journal of Marketing*, 57 (July), 53, 70.

**8** Vincent P. Barabba and Gerald Zaltman (1991), *Hearing the Voice of the Market*, Boston: Harvard Business School Press.

**9** Eric Schmuckler, "Red Flags Over Blue TV, *Mediaweek*, June 14, 1993; "Fifty ABC Affiliates Plan to Pre-empt 'NYPD Blue,'" *Wall Street Journal*, September 22, 1993; "'NYPD Blue' Debut Wins a Hefty Share of 27%," *Wall Street Journal*, September 23, 1993; Elizabeth Jensen, "Crusade Against ABC's 'NYPD Blue' Goes Local," *Wall Street Journal*, October 6, 1993; Elizabeth Jensen and Ellen Graham, "Stamping Out TV Violence: A Losing Fight," *Wall Street Journal*, October 26, 1993; Cyndee Miller, "Advertisers in Middle of the Battle Over 'Blue,'" *Marketing News*, May 9, 1994; Betsy Sharkey, "In the Blue," *Adweek (eastern edition)*, September 12, 1994.

**10** Alan R. Andreasen, (1991), "Consumer Behavior Research and Social Policy," in *Handbook of Consumer Behavior*, eds. Thomas S. Robertson and Harold H. Kassarjian, Englewood Cliffs: Prentice Hall, pp. 459–506.

**11** "Pharmacists Help Drug Promotions," *New York Times*, July 29, 1994; "Bristol-Myers Begins Campaign for Capoten Directed at Patients," *Wall Street Journal*, August 17, 1994.

**12** "How a Jury Decided That a Coffee Spill Is Worth $2.9 Million," *Wall Street Journal*, September 1, 1994.

**13** Francesco M. Nicosia and Robert N. Mayer (1976), "Toward a Sociology of Consumption," *Journal of Consumer Research*, 3 (September), 65–76.

**14** John F. Sherry Jr. (1995), *Contemporary Marketing and Consumer Behavior: An Anthropological Sourcebook,* Beverly Hills, CA: Sage.

# Chapter 2

**1** Gordon C. Bruner II (1985), "Recent Contributions to the Theory of Problem Recognition," in *1985 AMA Educators' Proceedings*, ed. Robert F. Lusch, Chicago: American Marketing Association, pp. 11–15; M. Joseph Sirgy, (1987), "A Social Cognition Model of Consumer Problem Recognition," *Journal of the Academy of Marketing Science*, 15 (Winter) 53–61.

**2** Peter H. Bloch, Daniel L. Sherrell, and Nancy M. Ridgeway (1986), "Consumer Search: An Extended Framework," *Journal of Consumer Research*, 13 (June), 119–126.

**3** Richard W. Olshavsky and Donald H. Granbois (1979), "Consumer Decision Making - Fact or Fiction?" *Journal of Consumer Research*, 6 (September), 93–100; Michael Ursic (1980), "Consumer Decision Making—Fact or Fiction?" *Journal of Consumer Research*, 7 (December), 331–333.

**4** Russell W. Belk (1974), "An Explanatory Assessment of Situational Effects in Buyer Behavior," *Journal of Marketing Research*, 11 (May), 156–163, and Russell W. Belk (1975), "Situational Variables and Consumer Behavior," *Journal of Consumer Research*, 2 (December), 157–164.

**5** Richard L. Oliver (1980), "A Cognitive Model of the Antecedents and Consequences of Satisfaction Decisions," *Journal of Marketing Research*, 17 (November), 460–469; Richard L. Oliver and Wayne S. DeSarbo (1988), "Response Determinants in Satisfaction Judgments," *Journal of Consumer Research*, 14 (March), 495–507.

**6** Bearden, William O. And Jesse E. Teel (1983), "Selected Determinants of Consumer Satisfaction and Complaint Reports," *Journal of Marketing Research*, 20 (February), 21–28; Jagdip Singh (1988), "Consumer Complaint Intentions and Behavior: Definitional and Taxonomical Issues," *Journal of Marketing*, 52 (January), 93–107.

**7** Jacob Jacoby, Carol Berning, and Thomas Dietvorst (1977), "What about Disposition?" *Journal of Marketing*, 41 (April), 22–28; James W. Hanson (1980), "A Proposed Paradigm for Consumer Product Disposition Processes," *Journal of Consumer Affairs*, 14 (Summer), 49–67.

**8** Kristin S. Palda (1966), "The Hypothesis of a Hierarchy of Effects: A Partial Evaluation," *Journal of Marketing Research*, 3 (February), 13–24; Michael L. Ray (1973), "Communication and the Hierarchy of Effects," ed. P. Clarke in *New Models for Mass Communication Research*, Beverly Hills: Sage, 1973, pp. 147–175; Thomas E. Barry (1987), "The Development of the Hierarchy of Effects: An Historical Perspective," *Current Issues & Research in Advertising*, 10 (2), 251–296.

**9** Herbert E. Krugman (1965), "The Impact of Television Advertising: Learning Without Involvement," *Public Opinion Quarterly*, 29 (Fall) pp. 349–356; Gilles Laurent and Jean-Noel Kapferer (1985), "Measuring Consumer Involvement Profiles," *Journal of Marketing Research*, 22 (February), 41–53; Judith L. Zaichkowsky (1986), "Conceptualizing Involvement," *Journal of Advertising*, 15, 4–14.

**10** Grant McCracken, (1986), "Culture and Consumption: A Theoretical Account of the Structure and Movement of the Cultural Meaning of Consumer Goods," *Journal of Consumer Research*, 13 (June), 71–81.

**11** Louis G. Pol (1991), "Demographic Contributions to Marketing: An Assessment," *Journal of the Academy of Marketing Science*, 19 (Winter), 53–60.

**12** Harold H. Kassarjian and Mary Jane Sheffet (1991), "Personality and Consumer Behavior: An Update," in *Perspectives in Consumer Behavior*, 4th edition, eds. Harold H. Kassarjian and Thomas S. Robertson, Englewood Cliffs, NJ: Prentice-Hall, pp. 281–303.

**13** Joseph T. Plummer (1974), "The Concept and Application of Life Style Segmentation," *Journal of Marketing*, 38 (January), 33–37; William D. Wells (1975), "Psychographics: A Critical Review," *Journal of Marketing Research*, 12 (May), 196–213.

**14** Hsiaofang Hwang (1995), "The Lifestyles of Exercisers and Non-Exercisers," unpublished Master's Thesis, School of Journalism and Mass Communications, University of Minnesota.

**15** William O. Bearden and Michael J. Etzel (1982), "Reference Group Influence on Product and Brand Purchase Decisions," *Journal of Consumer Research*, 9 (September), 183–194.

**16** Ernest Dichter (1964), *Handbook of Consumer Motivations: The Psychology of the World of Objects*, New York: McGraw-Hill.

**17** Richard L. Celsi and Jerry Olson (1988), "The Role of Involvement in Attention and Comprehension Processes," *Journal of Consumer Research*, 15 (September), 210–224.

**18** Mary Lu Carnevale, "FCC Proposes Crackdown on '800' Lines As More Companies Charge for Calls," *Wall Street Journal*, August 3, 1994; "Dial 1-800-Rip-off," *Philadelphia Inquirer*, August 25, 1994; "AT&T Wins, MCI Changes Its Billing to 800 Service," *Wall Street Journal*, January 5, 1995.

**19** James R. Bettman (1979), *An Information Processing Theory of Consumer Choice*, Reading, MA: Addison-Wesley; Walter R. Nord and J. Paul Peter (1980), "A Behavior Modification Perspective on Marketing," *Journal of Marketing* 44 (Spring), 36–47.

**20** William L. Wilkie and Edgar A. Pessemier (1973), "Issues in Marketing's Use of Multi-Attribute Models," *Journal of Marketing Research*, 10 (November), 428–441.

**21** John A. Howard and Jagdeth N. Sheth (1967), "Theory of Buyer Behavior" in *Changing Marketing Systems*, ed. Reed Moyer, Chicago: American Marketing Association, pp. 253–262 and John A. Howard and Jagdeth N. Sheth (1969), *The Theory of Buyer Behavior*, New York: Wiley.

# Chapter 3

**1** Peter C. Wilton, and Edgar A. Pessemier (1981), "Forecasting the Ultimate Acceptance of an Innovation: The Effects of Information," *Journal of Consumer Research*, 8 (September), 162–171; William J. Gregory, Robert B. Cialdini, and Kathleen M. Carpenter (1982), "Self-relevant Scenarios as Mediators of Likelihood Estimates and Compliance: Does Imagining Make it So?" *Journal of Personality and Social Psychology*, 43 (July), 89–99; Manohur U. Kalwani and Alvin J. Silk (1982), "On the Reliability and Predictive Validity of Purchase Intention Measurement," *Marketing Science*, 1 (Summer), 243–286; William J. Infosino (1986), "Forecasting New Product Sales From Likelihood of Purchase Ratings," *Marketing Science*, 5 (Fall), 372–384; Vicki G. Morwitz, Eric Johnson, and David Schmittlein (1993), "Does Measuring Intent Change Behavior?" *Journal of Consumer Research*, 20 (June), 46–61.

**2** Wendell R. Smith (1956), "Product Differentiation and Market Segmentation as Alternative Marketing Strategies," *Journal of Marketing*, 20 (1956), 3–8; Yoram Wind (1978), "Issues and Advances in Segmentation Research," *Journal of Marketing Research*, 15 (August), 317–337; Peter R. Dickson and James L. Ginter (1987), "Market Segmentation, Product Differentiation, and Marketing Strategy," *Journal of Marketing*, 51 (April), 1–10; David W. Stewart and Michael A. Kamins (1991), "Segmentation in Consumer and Marketing Research: Applications, Current Issues and Trends," *Advances in Consumer Research*, vol. 18, eds. Rebecca H. Holman and Michael R. Solomon, Provo, UT: Association for Consumer Research, pp. 176–178.

**3** Sources: John H. Cushman, Jr., "Lending-Bias Rules Create Quandary for Banks," *New York Times*, November 28, 1993; Keith Bradsher, "Minorities Get More Mortgages," *New York Times*, July 29, 1994; Yi-Hsin Chang, "Mortgage Denial Rate for Blacks Was Double the Level for Whites, Asians," *Wall Street Journal*, July 29, 1994; Ralph T. King, Jr., "Some Mortgage Firms Neglect Black Areas More Than Banks Do," *Wall Street Journal*, August 9, 1994; Albert R. Karr, "Regulators Issue Minority-Loan Plan; Revised Proposal Stirs Some Concerns," *Wall Street Journal*, September 27, 1994; Andrée Brooks, "Mortgage Outreach Efforts," *New York Times*, October 30, 1994.

**4** For representative articles that have discussed some of the background characteristics that can be used to segment consumer markets, see Joseph T. Plummer (1974), "The Concept and Application of Life Style Segmentation," *Journal of Marketing*, 38 (January), 33–37; Ronald E. Goldsmith, J. Dennis White, and Melvin T. Stith (1987), "Values of Middle-Class Blacks and Whites: A Replication and Extension," *Psychology & Marketing*, 4 (Summer), 135–144; Douglas M. Stayman and Rohit Deshpande (1989), "Situational Ethnicity and Consumer Behavior," *Journal of Consumer Research*, 16 (December), 361–371; Martha Farnesworth Richie (1989), "Psychographics for the 1990's," *American Demographics*, 11 (July), 24–31, 53–54; James C. Ward and Peter H. Reingen (1990), "Sociocognitive Analysis of Group Decision Making," *Journal of Consumer Research*, 17 (December), 245–262; Wagner A. Kamakura and Jose Afonso Mazzon (1991), "Value Segmentation: A Model for the Measurement of Values and Value Systems," *Journal of Consumer Research*, 18 (September), 208–218.

**5** Lewis Alpert and Ronald Gatty (1969), "Product Positioning by Behavioral Life Styles," *Journal of Marketing*, 33 (April), 65–69; John P. Maggard (1976), "Positioning Revisited," *Journal of Marketing*, 40 (January), 63–73; Robert E. Wilkes (1977), "Product Positioning by Multidimensional Scaling," *Journal of Advertising Research*, 17 (August), 15–22; Al Ries and Jack Trout (1981), *Positioning: The Battle for Your Mind*, New York: McGraw-Hill; David A. Aaker and J. Gary Shansby (1982), "Positioning Your Product," *Business Horizons*, (May–June), 36–62.

**6** Works on the importance of segmenting and positioning by the benefit offered to consumers are Russell I. Haley (1968), "Benefit Segmentation: A Decision-Oriented Research Tool," *Journal of Marketing*, 32 (July), 30–35; Russell I. Haley (1971) "Beyond Benefit Segmentation," *Journal of Advertising Research*, 11 (August) 3–8; Paul E. Green, Yoram Wind, and Arun K. Jain (1972), "Benefit Bundle Analysis," *Journal of Advertising Research*, (April), 31–36; Roger J. Calantone and Alan G. Sawyer (1978), "The Stability of Benefit Segments," *Journal of Marketing Research*, 16 (August), 395; Russell I. Haley (1984), "Benefit Segmentation—20 Years Later," *Journal of Consumer Marketing*, 1 (2), 5–13.

7 Russell S. Winer and William L. Moore (1989), "Evaluating the Effects of Marketing Mix Variables on Brand Positioning," *Journal of Advertising Research*, 39 (February–March), 39–45.

## Chapter 4

**1** Michael Clark (1974), "On the Concept of Sub-Culture," *The British Journal of Sociology*, 25, (December), 428–441.

**2** "The Hazards of Cross-Cultural Advertising. Translations, Manner and Customs, Usage," *Business America*, 7, April 2, 1984.

**3** Ian Stewart, "Singapore Reworks Ad Code: Officials Say West-

ern Influences Can Destroy Asian Family Values," *Advertising Age International* (supplement to *Advertising Age*), October 17, 1994.

**4** "Gaylord Adds Christian Video Channel Z to Stable," *Billboard*, May 21, 1994; Eric Boehlert, "Salem Builds Christian Radio Empire," *Billboard*, October 1, 1994; Deborah Evan Price, "EMI Buys Star Song, Creates Christian Group," *Billboard*, October 29, 1994; Lisa Gubernick and Robert LaFranco, "Rocking With God," *Forbes*, January 2, 1995; Nicholas Davidoff, "No Sex, No Drugs. But Rock 'N' Roll (Kind of), *New York Times Magazine*, February 5, 1995; Anita Sharpe, "Heavenly Niche: Fundamentalism Sells to the Mass Market, Same Moore is Finding," *Wall Street Journal*, February 6, 1995.

**5** Ray Serafin, "Auto Marketers Gas Up For World Car Drive," *Advertising Age International* (supplement to *Advertising Age*), January 16, 1995.

**6** Diana Walsh, "St. Nick's Look Has Changed Over Time," *San Francisco Chronicle*, December 25, 1994.

**7** Dennis W. Rook (1984), "Ritual Behavior and Consumer Symbolism," in *Advances in Consumer Research*, Vol. 11, ed. Thomas C. Kinnear, Ann Arbor, MI: Association for Consumer Research, 279–284; Dennis W. Rook (1985), "The Ritual Dimensions of Consumer Behavior," *Journal of Consumer Research*, 12 (December), 251–264; Mary A. Stansfield Tetreault and Robert E. Klein III (1990), "Ritual, Ritualized Behavior, and Habit: Refinements and Extensions of the Consumption Ritual Construct," in *Advances in Consumer Research*, Vol. 17, eds. Marvin Goldberg, Gerald Gorn, and Richard A.W. Pollay, Provo, UT: Association for Consumer Research, 31–38.

**8** Judith Waldrop, "Same Stuffing Next Year," *American Demographics*, (November 11, 1991).

**9** D. Nance, "When in Rome (Marketing and Advertising a Product Internationally," *Marketing*, 31 January 1993, 30–1.

**10** "Top Global Markets," (Special Report), *Advertising Age*, March 21, 1994, supplement *Advertising Age International*.

**11** Joel M. Ostrow, "Prices Soar at McD's: But Expansion Still Planned for Moscow," *Advertising Age*, November 12, 1990.

**12** Stewart Toy and Paula Dwyer, "Is Disney Headed for the Euro-Trash Heap?" *Business Week*, January 24, 1994.

**13** James Sterngold, "Tokyo's Magic Kingdom Outshines Its Role Model," *New York Times*, March 7, 1994; Robert Neff, "In Japan, They're Goofy About Disney," *Business Week*, March 12, 1990.

**14** "Selling in Europe: Borders Fade," *New York Times*, May 31, 1990.

**15** "Ethnic Marketing," *Marketing* (Canada, special report), July 4–11, 1994.

**16** Gary Levin, "Ads Going Global," *Advertising Age*, July 22, 1991.

**17** Douglas C. McGill, "Talking Business," *New York Times*, January 17, 1989.

**18** G.M. Zinkhan (1994), "International Advertising: A Research Agenda," *Journal of Advertising* (Special Issue: International Advertising), 23, (March), 11–15.

**19** "Changing Demographics: Global Marketers Court Middle Class Families as Women's Roles Expand," *Advertising Age International* (supplement to *Advertising Age*), October 17, 1994; Jack Russell, "Working Women Give Japan Culture Shock," *Advertising Age International* (supplement to *Advertising Age*), January

16, 1995; Milton Moskowitz, Michael Katz, and Robert Levering (1980), eds., *Everybody's Business: An Almanac (The Irreverant Guide to Corporate America)*, San Francisco: Harper & Row, 128–132; Adele Hast, editor-in-chief, *International Directory of Company Histories,* Vol. 5, pp. 216–217.

**20** Adrienne Ward Fawcett, "Friedan Sees Real Progress in Women's Ads," *Advertising Age*, October 4, 1993; Victoria Secunda, "By Youth Possessed: The Denial of Age in America," Wilson HQ1064. U5 S42, 1984 (in).

**21** Milton Rokeach (1973), *The Nature of Human Values,* New York: Free Press; Milton Rokeach (1979), *Understanding Human Values,* New York: Free Press.

**22** Lynn R. Kahle (1983), *Social Values and Social Change: Adaptation to Life in America,* New York: Praeger; Sharon E. Beatty, Lynn R. Kahle, Pamela Homer, and Shekhar Misra (1985), "Alternative Measurement Approaches to Consumer Values: The List of Values and the Rokeach Value Survey," *Psychology & Marketing,* 2 (3), 181–200; Lynn R. Kahle, Sharon E. Beatty, and Pamela Homer "Alternative Measurement Approaches to Consumer Values: The List of Values (LOV) and Values and Life Style (VALS)," *Journal of Consumer Research,* 13 (December), 405–409; Lynn R. Kahle and Patricia Kennedy (1988), "Using the List of Values (LOV) to Understand Consumers," *Journal of Consumer Marketing,* 2 (Fall), 49–56.

**23** Paula Kepos (1992), ed., *International Directory of Company Histories*, Vol. 6, Detroit, MI: St. James Press, 218–220.

**24** Suzanne Alexander, "Feisty Yankees Resist Wal-Mart's Drive to Set Up Shop in New England Towns," *Wall Street Journal*, September 16, 1993; "Wal-Mart Cancels Store in Massachusetts Town," *Wall Street Journal,* September 17, 1993; Bob Ortega, "Wal-Mart Loses a Case on Pricing," *Wall Street Journal*, October 13, 1993; Barnaby J. Feder, "Message for Mom and Pop: There's Life After Wal-Mart," *New York Times*, October 24, 1993; Bob Ortega, "Wal-Mart is Slowed by Problems of Price and Culture in Mexico," *Wall Street Journal*, July 29, 1994; Joseph Pereira and Bob Ortega, "Once Easily Turned Away by Local Foes, Wal-Mart Gets Tough in New England," *Wall Street Journal*, September 17, 1994; Bob Ortega, "Aging Activists Turn, Turn, Turn Attention to Wal-Mart Protests," *Wall Street Journal*, October 11, 1994; B. Saporito, "And the Winner Is—Wal-Mart," *Fortune,* May 2, 1994, 62–5+; M. Everett, "Drugstores Cowboys Shoot it Out (Wal-Mart Prescription Drug Prices Ruled Too Low; Consay, Ark.)," *Sales and Marketing Management*, 146, August 1994, 15; "Slinging Pebbles at Wal-Mart," *Economist*, 329, October 23, 1993, 76; Kenneth Stone, "When Wal-Mart Comes to Town," *New York Magazine*, April 2, 1989; Steven Koepp, "Make That Sale, Mr. Sam," *Time* May 18, 1987; "Walton's Mountain," *Nation's Business*, April 1988; "Wal-Mart: Will it Take Over the World?" *Fortune*, January 30, 1989.

## Chapter 5

**1** Representative articles about gender include Joan Meyers-Levy (1988), "The Influence of Sex Roles on Judgment," *Journal of Consumer Research,* 14 (March), 522–530; Eileen Fischer and Stephen J. Arnold (1990), "More Than a Labor of Love: Gender Roles and Christmas Gift Shopping," *Journal of Consumer Research,* 17 (December), 333–345; Joan Meyers-Levy and Brian Sternthal (1991), "Gender Differences in the Use of Message Cues," *Journal of Marketing Research,* 28 (February), 84–96; Joan Meyers-Levy and Durairaj Maheswaran (1991), "Exploring Differences in Males' and Females' Processing Strategies," *Journal of Consumer Research,*18 (June), 63–70.

**2** Eric Hollreiser, "Women and Cars," *Adweek's Marketing Week,* February 10, 1992; Andrea Heiman, "Beyond Thinking Pink: Cars Have Long Reflected Men's Needs. But Now Designers Have Women in Mind." *Los Angeles Times,* June 2, 1992; Leah Rickard, "The $65 Billion Woman: Carmakers Like Ford go Extra Mile to Make Vehicles Attractive Across Gender Lines," *Advertising Age,* October 4, 1993.

**3** Basic demographic statistics cited in this chapter are from William Lazer, (1994) *Handbook of Demographics for Marketing & Advertising: New Trends in the American Marketplace, 2nd edition,* New York: Lexington; and Peter Francese, (1995) "America at Mid-Decade," *American Demographics* (February), 23–31. Lazer's book and *American Demographics* are excellent sources of demographic information and insight for consumers and marketers alike.

**4** "Poll Finds More Working Women Comparison Shop Than Formerly," *Supermarket News,* February 28, 1983; Robert E. O'Neill, "How Consumers Shop," *Progressive Grocer,* December 1992; "Special Report: Marketing to Women," *Advertising Age,* October 4, 1993.

**5** Laura Zinn, "Real Men Buy Paper Towels, Too," *Business Week,* November 9, 1992; Keith J. Kelly, "Guys Show Their Muscle as Buyers of Groceries," *Advertising Age,* July 11, 1994.

**6** Carol S. Saunders, "Schools Ban Playing 'Milk Caps'" for Keeps," *New York Times,* January 22, 1995; Jean Seligman and Jeanne Gordon, "Is It 'Game Over' for Pog Players?" *Newsweek,* January 30, 1995.

**7** Paco Underhill (1994), "Kids in Stores," *American Demographics* (June), 22–27.

**8** Susan Mitchell (1993), "How to Talk to Young Adults," *American Demographics* (April), 50–54; Jennifer Steinhauer, "How Do You Turn on the Twentysomething Market?" *New York Times,* April 17, 1994.

**9** "What Media Hold Student Interest," *Advertising Age,* February 5, 1990; Susan Krafft (1991), "College Newspapers Score High-Grade Readers," *American Demographics* (June), 53; Stanley C. Hollander and Richard Germain (1992), *Was There a Pepsi Generation Before Pepsi Discovered It? Youth-Based Segmentation in Marketing,* Lincoln-wood, IL: NTC; Suzanne Alexander, "College 'Parties' Get High Marks as Sales Events," *The Wall Street Journal,* October 23, 1992; Patricia Winters and Scott Donation, "Coke Takes to Highway to Grab College Crowd," *Advertising Age,* March 29, 1993; Don Oldenburg, "College Credit," *The Washington Post,* September 16, 1993.

**10** Raymond Kotcher, "Gathering Moss," *Adweek - Eastern Edition,* October 5, 1992; Christy Fisher, "Boomers Scatter in Middle Age: Marketing Challenge Looms as Life Stages Diverge Sharply," *Advertising Age,* January 11, 1993; Kevin Goldman, "Advertisers Treat Boomers as Grown-ups," *The Wall Street Journal,* December 29, 1993; Kevin Goldman, "Forget Megabytes: Ads Push PCs as Hip," *The Wall Street Journal,* April 6, 1994; Peter Francese (1994), "Cellular Consumers," *American Demographics* (August), 30–36.

**11** For articles about the mature market, see John J. Burnett (1989), "Retirement Versus Age: Assessing the Efficacy of Retirement as a Segmentation Variable," *Journal of the Academy of Marketing Science,* 17 (Fall), 333–343; Charles D. Schewe and Anne L. Balazs (1990), *Marketing to an Aging Population: Selected Readings,* Chicago: American Marketing Association; Paula Fitgerald Bone (1991), "Identifying Mature Segments," *Journal of Consumer Marketing,* 8 (Fall), 19–32; George P. Moschis (1991), "Marketing to Older Adults," 8 (Fall), 33–42; Diane Crispell and William H. Frey (1993), "American Maturity,"

*American Demographics* (March), 31–42; Charles F. Longino Jr. (1994), "From Sunbelt to Sunspots," *American Demographics* (November), 22–31.

**12** Among the academic articles that investigate the effects of race and ethnicity are Melanie Wallendorf and Michael D. Reilly (1983), "Ethnic Migration, Assimilation, and Consumption," *Journal of Consumer Research,* 10 (December), 292–302; Joel Saegert, Robert Hoover, and Marye T. Hilger (1985) "Characteristics of Mexican-American Consumers," *Journal of Consumer Research,* 12 (June), 104–109; Rohit Deshpande, Wayne D. Hoyer, and Naveen Donthu (1986), "The Intensity of Ethnic Affiliation: A Study of the Sociology of Hispanic Consumption," *Journal of Consumer Research,* 13 (September), 214–220; Ronald J. Faber, Thomas C. O'Guinn, and John A. McCarty (1987), "Ethnicity, Acculturation, and the Importance of Product Attributes," *Psychology & Marketing,* 4 (Summer), 121–134; Ronald E. Goldsmith, J. Dennis White, and Melvin T. Stith (1987), "Values of Middle-Class Blacks and Whites: A Replication and Extension," *Psychology & Marketing,* 4 (Summer), 135–144; Jerome D. Williams and William J. Qualls (1989), "Middle-Class Black Consumers and Intensity of Ethnic Identification," *Psychology & Marketing,* 6 (Winter), 263–286; Douglas M. Stayman and Rohit Deshpande (1989), "Situational Ethnicity and Consumer Behavior," *Journal of Consumer Research,* 16 (December), 361–371; Van R. Wood and Roy Howell (1991), "A Note on Hispanic Values and Subcultural Research: An Alternative View," *Journal of the Academy of Marketing Science,* 19 (Winter), 61–68; Michel Laroche, Annanna Joy, Michael Hui, and Chankon Kim (1991), "An Examination of Ethnicity Measures: Convergent Validity and Cross-Cultural Equivalence," in *Advances in Consumer Research,* Vol. 18, ed. Rebecca H. Holman and Michael R. Solomon, Provo, UT: Association for Consumer Research, pp. 150–157; Geraldine Fenell, Joel Saegert, Francis Piron, and Rosemary Jiminez (1992), "Do Hispanics Constitute a Market Segment?" in *Advances in Consumer Research,* Vol. 19, ed. John F. Sherry, Jr. and Brian Sternthal, Provo, UT: Association for Consumer Research, pp 28–33; Johanna Zmud and Carlos Arce (1992), "The Ethnicity and Consumption Relationship," in *Advances in Consumer Research,* Vol. 19, ed. John F. Sherry, Jr., and Brian Sternthal, Provo, UT: Association for Consumer Research, pp. 443–449.

**13** Maria Mallory and Stephanie Anderson Forest, "Waking Up to a Major Market," *Business Week,* March 23, 1992; Bruce Horovitz, "Blacks Flex Buying Power: Advertising Studies Reveal Strength of African-American Consumers," *Los Angeles Times,* May 18, 1993; Ricardo A. Davis, "Advertisers Boost Minority Efforts," *Advertising Age,* August 16, 1993; Cyndee Miller, "Cosmetics Firms Finally Discover the Ethnic Market," *Marketing News,* August 30, 1993; Wendy Brandes, "Black-Oriented Radio Tunes Into Narrower Segments," *Wall Street Journal,* February 13, 1994; Deirdre Carmody, "An Enduring Voice for Black Women," *New York Times,* January 23, 1995.

**14** "Poll: Hispanics Stick to Brands (Asian American's Shop For Good Price, and African-Americans Look for Quality)," *Advertising Age,* February 15, 1993; William H. Frey and William P. O'Hare (1993), "Vivian lost Suburbios!" *American Demographics,* (April), 30–43; Scott Koslow, Prem N. Shamdasani, and Ellen E. Touchstone (1994), "Exploring Language Effects in Ethnic Advertising: A Sociolinguistic Perspective, " *Journal of Consumer Research,* 20 (March), 575–585; Judann Dagnoli, "Datawatch: Mexicans are Decidedly Brand Loyal," *Advertising Age International,* October 17, 1994; Leon E. Wynter, "Reaching Hispanics Across a Racial and Cultural Divide," *Wall Street Journal,* February 15, 1995; Daisann McLane, "The Cuban-American Princess," *New York Times Magazine,* February 26, 1995.

**15** Nejdet Delener and James P. Nellankavil (1990), "Informa-tional Sources and Media Usage: A Comparison Between Asian and Hispanic Subcultures," *Journal of Advertising Research,* 30 (June–July), 45–52; William P. O'Hare, William H. Frey and Dan Fost (1994), "Asians in the Suburbs," *American Demographics,* 16 (May), 32–38.

**16** Elizabeth C. Hirschman (1981), "American Jewish Ethnicity and Its Relationship to Some Selected Aspects of Consumer Behavior," *Journal of Marketing,* 45 (Summer), 102–110; Elizabeth C. Hirschman (1983), "Religious Affiliation and Consumption Processes: An Initial Paradigm," in *Research in Marketing,* ed. Jagdish N. Sheth, Greenwich, CT: JAI Press, pp. 131–170; Elizabeth C. Hirschman (1988), "Upper-Class WASPS as Consumers: A Humanistic Inquiry," in *Research in Consumer Behavior,* ed. Jagdish N. Sheth and Elizabeth C. Hirschman, Greenwich, CT: JAI Press, pp. 115–148; Priscilla LaBarbera (1988), "Consumer Behavior and Born Again Christianity," in *Research in Consumer Behavior,* ed. Jagdish N. Sheth and Elizabeth C. Hirschman, Greenwich, CT: JAI Press, pp. 193–222; Brad Edmonson (1988), "Bringing in the Sheaves," *American Demographics,* 10 (August), 28–32.

**17** Included among the work on social class are Richard P. Coleman (1983), "The Continuing Significance of Social Class to Marketing, " *Journal of Consumer Research,* 10 (December), 265–280; Donald W. Hendon, Emelda L. Williams, and Douglas E. Huffman (1988), "Social Class System Revisited," *Journal of Business Research,* 17 (November), 259–270; Elizabeth C. Hirschman (1990), "Secular Immortality and the American Ideology of Affluence," 17 (June), 31–42.

**18** Shawn McKenna (1992), *The Complete Guide to Regional Marketing,* Homewood, IL: Irwin Professional Publishing, 1992; Peter Franchese, Michael Mancini, and Barbara Clark O'Hare, "Rx for Cluster Headaches," April/May 1994, 48–57; S. Bradley, "Demographics: Going Where the Grass is Greener," *Brandweek,* August 22, 1994; Susan Mitchell (1995), "Birds of a Feather," *American Demographics,* 17 (February), 40–48.

**19** For studies of the family and household life cycle concept, see William D. Wells and George Gubar (1966), "Life Cycle Concept in Marketing Research," *Journal of Marketing Research,* 3 (November), 355–363; Ronald W. Stampfl (1978), "The Consumer Life Cycle," *Journal of Consumer Affairs,* 12 (Winter), 209–219; Mary C. Gilly and Ben M. Enis (1982), "Recycling the Family Life Cycle: A Proposal for Redefinition," in *Advances in Consumer Research,* Vol. 9, ed. Andrew A. Mitchell, Ann Arbor, MI: Association for Consumer Research, pp. 271–276; Janet Wagner and Sherman Hanna (1983), "The Effectiveness of Family Life Cycle Variables in Consumer Expenditure Research," *Journal of Consumer Research,* 10 (December) 281–291; Alan R. Andreasen (1984), Life Status Changes and Changes in Consumer Preferences and Satisfaction," *Journal of Consumer Research,* 7 (September), 112–120; Patrick E. Murphy and William A. Staples (1979), "A Modernized Family Life Cycle," *Journal of Consumer Research,* 6 (June), 12–22; Charles M. Schaninger and William D. Danko (1993), "A Conceptual and Empirical Comparison of Alternative Household Life Cycle Models," *Journal of Consumer Research,* 19 (March), 580–594.

**20** Christy Fisher, "It's All in the Family: Empty Nesters, Kids Moving Back Home," *Advertising Age,* April 27, 1992; Carrie Teegardin, "Unmarried Mothers are Multiplying," *Atlanta Constitution,* July 14, 1993; Elizabeth Shogren, "Traditional Family Nearly the Exception Census Finds," *Los Angeles Times,* August 30, 1994.

**21** See the articles by Bradley Johnson, "What's Behind the Numbers," Ricardo A. Davis "Sky's the Limit for Tour Operators: Attractive Due to DINK's Lifestyle, High Discretionary Income," and "The Gay Quandary: Advertising's Most Elusive, Yet Lucrative, Target Market Proves Difficult to Measure," in the Special Report on Marketing to Gays and Lesbians in *Advertising Age,* January 18, 1993. Also, C.A. Jaffe, "Target Marketing: Dealers Say Wooing Gay, Lesbian Customers is Good Business," *Automotive News,* January 31, 1994; Christy Fisher, "Local Print Bumps Into National Ad Walls," *Advertising Age,* May 30, 1994; Elliott, Stuart, "A Sharper View of Gay Consumers," *New York Times,* June 9, 1994; Stuart Elliott, "For Gay Consumers, Sales Pitches are Getting More Personal," *New York Times,* June 24, 1994, "Gays Celebrate and Business Tunes In," *Fortune,* June 27, 1994; Cyndee Miller, "Top Marketers Take Bolder Approach in Targeting Gays," *Marketing News,* July 4, 1994; Garry Boulard, "Numbers: No Matter What You Want to Say About Gay Income Levels, There's Now a Study to Back You Up," *The Advocate,* October 4, 1994.

**22** Jerry Adler and Debra Rosenberg, "The Endless Binge," *Newsweek,* December 19, 1994; Wendy Bounds, "Liquor Firm Liability Verdict Reversed," *Wall Street Journal,* January 65, 1995; William Celis III, "Tradition on the Wane: College Drinking," *New York Times,* February 5, 1995.

## Chapter 6

**1** For good introductions to personality, see Desmond S. Cartwright (1979), *Theories and Models of Personality,* Dubuque, IA: William C. Brown, Calvin S. Hall, Gardner Lindzey, John Loehin, and Martin Manosevitz, (1985), *Introduction to Theories of Personality,* New York: Wiley; Calvin S. Hall and Gardner Lindzey (1987), *Theories of Personality,* New York: John Wiley.

**2** Calvin S. Hall (1954), *A Primer of Freudian Psychology,* New York: New American Library.

**3** Karen Horney (1937), *The Neurotic Personality of Our Time,* Karen Horney (1939), *New Ways in Psychoanalysis,* New York: Norton, Karen Horney (1945), *Our Inner Conflicts,* New York: Norton.

**4** Joel B. Cohen (1967), "An Interpersonal Orientation to the Study of Consumer Behavior," *Journal of Marketing Research,* 6 (August), 270–278; Jon P. Noerager (1979), "An Assessment of CAD—A Personality Instrument Developed Specifically for Marketing Research," *Journal of Marketing Research,* 16 (February), 53–59; Arch G. Woodside and Ruth Andress (1975), "CAD Eight Years Later," *Journal of the Academy of Marketing Science,* 3 (Summer–Fall), 309–313.

**5** Dichter discusses his application of Freudian theories in Ernest Dichter (1964), *Handbook of Consumer Motivations: The Psychology of the World of Objects,* New York: McGraw-Hill. Martin Mayer offers a fascinating portrait of Dichter's work in advertising and consumer behavior research in the 1950s in Martin Mayer (1992 (1958)), *Madison Avenue U.S.A.,* Chicago: NTC Business Books.

**6** Laura Loro, "Do MCI's Ads Offer a Genius Child? Ask a Psychologist," *Advertising Age,* March 14, 1994; also see Carol Moog (1990), *Are They Selling Her Lips?,* New York: Morrow.

**7** Harold H. Kassarjian and Mary Jane Sheffet (1991), "Personality and Consumer Behavior: An Update," in *Perspectives in Consumer Behavior* 4th edition, eds. Harold H. Kassarjian and Thomas S. Robertson, Englewood Cliffs, NJ: Prentice Hall, pp. 281–303.

**8** Some examples include Kathryn E. A. Villani and Yoram Wind (1975), "On the Usage of 'Modified' Personality Trait Measures in Consumer Research," *Journal of Consumer Research,* 2 (December), 223–228; George Brooker (1975), "Representativeness of Shortened Personality Measures, *Journal of Consumer Research,* 5 (September), 143–145; George Brooker (1976), "The Self-Actualizing Socially Conscious Consumer," *Journal of Consumer Research,* 3 (September), 107–112; Charles M. Schaninger (1976), "Perceived Risk and Personality," *Journal of Consumer Research,* 3 (September), 95–100; Elizabeth C. Hirschman (1980), "Innovativeness, Novelty Seeking, and Consume Creativity," *Journal of Consumer Research,* 7 (December), 283–295; Russell W. Belk (1984), "Three Scales to Measure Constructs Related to Materialism: Reliability, Validity, and Relationship to Measures of Happiness," in *Advances in Consumer Research,* Vol. 17, ed. Thomas C. Kinnear, Ann Arbor: Association for Consumer Research, pp. 291–297; Russell W. Belk (1985), "Materialism: Trait Aspects of Living in the Material World," *Journal of Consumer Research,* 12 (December), 265–280; Morris Holbrook (1986), "Aims, Concepts, and Methods for the Representation of Individual Differences in Esthetic Responses to Design Features," *Journal of Consumer Research,* 13 (December), 337–347; Terence A. Shimp and Subhash Sharma (1987), "Consumer Ethnocentrism: Construction and Validation of the CETSCALE," *Journal of Marketing Research,* 24, (August), 280–290; William O. Bearden, Richard G. Netemeyer, and Jesse E. Teel (1989), "Measurement of Consumer Susceptibility to Interpersonal Influence," *Journal of Consumer Research,* 15 (March), 473–481; Ronald E. Goldsmith and Charles F. Hofacker (1991), "Measuring Consumer Innovativenss," *Journal of the Academy of Marketing Science,* 19, 209–221; Suresh Subramanian and Robert A. Mittellstaedt, (1991), "Conceptualizing Innovativeness as a Consumer Trait: Consequences and Alternatives," in *1991 American Marketing Association Educators' Proceedings,* eds. Mary C. Gilly and F. Robert Dwyer, Chicago: American Marketing Association, pp. 352–360; Marsha L. Richins and Scott M. Dawson (1992), "A Consumer Values Orientation for Materialism and Its Measurement: Scale Development and Validation," *Journal of Consumer Research,* 19 (December), 303–316.

**9** Kassarjian and Sheffet (1991) review these studies and report 'equivocal' results. For other perspectives, see John L. Lastovicka and Erich A. Joachimsthaler (1988), "Improving the Detection of Personality-Behavior Relationships in Consumer Research," *Journal of Consumer Research,* 14 (March), 583–587; Paul Albanese (1990), "Personality, Consumer Behavior, and Marketing Research: A New Theoretical and Empirical Approach," in *Research in Consumer Behavior,* 4, 1–49.

**10** E. Laird Landon, Jr. (1974), "Self Concept, Ideal Self Concept, and Consumer Purchase Intentions," *Journal of Consumer Research,* 1 (September), 44–51; M. Joseph Sirgy (1982), "Self-Concept in Consumer Behavior: A Critical Review," *Journal of Consumer Research,* 9 (December), 287–300; Barbara Stern (1988), "Sex Role Self-Concept Measures and Marketing: A Research Note," *Psychology & Marketing,* 5 (Spring), 85ff; John W. Schouten (1991), "Selves in Transition: Symbolic Consumption in Personal Rites of Passage and Identity Reconstruction," *Journal of Consumer Research,* 17 (March), 412–425; Kelly Tepper (1994), "The Role of Labeling Processes in Elderly Consumers' Responses to Age Segmentation Cues," *Journal of Consumer Research,* 20 (March), 503–519.

**11** Joseph T. Plummer (1984), "How Personality Makes a Difference," *Journal of Advertising Research,* 24(6), 27–31.

**12** Russell W. Belk (1988), "Possessions and the Extended Self," *Journal of Consumer Research,* 15 (September), 139–168; Joel B. Cohen (1989), "An Over-Extended Self?" *Journal of Consumer Research,* 16 (June), 125–128; Russell W. Belk (1989), "Extended Self and Extending Paradigmatic Perspective," *Journal of Consumer Research,* 16 (June), 129–132; Ronald Paul Hill and Mark Stamey (1990), "The Homeless in America: An Examination of Possessions and Consumption Behaviors," *Journal of Consumer Research,* 17 (December), 303–321; Glen David Mick and Michelle Demoss (1990), "Self-Gifts: Phenomenological Insights from Four Contexts," *Journal of Consumer Research,* 17 (December), 322–332; Ronald Paul Hill (1991), "Homeless Women, Special Possessions, and the Meaning of 'Home': An Ethnographic Case Study," *Journal of Consumer Research,* 18 (December), 298–310; Russell W. Belk (1992), "Moving Possessions: An Analysis Based on Personal Documents from the 1847–1869 Mormon Migration," *Journal of Consumer Research,* 19 (December), 339–341.

**13** Classic treatments of this topic include William D. Wells and Douglas J. Tigert (1971), "Activities, Interests, and Opinions," *Journal of Advertising Research,* 11 (August), 27–35; Ruth Ziff (1971), "Psychographics for Market Segmentation," *Journal of Advertising Research,* 11 (April), 3–10; Joseph T. Plummer (1974), "The Concept and Application of Life Style Segmentation," *Journal of Marketing,* 38 (January), 33–37; William D. Wells (1974), *Lifestyle & Psychographics,* Chicago: American Marketing Association; William D. Wells (1975), "Psychographics: A Critical Review," *Journal of Marketing Research,* 12 (May), 196–213. Three recent reviews are Barrie Gunter and Adrian Furnham (1992), *Consumer Profiles: An Introduction to Psychographics,* London: Routledge; Rebecca Pirto (1991), *Beyond Mind Games,* Ithaca: American Demographics Books; and Lynn R. Kahle and Larry Chiagouris *Values, Lifestyle, and Psychographics,* Hillsdale, NJ: Lawrence Erlbaum, in press.

**14** Some examples include Marvin E. Goldberg (1977), "Identifying Relevant Psychographic Segments: How Specifying Product Functions Can Help," *Journal of Consumer Research,* 3 (December), 163–169; Alladi Venkatesh (1980), "Changing Roles of Women—A Life-Style Analysis," *Journal of Consumer Research,* 7 (September), 189–197; John J. Burnett (1981), "Psychographic and Demographic Characteristics of Blood Donors," *Journal of Consumer Research,* 8 (June), 62–67; Jacob Hornik and Mary Jane Schlinger (1981), "Allocation of Time to Mass Media," *Journal of Consumer Research,* 7 (March), 343–355; Dorothy Leonard-Barton (1981) "Voluntary Simplicity Lifestyles and Energy Conservation," *Journal of Consumer Research,* 8 (December), 243–252; John L. Lastovicka, John P. Murry, Erich A. Joachimsthaler, Gurav Bhalla, and Jim Scheurich (1987), "A Lifestyle Typology to Model Young Male Drinking and Driving," *Journal of Consumer Research,* 14 (September), 257–263; John L. Lastovicka, John P. Murry, Erich A. Joachimsthaler (1990), "Evaluating the Measurement Validity of Lifestyle Typologies with Qualitative Measures and Multiplicative Factoring," *Journal of Marketing Research,* 27 (February), 11–23; Morris B. Holbrook (1993), "Nostalgia and Consumption Preferences: Some Emerging Patterns of Consumer Tastes," *Journal of Consumer Research,* 20 (September), 245–256.

**15** William D. Wells and Mike Swenson (1995), "Citizen Environmentalists," Unpublished paper, School of Journalism and Mass Communications, University of Minnesota,.

**16** Martha Farnsworth Riche (1989), "Psychographics for the 1990s," *American Demographics,* (July), 24ff. The WISH-TV example is from Riche's article; the others are from promotional materials provided by SRI.

**17** Alan King (1991), "The Rise and Fall of Lotus Marketplace," *Online,* 15 (July), 102–104; Brian Nielsen (1991), "Intellectual Freedom in an Electronic Age," 15 (July), 8–90; Mary J. Culnan (1993), "'How Did They Get My Name?': An Exploratory Investigation of Consumer Attitudes Toward Secondary Information Use," *MIS Quarterly,* 17 (September), 341–363; Paul Wang and Lisa A. Petrison (1993), "Direct Marketing Activities and Personal Privacy: A Consumer Survey," *Journal of Direct Marketing,* 7 (Winter), 7–19; Mitch Betts, "Subscriber Privacy for Sale," *Computerworld,* October 10, 1994; Claudia Montague (1994), "Privacy," *Marketing Tools,* (November/December), 40–52; Rich Wartzman, "A Research Company Got Consumer Data From Voting Rolls," *Wall Street Journal,* December 23, 1994; John D. Yeck (1995), "From the Practitioners," *Journal of Direct Marketing,* 9 (Winter), 2–4.

## Chapter 7

**1** The classic early treatments of reference groups are Herbert H. Hyman, (1942), "The Psychology of Status," *Archives of Psychology,* 38(No. 269); Tomatsu Shibutani (1955), "Reference Groups as Perspectives", *American Journal of Sociology,* 60, 562–569; and Robert K. Merton (1968), *Social Theory and Social Structure,* New York: Free Press.

**2** The work on consumer socialization includes Scott Ward (1974), "Consumer Socialization," *Journal of Consumer Research,* 1 (September), 1–14; George P. Moschis (1985), "The Role of Family Communication in Consumer Socialization of Children and Adolescents," *Journal of Consumer Research,* 11 (March), 898–913; Deborah Roedder John and John C. Whitney, Jr. (1986), "The Development of Consumer Knowledge in Children: A Cognitive Structure Approach," *Journal of Consumer Research,* 12 (March), 406–417; Carole M. Macklin (1987), "Preschoolers' Understanding of the Informational Function of Television Advertising," *Journal of Consumer Research,* 14 (September), 229–239; Les Carlson and Stanford Grossbart (1988), "Parental Style and Consumer Socialization of Children," *Journal of Consumer Research,* 15 (June), 77–94; and Stanford Grossbart, Les Carlson, and Ann Walsh (1991), "Consumer Socialization and Frequency of Shopping with Children," *Journal of the Academy of Marketing Science,* 19 (Summer), 155–164.

**3** Among the articles that discuss the transition from home to wider community and the effects of outside influences on consumption are Gilbert A. Churchill, Jr., And George P. Moschis (1979), "Television and Interpersonal Influences on Adolescent Consumer Learning," *Journal of Consumer Research,* 6 (June), 23–35; Russell W. Belk, Kenneth D. Bahn, and Robert N. Mayer (1982), "Developmental Recognition of Consumption Symbolism," *Journal of Consumer Research,* 9 (June), 4–17; Gerald J. Gorn and Marvin E. Goldberg (1982), "Behavioral Evidence of the Effects of Televised Food Messages on Children," *Journal of Consumer Research,* 9 (September), 200–205; Kenneth D. Bahn (1986), "How and When Do Brand Perceptions and Preferences First Form? A Cognitive Developmental Investigation," *Journal of Consumer Research,* 13 (December), 382–393; Ronald J. Faber and Thomas C. O'Guinn (1988), "Expanding the View of Consumer Socialization: A Nonutilitarian Mass-Mediated Perspective," in (E. Hirschman, ed.) *Research in Consumer Behavior,* Vol. three, Greenwich, CT: JAI Press, 1988, pp. 49–77; Deborah Roedder John and Mita Sujan (1990), "Age Differences in Product Categorization," *Journal of Consumer Research,* 16 (March), 452–460; Terry L. Childers and Akshay R. Rao (1992), "The Influence of Familial and Peer-based Reference Groups on Consumer Decisions," *Journal of Consumer Research,* 19 (September), 198–211; Oswald A. J. Mascarenhas and Mary J. Higby, (1993), "Peer, Parent, and Media Influences in Teen Apparel Shopping," *Journal of the Academy of Marketing Science,* 21 (Winter), 53–58.

**4** Daniel Boorstin (1974), *The Americans: The Democratic Experience,* New York: Vintage Books. For a perspective on the role of mass media in consumption communities, see David Prensky and Christine Wright-Isak, "Advertising, Values, and the Consumption Community," in *Values, Lifestyle, and Psychographics,* eds. Lynn R. Kahle and Larry Chiagouris, Hillsdale, NJ: Lawrence Erlbaum, in press.

**5** Lorne Manly, "Membership Clubs Gain Favor with Consumer Titles," *Folio: The Magazine for Magazine Management,* November 15, 1993; Stan Rapp and Thomas L. Collins, "The New Marketing: Sell and Socialize," *New York Times,* February 20, 1994; Joseph Weber, Jr., "How to Rope 'em With Plastic," *Business Week,* September 26, 1994; Kerry Dolan, "Getting a Charge Out of Rock 'n' Roll: Rolling Stones' Affinity Card," *Forbes,* December 19, 1994; Trip Gabriel, "Virtual Downtown," *New York Times,* January 22, 1995; John Perry Barlow, "Is There a There in Cyberspace?" *Utne Reader,* March–April 1995.

**6** See Howard Rheingold (1993), *The Virtual Community,* Reading, MA: Addison-Wesley; and Bruce MacEvoy, "Change Leaders and the New Media," in *Values, Lifestyle, and Psychographics,* eds. Lynn R. Kahle and Larry Chiagouris, Hillsdale, NJ: Lawrence Erlbaum, in press.

**7** Among the studies that examine the bases of influence are Robert E. Burnkrant and Alain Cousineau (1975), "Informational and Normative Social Influence in Buyer Behavior," *Journal of Consumer Research,* 2 (December), 206–215; C. Whan Park and V. Parker Lessig (1977), "Students and Housewives: Differences in Susceptibility to Reference Group Influence," *Journal of Consumer Research,* 4 (September), 102–110; Brian Sternthal, Ruby Roy Dholakia, and Clark Leavitt (1978), "The Persuasive Effect of Source Credibility," *Journal of Consumer Research,* 4 (March), 252–260; Peter H. Reingen, Brian L. Foster, Jacqueline Johnson Brown, and Stephen B. Seidman (1984), "Brand Congruence in Interpersonal Relations: A Social Network Analysis," *Journal of Consumer Research,* 11 (December), 771–783; William O. Bearden, Richard G. Netemeyer, and Jesse E. Teel (1989), "Measurement of Consumer Susceptibility to Interpersonal Influence," *Journal of Consumer Research,* 15 (March), 472–480; James C. Ward and Peter H. Reingen (1990), "Sociocognitive Analysis of Group Decision Making Among Consumers," *Journal of Consumer Research,* 17 (December), 245–262; Randall L. Rose, William O. Bearden, and Jesse E. Teel, (1992), "An Attributional Analysis of Resistance to Group Pressure Regarding Illicit Drug and Alcohol Consumption," *Journal of Consumer Research,* 19 (June), 1–13.

**8** William O. Bearden and Michael J. Etzel (1982), "Reference Group Influence on Product and Brand Purchase Decisions," *Journal of Consumer Research,* 9 (September), 183–194.

**9** Some of the articles that discuss consumer behavior in families include Harry L. Davis (1970), "Dimensions of Marital Roles in Consumer Decision Making," *Journal of Marketing Research,* 7 (May), 168–177; Harry L. Davis, (1976), Decision Making Within the Household," *Journal of Consumer Research,* 2 (March), 241–260; Harry L. Davis, (1977), "Decision Making Within the Household," in *Selected Aspects of Consumer Behavior: A Summary from the Perspective of Different Disciplines,* Washington, DC: National Science Foundation, 73–97; John Scanzoni (1977), "Changing Sex Roles and Emerging Directions in Family Decision Making," *Journal of Consumer Research,* 4 (December), 185–188; C. Whan Park (1982), "Joint Decisions in Home Purchasing: A Muddling Through Process," *Journal of Consumer Research,* 9 (September), 151–162; Rosann L. Spiro (1983), "Persuasion in Family Decisionmaking," *Journal of Consumer Research,* 10 (March), 393–402; Dennis L. Rosen and Donald H. Granbois (1983), "Determinants of Role Structure in Family Financial Management," 10 (September), 253–258; George Belch, Michael A. Belch, and Gayle Ceresino (1985), "Parental and Teenage Child Influences in Family Decision Making," *Journal of Business Research,* 13 (April), 163–176; Harry L. Davis, Stephen J. Hoch,

and E. K. Easton Ragsdale (1986), "An Anchoring and Adjustment Model of Spousal Predictions," *Journal of Consumer Research,* 13 (June), 25–37; Kim P. Corfman and Donald R. Lehmann (1987), "Models of Cooperative Group Decision-Making and Relative Influence: An Experimental Investigation of Family Purchase Decisions," *Journal of Consumer Research,* 14 (June), 1–13; William J. Qualls (1987), "Household Decision Behavior: The Impact of Husbands' and Wives' Sex Role Orientation," *Journal of Consumer Research,* 14 (September), 264–278; Ellen R. Foxman, Patriya S. Tansuhaj, and Karin M. Ekstrom (1989), "Family Members' Perceptions of Adolescents' Influence in family Decision Making," *Journal of Consumer Research,* 15 (March), 87–97; Michael B. Menasco and David J. Curry (1989), "Utility and Choice: An Empirical Study of Wife/Husband Decision Making," *Journal of Consumer Research,* 16 (June), 87–97; Sharon E. Beatty and Salil Talpade (1994), "Adolescent Influence in Family Decision Making: A Replication With Extension," *Journal of Consumer Research,* 21 (September), 332–341.

**10** Jerry E. Bishop, "TV Advertising Aimed at Kids Is Filled with Fat: Saturday Morning Television Commercials," *Wall Street Journal,* November 9, 1993; Stuart Elliott, "Parents' Fears About Toy Marketing: Children Transformed Into Consumer Monsters," *New York Times,* December 14, 1993; Kyle Pope, "How Children Decide on Gifts They Want, and Plot To Get Them," *Wall Street Journal,* December 23, 1993; Alice Z. Cuneo, "Not in My House, Parent Exclaims," *Advertising Age,* February 14, 1994; Alicia Lasek, "Misleading Ads, Wary Consumers," *Advertising Age,* February 14, 1994; Mark Schwed, "TV Commercials & Your Kids," *TV Guide,* February 18, 1995.

# Chapter 8

**1** Kurt Lewin (1935), *A Dynamic Theory of Personality,* New York: McGraw-Hill.

**2** This is called a double approach–avoidance conflict by Gerald Zaltman and Melanie Wallendorf (1979), *Consumer Behavior: Basic Findings and Management Implications,* New York: Wiley.

**3** See David C. McClelland (1955), *Studies in Motivation,* New York: Appleton-Century-Crofts; Calvin S. Hall and Gardner Lindzey (1987), *Theories of Personality,* New York: John Wiley; Paul T. Costa and Robert R. McCrae (1988), "From Catalog to Classification: Murray's Needs and the Five-Factor Model," *Journal of Personality and Social Psychology,* 55(2), 258–265.

**4** Abraham H. Maslow (1943), "A Theory of Human Motivation," *Psychological Review,* 50, 370–396; Abraham H. Maslow (1970), *Motivation and Personality,* 2nd edition, New York: Harper & Row; George Brooker (1976), "The Self-Actualizing Socially Conscious Consumer," *Journal of Consumer Research,* 3 (September), 107–112.

**5** Ernest Dichter (1964), *Handbook of Consumer Motivations: The Psychology of the World of Objects,* New York: McGraw-Hill is the classic work on motivational research. Discussions of Dichter's work include Rena Bartos, (1977), "Ernest Dichter: Motive Interpreter," *Journal of Advertising Research,* 17 (June), 8; Martin Mayer (1992 [1958]), *Madison Avenue U.S.A.,* Chicago: NTC Business Books. A recent work that uses this approach to understand advertising is Carol Moog (1990), *"Are They Selling Her Lips?",* New York: Morrow.

**6** Discussions of these kinds of research include Mason Haire (1950), "Projective Techniques in Marketing Research," *Journal of Marketing,* 14 (April), 649–656; James C. Anderson (1978), "The Validity of Haire's Shopping List Projective Technique," *Journal of Marketing,* 15 (November), 644–649; Sidney J. Levy (1985), "Dreams, Fairy Tales, Animals, and Cars," *Psychology and*

*Marketing,* 2 (Summer), 67–81; Jeffrey Durgee (1990), "Qualitative Methods for Developing Advertising That Makes Consumers Feel, 'Hey, That's Right for Me,'" *Journal of Consumer Marketing,* 7 (Winter), 15–21; Rebecca Piirto (1991), *Beyond Mind Games,* Ithaca: American Demographics Books; J. H. "Mike" Flynn, (1991), "Qualitative Research in Advertising," *Advances in Consumer Research,* Vol. 18, eds. Rebecca H. Holman and Michael R. Solomon, Provo, UT: Association for Consumer Research; David A. Aaker, V. Kumar, and George S. Day (1995), Marketing Research, 5th edition, New York: Wiley, pp. 280–283.

**7** Ronald Alsop, "Advertisers Put Consumers on the Couch," *Wall Street Journal,* May 13, 1988.

**8** Jonathan Gutman (1982), "A Means–End Chain Model Based on Consumer Categorization Processes," *Journal of Marketing,* 46 (Spring), 60–72, Thomas J. Reynolds and Jonathan Gutman (1988) "Laddering Theory, Method, Analysis, and Interpretation," *Journal of Advertising Research,* 28 )February–March), 11–34.

**9** Theodore Leavitt (1960), "Marketing Myopia," *Harvard Business Review,* (July–August), 45–56; Russell I. Haley (1968), "Benefit Segmentation: A Decision-Oriented Research Tool," *Journal of Marketing,* 32 (July), 30–35, and Paul E. Green, Yoram Wind, and Arun K. Jain (1972), "Benefit Bundle Analysis," *Journal of Advertising Research,* (April), 32–36.

**10** Some treatments of the benefits offered by associations include Peter B. Clark and James Q. Wilson (1961), "Incentive Systems: A Theory of Organizations," *Administrative Science Quarterly,* 6, 129–166; James Q. Wilson, (1971), *Political Organizations,* New York: Basic Books; Mayer N. Zald and David Jacobs (1978), "Compliance/Incentive Classifications of Organizations: Underlying Dimensions," *Administration and Society* 9, 403–424; David Knoke and David Prensky (1984), "What Relevance Do Organizational Theories Have for Voluntary Associations?" *Social Science Quarterly,* 65, 3–20. For some recent examples, see Donald M. Norris, "Market–Driven Success," *Association Management,* November 1991; Donald R. Levy, "Segment Your Members: The Needs of Association Members," *Association Management,* August 1992; Jan Carter, "Establishing a Marketing Function," *Association Management,* March 1993; Phil Hall, "Cutting the Cost of Keeping People Interested," *Marketing,* June 7, 1993; Stephanie Faul, "Adding Members, Building Bridges," *Association Management,* August 1993; Holly Townsend, "Magazine Must–Knows for the CEO," *Association Management,* September 1994; Bruce Watson, "Inside Club America: It's Not What You Do That Counts, It's What You Belong To," *Smithsonian,* April 1995; Carol A. Schwartz and Rebecca L. Turner (1995), *Encyclopedia of Associations,* Detroit: Gale Research.

**11** Some of the works that address this issue include Daniel Pope (1983), *The Making of Modern Advertising,* New York: Basic Books; Stephen Fox (1984), *The Mirror Makers: A History of American Advertising and Its Creators,* New York: William Morrow; Michael Schudson (1984), *Advertising, The Uneasy Persuasion,* New York: Basic Books; William Leiss, Stephen Kline, and Sut Jhally (1990), *Social Communication in Advertising,* New York: Routledge.

**12** Treatments of this issue include Diane Barthel (1988), *Putting on Appearances: Gender and Advertising,* Philadelphia: Temple; and Debra Lynn Stephens, Ronald Paul Hill, and Cynthia Hanson (1994), "The Beauty Myth and Female Consumers: The Controversial Role of Advertising," *Journal of Consumer Affairs,* 28 (Summer), 137–153. For articles about the particular controversy, see Don Dunn, "When Thinness Becomes Illness," *Business Week,* August 3, 1992; Louise Ague, "How Thin is Too Thin?" *People,* September 20, 1993; Stuart Elliott, "Ultrathin Models in Coca–Cola and Calvin Klein Campaigns Draw Fire and a Boycott Call," *New York Times,* April 26, 1994; Cyndee Miller, "'Give Them a Cheeseburger: Critics Assail Waif Look in Sprite, Calvin Klein Ads," *Marketing News,* June 6, 1994.

**13** See Morris B. Holbrook (1987), "Mirror, Mirror, on the Wall, What's Unfair in the Reflections of Advertising?" *Journal of Marketing,* 51 (July), 95–103; Richard W. Pollay (1986), "The Distorted Mirror: Reflections on the Unintended Consequences of Advertising," *Journal of Marketing,* 50 (April), 18–36; and (1987), "On the Value of Reflections on the Values in 'The Distorted Mirror.'" *Journal of Marketing,* 51 (July), 104–110.

## Chapter 9

**1** David Astor, "'Magic Eye' Creator Has Vision of Future," *Editor & Publisher,* August 20, 1994; M. Alexandra Nelson, "Dots of Illusion," *Popular Science,* September 1994; John Grossman, "In the Eye of the Beholder," *Inc.,* October 1994; Robert Dahlin, "Looking Through the Three Dimensions," *Publishers Weekly,* November 7, 1994; Steve Dougherty, "Hiding in Plain Sight," *People,* November 28, 1994.

**2** Several representative articles about schema are Joseph W. Alba and Lynn Hasher (1983), "Is Memory Schematic?" *Psychological Bulletin,* 93, 203–231; Ruth Ann Smith and Michael J. Houston (1985), "A Psychometric Assessment of Measures of Scripts in Consumer Memory," *Journal of Consumer Research,* 12 (September), 214–224; Mita Sujan and James R. Bettman (1989), "The Effects of Brand Positioning Strategies on Consumers' Brand and Category Perceptions: Some Insights from Schema Research," *Journal of Marketing Research,* 26 (March), 454–467.

**3** Bernard I. Levy (1984), "Research into the Psychological Meaning of Color," *American Journal of Art Therapy,* 23 (January), 58–62; Bruce Buchanan, Moshe Givon, and Arieh Goldman (1987), "Measurement of Discriminative Ability in Taste Tests: An Empirical Investigation," *Journal of Marketing Research,* 24 (May), 154–163; Jacob Hornik (1992), "Tactile Stimulation and Consumer Response," *Journal of Consumer Research,* 19 (December), 449–458; Naveen Donthu, Joseph Cherian, and Mukesh Bhargava, (1993), "Factors Influencing Recall of Outdoor Advertising," *Journal of Advertising Research,* 33 (May–June), 64–72.

**4** Bernice Kanner, "Color Schemes," *New York,* April 3, 1989; Wendy Bounds, "Mood is Indigo for Many Food Marketers," *Wall Street Journal,* September 2, 1993; Helen Mundell, "How the Color Mafia Chooses Your Clothes," *American Demographics,* (November) 21–23, (1993), Deborah L. Jacobs, "The Titans of Tint Make Their Picks," *New York Times,* May 29, 1994; Patrick M. Reilly, "Shoppers Buy Up a Bounty of Natural Beauty Products," *Wall Street Journal,* June 8, 1994; Suein L. Hwang, "Seeking Scents That No One Has Smelled," *Wall Street Journal,* August 10, 1994; Anthony Ramirez, "Bored to the Gills with Boutique Beers? How Does a Scratch-and-Sniff Magazine Campaign Sound?" *New York Times,* October 31, 1994; Jane M. Von Bergen, "Colors Can Affect Customers, A Designer Advises Retailers," *Philadelphia Inquirer,* January 25, 1995; Al Haas, "In Redoing the Continental, Lincoln Listened to Buyers," *Philadelphia Inquirer,* February 26, 1995; Jane Birnbaum, "In a Revolution of Paint Colors, Purple Is Coming Up Roses," *New York Times,* March 26, 1995; Paul M. Barrett, "Supreme Court Says a Distinctive Color Can Be Basis for a Product Trademark," *Wall Street Journal,* March 29, 1995; "Are the Flag's Colors Next?" *New York Times,* April 2, 1995.

**5** "Procter & Gamble Sues Look-Alikes," *Newark Star-Ledger,* September 8, 1994; "P&G Files Suit Against Its Own Customer

About Sale of Private-Label Products," *Wall Street Journal*, September 8, 1994; Jennifer Kent, "P&G Rival Agrees to Change Its Labels," *Cincinnati Post*, September 28, 1994; "P&G Wants Copycat Brands Off Shelves," *Columbus Dispatch*, November 21, 1994; Paul M. Barrett, "Color in the Court: Can Tints Be Trademarked?" *Wall Street Journal*, January 5, 1995; Evan Ramstad, "'Bookshelf' Dispute Threatens Jewish Software," *Philadelphia Inquirer*, March 4, 1995; "Microsoft Corp.," *Wall Street Journal*, March 6, 1995; Robert Frank, "Olympic Flame Singes Some Atlanta Businesses," *Wall Street Journal*, March 22, 1995; Paul M. Barrett, "Supreme Court Says a Distinctive Color Can Be Basis for a Product Trademark," *Wall Street Journal*, March 29, 1995; "P&G Wins Suit in Copyright Case," *Cincinnati Post*, April 8, 1995; Cliff Peale, "P&G Files Another Lawsuit in War Against Copy-Cats," *Cincinnati Post*, April 14, 1995.

**6** Timothy E. Moore (1982), "Subliminal Advertising: What You See Is What You Get," *Journal of Marketing,* 46 (Spring), 38–47; William E. Kilbourne, Scott Painton, and Danny Ridley (1985), "The Effect of Sexual Embedding on Responses to Magazine Advertisements," *Journal of Advertising,* 14(2), 48–56; Timothy E. Moore (1988), "The Case Against Subliminal Manipulation," *Psychology & Marketing,* 5 (Winter), 355–372; Anthony Greenwald, Eric R. Spangenberg, Anthony Pratkanis, and Jay Eskanazi (1991), "Double-blind Tests of Subliminal Self-help Audiotapes," *Psychological Science,* 2(2) 119–122; Eric R. Spangenberg, Carl Obermiller, and Anthony Greenwald (1992), "A Field Test of Subliminal Self-help Audiotapes: The Power of Expectancies," *Journal of Public Policy and Marketing,* 11 (Fall), 26–36; Stuart Rogers (1992–1993), "How a Publicity Blitz Created the Myth of Subliminal Advertising," *Public Relations Quaterly,* 37 (Winter), 12–17; Martha Rogers and Kirk H. Smith (1993), "Public Perceptions of Subliminal Advertising: Why Practitioners Shouldn't Ignore This Issue," *Journal of Advertising Research,* 33 (March–April), 10–18; Martha Rogers and Christine A. Seiler, "The Answer is No: A National Survey of Advertising Industry Practitioners and Their Clients About Whether They Use Subliminal Advertising," *Journal of Advertising Research,* 34 (March–April), 36–45.

**7** Among the works that investigate risk and risk reduction strategies are Charles M. Schaninger (1976), "Perceived Risk and Personality," *Journal of Consumer Research,* 3 (September), 95–100; Terence A. Shimp and William O. Bearden (1982), "Warranty and Other Extrinsic Cue Effects on Consumers' Risk Perceptions," *Journal of Consumer Research,* 9 (June), 38–46; Valerie S. Folkes (1988), "The Availability Heuristic and Perceived Risk," *Journal of Consumer Research,* 15 (June), 13–23; Keith B. Murray and John L. Schlacter (1990), "The Impact of Services versus Goods on Consumers' Assessment of Perceived Risk and Variability," *Journal of the Academy of Marketing Science,* 18 (Winter), 51–65; Keith B. Murray, (1991, "A Test of Service Marketing Theory: Consumer Information Acquisition Activities," *Journal of Marketing,* 55 (January), 10–25; Craig A. Kelley and Jeffrey S. Conant (1991), "Extended Warranties: Consumer and Manufacturer Perceptions," *Journal of Consumer Affairs,* 25 (Summer), 68–83; V-W. Mitchell, (1992), "Understanding Consumers' Behaviour: Can Perceived Risk Theory Help? *Management Decision,* 30(3), 26–31; Allen J. Klose (1993), "Commentary: Customer Service Insurance," *Journal of Services Marketing,* 7(1), 55–58; Grahame R. Dowling and Richard Staelin (1994), "A Model of Perceived Risk and Intended Risk-handling Activity," *Journal of Consumer Research,* 21 (June), 119–134; Dhruv Grewal, Jerry Gotlieb and Howard Marmorstein (1994), "The Moderating Effects of Message Framing and Source Credibility on the Price–Perceived Risk Relationship," *Journal of Consumer Research,* 21 (June), 145–153.

**8** Works that examine perceptions of quality include Valarie Zeithaml, (1988), "Consumer Perceptions of Price, Quality, and Value: A Means–End Model and Synthesis and Evidence," *Journal of Marketing,* 52 (July), 2–22; Kenneth G. DeBono and Michelle Packer (1991), "The Effects of Advertising Appeal on Perceptions of Product Quality," *Personality and Social Psychology Bulletin,* 17 (April), 194–200; William B. Dodds, Kent B. Monroe, and Dhruv Grewal (1991), "Effects of Price, Brand and Store Information on Buyers' Product Evaluations," *Journal of Marketing Research,* 28 (August), 307–319; William Boulding and Amna Kirmani (1993), "A Consumer-Side Experimental Examination of Signaling Theory: Do Consumers Perceive Warranties as Signals of Quality?" *Journal of Consumer Research,* 20 (June), 111–123.

**9** For a good introduction to legal issues, see Dorothy Cohen (1995), *Legal Issues in Marketing Decision Making*, Cincinnati: South-Western. Two works that address advertising deceptiveness are Ivan L. Preston (1990), "The Definition of Deceptiveness in Advertising and Other Commercial Speech," *Catholic University Law Review,* 39 (Summer), 1035–1081, and Ivan L. Preston and Jef. I Richards (1993), "A Role for Consumer Belief in FTC and Lanham Act Deceptive Advertising Cases," *American Business Law Journal,* 31 (May), 1–29. Discussions of specific product advertising and labeling include Bruce Silverglade, "To Stop Sneaky Ads, Stir UP the F.T.C.," *New York Times*, March 6, 1994; Laura Bird, "New Labels Will Tell Real Story on Juice Drinks," *Wall Street Journal*, May 3, 1994; Laurie McGinley, "FDA Expected to Propose Regulation Limiting Labeling of Foods as Healthy," *Wall Street Journal*, May 4, 1994; Marilyn Marter, "Digesting the Labels," *Philadelphia Inquirer*; Dick Mercer, "Tempest in a Soup Can," *Advertising Age*, October 17, 1994; Julia Miller, "Shoot Fast, Cut Back on Trickery: Ad Propping Today," *Advertising Age*, October 17, 1994,

## Chapter 10

**1** Eben Shapiro, "Molson Ice Ads Raise Hackles of Regulators," *Wall Street Journal*, February 25, 1994; James Bovard, "Beer Bust: Censorship of Commercial Speech Blocks the Pursuit of Happiness," *Barrons's*, November 21, 1994; Suein L. Hwang and Paul M. Barrett, "Court Allows Alcohol Levels On Beer Labels," *Wall Street Journal*, April 20, 1995.

**2** Gerald Gorn (1982), "The Effects of Music in Advertising on Choice Behavior: A Classical Conditioning Approach," *Journal of Marketing*, 46 (Winter), 94–101; Frances K. McSweeney and Calvin Bierley (1984), "Recent Developments in Classical Conditioning," *Journal of Consumer Research,* 11 (September), 619–631; Calvin Bierley, Frances K. McSweeney, and Renee Vannieuwkerk (1985), "Classical Conditioning of Preferences for Stimuli," *Journal of Consumer Research*, 12 (December), 316–323; Chris T. Allen and Thomas J. Madden (1985), "A Closer Look at Classical Conditioning," *Journal of Consumer Research*, 12 (December), 301–315; "Classical Conditioning of Consumer Attitudes: Four Experiments in an Advertising Context," *Journal of Consumer Research*, 14 (December), 334–339; Robert A. Rescorla, (1988), "Pavlovian Conditioning: It's Not What You Think It Is," *American Psychologist,* 43 (March), 151–160; Chris T. Allen and Chris A. Janiszewski (1989), "Assessing the Role of Contingency Awareness in Attitudinal Conditioning with Implications for Advertising Research," *Journal of Marketing Research*, 26 (February), 30–43; James J. Kellaris and Anthony D. Cox (1989), "The Effects of Background Music in Advertising: A Reassessment," *Journal of Consumer Research*, 15 (March), 113–118; Terence A. Shimp (1991), "Neo-Pavlovian Conditioning and its Implication for Consumer Theory and Research," in *Handbook of Consumer Behavior*, eds. Thomas S. Robertson and

Harold H. Kassarjian, Englewood Cliffs: Prentice-Hall, pp. 162–187; Elnora W. Stuart, Terence A. Shimp, and Randall W. Engle (1991), "A Program of Classical Conditioning Experiments Testing Variations in the Conditioned Stimulus and Contents," *Journal of Consumer Research*, 18 (June), 1–12.

**3** For a good overview of Skinner's work, see B.F. Skinner, "How to Teach Animals," *Scientific American*, December 1951 and B.F. Skinner (1953), *Science and Human Behavior*, New York: Free Press; and Iver H. Iversen (1992), "Skinner's Early Research: From Reflexology to Operant Conditioning," *American Psychologist*, 47 (November), 1318–1328. Marketing works that consider operant conditioning include Walter R. Nord and J. Paul Peter (1980), "A Behavior Modification Perspective on Marketing," *Journal of Marketing*, 44 (Spring), 36–47; Michael L Rothschild and William C. Gaidis (1981), "Behavioral Learning Theory: Its Relevance to Marketing and Promotions," *Journal of Marketing*, 45 (Spring), 70–78; J. Paul Peter and Walter R. Nord (1982), "A Clarification and Extension of Operant Conditioning Principles in Marketing," *Journal of Marketing*, 46 (Summer), 102–107; Gordon R. Foxall (1992), "The Behavioral Perspective Model of Purchase and Consumption: From Consumer Theory to Marketing Practice," *Journal of the Academy of Marketing Science*, 20 (Spring), 189–198.

**4** Among the many books and articles that have explored consumers' cognitive processing are James R. Bettman (1979), *An Information Processing Theory of Consumer Choice*, Reading, MA: Addison-Wesley; John G. Lynch and Thomas K. Srull (1982), "Memory and Attentional Factors in Consumer Choice: Concepts and Research Methods," *Journal of Consumer Research*, 9 (June), 18–37; Julie A. Edell and Richard Staelin (1983), "The Information Processing of Pictures in Print Advertisements," *Journal of Consumer Research*, 10 (June), 45–61; Eric J. Johnson and J. Edward Russo (1984), "Product Familiarity and Learning New Information," *Journal of Consumer Research*, 11 (June) 542–550; Terry Childers and Michael Houston (1984), "Conditions for a Picture-Superiority Effect on Consumer Memory," *Journal of Consumer Research*, 11 (September), 643–654; Joseph W. Alba and Amitava Chattopadhyay (1986), "Salience Effects in Brand Recall," *Journal of Marketing Research*, 23 (November), 363–370; Deborah J. MacInnis and Linda J. Price (1987), "The Role of Imagery in Information Processing: Review and Extensions," *Journal of Consumer Research*, 13 (March), 473–491; Michael Houston, Terry Childers, and Susan Heckler (1987), "Picture-Word Consistency and the Elaborative Processing of Attributes," *Journal of Marketing Research*, 24 (November), 359–369; Kevin Lane Keller (1987), "Memory Factors in Advertising: The Effect of Advertising Retrieval Cues on Brand Evaluations," *Journal of Consumer Research*, 14 (December), 316–333; Raymond R. Burke and Thomas K. Srull (1988), "Competitive Interference and Consumer Memory for Advertising," *Journal of Consumer Research*, 15 (June), 55–68; Julie A. Edell and Kevin Lane Keller (1989), "The Information Processing of Coordinated Media Campaigns," *Journal of Marketing Research*, 26 (May), 149–164; Joan Meyers-Levy and Brian Sternthal (1991), "Gender Differences in the Use of Message Cues," *Journal of Marketing Research*, 28 (February), 84–96; Joan Meyers-Levy and Durairaj Maheswaran (1991), "Exploring Differences in Males' and Females' Processing Strategies," *Journal of Consumer Research*, 18 (June), 63–70; Susan E. Heckler and Terry L. Childers (1992), "The Role of Expectancy and Relevancy in Memory for Verbal and Visual Information: What is Incongruency?" *Journal of Consumer Research*, 18 (March), 475–492;

**5** Gerri Hirshey, "Gambling Nation," *New York Times Magazine*, July 17, 1994; Edward Cone, "Taking No Chances," *Information Week*, December 12, 1994; Heidi Evans, "Bally's Grand Casino, For Elaine Cohen, Is Her One True Home," *Wall Street Journal*, December 28, 1994; William M. Bulkeley, "New On-Line Casinos May Thwart U.S. Laws," *Wall Street Journal*, May 10, 1995.

**6** Work that investigates the effect of repetition on consumer learning includes George E. Belch (1982), "The Effects of Television Commercial Repetition on Cognitive Response and Message Acceptance," *Journal of Consumer Research*, 9 (June), 56–65; Arno J. Rethans, John L. Swasy, and Lawrence J. Marks (1986), "Effects of Television Commercial Repetition, Receiver Knowledge, and Commercial Length: A Test of the Two-Factor Model," *Journal of Marketing Research*, 23 (February), 50–61; Rajeev Batra and Michael l. Ray (1986), "Situational Effects of Advertising Repetition: The Moderating Influence of Motivation, Ability, and Opportunity to Respond," *Journal of Consumer Research*, 12 (March), 432–445; Dena S. Cox and Anthony D. Cox (1988), "What *Does* Familiarity Breed? Complexity as a Moderator of Repetition Effects in Advertising Evaluation," *Journal of Consumer Research*, 15 (June), 111–116; H. Rao Unnava and Robert E. Burnkrant (1991), "Effects of Repeating Varied Ad Executions on Brand Name Memory," *Journal of Marketing Research*, 28 (November), 406–416.

**7** Two recent articles that discuss comparative advertisements and consumers' ability to discriminate among products are C. Whan Park, V. Parker Lessig, and D. H. Lee (1991), "The Level and Nature of Product Knowledge and Ad Format Strategies," *Current Issues and Research in Advertising*, 13(1), 125–154 and Thomas E. Barry (1993), "Comparative Advertising: What Have We Learned in Two Decades?" *Journal of Advertising Research*, 33 (March–April), 19–29.

**8** Among the works that have considered experience and prior knowledge are James R. Bettman and C. Whan Park (1980), "Effects of Prior Knowledge and Experience and Phase of the Choice Process on Consumer Decision Processes: A Protocol Analysis," *Journal of Consumer Research*, 7 (December), 234–248; Stephen J. Hoch and Young-Won Ha (1986), "Consumer Learning: Advertising and the Ambiguity of Product Experience," *Journal of Consumer Research*, 13 (September), 221–233; James R. Bettman and Mita Sujan (1987), "Effects of Framing on Evaluation of Comparable and Noncomparable Alternatives by Expert and Novice Consumers," *Journal of Consumer Research*, 14 (September), 141–154; Stephen J. Hoch and John Deighton (1989), "Managing What Consumers Learn from Experience," *Journal of Marketing*, 53 (April), 1–20; Carolyn L. Costley and Merrie Brucks (1992), "Selective Recall and Information Use in Consumer Preferences," *Journal of Consumer Research*, 18 (March), 464–474; Cynthia Huffman and Michael J. Houston (1993), "Goal-oriented Experiences and the Development of Knowledge," *Journal of Consumer Research*, 20 (September), 190–207. Examples of sampling programs can be found in issues of *Promo*, a magazine for those who work in the sales promotion industry, and in Bernice Kanner, "Try-It-Out Marketing Gains Ground," *New York Times*, January 23, 1995.

**9** Articles that have considered signs and symbols in marketing include David Glen Mick (1986), "Consumer Research and Semiotics: Exploring the Morphology of Signs, Symbols and Significance," *Journal of Consumer Research*, 13 (September), 196–213; Kim R. Robertson (1987), "Recall and Recognition Effects of Brand name Imagery," *Psychology and Marketing*, 4 (Spring), 3–15; Richard D. Zakia and Mihai Nadin (1987), "Semiotics, Advertising and Marketing," *Journal of Consumer Marketing*, 4 (Spring), 5–12; John F. Sherry, Jr., and Eduardo G. Camargo, (1987), "'May Your Life Be Marvelous': English Language Labeling and the Semiotics of Japanese Promotion," *Journal of Consumer Research*, 14 (September), 174–188; Teresa J. Domzal and Jerome B. Kernan (1992), "Reading Advertising: The What and

How of Product Meaning," *Journal of Consumer Marketing,* 9 (Summer), 48–64; Edward F. McQuarrie and David Glen Mick (1992), "On Resonance: A Critical Pluralistic Inquiry Into Advertising Rhetoric," *Journal of Consumer Research,* 19 (September), 180–197.

**10** J. Edward Russo, Richard Staelin, Catherine A. Nolan, Gary J. Russell, and Barbara L. Metcalf (1986), "Nutrition Information in the Supermarket," *Journal of Consumer Research,* 13 (June), 48–70; James R. Bettman, John Payne, and Richard Staelin (1986), "Cognitive Considerations in Designing Effective Labels for Presenting Risk Information," *Journal of Public Policy and Marketing,* 5(1), 1–28; J. Edward Russo (1987), "Toward Intelligent Product Information Systems for Consumers," *Journal of Consumer Policy,* 10, 109–138; Christine Moorman (1990), "The Effects of Stimulus and Consumer Characteristics on the Utilization of Nutrition Information," *Journal of Consumer Research,* 17 (December), 362–374; J. Craig Andrews, Richard G. Netemeyer, and Srinivas Durvasula (1991), "Effects of Consumption Frequency on Believability and Attitudes Toward Warning Labels," *Journal of Consumer Affairs,* 25 (Winter), 323–338; Todd Barlow and Michael S. Wogalter (1993), "Alcoholic Beverage Warnings in Magazine and Television Advertisements," *Journal of Consumer Research,* 20 (June), 147–156.

## Chapter 11

**1** For an excellent overview of attitudes, see Richard J. Lutz (1991), "The Role of Attitude Theory in Marketing," in *Perspectives in Consumer Behavior* (4th Edition), eds. Harold Kassarjian and Thomas Robertson, Englewood Cliffs, NJ: Prentice Hall, pp. 317–339.

**2** Daniel Katz (1960), "The Functional Approach to the Study of Attitudes," *Public Opinion Quarterly,* 24 (Summer), 163–204.

**3** For a comprehensive discussion of affect, see Joel B. Cohen and Charles S. Areni (1991), "Affect and Consumer Behavior," in *Handbook of Consumer Behavior,* eds. Thomas Robertson and Harold Kassarjian, Englewood Cliffs, NJ: Prentice Hall, pp. 188–240.

**4** Martin Fishbein (1963), "An Investigation of the Relationship Between Beliefs About an Object and the Attitude Toward That Object," *Human Relations,* 16, 233–240; Martin Fishbein and Icek Ajzen (1975), *Beliefs, Attitude, Intention, and Behavior: An Introduction to Theory and Research,* Reading, MA: Addison-Wesley; Icek Ajzen and Martin Fishbein (1980), *Understanding Attitudes and Predicting Social Behavior,* Englewood Cliffs, NJ: Prentice Hall. Other works that examine multi-attribute models include William L. Wilke and Edgar A. Pessemier (1973), "Issues in Marketing's Use of Multi-Attribute Models," *Journal of Marketing Research,* 10 (November), 428–441; James R. Bettman, Noel Capon, and Richard J. Lutz (1975), "Multi-attribute Measurement Models and Multi-attribute Theory: A Test of Construct Validity," *Journal of Consumer Research,* 1 (March), 1–14; Michael B. Mazis, Olli T. Ahtola, and R. Eugene Klippel (1975), "A Comparison of Four Multi-Attribute Models in the Prediction of Consumer Attitudes, *Journal of Consumer Research,* 2 (June), 38–52; David J. Curry, Michael B. Menasco, and James W. Van Ark (1991), "Multi-attribute Dyadic Choice: Models and Tests," *Journal of Marketing Research,* 28 (August), 259–267.

**5** See Michael J. Ryan and E. H. Bonfield (1980), "Fishbein's Intentions Model: A Test of External and Pragmatic Validity," *Journal of Marketing,* 44 (Spring), 82–95; Terence A. Shimp and Alican Kavas (1984), "The Theory of Reasoned Action Applied to Coupon Usage," *Journal of Consumer Research,* 11 (December), 795–809; Richard L. Oliver and William O. Bearden (1985),

"Crossover Effects in the Theory of Reasoned Action: A Moderating Influence Attempt," *Journal of Consumer Research,* 12 (December), 324–340; Blair H. Sheppard, Jon Hartwick, and Paul R. Warshaw (1986), "The Theory of Reasoned Action: A Meta–Analysis of Past Research with Recommendations for Modifications and Future Research," *Journal of Consumer Research,* 15 (September), 325–343; Richard P. Bagozzi, Hans Baumgartner, and Youjae Yi (1992), "State versus Action Orientation and the Theory of Reasoned Action: An Application to Coupon Usage," *Journal of Consumer Research,* 18 (March), 505–518.

**6** Among the many studies that investigate attitude-toward-the-ad are Terence A. Shimp (1981), "Attitude Toward the Ad as a Mediator of Consumer Brand Choice," *Journal of Advertising,* 10 (2), 9–15 ff.; Andrew A Mitchell and Jerry C. Olson (1981), "Are Product Attribute Beliefs the Only Mediator of Advertising Effects on Brand Attitude?" *Journal of Marketing Research,* 18 (August), 318–332; Rajeev Batra and Michael L. Ray (1986), "Affective Responses Mediating Acceptance of Advertising," *Journal of Marketing Research,* 13 (September), 234–249; Thomas J. Madden, Chris T. Allen, and Jacquelyn L. Twible (1988), "Attitude Toward the Ad: An Assessment of Diverse Measurement Indices Under Different Processing 'Sets,'" *Journal of Marketing Research,* 25 (August), 245–252; Pamela M. Homer (1990) "The Mediating Effect of Attitude toward the Ad: Some Additional Evidence" *Journal of Marketing Research,* 27 (February), 78–86; Thomas J. Olney, Morris B. Holbrook, and Rajeev Batra (1991), "Consumer Responses to Advertising: The Effect of Ad Content, Emotions, and Attitude toward the Ad on Viewing Time," *Journal of Consumer Research,* 17 (March), 440–453; Steven P. Brown and Douglas M. Stayman (1992), "Antecedents and Consequences of Attitude toward the Ad: A Meta-analysis," *Journal of Consumer Research,* 19 (June) 34–51; Amitava Chattopadhyay and Prakash Negungadi (1992), "Does Attitude Toward the Ad Endure? The Moderating Effects of Attention and Delay," *Journal of Consumer Research,* 19 (June), 26–33; Gabriel Biehal, Debra Stephens, and Eleonora Curlo (1992), "Attitude toward the Ad and Brand Choice," *Journal of Advertising,* 21 (September), 19–39.

**7** Classic statements concerning individuals' desire for consistency include Leon Festinger (1957), *A Theory of Cognitive Dissonance,* Stanford: Stanford University Press; Fritz Heider (1958), *The Psychology of Interpersonal Relations,* New York: Wiley; Muzafer Sherif and Carl I. Hovland (1961), *Social Judgment: Assimilation and Contrast Effects in Communication and Attitude Change,* New Haven: Yale; Harold H. Kelley (1967); "Attribution Theory in Social Psychology," in *Nebraska Symposium on Motivation,* ed. David Levine, Lincoln, NB; University of Nebraska Press, 192–238; Daryl Bem (1972), "Self Perception Theory," in *Advances in Experimental Social Psychology,* ed. Leonard Berkowitz, New York: Academic Press.

**8** William H. Cummings and M. Venkatesan (1976), "Cognitive Dissonance and Consumer Behavior: A Review of the Evidence," *Journal of Marketing Research,* 13 (August), 303–308.

**9** Richard W. Mizerski, Linda L. Golden, and Jerome B. Kernan (1979), "The Attribution Process in Consumer Decision Making," *Journal of Consumer Research,* 6 (September), 123–140; Donald R. Lichtenstein and William O. Bearden (1986), "Measurement and Structure of Kelley's Covariance Theory," *Journal of Consumer Research,* 13 (September), 290–296; Valerie S. Folkes (1988), "Recent Attribution Research in Consumer Behavior: A Review and New Directions," *Journal of Consumer Research,* 14 (March), 548–565; Valeri S. Folkes and Tina Kiesler (1991), "Social Cognition: Consumers' Inferences About the Self and Others," in *Handbook of Consumer Behavior,* eds. Thomas

Robertson and Harold Kassarjian, Englewood Cliffs, NJ: Prentice Hall, 281–315.

**10** A good overview of attitude change is Richard E. Petty, Rao H. Unnava, and Alan J. Strathman (1991), "Theories of Attitude Change," in *Handbook of Consumer Behavior,* eds. Thomas Robertson and Harold Kassarjian, Englewood Cliffs, NJ: Prentice Hall, 241–280. There has been a great deal of research investigating the effects of marketing communications on consumer attitudes. We mentioned some sources in the note on attitude-toward-the-ad and will mention more in the discussion of marketing communications in Chapter 15. A small, varied sample includes Scott B. Mackenzie (1986), "The Role of Attention in Mediating the Effect of Advertising on Attribute Importance," *Journal of Consumer Research,* 13 (September), 174–195; Robert E. Smith and William R. Swinyard (1988), "Cognitive Response to Advertising and Trial: Belief Strength, Belief Confidence and Product Curiosity," *Journal of Advertising,* 17 (November), 3–14; Paul W. Miniard, Sunil Bhatla, and Randall L. Rose (1990), "On the Formation and Relationship of Ad and Brand Attitudes: An Experimental and Causal Approach," *Journal of Marketing Research,* 27 (August), 290–303; Carolyn Tripp, Thomas D. Jensen, and Less Carlson, (1994), "The Effects of Multiple Product Endorsements by Celebrities on Consumers' Attitudes and Intentions," *Journal of Consumer Research,* 20 (March), 535–547.

**11** Jamie Murphy, "A Deadly Roundup at Sea," *Time,* August 4, 1986; "Swim With the Dolphins," *Newsweek,* April 23, 1990; "Tuna Without Guilt," *Time,* April 23, 1990; David Kiley, "Tuna Companies Market Morality Along with the Fish: Dolphin-Safe Labels," *Adweek's Marketing Week,* May 28, 1990; "Media-Wise and Dolphin Free," *Adweek's Marketing Week,* July 23, 1990; Jeffrey Ressner, "Ecologically Sound," *Rolling Stone,* May 31, 1990; Susan K. Reed, "A Filmmaker Crusades to Make the Seas Safe for Gentle Dolphin," *People,* August 6, 1990; Steve Weinstein, "Why Are Tuna Sales Soft?" *Progressive Grocer,* April 1991; Paul Rauber, "Trading Away the Environment," *Sierra,* January–February 1992; Nancy Marx Better, "Making a Difference," *Scholastic Update,* April 17, 1992; Dean Kuipers, "Pirates with a Difference," *Interview,* August 1992; Annetta Miller, "Teaching an Old Fish New Tricks: Trying To Make Tuna a Hot Product Again," *Newsweek,* August 16, 1993; Brad Warren, "The Downside of Dolphin-Safe," *Audobon,* November–December 1993; Natalie Blaslov, "Something's Fishy," *Ladies' Home Journal,* June 1994.

**12** Laurie Freeman, "Diaper Image Damaged," *Advertising Age,* June 11, 1990; Laurie Freeman, "P&G Seeks To Defend Its Diapers," *Advertising Age,* June 11, 1990; Elizabeth J. Moran, "Cost of Reusable vs. Disposable Diapers in Dispute," *Hospitals,* September 5, 1990; Jennifer Lawrence, "Diaper Drops Claim: State Probe Brings Change in Green Strategy," *Advertising Age,* October 22, 1990; Laurie Freeman, "Procter & Gamble: The Environmental Impact of Pampers Disposable Diapers," *Advertising Age,* January 29, 1991; Cynthia Crossen, "How 'Tactical Research' Muddied Diaper Debate," *Wall Street Journal,* May 17, 1994; Cynthia Crossen (1994), *Tainted Truth: The Manipulation of Fact in America,* New York: Simon & Schuster.

## Chapter 12

**1** See John A. Howard and Jagdeth N. Sheth (1967), "Theory of Buyer Behavior" in *Changing Marketing Systems,* ed. Reed Moyer, Chicago: American Marketing Association, 253–262 and Howard and Sheth (1969), *The Theory of Buyer Behavior,* New York: Wiley.

**2** Works that investigate information search include Howard Beales, Michael M. Mazis, Stephen C. Salop, and Richard Staelin (1981), "Consumer Search and Public Policy," *Journal of Consumer Research,* 8 (June), 11–22; David F. Midgely (1983), "Patterns of Interpersonal Information Seeking for the Purchase of a Symbolic Product," *Journal of Marketing Research,* 20 (February), 74–83; Merrie Brucks (1985), "The Effects of Product Class Knowledge on Information Search Behavior," *Journal of Marketing Research,* 12 (June), 1–16; Cathy J. Cobb and Wayne D. Hoyer (1985), "Direct Observation of Search Behavior," *Psychology & Marketing,* 2 (Fall), 161–179; Peter H. Bloch, Daniel L. Sherrell, and Nancy M. Ridgeway (1986), "Consumer Search: An Extended Framework," *Journal of Consumer Research,* 13 (June), 119–126; Gordon C. Bruner II (1987), "The Effect of Problem-Recognition Style on Information Seeking," *Journal of the Academy of Marketing Science,* 15 (Winter), 33–41; Girish Punj (1987), "Presearch Decision Making in Consumer Durable Purchases," *Journal of Consumer Marketing,* 4 (Winter), 71–82; Joel B. Cohen and Kunal Basu (1987), "Alternative Models of Categorization: Toward a Contingent Processing Framework," *Journal of Consumer Research,* 13 (March), 455–472; Sharon E. Beatty and Scott M. Smith (1987), "External Search Effort: An Investigation Across Several Categories," *Journal of Consumer Research,* 14 (June), 83–95; Itamar Simonson, Joel Huber, and John Payne (1988), "The Relationship Between Prior Brand Knowledge and Information Acquisition Order," *Journal of Consumer Research,* 14 (March), 566–578; Joel E. Urbany, Peter R. Dickson, and William L. Wilkie (1989), "Buyer Uncertainty and Information Search," *Journal of Consumer Research,* 16 (September), 208–215; Narasimhan Srinivasan and Brian T. Ratchford (1991), an Empirical Test of a Model of External Search for Automobiles," *Journal of Consumer Research,* 18 (September), 233–242; Julie L. Ozanne, Merrie Brucks, and Dhruv Grewal (1992), "A Study of Information Search Behavior During the Categorization of New Products," *Journal of Consumer Research,* 18 (March), 452–463; Dhruv Grewal and Howard Marmorstein (1994), "Market Price Variation, Perceived Price Variation, and Consumers' Price Search Decisions for Durable Goods," *Journal of Consumer Research,* 21 (December), 453–460; Jennifer Gregan-Paxton and Deborah Roedder John (1995), "Are Young Children Adaptive Decision Makers? A Study of Age Differences in Information Search Behavior," *Journal of Consumer Research,* 21 (March), 567–580.

**3** Rosalind Wright, "Crime on Campus," *Family Circle,* September 5, 1989; Denise Kalette, "New Law Ends Parents' Tragic Battle," *USA Today,* November 12, 1990; Carol Jouzaitis, "Law Tries to Uncover Campus Crime," *Chicago Tribune,* December 2, 1990; Stephen Burd, "U.S. Proposes Regulations on Disclosure of Graduation Rates and Campus Crime Data," *Chronicle of Higher Education,* July 22, 1992; Douglas Lederman, "Experts Say Disclosure Law Allows Colleges To Omit Categories That Could Give Clearer Picture of Crime," *Chronicle of Higher Education,* January 20, 1993; Ellen Graham, "Fortress Academia Sells Security," *Wall Street Journal,* October 25, 1993.

**4** Richard W. Olshavsky and Donald H. Granbois (1979), "Consumer Decision Making—Fact or Fiction?" *Journal of Consumer Research,* 6 (September), 93–100; John C. Mowen (1988), "Beyond Consumer Decision Making," *Journal of Consumer Marketing,* 5(1), 15–25.

**5** Work on the identification of alternatives includes Joseph W. Alba and Amitava Chattopadhyay (1985), "The Effects of Context and Part-Category Cues on the Recall of Competing Brands," *Journal of Marketing Research,* 22 (August) 340–349; John R. Hauser and Birger Wernerfelt (1990), "An Evaluation Cost Model of Consideration Sets," *Journal of Consumer Research,* 16 (March), 393–408; Wayne D. Hoyer and Steven P. Brown (1990), "Effects of Brand Awareness on Choice for a Common, Repeat-Purchase Product," *Journal of Consumer Research,* 17 (September), 141–148; Prakash Nedungadi (1990), "Recall and Consumer Consideration Sets: Influencing Choice Without Altering Brand Evaluations," *Journal of Consumer Research*, 17 (December), 263–276; John H. Roberts and James M. Lattin (1991), "Development and Testing of a Model of Consideration Set Composition," *Journal of Marketing Research*, 28 (November), 429–440; Juanita J. Brown and Albert R. Wildt (1992), "Consideration Set Measurement," *Journal of the Academy of Marketing Science*, 20 (Summer), 235–244; Frank R. Kardes, Gurumurthy Kalyanaram, Murali Chandrashekaran, and Ronald J. Dornoff (1993), "Brand Retrieval, Consideration Set Composition, Consumer Choice, and the Pioneering Advantage," *Journal of Consumer Research*, 20 (June), 62–75.

**6** Two excellent review articles on consumer decision making are James R. Bettman, Eric J. Johnson, and John W. Payne (1991), "Consumer Decision Making," in *Handbook of Consumer Behavior*, eds. Thomas Robertson and Harold Kassarjian, Englewood Cliffs, NJ: Prentice Hall, 50–84, and Robert J. Meyer and Barbara E. Kahn (1991), "Probabilistic Models of Consumer Choice Behavior," in *Handbook of Consumer Behavior,* eds. Thomas Robertson and Harold Kassarjian, Englewood Cliffs, NJ: Prentice Hall, 85–123. Other articles include: Amos Tversky (1972), "Elimination by Aspects: A Theory of Choice," *Psychological Review,* 79, 281–299; Peter L. Wright (1975), "Consumer Choice Strategies: Simplifying versus Optimizing," *Journal of Marketing Research,* 11, 60–67; James R. Bettman and Michel A. Zins (1977), "Constructive Processes in Consumer Choice, *Journal of Marketing Research,* 4 (September), 75–85; Eric J. Johnson and Robert J. Meyer, (1984), "Compensatory Choice Models of Noncompensatory Processes: The Effect of Varying Context," *Journal of Consumer Research,* 11 (June), 528–541; Mita Sujan, (1985), "Consumer Knowledge: Effects on Evaluation Strategies Mediating Consumer Judgments," *Journal of Consumer Research,* 12 (June), 31–46; Richard Thaler (1985), "Mental Accounting and Consumer Choice," *Marketing Science,* 4 (Summer), 199–214; Joseph W. Alba and Howard Marmorstein (1987), "The Effects of Frequency Knowledge on Consumer Decision Making," *Journal of Consumer Research,* 14 (June), 14–25; Noreen M. Klein and Stewart W. Bither (1987), "An Investigation of Utility-Directed Cutoff Selection, *Journal of Consumer Research,* 14 (September), 240–256; Gary T. Ford and Ruth Ann Smith (1987), "Inferential Beliefs in Consumer Evaluations: An Assessment of Alternative Processing Strategies," *Journal of Consumer Research,* 14 (December), 363–371; Christopher P. Puto (1987), "The Framing of Buying Decisions," *Journal of Consumer Research,* 14 (December), 301–315; William D. Diamond (1988), "The Effect of Probability and Consequence Levels on the Focus of Consumer Judgments in Risky Situations," *Journal of Consumer Research,* 15 (September), 280–283; Barbara E. Kahn and Rakesh K. Sarin (1988), "Modeling Ambiguity in Decisions Under Uncertainty," *Journal of Consumer Research,* 15 (September), 265–272; Irwin P. Levin and Gary J. Gaeth (1988), "How Consumers Are Affected by the Framing Attribute Information Before and After Consuming the Product," *Journal of Consumer Research,* 15 (December), 374–378; Scot Burton and Laure A. Babin (1989), "Decision-framing Helps Make the Sale," *Journal of Consumer Marketing,* 6 (Spring), 15–24; Noreen M. Klein and Manjit S. Yadav, (1989), "Contextual Effects on Effort and Accuracy in Choice: An Enquiry Into Adaptive Decision Making," *Journal of Consumer Research,* 15 (March, 411–421; Valerie S. Folkes (1989), "The Availability Heuristic and Perceived Risk," *Journal of Consumer Research,* 15 (June), 13–23; Joan Meyers-Levy and Alice M. Tybout (1989), "Schema Congruity as a Basis for Product Evaluation," *Journal of Consumer Research,* 16 (June), 39–55; Michael D. Johnson (1989), "The Differential Processing of Product Category and Noncomparable Choice Alter-

natives," *Journal of Consumer Research,* 16 (December), 300–309; Kim P. Corfman (1991), "Comparability and Comparison Levels Used in Choices Among Consumer Products," *Journal of Marketing Research,* 28 (August), 368–374; John C. Mowen and Gary J. Gaeth (1992), "The Evaluation Stage in Marketing Decisionmaking," *Journal of the Academy of Marketing Science,* 20 (Spring), 177–188; Durairaj Maheswaran, Diane M. Mackie, and Shelly Chaiken (1992), Brand Name as a Heuristic Cue: The Effects of Task Importance and Expectancy Confirmation on Consumer Judgments," *Journal of Consumer Psychology,* 1(4), 317–336; Pratibha A. Dabholkar (1994), "Incorporating Choice Into an Attitudinal Framework: Analyzing Models of Mental Comparison Processes," *Journal of Consumer Research,* 21 (June), 100–118.

**7** Among the articles that address the broader issue of consumers' use of nutrition and health information are Merrie Brucks, Andrew A. Mitchell, and Richard Staelin (1984), "The Effect of Nutrition Information Disclosures in Advertising: An Information Processing Approach," *Journal of Public Policy and Marketing,* 3, 1–27; Alan S. Levy, Odonna Mathews, Marilyn Stephenson, Janet E. Tenney, and Ramond E. Schucker (1985), "The Impact of a Nutrition Information Program on Food Purchases," *Journal of Public Policy and Marketing,* 4, 1–13; Edward J. Russo, Richard Staelin, Catherine A. Nolan, Gary J. Russell, and Barbara L. Metcalf (1986), "Nutrition Information in the Supermarket," *Journal of Consumer Research,* 13 (June), 48–70; Catherine A. Cole and Gary J. Gaeth (1990), "Cognitive and Age-Related Differences in the Ability to Use Nutritional Information in a Complex Environment," *Journal of Marketing Research,* 27 (May), 175–184; Christine Moorman (1990), "The Effects of Stimulus and Consumer Characteristics on the Utilization of Nutrition Information," *Journal of Consumer Research,* 17 (December), 362–374; Julie A. Caswell (1992), "Current Information Levels on Food Labels," *American Journal of Agricultural Economics,* 74 (December), 1196–1201, 1213–1216; Scot Burton and Abhijit Biswas (1993), "Preliminary Assessment of Changes in Labels Required by the Nutrition Labeling and Education Act of 1990," *Journal of Consumer Affairs,* 27 (Summer), 127–144; Christine Moorman and Erika Matulich (1993), "A Model of Consumers' Preventive Health Behaviors: The Role of Health Motivation and Health Ability," *Journal of Consumer Research,* 20 (September), 208–228.

**8** Betsy Frazao and Linda Cleveland, "Diet-Health Awareness About Fat and Cholesterol—Only a Start," *Food Review,* January–April 1994; Angela Shah, "FTC to Require Food Ads to Follow FDA Label Guides," *Wall Street Journal,* May 16, 1994; Paula Kurtzweil, "Food Label Close-Up," *FDA Consumer,* April 1994; Marilyn Marter, "Digesting the Labels," *Philadelphia Inquirer,* July 20, 1994; Yukimo Ono, "Today's Low-Fat Diet: Pretzels, Licorice," *Wall Street Journal,* March 14, 1995; Marilyn Marter, "Shoppers are Reading and Heeding the Labels," *Philadelphia Inquirer,* May 31, 1995.

## Chapter 13

**1** Among the important articles that were instrumental in developing the concept of involvement are Herbert E. Krugman (1965), "The Impact of Television Advertising: Learning Without Involvement," *Public Opinion Quarterly,* 29 (Fall), 349–356; Andrew Mitchell (1979), "Involvement: A Potentially Important Mediator of Consumer Behavior," in *Advances in Consumer Research,* Vol. 6, ed. William L. Wilke, Provo, UT: Association for Consumer Research, 191–196; John H. Antil (1984), "Conceptualization and Operationalization of Involvement," in *Advances in Consumer Research,* vol. 11, ed. Thomas C. Kinnear, Provo, UT: Association for Consumer Research, 203–209.

**2** Among the articles that have investigated the measurement of involvement are: Gilles Laurent and Jean-Noel Kapferer (1985), "Measuring Consumer Involvement Profiles," *Journal of Marketing Research,* 22 (February, 41–53; Raj Arora (1985), "Involvement: Its Measurement for Retail Store Research," *Journal of the Academy of Marketing Science,* 13 (Spring), 229–241; Judith Lynne Zaichkowsky (1985), "Measuring the Involvement Construct," *Journal of Consumer Research,* 12 (December), 341–352; J. Craig Andrews, Srinivas Durvasula, and Syed H. Akhter (1990), "A Frameword for Conceptualizing and Measuring the Involvement Construct in Advertising Research," *Journal of Advertising,* 19(4), 27–40; A. Dwayne Ball and Lori H. Tasaki (1992), "The Role and Measurement of Attachment in Consumer Behavior," *Journal of Consumer Psychology,* 1(2), 155–172.

**3** For work on factors that affect involvement, see such articles as Judith L. Zaichkowsky (1986), "Conceptualizing Involvement," *Journal of Advertising,* 15, 4–14; Marsha L. Richins and Peter H. Bloch (1986), "After the New Wears Off: The Temporal Context of Product Involvement," *Journal of Consumer Research,* 13(September) 280–285; Marsha L. Richins, Peter H. Bloch, and Edward F. McQuarrie (1992), "How Enduring and Situational Involvement Combine To Create Involvement Responses," *Journal of Consumer Psychology,* 1(2), 143–153.

**4** Among the articles that examine the effects of involvement are: Pradeep K. Korgaonkar and George P. Moschis (1982), "An Experimental Study: Cognitive Dissonance, Product Involvement, Expectations, Performance and Consumer Judgments of Product Performance," *Journal of Advertising,* 11, 32–44; Richard L. Celsi and Jerry C. Olson (1988), "The Role of Involvement in Attention and Comprehension Processes," *Journal of Consumer Research,* 15 (September), 210–224; Scott A. Hawkins and Stephen J. Hoch (1992), "Low Involvement Learning: Memory Without Evaluation," *Journal of Consumer Research,* 19 (September), 212–225; Jong-Won Park and Manoj Hastak (1994), "Memory-based Product Judgments: Effects of Involvement at Encoding and Retrieval, *Journal of Consumer Research,* 21 (December), 534–547.

**5** Douglas Lavin, "Cracking Down on Fraudulent Car Leases," *Wall Street Journal,* September 28, 1994; "Auto Leasing Industry To Offer More Disclosure," *Wall Street Journal,* October 25, 1994; S. Abraham Ravid, "Clarifying Those Complex Car Leases," *New York Times,* January 15, 1995; Jerry W. Boyd, "Car Hunters Arming Themselves with Information," *Philadelphia Inquirer,* March 26, 1995; Oscar Suris, "New Car Leases Come Loaded with Options," *Wall Street Journal,* April 12, 1995.

**6** Larry Jabbonsky and E. A. Wolfe, "Ready to Go: Upscale Iced Teas and Coffees Are Hot," *Beverage World,* September 1991; Larry Jabbonsky, "Pepsi Continues to Put Product and Flavor Extensions to the Test," *Beverage World,* March 31, 1992; Eric Sfiligoj, "Wake Up and Smell the Gatorade? Not Quite, But SunBolt Also Rises," *Beverage World,* June 30, 1994; Andrew Wallenstein, "Coca-Cola Still No. 1," *Advertising Age,* February 27, 1995; Andrew Wallenstein, "Coca-Cola's Sweet Return to Glory Days," *Advertising Age,* April 17, 1995.

## Chapter 14

**1** Investigations of situational influences include Joseph A. Cote, James McCullough, and Michael Reilly (1985), "Effects of Unexpected Situations on Behavior–Intention Differences: A Garbology Analysis," *Journal of Consumer Research,* 12 (September), 188–194; Meryl Paula Gardner (1985), "Mood States and Consumer Behavior: A Critical Review," *Journal of Consumer Research,* 12 (December), 281–300; Cathy J. Cobb and Wayne D. Hoyer (1986), "Planned Versus Impulse Purchase Behavior,"

*Journal of Retailing,* 62 (Winter), 384–409; C. Whan Park, Easwar S. Iyer, and Daniel C. Smith (1989), "The Effects of Situational Factors on In-Store Grocery Shopping," *Journal of Consumer Research,* 15 (March), 422–433; Easwar S. Iyer (1989), "Unplanned Purchasing: Knowledge of Shopping Environment and Time Pressure," *Journal of Retailing,* 65 (Spring), 40–57; Scott Dawson, Peter H. Bloch, and Nancy M. Ridgway (1990), "Shopping Motives, Emotional States, and Retail Outcomes," *Journal of Retailing,* 66 (Winter), 408–427; Jonathan K. Frenzen and Harry L. Davis (1990), "Purchasing Behavior in Embedded Markets," *Journal of Consumer Research,* 17 (June), 1–12; H. Bruce Lammers (1991), "The Effect of Free Samples on Immediate Consumer Purchase," *Journal of Consumer Marketing,* 8 (Spring), 31–37; Jacob Hornik (1992), "Tactile Stimulation and Consumer Response," *Journal of Consumer Research,* 19 (December), 449–458; Cele Otnes, Tina M. Lowrey, and Young Chan Kim (1993), "Gift Selection for Easy and Difficult Recipients: A Social Roles Interpretation," *Journal of Consumer Research,* 20 (September), 229–244.

**2** Lawrence Kutner, "When a Credit Card Habit Gets Out of Hand," *New York Times,* August 19, 1993; Marjorie Ingall, "Get Thee Back, Plastic!" *Sassy,* July 1994; Vanessa O'Connell, "A New Campus Stalker: Credit-Card Companies," *Money,* September 1994; Ken McEldowney, "Crash Course in 'Credit 101' Badly Needed," *Credit World,* September–October 1994; Robert Bryce, "Here's a Course in Personal Finance 101, the Hard Way," *New York Times,* April 30, 1995.

**3** Articles that address the effects of usage situations are Russell W. Belk (1974), "An Explanatory Assessment of Situational Effects in Buyer Behavior," *Journal of Marketing Research,* 11 (May), 156–163; Russell W. Belk (1975), "Situational Variables and Consumer Behavior," *Journal of Consumer Research,* 2 (December) 157–164; Kenneth E. Miller and James L. Ginter (1979), "An Investigation of Situational Variables in Brand Choice Behavior and Attitudes," *Journal of Marketing Research,* 16 (February), 111–123; Bruce E. Mattson (1982), "Situation Influences on Store Choice," *Journal of Retailing,* 58 (Fall), 46–58; Peter R. Dickson (1982), "Person–Situation: Segmentation's Missing Link," *Journal of Marketing,* 46 (Fall), 56–64; John F. Sherry, (1983), "Gift Giving in Anthropological Perspective," *Journal of Consumer Research,* 10 (September), 157–168; U.N. Umesh and Joseph A. Cote (1988), "Influence of Situational Variables on Brand-Choice Models," *Journal of Business Research,* 16(2), 91–99; David Glen Mick and Michelle DeMoss (1990), "Self-Gifts: Phenomenological Insights from Four Contexts," *Journal of Consumer Research,* 17 (December), 322–332; William R. Swinyard (1993), "The Effects of Mood, Involvement, and Quality of Store Experience on Shopping Intentions," *Journal of Consumer Research,* 20 (September), 217–280; Barry J. Babin, William R. Darden, and Mitch Griffin (1994), "Work and/or Fun: Measuring Hedonic and Utilitarian Shopping Value," *Journal of Consumer Research,* 20 (March), 644–656.

**4** Jerry Keller, "Applause and Anger: Beer Industry Efforts to Curb Drunk Driving," *Beverage World,* May 1994, Suart Elliott, "From a Leader in Moderation Messages, an Aggressive New Campaign Against Drunk Driving," *New York Times,* December 21, 1994.

**5** Some of the works that focus on consumers' assessment of their satisfaction and dissatisfaction are H. Keith Hunt (1977), *Conceptualization and Measurement of Consumer Satisfaction and Dissatisfaction,* Cambridge, MA: Marketing Sciences Institute; Richard L. Oliver (1980), "A Cognitive Model of the Antecedents and Consequences of Satisfaction Decisions," *Journal of Marketing Research,* 17 (November), 460–469; Gilbert A. Churchill and Carol F. Surprenant (1983), "An Investigation into the Determinants of Customer Satisfaction," *Journal of Marketing Research,* 19 (November), 491–504; Ralph L. Day and H. Keith Hunt (1983), *International Fair in Consumer Satisfaction and Complaining Behavior,* Bloomington, IN: Indiana University Division of Research; Claes Fornell and Robert A. Westbrook, (1984), "The Vicious Cycle of Consumer Complaints," *Journal of Marketing,* 48 (Summer), 68–78; Richard L. Oliver and Wayne S. Desarbo (1988), "Response Determinants in Satisfaction Judgments," *Journal of Consumer Research,* 14 (March), 495–507; Richard L. Oliver (1989), "Processing the Satisfaction Response in Consumption: A Suggested Framework and Research Propositions," *Journal of Consumer Satisfaction, Dissatisfaction and Complaining Behavior,* 2, 1–6; Daniel J. Howard and Thomas E. Barry (1990), "The Evaluative Consequences of Experiencing Unexpected Favorable Events," *Journal of Marketing Research,* 27 (February), 51–60; David K. Tse, Franco M. Nicosia, and Peter C. Wilton (1990), "Consumer Satisfaction as a Process," *Psychology & Marketing,* 7 (Fall), 177–194; Ann L. McGill (1991), "Predicting Consumers' Reactions to Product Failure: Do Responsibility Judgments Follow From Consumers' Causal Explanations?" *Marketing Letters,* 2 (January), 59–70; Ruth N. Bolton and James H. Drew (1991), "A Multistage Model of Customers' Assessments of Service, Quality and Value," *Journal of Consumer Research,* 17 (March), 375–384; Robert A. Westbrook and Richard L. Oliver (1991), The Dimensionality of Consumption Emotion Patterns and Consumer Satisfaction," *Journal of Consumer Research,* 18 (June), 84–91; Jagdip Singh, (1991), "Understanding the Structure of Consumers' Satisfaction Evaluations of Service Delivery," *Journal of the Academy of Marketing Science,* 19 (Summer), 223–244; Robert A. Peterson and William R. Wilson (1992), "Measuring Customer Satisfaction: Fact and Artifact," *Journal of the Academy of Marketing Science,* 20 (Winter), 61–72; Richard L. Oliver (1993), "Cognitive, Affective, and Attribute Bases of the Satisfaction Response," *Journal of Consumer Research,* 20 (December), 418–430; Haim Mano and Richard L. Oliver, (1993), "Assessing the Dimensionality and Structure of the Consumption Experience: Evaluation, Feeling, and Satisfaction," *Journal of Consumer Research,* 20 (December), 451–466; Michael D. Johnson, Eugene W. Anderson, and Claes Fornell (1995), "Rational and Adaptive Performance Expectations in a Customer Satisfaction Framework," *Journal of Consumer Research,* 21 (March), 695–707.

**6** Works on consumers' reactions to purchase and usage experiences include Mary C. Gilly and Betsy D. Gelb (1982), "Post-Purchase Consumer Processes and the Complaining Consumer," *Journal of Consumer Research,* 9 (December), 323–328; William O. Bearden and Jesse E. Teel (1983), "Selected Determinants of Consumer Satisfaction and Complaint Reports," *Journal of Marketing Research,* 20 (February), 21–28; Marsha L. Richins (1987), "A Multivariate Analysis of Responses to Dissatisfaction," *Journal of the Academy of Marketing Science,* 15 (Fall), 24–31; Alan R. Andreasen (1988), "Consumer Complaints and Redress: What We Know and What We Don't Know," in *The Frontier of Research in the Consumer Interest,* ed. E. Scott Maynes, Columbia, MO: American Council on Consumer Interests, 675–722; Jagdip Singh (1988), "Consumer Complaint Intentions and Behavior: Definitional and Taxonomical Issues," *Journal of Marketing,* 52 (January), 93–107; Jagdip Singh, (1989), Determinants of Consumers' Decisions to Seek Third Party Redress: An Empirical Study of Dissatisfied Patients," *Journal of Consumer Affairs,* 23 (Winter), 329–353; T. Bettina Cornwell, Alan David Bligh, and Emin Babakus (1991), "Complaint Behavior of Mexican-American Consumers to a Third-Party Agency," *Journal of Consumer Affairs,* 25 (Summer), 1–18.

**7** See such works as Alan J. Resnik and Robert R. Harmon

(1983), "Consumer Complaints and Managerial Response: A Holistic Approach," *Journal of Marketing,* 47 (Winter), 86–97; Nessim Hanna and John S. Wagle (1983), "Who Is Your Satisfied Customer?" *Journal of Consumer Marketing,* 6 (Winter), 53–62; Mary Jo Bitner, Bernard M. Booms, and Mary Stanfiled Tetreault (1990), "The Service Encounter: Diagnosing Favorable and Unfavorable Incidents," *Journal of Marketing,* 54 (January), 71–84; Cathy Goodwin and Ivan Ross (1990), "Consumer Evaluations of Responses to Complaints: What's Fair and Why," *Journal of Consumer Marketing,* 7 (Spring), 29–48; Craig A. Kelley and Jeffrey S. Conant (1991); "Extended Warranties: Consumer and Manufacturer Perceptions," *Journal of Consumer Affairs,* 25 (Summer), 568–583; Mary C. Gilly, William B. Stevenson, and Laura J. Yale (1991), "Dynamics of Complaint and Management in the Service Organization, *Journal of Consumer Affairs,* 25 (Winter), 295–322; Mary C. Gilly and Richard W. Hansen (1992), "Consumer Complaint Handling as a Strategic Marketing Tool," *Journal of Product and Brand Management,* 1 (Summer), 5–16; Jerry Plymire (1992), "Complaints as Opportunities," *Journal of Product and Brand Management,* 1 (Summer), 73–77; J. Joseph Cronin and Steven A. Taylor (1992), "Measuring Service Quality: A Reexamination and Extension," *Journal of Marketing,* 56 (July), 55–68; Terence A. Oliva, Richard L. Oliver, and Ian C. MacMillan (1992), "A Catastrophe Model for Developing Service Satisfaction Strategies," *Journal of Marketing,* 56 (July), 83–95; Scott W. Kelley (1992), "Developing Customer Orientation Among Service Employees," *Journal of the Academy of Marketing Science,* 20 (Winter), 27–36.

**8** Among the works that examine product disposition are Jacob Jacoby, Carol Berning, and Thomas Dietvorst (1977), "What about Disposition?" *Journal of Marketing,* 41 (April), 22–28; and James W. Hanson (1980), "A Proposed Paradigm for Consumer Product Disposition Processes," *Journal of Consumer Affairs,* 14 (Summer), 49–67; Michael Naughton, Frederick Sebold, and Thomas Mayer (1990), "Impacts of the California Beverage Container Recycling and Litter Reduction Act on Consumers," *Journal of Consumer Affairs,* 24 (Summer), 190–220; John A. McCarty and L.J. Shrum (1994), "The Recycling of Solid Wastes: Personal Values, Value Orientations, and Attitudes about Recycling as Antecedents of Recycling Behavior," *Journal of Business Research,* 30 (May), 53–62; L.J. Shrum, Tina M. Lowrey, and John A. McCarty (1994), "Recycling as a Marketing Problem: A Framework for Strategy Development," *Psychology & Marketing,* 11 (July–August), 393–416.

**9** See such examples as Russell W. Belk, John F. Sherry, Jr., and Melanie Wallendorf (1988), "A Naturalistic Inquiry Into Buyer and Seller Behavior at a Swap Meet," *Journal of Consumer Research,* 14 (March), 449–470; John F. Sherry, Jr. (1990), "A Sociocultural Analysis of a Midwestern American Flea Market," *Journal of Consumer Research,* 17 (June), 13–30; Kevin McCrohan and James D. Smith (1990), "Consumer Participation in the Informal Economy," *Journal of the Academy of Marketing Science,* 15 (Winter), 62–67.

## Chapter 15

**1** A recent work that examines this phenomenon is Arthur J. Kover (1995), "Copywriters' Implicit Theories of Communication: An Exploration," *Journal of Consumer Research*, 21 (March), 596–611.

**2** Carl Hovland and Walter Weiss (1951), "The Influence of Source Credibility on Communication Effectiveness," *Public Opinion Quarterly*, 15, 635–650, is the classic paper on source credibility. Others include Pamela M. Homer and Lynn R. Kahle (1990), "Source Expertise, Time of Source Identification, and Involvement in Persuasion: An Elaborative Processing Perspective," *Journal of Advertising*, 19(1), 30–39; Marvin E. Goldberg and Jon Hartwick (1990), "The Effects of Advertiser Reputation and Extremity of Advertising Claim on Advertising Effectiveness," *Journal of Consumer Research*, 17 (September), 172–179; S. Ratneshwar and Shelly Chaiken (1991), "Comprehension's Role in Persuasion: The Case of Its Moderating Effect on the Persuasive Impact of Source Cues," *Journal of Consumer Research*, 18 (June), 52–62; Elizabeth J. Wilson and Daniel L. Sherrel (1993), "Source Effects in Communication and Persuasion Research: A Meta-analysis of Effect Size," *Journal of the Academy of Marketing Science*, 21 (Spring), 101–112.

3 Robert J. Lavidge and Gary A. Steiner (1961), "A Model for Predictive Measurements of Advertising Effectiveness," *Journal of Marketing*, 25 (October), 59-62.

4 Kristin S. Palada (1966), "The Hypothesis of a Hierarchy of Effects: A Partial Evaluation," *Journal of Marketing Research,* 3 (February), 13–24; Michael L. Ray (1973), "Communication and the Hierarchy of Effects," in ed. P. Clarke, *New Models for Mass Communication Research,* Beverly Hills: Sage, 147–175; William J. McGuire (1978), "An Information Processing Model of Advertising Effectiveness," in *Behavioral and Management Science in Marketing,* ed. Harry J. Davis and Alvin Silk, New York: Ronald Press; Robert E. Smith and William R. Swinyard (1982), "Information Response Models: An Integrated Approach," *Journal of Marketing*, 46 (Winter), 81–93; Anthony G. Greenwald and Clark Leavitt (1984), "Audience Involvement in Advertising: Four Levels," *Journal of Consumer Research,* 11 (June), 581–592; Thomas E. Barry (1987), "The Development of the Hierarchy of Effects: An Historical Perspective," *Current Issues & Research in Advertising,* 10 (2), 251–296.

5 Don E. Schultz, Stanley I. Tannenbaum, and Robert E. Lauterborn (1993), *Integrated Marketing Communications: Pulling It Together & Making It Work*, Chicago: NTC; Donald Schultz, and Paul Wang, "Real World Results," *Marketing Tools*, April–May 1994; James Lucas and David Prensky, "Evaluating the Effectiveness of Place-Based Media," in *Measuring Advertising Effectiveness*, ed. William D. Wells, Hillsdale, NJ: Lawrence Erlbaum, in press.

6 Two good introductions to integrated marketing communications are Don E. Schultz, Stanley I. Tannenbaum, and Robert E. Lauterborn (1993), *Integrated Marketing Communications: Pulling It Together & Making It Work*, Chicago: NTC, and Esther Thorson and Geri Moore, *Integrated Marketing Communications: Synergy of Persuasive Voices*, Hillsdale, NJ: Lawrence Erlbaum, in press. The organizational issues are discussed in David Prensky, John McCarty, and James Lucas, "Integrated Marketing Communications: an Organizational Perspective," in *Integrated Marketing Communications: Synergy of Persuasive Voices*, eds. Esther Thorson and Geri Moore, Hillsdale, NJ: Lawrence Erlbaum, in press.

7 Bob Garfield, "Sominex Infomercial Issues a Wake-Up Call," *Advertising Age*, November 1, 1993; Julie Steenhuysen, "Adland's New Billion-Dollar Baby," *Advertising Age*, April 11, 1994; Michael McCarthy, "Media: Kodak's Big Picture," *Brandweek*, May 30, 1994; Kevin Goldman, "P&G Experiments with an Infomercial," *Wall Street Journal*, July 8, 1994; Phil Press, "Targeting Direct Response Television to the Desired Demographics," *Brandweek*, June 27, 1994; Stuart Elliott, "Infomercials Expand Their Reach Once Again, This Time To Extol the Virtues of Florida Citrus," *New York Times*, September 21, 1994; Kevin Goldman, "Apple Plans a Half-Hour Infomercial Aimed at Families," *Wall Street Journal*, November 4, 1994; Gary Levin and Joe Mandese, "Joe O'Donnell Betting on 24-Hour Infomercial Net," *Advertising Age*, November 7, 1994.

8 Among the many articles on types of advertising appeals are: Brian Sternthal and C. Samuel Craig (1973), "Humor in Advertising," *Journal of Marketing*, 37 (October), 12–18; William L. Wilke and Paul W. Farris (1975), "Comparative Advertising: Problems and Potential," *Journal of Marketing*, 39 (November), 7–15; Jessica Severn, George E. Belch, and Michael A. Belch (1990), "The Effects of Sexual and Non-sexual Advertising Appeals and Information Level on Cognitive Processing and Communication Effectiveness," *Journal of Advertising*, 19(1), 14–22; Cliff Scott, David M. Klein, and Jennings Bryant (1990), "Consumer Response to Humor in Advertising: A Series of Field Studies Using Behavioral Observation," *Journal of Consumer Research*, 16 (March), 498–501; Cornelia Pechmann and David W. Stewart (1990), "The Effects of Comparative Advertising on Attention, Memory, and Purchase Intention," *Journal of Consumer Research*, 17 (September), 180–191; Amitava Chattopadhyay and Kunal Basu (1990), "Humor in Advertising: The Moderating Role of Prior Brand Advertising," *Journal of Marketing Research*, 27 (November), 466–476; Darrel D. Muehling, Jeffrey J. Stoltman, and Stanford Grossbart (1990), "The Impact of Comparative Advertising on Levels of Message Involvement," *Journal of Advertising*, 19(4), 41–50; Michael S. LaTour, Robert E. Pitts, and David C. Snook-Luther (1990), "Female Nudity, Arousal, and Ad Response: An Experimental Investigation," *Journal of Advertising*, 19(4), 51–62; John F. Tanner, Jr., James B. Hunt, and David R. Eppright (1991), "The Protection Motivation Model: A Normative Model of Fear Appeals," *Journal of Marketing*, 55 (July), 36–45; Cornelia Pechmann and S. Ratneshwar (1991), "The Use of Comparative Advertising for Brand Positioning: Association versus Differentiation," *Journal of Consumer Research*, 18 (September), 145–160; Kathy L. Petit-O'Malley and Mark S. Johnson (1992), "Differentiative Comparative Advertising: Some Positive Results Revealed by Measurement of Simultaneous Effects on the Ad-Sponsoring and Comparison Brands," *Journal of Current Issues and Research in Advertising*, 14 (Spring), 35–44; Barbara Stern (1993), "Feminist Literary Criticism and the Deconstruction of Ads: A Postmodern View of Advertising and Consumer Responses," *Journal of Consumer Research*, 19 (March), 556–566.

9 The classic article is Richard E. Petty, John T. Cacioppo, and David Schumann (1982), "Central and Peripheral Routes to Advertising Effectiveness: The Moderating Role of Involvement," *Journal of Consumer Research*, 10 (September), 135–146. Other that have considered the issue include: Jerry C. Olson, Daniel R. Toy, and Philip A. Dover (1982), "Do Cognitive Responses Mediate the Effects of Advertising Content on Cognitive Structure?" *Journal of Consumer Research*, 9 (December), 245–262; John L. Swasy and James M. Munch (1985), "Examining the Target of Receiver Elaborations: Rhetorical Question Effects on Source Processing and Persuasion," *Journal of Consumer Research*, 11 (March), 877–886; Jerry B. Gotlieb and John E. Swan (1990), "An Application of the Elaboration Likelihood Model," *Journal of the Academy of Marketing Science*, 18 (Summer), 221–228; David W. Schumann, Richard E. Petty, and D. Scott Clemons, (1990), "Predicting the Effectiveness of Different Strategies of Advertising Variation: A Test of the Repetition-Variation Hypotheses," *Journal of Consumer Research*, 17 (September), 192–202; J. Craig Andrews and Terence A. Shimp (1990), "Effects of Involvement, Argument Strength, and Source Characteristics on Central and Peripheral Processing of Advertising," *Psychology & Marketing*, 7 (Fall), 195-214; Richard E. Petty, Rao Unnava, and Alan J. Strathman (1991), "Theories of Attitude Change," in *Handbook of Consumer Behavior*, eds. Thomas Robertson and Harold Kassarjian, Englewood Cliffs, NJ: Prentice-Hall, 241–280; Joan Meyers-Levy (1991), "Elaborating on Elaboration: The Distinction Between Relational and Item-specific Elaboration," *Journal of Consumer Research*, 18 (December), 358-367; Paul W. Miniard, Deepak

Sirdeshmukh, and Daniel E. Innis (1992), "Peripheral Persuasion and Brand Choice," *Journal of Consumer Research*, 19 (September), 226–239.

**10** William Wells, John Burnett, and Sandra Moriarty (1992) *Advertising: Principles and Practice,* 2nd edition, Englewood Cliffs, NJ: Prentice Hall.

**11** Laura Bird, "First Advertorials; Now Advernewscasts," *Wall Street Journal*, September 24, 1993; Laura Bird, "NBC Special Is One Long Prime-Time Ad," *Wall Street Journal*, January 24, 1994; Laura Bird, "'Custom' Magazines Stir Credibility Issues," *Wall Street Journal*, February 14, 1994; Thomas R. King, "Disney Draws Fire for Mock-Newscast Ads," *Wall Street Journal*, July 14, 1994; Kyle Pope, "Product Placements Creep Into Video Games," *Wall Street Journal*, December 5, 1994.

## Chapter 16

**1** The concept was introduced in William H. Whyte, Jr., "The Web of Word of Mouth," *Fortune*, November 1954. Other works include Ernest Dichter (1966), "How Word-of-Mouth Advertising Works," *Harvard Business Review*, 44 (November–December), 147–157; Fred D. Reynolds and William R. Darden (1971), "Mutually Adaptive Effects of Interpersonal Communication," *Journal of Marketing Research*, 8 (March), 449–454; Paul M. Herr, Frank R. Kardes, and John Kim (1991), "Effects of Word-of-Mouth and Product-Attribute Information on Persuasion: An Accessibility-Diagnosticity Perspective," *Journal of Consumer Research*, 17 (March), 454–462; Gloria Penn Thomas (1992), "The Influence of Processing Conversational Information on Inference, Argument Elaboration, and Memory," *Journal of Consumer Research*, 19 (June), 83–92.

**2** Richard Mizerski (1982), "An Attribution Explanation of the Disproportionate Influence of Unfavorable Information," *Journal of Consumer Research*, 9 (December), 301–310; Marsha L. Richins (1983), "Negative Word-of-Mouth by Dissatisfied Customers: A Pilot Study," *Journal of Marketing*, 47 (Winter), 68–78; Dorothy Leonard-Barton (1985), "Experts as Negative Opinion Leaders in the Diffusion of a Technological Innovation," *Journal of Consumer Research*, 11 (March), 914–926.

**3** Phil Frame, "Saturn Hopes Its Seat Problem Becomes a Case Study on Recalls," *Automotive News*, February 18, 1991; David Kiley, "Saturn Suffers Another Setback," *Marketing Week*, February 18, 1991; James B. Treece, "Getting Mileage From a Recall," Business Week, May 27, 1991; Kevin Goldman, "GM's Saturn Unit Handles Recall With Personal Touch But No Ads," *Wall Street Journal*, August 12, 1993; Phil Frame, "Saturn Throws Recall Party: Loaners, Food and Movies Help Soften Bad Effects," *Automotive News*, August 16, 1993; Ray Serafin, "Saturn Recall a Plus—for Saturn!" *Advertising Age*, August 16, 1993; Robert L. Simison, "How a Recall Becomes a Marketing Opportunity," *Wall Street Journal*, February 18, 1994.

**4** Mark S. Granovetter (1973), "The Strength of Weak Ties," *American Journal of Sociology*, 78 (May), 1360–1380; Jacqueline Johnson Brown and Peter H. Reingen (1987), "Social Ties and Word-of-Mouth Referral Behavior," *Journal of Consumer Research*, 14 (December), 350–362.

**5** Early works include Paul F. Lazarsfeld, Bernard Berelson, and Hazel Gaudet (1948), *The People's Choice,* New York: Columbia University Press. The classic discussions of the model are in Elihu Katz and Paul F. Lazarsfeld (1955). *Personal Influence: The Part Played by People in the Flow of Mass Communications,* Glencoe, Illinois: Free Press; and Elihu Katz (1957), "The Two-Step Flow of Communications: An Up-to-Date Report on an Hypothesis," *Public Opinion Quarterly*, 21 (Spring), 61–78.

**6** Lawrence Feick and Linda Price (1987), "The Market Maven: A Diffuser of Marketplace Information," *Journal of Marketing*, 51 (January), 83–97.

**7** Among the works that address aspects of the identification and measurement of flows of communications and opinion leadership are: Charles W. King and John O. Summers (1970), "Overlap of Opinion Leadership Across Consumer Product Categories," *Journal of Marketing Research*, 7 (February), 43–50; Peter H. Reingen, Brian L. Foster, Jacqueline Johnson Brown, and Stephen B. Seidman (1984), "Brand Congruence in Interpersonal Relations: A Social Network Approach," *Journal of Consumer Research*, 11 (December), 771–783; Terry L. Childers (1986), "Assessment of the Psychometric Properties of an Opinion Leadership Scale," *Journal of Marketing Research*, 23 (May), 184–188; Peter H. Reingen and Jerome B. Kernan (1986), "Analysis of Referral Networks in Marketing: Methods and Illustration," *Journal of Marketing Research*, 23 (November), 370–378; William O. Bearden, Richard Netemeyer, and Jesse Teel (1989), "Measurement of Consumer Susceptibility to Interpersonal Influence," *Journal of Consumer Research*, 15 (March), 472–480; William O. Bearden and Randall L. Rose (1990), "Attention to Social Comparison Information: An Individual Difference Factor Affecting Consumer Conformity," *Journal of Consumer Research*, 16 (March), 461–471; James C. Ward and Peter H. Reingen (1990), "Sociocognitive Analysis of Groups Decision Making among Consumers," *Journal of Consumer Research*, 17, (December), 245–262; Ronald E. Goldsmith and Rene Desborde (1991), "A Validity Study of a Measure of Opinion Leadership," *Journal of Business Research*, 22, 11–19.

**8** George Anders, "Managed Health Care Jeopardizes Outlook for Drug 'Detailers,'" *Wall Street Journal*, September 10, 1993; Elyse Tanouye, "Miles Under Probe for Paying Druggists to Advise Patients About Its Products," *Wall Street Journal*, May 31, 1994; Elyse Tanouye, "Owning Medco, Merck Takes Drug Marketing the Next Logical Step," *Wall Street Journal*, May 31, 1994; Gina Kolata, "Upjohn to Repay 8 States Over Drug Plan," *New York Times*, August 2, 1994.

**9** See Nicole Woolsey Biggart (1989), *Charismatic Capitalism: Direct Selling Organizations in America*, Chicago: University of Chicago Press, for an analysis of the social networks that make direct selling effective.

**10** Jeffrey Burroughs and Richard A. Feinberg (1987), "Using Response Latency to Assess Spokesperson Effectiveness," *Journal of Consumer Research*, 14 (September), 295–299; John Deighton, Daniel Romer, and Josh McQueen (1989), "Using Drama to Persuade," *Journal of Consumer Research*, 16 (December), 335–343; Grant McCracken (1989), "Who is the Celebrity Endorser? Cultural Foundations of the Endorsement Process," *Journal of Consumer Research*, 16 (December), 310–321; Michael A. Kamins (1990), "A Investigation into the 'Match-Up' Hypothesis in Celebrity Advertising: When Beauty May Be Only Skin-Deep," *Journal of Advertising*, 19(1), 4–13; Roobina Ohanian (1990), "Construction and Validation of a Scale to Measure Celebrity Endorsers' Perceived Expertise, Trustworthiness, and Attractiveness," *Journal of Advertising*, 19(3), 39-52; Roobina Ohanian (1991), "The Impact of Celebrity Spokespersons' Perceived Image on Consumers' Intention to Purchase," *Journal of Advertising Research*, 31 (February–March), 46–54; Mary Walker, Lynn Langmeyer, and Daniel Langmeyer (1992), "Celebrity Endorsers: Do You Get What You Pay For?" *Journal of Consumer Marketing*, 9 (Spring), 69–76; Gail Tom, Rebecca Clark, Laura Elmer, Edward Grech, Joseph Massetti, Jr., and Harmona Sandhhar (1992), "The Use of Created versus Celebrity Spokespersons in Advertisements," *Journal of Consumer Marketing*, 9 (Fall), 45–51; Barbara B. Stern (1994), "Classical and Vignette Television Advertising Dramas: Structural Models, Formal Analysis, and Consumer Effects," *Journal of Consumer Research*, 20 (March), 601–615; Barbara B. Stern (1994), "A Revised Communication Model for Advertising: Multiple Dimensions of the Source, the Message, and the Recipient," *Journal of Advertising*, 23 (June), 5–16; Marilyn Lavin (1995), "Creating Consumers in the 1930's: Irna Phillips and the Radio Soap Opera," *Journal of Consumer Research*, 22 (June), 75–89.

## Chapter 17

1 Thomas S. Robertson (1967), "The Process of Innovation and the Diffusion of Innovation," *Journal of Marketing*, 31 (January), 14–19; David H. Midgley and Grahame R. Dowling, "Innovativeness: The Concept and Its Measurement," *Journal of Consumer Research*, 4 (March), 229–242; Elizabeth C. Hirschman (1981), "Symbolism and Technology as Sources of the Generation of Innovations," in *Advances in Consumer Research*, Vol. 9, ed. Andrew Mitchell, Provo, UT: Association for Consumer Research, 537–541; Hubert Gatignon and Thomas S. Robertson (1991) "Innovative Decision Processes," in *Handbook of Consumer Behavior*, eds. Thomas S. Robertson and Harold H. Kassarjian, Englewood Cliffs, NJ: Prentice Hall, 316–348; David F. Midgley and Grahame R. Dowling (1993), "A Longitudinal Study of Product Form Innovation: The Interaction between Predispositions and Social Messages," *Journal of Consumer Research*, 19 (March), 611–625.

2 Everett M. Rogers (1983), *Diffusion of Innovations,* 3rd Edition, New York: Free Press; Hubert Gatignon and Thomas S. Robertson (1985), "A Propositional Inventory for New Diffusion Research," *Journal of Consumer Research*, 11 (March), 849–867; Vijay Mahajan, Eitan Muller, and Frank Bass (1990), "New Product Diffusion Models in Marketing: A Review and Directions for Research,: *Journal of Marketing*, 54 (January), 1–26; Fareena Sultan, John U. Farley, and Donald H. Lehmann (1990), "A Meta-Analysis of Applications of Diffusion Models," *Journal of Marketing Research*, 27 (February), 70–77; Rick Brown (1992), "Managing the 'S' Curves of Innovation," *Journal of Consumer Marketing*, 9 (Winter), 61–72.

3 Work that examines adopters includes Robert L. Anderson and David J. Ortinau (1988), "Exploring Consumers' Post-adoption Attitudes and Use Behaviors in Monitoring the Diffusion of a Technologically-Based Discontinuous Innovation," *Journal of Business Research*, 17, 283–298; Vijay Mahajan, Eitan Muller, and Rajendra K. Srivastava (1990), "Determination of Adopter Categories by Using Innovation Diffusion Models," *Journal of Marketing Research*, 27 (February), 37–50; Kenny K. Chan and Shekhar Misra (1990), "Characteristics of the Opinion Leader: A New Dimension," *Journal of Advertising*, 19(3), 53–60; Ronald E. Goldsmith and Charles F. Hofacker (1991), "Measuring Consumer Innovativeness," *Journal of the Academy of Marketing Science*, 19 (Summer), 209–222; Robert J. Fisher and Linda L. Price (1992),

"An Investigation into the Social Context of Early Adoption Behavior," *Journal of Consumer Research*, 19 (December), 477–486.

4 See pages 241–250 in Everett M. Rogers (1983), *Diffusion of Innovations,* 3rd Edition, New York: Free Press.

5 John Antil (1988), "New Product or Service Adoption: When Does It Happen?" *Journal of Consumer Marketing*, 5 (Spring), 5–15.

6 See pages 163–206 in Everett M. Rogers (1983), *Diffusion of Innovations,* 3rd Edition, New York: Free Press.

7 See pages 210–232 in Everett M. Rogers (1983), *Diffusion of Innovations,* 3rd Edition, New York: Free Press.

8 Bart Ziegler, "Interactive Services May Come at Expense of Other Features," *Wall Street Journal*, September 16, 1994; Kevin Goldman, "On-Line Catalog Service Takes Shopping to Cyberspace," *Wall Street Journal*, November 18, 1994; Clinton Wilder and Bruce Caldwell, "Online Force," *InformationWeek*, November 21, 1994; Bart Ziegler, "Share of Homes With PC's Rises to 31% in Poll," *Wall Street Journal*, February 6, 1995; G. Pascal Zachary, "NBC Agrees to Produce Programming For New Microsoft Electronic Network," *Wall Street Journal*, May 17, 1995.

9 Works that consider consumer resistance to innovation include: Jagdish N. Sheth (1981), "Psychology of Innovation Resistance: The Less Developed Concept (LCD) in Diffusion Research," in *Research in Marketing*, ed. Jagdish N. Sheth, Greenwich, CT: JAI Press; 273–282; S. Ram (1987), "A Model of Innovation Resistance," in *Advances in Consumer Research*, Vol. 14, eds. Melanie Wallendorf and Paul Anderson, Provo, UT: Association for Consumer Research, 208–212; S. Ram and Jagdish Sheth (1989) "Consumer Resistance to Innovations: The Marketing Problem and Its Solutions," *Journal of Consumer Marketing*, 6 (Spring), 5–14; Pam Scholder Ellen, William O. Bearden, and Subhash Sharma (1991), "Resistance to Technological Innovation: An Examination of the Role of Self-Efficacy and Performance Satisfaction," *Journal of the Academy of Marketing Science*, 19 (Fall), 297–308.

10 Matthew L. Wald, "Sparking Interest in G.M.'s Electric Car," *New York Times*, October 14, 1993; Oscar Suris, "Detroit Steps Up Push for Delay on Electric Cars," *Wall Street Journal*, February 7, 1994; James Bennet, "Chrysler, With Misgivings, Will Sell Electrical Mini-vans," *New York Times*, May 6, 1994; Oscar Suris, "Chrysler to Sell Electric Minivans in '98 in California, Giving in to Regulators," *Wall Street Journal*, May 6, 1994; Raymond Serafin and Cleveland Horton, "Electrical Vehicles Drive New Sales Approach," *Advertising Age*, May 16, 1994; William R. Diem, "California Positively Charged for EV's," *Automotive News*, December 5, 1994; David Woodruff, "Shocker at GM: People Like the Impact," *Business Week*, January 23, 1995; Gabriella Stern, "General Motors Says Saturn Division Is Likely to Market Electric Cars in U.S." *Wall Street Journal*, March 8, 1995; Ron Cogan, "Electric Vehicles: Technology Recreates the Automobile," Advertising Supplement to *Fortune*, June 26, 1995.

# ILLUSTRATION CREDITS

**Chapter 2.** Page 51, Box: "The Pleasures of Consumption: The Pleasures of Exercise" developed from Hsiaofang Hwang, "The Lifestyles of Exercisers and Non-Exercisers," unpublished Master's Thesis, School of Journalism and Mass Communications, University of Minnesota (1995). Reprinted with the permission of the author.

**Chapter 4.** Figure 4.3: "The Movement of Cultural Meaning" from Grant McCraken, "Culture and Consumption: A Theoretical Account of the Structure and Movement of the Cultural Meaning of Consumer Goods," *Journal of Consumer Research* 13 (June 1986): 72. Copyright © 1986 by The Journal of Consumer Research, Inc. Reprinted with the permission of The University of Chicago Press.

**Chapter 5.** Table 5.1: "Generations in Profile" from Peter Francese, "America at Mid-Decade," *American Demographics* (February 1995): 27. Copyright © 1995 by American Demographics, Inc. Reprinted with the permission of the publishers. Table 5.2: "Minority Markets" from Peter Francese, "America at Mid-Decade," *American Demographics* (February 1995): 26. Copyright © 1995 by American Demographics, Inc. Reprinted with the permission of the publishers. Figure 5.20: "A Contemporary View of the American Class Structure" from Richard P. Coleman, "The Continuing Significance of Social Class to Marketing," *Journal of Consumer Research* 10 (December 1983): 265-80. Copyright © 1983 by The Journal of Consumer Research, Inc. Reprinted with the permission of The University of Chicago Press. Table 5.3: "Regional Shifts" from Peter Francese," "America at Mid-Decade," *American Demographics* (February 1995): 28. Copyright © 1995 by American Demographics,

Inc. Reprinted with the permission of the publishers. Figure 5-23: "Standard PRIZM Social Groups." Copyright © 1995 by Claritas Inc. PRIZM is a registered trademark of Claritas Inc. Reprinted with the permission of Claritas Inc., 1525 Wilson Boulevard, #1000. Arlington, VA 22209-2411. Figure 5-24*a, b, c*: "Profiles of PRIZM Social Groups." Copyright © 1995 by Claritas Inc. PRIZM is a registered trademark of Claritas Inc. Reprinted with the permission of Claritas Inc., 1525 Wilson Boulevard, #1000. Arlington, VA 22209-2411. Figure 5-25: "PRIZM Profile for Midsize Import Sedans." Copyright © 1995 by Claritas Inc. PRIZM is a registered trademark of Claritas Inc. Reprinted with the permission of Claritas Inc., 1525 Wilson Boulevard, #1000. Arlington, VA 22209-2411. Table 5.4: "The Traditional Family Life-Cycle" from William D. Wells and George Gubar, "Life Cycle Concept in Marketing Research," *Journal of Marketing Research* 3 (November 1966): 353-363. Copyright © 1966 by American Marketing Association. Reprinted with the permission of the publishers. Table 5.5: "Household Types" from Peter Francese, "America at Mid-Decade," *American Demographics* (February 1995): 25. Copyright © 1995 by American Demographics, Inc. Reprinted with the permission of the publishers. Figure 5.26: "Am Extended Family Life Cycle Schema Account for Alternative Consumer Lifestyle Realities" from Patrick E. Murphy and William A. Staples, "A Modernized Family Life Cycle," *Journal of Consumer Research* 6 (June 1979): 17. Copyright © 1979 by The Journal of Consumer Research, Inc. Reprinted with the permission of The University of Chicago Press.

**Chapter 6.** Figure 6.8: "VALS 2." Reprinted with the permission of SRI International, 333 Ravenswood, Menlo Park, CA 94025. Text: Descriptions of Freud's five methods individuals use to balance conflicting demands; from Calvin S. Hall, *A Primer of Freudian Psychology.* Copyright © 1954 by Harper & Row, Publishers, Inc. Reprinted with the permission of HarperCollins Publishers, Inc. and Routledge. Table 6.3: "Summary of Personality Traits Measured by the Edwards Personal Preference Schedule" adapted from *Edwards Personal Preference Schedule.* Copyright 1953, 1954, © 1959 by The Psychological Corporation. Reprinted with the permission of the publishers. Table 6.6: "Examples of Activities, Interests, and Opinions Used to Measure Lifestyle and Psychographics," from the DDB Needham Life Style Study. Reprinted with the permission of DDB Needham Advertising Agency, Chicago. Page Box: "Pleasures of Consumption: Citizen Environmentalists" developed from William D. Wells and Mike Swenson, "Citizen Environmentalists," unpublished paper, School of Journalism and Mass Communications, University of Minnesota (1995). Reprinted with the permission of the authors.

**Chapter 7.** Figure 7.14: "Effects of Reference Groups on Product and Brand Purchase," adapted from William P. Bearden and Michael J. Etzel, "Reference Group Influence on Product and Brand Purchase Decisions," *Journal of Consumer Research* (September 1982): 185. Copyright © 1982 by The Journal of Consumer Research, Inc. Reprinted with the permission of The University of Chicago Press.

**Chapter 8.** Figure 8.9: "Maslow's hierarchy of human needs" adapted from Abraham H. Maslow, *Europsychian Management* (Homewood, Illinois: Richard D. Irwin, 1965) and Abraham H. Maslow, *Motivation and Personality, Second Edition.* Copyright 1954, © 1987 by Harper & Row, Publishers, Inc. Copyright © 1970 by Abraham H. Maslow. Reprinted with the permission of Richard D. Irwin, Inc. and HarperCollins Publishers, Inc. Table 8.1: "Examples of Needs and Products Identified by Dichter," from Ernest Dichter, *Handbook of Consumer Motivations: The Psychology of the World of Objects.* Copyright © 1964. Reprinted with the permission of McGraw-Hill, Inc.

**Chapter 13.** Figure 13.2: "Zaichowsky's scale to measure product involvement" from Judith Lynne Zaichowsky, "Measuring the Involvement Construct," *Journal of Consumer Research* 12 (December 1985): 350. Copyright © 1985 by The Journal of Consumer Research, Inc. Reprinted with the permission of The University of Chicago Press.

**Chapter 14.** Figure 14.7: "Dickson's Person-Situation Matrix for Suntan Lotion" from Peter R. Dickson, "Person-Situation: Segmentation's Missing Link," *Journal of Marketing* 46 (Fall 1982). Copyright © 1982 by American Marketing Association. Reprinted with the permission of the publishers. Figure 14.12: "Consumer's Disposal Options" from John Jacoby, Carol K. Berning, and Thomas F. Dietvorst, "What About Disposition?" *Journal of Marketing* 41 (April 1977): 23. Copyright © 1977 by American Marketing Association. Reprinted with the permission of the publishers.

**Chapter 17.** Figure 17.5: "Antil diagram of adoption models" from John H. Antil, "New Product of Service Adoption: When Does It Happen?," *Journal of Consumer Marketing* 5 (Spring 1988): 7. Copyright © 1988 by Grayson Associates, Inc. Reprinted with the permission of MCB University Press. Figure 17.6: "Rogers' stages in the innovation-decision process" and short description of each stage, adapted from Everett Rogers, *The Diffusion of Innovations, Third Edition,* Figure 5-1, page 165. Copyright © 1962, 1971, 1983 by The Free Press. Reprinted with the permission of The Free Press, an imprint of Simon & Schuster.

# PHOTO CREDITS

**Chapter 1.** Figure 1.1: Photofest. Figure 1.2: Courtesy Club Med Sales, Inc. Figure 1.3: Courtesy Senator Keneth Conrad. Figure 1.5: Courtesy The Dial Corporation. Figure 1.6: I.P.A./Stills/Retna Ltd. Figure 1.7: Photo by Cico Stupakof; courtesy Sears, Roebuck and Co., 1993. Figure 1.8: Courtesy Nike Corporation. Figure 1.9: Courtesy Argene Interiors. Figure 1.10: Courtesy Wyoming Public Television. Figure 1.11: Courtesy The American Cancer Society. Figure 1.12: Courtesy National Heart Savers Association. Figure 1.13: Advertisement prepared by Bozell, NY. Figure U1.1: Photofest.

**Chapter 2.** Figure 2.2: © 1995 Bally's Health and Tennis Corporation. Figure 2.3: © 1994 General Mills, Inc. Figure 2.4: Courtesy Barnetts Photos, Inc. Figure 2.5: Courtesy Lady Foot Locker. Figure 2.6: Courtesy the Ford Motor Company. Figure 2.7: Courtesy BMW of North America, Inc. Figure 2.9: © 1994 Toyota Motor Sales, USA, Inc. Figure 2.10: Courtesy Johnson & Johnson. Figure 2.11: Courtesy Evian Water. Figure 2.12: Courtesy McDonald's Corporation. Figure 2.13: Courtesy Bel-Tronics Limited. Figure 2.14: Courtesy Technics.

**Chapter 3.** Figure 3.1: © 1994 The Gillette Company. Figure 3.2: Courtesy Ford Motor Company. Figure 3.3 (left): Courtesy Waterman Pen Company. Figure 3.3 (right): © 1994 The Gillette Company. Figure 3.4: Courtesy Survey Sampling, Inc. Figure 3.6: Courtesy National Association of Home Builders. Figure 3.7: Courtesy Leo Burnett Company, Inc., and the GM Corp. Figure 3.8: © 1994 Rossignol Ski Company, Inc. Figure 3.10: Courtesy Twins Magazine. Figure 3.11: Courtesy Ford Motor Company. Figure 3.12: Courtesy AT & T Global Information Solutions. All rights reserved. Figure 3.13: Courtesy Volvo North America Corporation. Figure 3.14: © 1995 Helene Curtis. Figure 3.15: Courtesy Tourneau.

**Chapter 4.** Figure 4.2: Courtesy Gucci. Figure 4.3: Courtesy Burberry Stores. Figure 4.4: Courtesy Ford Motor Company. Figure 4.5: Paul Trummer/The Image Bank. Figure 4.6: Franklin Templeton Distributors, Inc. Figure 4.7: Stills/Retna ltd. Figure 4.8: Courtesy Godiva Choclatier. Figure 4.9: Courtesy of American Isuzu Motors, Inc. Figure 4.10: Courtesy DeBeers. Figure 4.13: Courtesy Coca-Cola Company. "Coca-cola" is a registered trademark of the Coca-Cola Company. © 1995 The Coca-Cola Company. Figure 4.14: Courtesy The Quaker Oats Company. Figure 4.15: Courtesy of Campbell Soup Company.

**Chapter 5.** Figure 5.1: © 1995 The Gillette Company, Inc. Figure 5.2 (left): Courtesy Sterling Health, Division of Sterling Winthrop, Inc. Figure 5.2 (right): Courtesy Avon. Figure 5.3: Courtesy General Mills, Inc. Figure 5.4: Courtesy Schieffelin & Somerset Company. Figure 5.5: Courtesy Mazda Motor of America, Inc. Figure 5.6: Courtesy Clorox Company. Figure 5.7: Courtesy The Kimberly-Clark Corporation. Figure 5.8: Magic Smoking Grill® is a trademark of Hasbro, Inc. © 1995 Hasbro, Inc., Pawtucket, Rhode Island. All rights reserved. Used with permission. Figure U5.1: J.G. Lyden. Figure 5.9: © 1995 MasterCard International Inc. Figure 5.10: Courtesy Daytona Beach Convention and Visitors Bureau. Figure 5.11: Courtesy The Clorox Co. Figure 5.12: Jerry Ohlinger's Movie Material Store. Figure 5.13: © 1994 Waterford Wedgwood U.S.A., Inc. Figure 5.14: © 1994 Maybelline Sales, Inc. Figure 5.15: Courtesy Univision. Figure 5.16: Kristi Yamaguchi © 1995 National Fluid Milk

Processor Promotion Board. Figure 5.18: Reproduced with permission of Schering-Plough Healthcare Products, Inc. Figure 5.23: Courtesy ADBANK.

**Chapter 6.** Figure 6.2: © 1992 Birkenstock. Figure 6.4: Courtesy The Ford Motor Company. Figure 6.5: Courtesy Coca-Cola Company. "Coca-cola" is a registered trademark of the Coca-Cola Company. © 1995 The Coca-Cola Company. Figure 6.6: Courtesy Chrysler Corporation. Figure 6.7: Stewart Cohen/Tony Stone Images/New York, Inc. Figure 6.8: Photofest.

**Chapter 7.** Figure 7.2: Mitch Kezar/Tony Stone Images/New York, Inc. Figure 7.3: John Pinderhughes/The Stock Market. Figure 7.4: Michael Heron/The Stock Market. Figure 7.5 (left): © Beltra/Vanderville/Gamma Liaison. Figure 7.5 (right): Andy Schwartz/Photofest. Figure 7.6: © 1995 Whirlpool Corporation. ®Registered trademark of Whirlpool Corporation. Figure 7.7: Courtesy alien Sport, Inc. Figure 7.8: Courtesy Dana Perfumes Corporation, Renaissance Cosmetics, Inc.

**Chapter 8.** Figure 8.2: © 1994 Carter-Wallace, Inc. Figure 8.3: © 1994 Coors Brewing Company, Golden Colorado. Figure 8.4: Courtesy Upjohn Company, Kalamazoo, Michigan. Figure 8.5: Courtesy of the National Pork Producers Council, Des Moines, Iowa. Figure 8.7: Courtesy USDA. Figure 8.9: © 1995 Ansell, Inc. Figure 8.12: © 1995 Dreyfus Service Corporation. Reprinted with permission. Figure 8.13: © American Association of Advertising Agencies.

**Chapter 9.** Figure 9.2: © 1995 Gerber Products Company. Figure 9.3: Courtesy Morton International, Inc. Figure 9.4: © 1995 Neutrogena Corporation. Figure 9.6: Courtesy The Paddington Corporation. Figure 9.7: © 1994 L&F Products. Figure 9.9: 7-Up is a registered trademark of Dr. Pepper/Seven-Up Corporation. Reprinted with permission. Figure 9.10: Courtesy Summer Infant Products, Inc. Figure 9.11: Courtesy USDA. Figure 9.12: Courtesy Jockey International, Inc. Jockey for Her is a registered trademark of Jockey International, Inc.

**Chapter 10.** Figure 10.7: Courtesy Colgate-Palmolive Co. Figure 10.8: Courtesy Land O'Lakes. Figure 10.9: Reproduced with permission of the Hearst Corporation. Figure 10.10: Courtesy Hearst Corporation and The Children's Hospital of Pittsburgh and the American Association of Poison Control Centers.

**Chapter 11.** Figure 11.1: © 1995 SmithKline Beecham Consumer Healthcare. Figure 11.2: © 1995 Nestlé Frozen Food Company. Figure 11.3: Courtesy US De-

partment of Transportation. Figure 11.5: © 1995 Apple Computer, Inc. Figure 11.7: © 1994 Jordache Enterprises, Inc. Figure 11.8: Courtesy McNeil Consumer Products Company. Figure 11.9: Courtesy A&P. Figure 11.10: Courtesy ABC Canada Literacy Foundation. Figure 11.11: Courtesy Goods for Guns Foundation, Inc.

**Chapter 12.** Figure 12.2: Courtesy Clearly Canadian. Figure 12.3: Courtesy Marshalls. Figure 12.7: Courtesy World Publications. Figure 12.9: Courtesy Stanley Kaplan. Figure 12.10: Courtesy Smartel, Inc. Figure 12.11: Courtesy Blockbuster Entertainment, Inc. Figure 12.12: Courtesy General Electric Co. Figure 12.13: Courtesy National Food Processors Association, Washington, D.C.

**Chapter 13.** Figure 13.1: Courtesy Gucci. Figure 13.3: © 1995 Zima Beverage Co. Figure 13.4: Courtesy Toyota Motor Sales, USA, Inc. Figure 13.5: © 1995 Graco Children's Products, Inc. Figure 13.6: Courtesy Consumer Reports. Figure 13.7: Courtesy Jaguar Cars Ltd. Figure 13.8: Courtesy Miller Brewing Company. Figure 13.9: Courtesy Subway. Figure 13.10: © 1995 Hershey Foods Corporation. Figure 13.11: Courtesy Department of Sanitation.

**Chapter 14.** Figure 14.2: Courtesy of International Business Machines Corporation. Figure 14.3: Courtesy Omaha Steaks International. Figure 14-4: Courtesy Ikea. Figure 14.5: Courtesy CVS, Inc. Figure 14.6: Courtesy Zanetti. Figure 14.8: Courtesy Anheuser-Busch Company, Inc. Figure 14.10: V 1994 GM Corp. All rights reserved. Figure 14.12: Courtesy Hewlett Packard Company.

**Chapter 15.** Figure 15.2: Photofest. Figure 15.3: Courtesy ADBANK. Figure 15.7: Culver Pictures, Inc. Figure 15.8: © 1995 Neutrogena Corporation. Figure 15.9: Courtesy Intuit, Inc. Figure 15.11: Courtesy Coca-Cola Company. "Coca-cola" is a registered trademark of the Coca-Cola Company. © 1995 The Coca-Cola Company. Figure 15.12: Courtesy COSMAIR, Inc.

**Chapter 16.** Figure 16.1: Courtesy Johnson & Johnson. Figure 16.2: Peter Correz/Tony Stone Images/New York, Inc. Figure 16.7: Courtesy MAC Cosmetics. Figure 16.8: © 1994 GM Corp. All rights reserved. Figure 16.9: © 1995 Amway Corporation.

**Chapter 17.** Figure 17.1: Courtesy Smith & Wesson. Figure 17.3: Courtesy Hewlett Packard Company. Figure 17.7: Courtesy General Motors. Figure 17.8: © 1995 Sony Corporation. Figure 17.9: Courtesy Pipeline USA.

# COMPANY INDEX

## A

ABC Canada, 333
ABC television network, 23-24
Absolut voda, 293, 496
Acura, 92, 416, 501
Adidas, 449
Alligator Records, 469
Allstate, 303
American Cancer Society, 14-15, 18
American Express, 151, 161, 332
American Family Association, 24
American Medical Association (AMA), 25
American Society of Association Executives, 243
America On-line, 416, 498
Anheuser-Busch, 147, 290, 407, 449
Apple Computer, 122, 440
Arizona, 185
Arm and Hammer, 302
Aromapower Diet, 295
Arthur D. Little, 335
AT&T, 56, 90, 161, 264, 292
Avon, 132, 332, 442

## B

Bacardi, 407
Bath & Body Works, 266
Baume & Mercer, 93
Bel-Tronics Limited, 55
Birkenstock, 173
Black Entertainment Network, 146
Blockbuster Video, 361
Bloomingdale's, 277
BMW, 73, 188
Body Shop, 266
Borden, 232
Boston Chicken, 260
Boycott Anorexic Marketing, 248

Bradlee's, 334
Budweiser, 88, 188

## C

Cable News Network (CNN), 135
CACI Marketing Systems, 154
Calvin Klein, 206, 248, 289
Cambridge Builders, 77
Campari, 161
Campbell Soup, 119, 278
CarBargains program, 380
CarMax, 381
Carrefours, 399
CBS television network, 440
Champion, 295
Chevrolet, 141, 188, 256, 415
Chrysler Corporation, 184, 215, 383
Circuit City, 381, 442
Clairol, 345
Claritas, 154
Clearasil, 132
Clearly Canadian, 345
Clorox, 142
Club Med, 6
Coca-Cola, 88, 116, 141, 179, 204, 248, 269, 270, 275, 292, 385, 386, 387, 389, 443, 444, 446, 449
Colgate, 301
Columbia House of Music, 459
Combat, 240, 241
CompUSA, 276
Compuserve, 416, 498
Continental Airlines, 295
Coors Brewing Company, 148, 230, 290, 407
Craftsman, 240
Crowne Plaza Hotels, 73
CVS, 403

## D

DDB Needham Lifestyle Survey, 51-52, 188
DeBeers, 113
Depends Undergarments, 137
Devon, 213
Dewar's Scotch, 133
Dial soap, 11
Diet Rite, 256
Discovery Channel, 189
Disney Corporation, 13, 114, 449
Domino's Pizza, 496
Dove Ice Cream Bars, 278
Dr. Pepper, 389
Dr. Scholls, 152
Dreyfus, 245
Duracell, 293

## E

Easy Spirit, 276
Evian, 51
Excedrin, 364

## F

Family Channel Christian cable network, 150
Federal Express, 401, 402
Ford Motor Company, 42, 69, 89, 108, 116, 144, 188, 215, 273, 315, 382
Fox Network, 146
Franklin Templeton Group, 109
Frito-Lay, 449

## G

Gap, 442
Gateway, 319, 416
Gatorade, 389
Gemstar Development, 440
General Electric, 362, 363, 416

General Foods, 88, 269
General Mills, 40, 132, 133, 185
General Motors, 148, 316, 440, 449, 475, 502
Gerber, 117
Gillette, 68, 69, 132
Glenfiddich scotch, 188
Godiva, 111
Graco, 382
Green Giant, 293
Gucci, 107, 373

**H**
Harley-Davidson, 100, 121-122
Healthy Choice, 248
Heinz, 331-332
Helene Curtis, 275
Hersheys, 388
Hertz, 276
Hewlett Packard, 418, 488
Holiday Inn, 73
Home Box Office (HBO), 22
Home Shopping Network, 404
Honda, 226, 237, 501
Huggies, 137
Hyundai, 180, 329

**I**
IBM, 116, 150, 276, 399
Ikea, 161
Internet's World Wide Web, 405, 439
Isuzu, 112, 363

**J**
Jaguar, 384
J & B Scotch, 268
J. D. Powers, 226
Jeep, 184
Jell-O, 330
Jenny Craig, 248, 449
Jim Smith Society, 243
Jockey International, 279
Johnson & Johnson, 49, 330
Jolt Cola, 389
Jordache, 325

**K**
KayBee Toys, 334
Kellogg, 104, 263, 365
Kentucky Bourbon Circle, 475
Kentucky Fried Chicken, 118
Kingsford, 447
Kmart, 123, 206, 277
Knight Publishing Company, 74
Kodak, 292, 440
KPC Research, 74
Kraft Foods, 232

**L**
L.A. Gear, 449
Land-O-Lakes, 303

Lands' End, 274
La-Z-Boy, 226
L'Eggs, 291
Levi Strauss, 76, 401
LifeStyles, 238
The Limited, 85
Lincoln-Mercury, 266
L'Oréal, 276
Lysol, 273

**M**
Macintosh, 320, 321
Magic Eye, 258-259
Make-up Art Cosmetics (MAC), 473
Marlboro, 109, 110
Marshalls, 346
Mary Kay Cosmetics, 88
MasterCard, 140
Maybelline, 146, 437
Mazda, 135, 215
McDonald's, 53, 114, 115, 116, 122, 153, 298, 299, 403, 405, 445
MCI, 56, 90, 161, 475, 496
McNeil, 274, 303, 330
Mercedes-Benz, 73, 88, 150, 266, 276
Merrill Lynch, 303
Microsoft, 268
Miles, Inc., 474
Miller Brewing Company, 161, 290, 293, 376
Mirage Resorts, 449
Mistic, 345
Monsanto, 269
Morton Salt, 263
Mott, 204
MTV, 140, 289

**N**
Nabisco, 84, 185
National Cable Television Association, 21
National Heart Savers Association, 20
National Organization of Mall Walkers, 243
National Parent-Teachers Association (PTA), 25, 219
National Public Radio (NPR), 189
NBC television network, 9, 449
Neiman Marcus, 414
Nescafe, 256
Nestle, 256
Neutrogena, 438
Nike, 16, 141, 289, 292, 300, 329, 476
Nissan, 501
Nordstrom's, 274
Nynex, 232

**O**
Ocean Spray, 279
Olympic Restaurant, 269

Owens-Corning, 269
Oxy 10, 132

**P**
Packard Bell, 319, 444
Papermate, 70
Parkay, 293
PBS television network, 17
Pepsi-Cola, 88, 116, 117, 141, 275, 289, 385, 386, 387, 389, 501
Perdue chicken, 148
Philip Morris, 7
Pipeline USA, 500
Play It Again Sports, 419
Playschool, 138
Pontiac, 178
Price Club, 399
PRIZM, 154, 155-158
Proctor & Gamble, 71, 75, 76, 85, 116, 268, 293, 302, 331, 332, 335, 440
Prodigy, 180, 498
Program Fitness, 430
Prudential, 292

**Q**
Quaker Oats, 116
Qualitex, 269
Quicken, 440, 441

**R**
Ragu, 436
Ralph Lauren, 246
Range Rover, 363
Ray-Ban, 289, 449
Reebok, 141, 289
R. J. Reynolds, 163
Rolls-Royce, 85
Rossignol, 81
Ross Laboratories, 85

**S**
Saks Fifth Avenue, 277
Samuel Adams Beer, 266
Saturn, 381, 461
Seagrams, 407
Sears, 15, 123, 319, 442
7-Eleven, 416-417
7-Up, 275
Singer, 116, 117
Slice, 275
Smartfoods, 303
Smith Kline Beecham, 440
Snapple, 185
Snickers, 444
Soloflex, 273, 430
Sony, 319
Stanford Research Institute (SRI), 190, 191
State Farm, 300
Stouffers, 317

Strategic Mapping, 154
Stridex, 132
Suave, 93
Subway, 387
SunBolt, 389
Survey Sampling, Inc., 74

**T**
Taster's Choice, 256
Technics, 57
Telemundo, 148
Texaco, 303
Thing Enterprises, 259
Tilex, 136
Touchstone Pictures, 13
Toyota, 47, 256, 316, 379, 501
Toys Я Us, 334
Tretorn, 41

Tropicana, 110, 330
Tums, 315, 316
Tupperware, 88
*Twins* magazine, 85
Tylenol, 274, 330

**U**
Unilever, 102
Univision, 148
Upjohn Company, 231, 474

**V**
Vertical Clubs, 39
VH1, 140
Vicks, 119
Viewers for Quality Television, 24
Virginia Slims, 110
Volvo, 91, 364

**W**
Wal-Mart, 122-123, 380, 419
Walt Disney Studios, 449
Waterford, 144
Waterman Pen, 70, 331
Weather Channel, 135
Weight Watchers, 248
Wendy's, 267, 297, 298
Werner, 305
Whirlpool, 210
Wisk, 323, 363
World Pog Federation, 139
World Wide Web, 405, 436, 439
Wrigley's, 300

**Z**
Zanetti, 406
Zima, 376

# Name Index

**A**
Ajzen, Icek, 323, 324
Alger, Horatio, 109
Anderson, Louie, 417

**B**
Baccei, Thomas, 259
Baker, Anita, 146
Barkley, Charles, 445
Bearden, William O., 216
Bennett, Tony, 289
Bird, Larry, 445
Bochco, Steven, 24
Boorstin, Daniel, 206
Butler, Brett, 417

**C**
Chase, Chevy, 449
Cohen, Joel B., 179
Conick, Harry, Jr., 209
Crow, Sheryl, 184, 205

**D**
Dichter, Ernest, 179, 239
Dickinson, Peter R., 408

**E**
Elizabeth II (q. of England), 118
Etheridge, Melissa, 316
Etzel, Michael J., 216

**F**
Fishbein, Martin, 321, 323, 324, 331
Forbes, Malcolm, 100
Franklin, Benjamin, 109

Freud, Sigmund, 174, 175, 176, 177, 236, 239

**G**
Gottfried, Gilbert, 417
Grant, Amy, 316
Gubar, George, 159

**H**
Horney, Karen, 178
Hwang, Hsiaofang, 51

**J**
Joplin, Janis, 266
Jordan, Michael, 329, 445

**K**
Kahle, Lynn, 121
Kennedy, John F., 277
Klein, Calvin, 206
Kroc, Ray, 122

**L**
LaBudde, Sam, 331
Lavidge, Robert, 432, 433
Letterman, David, 114, 141
Lewis, Jerry, 332

**M**
Madonna, 205
Manilow, Barry, 184
Maslow, Abraham, 236-237
Mateo, Fernando, 334
McLean, Jim, 211
McMenamy, Kristin, 248

Moss, Kate, 248
Murray, Henry, 236

**P**
Packard, Vance, 269
Pavlov, I., 291

**R**
Reagan, Ronald, 118
Reno, Janet, 25
Riley, Pat, 460
Robertson, Thomas S., 486, 492
Rogers, Everett, 489, 493-495
Ross, Jerry, 331
Rubin, Joel, 331

**S**
Schwarzenegger, Arnold, 25
Skinner, B. F., 291, 294, 295
Steiner, Gary, 432, 433
Swenson, Mike, 189

**T**
Thomas, Dave, 297, 298
Truett, Bill, 74

**W**
Walton, Sam, 123
Weber, Ernst, 263
Wells, William D., 159, 189
White, Barry, 146

**Y**
Yamaguchi, Kristi, 149

**Z**
Zaichowsky, Judith Lynne, 375

# SUBJECT INDEX

**A**

Absolute threshold, selective perception, 262
Accessibility of market, target market, 79-80
Access to funds, purchase and use, 400-401
Access to product, purchase and use, 400-401
Acculturation, defined, 103
Acquired need, defined, 228
Activation, cognitive learning theory, 298
Activities, interests, and opinions (AIO), lifestyle and psychographics measurement, 188-189
Actors:
  in consumer behavior, 9-21
    consumer, 10-13
    marketers, 13-17
    overview, 9-10
    public policy actor, 17-21
  defined, 9
Actual self:
  consumer behavior and, 185
  defined, 182
Adoption:
  barriers to, 498-502
  process described, 492-498
Advertising. *See also* Interpersonal communication; Marketing communication
  alcohol content and, 290
  attitude-toward-the-ad models, 325
  children and, 11, 139, 219-220
  deceptive, public policy and, 278
  defined, 436

gay market, household characteristics, 161-162
  imitation and, 268-269
  marketing communication, integrated, 437-438
  needs creation and, 246-249
  selective perception, 262
  subliminal perception, 269-270
Affect, attitude models, 320
Affinity, defined, 209
African-Americans:
  demographic subculture, 145-146
  market segmentation and, 72
Age level, demographic subcultures, 136-144
Alcohol abuse:
  college drinking, 163-164
  driving and, 407, 409
Alcohol content, advertising and, 290
Alternatives evaluation:
  consumer purchase activity, 40, 48
  decision making, 354-361, 362-364
  involvement level
    high involvement purchase, 381
    low involvement purchase, 386-387
Alternatives search:
  consumer purchase activity, 40
  decision making, 349-354, 362
  involvement level, 377
    high involvement purchase, 379-380
    low involvement purchase, 386
American Academy of Pediatrics, 219
American Association of School Administrators, 219
American Automobile Association (AAA), 380

Anorexia, 248
Anthropology, consumer behavior and, 29
Aperture, marketing communication, 447-448
Approach-approach conflict:
  decision making, 359
  defined, 232
Approach-avoidance conflict, defined, 233-234
Asian-Americans:
  demographic subculture, 148-149
  subculture and, 105
Aspiration group:
  interpersonal communication, 462
  reference groups, 216
Associative networks, cognitive learning theory, 298
Attitude, 311-339
  changing of, 328-335
  defined, 313
  formation of, 313-319
    behavioral processes, 56-58
    market segmentation and, 82
  measurement of, 325-327
  models of, 319-325
Attitude scales, described, 327
Attitude-toward-object model, 322-323
Attitude-toward-the-ad models, described, 325
Attribution theory, attitude change and, 329
Authorities, opinion leadership, 467-468
Automatic teller machines, 400-401, 496
Avoidance-avoidance conflict, defined, 234-235

**B**

Baby boomers:
  defined, 137
  demographic subcultures, 141-143
  lifestyle and psychographics, 187
Baby busters:
  defined, 137
  demographic subcultures, 139-141
Background characteristics. *See* Consumer background characteristics
Behavioral learning theory:
  described, 290-295
  marketing applications, 300-304
Behavioral processes:
  attitude formation, 56-58
  consumer purchase activity, 46, 53-58
  decision making, 58
  learning, 56
  market segmentation and, 82
  motivation, 53-54
  perception, 54-56
Beliefs, attitude models, 319-320
Benefit addition, attitude change and, 330
Better Business Bureau, 382
Brand experience perspective, marketing communication, 434-436
Brand image:
  positioning and, 275-276
  risk reduction strategies, 274
Brand loyalty:
  decision making and, 364
  risk reduction strategies, 273-274
Brand name:
  decision making, 354, 359
  marketers and, 16

**C**

CAD scale, 179
CarBargains program, 380
Cause-related marketing, described, 332
Celebrities, reference groups and, 205-206, 216
Celebrity advertising:
  interpersonal communication, 473
  marketing communication, 445
Center for the Study of Services in Washington, 380
Children:
  advertising and, 11
  demographic subcultures, 138-139
  family life cycle, 157-161
  television viewing and, 219-220
Christianity. *See* Religion
Classical conditioning, described, 291-293

Closure, perceptual organization, 267-268
Clubs:
  consumer benefits identification and, 243-244
  reference groups, 215
Cognitive dissonance theory, attitude change and, 329
Cognitive learning theory:
  described, 296-300
  marketing applications, 300-304
Cohorts, defined, 138
College market:
  alcohol abuse, 163-164
  crime, public policy and, 352
  demographic subcultures, 140-141
Color:
  cross-cultural analysis, 117
  perceived quality, 276
  perception and, 265-266
Communication, defined, 427. *See also* Interpersonal communication; Marketing communication; Opinion leadership
Comparative advertising, marketing communication, 445
Compatibility, new product planning, 496
Compensatory decision rule, alternatives evaluation, 357
Complexity, new product planning, 496
Conative component, attitude models, 320
Concentrated market segmentation strategy, defined, 83-84
Conditioning. *See* Behavioral learning theory
Condoms, 238
Confidence. *See* Consumer confidence
Conjunctive decision rule, alternatives evaluation, 358
Consideration set, decision making, alternatives search, 353
Consistency, attitude change and, 328-329
Consumer:
  consumer behavior actor, 10-13
  defined, 5, 9
Consumer background characteristics, 45, 46-52
  culture and values, 46-48
  defined, 45
  demographics, 48-50
  goals and, 230
  involvement level and, 374, 375
  lifestyle and psychographics, 192-193
  market segmentation and, 82
  perception and, 260-261

personality, lifestyle, and psychographics, 50-52
  reference groups, 52, 102, 202
Consumer behavior:
  actors in, 9-21
    consumer, 10-13
    marketers, 13-17
    overview, 9-10
    public policy actor, 17-21
  analytic approach to, 8-9
  anthropology and, 29
  defined, 4-8
  economics and, 28
  lifestyle and psychographics, 185-193
  marketing strategy and, 67-71
  market segmentation and, 80-83
  organizational behavior and, 29
  psychoanalytic theory and, 177-178
  psychology and, 27-28
  self-concept theory and, 183-185
  sociology and, 28-29
  television viewing as, 22-24
  trait theory and, 180-182
Consumer behavioral processes. *See* Behavioral processes
Consumer benefits identification:
  marketers and, 243-244
  means-end chains and laddering, 242-243
  motivational research, 239-241
Consumer confidence, risk reduction strategies, 272-275
Consumer education:
  decision making, alternatives search, 349-354
  risk reduction strategies, 272-273
Consumerism, public policy and, 277-279
Consumer mood, purchase and use, 403
Consumer motivation. *See* Motivation
Consumer need. *See* Need
Consumer purchase activity, 37-44
  alternatives evaluation, 40
  alternatives search, 40
  consumption experience evaluation, 41-42
  disposal and end use, 43-44
  feedback, 43
  needs recognition, 37-40
  purchase and use, 40-41
  steps in, 38, 39
  variations in, 44-46
Consumer Resource Network, 440
Consumer satisfaction or dissatisfaction, postpurchase activities, 411-417
Consumer socialization, reference groups and, 203-207

Consumption community, defined, 206
Consumption experience evaluation:
    consumer purchase activity, 41-42
    involvement level
        high involvement purchase, 381-
            382
        low involvement purchase, 389
Continuous innovation, new product
    planning, 487
Creative strategy, marketing commu-
    nication, 445-446
Credibility:
    marketing communication, 428-429
    reference groups and, 211
Credit cards:
    access to funds, purchase and use,
        400-401
    purchase and use, 400-401
Crime, public policy and, 352
Crime Awareness and Campus Secu-
    rity Act of 1990, 352
Cross-cultural analysis, international
    marketing and, 117-120
Culture, 101-108
    components of, 105-113
    consumer background characteris-
        tics, 46-48
    defined, 46, 101
    geography and, 152-154
    international marketing and, 113-
        120. See also International mar-
            keting
    lifestyle and psychographics, 186
    market segmentation and, 82
    nature of, 101-104
    perception and, 260-261
    subcultures, 104-105
    values and, 108-109
Custom:
    cross-cultural analysis, 117
    culture and, 101, 102, 110
Customer service, 416
Customized market:
    defined, 75, 76
    purchase and use, 401

D
Deceptive advertising, public policy
    and, 278, 448-449
Decision making, 341-369
    alternatives evaluation, 354-361
    alternatives search, 349-354
    attitude function, 318
    behavioral processes, 58
    defined, 343
    involvement level, 378
        high involvement purchase, 378-
            385
        low involvement purchase, 385-
            390

levels of, 343-347
    marketer's influence on, 361-363
    market segmentation and, 82
    motivation and, 244-246
    perceived risk and, 271-272
    perception and, 257
    process of, 347-349
    public policy and, 364-365
Decision rule, alternatives evaluation,
    356-361
Decoding, marketing communication,
    431
Demographics:
    consumer purchase activity, 45, 48-
        50
    lifestyle and psychographics, 186
    market segmentation and, 82
Demographic subcultures, 129-167
    age level, 136-144
    bases of, 131-134
    gender, 134-136
    geography, 152-154
    household characteristics, 154-162
    public policy and, 162-164
    race and ethnicity, 144-149
    reference groups and, 210
    religion, 149-150
    social class, 150-152
Depth interview:
    attitude measurement, 326
    motivational research, 240
Diapers, attitude change and, 334-335
Dickinson person-situation matrix,
    408
Differential threshold, selective per-
    ception, 262-263
Differentiated market segmentation
    strategy, defined, 85
Diffusion of innovation, new product
    planning, 489-491
Direct response, marketing communi-
    cation, integrated, 438-440
Discontinuous innovation, new prod-
    uct planning, 488
Discrimination, market segmentation
    and, 72
Discrimination group:
    negative reference group, 216
    reference groups, 216
Disjunctive decision rule, alternatives
    evaluation, 358-359
Displacement, psychoanalytic theory,
    177
Disposal and end use:
    consumer purchase activity, 43-44
    involvement level
        high involvement purchase, 384-
            385
        low involvement purchase, 390
    options in, 417-419

Distribution channel, marketing mix,
    92-93
Driving, alcohol abuse and, 407, 409
Dynamically continuous innovation,
    new product planning, 487-488

E
Early adopters, new product planning,
    490
Early majority, new product planning,
    490-491
Economic and social welfare issues,
    public policy and, 26
Economics, consumer behavior and,
    28
Education, social class and, 151. See
    also Consumer education
Edwards Personal Preference Sched-
    ule (EPPS), 180, 181, 236
Ego, psychoanalytic theory, 175
Ego-defensive function, of attitude,
    316-317
Elaboration likelihood model (ELM),
    marketing communication, 446-
    447
Elaborative rehearsal, memory, 298
Elimination by aspect decision rule, al-
    ternatives evaluation, 358
Embedding, subliminal perception,
    270
Enabling conditions, purchase and
    use, 400-401
Encoding, marketing communication,
    428
Enculturation, defined, 103
Enduring involvement, defined, 377
Environmentalism:
    attitude change and, 331-332, 334-
        335
    product disposal, 419
    product packaging and labeling, 279
Equity issue, public policy, 26, 449-450
Ethics, public policy and, 24-26
Ethnic differences:
    demographic subcultures, 144-149
    market segmentation and, 72
    subcultures, 104-105
Ethnocentrism, defined, 114
Evaluation, of consumption experi-
    ence, consumer purchase activity,
    41-42. See also Alternatives evalu-
    ation
Evaluative criteria, decision making,
    alternatives evaluation, 354-356.
    See also Alternatives evaluation
Evoked set, decision making, alterna-
    tives search, 353
Exchange, defined, 5-7
Experience, learning theory and, 303

Extensive decision making, described, 345-346

**F**

Factual message, marketing communication, 445
Fairness issue, public policy, 25-26, 448-449
Fair Packaging and Labeling Act of 1966, 278-279
Familiarity, retrieval, cognitive learning theory, 298-299
Family:
    consumer socialization and, 203-204
    household characteristics, demographic subculture, 154-162
    as reference group, 217-220
Family life cycle, household characteristics, 157-161
Fashion:
    culture and, 104, 107
    needs creation and, 246
    public policy and, 248
Fear appeals, marketing communication, 445-446
Federal Communications Commission (FCC), 19, 23, 56, 139
Feedback:
    consumer purchase activity, 43, 48
    consumer satisfaction or dissatisfaction, 411-417
    direct response, 439
    involvement level
        high involvement purchase, 382-383
        low involvement purchase, 389-390
    marketing communication, 431-432
Female market:
    demographic subcultures, 134-135
    handgun advertising, 486
Figure and ground relationships, perceptual organization, 267
Financial risk, defined, 272
Florida Citrus Commission, 440
Focus groups, attitude measurement, 326
Food Marketing Institute, 365
Foot-in-the-door technique, attitude change and, 329
Forecasting, target markets, 80
Form, retrieval, cognitive learning theory, 300
Formal reference group, defined, 209
Freudian personality theory, 174-179, 236, 239
Functional risk, defined, 272

**G**

Gambling, learning theory and, 301-302

Gay market, household characteristics, 161-162
Gender, demographic subcultures, 134-136
Generalized exchange, defined, 7
Generational differences. *See* Age level
Generation X, demographic subcultures, 139-141
Generic competitor, defined, 21
Geodermographics, defined, 153-154
Geography:
    demographic subculture, 152-154
    gay market, 161
Gestalt psychology, perceptual organization, 266-267
Global marketing strategy, international markets, 116
Goal:
    defined, 227
    motivation and, 229-232
Goals, conflicts among, 232-235
Good Housekeeping Seal, 303
Government, international marketing and, 115. *See also* Politics; Public policy
Greenpeace, 331
Green Seal, 419
Guarantees, risk reduction strategies, 273-274

**H**

Habit, low involvement purchase, 387
Handguns, 486
Harvard Alcohol Project, 407
Hero worship, 177
Heuristics, decision rule, alternatives evaluation, 356
Hierarchy of effects model, marketing communication, 432-434
High involvement purchase. *See* Involvement level
Hispanics:
    demographic subculture, 147-148
    market segmentation and, 72
    subculture and, 104, 105
Home shopping:
    marketing communication, 439
    purchase and use influence of, 404-405
Homosexuality, gay market, household characteristics, 161-162
Household characteristics, demographic subculture, 154-162. *See also* Family
Humor, marketing communication, 446

**I**

Id, psychoanalytic theory, 175
Ideal self:
    consumer behavior and, 185
    defined, 182
Identification, psychoanalytic theory, 176
Identification groups, reference groups and, 214-215
Image, reference groups and, 212
Imitation, advertising and, 268-269
Individual referent, defined, 209
Inept set, decision making, alternatives search, 353
Inert set, decision making, alternatives search, 353
Infomercials, 430, 439-440
Informal reference group, defined, 209
Information content, interpersonal communication, 458
Information processing, cognitive learning theory, 296-297
Innate need, defined, 228
Innovation. *See* New product planning
Innovators, new product planning, 490
Instrumental conditioning, learning theory and, 294-295
Instrumental values, defined, 121
Intangible product, defined, 8
Integrated marketing communication, 436-442. *See also* Marketing communication
International marketing, 113-120
    cross-cultural analysis and, 117-120
    cultural factors and, 114-115
    market segmentation strategies and, 115-116
    perception and, 265
Interpersonal communication, 455-477. *See also* Advertising; Marketing communication
    defined, 457
    information content, 458
    marketer use of, 473-477
    opinion leadership, 466-473
    partner type, 461-462
    product type, 462-463
    receiver's purpose, 458-459
    source evaluation, 460-461
    source's purpose, 459
    theory, 464-466
    word-of-mouth communication, 457-458
Interpretation of imagery, perception and, 271-277
Involvement level:
    consumer purchase activity, 44-45
    decision making and, 344-347, 359
    effects of, 377-378
    factors affecting, 374-377

high involvement purchase, 378-385
low involvement purchase, 385-390
measurement of, 375
motivation and, 373-374

**J**

Just noticeable difference (JND), selective perception, 263-264

**K**

Key informant method, opinion leadership measurement, 471
Knowledge function, of attitude, 317-
319

**L**

Labeling. *See* Product packaging and
labeling
Laddering, means-end chains and lad-
dering, 242-243
Laggards, new product planning, 491
Language:
    cross-cultural analysis, 117
    culture and, 101, 102
Late majority, new product planning,
491
Law, culture and, 101, 102, 110, 112
Learning, 285-309
    attitude formation, 313-314
    behavioral learning theory, 290-295
    behavioral processes, 56
    characteristics of, 288-290
    cognitive learning theory, 296-300
    culture and, 103
    defined, 287
    marketing applications of, 300-304
    market segmentation and, 82
    public policy and, 304-306
Lexicographic decision rule, alterna-
tives evaluation, 358
Lifestyle analysis, defined, 186
Lifestyle and psychographics, 185-193
    background characteristics and,
        192-193
    consumer background characteris-
        tics, 50-52
    market segmentation and, 82
    measurement approaches, 188-191
        activities, interests, and opinions
            (AIO), 188-189
        VALS program, 190-191
    overview of, 185-188
    public policy and, 191-192
Limited decision making, described,
347
Line extension, new product planning,
487
List of Values (LOV):
    described, 121-122
    motivation and, 236

Localized marketing strategy, interna-
tional markets, 116
Local opinion leadership, 468-469
Long-term memory, defined, 298

**M**

Male market, demographic subcultures, 136
Marine Mammal Protection Act of
1972, 331
Marketers, 65-97
    consumer behavior actor, 13-
        17
    consumer benefits identification
        and, 243-244
    consumer goals and, 231-232
    consumer satisfaction or dissatisfac-
        tion, 414-417
    decision making influence of, 361-
        363
    defined, 9
    interpersonal communication and,
        473-477
    marketing mix, 90-93
    marketing strategy, 67-71
    market segmentation, 71-87
    needs creation and, 246-249
    product positioning, 87-90
    public policy and, 19-20
    purchase and use influence of, 404-
        405
Marketing communication, 425-453.
    *See also* Advertising; Interper-
    sonal communication
    consumer and, 432-436
        brand experience perspective,
            434-436
        hierarchy of effects model, 432-
            434
    defined, 427
    feedback, 431-432
    integrated, 436-442
        advertising, 437-438
        defined, 436
        direct response, 438-440
        personal selling, 442
        publicity, 440-441
    medium, 429-431
    message, 429
    overview of, 427-428
    public policy, 448-450
    receiver, 431
    source, 428-429
    strategies for, 442-448
        media strategy, 447-448
        message strategy, 443-447
Marketing concept:
    applications of, 15
    defined, 13

Marketing mix:
    activities in, 90-93
    defined, 14, 69-70
Marketing strategy, 67-71
    benefits of, 70-71
    components in, 68-70
    defined, 14, 67
Market maven, defined, 468
Market segmentation, 71-87
    consumer behavior and, 80-83
    defined, 14, 68, 73
    overview of, 71
    product positioning and, 90
    public policy and, 72
    results of, 74-79
    strategy in
        domestic markets, 83-87
        international markets, 115-116
    target selection, 79-80
Maslow's hierarchy of needs, 236-
237
Mass market, defined, 75, 76-77
Material artifacts, culture and, 101,
102, 112-113
Mature market:
    defined, 137-138
    demographic subcultures, 143-144
Means-end chains and laddering, con-
sumer benefits identification, 242-
243
Media. *See also* Television viewing
    demographic subcultures, 141,
        146
    politics and, 25
    reference groups and, 204-207
    social class and, 151-152
    violence and, 12-13, 19, 23-24, 25
Media strategy, marketing communi-
cation, 447-448
Medium, marketing communication,
429-431
Membership reference group, de-
fined, 208
Memory, cognitive learning theory,
296-300
Message, marketing communication,
429
Message strategy, marketing commu-
nication, 443-447
Mirror controversy, needs creation
and, 248-249
Mood, of consumer, purchase and
use, 403
Mothers Against Drunk Driving, 407
Motivation, 225-253
    approaches to, 236-238
    behavioral processes, 53-54
    consumer benefits identification,
        239-244
        marketers and, 243-244

Motivation *continued*
    means-end chains and laddering, 242-243
    motivational research, 239-241
    decision making and, 244-246
    defined, 227
    goals and, 229-235
    involvement level and, 373-374
    market segmentation and, 82
    needs and, 228-229
    needs creation and, 246-249
    psychoanalytic theory, 179
Motivational research, consumer benefits identification, 239-241
Multiattribute attitude models, described, 321-325
Multiattribute compensatory decision rule, alternatives evaluation, 359
Multi-step theory of communication, interpersonal communication, 465-466
Music, cognitive learning theory, 300
Myth, culture and, 101, 102, 109-110

N
National Association of Attorneys General, 56
National Food Processors Association, 365
National Parent-Teachers Association (PTA), 25, 219
Need:
    creation of, marketers and, 246-249
    defined, 227
    Maslow's hierarchy of needs, 236-237
    types of, 228-229
Needs recognition:
    consumer purchase activity, 37-40
    decision making, 347
    involvement level
        high involvement purchase, 378-379
        low involvement purchase, 385-386
Negative reference group:
    defined, 209
    discrimination group, 216
    separation from, 215
Negative reinforcement, defined, 294-295
Neo-Freudian personality theory, 178-179
New product planning, 483-506
    adoption barriers, 498-502
    adoption process, 492-498
    diffusion of innovation, 489-491
    innovation types, 485-489
    public policy and, 501-502

Noncompensatory decision rule, alternatives evaluation, 356-357
Nonmembership reference group, defined, 208-209
Nonprofit organizations:
    consumer behavior actor, 17
    defined, 14-15
Normative influence, reference groups and, 212
Nutrition Labeling and Education Act of 1994, 279, 364-365

O
Objective perception, defined, 259
Observability, new product planning, 498
Observation, attitude measurement, 326
On-line shopping:
    marketing communication, 439, 497-498
    purchase and use influence of, 405
Operant conditioning, learning theory and, 294-295
Opinion leadership, 466-473. *See also* Advertising; Interpersonal communication; Marketing communication
    authorities, 467-468
    creation of, 474-475
    defined, 466
    local leaders, 468-469
    marketer use of, 473-477
    measurement of, 469-473
    trend setters, 468
    word-of-mouth communication compared, 467
Organizational behavior, consumer behavior and, 29
Organizational buying, defined, 10

P
Packaging. *See* Product packaging and labeling
Partnership for a Drug Free America, 302
Patents, advertising and imitation, 268-269
Perceived quality, perception, interpretation of imagery, 276-277
Perceived risk. *See also* Risk
    decision making and, 271-272
    new product planning, 501
Perception, 255-283
    behavioral processes, 54-56
    defined, 257
    interpretation of imagery, 271-277
        perceived quality, 276-277
        perceived risk, 271-272

positioning and brand image, 275-276
    risk reduction strategies, 272-275
    learning and, 289, 290
    market segmentation and, 82
    organization of stimuli, 265-269
    overview of, 257-260
    public policy and, 277-279
    schema and, 260-261
    selective perception, 262-264
    subliminal, 269-270
Perceptual map, positioning, interpretation of imagery, 275-276
Personality, 171-185. *See also* Psychology
    consumer background characteristics, 50-52
    defined, 172
    market segmentation and, 82
    motivation and, 236, 240. *See also* Motivation
    needs and, 228
    overview of, 171-172
    perception and, 259-260
    theories of, 174-185
        Freudian, 174-179
        Neo-Freudian, 178-179
        self-concept theory, 182-185
        trait and type theory, 179-182
        traits and types, 173
Personal selling, marketing communication, integrated, 442
Pharmaceuticals, interpersonal communication, 474
Physical attributes, purchase and use, 399-400
Physical risk, defined, 272
Place, marketing mix, 92-93
Poison control, warning labels, 304, 305
Policy makers, defined, 18-19
Politics. *See also* Public policy
    consumers and, 8
    demographic subcultures, 142
    media and, 25, 219-220
    public policy actor, 9-10
    trade association, 19-21
Positioning, perception, interpretation of imagery, 275-276
Positive reference group:
    aspiration groups, 216
    defined, 209
    identification with, 214-215
    interpersonal communication, 461-462
    local opinion leaders, 468-469
Positive reinforcement, defined, 294
Postpurchase activities, 409-419. *See also* Consumption experience evaluation

consumer satisfaction or dissatisfaction, 411-417
    preparation to buy again, 409-411
    product disposal, 417-419
Price:
    automobiles, 380
    decision making, 359
    involvement level and, 373
    marketing mix, 92
    new product planning, 499-500
    perceived quality, 276-277
    public policy and, 123
    risk reduction strategies, 275
Primary demand, defined, 232
Privacy rights, lifestyle and psychographics, 191-192
PRIZM, 154, 155-158
Product:
    defined, 7-8
    interpersonal communication, 462-463
    involvement level and, 374
    marketing mix, 91-92
    new product planning, 483-506. See also New product planning
Product life cycle, new product planning, 491
Product line, market segmentation strategy, 84
Product packaging and labeling:
    attitude change and, 330
    learning theory and, 302-303
    low involvement purchase, 388
    public policy and, 278-279, 290, 304-305, 364-365
Product positioning:
    defined, 68-69, 87
    market segmentation and, 90
    process of, 87-90
Professional associations:
    consumer benefits identification and, 243-244
    reference groups, 215
Projection, psychoanalytic theory, 177
Projective techniques:
    attitude measurement, 326-327
    motivational research, 240, 241
Promotion, marketing mix, 92
Proximity, perceptual organization, 268
Psychoanalytic theory of personality, 174-179
Psychographic analysis. See also Lifestyle and psychographics
    defined, 186
    needs and, 228
Psychological barriers, new product planning, 501
Psychological risk, defined, 272

Psychological testing, attitude measurement, 326-327
Psychology. See also Personality
    consumer behavior and, 27-28
    Gestalt psychology, perceptual organization, 266-267
    lifestyle and psychographics, 186
Public health:
    advertising and, 11-12
    goal conflict and, 235
Publicity, marketing communication, integrated, 440-441
Public policy. See also Politics
    advertising and, 268-269
    attitude change and, 332-335
    automobile prices, 380
    children, 138-139, 219-220
    crime and, 352
    decision making and, 364-365
    demographic subculture and, 162-164
    ethics and, 24-26
    interpersonal communication, 474
    learning and, 304-306
    lifestyle and psychographics, 191-192
    marketing communication, 448-450
    market segmentation and, 72
    needs creation and, 248-249
    new product planning and, 501-502
    perception and, 277-279
    pricing and, 123
    seat belt use, 318
    telephone numbers, 54-56
    television viewing and, 23-24
Public policy actors:
    attitude function and, 318-319
    consumer behavior actors, 17-21
    consumer goals and, 231-232, 235
    consumption and, 12
    defined, 9, 10
Punishment, defined, 295
Purchase and use, 395-423
    activities in, 397-398
    consumer purchase activity, 40-41
    influences on, 398-409
        marketer's influences, 404-405
        situational influences, 399-403
        usage influences, 405-409
    involvement level
        high involvement purchase, 381
        low involvement purchase, 387-389
    postpurchase activities, 409-419
Purchase environment, high involvement purchase, 381

Qualitative investigation, attitude measurement, 326-327

Quality, perception, interpretation of imagery, 276-277

Race differences:
    demographic subcultures, 144-149
    market segmentation and, 72
    subcultures, 104-105
Rationality of consumer, decision making, alternatives search, 352-353
Rationalization, psychoanalytic theory, 177
Recalls, 461
Receiver:
    interpersonal communication, 458-459
    marketing communication, 431
Recycling:
    attitude formation, 314
    high involvement purchase, 384-385
    low involvement purchase, 390
Reference groups, 201-223
    attitude models, 325
    consumer background characteristics, 52
    consumer socialization and, 203-207
    defined, 201
    family as, 217-220
    influence of, 211-217
    interpersonal communication, 461-462
    local opinion leaders, 468-469
    market segmentation and, 82
    motivation and, 227
    overview of, 201-203
    types of, 207-211
Reinforcement, learning theory and, 294-295
Reinforcement schedule, described, 295
Relative advantage, new product planning, 495-496
Relevance, retrieval, cognitive learning theory, 299
Religion:
    attitude function, 316
    demographic subculture, 149-150
    marketing and, 107-108
    Maslow's hierarchy of needs and, 237
Religious organizations, reference groups, 215
Repair services, 416
Repeat, postpurchase activities, 410-411
Repetition:
    behavioral learning theory, 293
    cognitive learning theory, 300
    marketing applications, 302

Repression, psychoanalytic theory, 176-177

Retail environment, purchase and use, 399-400

Retrieval, cognitive learning theory, 298-300

Rewards, learning and, 301-302

Risk. *See also* Perceived risk
decision making and, 345
interpersonal communication, 463
involvement level and, 377
new product planning, 501
perceived risk, decision making and, 271-272
reduction strategies, 272-275

Ritual, culture and, 101, 102, 110

Rokeach Value Survey, described, 121

Routine decision making, described, 347

**S**

Safety issue, public policy and, 26

Salespeople, purchase and use, 402-403

Satisfaction or dissatisfaction, postpurchase activities, 411-417

Schema, perception and, 260-261

Search for alternatives. *See* Alternatives search

Seat belt use, public policy, 318

Segmented market, defined, 75, 77-79

Selective demand, defined, 232

Selective perception, described, 262-264

Self-concept theory, of personality, 182-185

Self-designating method, opinion leadership measurement, 469-471

Self-perception, attitude change and, 329

Selling, exchange contrasted, 7

Sensation, perception and, 257

Sensory memory, defined, 297

Sensory receptor, perception and, 257

Sensory threshold, selective perception, 262

Separation groups, reference groups, 215

Sex appeal, marketing communication, 446

Sex role, handgun advertising, 486

Short-term memory, defined, 297

Sierra Club, 243, 331

Similarity, perceptual organization, 268

Situational effects, involvement level and, 374, 377

Situational influences, purchase and use, 399-403

Size of market, target market, 79-80

Small business, consumer behavior actor, 16-17

Smell, perception and, 266

Social action organization, defined, 19

Social category reference group, defined, 210

Social class:
demographic subculture, 150-152
lifestyle and psychographics, 186

Social interaction, purchase and use, 402-403

Socialization, consumer, reference groups and, 203-207

Social marketing:
defined, 26
described, 332-334

Social risk, defined, 272

Socioeconomic class, income, 144, 148

Sociology, consumer behavior and, 28-29

Sociometric method, opinion leadership measurement, 471-473

Sound, perception and, 266

Source:
interpersonal communication, 459
marketing communication, 428-429

Source credibility:
interpersonal communication, 459
marketing communication, 428-429

Source evaluation, interpersonal communication, 460-461

Space, cross-cultural analysis, 118

Stability of market, target market, 79-80

Stimuli, perception and, 257

Stimulus discrimination:
learning theory and, 293
marketing applications, 302-303

Stimulus generalization:
learning theory and, 293
marketing applications, 302-303

Store image, risk reduction strategies, 274-275

Strategic business unit (SBU), defined, 16

Subcultures. *See also* Demographic subcultures
described, 104-105
values and, 120

Subjective norm, attitude models, 324

Subjective perception, defined, 259

Subliminal perception, described, 269-270

Superego, psychoanalytic theory, 175

Symbols, learning theory and, 291-292, 293, 297, 303-304

**T**

Tangible product, defined, 8

Technology:

culture and, 104

international marketing and, 114-115

new products, 486. *See also* New product planning

Telephone numbers, public policy, 54-56

Television viewing. *See also* Media
children and, 219-220
as consumer behavior, 22-24
demographic subcultures, 135, 140, 143, 145-146, 148, 163
lifestyle and psychographics, 189
reference groups and, 205

Television Violence Act of 1990, 19

Terminal values, defined, 121

Thematic Apperception Test (TAT), 327

Theory-of-reasoned-action model, attitude models, 323-325

Time, cross-cultural analysis, 117-118

Tobacco industry, warning labels, 304, 305

Total Quality Management (TQM), 414

Trade association, defined, 19-21

Trademarks, advertising and imitation, 268-269

Traditional family life cycle, household characteristics, 157-161

Traits, personality, 173

Trait theory, personality, 179-182

Trend setters, opinion leadership, 468

Trial, postpurchase activities, 409-410

Trialability, new product planning, 496-497

Tricomponent attitude model, described, 319-321

Two-step theory of communication, interpersonal communication, 464-465

Types, personality, 173

**U**

Undifferentiated market segmentation strategy, defined, 84

United States Bureau of Alcohol, Tobacco and Firearms, 290

United States Consumer Product Safety Commission, 278

United States Department of Agriculture, 235

United States Environmental Protection Agency (EPA), 419

United States Federal Trade Commission (FTC), 278, 279, 334

United States Food and Drug Administration (FDA), 278, 303, 365

United States Patent and Trademark Office, 269

United States Supreme Court, 290
Usage influences:
  new product planning, 499
  purchase and use, 405-409
Utilitarian function, of attitude, 315

**V**
Valence, defined, 230
VALS program, lifestyle and psycho-
  graphics measurement, 190-191
Value barrier, new product planning,
  499-500

Value-expressive function, of attitude,
  316
Values:
  consumer background characteris-
    tics, 46-48
  culture and, 101, 102, 108-109
  defined, 46
  market segmentation and, 82
  measurement of, 120-123
Vietnam War, 142
Violence, media and, 12-13, 19, 23-24,
  25

**W**
Warning labels, public policy and, 304-
  305
Wheeler Lea Amendments of 1938,
  278
Women. *See* Female market
Word-of-mouth communication, defined, 457-458. *See also* Interpersonal communication

**Z**
Zero-emission vehicles, 501-502